Edited by Joseph Prokopenko

Management
development

A guide for the profession

Edited by Joseph Prokopenko

Management development

A guide for the profession

INTERNATIONAL LABOUR OFFICE · GENEVA

Prokopenko, J. (ed.)
Management development: A guide for the profession
Geneva, International Labour Office, 1998
/Trainers' manual/, /Management development/, /Teaching and training material/, /Management/, /Management technique/, /Manager/, /Supervisor/. 12.04.2
ISBN 92-2-109196-1

ILO Cataloguing in Publication Data

Printed in England   STO/ALD

PREFACE

The end of the twentieth century is distinguished by the rapid growth in awareness of the critical importance of human talent in business, civil services and social activities. Terms like "knowledge management" and the more precise "intellectual capital management" have appeared recently. These terms suggest that, in the future, managers could be primarily involved with the management of people's talent and intellectual capabilities.

The main difference between success and failure is decided more often than not by the quality of management of intellectual capital. This is the main difference between managers of the 1970s and 1980s, who were more oriented towards asset management, and contemporary managers, who focus on the development and effective use of human capital. After the turn of the century this trend is expected to be even more pronounced.

To prepare managers for these new challenges and realities, management training and development approaches and systems should be adjusted accordingly. This book is about improving management training and development in order to improve the quality of managers by preparing them for the more dynamic and challenging future.

This book is the result of many years of research and analysis on management practices around the world, and reflects the International Labour Office's long-term experience in promoting management development through its technical cooperation and advisory services. It has been prepared within the framework of the ILO Management and Enterprise Development Programme and reflects the results of intensive studies of multinational teams of human resource development professionals and their analysis of the latest trends in the management training and development fields in the 1990s.

An earlier publication — *Introductory course in teaching and training methods for management development*, first published in 1972 — was used successfully in training trainers the world over, but has now become obsolete. Our intention is to replace that publication with this new guide as a basic management development reference work. As the reader may know, the ILO Management Development Programme has already issued many publications including *Management consulting: A guide to the profession*, edited by M. Kubr; *Management research: Guide for institutions and professionals*, by R. Bennett; *Case Method in management development*, by J. I. Reynolds; *Diagnosing management training and development needs: Concepts and techniques*, by M. Kubr and J. Prokopenko; Management self-development, by T. Boydell; and *Library and information services of management development institutions*, edited by K. Vernon. The Programme has also published various monographs such as *The application of action learning: A practical guide*, by G. Boulden and A. Lawlor, and *Management implications of structural adjustment*, by J. Prokopenko. This guide, therefore, is based on experience acquired through developing and using these ILO publications. It also reflects management trainers' and consultants' experience from different countries throughout the world.

This guide describes the complete management development cycle, starting from enterprise problems and management training needs analysis, through setting objectives, programme design and implementation, selecting training methods and techniques and programme evaluation. It takes account of modern trends in management development approaches, such as the move away from teaching towards learning organizations and expanded training methodology and techniques. An important part of this guide is devoted to trainers and management development professionals. Examples of applications of different types of programme are also provided.

A proper balance has been achieved between concepts and ideas on the one hand and practical suggestions to trainers on the other (e.g. how to analyse training needs, how to set training objectives, how to plan and prepare and how to arouse participants' interest or make the best use of training methods and techniques). Where appropriate, specific exercises, cases, tables and figures, etc., for use in training of trainers programmes have been provided.

This book's main target group comprises management development professionals and trainers, management consultants and training organizers, specialists of management training and development centres, policy makers in personnel development, ILO experts, consultants and project and programme staff.

Although the principal target group is the management development professional, the book could be of interest to practising managers who want to deepen their knowledge of management development concepts and techniques. It could also be suitable for use as reading in training of trainers programmes.

While still under preparation, this book attracted the attention of the ILO's major institutional clients and individual management development professionals and consultants. One of them, the Czech National Training Fund, with which the ILO has close cooperation, has sponsored the translation and publication of this manuscript by Grada Publishers in Prague.

With its up-to-date management development strategies, approaches, methodologies and techniques, we believe that this new guide will be an important contribution to ILO constituents as well as to the broader market of management development specialists.

Joseph Prokopenko,
Head, Research and
Programme Development
on Entrepreneurship and
Management Development

CONTENTS

Part I   Management development in perspective

Figures

Tables

Boxes

AUTHORS AND ACKNOWLEDGEMENTS

Twenty-two authors from many different countries including Australia, France, Ireland, Italy, Norway, Switzerland, the United Kingdom and the United States have contributed to this guide. Among them are seven former and present ILO officials specializing in this area. The authors also represent the best business schools, universities and consulting companies, recognized for their experience and contributions to management development (for example, Ashridge Management College, United Kingdom, Durham University and the Institute of Management Development (IMD) in Switzerland) and which have accumulated vast experience in developing training and consulting methodology.

Derek F. Abell, co-author with Milan Kubr of Chapter 1, "Managers and their competences", and author of Chapter 4, "Management education and training programmes: An overview", is a Professor at the IMD in Lausanne (Switzerland). Formerly he was Dean of IMEDE and a member of the Harvard Business School faculty. Professor Abell is the author of a number of books and articles and is a well-known consultant in the field of strategic planning for different governments. He has developed and taught numerous executive seminars for large and small companies.

Aamir Ali, author of Chapter 15, "Lectures and presentation methods", was an ILO official for almost 40 years, serving in many countries, his last post being Director of the Personnel Department. He is a well-known author, speaker and trainer on effective writing, speaking, conducting meetings and communication skills. He is also known for his wide knowledge of literature and cultural matters.

Lester R. Bittel, author of Chapter 20, "Planning, implementing and evaluating a supervisory development programme", and Chapter 21, "Management development for scientific and engineering personnel", is Emeritus Professor of Management, James Madison University (United States) and a Virginia Eminent Scholar. He is a management and organization development consultant and well-known author on supervisory and management development. Professor Bittel has received a number of awards for his contributions to the field of management development.

Olle Bovin, author of Chapter 18, "Towards a learning organization", is an international consultant and Director of International Leadership Olle Bovin SA, specializing in advising large corporations on implementing changes and result-oriented improvement programmes. He worked with Atlas Copco, Kockums and Bofors (Sweden) as Training and Development Manager, Personnel Manager, and at Hewlett Packard (Geneva) as the European Training and Development Manager. He was Chairman of the European Foundation for Management Development (EFMD) Corporate Members Steering Committee and is a founding member of the International Management Development Network INTERMAN. He has written a number of publications on management and leadership development.

Tom Boydell, author of Chapter 10, "Self-development methods", is a Director of Transform Development Consultants, Sheffield (United Kingdom). He is a former Senior Lecturer in management at Sheffield City Polytechnic and training adviser to the Iron and Steel Industry Training Board. He has extensive experience in management training and development and in management consulting to many governments and private organizations and companies. He has written many publications on management training, self-development, experiential learning, training needs identification and total quality management.

John Butler, author of Chapter 7, "Training programme design", is Chief of Training at the Ministry of Labour and Social Affairs, Bahrain. Previously he was Manager of Management Development at the Training and Employment Authority, Ireland. He is experienced in training programme design, development and management of training both in public and private organizations, including international positions.

Francesco Campagna, author of Chapter 8, "Programme implementation and monitoring", is Chief of the Training Support Service and Senior Lecturer at the ILO's International Training Centre at Turin (Italy), a Programme Manager for UNDP and for other UN agencies and also a researcher and training programme designer. He has also worked at the ILO and UNESCO as researcher, training expert and chief technical adviser, and as a development engineer with Lotus Cars Ltd. (Switzerland) and with Fiat-Abarth cars (Italy). He has published a number of modular training series and management development and training of trainers packages.

Brian Delahaye, co-author with **Barry Smith** of two chapters — Chapter 25, "The management development professional" and Chapter 28, "Programmes for the training of trainers" — has been a Senior Lecturer in human resource management at Queensland University of Technology (Australia) for the last 10 years. Previously he spent 16 years with Telecom Australia including six years in training and development. He has published a number of articles and training manuals on self-directed learning, management development and team-building.

Mark Easterby-Smith, author of Chapter 9, "Training evaluation and follow-up", is Director of the Management Teacher Development Unit, The Management

School, Lancaster University (United Kingdom). Previously he worked at Durham University Business School and Newcastle-upon-Tyne Polytechnic. He has extensive experience in trainers' programme design, management development, human resource development, international management education and international consulting for government enterprises and management institutions. He has authored a number of important publications on management training and development, cultural and organizational changes and action learning.

Valerie J. Hammond, author of Chapter 22, "Training and development of women for managerial jobs", is Chief Executive of Roffer Park Management Institute (United Kingdom). She deals with such topics as management performance, future management profiles, management development, organization culture, business ethics and women in management. Previously she was Director of Ashridge Management Research Group and earlier worked for the Rank Organization, ICL Friden, Mobil Data Services Ltd., and the Petroleum Industry Training Board. She has authored many publications on leadership, human resource development and women's participation in management.

Tor Hernes, author of Chapter 12, "Group work and discussion methods", and Chapter 13, "Simulation methods", also assisted in the technical editing of most of the chapters and contributed original material (examples, cases and concepts) to a few of them. He is an Associate Professor of Management at the University of Tromsö (Norway), and an international consultant in management and organization development. Mr. Hernes worked with the ILO as a manager of construction management projects, and as senior researcher. He has carried out a number of consulting assignments for the UNDP and private organizations. He has published a number of articles and training materials on management development and project management.

Milan Kubr, co-author with **Derek Abell** of Chapter 1, "Managers and their competences" and author of Chapter 26, "Using consulting for management development", has greatly contributed to the design and editing of this book. He is an international consultant in management and human resource development and a former Chief of the ILO Entrepreneurship and Management Development Branch (Geneva). As a consultant he has worked with several governments and public and private enterprises as well as international organizations and funding agencies on management development, human resource management and institution building, particularly for economies in transition. He is the author and editor of many publications on management and human resource development, management consulting and institutional strategies.

Roger Lewis, author of Chapter 19, "Open and distance learning", is Professor of Learning Development at the University of Humberside (United Kingdom). He worked previously for a number of institutions such as the Open University, the

National Extension College, The Open Tech Unit of the Manpower Services Commission and the Open College. He has published a number of papers on open learning and adult education.

Alan Mumford, author of Chapter 2, "How managers learn", and Chapter 11, "Experiential and action learning", is Professor in Management Development at the International Management Centre (United Kingdom) and a part-time private consultant. He is also a Companion of the Institute of Personnel Management. His experience in management development has been exceptionally wide and he is particularly well known for his work in experiential and action learning, improving management performance through effective learning processes. He has published numerous articles and books on management development strategies and approaches.

Joseph Prokopenko, editor-in-chief of this guide, project manager and authors' team leader, contributed Chapter 6, "Problem identification and training needs assessment", and Chapter 17, "How to make the best use of available methods and techniques". He is Head of Research and Development with the Entrepreneurship and Management Development Branch of the ILO, Geneva. Prior to working with the ILO he was a aviation designer and a senior researcher at the Ukrainian Academy of Science. He has published more than 80 publications in the fields of macro-economics and industrial policies, structural adjustment, privatization, management of R & D, productivity improvement, management and human resource development.

John I. Reynolds, author of Chapter 14, "Case method", was Emeritus Professor and Professor of Management at Harvard Business School and Texas A & M University. Dr. Reynolds was a well-known case-study writer, consultant and promoter of the case-study method in management development world-wide. He was an expert and consultant to UN agencies and the ILO in many developed and developing countries. He wrote a number of publications and teaching cases.

Philip Sadler, author of Chapter 3, "Concepts and components of management development", also made contributions to other chapters. He is an independent consultant and Chairperson of the Association for Management Development (United Kingdom). He spent ten years in personnel research with the British Ministry of Defence followed by a period working at the National Economic Development Office, at Ashridge Management College as Director of Research, as Principal of the College and subsequently as Chief Executive of the Ashridge Group of Management Centres. He also spent six years as Vice-President of EFMD (European Federation for Management Development). He has authored many publications on management and organization development.

Barry Smith, author of Chapter 16, "Audiovisual, computer and communication technologies", and co-author with **Brian Delahaye** of Chapter 25, "The management development professional", and Chapter 28, "Programmes for the training of trainers", is a Senior Lecturer at the School of Human Resource Management and Labour Relations at the Queensland University of Technology, Brisbane (Australia). He has published extensively on management development and training delivery. He is a consultant of both public and private organizations.

Harald Stokkeland, principal author (assisted by **R. Weitz** and **L. Lawson**) of Chapter 23, "Management development for public service organizations", is Adviser to the Norwegian Council for Management Development (STILO), Ministry of Administration. He previously worked for the World Health Organization, and at the Norwegian School of Local Government, Public and Social Administration as Lecturer in leadership and human resource development. He also did research for the Institute of Political Science, University of Oslo and carried out a number of consulting assignments.

Arturo L. Tolentino, author of Chapter 24, "Training and development of entrepreneur-managers of small enterprises", is Senior Research and Programme Development Officer in the Entrepreneurship and Management Development Branch of the ILO. He is responsible for research and technical advice to ILO constituencies on productivity improvement, enterprise and management development and promotion of small and medium-sized enterprises. He has extensive experience as the ILO Regional Adviser for Southern Africa on management and small enterprise development and as the Managing Director of the Philippine Productivity and Development Centre where he initiated various programmes for improving productivity and training of small enterprises.

John B. Wallace, author of Chapter 27, "Self-development for the trainer", is Director of the Small Business Institute, Marshall University (United States), dealing with experimental leadership development programmes for small and medium-sized firms. Prior to this he was Head of Research and Programme Development of the Management Development Branch, ILO; Chairman of the Department of Management Science, University of Nairobi; and Vice-President of the Computer Management Corporation (United States). He has also held a number of consulting assignments and published a number of papers, articles and books on management and human resource development.

Gordon S.C. Wills, author of Chapter 5, "Future perspectives of management development", is Principal of the International Management Centre, Buckingham (United Kingdom), Deputy Chairman, MCB University Press, Professor of Customer Policy at Cranfield Institute of Technology, and Professor of Management at Bradford University. He has worked for the Royal Air Force, ICI, Sales Research Services, and held a number of directorships in companies and research organizations. He has written over 30 books and 200 articles in the fields of management, education and organizational improvement.

Management development

We would like to thank all the authors and their assistants and the ILO editorial team for their contributions to this guide. Special appreciation is extended to Mr. Milan Kubr, who provided an invaluable contribution to the design and editing of this book as well as professional and moral support during this project. He was also the main driving force in the adaptation and translation of this book into Czech.

INTRODUCTION

It is broadly recognized, not only in the professional literature but in practice in the most successful companies worldwide, that human capital and human resource development is becoming the key factor for enterprise competitiveness and survival in market-oriented economies.

Globalization, structural adjustment, decentralization, privatization, the proliferation of flatter, project-oriented organizational structures (as opposed to vertical, hierarchical ones), all emphasize the critical importance of the development of human talent. Indeed, delegation of decision-making down the hierarchical and profit-centred structures of enterprises demands greater initiative, dynamism, responsibility, vision, entrepreneurship and professionalism from company managers, including supervisors at the shop-floor level.

The new, broader and integrative management responsibilities require new skills and attitudes and more efficient methods. These are the challenges facing management training and development professionals and institutions. The approaches and methodologies of management development and its institutions, therefore, will have to adjust to meet these challenges. The following global trends give an indication of the types of change that will be called for:

- a shift away from academic training toward developing practical abilities;
- a shift away from a fragmented approach to training towards a more focused one, where training becomes an integrated part of company strategy and its effectiveness is measured;
- a shift away from a trainer-centred towards a trainee-oriented learning process;
- a shift away from a teaching to a learning process and from individual training to learning organizations;
- a shift away from standardized programmes and formal training to self-development and flexible, result-oriented, learner-controlled training systems;
- a shift away from viewing training as a cost to realizing that it is an investment; and
- a shift away from outside training programmes to in-company, task-oriented management development.

This list is by no means complete, but it does give an indication of the need to update management training and development approaches, methods, techniques and institutional mechanisms if we are to cope with these changes and new management practices.

The main objective of this guide, therefore, is to provide an international state-of-the-art guide for managers, management consultants and management professionals based on a solid theoretical approach and reflecting the best practice as applied by business firms, public organizations, training and development institutions, business and management schools and management consultants in various countries.

Plan of the book

This book consists of five parts which extensively cover the most important areas — both conceptual and practical — of management training and development. It reflects the evolution of development concepts, approaches, methods and techniques, as well as the latest developments resulting from globalization, growing competitiveness, changes in managerial practices and organizational structures.

Part I (Chapters 1-5), "Management development in perspective", deals with general management development and training concepts. Chapter 1 discusses the nature of a manager's job and the content and structure of managerial competence and skills. Chapter 2 explains how managers learn and the nature and content of the learning process. Chapter 3 illustrates the main concepts and components of management development, including formal education, major training approaches, modern trends and shifts from formal management education to learning organizations. Chapter 4 provides an overview of the most common management education programmes and profiles of leading institutions. The last chapter in this part, Chapter 5, discusses the future of management development, its investment directions, marketing approaches, changes in managerial and informational resources, privatization and its impact on training trends, and shift from fragmented approaches to management training towards a total development perspective closely linked with organization and business strategies.

Part II (Chapters 6-9), "The management development cycle", describes the management training and development process and the ongoing, flexible, results-oriented systems that help human resource development professionals link management development objectives with present and future enterprise problems and strategies. It also addresses the issue of cost-effectiveness. Chapter 6 deals with problem identification and needs assessment. It offers proposals on how managers can select the most appropriate approaches and techniques depending on levels of management, organizational structures and the nature of the problem and development needs. Chapter 7 illustrates how to set training objectives and design training programmes, and covers the issue of logistics relating to programme implementation. The latter are also discussed in detail in Chapter 8. The last chapter of this part, Chapter 9, discusses the concepts and techniques for training evaluation and follow-up, thus concluding the management development cycle.

Part III (Chapters 10-17), "Compendium of methods and techniques", illustrates the most important and frequently used business school practices and training and development methods and techniques. This part begins with Chapter 10, a description of management self-development methods that emphasizes the idea that the most important actors in management development are the managers themselves. This trend will become stronger in the future. Chapter 11 analyses the most important modern trends in management development: experiential and action learning. Here the importance of learning from experience and practical actions is stressed. Other noteworthy methods discussed in Part III are group work and discussions (Chapter 12), simulation (Chapter 13), case method (Chapter 14), and cognitive presentation methods such as lecturing (Chapter 15). An overview of the most common audiovisual and communication training technologies is also provided (Chapter 16). The last chapter in this section provides know-how on issues of critical importance, namely the selection and effective use of available training methods and techniques. Chapter 17 also contains much practical information and many recommendations.

Part IV (Chapters 18-24), "Management development in practice", provides a number of practical examples of management development and training approaches and programmes for different sectors and target groups. Chapter 18 discusses moving a company towards being a learning organization adaptable to the changing business environment. Chapter 19 describes the methods, advantages and processes of using open and distance learning for managers who, for whatever reason, cannot utilize full-time formal programmes. Chapter 20 focuses on planning, implementing and evaluating supervisory training, and also describes the ILO Modular Programme for Supervisory Development, which has become the main approach for promoting supervisory result-oriented training around the world. Chapter 21 deals with the specifics of training and developing scientific and engineering personnel. It discusses typical career paths, competence profiles, programme designs and implementation. Chapter 22 discusses the development of women managers and certain negative and positive aspects of the corporate culture as they relate to training. There is also a chapter dealing with management development in public service organizations based on the experience of an international organization (Chapter 23), and a chapter describing approaches and methods of training and developing small enterprise managers and entrepreneurs (Chapter 24).

Part V (Chapters 25-28), "Developing effective trainers", addresses the strategies and needs of management development professionals themselves. Chapter 25 discusses the nature and profile of management development professionals, their major job components and developmental roles. Chapter 26 explains the growing role of management consultants as trainers and how management consulting contributes to management development. Chapter 27 emphasizes the role of trainers' self-development and provides illustrations of the methods and techniques broadly used by successful trainers for their own development. This chapter also provides several simple and effective instruments for self-assessment and diagnosis of trainers' learning needs. The last chapter, Chapter 28, describes possible training programmes in the modular format for trainers and explains how to design and implement trainers' training programmes.

The chapters comprising this book, with their many illustrations, tables, examples, questionnaires and checklists, along with the index containing the principal professional terms and references in management training and development, are highly practical and certainly warrant the word "guide" in the title.

MANAGEMENT DEVELOPMENT
IN PERSPECTIVE

MANAGERS AND THEIR COMPETENCES

1

Milan Kubr and Derek Abell

The purpose of management training and development is to develop more competent and more effective managers. Therefore, before starting to discuss the concepts and methods of management development in detail, it will be useful to look at who the managers are, what they do, and the meaning of concepts such as "managerial competence" or "managerial effectiveness".

1.1 Who is a manager?

In its conventional conception, management as a special function and activity has its roots in the growth and expansion of private business. A manager is someone who operates and runs the business organization on behalf and in the interest of one or more private owners of this organization. In a smaller business and in many larger businesses, the exclusive or principal owner may also be the exclusive or principal manager. However, the historical trend has been towards a separation of the management function from the ownership function and towards the growth of a category of salaried employees called managers. In today's business, most larger organizations are managed by individuals who have no direct ownership interest in the business, or only a relatively small stake by owning a few shares. Even family-owned businesses tend to be less and less family-managed.

The man or the woman on the top (general manager, managing director, chief executive, etc.) is a manager *par excellence* and is responsible for taking and implementing the decisions involved in operating the organization. He or she reports to the owner, or a body representing owners. There are, then, further sorts and categories of managers whose responsibilities are confined to functions, units and levels within an organization.

More recently, the term manager started being used (in particular in Anglo-Saxon countries) more loosely to denominate any individual responsible for operating an organization or a service, be it in business, in public administration or in social sectors and non-profit organizations. One of the reasons for this has been the growing glamour of being called "a manager". Another, more important reason has been the desire to use business-sector approaches and experiences in enhancing effectiveness and efficiency in other than business services and sectors. Therefore, in using the term manager, and in discussing concepts such as management development, it is necessary to keep in mind the perspective chosen. It is necessary to find out what a person actually does, not merely what his or her position is called. While experience with the training and development of business managers is generally regarded as useful to the training and development of any managers, there may be sectoral and other differences that need to be respected.

1.2 What managers do

Generally speaking, management is concerned with directing and running *human organizations* and making sure that people who belong to an organization act together and effectively meet its objectives. Management is often described as "doing things with and through other people". Management is also concerned with applying and utilizing all other resources of an organization in addition to human resources, including material and natural resources, finance, information and technology, and with the relationships to an organization's external environment.

In 1916, Henri Fayol described the management function as one involving planning, organization, coordination and control. Since Fayol's time, many variations of the basic management functions and activities have been described by various authors. It has been pointed out that a manager's job also involves staffing, directing, reporting and budgeting. More recently, functions such as problem-solving, decision-making, managing change, providing a vision of the future, leading, motivating, innovating, implementing and representing the organization have been stressed.

To be of practical use, management development must be in tune with what managers are expected to achieve, what they actually do, the numerous different roles they play and how well they perform. A mere listing of general functions or broad area of responsibilities will not suffice. Management development professionals need to discover managers' objectives, what they actually accomplish and how they spend their time before making any conclusions regarding what managers should know and be able to do. The design of training programmes must recognize the nature and needs of real managerial work, and reflect this in terms of content, methods and training objectives. In order to improve managerial competence, the objectives of training programmes are now often being expressed in behavioural terms. Increasingly, management development professionals are focusing on productive managerial behaviour and expected results rather than on specific sets of skills. Consequently, attention is being given to behavioural development and motivation, and not only to the acquisition and refinement of particular skills. As a result, learning methods being used involve active processes which move towards the abstract from a solid basis in concrete experience. This can only be achieved by consistently proceeding to a thorough assessment of the training and development needs of the target group. This assessment cannot be a mere collection of accidental observations or wishes expressed by the participants. It is thus useful to refer to generic concepts and models, viewing managerial functions and competences from a wider perspective of total organizational systems and the contemporary business environment.

1.3 Managerial competence and changes in business practice

The current, increasingly complex, rapidly changing and often hectic business practice requires much from business managers. In this section we shall successively examine the following topics:

- the nature of the manager's functions;
- changes in responsibilities over career spans; and
- environmental and organizational changes.

(A) The nature of the manager's functions

Managerial competence involves the ability to perform a job, or a range of jobs, and to attain certain performance levels. This requires possession of information, which could include knowledge relating to the economic, business and management environment; technology; a particular organization and its structure and culture; management concepts, systems, principles and methods; social, psychological, cultural and political factors; and so on. It also requires certain skills, such as technical subject skills; general management and organizational skills; analytical and conceptual skills; social, cultural and, increasingly, intercultural skills; management of people and communication skills; leadership skills; and political skills. In the emerging global business environment, particularly important competences will include negotiating skills and language abilities as well as the ability to use modern communication and information technologies.

Acquisition of knowledge and skills depends very much both on the learning opportunities provided by a particular sort of practical experience, and on the manager's ability to learn from this experience. Furthermore, successful managers usually share certain traits and attitudes. The knowledge, skills and experience, and the traits and attitudes required of a manager differ by level of responsibility, by function, by industry, by cultural setting and from one organization to another. These requirements may be considered under the following four major headings:

- Analytical/conceptual abilities;
- Managerial process skills;
- Personal traits or attributes; and
- "Industry or sector know-how".

Analytical/conceptual abilities

We may think of analytical and conceptual abilities in terms of a hierarchy. At the lowest hierarchical level a set of management "techniques" dominates heavily over conceptual skills. These techniques are essentially the "basic vocabulary" of management — it would be hard to be a good manager without these basic tools of the trade. For example, accounting, financial analysis and a general aptitude for numbers are among these essential techniques.

At the next level are a set of concepts and analytical approaches to the management of *individual* functions. These include marketing, finance, manufacturing, technology management, management control systems and human resource management.

Further up the scale, the manager needs to develop an understanding of the inter-relationships *among* the functions and cultures (both organizational and traditional). This may take two forms. On the one hand, managers must be able to relate the requirements of any one function and culture to the overall strategic priorities of the enterprise. On the other hand, they must be able to integrate the activities of any one function with another. Interfaces between marketing, manufacturing, R & D and finance are of particular importance in terms both of managing ongoing operations and of introducing new products or services in a timely fashion. At even higher hierarchical levels, analytical and conceptual skills must be acquired with respect to developing an overall strategic direction for the enterprise, and for understanding the complex environmental and competitive forces within the industry which shape the future of the firm and its global networks and strategic alliances.

Managerial process skills

Whereas analytical and conceptual abilities allow the manager to decide *what* to do, managerial process skills are more concerned with *how* to do it. Among the most important skills are "people" skills in general, negotiating skills, communication skills (including listening, "outward" oral and written communications and the use of modern information technology), appraisal skills and skills related to organizing time and setting priorities. On a broader level, managers must develop skills in understanding the "political" process of a company and its interaction with the social environment and local community, and in acting effectively within such a context.

Personal traits or attributes

There are certainly many different personal attributes distinguishing good and bad managers, and many authors make a difference between "leadership" and "management" to distinguish the characteristics of those who carry the ultimate responsibility for the success or failure of an enterprise.

The following attributes appear, however, on most lists attempting to define the characteristics needed:

- *industriousness* — that inner energy which drives the manager forward;
- *thoroughness* — the ability to look after the details without losing sight of the "big picture";
- *follow-through* — emphasis on seeing the final result;
- *creativity* — the ability to think "laterally" and synthetically;
- *cultural flexibility and awareness* — the ability to step out of one's own cultural background and, particularly as a result of globalization, the ability to communicate in multiple languages;
- *team-playing ability* — the ability to work, and network, with others and engage their capabilities;
- *self-confidence and self-awareness* — a realistic sense of self and one's own strengths and weaknesses;
- *personal charisma* — the ability to inspire others;
- *individual values* — a well-developed sense of what is right and wrong and how to act in ambiguous circumstances.

While certain characteristics are clearly needed for certain types of job, it has been impossible to develop universal personality models and prove that a person fitting the model will have guaranteed success in a given managerial position. Nevertheless, in practice it is often found useful to consider selected personality traits, aptitudes and attitudes particularly relevant to the job in question.

For example, a general manager who is permanently in contact with other managers and employees and has to do a great deal of negotiation, task explanation and persuasion cannot be someone who is timid and shy, resents dealing with unpopular issues, dislikes frequent social contacts with other people, is ignorant of other cultures and unable to communicate in other languages. A financial manager, in addition to a positive attitude to working with great amounts of data, must have a great deal of perseverance and patience, be able to think and work systematically without, however, becoming a hair-splitter or someone for whom figures have become more important than people and the enterprise, and be able to understand legal differences between financial markets of various foreign partners.

Personality traits could be defined as characteristic ways in which the person responds to equivalent sets of stimuli. Such traits determine how a person will react to any general set of events which allows the trait to be expressed. Thus, traits define a typical thought pattern and resultant behaviour characteristic of a person in a variety of situations. Examples of personality traits are: propensity to take initiative, flexibility, adaptability, self-confidence, shyness, aggressiveness, tolerance, perseverance, patience and the like.

Attitudes consist of feelings or statements for or against issues. In business and management, attitudes are the individuals' predispositions to view their jobs, other people, and the work and business environment in a certain way. Managers' attitudes are reflected in their behaviour. For example, managers who do not believe in the usefulness of teamwork and the necessity of consulting their staff will tend to make their own decisions even when dealing with problems which clearly require collective wisdom and a participative approach. A manager who believes that Anglo-Saxons are more pragmatic and efficient than Latin Americans is likely to be influenced by this attitude when choosing collaborators. Attitudes reflect values that a person holds. Values, and the resulting attitudes, are moulded by the person's total life experience and socialization in a particular family, school, ethnic, cultural and work environment. Values are concerned with matters of human preference and result from choices between competing interests. Often they are irrational and emotionally rooted.

The basic question concerning attitudes is whether it is possible to influence them by training and development. Indeed, if attitudes could not be changed, they should be considered in describing the requirements of a particular job and in choosing a manager, but could be ignored in determining training needs. There is no single and unique answer to this question. Experience shows that attitudes do not change easily, but may change under certain circumstances on the basis of one's own experience and feedback from other people, if the individual concerned has enough will, talent and interest to understand and modify his or her attitudes.

In describing managerial competence the above-mentioned attributes can be grouped into two broad areas: technical and behavioural. The technical area includes knowledge, skills, aptitudes and attitudes concerning technological, economic, financial, structural and procedural aspects of the job. The behavioural area includes all people-related aspects affecting the manager's communication and dealings with people as individuals or social groups within and outside the organization. The terms "hard" and "soft" aspects of management are also used. This grouping is meaningful because it reflects the two fundamental sides of every management job: the technical side and the human side. Different management development approaches and techniques can be chosen for developing technical and people-related skills.

"Industry or sector know-how"

"Industry or sector know-how" usually takes three particular forms. First is the substantive knowledge of the product or service and everything related to its development, underlying technologies, manufacture, distribution, marketing, and service; second is an intimate understanding of the major environmental and competitive forces at work in the industry; and third is the development of personal networks of the people who are related in some way to the industry or sector. Such personal networks are part of the essential capital built up by managers during their career.

(B) Changes in responsibilities over career spans

The changes in roles and responsibilities experienced by a manager during his or her career provide a basis for differentiating between various development needs. In general there are six main career stages at which management development may be provided. These are:

- prior to any real management or organizational experience;
- during or following the first one-to-five years of experience;
- when changing from specialist to more generalist responsibilities;
- just before or after taking charge of an autonomous business unit (e.g. major department, line of business, division or geographic area);
- following five-to-ten years of experience in senior management; and
- at the top management and board level.

At each of these stages there is some balance between *preparatory* education and *experience sharing* aimed at enriching individual experience by contact with others who have had similar, but not identical tasks and responsibilities in different settings. At the earlier career stages, preparatory education predominates; at the later stages, managers are more likely to come together to share experiences and gain new insights.

Prior to management experience. Educational needs for those without prior management experience are numerous. However, the handicap of not having worked in an actual organization severely limits the educational possibilities. Most university-level programmes therefore emphasize the underlying quantitative, economic, social science and financial disciplines of management, and provide a broad descriptive view or "survey" of functional concepts and practices. Broader, more complex strategic issues or organizational processes and implementation problems are more difficult to tackle, and are not likely to be germane to the first job after graduation.

During or following the first one-to-five years. In their mid-to-late twenties, it already begins to be possible to separate the high-potential young managers from those who may progress less quickly or who will level off at a relatively early stage. MBA education or shorter programmes in companies for high-potential young managers aim at providing a broad comprehensive view of management — strengthening functional skills, broadening to include functional and interfunctional issues beyond personal on-the-job experience and opening the door to the world of leadership.

Specialist to generalist transition. Managers destined for higher responsibilities confront an important mid-career transition usually at some point in the early-to-late thirties age bracket. Most have spent the first five-to-ten years of their professional managerial career climbing the first ladder of relatively specialized responsibilities. This may be in sales or marketing, finance, engineering, manufacturing, R & D or human resource management — the common denominator is the primarily functional orientation.

The good ones emerge at the upper end of this first ladder to find that a second ladder then has to be scaled. This second ladder is fundamentally different in terms of breadth and scope of tasks, since it demands: (a) more ability to view a business in its totality; (b) integrative capabilities; (c) abilities to work more at the interface between upper level management and subordinates and between the members of the company networks both local and global; and, in many cases, (d) increased leadership capability. One important distinction is that managers on the first ladder usually work within defined processes and systems; managers on the second ladder often have to redefine processes and systems within which others work.

Some of these managers go on to general management responsibilities; others take on higher-level functional responsibilities. But the difference is in fact not that significant, since running a large plant, branch sales operations or R & D establishment all require multifunctional integrative capabilities and a "view of the whole".

Management development can play a critical role in this transition process, supplying functional capabilities beyond those acquired on the job, improved strategic and operational understanding, and broadening of horizons generally.

The years directly before or after initial general management experience. Although there are considerable age variations, usually the late thirties or early forties bring the rising manager to his or her first real generalist responsibility. Management education may be useful immediately prior to such an appointment, but many find that it is even more useful after two or three years of experience. Thus the purpose is less preparatory than an opportunity to compare and exchange experience with others who have had similar but perhaps contrasting experiences in other branches or countries. It also serves to consolidate formally what has been learned by experience.

Following five-to-ten years of experience in senior management. Senior managers with considerable experience have fundamentally different "education" (or rather, development) needs from those who are still climbing the ladder towards senior responsibilities. In the main, the need is to "stand back" from the job and get a new perspective on management issues, threats and opportunities which are likely to affect the future fundamentally. At this stage, fundamental training and development in management gives way almost entirely to the exchange of ideas and experience around topics which are often neglected or pushed aside by everyday pressures on the job — such as broad political, environmental, economic and social concerns, new ways to think about strategic and organizational issues, and a re-evaluation of one's own role as an organizational leader.

Top management and board level. It is often said that top corporate managers or board members do not attend management development programmes. This is only partly true. What is true is that time is usually short, and interests and needs are different. The distinguishing features of development at this level are:

- emphasis on self-development;
- training events which last a few hours to a few days;
- a substantial proportion of time devoted to experience-sharing and discussion with *peers*;
- an interest in hearing truly new and innovative ideas concerning management and/or being exposed to leading personalities;
- a desire to see relevance to one's own particular situation, rather than general learning.

(C) Environmental and organizational changes

A third frame of reference is the changing organizational context within which managers work. Fundamental changes are taking place in managerial responsibilities as organizations attempt to become more market driven, entrepreneurial, international and network-oriented. In most organizations, general management tasks are being pushed to lower organizational levels in response to increased market segmentation, greater corporate diversification and the need to release managerial energy at lower levels via decentralization and delegation. Leadership is thus more widely distributed, exercised at multiple vantage points several levels below the top, and requires more individuals with broad perspectives, integrative capabilities, horizontal management skills and the ability to take the initiative.

The growing requirement is not only to "run" a business, but to change it as competition sharpens, new technology burgeons, industry lines blur and time is compressed. Successful managers and leaders are preoccupied with corporate renewal as opposed to custodianship and administration.

Old organizations and new organizations. Let us describe two stereotypes. "Old" organizations were common in less competitive times. Many still exist, but will die unless they change. "New" organizations are relatively rare, but many firms are trying to change in this direction. They have a much higher chance of succeeding in today's business environment of ferocious competition, rapid change, instability and global scope. The new organization totally differs in structure, form, processes and vitality from its predecessor. Changing an organization from "old" to "new" is one of management's greatest challenges today.

The old organizations depended for success on a durable competitive advantage in a defined market, or localized and restricted competition. The new organizations, by contrast, acknowledge that their product or service superiority will be short-term due to global competition and rapid technological change. Constant innovation and renewal are essential to maintaining uniqueness.

With a durable advantage, an old organization's people had well-defined jobs. Their task was learning to do their jobs better roughly like rowing a boat, or learning to march in step. Because neither markets nor customer demands changed much, there was very little real competition.

Old organizations had well-defined boxes on an organization chart, and everybody knew exactly what each box meant. These organizations did not like people to do things outside of their boxes, because when people marched out of step, it upset others trying to march in step. Consequently, these organizations enforced discipline through hierarchy and "top-down" management. Senior management set the rules, and the rest obeyed. The result, all too often, was a not-too-subtle interdiction of both initiative and personal responsibility.

These old organizations are breaking down. Why? Because if everybody is doing a well-defined task and job requirements change, people do not know what to do any more — nor do their bosses. Today's fast-moving, more globalized and competitive markets will not let you hide this kind of ignorance inside your organization.

Responding to increased competition and internationalization, many organizations have diversified into new product and service lines. Or they have increasingly segmented their markets and focused their offerings. To manage these businesses effectively, organizations have been restructured into divisions that emphasize the networking of strategic business alliances. Instead of the traditional pyramid with the boss at the top, organizations have become "flatter", with multiple "bosses" at middle management levels. Leadership is distributed more broadly and pushed further down the organization.

As well as using decentralized structures to focus on different business lines and market segments, the new organizations tend to have these attributes:

- *Market driven.* New organizations must respond quickly and flexibly to changing market needs and competitive initiatives and be more responsive to customers throughout the organization.

- *Entrepreneurial.* New organizations need an entrepreneurial climate which will actively encourage initiative and innovation further down the hierarchy. Increasingly, the competitive and global environment demands intercultural teamwork across functions and countries. The whole team must participate in conceiving and implementing initiatives like just-in-time manufacturing, global marketing or strategy-based information systems. An entrepreneurial climate encourages people to embrace change as a way of life, and carries not only a "bias towards action" but a bias towards individual responsibility.

- *Horizontal decision-making.* This contrasts with the hierarchy of the "old" organization. Responsibility is no longer necessarily tied to authority over the resources needed to do the job. Business segment managers, or "programme managers" must negotiate the allocation of major resources with their peers in functional management.

These organizational changes are having a fundamental impact on management education needs. Among the most important implications are:

- strongly increased demand for "generalist" management education, since more people at lower levels now need a broad view of the enterprise and its business environment, and how its various component parts interact and must be integrated together;

- increased attention to the "action" dimensions of management — in particular the abilities to take the initiative, think and act entrepreneurially, be innovative and implement as well as develop strategies;

- increased ability to comprehend and act on changes in the external environment of the firm both locally and internationally, and to negotiate with a wide variety of other organizations in that environment, e.g. alliance partners, suppliers, distributors, trade unions and government representatives and other stakeholders;

- greater concern for "negotiated" solutions up, down and sideways in the enterprise, as opposed to hierarchical command; and

- more need for "leaders" — less need for "administrative managers".

1.4 Competence modelling and management standards

In the previous section we reviewed a number of general characteristics usually stressed by various authors when describing the nature of management, the changes that are due to career progression, or the new requirements reflecting current trends in global business and in society. We realize that the reader could easily point out that some characteristics significant from his or her perspective have been left out or underrated, while other characteristics are in fact less important than stated.

There are two reasons for this. The first one is the extreme diversity of organizational contexts and managerial jobs. Whenever we use the term "manager" as a generic term, without specifying the organizational environment and the set of activities to be managed by a particular person, we are making statements at a high level of generalization and taking a great risk that these statements will not apply to a particular organizational context, or will be so general that they will lose any practical meaning.

The second reason is the difficulty involved in defining and assessing management performance objectively. Managers are developed not to be more competent in general, but to acquire competences needed to achieve a required level of performance in particular organizations. This implies that a manager's personal performance or effectiveness cannot be assessed outside an organizational context and actually requires the assessment of performance of a business or another organizational unit for which the manager is responsible. A manager who performs brilliantly in one organizational setting may turn out to be a mediocre performer in other conditions.

What, however, is excellent or satisfactory organizational performance? How and by whom can it be determined? It could be argued that in a stabilized environment it is possible to use common measures such as profitability or return on investment. Interfirm comparison or benchmarking can also be used. But what should the criteria be in changing environments? What criteria should be applied in organizations aiming at a high pace of innovation, radical restructuring, rapid business expansion and superior performance? Hence the final judgement must be subjective. Someone (higher management, a company owner, a board of directors, etc.) will have to judge whether a manager's competence has met the expectations in a given organizational and business context by achieving expected (required, planned, etc.) performance.

Aware of these criteria and constraints, management development professionals tend to adjust the contents, the methods and the organization of management development to the requirements of individual organizations and managers. At the same time, the profession has been looking for common ground and a conceptual framework, including the identification and description of generic competences common to larger groups or categories of managers who have achieved certain levels of performance as individuals in their organizations. This path has been called *competence modelling* (in"British English"or competency modeling in "American English" terminology).

Competence modelling is not a new field. In establishing training objectives for a particular programme, designers normally think in terms of participant competences before and after the programme. However, a major conceptual contribution to competence modelling was made in the 1970s by the American research and consulting firm in the human resource field McBer and Company, managed by Richard Boyatzis. Developments that have followed are due mainly to the Training Commission, the Management Charter Initiative (MCI) and other organizations interested in promoting management development in the United Kingdom. Models of managerial competences have also been used, in various variants, in a number of larger business companies and by consultants in human resource development.

A typical competence model is derived from observation and analysis of actual managerial behaviour and performance. While a job description would describe the tasks or activities to be performed, a competence model describes the competences required by that job. It usually defines (1) the sorts of competences and (2) the levels at which each competence is required. A total approach is emphasized since a manager's competences cannot be understood and judged by looking at one of his or her competences out of context of other competences. The list of 18 competences defined as the underlying characteristics of a manager causally related to superior performance on the job, provided in the McBer model and applied by the American Management Association (AMA) in designing and delivering management training programmes, is reproduced in box 1.1.

A somewhat different direction was chosen by the MCI and other British organizations. It is based on a wider common definition of competence introduced by the system of National Vocational Qualifications (NVQs), where competences are related to the expectations of employment and focus on work roles. In this model, competence is defined as "the ability to perform the activities within an occupational area to the levels of performance expected in employment". Managerial competences at the lower and middle management levels, corresponding to NVQs levels 3 to 5, are grouped under four "key roles" as follows: (1) managing operations, (2) managing finance, (3) managing people and (4) managing information. Within each key role, competences are broken down into units and elements as shown in figure 1.1. For each element, the model also indicates performance criteria, evidence and knowledge required. A different grouping of competences under four key roles was proposed at senior management level: (1) reading and influencing the environment, (2) setting the strategy and gaining commitment, (3) planning, implementation and control, and (4) evaluating and improving performance. (See figure 1.1.)

A unique feature of the current British approach to the modelling of managerial competence is that the MCI models described above have been adopted as *national standards* of performance for managers and supervisors. They permit managers and supervisors who can demonstrate competence and performance at work to gain a National Vocational Qualification at the appropriate level from an officially recognized awarding body. They can be used as checklists and benchmarks in

Box 1.1. A competence model used by the AMA

Goal and action management cluster

Efficiency orientation — Concern with doing something better (in comparison with previous personal performance, others' performance, or a standard of excellence).

Proactivity — Disposition toward taking action to accomplish something, e.g. instigating activity for a specific purpose.

Concern with impact — Concern with the symbols and implements of power in order to have impact on others.

Diagnostic use of concepts — Use of a person's previously held concepts to explain and interpret situations.

Directing subordinates cluster

Use of unilateral power — Use of forms of influence to obtain compliance.

Developing others — Ability to provide performance feedback and other needed help to improve performance.

Spontaneity — Ability to express oneself freely and easily.

Human resource management cluster

Accurate self-assessment — Realistic and grounded view of oneself.

Self-control — Ability to inhibit personal needs in service of organizational goals.

Stamina and adaptability — The energy to sustain long hours of work and the flexibility orientation to adapt to changes in life and the organizational environment.

Perceptual objectivity — Ability to be relatively objective rather than limited by excessive subjectivity or personal biases.

Positive regard — Ability to express a positive belief in others.

Managing group process — Ability to stimulate others to work effectively in a group setting.

Use of socialized power — Use of influence to build alliances, networks, or coalitions.

Leadership cluster

Self-confidence — Ability consistently to display decisiveness or presence.

Conceptualization — Use of concepts *de novo* to identify a pattern in an assortment of information.

Logical thought — A thought process in which a person orders events in a causal sequence.

Use of oral presentations — Ability to make effective oral presentations to others.

Source: Powers, 1987.

analysing management development needs, designing training programmes, assessing competence and performance, producing job descriptions, recruiting new managers and so on. Their use has been voluntary.

However, experience with using competence models as national, sectoral or even organizational management standards has been limited. Supporters have stressed benefits such as the codification of best practice; the possibility to use standards as role models, objectives and yardsticks; the assistance thus provided to smaller and weaker organizations; and the mobilization of resources and energies towards wider national or sectoral goals. Critics refer to the impossibility to produce other than

Figure 1.1. The MCI model of competences

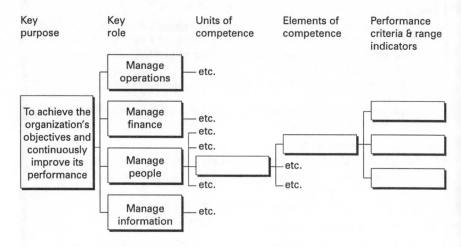

Source: Management Charter Initiative, 1992, p. 5.

general and superficial standards for the extremely heterogeneous and diversified population of management positions and personalities. They point out that the competence framework has been past-focused and has failed to capture innovative, creative, international, entrepreneurial and similar managerial qualities required in the run-up to the next millennium. This speaks for a very cautious application of this approach, in particular in using competence models as national or sectoral standards.

Despite the attempts here to provide definitions of managers, their responsibilities and their skills and competences profile, it is necessary to keep in mind that flexibility should be allowed for these definitions. Business practices, organizational structures and consumer preferences are changing rapidly, and it would be naïve to believe that such changes do not significantly affect the body of concepts relating to management, managers, their jobs and their competences. As a result, management development professionals must judge when, where and how to introduce the appropriate adjustments to reflect reality.

HOW MANAGERS LEARN

2

Alan Mumford

2.1 Learning from real work

Most managers say that they have "learned from experience" or "learned the hard way". Trainers are especially familiar with this kind of statement, because it is often given as a reason for not participating in, or denying the value of, management courses. There are various reasons why managers take this view.

One reason is that for many managers, training off the job through courses is a rare experience. For most managers the statement that they have "learned from experience" is literally true.

Also learning from experience is given such high value by most managers because of the nature of managerial work — complex, reactive, bitty, turbulent and subject to constant change. Managers have long believed that you can only learn to be a manager by being a manager. Those parts of the managerial process which can be identified, boxed and delivered by training programmes, though sometimes recognized as useful or even necessary by some managers, are all too often seen as insufficient and unreal by others.

The difficulty which trainers have traditionally fought to overcome is that managers' claims about learning from experience do not reflect the reality of how inefficient and ineffective much learning from the job actually is. Managers naturally give primacy to effective task performance, not to learning from performance on the job. Indeed these words understate the dedication and commitment of managers to "get things done" and not to stand around thinking about what to do, how to do it, and how successful the doing of it has been. This primacy of concern for doing the job would not matter so much if it were not accompanied by a failure: not the failure to give learning a second place, but the failure to give learning an effective place at all. So, conscious of the inefficiency and ineffectiveness of much learning on the job, and aware of the missed opportunities for learning within a job and around specific tasks or projects, trainers attempt to supplement (and indeed often to replace) these activities with carefully contrived learning situations. A major reason for creating learning processes away from work is that total concentration on learning objectives will often produce a more effective learning process.

This guide aims, among other things, to explain how an effective training process can be created off the job. However, trainers and educators have given themselves a problem by separating learning on the job and learning away from the job. Although over the last 20 years there has been an increasing effort to incorporate simulations of managerial work, or, indeed, to include real pieces of work in training events, there seems not to have been a real integration in most trainers' minds between the nature of managerial work and the carefully designed tutorial processes on courses. It is an uncomfortable realization for most trainers (and therefore one which many of them would prefer not to face) that their work represents only a tiny part of the learning — and sometimes not the most effective part — which any manager will acquire in her or his career, even though it is uniquely designed as a learning experience.

There are two major consequences for trainers who are prepared to consider this evidence. The first is that, in most cases, training processes, in terms of content and process, should be designed to follow as closely as possible the way in which managers carry out their jobs in real life. The major case for this approach is provided in Chapter 11 on action learning. The second consequence is that any significant training event (i.e. more than one day of lectures) ought to contain processes which enable managers to continue to learn when they return to their jobs after the structured learning event is over. The remainder of this chapter gives particular emphasis to structured learning activities designed and implemented by trainers, but returns from time to time to the application of learning principles to on-the-job experiences.

2.2 Learning is an individual activity

Most trainers recognize that managers can be discouraged by any purely cognitive process, be it a lecture, a case-study or the syndicate method. Trainers are increasingly turning to more active methods that offer simulations of management experiences. Thus, in the 1960s and early 1970s, there were the popular business games or Lego towers or other such processes. Then there was a wave of experiential learning activities, derived from T-groups or sensitivity training from the United States, in which participants on training courses were asked not only to reveal their own innermost thoughts, but to comment on the thoughts and demonstrated behaviour of others.

There was only one thing which these successive approaches to management training had in common: they generalized about managers as a group. Until relatively recently, behind both the generalizations about teaching practice and the actual behaviour of most trainers was the belief that, from a learning point of view, managers were a homogeneous group (all managers learn most effectively by ...). When it became clear that this was not true (some managers respond well to experiences that others hate), a more realistic, but still rather despairing solution was offered.

There are different training methods on offer, but many trainers offer only a limited range. In practice, the greater the variety of teaching methods proposed the less managers are likely to be bored during the course.

Like other people, managers have their likes and dislikes. Some prefer opera to ballet, others prefer westerns to thrillers, or American football to rugby. Equally, in their managerial lives, managers differ in their behaviour and in their concept of managerial styles. Some are thoughtful, receptive, analytical, and seek to gain agreement. Others are equally thoughtful and analytical, but express themselves directly in a form seen by some as autocratic. So it is not surprising that different people have different reactions to the same learning experience. Some managers will respond enthusiastically to the charismatic performance at a huge seminar of American guru Tom Peters, while others will come away grumbling that nothing was said of practical value to them and their particular organization. Some managers will be excited by, and learn from, the experience of leading a group of managers in the middle of the night across country to find a hidden treasure. Others will say they have learned nothing about leadership from such a childish game.

Of course, trainers may have different views about how important those differences are. Figure 2.1 shows how different influences — or different pressures — affect a learner's willingness to learn, and subsequently to implement the learning.

Figure 2.1. Influences on learning

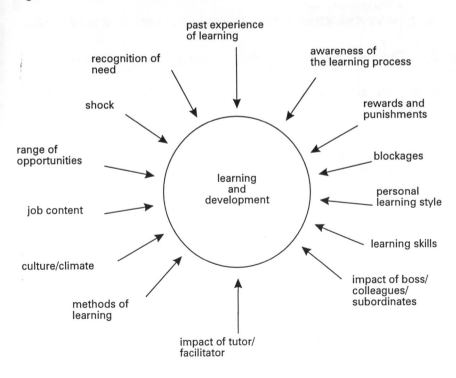

The reader may now find it valuable to pause, analyse and reflect while going through the exercises in box 2.1.

Box 2.1. Learning exercises 1-3

Exercise 1
- Review your past learning experiences. Select two which you see as highly successful, helpful or influential. Select two more which you see as unhelpful and unsuccessful.
- Which of these experiences took place on the job, and which on courses?
- To what do you attribute the success or failure of those learning experiences?

Exercise 2
- Do you agree or disagree with what has been written so far in this chapter?
- To what extent have you tried to move into real managerial work or simulations of it in your training activity?
- Do you agree that generalization has been a major problem in the provision of effective training?

Exercise 3
- Review figure 2.1 on influences on learning.
- On a scale of 0 to 10, assess the importance of each of the influences on yourself as a learner.
- On a scale of 0 to 10, assess each of the influences on the organization for which you do most work as a trainer.

2.3 Definition of learning: Theories of learning

Few trainers and educators have explicit theories of learning in the sense of a coherent articulated set of concepts used in their training practices. Most of them base their work on a set of guiding beliefs, acquired from experience or technically oriented training on training methods. The process by which they acquire these beliefs is described by the learning cycle theory given later.

Early learning theory in management development drew heavily on the concepts produced by psychologists who dealt initially with child learning and later with operative skills training. The list produced by Burgoyne and Stuart (1977) sets out what they called "Schools of thought on learning theory":

Conditioning
Trait modification
Information transfer
Cybernetic
Cognitive
Experiential social influence
Pragmatic

While a great deal of management education was clearly driven by a cognitive theory of learning, the more adventurous parts of management education and most of the training world operated — consciously or unconsciously — using experiential learning theory. Unfortunately, some interpretations of experiential theory do not appreciate the extent to which it embraces cognitive processes as well as simple actions which could be described as experience.

The first theorist to influence a changed approach to management training was Malcolm Knowles (1985). Although his books were concerned with adult learning, not managerial learning as such, his description was powerfully realistic for people working with managers. He describes traditional processes of teaching children, and indeed the extension of these into higher education, as pedagogy. He originally placed the effective processes of adult learning as andragogy (the theory of adult learning) — in opposition to pedagogy. Later he came to regard the two models as parallel rather than antithetical. The main features of his theory are:

- The learner is self-directed but has a conditioned expectation to be dependent and to be taught.

- The learner comes with experience, which means that for many kinds of learning, adults are themselves the richest resources for one another, and also that there is a wide range of experience in most groups of learners.

- They are ready to learn when they have a need to perform more effectively in some aspect of their lives.

- For the most part adults do not learn for the sake of learning; they learn in order to be able to perform a task, solve a problem, or live in a more satisfying way.

In some respects the two major theoretical expressions of Reg Revans (1980) link Knowles and our next theorist, David Kolb. Revans identified a difference between what he described as programmed knowledge and the questioning approach. Programmed knowledge (P) is learning from what someone else has learned, this information being provided in the form of books, papers, studies, lectures. Questioning (Q) is learning from your own processes of action and reflection. This led him to focus for learning purposes on real work instead of on the delivery of programmed knowledge or simulations of managerial work. Like Knowles, Revans said essentially that managers are less interested in being taught than they are in resolving problems and learning from that resolution. This focus led Revans to the creation of the process he called "action learning". Revans also produced a theoretical statement of learning as an example of the scientific approach. This was his "system beta", involving the assembly of data, the development of a theory, experimentation, the comparison of results derived from the experiment, and the final evaluation of the theory.

While Revans's action-learning approach has become increasingly popular, his "system beta" has been less influential than the more explicit experiential learning theory advanced by David Kolb (1984). Kolb's unique contribution was not the learning cycle (see figure 11.1), which consists of a continuous process of concrete experience, reflective observation, abstract conceptualization and active experimentation , but the view that individuals differed in their propensity to learn at different stages of the learning cycle — the concept of learning styles. Through his learning styles inventory (LSI), it is possible to identify an individual's preferred approach to learning: accommodators, divergers, assimilators, and convergers.

Accommodators give greatest emphasis to doing things, carrying out plans and tasks, and getting involved in new experiences. They adapt to changes in their immediate circumstances.

Divergers have imaginative ability and awareness of meaning and values. They use different perspectives and organize many relationships into a whole. They respond well to situations requiring alternative ideas and implications.

Assimilators rely on inductive reasoning and the ability to create theoretical models, assimilating disparate observations into an integrated explanation.

Convergers use problem-solving and a practical application of ideas focusing knowledge to produce single answer solutions to specific problems.

Kolb has not proposed an alternative to cognitive or behavioural theories of learning. He combines experience, perception, cognition and behaviour in one theory. Thus his definition of learning is "the process whereby knowledge is created through the transformation of experience". That transformation is achieved through the learning cycle.

Since Kolb's definition insufficiently recognizes the crucial issue of whether learning involves doing as well as knowing, we would suggest the following definition:

A learner knows something he or she did not know earlier, and can show it. A learner is able to do something she or he was not able to do before.

At this point it would be useful to check and reflect on your own ideas about the theories of learning in the light of the questions in box 2.2.

Box 2.2. Learning exercise 4

- Do you agree with the connection as drawn in this section between the three major theorists reviewed?
- Do you agree with the major theoretical components of each of the individuals reviewed?
- How far do any or all of the theories relate to your own view of the way in which managers learn?
- In what ways, if any, might you go about changing the way in which you do things as a result of looking at these theories?
- How far does your personal experience relate to any or all of these theories? (See, for example, your answers to exercise 1 in box 2.1.)

The questions of *how* and *why* managers learn are closely connected, and in turn lead to the question *what* they learn. Perhaps the most interesting theoretical distinctions here are those concerned with different types of learning. Argyris (1982) distinguishes between single-loop learning and double-loop learning. Pedler and Boydell (1986) talk about the difference between learning which involves increases in knowledge or an existing skill, and development. They describe the latter as "a different state of being or functioning". This is very close to double-loop learning, which involves challenging the present rather than merely improving performance in it. For Argyris single-loop learning is appropriate for routine and programmed issues, whereas double-loop learning causes individuals to look at values and assumptions, and to change the nature of the organizational world. Other writers outside the managerial field have also described different levels of learning.

2.4 Application of the learning cycle and learning styles

The essential propositions of the main learning theories we have just discussed are:

- Managers will tend to want to learn things which are relevant to immediate (and near future) job performance.
- The most effective learning processes will centre on the content of managerial jobs.
- There is a desirable learning cycle describing any learning experience, i.e. the processes through which managers should go in thinking about that experience.
- Individuals differ in their initial interest and willingness to learn through the thinking processes involved at different stages of the cycle.
- Both the general nature of management and the particular nature of the environment around each individual will have an impact on achieved learning.

In this section, we are concerned with the application of the learning cycle and of learning styles. The benefits to be obtained include:

- the opportunity to design learning experiences which encompass the total learning cycle, rather than part of it, and to design activities within a total programme which also take learners through the complete cycle;
- the increased potential to design or select events and programmes to suit the predominant needs of managers, or to meet a preferred learning approach; and
- an improved understanding by managers of their own learning processes, thereby providing for one of the major untackled objectives of structured learning experiences — the ability to continue them away from the domain of the trainer.

The design of this chapter provides an illustration of the learning cycle. The sequence we have gone through comprises:

- the experience of reading the early part of the chapter and then conducting an exercise — a different sort of "experience";
- the collection and review of data — the second stage in the cycle; and
- the exercises in boxes, which were directed in part at enabling the reader to draw conclusions from this information.

In some but not all sections, readers were invited to decide on some direct action which might be taken. In fact, readers have been taken through the essence of the experiential learning theory, and the stages of Kolb's learning cycle (see figure 2.2 and 11.1). The Honey and Mumford versions of the learning cycle and learning styles have different descriptions (activists, reflectors, theorists, and pragmatists).

Activists learn best from activities in which they can engross themselves — in here-and-now activities — not from solitary work such as reading or thinking.

Reflectors learn from activities that provide them with the opportunity to review what has happened and what they have learned.

Theorists learn from activities that form part of a system, a model, a concept or a theory.

Pragmatists learn from activities when the subject matter is obviously linked to the problems or opportunities on the job.

These descriptions are more useful when working with managers, because they are closer to their normal task processes.

Figure 2.2. Combined learning and task cycle

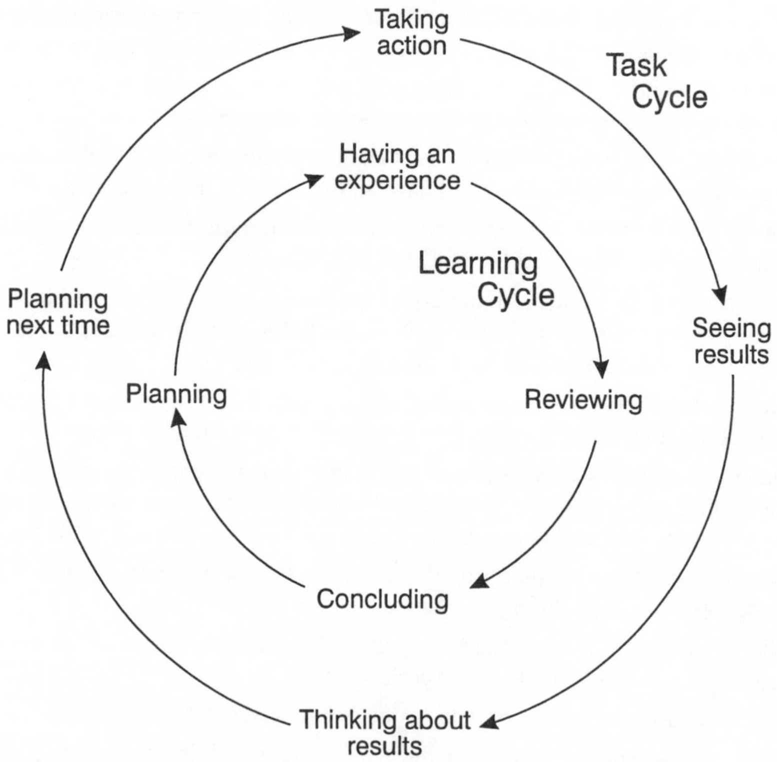

> **Box 2.3. Learning exercise 5**
>
> *Learning cycle and learning styles*
> - How much do I consciously use the learning cycle in the design of programmes or counselling of individuals?
> - Am I convinced in principle that there might be something I could do with such activities by using the learning cycle?
> - Should I learn more about learning styles in order to test their potential application?

2.5 People who help development

Managers are much influenced by the people around them. The impact of those people can be positive or negative and the kind of learning involved can cover a variety of content, function and process. The management development literature has always given great attention to the role of the learner's boss, but attention has been almost entirely centred on the formal contributions of the boss to the management development system, such as appraisal. At one time it looked as if "the manager as coach" would become a main feature of formal management development, but this has not happened. In our research we found evidence that managers are helped to learn by others more frequently through informal than formal processes. For example, though few of the directors we interviewed had ever been "coached" formally, a number of them had learned from discussing real problems with colleagues and bosses — discussions which they had never considered as learning processes until asked about them.

In the 1970s a newly identified helper in management development appeared in the literature — the mentor. Of course, the mentor had long been present in the classical literature, and informally in the experience of managers. The idea of a mentor as a senior respected person helping someone else became identified as a major potential contributor. The idea of a mentor, when the word is properly used, is certainly helpful, and again not least because it focuses attention on opportunities for learning on the job. Unfortunately the word has been misused to describe bosses as well as others. What a boss can and should do for a subordinate differs considerably from what a mentor — the helpful outsider — can and should do.

There are great possibilities for improving management development by the more effective identification, training and use of a variety of helpers:

On the job
- Boss
- Professional advisers - internal and external
- Mentors
- Colleagues
- Subordinates
- Management development committee

Off the job

- Tutors/trainers/facilitators
- Consultants
- Friends
- Family members
- Competitors
- Colleagues
- Mentors

As can be seen from this list, trainers are only one of a variety of possible helpers. Of course, trainers have the opportunity to be quite powerful and influential at certain stages and in certain roles. In particular, they have the opportunity to develop their roles beyond what many of them do as course runners or scheme designers. Two such opportunities are:

- To become knowledgeable about and facilitators of the total range of learning opportunities and processes in their organizations.
- To become the initiators of the processes for improving the ways in which other people give help on management development.

Box 2.4. Learning exercise 6

Helpers in development
- Which people have been most helpful in my own development?
- In what circumstances and how was the help offered?
- Who are the most effective helpers in the development of others in my organization?
- Are there steps I might take to improve the capacity of managers to help with the development of others?

2.6 Improving the processes of learning

We have now drawn together three major aspects of how managers learn. The way in which they interact is shown, unfortunately in a one-dimensional form, in figure 2.3.

There is tension between managers' major interest in completing their work satisfactorily, and encouraging them to learn from doing that work. Our attempts to encourage managers in this will inevitably focus on the reviewing or reflective stage of the learning cycle.

The process of formal and informal learning and the principle of the learning cycle can be joined together in the learning contract or learning agreement. The crucial idea is for the individual to specify in advance of a learning experience:

Figure 2.3. Interaction and learning

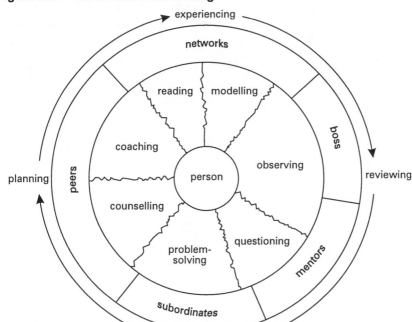

- what she or he claims to achieve through it;
- how it is to be achieved; and
- how that achievement is to be monitored and assessed.

Another process explicitly encouraging the review-and-reflect learning stage is that of a learning log, or learning diary. Predictably, it is a process used much more willingly by reflectors than by activists! Although very powerful and useful on formal programmes, much more work needs to be done to make the idea acceptable and useable by managers of outside programmes. As a rule, senior managers find it very difficult to keep a learning log in relation to their normal work activities.

There is a constant struggle by trainers to find ways of enabling managers to identify opportunities for learning and make more effective use of them both on the job and on courses. A major concern must be to help managers not only to recognize but to use opportunities. The most recent research shows that management development professionals could also help managers better to understand the following approaches available to them for learning from experience: intuitive, incidental, retrospective and prospective.

Details of these four approaches, and the circumstances in which they are applied, are given in Chapter 11 on action learning, where it is also indicated that much remains to be done to discover and develop ways of increasing our understanding of how managers learn.

CONCEPTS AND COMPONENTS OF MANAGEMENT DEVELOPMENT   3

Philip Sadler

Management development has a deceptively simple sound to it. Clearly it means developing the ability of people to manage in their organizational environment. What more is there to be said? Why has so much been written about the subject? What are the problems?

Of course, it is a highly complex subject, fraught with both conceptual and practical difficulties. It involves unravelling the intricate nature of managerial work and identifying and using processes which facilitate learning. It requires a deep knowledge and understanding of how organizations function, of how they change, and of the ways in which management development can effectively assist and support the process of organizational change.

The aim of this chapter is to give an overview of this complex subject without, at this stage, going into much detail, which will be done in other chapters of this book. We shall start by reviewing the following key approaches and components of the total management development process:

- formal education and training
- action learning
- career planning
- learning from experience
- organization development
- open and distance learning
- self-development ·
- management consulting.

This review will be followed by a discussion of critical conditions for management development. The chapter will close with a description of a historical trend from fragmented training towards a learning organization concept.

3.1 Formal education and training methods

(A) Formal education and training

The distinction between education and training is not a precise one. Programmes which lead to formal qualifications such as an MBA degree, dealing with basic management disciplines such as economics and psychology, tend to be lumped together under the heading *management education.* These are usually longer rather than shorter in duration. Short courses which do not lead to qualifications, and which focus on skills and techniques, tend to be described as *management training* programmes.

The objectives of formal training programmes vary considerably. They include:

- *Acquisition of knowledge.* This knowledge can be very specific at one extreme, relating to such things as the particular systems and procedures of the manager's own organization, or highly general at the other, such as knowledge of global economic trends. It may focus on a particular managerial function such as production or personnel management, or may embrace knowledge from several different fields.

- *Learning of techniques.* Closely related to the acquisition of knowledge is the learning of particular techniques — for example, how to carry out statistical quality control, how to draw up a plan, a budget and a profit and loss account, how to administer a psychological test, or how to conduct an employment interview. The acquisition of knowledge and the learning of techniques have in common the relative ease with which the learning process can be validated. Either the participants know at the end of the course the things they are expected to know or they do not. Either they can apply the technique or they cannot.

- *Developing interpersonal skills and related behaviour patterns.* Here the training is less structured and the outcomes less tangible and less capable of being measured precisely. Under this heading are skills of leadership, of communication, motivation, negotiation, influence and persuasion, and more complex skills such as managing change, etc.

- *Developing latent qualities within the individual.* This category includes a group of training programmes which are truly developmental in the sense that they have as their objective the empowerment of the individual by bringing out and sharpening certain inherent qualities. Examples include assertiveness training, creativity workshops, and programmes designed, for example, to develop vision and strategic thinking.

- *Changing attitudes, engendering commitment.* Included in this last category are programmes such as ones designed to create a feeling of common identity among managers from different sites or functions of a large organization; courses intended to "broaden" managers' horizons through the cross-fertilization of ideas with managers from other organizations; courses intended to give managers insight into values in other cultures; and courses designed to facilitate men and women working together.

Some courses will be confined to achieving one of these objectives, others will embrace two or three of them at the same time. So-called *general management* courses will usually aim simultaneously to impart knowledge of basic disciplines such as economics, functional knowledge and knowledge relating to the organization's environment; techniques such as linear programming; and skills such as running meetings; as well as to develop the individuals in respect of such qualities as creativity.

Target audiences

The objectives of programmes also differ in relation to the target audience. Target groups may be defined in terms of the level of management within the hierarchy, the function from which the manager is drawn, or the extent to which they are seen as having "fast track" potential. Some courses are designed specifically for managers in public sector organizations.

Open versus tailored programmes

Training courses offered by external institutions can also be broadly classified into "open", or "public", programmes on the one hand and "closed", "tailored", "customized" or "bespoke" programmes on the other. These terms are largely self-explanatory. Public programmes are normally designed by the external institution concerned and offered to the open market, usually by issuing some form of prospectus or catalogue of courses. Business and public sector organizations now receive regularly an "avalanche" of direct mail promoting such courses. Choosing between them can be both extremely time-consuming and risky. It is not always certain that all the benefits described in glowing terms can be realized in practice.

Tailored programmes

Training programmes tailored to the needs of particular organizations vary according to how individually designed they are. At one extreme the course is essentially a standard public course where all the places are taken up by managers from a single organization, which means there is nothing tailored. At the other extreme the design of the programme, the content, methods, cases and materials are all specially developed to meet identified training needs. In between are courses where the structure of the programme is given, but special cases and exercises relevant to the particular organization and its needs are developed.

Tailored programmes can involve genuinely joint activities between the external institution and the client organization. This partnership can include needs analysis, programme design, development of learning materials, tutorial teams, as well as implementation and programme results evaluation.

In-company training programmes

By far the greater number of management training programmes are conducted by employing organizations for their own managers. It is often the case, however, that the actual sessions within these programmes are led by business school professors, management consultants or others of relevant expertise drawn from outside the company. The more senior the participants in the programme, the more likely this is to be the case. Other sessions will normally be shared by professional trainers and company management. In practice, companies vary as to whether they maintain their own management training centres. Many major companies have considerable in-company training programmes but prefer to use hotels or conference centres. Others maintain centres with facilities which match those of the major business schools.

(B) Action learning

This method of management development, pioneered by Reg Revans, can be seen as standing midway between formal courses and learning from experience on the job. The argument behind the method is that in a period of rapid change, organizations which fail to adapt soon encounter problems. Adaptation is achieved by learning, but in formal courses of the traditional kind the emphasis is, Revans believes, on making managers proficient in the expertise which has proved successful in the past. Such courses cannot help managers resolve problems and situations which have not been previously encountered. Action learning concentrates on searching the unfamiliar and learning to pose useful and discriminating questions in conditions of ignorance, risk and confusion. It helps managers cope with the novel and unfamiliar by requiring them to tackle real problems that have so far defied solution. It is seen as supplementing conventional courses rather than replacing them. The main principles of action learning are as follows:

- It focuses on the task.
- It does not reject formal instruction, though it recognizes that such instruction cannot stimulate questioning in new fields.
- Managerial learning should develop the ability to carry out the solution as well as specify it.
- The desire to learn is reinforced by the threat of urgent problems (or the promise of enticing opportunities).
- In learning new behaviour, managers must tackle real problems (preferably ill-defined), receive constant feedback, and face some risk of penalty for failure.
- Lasting behavioural change is more likely to result from reinterpreting past experience achieved through exchanges with other managers than from the acquisition of fresh knowledge.
- The role of the management trainer or facilitator is to create the conditions in which managers may learn with and from each other and to facilitate learning.

In summary, action learning has three major objectives: (1) to solve a problem in the real world; (2) to help managers learn how to solve ill-structured problems; and (3) to encourage management development practitioners to shift from teaching to helping managers to learn how to learn.

A detailed description of the action-learning method is provided in Chapter 11.

(C) Career planning

The systematic interweaving of management development with career and management succession planning involves a set of inter-linked activities including those listed below.

A systematic evaluation and grading of jobs based on their content

Job evaluation and grading is usually first introduced as a basis for company-wide salary determination, but it is equally relevant to management development, providing a common language to describe and group jobs according to their content. Increasingly such processes involve using the concept of management competence, and competence models or standards.

A system for performance appraisal

Performance appraisal systems have varied uses — for example, to facilitate objective wage setting, to provide an equitable basis for differential compensation or for counselling individuals on performance issues. They also have an important part to play in the process of management development by providing on the one hand a continuing record of an individual's level of achievement and on the other a means of identifying gaps in competence and hence the individual's needs for development.

A system for the assessment of potential

No career planning can avoid decisions about the potential of individual managers. These decisions must be translated into actions such as promotion or rotation of personnel. The potential assessment is less concerned with what a manager has achieved and more concerned with *how* he or she has achieved it. Also the assessment of potential usually involves the use of objective tests to measure such factors as intelligence, personality traits, character qualities and various aptitudes. Such tests form part of the apparatus of *assessment centres* which will also usually involve in-depth interviews with senior executives and with professional assessors — usually qualified occupational psychologists.

A system of development lists

The outcome of the previous three activities makes it possible to draw up development lists which then form the basis for future career planning and development. Jobs can be divided into a number of broad bands, each of which includes three or four distinct salary grades. A typical development list would consist of the individuals in any one of these broad bands who are regarded as having the potential to reach the next highest level within a specified period of time — say five years. The people on these lists are then provided with access to the development opportunities — whatever form these may take — which are seen as likely to facilitate their transition to the next level. These opportunities range from special assignments such as a period as personal assistant to the organization's chairman, through careful selection of posts to be filled, so as to provide a broad cross-functional and cross-cultural basis of experience, to attendance on special "high fliers" training programmes.

Management resource planning or succession planning

The normal vehicle for this process is a meeting or conference at corporate level, at which the information derived from job grading, performance appraisal and assessment of potential will be examined and attention focused in particular on the individuals whose names appear on the management development lists. Normally such a meeting will be run by the chief executive, closely supported by the personnel director and attended by the top line managers in charge of divisions. Frequently companies also employ specialist management development staff who will play a key role in the process. Increasingly the internal "professionals" will be supplemented by one or more external consultants.

The focus of the meeting will be the match (or mismatch) between the major strategies of the business and likely future organizational changes on the one hand and the quantity and quality of the managerial resources likely to be available to the company over the same time period — usually three to five years. The outcomes of the review will be the individual appointments, promotions, attachments, nominations for training courses and so on for the coming 12 months.

Flexibility in career development

However, excessively detailed and rigid career planning has become unrealistic and belongs to the past. The current business environment requires considerable flexibility and adaptability of individual management jobs and total management systems. This has a strong impact on career patterns. Managers have to be developed in ways that make them available for a wider array of new positions, including positions that could not be anticipated in outlining their future career paths. More open career planning also assumes that, for some managers, their whole career cannot be with the same company, thus helping individuals to maintain a necessary degree of employability.

(D) Learning from experience "on the job"

The frequently expressed view that "experience is the best teacher" is strongly supported by a major research project carried out by the Center for Creative Leadership (CCL) in the United States (see McCall et al., 1988). The CCL researchers argue that their findings concerning what kinds of experience lead to what kinds of learning can be used to make development on the job much more systematic than it has been in the past. They cite broad categories of experience and factors affecting experience that executives generally report as being potentially developmental. They are:

Challenging jobs

These include start-ups, fixing troubled operations, dealing with crises and working against tight deadlines. The lessons learned include how to cope with pressure and stress, how to learn new skills and techniques rapidly, and how to deal with problem subordinates.

Experience of other people (mostly bosses)

These people serve mainly as models of values — either by representing what to be or do, or what not to be or do.

Hardships

Hardships help people learn their limits. Things like making serious mistakes, having to lay off employees or close plants and enduring the traumas of personal life cause managers to pause and reflect on what is desirable and also what is possible.

Training

Training others is self-development. Participating in training will provide an opportunity to build self-confidence by comparing oneself with other managers.

Related off-the-job learning opportunities

Community service provides possible learning opportunities. For experience to be developmental, the researchers concluded that at least five of the following challenges needed to be present in the on-the-job learning process:

- Dealing with cases where success and failure are obvious to others.
- Handling a deteriorating situation that calls for dynamic "take charge" leadership, when the manager is left alone to cope.
- Working with new, difficult, or unusually large numbers of people.
- Working under unusually severe pressure.
- Having to influence people, activities and factors over which the manager has no direct control.
- Coping with change, uncertainty, ambiguity, the new and unfamiliar, uncontrollable events, paradoxes.
- Performing while being closely watched by people whose opinions count.
- Exercising team leadership in demanding circumstances.
- Handling a task with a major strategic component or which is intellectually stretching in some other way.
- Interacting with a particularly effective (or particularly ineffective) boss.
- Dealing with a situation in which something important is missing, e.g. top management support, adequate resources, key skills or knowledge.

Specific developmental assignments

The researchers also point out 88 specific assignments which are particularly important in management development on the basis of experience. These are divided into five groups as follows:

- Small projects and start-ups which mainly emphasize persuasion, learning new things quickly, working under time pressure and working with new people.

- Small scope "jumps" and fix-its, emphasizing team-building, individual responsibility and dealing with the boss and time pressures as well as emotion.

- Small strategic assignments, emphasizing intellectual demands and influencing skills.

- Course work and coaching assignments, i.e. teaching or coaching others, which emphasizes awareness of gaps in one's own knowledge or skill, or ability to communicate to others one's own expertise, as well as intellectual pressure.

- Activities away from work, emphasizing individual leadership and working with new people.

Once developmental assignments have been identified, there needs to be some method for giving specific assignments to particular managers. This can be done in several ways. First, given the requisite information about developmental opportunities, many managers will volunteer for assignments that will match their own perception of their developmental needs.

Secondly, a useful strategy to follow is systematically to give career managers early exposure to one or two assignments in each of the five areas over a given period of time.

Thirdly, when selecting a manager to fill a job assignment which comes up, the developmental challenges created by the assignment should be matched with the developmental needs of the managers available to be assigned.

Fourthly, having identified a specific developmental need, a strategy of targeted development can be followed, in which that need is addressed by a series of assignments.

When managers are given developmental assignments, it would be wrong to assume that learning will take place automatically. It is likely that managers will rely on past habits and old skills to get by.

If managers are to learn, they should be consciously making some kind of transition and accept that this will involve giving up or modifying some past behaviour patterns and adopting new ones. Given awareness of the transition, managers can then be helped not only to cope with it but to learn from the experience.

(E) Organization development

The term *organization development* (OD) is used to describe a planned process of organizational change designed to assist the organization in achieving its strategic goals. It concerns such aspects of the organization as structure, systems and procedures, values and culture, management style, teamworking and conflict resolution.

The first stage in an OD programme is normally the diagnostic stage in which answers are sought to such questions as:

- Where are we now?
- Where do we want to go?
- What are the forces helping or preventing us from getting there?
- What do we have to change in order to enable us to get there?

The diagnosis may be made with or without outside assistance although frank, objective answers to searching questions are usually more forthcoming when uninvolved third parties intervene. It is increasingly common to use employee opinion surveys as a key diagnostic tool. Other approaches include in-depth interviews with a sample of employees, discussion groups and interviews with customers or suppliers.

The second stage of the process involves planning the action to be taken in order to achieve the requisite changes. These actions can include structural changes, changes to systems and procedures, training programmes, the development of mission statements and the building of cohesive work groups. The objectives of such changes will vary considerably from one situation to another but can include such outcomes as:

- Free and open communication and feedback.
- Constructive use of conflict.
- Increased cooperation between work teams.
- Greater trust between management and shop-floor.
- Encouragement of innovation and enterprise.
- Heightened commitment to the organization and its objectives.
- Increased job satisfaction.
- Improved customer service.
- Improved quality of product or service.
- Greater retention of key personnel.
- A reduction in the incidence of industrial disputes.

The third stage is implementation. It is inherent in the nature of the OD process that involvement in implementation is essential to its success. The ideas and theories on which OD is based strongly indicate that imposed change is relatively ineffective and short-term in achieving the desired results. It is common practice, therefore, to set up task forces of employees drawn from different functions and different levels (often referred to as "diagonal" groups) to implement organizational change. They will work with the full support of top management and often with the assistance of external consultants playing the role of "facilitator" or "change agent". This process is a very different one from the traditional approach to organizational problems -

call in consultants, throw the problem at them, receive a set of recommendations and impose them on a suspicious and bewildered workforce.

The role of "consultant" in the OD process is different from the conventional consultant role. His or her job is not to solve the problem facing the organization but to *facilitate* the solving of it by the managers and other employees. The descriptive term "process consultancy" is used to indicate concern not with the content of a workshop (for example, designing more satisfying jobs) but with the *processes* of human interaction, conflict resolution, decision-making and the dynamics of group working generally.

The final stages are evaluation and consolidation. Have the objectives been achieved? Here again, employee opinion surveys can provide valuable feedback in addition to such things as measures of quality, of satisfaction, of industrial stoppages or labour turnover. Once objectives have been achieved to management's satisfaction, steps need to be taken to ensure that what has been gained is not lost again. The book *Whatever happened to Shell's new philosophy of management?* (Blackler and Brown, 1980) gives an excellent example of how a massive OD programme was, in the final analysis, wasted because of failure to follow through and set up adequate and effective systems for the maintenance and further development of the new climate and culture.

Richard Beckhard (1969), a leading protagonist of OD, lists eight characteristics of a successful OD programme:

- It is a *planned* programme which involves the *whole organization* or a relatively autonomous sub-unit.
- It is designed to lead to the achievement of specific strategic objectives.
- Top management is fully committed to supporting the programme.
- It is sustained over time (it usually takes two to three years before real results are achieved).
- The programme is designed from the outset to lead to *action*.
- Emphasis is placed on changing attitudes, perceptions and behaviour as well as structure and systems.
- It relies on a learning process which is based on experience.
- It is carried through by groups of employees at different levels of the organization.

Organization development and management development

As indeed the term organization development implies, its focus is on the organization, not the manager. The common ground between organization development and management development lies in the notion of the *learning organization* (see Chapter 18). From the standpoint of human resource development, specialities of organization development will involve some activities — in particular the design or modification of organization structure — which are conceptually quite distinct from management development. Similarly, management development will involve some training activities, which are conceptually quite distinct from organization development. In the overlapping area between the two lies an activity such as team-building, which contributes both to the organization's and to the manager's development.

(F) Open and distance learning

The growing use of open and distance learning approaches in management development reflects the attractiveness of the idea that managers should be able to learn at times, at places and at a pace to suit themselves. It is also widely believed that most managers, being mature, experienced people are not excited by traditional, formal methods of learning. Being primarily people of action, they will favour learning close to the job rather than attending long training courses at external institutions. Some may also be stimulated by the use of modern multimedia communication techniques.

Coffey (1977) defines open learning systems as having removed constraints which would otherwise make them closed. He puts forward constraints of two kinds:

1. *Administrative*. Students must attend at specific places and at specific times or must complete a course of education or training within a specified period of time.

2. *Educational*. For example, minimum qualifications for entry and lack of flexibility concerning learning objectives, methods and sequence.

The following features of distance learning programmes are often mentioned by different specialists:

● Separation of teacher and learner.

● A relationship with an educational or training institution which separates the process from private study.

● The use of communication media of various kinds to link the learner with the tutorial system.

● The use of two-way communication, so that the learner and tutor enjoy a benefit from dialogue.

● Learning mostly on an individual basis but occasionally in groups.

● Elements of a more "industrialized" approach to education.

Considerable effort has been put into developing appropriate teaching material and there is also increasing use of computer-based packages and interactive video systems. A more detailed discussion of open and distance learning systems is presented in Chapter 19.

(G) Management self-development

Management self-development is another way of assisting managers to hone their management skills and perspectives at a time, place and pace appropriate to their individual circumstances and motivation. Unlike other approaches where attention has to be paid to schedules, assignments, group interaction and formal evaluation, this approach provides the manager with considerable scope for variation and flexibility.

However, despite more flexibility and freedom, self-development requires a great degree of personal discipline and commitment in completing a programme and achieving learning objectives within a reasonable time. To paraphrase the old saying associated with learning, "the amount you get out of management self-development is directly related to the amount of time, effort and commitment you put in". There are no short cuts.

The motivation to pursue management knowledge through self-development must first come from within, before the programme is started. In assessing whether or not one is able to complete successfully a management self-development programme one must ask oneself a few very difficult questions:

- Do I have the time that is required on a daily and weekly basis?

- Are my personal and professional obligations sufficiently under my control to devote myself to the required schedule?

- What is my past experience with self-development activities in general, such as resolutions concerning exercise, dieting and so on?

- What is my motivation for pursuing management self-development? Am I pursuing this to please, impress or influence someone? Or am I pursuing this course of study because, given my special circumstances, it is the only realistic way of acquiring this body of knowledge?

Once the decision is made that one is prepared to see this process successfully completed, one has to decide which of the various management self-development methods (see table 3.1) is most appropriate for one's level of education, interest and motivation.

(H) Management consulting

The original purpose of management consulting was different from the purpose of management development. Instead of training and developing a manager, a management consultant was providing advice on how to solve a particular management problem, or even working out a problem solution individually and submitting this solution to the manager.

However, managers and consultants alike were becoming increasingly aware of the limits of this way of using consultants. If the client-manager fails to collaborate closely with the consultant, the consultant cannot make full use of the client's experience and know-how in looking for the best solution. The client regards the solution thus produced as someone else's product and does not feel committed to it. The client has learned little or nothing about the consultant's approach and method, and may have to call the consultant again to deal with the same sort of problem.

The solution has been found in various modes of client participation in consulting assignments and in linking management consulting and management development.

Table 3.1. Summary of self-development methods

Methods and activities	Characteristics of a developed person (art of management)												Qualities of an effective manager (science of management)											Tools for learning to develop from everyday work and life experience	Qualities needed for self-development				Skills required for self-development					
	Health			Skills			Action			Identity																							
	Mental health	Emotional health	Physical health	Mental skills	Expressive and social skills	Physical skills	Making decisions	Keeping going	Taking initiatives	Self-knowledge	Feeling about self	Purpose in life	Command of basic facts	Relevant professional knowledge	Sensitivity to events	Decision-making	Social skills	Emotional resilience	Proactivity	Creativity	Mental agility	Balanced learning habits	Self-knowledge	Tools for learning to develop from everyday work and life experience	Courage	Openness	Faith	Hope	Initiating	Responding	Looking forward	Looking back	Theorizing	Practical movement
1. Personal journal	•	•	•	•	•	•	•	•	•	•	•	•	•	•	•	•	•	•	•	•	•	•	•	•	•	•	•	•	•	•	•	•	•	•
2. Backward review	•	•	•	•	•	•	•	•	•	•	•	•	•	•	•	•	•	•	•	•	•	•	•	•	•	•	•	•	•	•	•	•	•	•
3. Reflecting on things that happen	•	•	•	•	•	•	•	•	•	•	•	•	•	•	•	•	•	•	•	•	•	•	•	•	•	•	•	•	•	•	•	•	•	•
4. Listening to your inner self and self-counselling; intuition	•	•	•	•	•	•	•	•	•	•	•	•			•	•	•	•	•	•	•	•	•	•	•	•	•	•	•	•	•	•	•	•
5. Courage to try out new things								•	•									•	•	•	•	•	•	•	•				•					
6. Experimenting with new behaviours								•	•										•	•	•	•	•		•	•	•	•	•	•				
7. Improving your will-power								•	•									•	•			•	•	•	•				•					
8. Keeping an open mind	•						•													•	•	•	•			•				•				
9. Working with your higher and lower selves					•		•	•							•		•	•	•			•	•	•	•	•	•	•	•	•				
10. Reading				•									•	•																			•	
11. Note taking				•									•	•										•								•	•	
12. Repertory grid				•						•					•							•	•	•									•	
13. Ways of remembering things				•									•	•								•		•										
14. Improving your ability to think logically	•			•			•									•						•		•							•		•	
15. Courses, including correspondence	•	•	•	•	•	•	•	•	•	•	•	•	•	•	•	•	•	•	•	•	•	•	•	•	•	•	•	•	•	•	•	•	•	•
16. Packages and programmed learning	•	•	•	•	•	•	•	•	•	•	•	•	•	•	•	•	•	•	•	•	•	•	•	•	•	•	•	•	•	•	•	•	•	•
17. Special projects				•									•	•								•												•
18. Joining associations and professional bodies				•										•								•												
19. Writing for journals				•	•									•								•												
20. Teaching and training others				•	•				•	•	•	•	•	•	•	•	•	•	•	•	•	•	•		•	•	•	•	•	•	•	•	•	•
21. Working with physical fitness, relaxation and meditation	•	•	•	·		•				•	•							•				•	•											
22. Working with your size, shape and appearance				·	•	•				•	•				•		•						•											
23. Working with people who are different	•	•		·	•					•	•				•		•	•					•			•								
24. Working with your temperament				·	•					•	•				•		•						•											
25. Working with your managerial style				·	•					•	•				•		•						•						•	•	•	•	•	•
26. Working with a speaking partner	•	•	•	•	•	•	•	•	•	•	•	•	•	•	•	•	•	•	•	•	•	•	•	•	•	•	•	•	•	•	•	•	•	•
27. Group approaches	•	•	•	•	•	•	•	•	•	•	•	•	•	•	•	•	•	•	•	•	•	•	•	•	•	•	•	•	•	•	•	•	•	•

Source: Boydell, 1985, p. 65.

Modern consulting styles facilitate and encourage the client manager's learning in various ways. The client must be more than an attentive observer of the consulting process: he or she becomes an active participant, who works together with the consultant, sharing ideas, knowledge, information, judgement, feelings, feedback, experiences and assessment of results. Increasingly, consulting projects pursue distinct learning objectives. The consulting practice has developed a wide array of methodological approaches, and the clients are thus in a position to choose among alternatives that fit their own personal and organizational learning needs and objectives.

Consulting is also used to identify training needs and prepare management and human resource development programmes, either internal or external. Conversely, consulting projects may be generated by management courses and workshops, with the aim of assisting course graduates to apply particular approaches or techniques in their organizations.

Finally, a rapidly increasing number of management and business consulting firms also act as independent providers of external or tailored management training courses and workshops (see Chapters 4 and 26).

3.2 Conditions for effective management development

In recent years a consensus has begun to emerge about the most important conditions for effective management development. Briefly, these are that management education and training are perceived within the enterprise, especially by senior managers, as key activities; education and training needs are derived primarily from the strategic plan for the business; the design of education and training programmes and the selection of learning methods take into account the nature of managerial work; decisions about education and training take into account the needs and capacities of individual managers; education and training are seen as a continuous process in which job experience, career progression and opportunities for learning are linked together; and management education and training are systematically reviewed and evaluated to establish their cost-effectiveness. Each of these characteristics will be considered in turn.

(A) Management development as a key business activity

First, the commitment of top management to management development can be demonstrated in various ways. Increasingly, for example, the executives responsible for management development take an active part in in-company training programmes, and lecture at the business schools where they become honorary or visiting fellows. They also accept that they still have things to learn themselves and find time to attend seminars to keep abreast of new developments in management.

Secondly, the executives responsible for management development are among the most able executives in the business with great potential for promotion. They are assigned to conduct training long enough to become management development professionals and receive adequate preparation for this task. Their posts are so located in the organization structure that they provide weight, authority and status to management development activities.

Thirdly, adequate resources are allocated to the management development function and the temptation to cut this allocation back in leaner times is strongly resisted.

(B) Management development in relation to corporate strategy and change

Enterprises do not remain static. They grow, they diversify, they expand overseas, they restructure themselves. They also acquire subsidiaries and effect mergers. Not all these things will, of course, be planned or foreseen, certainly not in detail or in precise timing and sequence. In the well-managed enterprise, however, they will reflect a corporate purpose or policy and a strategy for bringing it to fruition, which has profound implications for both the quantity and quality of managers required. In quantitative terms, this means having managers at each level to meet the changing needs of the enterprise. More importantly, in qualitative terms these managers must be capable of meeting the challenges, both internal and external, that the future will bring. It is the gap between today's level of managerial competence and the demands likely to be made on management in the future which defines training and development needs. At the individual level, it requires an appraisal of current performance and an assessment of the existing levels of knowledge, skill and other forms of competence possessed by individuals for comparison with the expected future requirements for managerial performance, knowledge and skills. At the level of the management team, it requires an objective assessment of the collective capability of the management of a firm or an enterprise division in such matters as achieving innovation, adapting to change, securing financial control, launching new products or services, and meeting competition - all those matters in fact which reflect the functioning of a management team rather than the performance of individuals.

Inevitably, such an assessment is likely to identify not only education and training needs in the areas of interpersonal skills, communications, leadership, planning and handling information, but also in the less obvious fields of values and attitudes. For example, the failure of a management team to innovate successfully may reflect, more than anything else, a shared culture in which "playing it safe", avoiding risk and prizing security are the dominant values. The need to change such a value system constitutes an important training need just as much as the need to improve communications.

(C) Management development related to individual need and potential for development

Where management development is sponsored by business, the anticipated outcomes will be stated in terms of benefits for the business. In order to achieve this, the needs of managers must be studied as well as those of the organization. The evidence suggests that two things are fundamental. First, managers should be able to perceive development programmes as a way of achieving the things they variously want to attain, such as personal development, career advancement, a sense of belonging, recognition, esteem, status or other forms of satisfaction. If attendance at courses is unrelated to these needs, then managers will either find reasons for not attending them, or will attend them for the wrong reasons, such as taking an extra vacation at the company's expense.

Secondly, managers must be motivated to learn. This state of mind is quite different from merely being willing to be taught. It implies an active, searching, enquiring approach to learning, and one which, having been developed while attending a course, is capable of continuing back on the job, making a reality of the precept that management education is a continuous process.

Assessing the potential of the individual for development is a more difficult problem and the weaknesses of traditional approaches are well documented. Appraisal of the individual's personal qualities and potential for higher management by an immediate superior is a highly subjective process, in which personal bias and prejudice tend to cloud the issue. Once individuals are assessed as having high potential, they become marked out as favoured, collect the best jobs and attend the most prestigious management courses until they arrive, through the reliable mechanism of the self-fulfilling prophecy, in top management jobs. At this stage it may be difficult to convince them that such a system does not necessarily produce the best senior managers. It is no answer, however, to rely solely on measured performance in relation to well-defined objectives or targets as a means of identifying potential top and senior managers. The requirements of jobs change a great deal between levels and functions, and there is no reason to expect that the best field sales manager in the company (as measured by sales results) will one day make a good marketing director, let alone a good chief executive.

To avoid such difficulties, companies are increasingly looking to the assessment centre techniques referred to earlier in this chapter, not only to assess potential, but also to monitor the development of potential over time.

(D) Management development as a continuous process

People tend to see education and training as processes which happen to them and in which they have a more or less passive role. They also see formal courses of education and training largely as episodic processes, which begin on the first day of a programme and end on the last day, freeing the manager to return to the real world, and get on with the job until it is time for the next course. "Learning", however, is not something that happens to people; it is something they do and something they can be active rather than passive about. Courses provide opportunities for learning, but so does the job itself, and so do other processes and activities, inside the organization or away from it, in which the individual manager becomes involved. Learning, therefore, does not begin when the course begins, nor stop when the course finishes. It proceeds continuously over time, changing from the informal to the more formal modes and back again.

In order to make this concept operational, however, certain conditions have to be satisfied. First, managers must not only be motivated to learn and be offered learning opportunities, they must also know how to take advantage of them, which means *learning how to learn*. Secondly, few people are capable of sustained learning without supporting relationships and a means of achieving knowledge of results and a sense of progress.

Increasingly, these conditions are being created by means of close and continuing relationships, between an organization and its managers on the one hand, and an external centre of management education on the other. This again reduces the episodic nature of management education and gives it a continuity extending beyond the boundaries of formal education programmes, whether these take place within the company or externally.

The management development cycle (figure 3.1), consisting of five major blocks, provides a good demonstration of the continuity of the management development process both for an individual manager and for an organization.

(E) Evaluation and review

The evaluation of management development programmes (block V in figure 3.1; Kubr and Prokopenko, 1989) is especially difficult, because it is not normally possible to establish absolutely precise criteria of management performance. As in other instances where judgement has to be exercised in conditions of uncertainty, however, the provision of relevant data can be an important aid to decision-making. The relevant data in the case of management training include course participants' perceptions of the relevance of training programmes and their impact on performance, assessments of change in performance by superiors, measures of attitude change, and such performance measures as are available in a given managerial situation. The art of training evaluation (see Chapter 9) has developed considerably in the past decade or so and organizations with large training budgets can avail themselves of the most up-to-date specialist knowledge in this field.

3.3 From fragmented training to a learning organization

The concept of the learning organization links learning which takes place at the level of the individual to learning (and hence development) on the part of the organization as a whole by such processes as the transfer of learning to others. By integrating separate individual learning into group and later into whole organization learning processes, training methods themselves have been changed from mere teaching methods into more sophisticated change and learning systems.

Figure 3.1. Model of the management development cycle

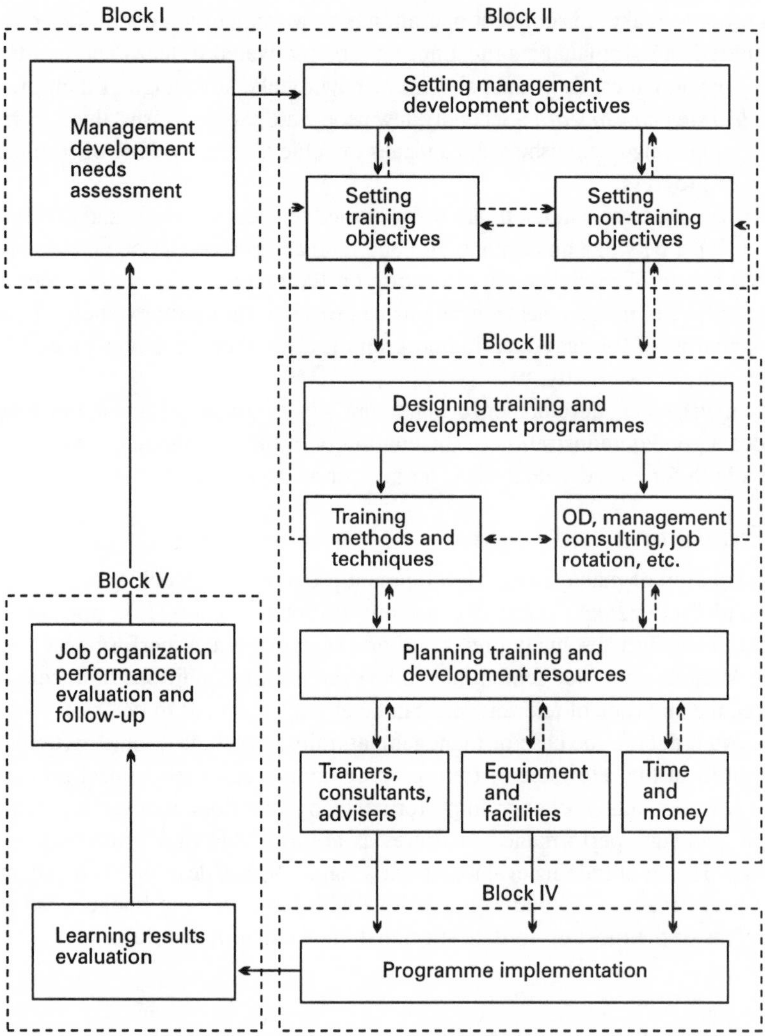

Source: Kubr and Prokopenko, 1989, p. 51.

Research carried out by the Ashridge Management Research Group (Barham, Fraser and Heath, 1988) suggests four identifiable approaches to management development. Organizations may pass through them as a series of stages toward greater effectiveness or they may prefer one approach to the others. Also, different parts of an organization may simultaneously follow different approaches, though a movement towards the third and fourth approaches would normally seem most likely to contribute to improved business performance.

These four approaches are: fragmented, formalized, focused and a fully integrated learning organization.

(A) Fragmented approach

Under the fragmented approach, training and development activities are peripheral rather than central to the organization. The main characteristics of this approach are as follows:

- Training and development are not linked to organizational goals.
- Development is seen as a cost rather than as an investment.
- The focus is on training courses (a discontinuous process) rather than on development (a continuous process).
- Training is directive when it does occur and it is carried out almost exclusively by trainers.
- Emphasis is on courses which lead to the acquisition of knowledge.
- Formal delivery methods, most of them passive, are used on training courses.
- Course attendance is frequently cancelled due to other pressures or lack of commitment by bosses.
- Learning is rarely implemented back at work.
- People are often sent on courses because it is their turn or as a reward for good performance.

(B) Formalized approach

This approach is more systematic and better organized than a fragmented one. Its main features are as follows:

- There is more concern about individual career development.
- There are attempts to link training with individual needs.
- Line managers become more involved in training and development and the appraisal of their subordinates' needs.
- Sometimes pre- and post-course activities are provided to facilitate the transfer of off-the-job learning.
- Training is mainly carried out off the job but the value of on-the-job learning gains some recognition.
- Training is carried out mainly by trainers, but demands a greater range of skills from the trainers to meet the breadth of the courses offered.
- The emphasis is still on knowledge-based training but skill training is involved.

This approach to training is linked with organizational systems which ensure that training activity takes place with some regularity. Managers are normally directed to the training believed by superiors to be necessary and there may be little freedom of choice. The formalized structure tends to be associated with a hierarchical structure, but it does attempt to release the potential of training and development as a means of ensuring that human resource requirements, and to some extent personal aspirations, are met.

(C) Focused approach

In this approach training and development are seen as making a vital contribution to the development of the organization, since it is more result-oriented. The main features of this approach are that:

- Learning is linked both to organizational strategy and to individual goals and aspirations.
- Continuous learning by individuals is perceived as a necessity for organizational survival.
- Training and development are regarded as competitive weapons.
- The main responsibility for training and development lies with line management.
- There is increasing emphasis on on-the-job development.
- There is more emphasis on learning as a process.
- Trainers adopt a wider role as human resource development consultants.
- Specialist training courses are available across the knowledge/skill/issue/value spectrum.
- New, more participative methods of learning are used, such as open and distance learning and self-development programmes.
- There is concern to measure the effectiveness of training and development.

Thus the focused approach concentrates much more on the organization's objectives, while the mutual benefit to the individual and the organization are clearly linked. It still reflects the assumption that the benefit to the organization comes through the development of the individual, but there is a move away from formal training to continuous personal development. There is more explicit recognition that the organizational environment has an important part to play in development, particularly of attitudinal and leadership factors.

This approach is described as focused, because training and development activities are driven by both the strategic goals of the organization *and* the needs of the individuals. It contrasts with the earlier approaches in that it goes beyond problem-solving to positive growth. It represents a switch from a teacher-centred to a learner-centred approach, from an emphasis on training to learning.

(D) A fully integrated learning organization approach

This is the logical outcome of a further development of the focused approach and may be considered more as an ideal than as a widely implemented approach. In the fully integrated approach to management development, the following features could be found:

- Every significant event in the life of the organization is seen as a potential learning experience.
- At all levels there is a ceaseless search to improve things, to introduce beneficial change.
- Daily experience is treated creatively as a step towards innovation and securing competitive advantage.
- Experience is reflected upon, conclusions drawn and new ideas tested out; learning is turned into action.
- People are encouraged to take constructive risks.
- Ideas, energy and knowledge flow upwards from the shop-floor as well as downwards from top management.
- Individuals develop, but they do so in an organizational context.
- The management skills they acquire are firmly integrated with the process of the business.
- Strategy is not seen as a separate discipline; it is the way all the functions work together.

Something separate called human resource management or management development is hardly required, since these activities are fully integrated into the daily life of the organization. It has become a learning organization (see Chapter 18) which has developed mechanisms, through restructuring and changing organizational culture, that enable it to monitor and learn from its internal and external environment.

Appendix 1: Important sources which could provide information regarding the reputation of management development institutions and programmes

African Association for Public Administration and Management,
PO Box 60087, Addis Ababa, Ethiopia.

American Assembly of Collegiate Schools of Business,
605 Ballas Road, Suite 220, St. Louis, Missouri 63141, United States.

Arab Organization of Administrative Services,
PO Box 17159, Amman, Jordan.

Asian Productivity Organization,
Aoyama Daiichi Mansions, 4-14 Akasaka, 8-Chome, Tokyo, 107, Japan.

Association of Deans of South-East Asian Graduate Schools of Management,
MCC, PO Box 898, Makati, Metro Manila, Philippines.

Association of Indian Management Schools, Indian Institute of Management,
Bennerghatta Road, Bangalore, 560076 India.

Association des Institutions de Formation et de Perfectionnement en
Management d'Afrique, c/o CIGE 07, Boîte postale 322,
Abidjan 07, Côte d'Ivoire.

Association of Management Development Institutions in South Asia,
Bella Vista, Hyderabad, 500049, India.

Association of Management Training Institutions of Eastern and Southern
Africa, Njiro Hill, PO Box 3030, Arusha, United Republic of Tanzania.

Canadian Federation of Deans of Management and Administration Studies,
275 Nicholas St., Ottawa, Ontario K1N 6N5, Canada.

Caribbean Management Development Association,
27 Block C Garrison, St. Michael, Barbados.

Consejo Latinoamericano de Escuelas de Administración,
Escuela de Administración de Negocios para Graduos,
Casilla postal 1846, Lima 100, Peru.

European Foundation for Management Development,
Rue Washington 40, B-1050 Brussels, Belgium.

National Association of Schools of Public Affairs and Administration,
1120 G Street N.W., Washington D.C. 20005, United States

West African Management Development Institution Network,
c/o ASCON Topo-Badagry, Lagos, Nigeria.

MANAGEMENT EDUCATION AND TRAINING PROGRAMMES: AN OVERVIEW

4

Derek F. Abell

Management education and development has its advocates and its detractors. In recent years particularly, articles in the press lauding the achievements of leading management schools and their graduates have often been countered by others which point to shortcomings — real or imaginary. Why is it, the critics ask, that the United States, with its long history of management education, and close to 70,000 MBA graduates annually, is suffering so many business reversals? And why do Germany and Japan, with much shorter traditions of management education, do so well?

The purpose of this chapter is to describe and evaluate the actual state of formal management education and training — their good and bad sides. We shall begin with a short historical overview. This will be followed by a description of the principal groups of programme providers and an examination of factors affecting their profiles.

4.1 Historical perspectives

It is useful to open the discussion of how needs for management development are met by providing some historical perspectives.

Until the 1920s, in the United States, and until after the Second World War in Western Europe, management education institutions as we know them today simply did not exist. We are talking therefore about a phenomenon which is still in the early stages of its development. In many developing countries, management schools are only now coming into being. There is the growing recognition that management is a profession; as in other professions, the knowledge, skills and attitudes required can be learned systematically, and not left to chance.

Prior to this realization, management was learned "on-the-job" — by the process commonly referred to as "the school of hard knocks". Indeed, it was often believed that managers were born rather than made — and this was frequently true, because management at the top level was frequently handed down from father to son.

Formal education for future managers, if it existed at all, took a wide variety of forms. University degrees in "classical" subjects such as history, literature or politics were presumed to provide as good an intellectual base for managing as degrees in law, economics or science. Not infrequently, entrepreneurs emerged because of their bright ideas, creativity and effort, and learned to manage through necessity. It is important to recognize that this approach was quite satisfactory for those earlier times. The institutions themselves were relatively simple, and "pyramidal".

It was only with the onset of the great waves of growth and diversification in terms of products, markets and geographical spread that these old ways of recruiting and developing managers broke down and new ways started to develop. The most obvious recruiting ground for top management was at the level of more specialized jobs one step down. This was not unreasonable, but the people moving into the top jobs had a very one-sided experience of management. It was not unusual for chief executives to be strong in accounting, finance, engineering or operations — depending on their previous background — and weak in other areas such as marketing or customer care.

Further diversification led to new channels of on-the-job development for managers as companies split into divisions. The job of divisional general manager became a schooling point for people moving on to top corporate jobs. This was also reasonably satisfactory, but not perfect because experience was often restricted at the divisional level to one sector and one country; top corporate jobs required more industrial breadth and international diversity.

All of these changes have spawned the present complex variety of modes of management development. These may include formal education not only at the beginning of a managerial career, but also at key stages throughout, as well as carefully tailored assignments designed to provide the maximum development opportunities. The possible combinations and permutations are many, but a few main patterns may nevertheless be defined.

(A) Company training programmes

Young potential managers are hired directly from schools or universities into commercial apprenticeships or graduate training schemes respectively. From their mid- to late twenties, high-potential individuals are given the opportunity to attend short "in-company" management training programmes organized by the company itself. High performance on the job is rewarded with expanded managerial responsibility and development opportunities, and at some point the individual may be sent to one or more "external" executive programmes in a business school.

This remains, especially in Europe, the most common pattern of management development. Over the course of their careers, individuals may find themselves involved in a complementary set of in-company and external management programme experiences, all of which aim to enrich the main form of development — management responsibility itself.

(B) The MBA route

An alternative management development route is provided by an MBA experience. Still much less common in Europe than in the United States, its popularity is nevertheless increasing quite rapidly. The MBA may take three essential forms: either a full-time two-year course (more typical in the United States), or a one-year full-time course (more common in Europe), or a part-time "executive MBA" combining periods of work and short periods of education spread over one to two years.

Whichever the variant, the basic intention is the same, i.e. to take a high-potential young executive, typically in the 25 to 30 age range (or 25 to the late thirties for executive MBA programmes), and provide a thorough professional management education following several years of university education including practical managerial work in an organization. The MBA frequently provides its recipient with the opportunity to make a significant change in his or her career path — either from one sector to another (which often takes the form of moving from industrial responsibilities to careers in management consulting or financial services), or from functional responsibilities to more generalist responsibilities.

(C) Management training and development programmes

Many successful managers today have neither experienced a company training programme, nor an MBA course. Instead they have come to positions of responsibility in their companies and have their first, and often only, formal schooling in management via management or executive development programmes. These may be internal or external to the company, or a combination of both. Many managers, of course, especially in smaller organizations, still receive no professional management education. What they learn, they learn from experience alone.

Between these three broad patterns are an almost infinite number of permutations and combinations of all three. The main point to bear in mind, as we focus in subsequent sections on the supply of management education, is that education programmes are always complementary to experience itself, and in terms of what can be acquired over a career, often play a subsidiary role to on-the-job learning.

4.2 Overview of current supply

Just as the demand for management education is highly segmented, the supply is highly differentiated — both in terms of basic educational approach and of quality. For the potential candidate or corporate sponsor, choices are often difficult to make, since the institutions themselves often do not clearly "position" themselves in the marketplace, nor are the basic dimensions of difference (and therefore of choice) well understood by the buyers.

Perhaps the first thing to realize is that, although initially management education was the preserve of a few well-known "business schools", today it is offered by an increasingly wide range of institutions, individual entrepreneurs and corporations which run their own "internal" programmes. In this mosaic of supply, management schools have a relatively small and decreasing share — even though they still play a dominant role in certain areas, e.g. MBA education, and "long" executive education programmes.

The following are among the most important providers of management education and development today:

- companies, or consortia of companies, running their own internal programmes;

- management departments within universities;

- private non-university-based management institutions or schools (often with corporate and/or alumni sponsorship);

- management seminar and conference organizers, either dedicated to conference activities, or as a sideline to another related activity such as publishing;

- management consulting firms; and

- private individuals acting as independent programme organizers.

The "core" activity of the providing organization inevitably has an important effect on the type and quality of education offered, and a word about each is in order.

(A) Company "internal" programmes

Nearly all large multinational companies, and many others too, today have an extensive offering of internal programmes. These range from introductory courses in basic management functions and disciplines for incoming young recruits to general management courses for senior and top management.

A growing trend seems to be for companies to join together in "consortia programmes" (i.e. in groups of anything between two and ten members) to organize management education programmes jointly. While it is often difficult to agree on the target participants, programme duration and outlines, such programmes have the benefit of allowing corporations to compare performance and share experiences about issues of common concern.

Some of the most advanced corporations have put in place a complete "ladder" of programmes corresponding to various management functions and levels of responsibility. These are then sequenced with career assignments, consortia activities, and "external" programmes in management schools to provide synchronized and "lifelong" management development opportunities.

On the positive side, internal company programmes tend to be closely allied to management practice — and particularly to the company's own problems and specific culture. Their physical facilities are often very good and some of them exceed in scale and quality those of the best management schools. On the negative side, few if any corporations have permanent teaching staff who can rank with the best in leading management schools. They therefore quite often "borrow" faculty resources from management schools. Further, corporations do not make many direct contributions to the production of new teaching materials or research in these management schools.

Companies vary regarding whether or not they maintain their own management training facilities. There are a number of major companies which have significant in-company training programmes but which use hotels or conference centres. Others, such as IBM, maintain centres which rival the major business schools in terms of size and facilities. The arguments in favour of a company having its own centre are as follows:

- Facilities are firmly under the company's control and can be tailored precisely to the company's needs.

- The ambience or climate of the centre will reflect the company's culture and reinforce desired cultural attributes.

- The centre can be used for top management meetings and for a range of other company functions.

- The centre symbolizes the company's lasting commitment to management development.

- Positions on the tutorial staff of the centre are in themselves important developmental opportunities for managers within the company.

Arguments against include:

- Such centres are expensive to maintain. In order to justify the expenditure, courses are often laid on not because training needs have been clearly identified, but because of the need to maximize utilization of the centre.

- Company training centres can become comfortable "ivory towers" in which the conventional wisdom goes unchallenged and new ideas seldom get an airing.

Companies increasingly try to avoid these dangers by establishing their management training centres as profit centres. Business units sending managers on courses are charged the economic cost of providing the training, while the manager of the centre is financially responsible for breaking even or showing a surplus. In many cases the centre manager has the flexibility of being able to sell any surplus capacity on the outside market for whatever price can be obtained.

(B) Management departments within universities

With a few notable exceptions, universities were relatively late entrants into management education — and some still have not really differentiated the teaching of social sciences and social science methodologies such as economics, quantitative methods and the like (the underlying discipline of management) from the teaching of management itself.

Universities typically concentrate on the teaching of "undergraduates" and from that starting point have moved on to MBA teaching. Only a few of the more prestigious universities have been able to take the additional step of teaching practising executives, and only a very few successfully offer executive education programmes for top managers. This is to be expected because university teachers devoted primarily to undergraduate teaching are unlikely to accumulate the breadth of practical experience, combined with a broad research and academic background, to be fully credible to top management.

It should be added, however, that some of the best management education available is provided by a few leading universities, namely those that engage in extensive management research, working closely with the business world, and have a history of management education at the MBA and executive levels.

(C) Non-university-based management institutions

In Europe particularly, the relatively cautious response of universities to entry into executive education led to the establishment of management institutions sponsored initially by corporations or by chambers of commerce. These institutions had two immediate advantages: they were necessarily forced to be practically oriented and relevant, since they had to meet the needs of their sponsors; they were able to be much more entrepreneurial in spirit and action than some of their university-based counterparts — where the shift towards practice-oriented teaching and research was (and still is) resisted by the more conservative "academic" forces in the university system.

As a result, some of these non-university-based "private" institutions have become major forces for change and development in management education, and leaders in their own right. It should be added, however, that such management schools span a wide range of quality, and while the best compete for leadership with the very best university-based institutions, others leave much to be desired.

(D) Management seminar and conference organizers

The main difference between seminar organizers and management schools is that the former are largely marketing organizations with no faculty or academic resources of their own. Faculty, guest lecturers and speakers are hired "for the occasion" as are, in most cases, the physical facilities needed. Hotels are the most common venue.

Earlier, the organizers of such seminars concentrated mainly on one or two day "events" often bringing together one or two academic or business celebrities, and anything from 50 to several hundred managers. Recently, these organizations have diversified and offer longer management programmes of one or even several weeks duration — and are therefore becoming direct competitors of management schools. Their advantage is that they can bring in "star" speakers by offering them attractive fees. Their disadvantage is that in the absence of any ongoing faculty or staff of their own, most of the longer programmes being offered lack the cohesion, integration and learning effect found among teachers in the best schools.

Conference organizers are predominantly spin-offs of large publishing firms — either newspapers or business-oriented magazines for the most part. They have exhibited very rapid growth in the last decade, and now account for a substantial portion of the "educational" time which managers spend away from the job. The typical conference lasts one to three days, and usually focuses on one issue or set of related issues, using a mixture of speakers and "panels" as the main approach.

(E) Management consulting firms

In recent years the consulting profession has shifted progressively from analysis to a much greater concern for implementation and the client's involvement in the consultant's work. As a result, consultants are increasingly being asked to confront human resource questions, including staff and management development.

Some have taken this a step further to become providers of management courses, workshops and seminars to clients, either singly or on a multi-client basis. Those with substantial ongoing consulting experience, who take the time and effort to "boil out" conceptual ideas and insights, and disseminate these insights internally and externally, have the potential to offer high quality educational programmes. Their strength is their close contact with real business problems at a high level; their weakness is a lack of time to turn this into teachable material, and lack of skill in the educational process itself. Few consultants easily or quickly make the transition from consultancy to very high quality and credible executive teaching or research.

(F) Private individuals or groups

A number of private individuals, in most cases ex-professors from leading management schools, have "consulting" companies specializing in management education nearly all of which is in the form of programmes tailored to the needs of specific companies. Acting as "impresarios" they hire other professors on a part-time basis to work with them on specific assignments. The quality of the best programmes offered in this way can be comparable to those offered by the best management schools. Careful selection of a faculty team, by "cherry picking" from the best management schools, can produce high quality education.

4.3 Profiles of leading institutions and programmes

Management education and training institutions differ on a large number of points. Among the most important real differentiating features are the following:

- age and level of participants targeted;
- theoretical versus practical orientation;
- teaching versus research orientation;
- degree of integration across courses;
- emphasis on long versus short programmes;
- internationality; and
- overall quality.

(A) Age and level of participants

Some universities, as already noted, engage only in education for undergraduates. Many other universities combine undergraduate and MBA teaching. A smaller but growing number offer education for undergraduates, MBAs and practising execu-tives. Non-university management institutions often combine only MBA and executive education. Other providers focus on executive education. A few have tried to enter the MBA market, but this has invariably raised questions about certification standards.

(B) Theoretical versus practical orientation

As prototypes, Harvard Business School is usually thought of as being at the practical end of the spectrum, while schools like the Sloan School at MIT and the University of Chicago Business School are usually seen as having a more theoretical approach. In reality the best schools mix practice and theory, but with different emphases.

It is only a mild oversimplification to say that institutions which are practice-oriented start with real management problems and derive concepts and theories from the study of these problems in the classroom and in the process of research. Institutions which are more theoretically oriented start with concepts and theory, and look to see how these theories can be applied in practice.

(C) Teaching versus research orientation

It is common knowledge that excellent teachers are usually active in adding new conceptual insight to their fields as well; they combine teaching with research, and if the teaching is practically oriented, the research will be too.

In many university institutions, however, there is a basic dichotomy between teaching and research, going so far in some cases that there is a separate research staff with few if any responsibilities towards students. In the extreme, this runs the risk that the research is not rooted in practical managerial problems, while teachers become simply communicators of other people's ideas, rather than developing as well as teaching new ways of looking at the complex world of management.

While research must be regarded, therefore, as fundamental to quality education, an over-emphasis on research at the expense of teaching is a serious problem in many university management institutions. This has its roots in a lack of market orientation on the part of the institution and its leadership, undue weight being given to "academic" publications in the hiring and promotion process and a self-perpetuating process by which senior faculty members, not understanding practice themselves, promote others after their own image.

(D) Integration across courses

Management itself, and especially general management, requires a broad, integrated view of the enterprise and the interrelationships among its functional parts. Manage-ment problems can seldom be viewed with detachment. Thus the practice of teaching specialized courses without reference to what is going on in other courses or other parts of the curriculum is fundamentally at odds with the management process itself.

Some institutions, unhappily a minority, recognize this and consciously try to avoid creating artificial barriers between one course and another, and one instructor and another. Departmental organization lines are not "watertight", and instructors cluster in a variety of cross-functional ways to assure an integrated and team approach to the teaching effort. Others assign faculty members in ways which promote teaching and research compartmentalization — thus failing to address the true integrative nature of most real management problems.

(E) Long versus short programmes

A Managing Director at Nestlé, which was one of the founding companies of IMEDE (Lausanne), was fond of saying: "We believe in instant coffee, but not in instant management education". Institutions vary substantially in their belief on the appropriate length of management education programmes. The Advanced Management Program at the Harvard Business School runs for 12 weeks; at Stanford the equivalent programme is ten weeks; at IMEDE it used to be three weeks, while at IMI (Geneva) it was one week.

These differences can be explained partly in terms of the scope of objectives, but partly also in terms of learning methodology. The greater the emphasis on participant involvement and participant-based learning as opposed to "straight lecturing", the deeper the educational experience is likely to be. Learning by self-discovery just takes longer. Some argue that the added time-investment is amply repaid in terms of effectiveness.

(F) Internationality

The internationality of a school can be judged by three main factors: the internationality of its study body, the internationality of its faculty members and the internationality of the subject matter being addressed. All three must be present for a truly international educational experience.

When, for example, a foreign professor tackles a relatively pedestrian accounting problem with a class of participants from highly diverse cultural backgrounds, the result is likely to be international learning. When a domestic professor teaches an international business case to a group of purely domestic students, the result may be more domestic than international, since there is insufficient cultural diversity or experience to bring the discussion alive.

From this perspective, institutions could be divided broadly into the following three categories:

- A very few truly international institutions combine highly diverse student bodies with international faculty members, and an emphasis on international business. There are probably not more than a handful of such institutions in the world today.

- A substantially larger number of first-class "national" institutions enrol primarily domestic students and use mostly local faculty members. They may teach international management problems to a greater or lesser extent. Many of these

national institutions are making large efforts now to internationalize more —
often by exchanging students and faculty members with schools in other countries.

- The rest, which is the large majority, tend to be either second- or third-level
  national institutions, or regionally oriented.

(G) Quality

Any review of differences between institutions would be incomplete without some
discussion of quality differences. Quality depends on three main factors: quality
and diversity of the participant body; quality of the faculty — of its thinking,
contributions to research, and dedication and skill in teaching; and quality of the
educational process itself.

Quality is extremely difficult to measure by any of these three factors, and
particularly by the third one — quality of the educational process. Some people
prefer to take a long-term, results-oriented view of this, and ask what happens to the
institutions' alumni 10, 15 or 20 years after graduation. If an institution finds that
its alumni are consistently occupying a good percentage of important leadership jobs,
it probably means more than its ranking by faculty members and deans, which is
often based on the quantity of the faculty's research output rather than the achievements of its graduates.

FUTURE PERSPECTIVES OF MANAGEMENT DEVELOPMENT

5

Gordon S.C. Wills

This guide is fundamentally concerned with the more effective design and delivery of management development activities. Therefore it must be forward looking. As the professional practice of management development evolves, it will reflect managerial practices that are themselves undergoing substantial changes. These include the globalization of business management worldwide, structural changes and decentralization, growing technological capabilities, the networking of information and managerial skills, and dramatic changes in managerial roles and profiles. These changes, which raise fresh challenges for managers and management development, require provision of the skills to meet the new expectations. Successful managers of tomorrow will have a distinctly different profile from those of yesterday and today.

The chapter will focus on the following eight themes:

- How much will be invested in management development in the years ahead?
- How can management development best be marketed?
- How can management development become a truly continuous process?
- What material and information resources will be needed?
- Who will be the best tutors?
- How will the provision of management training be privatized?
- What will replace conventional wisdom?
- What is the overall outlook for management development?

5.1 Investment in the years ahead

There are few areas of organizational activity with better scope for good investment returns than management development, provided such development does two things: it must benefit both the manager's career and the organization's stakeholders. Since it is the stakeholders' funds that are to be invested, they will want — indeed demand — a good return for that investment through organizational performance.

Furthermore, since the individual manager can and will move elsewhere, the stakeholders will expect their return to be realized over a fairly short time-scale. Driving the investment forward will be the certain knowledge that competitors are also developing their managers, and superiority not parity of managerial performance must be attained. The manager and the management development staff together must ensure that management development is as obviously beneficial as a new computer system, manufacturing facility or advertising campaign.

Soft development goals like "developing the team" must be linked to hard goals like "in order to win the next competitive negotiation with a major potential customer by taking business away from a key competitor". The net gain on such new business can be directly offset against the team development undertaken, and the flow of improved performance into the future can be seen as an additional bonus of considerable magnitude. In this manner, management development is seen as a project or task-related activity. The opportunity to incorporate management development into normal operational activity may present itself accidentally, but when it does, it provides immediate scope for expert tutorial support quite outside of the regular training budget.

How much will be invested in management development in this way is a function of the vision and competence of the line and management development managers involved. Management development here is operating in a profit-centred framework, as an investment in the sale. Within this framework, likely returns on the investment can be used to generate extensive extra funding. Management development must either reduce costs or increase productivity in a way that is quantifiable.

The essence of this future perspective, therefore, is that the demand for managerial excellence will drive the growth of management development. Management development practitioners should win friends and influence line managers by meeting those demands, rather than advancing their own professional careers.

In the future, the source of real funding will be where the action is — in line management and at board level, to resolve company problems and to implement its strategy. Movement in this direction will constitute a major step forward in the development of human asset accounting.

5.2 Marketing of management development

The first question to be asked is: How do management development professionals break through to the consciousness of the line manager? Management development professionals must demonstrate how these key individuals can find the time away from their present business roles to undertake such development. They must be convinced that management development for engineering graduates entering a multinational company will be cost beneficial in terms of fewer departures during training or immediately thereafter.

Management development

The management development experience must begin by respecting the line manager's objectives. Curriculum and scheduling must not challenge these objectives. The programme must be designed to ensure that the outputs for which the line manager is accountable are delivered, with the fullest possible additional benefits gained *en route*.

This means working in project teams, on real tasks of key concern to the organization. This achieves a level of workplace learning unequalled in any off-the-job situation. It brings urgency, visibility, team work and new experiences at the workplace with other professionals. Most of all from a learning perspective, it brings reinforcement of ideas by testing them through their application to an ongoing management situation.

Other developments will be going on back in the normal work role. The classic wisecrack concerning management development programmes — "Who learns most when someone goes on a programme, the person who goes or the ones who stay behind?" — will take on a new meaning. An infinitely sharper focus will emerge in respect of time management and its direct link with delegation. Stress will be tackled and managed. Project management competences will be improved. Competences will not be taught as such, they will be learned as the situation calls for them. The design of the management development activities will ensure that the opportunity is given again and again for them to be focused upon.

Balancing marketing and "product development" will be essential. Excellent management schools *combine* marketing and product development in the easiest and most natural way — the school's faculty staff spend several days each week working with managers and their organizations on research projects, case writing, student project work, diagnostics related to educational programme design, consulting assignments, and the like. The faculty staff themselves thus become the chief marketing *and* product development arm of the institution. What is even more important perhaps is that their main point of reference and contact in enterprises is senior line management. There is something unsatisfactory about institutions where the faculty members remain largely on the campus while marketing "staff" make contact, largely with human resource counterparts, in firms, while plying the market with large numbers of brochures and advertising messages.

However, marketing of management development is also about pricing, promotion and distribution. There are few managers who, given the choice between a cheap and an expensive programme of management development, would choose the cheaper one. Price is seen as an indicator of quality and, except in mercifully few cases, it is. The price must include a sufficient margin to meet adequate preparation costs, including a detailed discussion of the task being focused on. It must include a margin for the proper support of managers and the provision of the best tutorial services throughout, which must be customized or tailored to be most effective. The price must also allow for evaluation and follow-up of the implementation stage of action plans.

Management development is a process of self-actualization. Everything that is said about it and communicated about it must be consonant with, and be seen to be, enhancing the managerial self. Accordingly, conventional marketing variables must be well managed. The brochure advertising the programme must be well presented. The facilities must be presented positively. The back-up services must be professional. No skimping is permissible. At the same time, management development is not a holiday or, heaven forbid, a reward. There is much to be said for golf, riding and swimming as ways to unwind from a high-stress management development programme of activity, but they should not be confused with the purpose at hand — to get a return on the investment.

Finally, from the marketing perspective, how should management development be geographically distributed? Managers often travel out of their own culture, often across the world to receive training in issues unrelated to their own environment. Better by far for the tutors to travel to the other culture and put their own perspective to the test. Unfortunately, many management development specialists build training factories to which managers are expected to travel. Cash-and-carry retailing of management development like this has its merits, but it is increasingly less significant.

5.3 Management development as a continuous process

As has already been mentioned, management development is a continuous process and in future we can expect greater attention to be given to that continuity. As the trend in industrialized countries towards becoming learning organizations (see Chapter 18) demonstrates, companies will be increasingly responsible for facilitating and encouraging management development. It is still the case that a manager is regarded as being "well enough developed" after having gained an MBA, for example, or followed an extended executive programme. Certainly the individual will have a much greater understanding of the body of knowledge about management. But the needed synthesis of management development opportunities and training with real issues must provide a much better understanding of the continuing role that professional journals and books can play, as well as the continuing learning opportunities available from the challenges at the workplace.

Mentoring, self-development and task groups are particular approaches to continuing development that have become widespread. By far the most potent force for continuing development outside the workplace, however, has to be professional groupings such as management training and consulting associates, courses, etc. They can — and will in the future — become more committed to safeguarding high professional standards either through legal frameworks, or by powerful marketing within their networks.

Associations of management institutes' alumni can also play a similar role to the professions, as they break away from their preoccupation with contact networks and fund-raising to tackle a real task of this nature.

There seems to be very good reason to anticipate that the increasing level of joint ventures between tertiary institutions and the professions worldwide may give rise to an eventual fusion of the two. Professions may well come to base themselves on university campuses; and universities to take city centre facilities to get closer to the focus of action.

The success of institutions in playing a key part in continuing management development outside the workplace will depend on the same range of factors as enabled them to participate in the management development process originally. What benefits are to be provided? If the benefits are social, only those seeking sociability will be active. If they are to be developmental in an intellectual, managerial way with a pragmatic focus on investment returns, something more than nostalgia or loyalty must be relied on. Short management development encounters are unlikely to be of great attraction except as vehicles for renewing contacts, networking, or for special conferences or workshops. Depending on the managerial grouping concerned, offerings must be thoughtfully created and managed in line with their preferred learning styles.

However, until line management commitment to continuing management development at the workplace matches the quality of major training programmes, little can or will emerge. It is a considerable educational design challenge. The present yardstick in weeks or days of participation in formal courses concerned with updating is almost an irrelevance. As this guide exemplifies, the quality of what occurs on such courses is of far greater significance than their duration.

Accordingly, it must be envisaged that continuous management development will mainly occur at the workplace. Senior line managers will increasingly be trained and developed to see the way they lead, organize, delegate, supervise, monitor and control the activities of their colleagues as management development. Their heightened consciousness will of itself raise the level of development. Project teams will be put together with development as much in mind as getting the job done well.

5.4 Material and information resources

Most management development occurs in physical facilities created for another purpose, i.e. the workplace. The majority of off-the-job management development takes place in hotels and centres not dedicated solely to such activity. Physical facilities are only likely to be a constraint when it is deemed indispensable for the development to take place within centres dedicated to that purpose. Usually board and meeting rooms and hotel facilities can provide appropriate venues, and the necessary equipment can be found.

The greatest obstacle to ensuring that development goes on has not been the lack of suitable physical facilities; rather, it has been difficulty accessing the relevant literature. However, the advent of quality screened services such as *ANBAR Management Abstracts*, with 24-hour fax delivery worldwide and a multitude of other information and intelligence databases, has overcome many of these difficulties. Distance learning and programme "packages" also provide ready availability of a carefully selected management development library. Finally, satellite television makes it possible for distance learning to extend way beyond the correspondence course into an interactive relationship with tutors thousands of miles away (see Chapter 19).

5.5 Getting the best tutorial inputs

There is a perceived shortage of full-time management development tutors and experts. But what is the real situation? It is true that there are very few databases that bring together those offering tutorial services and those in need. Where they do exist, however, the outcome has typically been an under-utilization of the tutors — an excess of supply over demand. Most of the shortages are highly localized, and frequently artificial and structural, because what is missing is an adequate mechanism for bringing supplier and user together by increasing their mobility. What is demonstrably true is that the quality of teaching and facilitating skills is often less than satisfactory because of a lack of sufficient training, development, coaching and mentoring of the tutors themselves. There is a considerable supply of tutors available, but appropriate training is seldom required as a prerequisite for their involvement in management development. Most industrialized countries do not allow teachers to teach in schools unless they have university-level qualifications, nor do they allow untrained accountants or doctors to practise. How long will it be before management development practitioners need to be licensed? Maybe that requirement is long overdue, but there is no focus of pressure to bring it about. Only the professions and the tutors involved could bring this to fruition.

How good are workplace managers as tutors or as managerial helpers and mentors? The general impression seems to be that they are good, with occasional appalling exceptions. Indeed, good management is achieved through working with others, delegating, monitoring and controlling. The senior line manager as a rule knows the field of expertise well and the realities of the process of managing within it, or he or she would not survive long in the role. So, being a tutor-manager is like being a parent, but with two very important elements of significant difference from the parent: managers have been chosen for their jobs, and their subordinates can leave and work elsewhere.

If managers are potentially good tutors, it is only a short step to contemplating that they could and should be one of the richest sources of tutorial support for off-the-job training too. Experience increasingly shows this to be the case, and it can be accomplished with great credibility provided they are assisted in the structuring of the learning and tutorial situations.

Some areas of tutorial support are wholly natural for line managers, such as team working, motivation, and strategic planning and management. In other areas, such as enabling managers to understand and better contribute to and act upon financial or social information, detailed support is often required. So the future perspective is not simply of more line managers undertaking tutorial work off the job. It is important to involve them in team teaching situations as counterparts to external faculty experts, in the development of relevant resource materials and examples, and in dealing with challenging specific questions about enterprise realities. The clinching argument of such involvement is that it could be a subtle way to ensure that the senior managers themselves are developed. It also has the great merit of making senior managers aware of the shortcomings of task-focused management development, and forcing them to generalize, conceptualize, compare and evaluate their own experience.

Finally, good tutorials come from fellow managers — not fellow managers in a tutorial role, or a boss or a professional trainer, but simply from another participant in the programme or in the office. Every organization finds out very rapidly which colleagues are most helpful and encouraging. On the job, the most able line managers use such tutorial potential not only in the way they construct task teams, but even in office layouts and reporting relationships. They will also organize off-the-job departmental events such as setting the planning cycle, analysing out-turns, debating customer-care relationships and the like.

5.6 Privatizing the provision of management education and training

In many countries, significant past initiatives to ensure the provision of management education and training to emerging local businesses as well as to the public sector came from government. Therefore many management institutes and centres were first established and operated as government institutions, with all or most finance provided through government allocations and technical assistance funds.

The current trend towards increasing and strengthening the role of the private sector in economic development has many implications for the providers of management education and training. An obvious consequence is increased demand from the private sector, including the special training needs and requirements of enterprises that have been privatized. In many countries, this will continue to be a major market for many years to come. On the other hand, changes within the reduced and restructured public sector will also boost demand for management development thanks to the growing understanding that no country can fare for long without highly competent and efficient public services.

To cope with these changes, government-established management institutes have to review their value systems, organizational cultures and work styles. They will have to become market- and client-oriented, cost- and profit-minded, versed in financial management and marketing, and increasingly flexible and adaptable. Many of the great institutions that have been developed under the aegis of public financing will need to take a radical view of their future in order to survive and thrive.

The decision to transfer a government-owned and government-sponsored institution to the private sector should be consistent with national development policies, conditions and resources. In one case an institution may be well suited for privatization, while in another case it may be better to close it down and encourage the creation of a new provider of training services as a completely different entity, not a successor of a former government institute. For example, in one country, the government took over the national productivity centre with very critical functions in management development at the country level, and placed it within the premises of the Ministry of Labour. In a very short time this ministry transformed the centre into another department, forcing its staff to assist the ministerial bureaucracy in preparation of different papers, reports and documents. The centre became the "garbage basket" where the ministry put people it had decided to get rid of. Very soon the main corporate clients had stopped using the services of the training centre and the best specialists left for other jobs. Finally, the government realized the problem and decided to close the centre down as part of the restructuring of public administration: it would be impossible to transform it into something useful and efficient within the previous organizational culture. There was a decision to set up a new, non-governmental centre.

In a third case, it may be decided to maintain the public status and ownership, but phase out the provision of government allocations, or combine it with cost recovery and motivation for performance and efficiency. For example, it is often more effective to allocate government funds for assistance in training to the consumer of the training rather than to the institutional provider. In this case the consumer has the right to select the best training provider and introduce more competition among the suppliers. This would force public training institutions to commercialize their services and increase the quality of training.

In all instances, private sector clients ought to be made aware of their responsibility for the development of managerial resources, and of the necessity to take over, improve and pursue activities in the management education and training field that were originally initiated in the public sector. Options have to be sought with imagination and responsibility, with the ultimate purpose in mind.

5.7 Beyond conventional wisdom

For more than 50 years, management literature has contained analyses of what managers do at work. One future perspective must therefore be that as management development becomes more customer-oriented, the curriculum will not simply focus on task challenges, but also on the competences and skills required to accomplish them effectively. The work of Boyatzis (1987) and Burgoyne (1988) are powerful indicators of the directions in which we can expect to see movement to overturn the conventional wisdom.

There is another vitally important issue that has, however, been frequently overlooked. Managers almost always work in teams. The notion of the all-knowing executive is seldom accepted in the workplace. Although authority is frequently vested in a single individual, few wise managers exercise it on their own without canvassing of views and the expertise of others.

As such, theories of general management that incorporate but also go beyond the direct tutorial propositions of business policy integration can be expected to predominate. The formal tutorial imparting of core areas of knowledge, so that managers can reach basic levels of competence across the board, is already being increasingly challenged. There is growing evidence that the following trends will dominate the future scene of management development:

- It will aim more to help managers understand the conceptual frameworks and professional disciplines involved rather than the technical expertise used.

- It will seek to foster trust and understanding among diverse professions working within management teams.

- It will work on real issues that frequently cross professional and national boundaries (Hams, 1987).

- It will be focused on achieving results as well as leading managers to consider the options available.

Classical business integration policy must be attempted through the medium of corporate planning and strategy formulation, and by acting upon the need to set priorities and allocate scarce resources when several possible routes can be followed. The process of selecting choices can be much more widely shared as part of the process of management development and effective action.

The traditional assumptions of teaching strategy, namely that integration involves mainly products and markets, need to be extended to encompass funds flows, information/intelligences, logistics and human resources. Perhaps most importantly, they need to comprehend multinationalism and the process of change-management. The challenge of doing the same thing as hitherto is seen as less of a challenge for management development than improving upon it, or shifting our assumptions altogether about how to do it or whether to do it at all.

Against such perspectives on the processes of general management, how can the body of knowledge best be taught and how can it best be learned? Not, as one can clearly see, according to the conventional methods; not from Chapters 1 to 30 of a textbook; nor from a collated selection of case-studies. It would seem more likely that the new curriculum will be as follows: managers must come to understand the core areas of the business, the interfaces between them and their integration. They must identify and practise the skills of working in a team of diverse professionals who trust each other and are out to win in real management tasks. It is a team process that learns to evaluate, link and feed back into the process, specifically to improve team performance. Management development, then, will not be about a solo performance; it must develop the whole team using the whole range of participative training methods and techniques available.

5.8 Towards a total development perspective

For a final perspective, it is surely right that we should look towards the total system that is management development. Separate institutionalization — which has given us university business schools, professional institutes, independent colleges and centres, and management development consulting firms and others — places all the burden on the manager to build an optimum mixture. The future must surely hold the possibility that the discrete offerings will come together in a total management development process without reference to current institutional structures. Only in this way can the contextual development of managers at work gain the proper recognition of the opportunities it provides — and sufficient attention be given to it as a mechanism for increasing productivity.

As an example let us take training in finance. The most frequent option used is the one which most recent analyses have shown to be the least effective and most expensive. Individual managers have been released to go on courses to study broadly under the title "finance for the non-financial manager". Sometimes outside tutors are brought in to offer such training on site. Seldom, however, is account taken of the learning needs of the whole organization, nor of who gains or loses most by not being properly informed. The total model could perhaps focus on the issue in this way:

- Who in an organization knows most about financial management professionally?
- Who knows best what each individual manager needs to know?
- What is the best way of ensuring that managers all learn what is needed?

It is, however, difficult to get such a total model into operation. Quite often, the manager who feels inadequate in the field of financial management is reluctant to admit it publicly and professionally. Those who are experts in financial management elsewhere are not aware of the problems and difficulties being encountered, despite the fact that the greatest cause for concern of senior financial management in the organization is that their colleagues feel inadequate in this field.

Several organizations have recognized this now, and placed professionally qualified financial managers at the heart of their operating activities, reporting to appropriate line managers rather than to the specific accounting or financing function. The results have frequently been a dramatic improvement in management understanding of financial issues throughout the team. There are, however, moments when the financial managers themselves need refreshing, updating and even being given an opportunity to interact with academia. There will also be occasions when a major new direction or systems implementation makes it vital to call in consultants to show how to share the management development load.

A total development perspective will need a sharp focus. The fundamental question has to be: who or which group in an organization can be expected to adopt the total development perspective? It cannot be the line managers alone because, although they are the main clients for management development, they can never hope to know enough. But they will be the deciders. The budget will be allocated by them, not by the management or human resource development professional.

The annual audit of management development and any minimum development requirements must not be perceived as formal days "off the job" per person or as a percentage of the payroll for training. The total development perspective will be nothing less than its name implies. What has my job and workplace development taught me? How have my colleagues helped me to learn? How have I filled gaps in that learning by going "off the job"? Have I had the opportunity to retreat and think as needs required? What practical use could be made of what I have learned? Managers' consciousness of developing in all the unseen ways, as well as the readily observable ways, must be maximized.

PART II

THE MANAGEMENT DEVELOPMENT CYCLE

PROBLEM IDENTIFICATION AND TRAINING-NEEDS ASSESSMENT

6

Joseph Prokopenko

Training should always be results-oriented. Since the main result of good management is improved organizational performance, any meaningful assessment of training needs should start with the identification of organization (performance) problems. The final purpose of needs assessment is to find out what training and development managers should receive, and what conditions ought to be created in order to make sure that this training and development will have a positive impact on organizational performance.

However, it is often not possible to improve organizational performance by training alone. There may be problems that require both training and non-training solutions. In this connection, the first important conceptual and practical task of trainers or consultants in a needs-assessment survey is to identify organizational performance problems and to distinguish the training and non-training needs and solutions.

6.1 General concepts and dimensions for needs assessment

(A) Basic model

To tackle the above-mentioned task, consider the five different situations illustrated in figure 6.1 (Kubr and Prokopenko, 1989). It shows that in defining training needs we have to start by identifying and comparing two levels of performance: the standard (desired, optimum, future, planned) performance level (Ps) and the current (existing, real) performance (Pc). The difference between these two levels is the performance gap (Pg). This relationship is shown in case X.

As mentioned, to improve performance we normally have to deal with certain non-training and training needs. In case A no training is necessary to fill the performance gap and to attain the performance standard, since the manager's current competence (Cc) is sufficiently high. Only non-training needs (Nnt) have been identified and corresponding non-training interventions or measures are required, such as changing the work environment, organization, incentives and so on.

Figure 6.1. Basic model of the training development needs concept

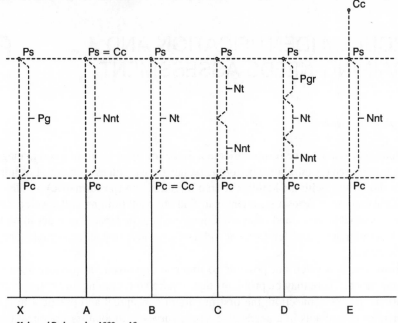

Source: Kubr and Prokopenko, 1989, p. 18.

Case B is the opposite of case A. Here the current competence (Cc) is not high enough. The performance gap is equal to training needs (Nt) and can be closed by training alone.

In management practice, cases A and B are rather the exception. The situation encountered most frequently is that shown in case C. Here, to fill the performance gap it is necessary to apply a package of both training and non-training interventions. The safest way to approach needs diagnosis is to assume that we are facing case C.

Case D is one that managers and trainers hope to avoid. Here, training and non-training interventions are not sufficient to fill the whole performance gap. There will be a residual performance gap (Pgr), which can be due to various factors such as geographic location and high transport costs; or the competence of the owner or manager of the business can no longer be increased and there is no possibility of removing him or her from this position in the short run, etc.

As a matter of interest, we also show case E. Here the job holder is already more competent than necessary and the performance gap can be filled by applying a set of non-training measures. However, even when the standard is reached, there will still be some difference between the incumbent's individual potential and the standard performance requirements of the job or the organization. This gap may continue to exist unless a new higher performance standard can be established, or another more challenging position found for the current job holder in order to fully use his or her potential.

(B) Defining the gap between current and desired performance

The identification of current performance starts by fact-finding, which consists of collecting information indicative of performance, describing and measuring it. For example, the plant utilization may be chosen and measured as a global indicator of performance. The related competence problems of production managers may be in areas of production scheduling and control, maintenance management, quality improvement and purchasing. Factors other than the production managers' competence (calling for non-training solutions) may include a shortage of foreign exchange, the absence of any bonus systems for stimulating better utilization of plant, and so on.

Without assessment of the desired or standard state of affairs — of standard competence and/or performance — we would have no starting-point, no base from which any training and other needs could be identified and compared. In the above-mentioned case, is the utilization of plant substandard or satisfactory? Are equipment breakdowns or stoppages within acceptable limits? The only way in which this assessment can be done is by comparing our findings on the current state of affairs (absolute data) with established standards.

To judge current competence and performance, the following types of standards could be used:

- standards achieved by some other organizations, serving as models ("excellent" companies, organizations representing a "solid" standard without being the top performers, etc.);

- sectoral or national standards, reflecting agreed levels of "good practice" in particular industries, services, etc. (e.g. standards recommended by trade associations, centres for inter-firm comparison, or consulting firms);

- standards established as performance targets or quotas (planned standards), to which actual performance in the current period of time can be compared;

- standards used and achieved by the same organization in the past (in order to show trends in performance improvement or deterioration).

(C) Structure of the needs

In applying the approaches described above, it is useful to be able to refer to clear and generally acceptable ways of structuring the training and development needs. This helps to avoid confusion in what is meant by needs, and endless debates on the differences between performance and competence, and so on. In particular, it is useful to differentiate between the levels of organizational performance, individual behaviour and performance, and competence. This is consistent with the postulate that training must be performance and results oriented.

Organizational performance

Training needs can and should if possible be expressed in terms of required changes in organizational performance levels, bearing in mind that other factors may have to be identified, and tackled, in addition to training needs *per se.* The trainer's task is to identify the difference between existing and desired performance, and determine whether and how this difference can be reduced by training. This mental approach applies also if the purpose is to prepare managers for future opportunities and future performances rather than merely trying to redress insufficient past and current performance.

Individual behaviour and performance

The next level is that of managerial behaviour taken in the broadest sense of the term, beyond interpersonal relations and communication. Managers affect organizational performance by the achievement of certain performance levels as individuals, which also includes helping and motivating others to improve their individual performances. This requires changes in behaviour, which can be in any area of the manager's activity, style and interpersonal relations. They can be either strictly technical, or behavioural, or both. For example, a manager starts consulting direct collaborators on significant and not trivial issues. This is a change in behaviour which may result in better utilization of collective experience and wisdom, and may contribute to better organizational performance. Some educators regard changes in individual behaviour and in the resulting individual performance as the best way of describing training needs and objectives. However, we already know that in judging managers it may be difficult if not impossible to separate individual performance from the performance of the given organizational unit.

Competence

This brings us to individual competence. The concept and structure of competence, as well as typical managerial competences, were described in Chapter 1, sections 3 and 4 in sufficient detail. We know that at the competence level, training needs are usually defined as a difference between existing and required competences, which may be in the knowledge, traits and attitudes, or skills areas. We have seen that the spectrum of managerial competences is extremely broad and that competences can be grouped and categorized in many different ways. Competence models and standards are in use in some countries and organizations, but many trainers prefer to use their own classifications and checklists in determining training needs.

It is useful to see that different training and development contexts will require different approaches. In preparing standard and open training programmes, preparatory work will focus on a wider range of competence problems and gaps common to groups of managers who constitute the target population. There will be a distinct and structured needs-assessment phase, which under normal circumstances will precede and direct the course design that will follow. Conversely, in individualized ad hoc training aimed to solve a distinct performance problem, a different approach will be preferable. The focus will be on selected competences of individuals or small groups. For example, in an action-learning programme, individual and group needs will be defined in connection with new tasks that are to be tackled, and met virtually immediately. This improvement in competence should be reflected in immediate change as regards action and behaviour, and in resulting better performance. The same cycle may be repeated many times as the project proceeds.

(D)   The management structure and career dimensions

Managerial jobs are part of a management system and it is important to keep this in mind when describing performance, behaviour, competence and training needs of individual managers. For example, in most medium-sized to large business organizations we could normally find three basic echelons of the management structure: lower, middle and higher management.

In addition to vertical there is normally some horizontal structuring resulting in specialization by functions, sectors, divisions, products, and the like. While the person at the top level of the organization would be responsible for total management, i.e. for all functions and aspects, those assisting the top manager in a large enterprise as deputies or vice-presidents would normally specialize in areas such as finance, marketing, research and development, production, human resources, and so on. As we move down the hierarchy, this specialization of managerial positions tends to be even more pronounced. The scope of competence and the nature of training needs are different at each echelon of the hierarchy, as shown in figure 6.2.

Figure 6.2.   Competence structure at various levels of management heirarchy

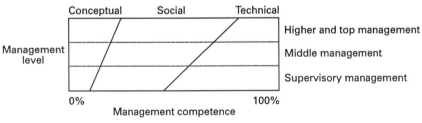

Source: Kubr and Prokopenko, 1989, p. 28.

It is therefore necessary to find out how a particular organization describes the work content, responsibility and competence required for the various positions at each echelon of the hierarchy. Such a description may be available from documentation (statutes, mission statements, organization manuals and charts, internal instructions, job descriptions), or we may find that it does not exist or is incomplete. In the latter case it may be appropriate to analyse the organization's mission and objectives and bring its documentation up to date, which is the development need in itself.

As for managerial career training needs, these should be related not only to the manager's role in the structure, but also to the specific pattern of his or her managerial career. Thus, the assessment of training needs will keep in mind, as much as possible, the manager's future career prospects. Career planning therefore becomes one of the essential techniques for individual needs assessment.

Needs at different levels

The assessment of management training and development needs can be undertaken at different levels of generalization. This distinction is important since different levels require different methodological and organizational approaches in the needs assessment.

- *Individual level*. This is the starting-point and basic building-block of any needs assessment. Every manager has unique needs owing to the particular combination of his or her job profile, educational and cultural background, experience and personality. Emphasis on individual needs assessment makes it possible to have development programmes that are tailored to individual needs and aim at results that are visible and understandable to each individual concerned and for which he or she can feel responsible.

- *Group and team level*. To identify and meet needs, we also have to group managers for the following reasons: (i) while some of their needs are individual and unique, other needs are common; and (ii) as mentioned above, managers do not work as isolated individuals, but in groups and teams: this brings out needs that could not be identified in dealing with each individual separately. Also, needs that concern relations and interaction with other managers and workers often have to be treated through collective training and development.

- *Organization level*. This level is particularly important for relating management development and training needs to organizational systems, their problems, objectives and performance improvement programmes. In practice, most needs assessment exercises take place at the organization level and include the two previous levels as their components.

Present and future needs

Present (short-term, current) needs can be established by comparing the real present performance of managers with a standard that should be attained immediately or in a relatively short time. For example, performance may be substandard, and corrective measures are required as soon as possible to redress the situation. In another case, some change in the environment or in the organization itself may be occurring (e.g. computerized production control is being introduced) that requires virtually immediate training so that managers develop new competences in parallel and in accordance with this change.

Future (long-term) needs are linked with future projections and long-range objectives. The underlying idea is that the existing managerial population should not only be made more efficient in the short run but should also be prepared to face new situations likely to develop in the future.

Thus present and future needs should be indicated separately in diagnoses of training needs.

(E)   Qualitative and quantitative needs

The final dimension of needs concerns their qualitative and quantitative aspects. Qualitative needs reflect the content of managerial jobs and competence, and of the required changes. They define the main problem and/or functional areas (accounting, leadership, motivation, maintenance, etc.) and the sorts of additional knowledge and skill that have to be developed, or attitudinal and behavioural changes to be achieved, in identified areas. In other words, qualitative needs help to identify programme subjects or disciplines as well as objectives of qualitative change to be achieved through training and development interventions.

Quantitative needs do not exist independently of qualitative needs. They indicate how many managers have identical or similar qualitative needs, and what volume of developmental effort and what resources will be required to achieve a defined qualitative change. Thus the main indicators of quantitative needs are numbers of managerial posts, numbers of managers to be trained, developed and replaced, time allocated to training, the volume of training and development activities, and the human, material and financial resources required.

6.2 Results-oriented needs-assessment process

After discussing the most important elements and dimensions of the needs-assessment concept, we would like to consider the needs-assessment process and its main stages. Result-orientation of needs assessment means that we have to direct the whole assessment exercise to improve individual managers' performance and that of their unit or organization after the training programme. This approach has been extensively applied in so-called "performance-based" or "performance-oriented" training. However, performance-based training does little to prepare people for future jobs with more complex responsibilities.

This does not mean that the concept of results-oriented training and needs assessment will have to be abandoned. What is increasingly required is a broader conception of "results". However, "results" are, more and more, being thought of as embracing both immediate and future results. Future training needs (i.e. those related to future results) are receiving growing attention. They are related to expected or envisaged future changes in technology, new areas of business, new types of customer service, innovative ways of cooperating with foreign partners, and so on.

This approach is shown in a model form in figure 6.3. In this model, the starting-point (step 1) is to identify the existing (or potential) organizational problems (in productivity, profitability, quality, marketing, etc.), the degree of their urgency and the order of priority in which they will have to be tackled. Step 2 is to trace and identify the main causes and areas of the problems. Here we could identify causes such as lack of communication, discipline and poor morale, wrong or inefficient equipment and facilities, problems with excessively complex organizational design and cumbersome procedures, and so on.

At the same time we could identify precisely the main areas (technical, functional, geographic, etc.) where the problems arise. It could be the marketing department, assembly line, financial or planning department or a workshop.

Step 3 is building awareness and recognition of the problems and their causes and the areas affected by them. During this stage, it is important to identify precisely those managers at different levels and in different parts of the organization who "have created" these problems or tolerated their existence in some way. This step enables us to avoid total analysis of the training needs of all the management teams in an organization, and to concentrate only on those individuals who are the sources of the problems

When the problem areas and the particular managers responsible for them have been identified, step 4 is to analyse each job (including the job requirements and the actual behaviour of the job holder) and compare it with the performance standards and the results of performance appraisals (step 5). The results of this comparison will show the gap between performance standards and actual achievements, expressed in terms of missing competence, which in turn will have to be broken down into specific skills, knowledge, attitudes and managerial behaviour, as well as other organizational factors and forces that co-determine managerial behaviour and effectiveness (step 6).

This analytical exercise will be pursued in step 7 by separating non-training needs from training needs and suggesting the required non-training solutions (interventions) in addition to training solutions.

The assessment of training needs has thus been completed. In step 8, the conclusions reached are translated into specific objectives and programmes for training and actions.

To go through the whole process of management training-needs assessment, one ought to possess certain methods and techniques, which could now number well over 50. It is impossible to describe in detail all these methods and techniques, and not even necessary since there are many publications on them. However, what is more important is to help the management development professionals to orient themselves in this jungle of techniques. For this purpose we suggest breaking them down into two major groups — generic approaches and techniques for needs assessment.

Figure 6.3. Model of results-oriented needs assessment

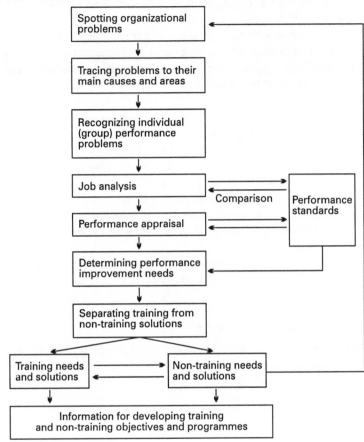

Source: Kubr and Prokopenko, 1989, p. 45.

6.3 Generic approaches to needs assessment

Under generic approaches to needs assessment, the most important ones will be discussed below. These are:

- problem identification and analysis;
- comparison; and
- expert opinion.

(A) Problem identification and analysis

First of all, any training and development need can be regarded as a management or organizational problem, and needs assessment as problem identification. A training need is a problem in its own right, which has its own characteristics, causes and solutions. In addition, it is often part of a wider and more complex personnel or organizational problem, and may be interwoven with other problems, more or less complex and significant.

How is a problem defined? A problem is normally defined as a difference or discrepancy between what is (or will be) actually happening and what should (or might) be happening. A problem can also be an uncertain or disturbed situation. Any problem can be identified by the following five principal dimensions or characteristics (Kubr, 1996):

(1) *substance or identity:* low performance, growing costs, shortage of competent staff, lack of new ideas, etc.;

(2) *location:* divisions, departments, plants, buildings, offices, etc.;

(3) *problem "ownership"* (people affected by the existence of the problem and primarily interested in resolving it): managers, staff, specialists, supervisors, workers, secretaries, the whole organization;

(4) *magnitude* (in absolute and relative terms): importance of the problem to the unit and whole organization, e.g. in terms of waste, idle capacity, money lost, potential savings, etc.;

(5) *time perspective:* since when has the problem existed? When was it first observed? Has it been recurrent? Has it been growing, diminishing or stabilizing, etc.?

Steps in problem-solving

The process of problem-solving can be broken down into several steps:

- creating awareness;
- defining and describing the problem;
- finding and analysing facts;
- establishing and verifying real causes;
- developing alternative solutions;
- choosing the optimum solution; and
- implementing the solution chosen.

A short description of these steps is given below.

Creating awareness. The process starts with the realization that something is going wrong, or not as planned or expected, or not as well as in other organizations. This may be only a feeling, or a finding based on hard data measuring profitability, productivity, quality, market position, deviations from long-term objectives, etc. For example, a high (or increasing) personnel turnover (the ratio of staff leaving in relation to the total number of personnel in the organization) might be an indicator of poor employee morale, as well as involving increased costs of recruiting new personnel. The failure to achieve the long-term organizational objectives could be identified through a strategic audit, which includes a systematic examination and appraisal of how an organization fits into its environment and opportunities. For this purpose, such measurement tools as ratio and variance analysis can be used.

Defining and describing the problem. In this step the symptoms and signals indicative of potential problems are reworded into specific and precise statements of deviations that name the object, the kind of malfunction whose cause is to be discovered and explained, or the conditions and people who have created and are sustaining the problem. The objective is to go beneath the symptoms and identify the "real" problems.

Finding and analysing facts. The main purpose of this phase is to gather and analyse necessary facts in order to solve the problem. This includes the definition of data content, degree of detail, time reference, extent of coverage, and criteria for classification and tabulation. There are three main sources of facts:

- records (files, reports, publications, computer files, etc.);
- events and conditions (actions and processes to be observed); and
- memory (information stored in the minds of people).

The following techniques are widely used for collecting data needed for problem-solving: retrieval of recorded data or special recording; observation; interviews; questionnaires; data-gathering meetings and workshops; attitude surveys; document gathering; charting; estimates; corporate audit, etc. Analysis of facts and data aims to describe a problem correctly, identifying its nature, events and causes, and establishing how to develop solutions and solve the problem. It helps also to identify relationships, proportions and trends. For this purpose a variety of statistical techniques can be used, including averages, dispersion, frequency distribution, correlation and regression, etc.

Establishing and verifying real causes. An important feature of fact and data analysis is causal analysis, which aims to discover causal relationships between conditions and events. When the causes of certain situations or problems are known, action can focus on these causes to influence them. To analyse the causes, it is essential to proceed systematically by examining whether a hypothetical cause could really have created the problem effect observed. The principal task is to identify the forces and factors which are causing the problem.

The exercise starts with some preliminary knowledge or assumptions on what the causes might be. It is useful to formulate several hypotheses about possible causes, and to keep an open mind when investigating the alternatives. Verification aims to prove that a likely cause did produce the observed effect.

Developing alternative solutions. After the necessary facts, causes and problem statements are verified, it is time to start to work on developing solutions. This phase aims at developing and selecting the effective solution to the problem, as well as a plan for implementing the solution. The effective solution is the one which has sufficient technical quality to resolve the problem, and has the best chance of being accepted and supported by those who are to implement it; acceptance here means readiness to invest time and energy with sufficient confidence of success. The solution should meet the criteria of efficiency, adaptability, cost, time and reliability.

Choosing the optimum solution. Once alternative solutions have been developed and refined, they should be evaluated to determine the preferred solution. It is important to start this process with a preliminary evaluation, to reduce the number of alternatives on which a more comprehensive evaluation will be made. Each alternative solution should be evaluated against all the other solutions, using the same criteria. In this way it is easy to eliminate those that do not promise the desired improvement. When analysing the alternatives, economic, operational, technical, scheduling and legal criteria, among others, should be borne in mind. Other factors to consider include organizational culture, attitudes, traditions, values and so forth, of the workers, managers and customers who will be affected by the implementation of the solution.

Implementing the solution. During implementation, unexpected new problems may be uncovered and the "optimum" solution originally envisaged may need adjustment to new conditions. A creative and open-minded approach to implementation is therefore necessary. However, the development of a plan for implementation and gaining and commitment of those participating in implementation are of crucial importance. The plan for implementing the desired solution could be made an important consideration when establishing training objectives and identifying non-training interventions.

(B) Comparison

Comparison is inherent in the very concept of training and development needs. When dealing with needs, we are constantly comparing at least two — but often more — different conditions. Therefore, comparison is extensively used in needs-assessment techniques, as indeed in any other problem identification and diagnosis. When training and development needs are diagnosed, factors and conditions affecting competence and its applications are being compared in addition to, and in parallel with, competence and performance.

The simplest case of comparison is one where there is an accepted standard against which current competence and/or performance can be assessed. It may be a job description, a competence profile, a technical performance standard, or an output and performance plan of a unit or a whole organization. It is useful to look for these standards in preparing for training-needs assessment and to make wide use of them in order to enhance the objectivity of the exercise.

The use of future-oriented models of managerial competence is quite popular in management education and training circles. By comparing the profiles of current managers with expected future profiles, it is possible to get some ideas on the sort of training and development that will be required. For example, such an exercise would be used for revising training policies, reorienting training programmes and institutions, and providing managers with an idea of what they may expect in the future.

In assessing both current and future needs, the achievements and practices of enterprises in other countries are often used as references. For example, a leading and innovative international firm may be used as a standard, or a particular feature of Japanese management (e.g. quality management) or the management of Japanese firms as a whole may be used as a benchmark for comparison. An enterprise in a less developed country may be interested in achievements of comparable enterprises operating in relatively more advanced developing countries.

An important issue in making comparisons and evaluating the intensity or span of any management development or training problem is the measurement of skills, knowledge, attitudes, behaviour and so on. This can be done with the help of varying rating techniques, which is a universal tool for quantitative measurement and comparison under any kind of needs-assessment method.

(C)   Expert opinion

In diagnosing management training and development needs, we are constantly faced with the question of whether and how to use "hard" data (precisely defined, identified by scientific techniques and quantified), or "soft" data (opinions, impressions, feelings, predictions of what "should have been achieved" or "might happen" or "might be required" in the future). The possibility of basing all needs assessment on hard data is limited by the nature of the needs.

The choices involved in such an exercise are not possible without expert opinion (judgement). By definition, such expert opinion will be subjective, and will be based on both rational and intuitive mental processes.

The more complex and uncertain the management setting within which the training and development needs are being diagnosed, the greater will be the role of expert opinion. Typically, studies of future training and development needs will use expert opinion as their principal tool for examining future trends and identifying the most likely, but not certain, implications for management education, training and development.

The expert opinion can be tapped and used through various needs-assessment techniques. They range from simple interviewing of one or more experts, and collective consultations and task groups, to research studies using the Delphi technique, whereby a number of experts are questioned through an iterative process of gradual reviews and approximations. In using these techniques, analysts should always ask themselves whether they are identifying facts or opinions, whose opinions they are, and what their basis is (scientific knowledge, practical management experience, a biased or unbiased view of the business reality, conservative assessment of trends or wishful thinking, etc.).

Consulting a small number of selected experts may be a useful preparatory step in planning and structuring a needs analysis, and when an analyst is to prepare a survey of needs in an environment which is new to him or her. The key informants should be carefully chosen individuals who are knowledgeable about current and emerging trends in the given sector, concerning questions such as supply and shortages of particular skill categories, changes in demand for particular skills, changes in the nature of skills and resulting changes in training requirements.

The choice of the experts who should be able to give meaningful advice and to be consulted is infinitely more important than the choice of the techniques to be used for tapping expertise. There could be four major categories of experienced managers and specialists in which likely experts could be looked for. First, there are the managers who constitute the target population, that is, those whose needs are being diagnosed. Technically they have the most appropriate practical experience and knowledge of the facts, and are well placed to judge the context in which they operate. More importantly, they are emotionally involved in the situation under scrutiny and will expect their expert opinion to be sought, in addition to facts indicative of the presence or absence of certain competences. Thus, managers in this group will play a double role as the objects and subjects of the needs assessment, or, in other terms, as those who are being assessed and those who are making the assessment.

Secondly, there are managers from outside the target population who are close enough to be of help. For example, higher management could be interviewed for an expert opinion on the training of lower-level managers and supervisors. Managers in client enterprises could also provide useful information on the training needs of their suppliers.

Thirdly, the managers' expert opinion will have to be tapped in broader (sectoral, national, etc.) forward-looking studies and surveys of needs. Finally, professional experts — management trainers, teachers and consultants, accountants, economists, sociologists, lawyers, political scientists, development planners and other professionals — are another major source of expertise in assessing needs.

Managers have been the clients of trainers and management consultants as course participants or users of consulting services, or else these professionals have done research and gathered experience on various aspects of the environment in which managers operate, and on management functions, methods and processes.

6.4 Tools and techniques for needs assessment

Since it is impossible to discuss in detail all commonly used assessment tools and techniques in the scope of this chapter, we will provide just a brief review indicating some important sources for those who would like to get more information. First, it would be useful to classify these techniques into three major categories based on the target group:

- individual needs assessment;
- group needs assessment; and
- organizational needs assessment.

This is important since it enables the most efficient assessment techniques to be selected for each target group.

(A) Individual needs-assessment techniques

Job analysis and job descriptions, although not strictly speaking techniques for needs assessment, should be mentioned as an important tool for defining the scope, content and qualification requirements of management jobs. They serve as the "basic building blocks" in needs assessment and may be used in conjunction with several other techniques.

If job analysis is the process of assembling, recording and interpreting information relating to essential characteristics of individual jobs in order to uncover the nature of tasks, working conditions, responsibilities and skills requested, then a job description is the end-product of job analysis and summarizes the essential information (job elements, responsibilities, skills, etc.) in simple descriptive language and uniform phraseology to facilitate comparison of different jobs. A *competence model*, for example, is a variant of a job description that describes the key capabilities required to perform a job. Competence models of managerial positions typically focus on elements of managerial behaviour and the underlying behavioural skills.

Texts and examinations are a means of observing and describing how an individual performed in a specific controlled situation. The test sets the verbal or numerical tasks that are used to refer to different kinds of information about the person who takes the test. It is one of the simplest and most direct methods of assessing training needs by asking specific questions and evaluation answers. Tests could include "question and answer" tests, objective oral tests, essay tests, performance tests, in-tray (in-basket) exercises, psychological tests and the like (Kubr and Prokopenko, 1989).

Questionnaires ask the respondent to supply written information related to his or her job and training needs. Usually, a manager is asked to complete the questionnaire alone; however, the immediate supervisor may sometimes be asked to assist or to verify the responses. There are closed-form and open-ended questionnaires.

The first type provides a list of items to be ticked, alternative answers to be selected, and blanks to be filled in. It could also have a scaled structure or require "yes/no" responses. The second type (open-ended) offers an opportunity to give a more complete and comprehensive picture of a situation. It encourages managers to go beyond the factual material and data, and to convey their attitudes, feelings, opinions and ideas.

Interviewing, a universal and powerful fact-finding technique, is used for many different purposes and in many different ways. Interviewing is undoubtedly the principal technique used in diagnosing management development needs; it may be used alone or in combination with other techniques.

The purpose of interviews is to gather relevant information in face-to-face contacts. This information may concern events, work results, knowledge, behaviour, attitudes, opinions, values, habits, perceptions, and so on. A properly prepared and conducted interview produces a considerable amount of information on numerous problems in addition to training and development needs. Unlike the average conversation, the interview focuses upon a specific subject that is relevant to a specific situation. Sometimes it is the only feasible method of getting the necessary data. However, in most cases the interview is used in combination with other needs-identification techniques. For example, interviews often supplement survey question-naires.

Observation is very useful, because many training and development problems become apparent only through systematic and careful observation of work and management processes, i.e. what is actually happening in the organization. For example, observing a regular management meeting, watching a manager dealing with people or problems, or observing a manager full-time for a working day — all these are sources of invaluable information on organizational and management problems, and — possibly — on related training needs.

Observation techniques are particularly useful for analysing managerial behaviour and working (rather than organizational and administrative) relationships between individuals and teams in the same unit, as well as among various units within the organization. It is possible to obtain qualitative information (what is actually happening and what positions and attitudes prevail in various situations), as well as quantitative information (e.g. frequency of particular contacts or relative importance of collaborative relationships), that lends itself readily to various analyses.

Critical incidents are those particular and distinct events in the life of the organization that are different from the ordinary daily routine. It is assumed that in facing and handling these events, managers will supply and demonstrate certain skills, or will be unable to take appropriate action since they are ill-prepared for such a situation. When this technique is used, managers are asked to recollect and describe particularly difficult situations and problems they have had to face within, say the last four to six weeks and then to discuss and analyse how they handled them.

The diary method is a variant of the previous two, i.e. of observing and critical incidents. In this case it is the manager who records activities under various headings. The coverage can be exhaustive (a complete range of activities over a given period of time), selective (certain preselected sorts of activities are recorded, e.g. activities lasting more than 30 minutes) or be confined to events regarded as critical incidents.

Management by objectives (MBO), in addition to its use as a management technique, can also be used to identify management development and training needs. In this system, a set of objectives is assigned to a unit or individual for a given period (for example, six or 12 months). This assignment is based on joint assessment and consultation on what could and should be achieved; thus the method is participative. The objectives focus on six to ten key results to be achieved. These are "milestones", or specific "achievables" or "deliverables", rather than levels of standard effective-ness that will be acceptable on a continuing basis.

Self-assessment is a conceptual approach to needs assessment rather than a technique. Professional managers who enjoy their job and have a developed sense of responsibility continuously assess themselves without being invited to do so. They may also take corrective action, learn new methods and change their behaviour, without passing through any explicit exercise of needs assessment or attending a course.

In managerial practice it is essential that people have a maximum of self-insight and self-understanding, including insight into reactions to problem situations and to their own strengths and weaknesses. Self-insight is normally achieved through systematic self-study in a variety of situations, and by being alert to signals that may indicate problems in an individual manager's behaviour and performance. Various techniques, such as the critical incidents and the diary method can help the manager in self-assessment (Brearley and Sewell, 1990).

Career planning aims at matching individual potential for promotion and individual aspirations with organizational needs and opportunities. Its principal product, an individual career plan, suggests a career path that is both feasible and desirable from the individual's and the organization's point of view, as well as conditions to be met in pursuing this path.

Further training and development has a prominent place among these conditions. In particular, career planning indicates what training and development would be necessary for career advancement (promotion to a higher-level position), altering the career path (transfer to another type of work), or staying in the current position (no transfer, but broadening the scope of the function).

Assessment centres use a basic approach exposing the manager to a range of exercises, tests, simulated situations, and so on, in a structured environment within the centre for a few days. These exercises are designed to provoke behaviour that is relevant to skills critical for success in a target job. The individual's reactions are watched by competent observers with practical management experience and evaluated in terms of the individual's managerial potential and/or training and development needs. As a rule, assessment centres are used for early identification of high-potential ("fast-track") talents; assessing an individual's experience, diagnosing strengths and weaknesses and suggesting a tailor-made training and development programme; encouraging self-development and stimulating interest in training by providing direct feedback to the person being assessed.

Assessment centres use a combination of techniques such as in-depth interviews, in-basket exercises, role-playing, management games, individual and peer evaluation, group evaluation, group discussion, work group exercises, fact-finding and problem-solving, questionnaires, tests and analysis of educational records.

Action learning is both a practical problem-solving method and a management development method. A manager who engages in an action-learning exercise works at the diagnosis and solution of a real organizational problem. As a rule, this would be an "open-ended" problem, i.e. one which does not have a single straightforward solution but can be approached and solved in various ways and whose solution requires considerable judgement and "people skills", in addition to the application of management techniques.

The contribution to needs assessment can be considerable and straightforward. The process of action learning identifies training needs at all its stages. First, these can be the needs of the individual undertaking the project — new information, knowledge or skills, that are required in order to pursue the project successfully. In action learning, these needs are not recorded for later action, but are immediately met in the course of the project. This provides the opportunity for immediate application and feedback, and for correcting and supplementing the training provided if necessary. Second, action learning also generates information on those training needs of the client which become apparent in working on the project, or are defined as conditions of implementing the proposed solutions.

Performance appraisal is the process of evaluating the manager's effectiveness against predetermined, job-related performance standards or objectives usually set by job descriptions or other specific requirements (e.g. business plans). It aims to determine the relationship between the individual effort and results, as well as between individual results and the attainment of organizational (enterprise, plant, unit) objectives. Performance appraisal aims to evaluate all factors together in order to distinguish what a particular manager has contributed as an individual. However, the focus on organizational performance as the principal criterion or basis for assessing individual managers' performance has always to be very strong in order to stress the ultimate purpose of the manager's total endeavour, including efforts in training and self-development.

(B)   Techniques for assessing group needs

Group techniques are used to: (i) identify those training and development needs that reveal themselves best, or only, when individuals are at work, communicate and interact in a team; (ii) find out about needs that are common to the members of the group; and (iii) obtain the group's collective opinion and consensus on what the needs are and in what order of priority they should be met. An overview of some of the commonly used techniques to assess group management training needs is given below. It should be noted, however, that some techniques listed as individual techniques can also be applied to groups (like action learning).

Meetings of management teams bring together the most natural and logical groups for assessing training and development needs. These are more or less permanent groups of people who have developed certain characteristic patterns in working together on a variety of topics over a fairly long period. Typically, they include the top management team (e.g. the president, general manager or director-general, with deputies and main functional or division directors), functional management teams (a functional vice-president with specialist managers, etc.), and middle- and lower-level management teams.

Observation of the meeting process reveals such information as who plays what role, who is listened to, who does not listen, who normally disagrees with whom, whose views are ignored by the group, and who has the main impact on the final outcome and why. It also becomes evident whether the meeting serves for collective diagnosis and synthesis, or is used merely to formally endorse conclusions already reached by someone before the meeting.

Group meetings and discussions of various sizes and composition are a very common communication and management tool in any type of organization. The assessment of training needs can be a by-product of group work organized for another purpose (e.g. for consulting the group on changes in production scheduling and stock control). Alternatively, a group can gather specifically to discuss training and development needs. As in the previous case, the assessment of training and development needs can focus on technical aspects, on group dynamics involving mainly behavioural issues, or both.

Syndicates are small groups (of about ten people), whose members come from various organizations and represent various areas of expertise. Their purpose is to serve as a tool for collectively exploring various possible solutions to management and business problems, and learning from other members' experience. Often syndicates are established within the framework of a management training programme or conference to deal with specific problems which may have been identified by the managers themselves, or assigned to the syndicates by the course director for learning purposes. Syndicates can be quite useful for examining training and development needs by groups of managers who can contribute various experiences, insights and approaches.

Training problems can be presented to the syndicates as an issue on which they should work, or they can deal with training issues in connection with other, "non-training" problems. As in the previous cases, observing syndicates at work, and assessing the quality of their "product", provides training professionals with information on the participants' training and development needs.

Group projects like group meetings, can serve a wide range of purposes. In business practice, the following two tend to prevail: (i) a temporary group is established on a part-time basis, with the agreement and support of senior management (a senior member of the management team may be the group leader and various managers can be group members) to deal with a significant organizational problem; (ii) a group is established with the combined objective of working on a practical problem and of learning specific skills in the course of this process (a group form of action learning). In both cases, the task is distinct, important and complex enough to be defined as a project. The group will have to work at it as a collective, over a period of time.

In the course of the project, the group itself can gradually define, and redefine, its own or other managers' and staff members' training needs, and the interventions required for progressing with the project and putting its results fully into effect. If an action-learning objective is pursued simultaneously, the information on training needs uncovered would be handled in a similar way as in individual action learning.

Group creativity techniques use creative thinking to relate things or ideas which were previously unrelated. The basic philosophy of creative thinking is to suspend the normal logical process of looking for solutions and to concentrate in the early stages on looking at alternatives. This approach is particularly relevant to those management problems which have a number of potential solutions but no specifically right answers. These techniques could be useful for assessing training and development needs.

Simulations can be used not only for training itself but as a tool for identification of management training and development needs. Even when these methods are not used intentionally for this purpose, an attentive trainer can nevertheless derive valuable information on many aspects of management skills, knowledge, attitudes and shortcomings in a situation that is close to actual practice. Alternatively, an observer may be present during the training sessions to collect and evaluate this information.

Among the simulation methods, role-playing is perhaps the method that is most appropriate for identifying training needs. In a role-play, participants assume an identity other than their own, and try to cope with real or hypothetical problems, mostly in human relations, personnel or communications. Playing their roles, managers try to behave in a way they believe characteristic of these roles and specific situations. Role-playing allows a player to simulate reality, make and detect mistakes, try out alternative responses, and so on.

Business games are another simulation technique which could be used not only for management development, but training-needs assessment as well. In this technique participants are grouped in teams, consider a sequence of steps in dealing with problems, make decisions and receive feedback which reflects the action taken by the opposite team. It is a form of sequential decision-making exercise structured around a hypothetical model of an organization simulation in which participants assume roles as managers of the operations involved.

The case method simulates the analytical and synthetic work involved in preparing and proposing solutions to business problems. Since many case-studies are usually very close to real life (most of them describe actual business events), the trainer (or a separate instructor charged with observing) can detect gaps in knowledge and experience that prevent participants from viewing the problems from the correct angle (i.e. proceeding methodically from facts to solutions, and making full use of information and opinions contributed by others).

Behaviour modelling and analysis aims to modify the organizational behaviour of managers by increasing their behavioural repertoire. This can be done by providing them with information on alternative and more effective forms of behaviour relevant to their jobs. The technique can be applied both to individuals and to teams or groups of managers. Observation and analysis of different behaviour during this exercise could provide a lot of useful information for training needs assessment.

(C)   Techniques for assessing organizational needs

The techniques reviewed below tend to take a broad view of the organization, or its major parts and its problems. The focus is on facts and problems affecting business strategy and performance, relations with the environment, corporate culture, management systems and processes, and management style. A common advantage of these techniques is that they relate the assessment of training needs to wider organizational concerns, although there are differences in the method and degree of establishing this relationship. Therefore they are well suited to identifying both training and non-training needs, and the relationship between these two types of needs. Again, as in previous cases, some of these techniques could be also used for assessing individual and group level needs.

Analysis of records and reports taps this prolific source of information, which should exist in any organization. An obvious source related to training needs is personnel and staff development documentation, covering issues such as personal files, application forms, past performance evaluation records, requests for transfer, promotions, disciplinary measures, demotions, labour disputes, complaints and grievances, terminations, exit interviews, sick leave, overtime, training reports, and so forth.

Records and reports related to activities and performance globally (financial statements, operating performance reports, documents on quality issues) and by specific technical functions or processes (production, research and development, marketing, finance) can be equally significant. Thorough and consistent collection and examination of organizational records and reports is therefore an essential, and universal, technique of needs assessment.

Analysis of future trends and opportunities is very important when assessing management training and development needs, which is itself an essentially future-oriented activity. Even in dealing with short-term needs which require virtually immediate action, it is important to know enough about trends — for example, to avoid spending money on an activity or product that will have to be phased out. As regards future needs, they can be considered only in the light of trends and opportunities at the level of the organization, the sector, the whole national economy, global markets, new telecommunication technologies, and the like.

An environmental analysis should be the first step in any analysis of future trends and opportunities. The main questions to be asked are: What are our future development prospects? What should be our future strategies? What new skills will be required so that we can cope with future problems and opportunities? What current skill gaps could jeopardize our market position and chances in the future? What skills will no longer be needed? What roles will training and development have to play in the future and what will be the resource implications?

Inter-firm comparison is a variant of the universal comparison technique discussed earlier. It reveals how a firm's performance compares with that of other similar organizations. Further analysis can discover and explain the reasons for differences in performance, and suggest action needed for improvement. Comparison techniques can refer to examples, models and standards in other organizations, sectors and even countries.

Inter-firm comparison usually starts by examining global indicators of performance such as profitability, return on investment, turnover, cost of sales or productivity. These ratios are then broken down and supplemented by a number of operating ratios, indicative of more specific and detailed relationships in the use of resources, including human potential. This information could provide excellent data to formulate management training and development needs, particularly for top managers.

Benchmarking has emerged recently as a method whereby companies focus on key improvement areas, identify and study best practices by others in these areas, and implement new processes and systems to enhance their own productivity and quality. Pioneered by the Xerox Company in the late 1970s, benchmarking is currently practised in many different ways. A benchmarking exercise may determine that differences in performances are affected by differences in competence, and may thus reveal training needs that ought to be met in order to attain the new performance target. This approach to training-needs identification is very selective and strongly action-oriented.

A management (diagnostic) survey is a fact-finding and analytical exercise whose main purpose is to provide an overall picture of the organization's performance and effectiveness, strengths and weaknesses, development potential and possible improvements. There are two principal types of management (diagnostic) survey. The first is carried out by management consultants in preparing specific consulting projects. It is relatively short (one to four days, or five to ten days if a more complex assignment is being prepared) and is completed by a diagnostic report, or a proposal to the client to undertake a consulting project. The second type of survey is a detailed in-depth study that is usually carried out in preparation for important decisions on the future of the business. The consultant's mandate is to help the client to prepare correct decisions and to act as an objective and neutral expert who gives a professional opinion on the health, strengths, weaknesses and prospects of the business.

Management surveys provide good orientation and an introduction to an assessment of training and development needs, by identifying the main problem areas where corrective action is required. They also make suggestions on the orientation of further diagnostic and problem-solving efforts.

A management or human resource development audit is a fact-finding and evaluation exercise which provides a comprehensive picture of management development within an organization. Normally the audit starts by identifying official management development policy (e.g. by reviewing policy documents and interviewing top management). Questionnaires are then issued to a representative sample of managers throughout the organization to reveal (a) what happens in practice as opposed to plans, (b) what the managers' evaluation is of the effectiveness of existing programmes, and (c) what changes they would like to see introduced. The central issues examined involve training and development, staff appraisal and career development.

Attitude surveys, the main purpose of which is to determine the opinions and feelings of large groups of individuals in respect of an issue or set of issues, can lead to a better understanding of the causes of different problems, anticipate undesired events, identify some management development and training needs, and generally improve the quality of the decision-making process and management style. Attitude surveys are more often used to identify probable causes of dissatisfaction, such as inadequate supervision, wrongly focused wage policy and administration, interpersonal clashes, uninteresting work, and so on.

The management climate survey is a technique that aims at measuring how people view and react to the organization's culture, values and norms, and other aspects of the organization's health. Normally, people behave in accordance with their understanding of these norms and values. Their perceptions affect the management team's performance, as well as the individuals' motivation and, as a result, organizational effectiveness. Thus, any discrepancies between real and perceived organizational norms and values among managers and employees could be considered as important pieces of information on existing management development and training needs.

Organization development has been defined in many different ways. The most common and constructive one defines OD as a planned activity or organization-wide effort managed from the top, and directed to increase organizational effectiveness and health through interventions in the organization's processes using knowledge and techniques from the behavioural sciences. OD aims to help members of an organization to interact more effectively in pursuit of organizational goals. It is intentionally based on an awareness of human behaviour and organizational dynamics, provides for harmonizing individual and organization goals, and promotes participative management. Indeed, much of an organization's inefficiency can usually be traced to employees' lack of interest in, or even hostility to, the organization.

One of the important stages of OD is a diagnosis and evaluation of the change process, which could supply interesting and practical information on present and future organizational and management weaknesses, problems and further management training and development needs.

Re-engineering, restructuring and performance improvement programmes also exist in many variants and their detailed description would be beyond the scope of this guide. The reader may refer to special publications and documentation of consulting firms. These programmes have always paid some attention to human resources and the necessity to identify and meet training needs in order to restructure a company, re-engineer its major processes, or achieve the targets set in a performance-improvement programme. However, in many cases this programme element has been assigned secondary importance. In the current period we are witnessing a major change. Management and human resource development is increasingly regarded and treated as a key area of organizational performance improvement. A common feature of these diverse programmes is the growing attention paid to a precise and focused (though not narrow) identification of training and development needs, and to measures whereby these needs can be met within the given programme of extensive organizational change. As a rule, a range of needs-assessment techniques described in the previous paragraphs would be applied in such cases.

6.5 How to select and use needs-assessment techniques

As we have stressed above, to be effective several techniques have to be combined in most cases, and it would be risky to draw conclusions from information collected and analysed through only one technique. To facilitate the choice of techniques appropriate to different situations, it is useful to classify (or categorize) by several criteria. As no formally agreed categorization is available, we present below tables 6.1 and 6.2 in which certain criteria are applied to all techniques covered, thus pointing out some of their common features and differences. We also suggest some important dimensions which should be taken into consideration in selecting needs-assessment techniques.

In table 6.2, the tecnniques are assessed from the viewpoint of their suitability for finding out about:

(1)   knowledge;
(2)   skills;
(3)   attitudes;
(4)   managerial behaviour.

Needs-assessment cycle

Table 6.1 shows how the various needs-assessment techniques are suitable for different elements of the assessment cycle such as:

● spotting organizational problems;

● tracing problem areas and causes;

● recognizing individual (or group) performance problems;

● determining management development needs; and

● separating training from non-training needs.

The nature of needs-assessment purposes and activities for each element of the cycle requires only those techniques which are best suited to these purposes. For example, among the best techniques to spot organizational problems — the very first step in results-oriented assessment of management development needs — are such techniques as reports and records analysis, inter-firm comparisons, creativity techniques (brainstorming), etc. Using this table, the management development practitioner could first select the best set of needs-assessment techniques for particular steps, and then choose among selected techniques those which are simpler to practise and which correspond better to specific purposes of needs analysis.

In using any of these checklists, and any general rating of techniques concerning their suitability for dealing with one or another dimension of the problem at hand, personal and organizational preferences will play an important role. In particular, the user has to feel comfortable with the technique — he or she must regard it as a

Table 6.1. Needs-assessment techniques: The needs-assessment cycle

Needs-assessment technique	Dimension of needs assessment				
	Spotting organizational problems	Tracing problem areas and causes	Recognizing individual (or group) performance problems	Determining management development needs	Separating training from non-training needs
	(1)	(2)	(3)	(4)	(5)
Generic approaches					
Problem analysis	XXX	XXX	XX	X	X
Comparison			X	XX	XX
Expert opinion	XXX	XX	XX	XXX	XXX
Individual techniques					
Job analysis			XXX	XXX	XX
Job description			XXX	XX	XX
Tests and examinations			X	XX	XXX
Questionnaires	X	X	XX	XXX	XX
Interviews	X	X	XX	XXX	XX
Observatios	X	XX	XX	XX	X
Critical incidents	XX	XX	XX	X	X
Diary method	X	XX	XX	X	XX
Management by objectives	XX	XX	XX	XX	X
Action learning	XXX	XXX	XX	XX	X
Performance appraisal			XXX	XXX	XX
Self-assessment			XX	XXX	XXX
Career planning			XX	XX	XXX
Assessment centre			X	XX	XXX
Group techniques					
Meetings of management teams	XX	XXX	XX	X	X
Group meetings and discussions	X	X	XX	X	X
Syndicates	XX	XX	XX	X	X
Nominal group technique	X	XXX	XX	X	
Group projects		XX	XX	XX	X
Group creativity techniques	XXX	XXX	XX	XX	X
Simulation training techniques	X	X	XXX	XX	XX
Case method		XX	XXX	X	
Behavior modelling (analysis)	XX	XX	XX	X	X
Organizational techniques					
Records and reports analysis	XXX	XX	XX	XX	X
Future trends and opportunities	XXX	X			
Inter-firm comparison	XX	XX	X		
Management (diagnostic) surveys	XX	XX	X	XX	
Management development audits			X	XXX	XX
Attitude surveys	XXX	X	XX		
Management climate surveys	XX	XXX	XX	XX	
Organization development	XXX	XXX	XX	XX	X
Structured performance improvement programmes	XXX	XXX	XX	XX	X

Key: X - good; XX - very good; XXX - excellent

Source: Kubr and Prokopenko, 1989, p. 296, and Prokopenko and North, 1996, p. A-25.

good and practical one, and be able to use it without difficulty. The clients (the managers whose needs are assessed) must not resent the technique (e.g. because it is too intrusive) or regard it as trivial and unproductive. Practical experience and common sense are your best advisers in choosing techniques.

Table 6.2. Needs-assessment techniques: Type of training and development needs

Needs-assessment technique	Dimension of needs assessment			
	Knowledge (1)	Skills (2)	Attitude (3)	Managerial behaviour (4)
Generic approaches				
Problem analysis	X	XX	XX	XXX
Comparison			XX	XX
Expert opinion	XXX	XXX	XX	XX
Individual techniques				
Job analysis	X	XX	X	
Job description	X	XX	X	
Tests and examinations	XXX	XXX	X	
Questionnaires	XX	XX	XXX	X
Interviews	XX	X	XXX	X
Observations		XX	XXX	XXX
Critical incidents	X	XX	XX	XX
Diary method	X	X	XX	XXX
Management by objectives	X	XX	X	
Action learning	X	XX	XX	XX
Performance appraisal	XXX	XXX	X	XX
Self-assessment	XX	XX	XXX	XX
Career planning	X	XX	XX	X
Assessment centre	XX	XX	XX	X
Group techniques				
Meetings of management teams	X	XX	XX	X
Group meetings and discussions	X	X	XXX	X
Syndicates	X	XX	XX	X
Nominal group technique	X	XX	XX	
Group projects	X	XX	XX	XX
Group creativity techniques	XX	XXX	XXX	XX
Simulation training techniques	X	XXX	XX	X
Case method			XX	XXX
Behaviour modelling (analysis)			XXX	XXX
Organizational techniques				
Records and reports analysis		XXX	XX	XXX
Future trends and opportunities	XX	X	X	
Inter-firm comparison		XX		XX
Management (diagnostic) surveys		X	XX	X
Management development audits	XX	XXX	X	X
Attitude surveys			XXX	X
Management climate surveys		XX	XX	X
Organization development		XX	XXX	XX
Structured performance improvement programmes	X	XX	XX	XX

Key: X - good; XX - very good; XXX - excellent

Source: Kubr and Prokopenko, 1989, p. 297.

6.6 How to use rating techniques

As shown in box 6.1, there are two general classes of rating techniques used in needs assessment: comparative and absolute.

Box 6.1. Rating techniques

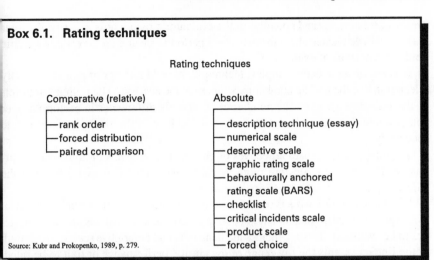

Rating techniques

Comparative (relative)	Absolute

Comparative (relative)
— rank order
— forced distribution
— paired comparison

Absolute
— description technique (essay)
— numerical scale
— descriptive scale
— graphic rating scale
— behaviourally anchored
   rating scale (BARS)
— checklist
— critical incidents scale
— product scale
— forced choice

Source: Kubr and Prokopenko, 1989, p. 279.

(A)   Comparative rating techniques

Comparative (or relative) techniques are used to compare the performance of two or more managers with one another.

The *rank order* (or ranking) technique involves the comparison of each member within a group, for example, from the highest to the lowest. This ranking can be improved by alternative ranking, when evaluators choose the top and bottom employees first, then select the next highest and next lowest, and move towards the middle.

Forced distribution begins by setting up categories from poor to good with the restriction that only a certain percentage of the managers concerned can be assigned to each category. This forces the rater to distribute the managers according to a pre-scaled scheme (or curve). A variation of the forced-distribution technique is the so-called equal-interval technique, which assumes that managers with similar abilities or traits can be placed in the same group. The point-allocation technique (PAT) is another alternative of forced distribution. Here each rater is given a number of points per manager in a group, and the total points for all managers actually rated must not exceed the number of points allocated to the rater. The points are allocated to a criterion (e.g. planning, decision-making authority).

Paired comparison makes the ranking easier and more reliable. Each manager is compared with all other managers in the group, and an explicit judgement is made as to who is a better performer according to a certain criterion.

(B)   Absolute rating techniques

These techniques assign absolute values to the characteristics or performance levels on a fixed scale without any reference or comparison to other people.

Description technique consists of a description, in writing, of a manager's strengths, weaknesses and potential in the evaluator's own words. Clearly, the rater must be knowledgeable about the manager's performance and an expert in a specific field (or criterion) of evaluation.

Numerical scale is the simplest technique. An odd number of points is usually selected so that the middle number may represent the average. The number of points on the scale depends upon the number of observable differences in performance or competence that are to be rated, and on the ability of the raters to discriminate accurately.

A *descriptive scale* uses adjectives or phrases to rate levels of ability or performance. Descriptive scales are more versatile than numerical scales because the adjectives or phrases can be varied to suit the situation.

The *graphic rating scale* is one of the oldest quantitative performance-appraisal techniques. It usually contains a number of job performance qualities and characteristics to be evaluated. It also combines the numerical and descriptive scales. The length of the line represents the full range of the ability, performance or trait to be rated. The analyst should consider both the numerical scale and the descriptive phrases.

A *Behaviourally Anchored Rating Scale* (BARS), sometimes called "Behavioural Expectation Scale" (BES), is based on the critical incident approach. Here the descriptions of actual good and bad performance, supported by incidents, are grouped into five to ten dimensions. An advantage of BARS is that it concentrates on the behaviour of the manager rather than his or her personality.

A *checklist* is a set of adjectives or descriptive statements. It is actually marked on a two-point rating scale — "yes" or "no". The rater marks the item with a tick only when the manager possesses the trait listed. A rating score from the checklist is given by the number of ticks (e.g. six positive checks out of ten possible).

An advanced variation of the checklist is a weighted checklist. This lists various types and levels of skills for a particular job or group of jobs. Weights are assigned to each item by a group of experts based on how significant the item is to successful performance. The rater indicates the extent to which each statement describes the manager being evaluated. The marks awarded and their corresponding weights are summed up for each manager.

A *critical incidents scale* is a sort of behaviourally oriented checklist. Critical requirements here include those which have been demonstrated to have made the difference between success and failure in carrying out an important part of the job assigned in a significant number of instances.

A *product scale* (or direct index) is used when a product (or other output) is to be rated as an indication of performance, since products are usually tangible and measurable things. The technique focuses attention on the specific accomplishment or results achieved by the manager. With this approach, managers are evaluated solely on the basis of the results actually achieved. For each managerial job, several measures of output of results are identified and combined to form a numerical index. It could be, for example, product output, sales volume, market share, productivity or profit.

Forced choice is a method of rating which uses two to five descriptions of behaviour in each section; both favourable and unfavourable statements may be used in the same section. The rater has to select the statement that is most characteristic and the one that is least characteristic. As a rule, this technique uses sets of four statements, known as tetrads, so constructed that each one contains two favourable and two unfavourable characteristics. Only one of the favourable statements in each tetrad will yield a point on the report if it is chosen as "most characteristic" of the person rated. Similarly, only one of the unfavourable statements will yield a point if it is selected as "least characteristic". In other words, although the favourable items in each pair appear equally favourable to the rater (and the unfavourable items equally favourable), only one item in each pair has been demonstrated to discriminate between good and poor performers.

(C) How to select rating techniques

The effective use of techniques depends not only upon the skills of the evaluator but also on the right choice of technique. Tables 6.3 and 6.4 can assist the practitioner in choosing the best set of rating techniques depending upon the tasks and the dimensions of needs analysis.

Table 6.3. Rating techniques: The needs-assessment cycle

Rating technique	Dimension of needs assessment				
	Spotting organizational problems	Tracing problem areas and causes	Recognizing individual (or group) performance problems	Determining management development needs	Separating training from non-training needs
	(1)	(2)	(3)	(4)	(5)
Comparative			XX		
Rank order		X	XX	X	
Forced distribution		X	XX		
Paired comparison		X			
Absolute					
Essay (description)		X	X		
Numerical scale		X	XX	XX	X
Descriptive scale		X	X	XX	X
Graphic rating scale		X	XX	XX	X
BARS		X	X	XX	
Checklist		X	X	XX	XX
Critical incidents scale	X	X	XX	XXX	X
Product scale	X	X	X	XX	
Forced choice		X	X	XX	

Key: X - good;   XX - very good;   XXX - excellent

Source: Kubr and Prokopenko, 1989, p. 279.

Table 6.4.   Rating techniques: Type of development needs

Rating technique	Dimension of needs assessment			
	Knowledge (1)	Skills (2)	Attitude (3)	Actual behaviour (4)
Comparative				
Rank order	X	XX	X	X
Forced distribution	X	XX	X	X
Paired comparison	X	XX	X	X
Absolute				
Essay (description)	XX	XX	X	X
Numerical scale	X	XX	X	XXX
Descriptive scale	X	X	XX	XXX
Graphic rating scale	XX	XX	X	X
BARS	XX	X	XX	XXX
Checklist	XX	X	X	X
Critical incidents scale	X	XX	XX	XX
Product scale	X	XX	X	X
Forced choice	X	XX	X	X

Key: X - good;   XX - very good;   XXX - excellent

Source: Kubr and Prokopenko, 1989, p. 291.

TRAINING PROGRAMME DESIGN

7

John Butler

Programme design can be described as the process of developing training curricula and materials to meet training and development needs. Effective programme design therefore should be oriented towards job performance rather than towards subject-matter content or training staff preferences.

Programme design has three major phases:

Preparation or training-needs identification phase — where required job performance is compared with current job performance and the resulting gap identified. This "gap" or discrepancy is further analysed to determine what can be reduced or eliminated by training. This tells us what training objectives should be.

Development phase — where training programme units are outlined in terms of job tasks, and the content and sequence of individual sessions is developed. This tells us how the training will be done.

Improvement phase — where each individual training unit and the total programme is evaluated against session objectives to determine where further improvements can be made.

In order to optimize training and development activities two points should be considered during the design stage: (1) the effectiveness of training and (2) the efficiency of training.

The effectiveness is concerned with whether the training achieves its objectives in terms of learning objectives and transfer of skills to the job. In this context we ask whether a certain development could best be learned through a certain method — lecture, case-study, role-play, etc.

The efficiency is concerned with the cost and time required to deliver training to the level of agreed effectiveness. Thus, the efficiency of training is a feature of the training media used. In this context we ask whether a module should be conducted through a lecture, audio-video aids, computer-based training, etc.

Thus, if the effectiveness of training is a function of instructional technology, the efficiency of training is a function of delivery technology. Besides, the programme design should also be based upon and reflect in its elements the training cycle — starting from needs analysis and finishing with the evaluation of training results.

7.1 Main elements of programme design

The main elements of programme design are:

- needs analysis
- learner analysis
- setting objectives
- designing the training curriculum
- selection of training and development methods
- selection of training and development media
- evaluation

Training-needs analysis helps to identify and prioritize the most critical problems and needs, and to determine which of them could be solved by training and/or by organizational development intervention (see Chapter 6).

Learner analysis is important to identify individual needs and learning potential or trainability of trainees.

The setting of clear and precise objectives is important to specify the nature, dimensions and the volume of the knowledge, attitude and skill which should be changed during the training. Often, the objectives indicate job standards or performance parameters to be achieved.

Designing the training curriculum deals with selecting, producing, sequencing and reviewing the training modules.

Selection of the appropriate training and development methods is important to ensure that effective training is carried out in accordance with the curriculum and the objectives.

Selection of the appropriate training media ensures that the training is delivered in the most efficient manner possible.

Training results evaluation serves to monitor the programme implementation and ensure whether the training objectives have been achieved and, if not, why not and what types of corrective action are necessary.

With regard to the phases outlined in the introduction, the preparation phase would include:

- needs analysis
- learner analysis
- setting general objectives (including performance targets)

The development phase would include:

- setting detailed objectives
- designing the training curriculum
- selection of training and development methods
- selection of training and development media

The improvement phase would include evaluation with feedback and necessary interventions in the first two phases, particularly for medium- and long-term training programmes.

Since Chapters 6 and 9 cover the first and third phases, this chapter will concentrate mainly on the development phase.

(A) Learner analysis

If the needs analysis indicates among other things the expected outcome of a successful training programme, the analysis of the learners could provide essential information on their trainability, the possible length of the training and the extent of training to be carried out. Fundamental differences between people usually influence their learning capabilities and hence influence programme design. These differences could be analysed in the following areas:

- intellectual ability
- prior knowledge or expertise in the area to be taught
- motivation to learn

Intellectual ability could be reflected in the learners' capability to plan their own learning, and conceptual and intellectual readiness to cope with learning tasks and materials. Can the learner select the most important aspects of the course material, devote sufficient time and attention to critical programme elements and ignore the unimportant ones? Can the learner connect and interrelate new knowledge to existing and familiar knowledge which is particularly important for managers in order to integrate and conceptualize fragmented facts, derive trends and practical conclusions? All these depend upon the intellectual abilities of the trainees.

Prior knowledge or expertise in the area to be taught obviously influences the breadth and depth of the course level, the content and the pace of instruction. If the course level is too low and/or the pace of instruction too slow or vice versa, the trainees will become frustrated. This is often a problem on programmes for managers with widely divergent knowledge and expertise, particularly if they are drawn from various organizations, departments and functions. In such a situation, specific skill-training modules should be provided separately from the main course, and the latter should be confined to specific organization issues. For example, the fundamentals of budgeting should be covered as a separate programme only for individuals requiring it, but the budgeting system itself for the whole organization could be provided as part of the main body of the course.

In cases where a divergence of prior knowledge and expertise still exists, there is an opportunity for team-building by selecting groups of people with varying expertise to work on selected work-related issues and projects, and thus facilitate the exchange of experience, as well as the use of the synergetic effect to enrich the learning.

Motivation influences the effectiveness of learning and depends greatly upon such factors as the value that learners place on the learning task or objective in relation to their present job and their future career, their perception of their own knowledge and trainability, and the difficulty of the task or objective.

If a task is perceived as very difficult or very easy, learners will put in very little effort. The learners' overestimation of the own abilities could also reduce their efforts in the learning process. Finally, if the project design is not based on their interests and identified individual needs, the learners are not going to pay full attention to the programme. The design should prove and be seen by learners to be based on all these three considerations.

The learners' analysis could play an important part in the decision on the level of training and development support required for the programme. A basic principle in this regard is that one should never do for learners what they are able and should do for themselves.

Three main levels of support can be distinguished. The lowest level only provides information and sets the goals to be achieved based on information obtained from the needs analysis. The medium level activates the learners' intellectual ability and motivation, and lets them do the actual learning. The highest level requires the trainers' intervention to fill the gaps between the objectives and the abilities of the learners.

(B) Setting detailed objectives

Training objectives are normally derived by comparing actual and expected job performance through training and development needs analysis. Training objectives can be conveniently classified into the following two categories:

- *Programme objectives*, which include training objectives for the whole training programme; and
- *Session objectives*, which include training objectives for individual training sessions.

In long training programmes a third category — *unit objectives* — may also be introduced, where the programme is divided into units, before being further divided into individual training sessions.

An example of programme objectives for a training programme on performance appraisal may be as follows:

At the end of the training programmes trainees will be able to:

- describe performance appraisal and its advantages;
- describe and conduct the steps of a formal appraisal system;
- set performance standards and evaluate the actual work carried out; and
- plan and conduct the performance interview and place emphasis on problem solving, goal setting and improving performance.

An example of a session objective for a session of the above programme on the topic of goal setting may be as follows:

- At the end of the training session the trainees will be able to set work performance goals for their subordinates for a specific period, outlining the items to be achieved and the performance standards required. The goals will be agreed with each subordinate and, in setting the goals, the manager will have access to information on past work performance and future plans.

Objectives are important to serve as the yardstick of the achievement and its measurement. They should prescribe what the learner will be able to do at the end of the session. It helps the programme designer to know precisely what to test and to design the evaluation methods.

Elements of a performance-based objective

This objective must be:

- specific — related to definite action;
- measurable — describing the quality or quantity required;
- attainable — possible to achieve, not just a target;
- relevant — to do with the behaviour required; and
- time-related — performed at or within a specified time.

In order to explain these characteristics better we can relate them to the objectives of the training programme, for example, on performance appraisal.

Specific. There are a number of areas related to definite actions, such as describing performance appraisal and its advantages, conducting the steps of a formal appraisal system, etc.

Measurable. It should be possible to evaluate by questions or other tests whether the trainee can describe the performance appraisal system and its advantages, and outline the steps that need to be taken to conduct a formal performance appraisal. It should also be possible to measure the trainee's skills in applying the performance interview techniques.

Attainable. The objectives, in this case, are a combination of the knowledge and skills objectives, information about appraisal planning, information on conducting the performance interview, attitude objectives, and using performance appraisal results in practice.

Relevant. If the company does not currently practise performance appraisal nor plan to do so in the future, the objectives of this course will not be related to the behaviour and skills required by the job and hence the learning itself will not be successful.

Time-related. The skills, knowledge and attitudes are to be acquired during the course. In addition, as part of this programme, trainees are recommended to apply their knowledge back on the job within a specified period. For example, each trainee (manager) will carry out an appraisal interview with all his or her subordinates within two weeks of returning to work. Many training programmes now incorporate the development of an action plan for transferring the acquired skill knowledge and attitude back to the job.

Another example which highlights the elements of performance-based objectives is the goal-setting session, where individuals are actually trained to establish performance-based objectives that reflect all the basic qualities such as specificity (items to be defined), measurability (standards to be achieved), attainability (corresponding to the learners' trainability), relevance (directly related to the learners' job functions), and being time-related (specific training period is indicated).

Structure of an objective

Structurally, training objectives can be divided into three parts:

(1)   *The statement of terminal behaviour.* This is a well-defined behavioural statement using an action verb, which gives the trainees a clear goal — a statement explaining where they are going in terms of behaviour modification.

Examples of action verbs: solve, prove, change, choose. Examples of a statement of terminal behaviour:

- at the end of the training the trainee will be able to run the 100 metre sprint; or

- at the end of the training the trainee will be able to prepare the annual budget on a spreadsheet.

(2)   *The standards to be achieved.* These standards will state how well, how many or within what time limit the activity will be performed.

Considering our two examples above, standards may be:

- within 20 seconds; or

- with no errors and within two hours.

(3)   *The conditions in which the objectives will be implemented.* Description of the environment; what will be given to help or hinder the achievement of objectives.

Again considering the two examples above, the conditions may be:

- on a grass track, wearing spiked shoes; or

- using a personal computer with X software and the provision of all the relevant budgetary information.

With different conditions therefore, different results will be achieved. For example, unless the relevant budgetary information is supplied, the trainee may not be able to prepare the spreadsheet; further, the task may be possible, but the trainee may not be able to achieve it in two hours with no errors.

(C)   Designing the training curriculum

This stage involves the selecting, producing, sequencing and reviewing of training modules to meet the identified programme objectives.

Selecting

In this area we are concerned with selecting subject areas and prioritizing the content under the following headings:

- *What the learner must know* — items essential to the programme objectives.

- *What the learner should know* — items which supplement the essential materials and should be included if sufficient time is available.

- *What the learner could know* — items which are interesting and relevant but not essential.

Because of the scope of a manager's job there is a temptation to include a wide range of items, as they may be of benefit to the manager either now or in the future. If this is allowed, the management development programme not only becomes very long, but may also become very diluted, with no real core or focus as well as being expensive. Such an approach will also adversely affect the reputation of management development within the organization; when the programme is evaluated, the real benefits will be less evident than the excess costs both in money and organization time.

Sequencing

This can be approached in a number of ways. For example, to start with, the need for certain knowledge should be identified before other knowledge can be discussed. Although not necessary for understanding, materials may be available which can make learning of a segment easier if they precede it. If the variation in learning difficulty is great, and should the learning of the easier parts help in learning the more difficult materials, a sequence developed around the concept of moving from the easier to the more difficult tasks may be better.

Normally a mixture of the above approaches may be the best. As the purpose of the programme is achievement by the trainee of the programme objectives, pedagogical logic or learning-effectiveness considerations must carry a higher priority than subject-matter logic.

Production of training modules

It is recommended that the first step in the modules' production would be the preparation of a plan for each individual training session, which could use any type of training method, e.g. lecture, role-play, case-study, etc. Preparation of the session plan has a number of important advantages among which the following should be emphasized:

- a standard format for the session plan facilitates the maintenance of a consistent approach by different trainers in their part of the programme;

- the session plan forms an important link between the programme objectives, based on the needs analysis, and the actual training process;

- the session plan helps the programme designer to ensure that no important elements of the training process or the subject-matter are omitted;

- it also helps the trainer to continue with the session if any deviations occur, as well as to fill in gaps for sessions that were omitted for different reasons;
- finally, the plan could also help a new or substitute trainer who has to take over the conducting of a session.

The most important elements to be included in a session plan are the following:

- *the title* of the subject to be covered in the training session;
- *the duration* of the training session;
- *the location* and address of the session, specifying lecture room, discussion room, computer laboratory, etc.;
- *the objectives* to be achieved in the training session in line with those of the overall programme;
- *the key points* to be covered in the training session;
- *the training equipment* and audiovisual aids required for the session;
- *the session outline* indicating the sequence of the subjects and their elements, the points to be covered and the methods and media to be utilized; and
- *the evaluation outline* to indicate how the session is to be assessed in meeting its objectives.

Reviewing

After arranging all the components in an appropriate sequence, the programme designer should add up the time required. Normally it will be found that the time required exceeds what is available. As a rule it will not be enough just to make changes in the timetable; it will also be necessary to revise the objectives, making them more realistic within the given time constraints. This revision should be carried out in agreement with the programme client since it may involve a reduction in the achievement level agreed in advance.

The programme designer may also review training and development media to maintain or even improve efficiency in the new circumstances of the revised programme.

By using this approach, it is easier to drop the breadth of impact knowledge in favour of in-depth analysis of a smaller portion of the subject.

(D)   Selection of training and development methods

Training and development methods are important means to support the learning process. There is a need for continuous improvement in the overall organization and methodology of management development programmes, particularly training methods and techniques.

Factors to consider in the selection of methods

Human factors. The learner: intellectual ability, prior knowledge or expertise in the area to be taught, and motivation. The trainer: knowledge, managerial and teaching experience and personality, etc.

A trainer-manager with expert knowledge in his or her field, but with little or no teaching experience normally prefers to use small discussion groups rather than lecturing.

Programme objectives. As a rule, management training objectives are defined in terms of changes to be effected in knowledge, attitudes and skills, which should in turn lead to improved managerial behaviour. Where training is intended to improve multiple skills, as is usual for management programmes, a combination of different cognitive and participative teaching methods could be used.

Subject areas. Various subject areas (e.g. finance, marketing, etc.) have their own specific features. However, for a practical manager, the purpose is not only to know the technique itself, but to be able to apply it. This practical ability can be developed through case-studies, business games, simulation exercises, practical projects, etc.

Time and material factors

The following time and material factors should be taken into consideration when designing the programme:

- the preparation time, which varies for different subjects and training methods;
- the length of the course, which could provide an idea on how to combine different kinds of methods effectively and when to use them;
- the time of day when the programme is conducted. For example, the morning is the best time for lecturing, the afternoon for participative methods; and
- the teaching facilities available. Some methods require small teams and premises and others need large premises, each with relevant training equipment. The lack of adequately equipped facilities could influence the training methods selection.

The relationship between the principles of effective learning and teaching methods

Motivation. Learning is always better if the presentation methods are interesting, emphasize applicability and show the benefits to be drawn from application.

Active involvement. The deeper the participants' involvement, the more they learn. This is particularly true in the case of managers, who will wish to relate the course content to their past experience and future applications. Active involvement facilitates the development of new knowledge through the exchange of experience and better reflection. It also facilitates supervisory human relations and team-building skills.

Individual approach. The needs of individuals and their specific trainability as well as those of the total group must be considered when selecting the training methods. For example, some people learn best through practice, others through reading and discussions.

Sequencing and structuring. Some methods are better than others for introducing new ideas or developing practical skills. Thus, by correctly sequencing them in accordance with session objectives the general effectiveness of the learning process is increased.

Feedback. The trainer must receive feedback on the participants' competence, behaviour, what was actually learned and the participants' ability to apply it effectively. Strong feedback is provided by participation in role-playing, case-studies, business games and sensitivity training. Practical exercises, consulting assignments and application projects also provide feedback on the practical application of training results. These feedbacks are of crucial importance to trainers in order to correct in time the programme, the pace of learning and its methodology.

Transfer. This principle requires that development helps the individual not only to learn, but also to transfer what he or she has learned to the job and systematically apply it. There are two types of transfer: *near transfer* where the training content and programme exercises are the same as or close to what will be found on the job, and *far transfer* where the actual job situation is very different from the training programme content. The latter is generally true with regard to management development programmes attended by participants from a variety of different companies and positions, or when managers are preparing the new posts.

Management programmes in the latter case should concentrate on concepts and principles which have a wider application and use a broad range of exercises to enable the techniques, concepts or principles taught during the course to have a wide range of applications.

(E)   Selection of training and development media

Once the training content has been decided and the appropriate training methods selected to support the learning process, the next step is to select the appropriate media for delivery of the training in the most efficient manner and at minimum cost. In this context there is often a danger that trainers will preselect a certain training design to meet the requirements of the media, and not vice versa.

For example, a trainer may have a preference for videos, and design a training programme around videos. In another case, a company manager may decide that to keep up with new technology, the company must build its training programme around the medium of computer-based training. Both these media are very successful in appropriate situations, but will not suit in most cases; even where they are suitable, the actual costs, in comparison to other media, may be prohibitive.

It should also be remembered that whereas the media selected will affect the efficiency and cost of training, it will not necessarily influence the effectiveness of training. For example, there will be little difference in the delivery of the content of training between a lecture given in person or showing a videotape of the same lecture. There will, however, be a difference in cost and availability, particularly if the lecturer is a busy person who charges a large fee for personal appearances. Thus, it is important to review the most important factors influencing training media selection when designing the programme.

Factors in selecting media

Need for interactivity between instruction and learner. Some training tasks or trainees require a high level of interaction. An example of media that provide a high level of interaction is a live trainer sometimes assisted by computers.

Changes in content. The possibility and scope of changes in content must be reviewed before the media is selected and the programme material prepared. For example, where training materials are selected to meet training needs and some of the content then becomes obsolete, the materials need to be replaced or modified.

Cost and convenience factors. The first is *Location.* In organizations which have employees spread over a large geographical area, trainers must decide whether to bring the learner to the training site or the training process to the learner. This would certainly influence the media selection. The programme designer should compare the costs and benefits between the above-mentioned two alternatives, taking into consideration transport, hotels, availability of media and training equipment.

The second is the *Number of managers to be trained.* If a large number of managers are to be trained, investment in initial media development suited to the programme content and trainees' needs may be justified and training costs should be compared with expected training effectiveness.

Third, *When training is to be carried out.* If the training has to be carried out for a group of employees within a short period of time, the selection of media will reflect the time constraints imposed.

Fourth, *Company conditions.* Many companies have difficulty in releasing employees for training programmes. Additional problems occur if a company operates a shift-work system, and training must be organized in line with constraints imposed by the work schedule. It is necessary to consider media to suit this situation. For example, flexible learning systems like computer-based training have the advantage of permitting learners to learn at their own pace, in their own time and at their own location.

Fifth, *Company preferences.* Though it is already recommended that media decisions should be made to suit the training programme objectives after a full analysis of the alternatives, it may sometimes be more appropriate for a particular company to select readily available media because they have already had experience using it and have the necessary hardware. This should be weighed against the costs and effects of introducing the new media.

Sixth, *Fear of attending courses.* The fear of exposing their lack of expertise could also influence the media selection. For example, individualized learning using books or flexible learning systems can address this need and bring the individual to a level of acceptable expertise without embarrassment in front of other trainees.

(F)   Evaluation

The last step in the process of programme design is preparing evaluation instruments. This is critically important because it determines if the learner has achieved the objectives of the programme and also highlights areas where the programme should be revised. Though the area of evaluation is covered in more depth in Chapter 9, at this point it should be mentioned briefly in regard to how it relates to the programme design process. It is useful to think about the training evaluation process in terms of four main levels of evaluation.

The reaction level is obtained from the reaction of the learners after each training session, each module or at the end of the course. This provides an immediate feedback from the learners on areas such as the course content, its relevance to the job, the quality of presentation, the training climate, where improvements could be made, and so on. This immediate feedback assists the trainer in steering the course adequately. However, it is of limited value since it does not measure actual learning, nor can it measure the application of new concepts on the job. Thus, evaluation at this level can only answer the questions "How do trainees learn?" and "Are they happy or not?".

Learning level measures the amount of learning that trainees have acquired during the training programme. It would also answer questions on what and how well they have learned during the course. Learning will be measured against programme learning objectives for individual sessions and for the total training programme. The design of evaluation procedures will cover knowledge, skill and attitude learning, and it forms part of the programme design process.

Job behaviour level measures whether learners have transferred and applied their learning to the job. This is more difficult to measure, since it should happen out of the programme context and in the actual job setting. The best way to do this is for trainers to visit learners (or some of them) in their work situations before and after the training programme to discuss any changes in their job performance with them and their managers.

Functioning level measures the change in department or organization performance which can be credited to the training. It is difficult to estimate because many other factors than training affect performance. However, there are some statistical and analytical methods which can be used to eliminate the influence of those other factors.

7.2   Programme logistics

Programme design also includes a number of areas which support the training activity and without which it will not take place or would be ineffective. These are:
- planning
- budgeting

- timing
- staffing
- facilities
- programme promotion and marketing

Below are some checklists to ensure that all critical items are taken into consideration at the design stage.

(A)   Planning

This is basically the overview or a master checklist ensuring that all relevant areas have been covered.

Programme planning checklist

- Needs analysis.
- Should needs be fulfilled through external courses?
- If external courses required, identify appropriate one.
- If internal programme required then:
  — design training programme
  — identify staff and resources
  — prepare programme budget
  — decide on course timing
  — decide on course location
  — decide on course accommodation and hotel reservations
  — decide on trainers (internal and external)
  — promote course to potential trainees and their supervisors
  — check out training facilities
  — conduct training programme
  — evaluate training programme

(B)   Preparing the programme budget

The following worksheet outlines the main budget items with regard to training.

Budget items

Staff salaries:
  clerical
  professional
  outside consultants

Equipment
Promotional material

Staff benefits:
  clerical
  professional

Facilities:
  meeting rooms
  staff work rooms
  hospitality areas

Instructional materials:
  films
  videotapes
  videodiscs
  audiotapes
  35mm slides
  overhead transparencies
  manuals
  hand-outs
  computer programmes
  books and articles
  other

Accommodation for staff participants:
  means, coffee breaks, receptions
  staff
  participants
  timing

Travel:
  staff
  in-house
  external consultants
  participants

General overheads:
  administrative costs
  utilities
  maintenance
  other

TOTAL COSTS

(C)   Timing of programmes

Some factors which affect the timing of programmes and should be taken into consideration at the design stage are as follows:

Availability of potential trainees. Generally speaking, holiday periods are not very popular for training courses because many potential trainees are not available. However, some universities schedule programmes at this time, as training resources become available. Other organizations commence programmes after the holiday period or after the beginning of the financial year in line with the availability of training budgets and/or a reduction in the volume of urgent work.

Availability of trainers and facilities. Management development programmes will — in addition to company trainers — also utilize outside trainers and consultants. Their availability may be limited and therefore often determine when the programme can be conducted. Availability of outside training and residential facilities are also important in programming training.

Lead time for programme. In many cases the actual logistics of planning, designing, promoting and providing training resources and faculty staff, means that a minimum lead time exists before a successful programme can commence. This time depends on the number of participants, their jobs, location, programme complexity, professionalism of the training and support staff, etc., and should be well assessed during the design stage.

(D)   Staffing

The planner also needs to consider the availability of: (i) staff members, either training or management staff; (ii) outside consultants or guest speakers; and (iii) administration and support staff.

(E)   Facilities

A seminar facility checklist as well as factors to be considered in choosing meeting rooms are suggested below.

● Availability on seminar dates

● Cost (rooms, meals, seminar rooms, equipment, etc.)

● Transport (public or own car; if public, consider convenience, frequency and cost)

● Seminar room (size, appearance, lighting, decor, outlook, sound protection, ventilation and other comfort conditions)

● Supporting services (food, sleeping accommodation, recreation, public telephone, quality of service, etc.)

● General (scenic outlook, general decor, cleanliness, experience in hosting seminars, etc.)

● Factors to consider in choosing meeting rooms (room size, room structure, windows, furnishing, acoustics, colour scheme, floor coverings, lighting, electrical outlets, glare, temperature, ventilation, noise, computer hook-in)

(F)   Promotion of programmes

Promotion involves developing strategies and materials aimed at generating enrolments for training programmes. Examples of promotional materials used to foster interest in training programmes could be as follows:

● brochures

● direct mail

● newsletter/newspaper

● personal contacts

● leaflets

● posters

● magazine advertisements

● television and radio advertising.

Appendix 1: Some examples of checklists

Some control questions and checklists are provided below. They should not be considered as final instruments for needs analysis, which in reality are more detailed and complex. These are just examples of the most important components which should not be overlooked during the programme design.

Checklist for needs analysis

- Has the problem been properly analysed and emphasis placed on causes rather than effects?
- Have training needs and non-training needs been properly segregated?
- Have priority training needs been identified?

Checklist for learners' analysis

- Do the learners have the ability to undergo the training programme and learn from it?
- Will the learners be able to apply their learning on the job?
- What is the learners' current level of skill and knowledge in the area to be taught?
- Are the learners motivated to attend the training programme?
- Are they motivated to apply sufficient effort as required by the programme?
- Are they motivated to apply the learning on the job?
- Are the levels of intellectual ability, prior knowledge, experience and motivation very different among the learners?
- What level of support should be provided to the learners in given specific situations (lowest, higher, or highest level)?

Checklist for setting objectives

- Do the programme objectives relate to the identified training needs?
- Are individual session objectives or unit objectives compatible with and do they contribute sufficiently to the overall programme objectives?
- Do all objectives have a statement of terminal behaviour containing an action verb (what the trainee should be able to do)?
- Where possible, have the standards to be achieved been clearly outlined?
- Have the critical conditions to achieve objectives been identified?

Checklist for designing the training curriculum

- Was content *selection* based on the following priorities: what the learner must know; what the learner should know; what the learner could know?
- Has the *sequencing* of the programme been based on learning-process logic or subject-matter logic?
- Have *session plans* been produced for all sessions and in an accepted standard format?
- Have all training materials been *reviewed* with regard to their duration and content and the trainees' ability to achieve the session and programme objectives? Where changes

are necessary that may affect the programme objectives, have they been agreed with the client? Have any changes diluted any particular area which may be best omitted totally from the programme?

Checklist for selection of training and development methods

Have the following factors been considered while selecting the training methods?

- human factors;
- programme objectives;
- course content;
- time and material factors;
- trainees' motivation to learn;
- active involvement of trainees in the learning process;
- needs of individuals as well as of the total group;
- the sequence and structure of the programme;
- feedback to trainer and trainees;
- transfer of learning to the job.

Checklist for selection of training and development media

Have the following factors been considered while selecting the media?

- the need for interaction between instruction and learner;
- the number of changes of media which may be necessary over time;
- cost and convenience factors
  — location;
  — numbers to be trained;
  — timing of training;
  — company conditions;
  — company preferences;
  — fear of attending courses.

Checklist for evaluation

- Is an evaluation system in place which relates to the programme objectives and the training needs?
- Does the evaluation system operate at any of the following?
  — Reaction level.
  — Learning level.
  — Job behaviour level.
  — Functioning level.
- Is a system in place to ensure that information gained through evaluation is fed back to learners and their superiors, and is it also used to improve the training programme?

PROGRAMME IMPLEMENTATION AND MONITORING

8

Francesco Campagna

Programme implementation consists of three main activities:
- planning programme implementation;
- preparing and organizing programme activities; and
- executing the programme.

The purpose of this chapter is to provide practical guidelines for each of these activities. Figure 8.1 illustrates the inputs required and the outputs generated by each activity. A programme director can monitor programme implementation by organizing and checking the timeliness, quantity and quality of each activity's output.

8.1 Planning programme implementation

Planning programme implementation consists of two major activities:
- identifying the inputs or information necessary for the planning process; and
- planning programme outputs, or what is expected from programme implementation.

(A) Inputs for planning

Planning programme implementation cannot be done without essential information, or "inputs". Let us review the most important inputs required for planning the programme based on the programme design (see Chapter 7).

The first planning input is the curriculum, which is actually an output from the programme design. A curriculum should contain a description of the target population, the objectives to be achieved, the prerequisites for entering the programme, the description of content, the choice of methods and means, and the means of monitoring and evaluating the results.

Programme implementation planning should take into consideration company management development policy, which could be collected from company docu-

Figure 8.1. The programme implementation activities

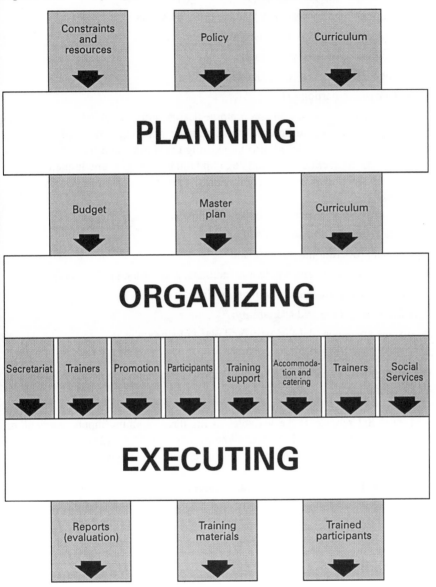

ments or by interviewing top management. This policy should indicate the most important procedures, for example, whether training should:

● stand alone or be combined with consulting and organizational changes;

● take place on an ad hoc, periodic or continual basis;

- take place within the company;
- be implemented by company trainers or by outsiders;
- take place during or outside working hours;
- be residential or non-residential;
- be subcontracted to a specialized institution;
- be charged to participants.

When there is no policy, the programme design should establish and reflect all necessary information to be used in programme planning. The implementation procedure will be influenced also by existing constraints and the availability of resources. The most critical task will be to find the best programme implementation balance between curriculum requirements, existing constraints and available resources.

Training resources may be divided as follows:

- human (trainers and support staff);
- financial (operational budget); and
- material (teaching and residential facilities, and training equipment).

The following are examples of constraints:

- participants' time and availability;
- distance between place of work and place of study;
- size of group (number of participants); and
- heterogeneity of participants' needs, language, experience, motivation, economic possibilities.

Figure 8.2 represents the variables of the three planning inputs: curriculum, resources and constraints in a three-dimensional grid. The grid contains 3 x 4 x 4 = 48 combinations which may help to identify critical planning issues more systematically.

Figures 8.3, 8.4 and 8.5 illustrate examples of identifying critical issues by combining two variables (figures 8.3 and 8.4) and by combining three variables (figure 8.5).

(B) Planning outputs

Now that we have identified the three major inputs needed for the planning of programme implementation, let us see how to process these inputs in order to generate useful outputs. The main task of planning the programme implementation is to produce a master plan and to identify and mobilize resources for implementing it. These are the two major outputs of planning. Both the master plan and the budget are required by the organizers for preparing programme activities (see figure 8.3).

Figure 8.2.   Variables of the planning inputs

Example 1

Select a trainer
(HUMAN RESOURCES)
who

1. is competent to deal
   with the OBJECTIVE
2. is able to deal with
   the TARGET GROUP
3. masters the METHODS
4. is able to use audio-
   visual aids (MEANS)

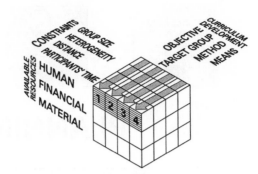

Example 2

Participants have a long
DISTANCE to travel.

Can they pay for their travel?

or

Are FINANCIAL RESOURCES
available to pay participants'
travel?

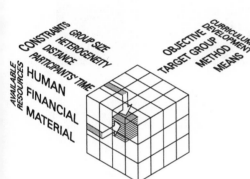

Example 3

International seminar:

Participants are
HETEROGENEOUS
in languages.

The CURRICULUM includes a
videotape (MEANS) to be
presented by a lecturer.

Are MATERIAL RESOURCES
available to project the video
simultaneously in different languages?

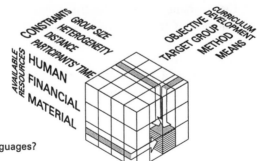

1. The master plan

Whatever training events are going to be planned (a conference, seminar, workshop or meeting), they all have the following in common:

- an objective, curriculum, subject-matter, etc.;
- participants (target group);

Figure 8.3. The planning stage of the programme implementation

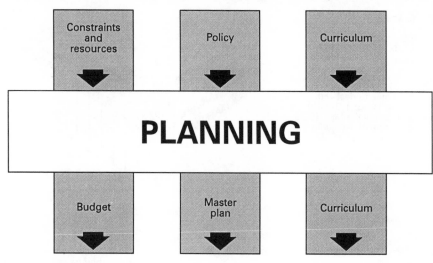

- trainers (resource persons);
- a time;
- a place;
- means and facilities; and
- an organizer.

The programme master plan (see Appendix 1) helps the organizer to prepare a great number of activities systematically without having to depend on memory or improvisation. It also allows the programme director to monitor the progress of preparatory activities.

Let us look at each of the main items in conjunction with imposed external constraints and available resources.

2. The curriculum

This is the central reference point for planning activities:

- A description of the target population and of the necessary prerequisites is required in order to get the right participants for the programme.
- A description of the objectives and content will be required to select the most experienced trainers, to set the time frame for programme schedules, printing the hand-outs, etc.
- A description of methods and means will help in organizing appropriate places and facilities.

Participants

- How will potential participants be identified?
- What means should be used to inform them?
- How much advance notice should they be given?
- How should participants be selected (if applicable)?
- How should fees be collected?

Trainers

- How will competent, qualified trainers be obtained within the budget limits?
- How will trainers be briefed about the objectives, target population, timing and availability of resources?

Time

- When should the training event take place?
- What should be its duration?
- When should programme publicity be sent out?
- What should be the deadline for participants' enrolment?
- When are suitable trainers available?
- When should trainers be briefed and appointed?
- When should programme material be printed?
- When should facilities and resources be prepared?

Place

- Where are participants coming from?
- Where should the training event take place?
- Where should programme material be printed?
- Where should participants, trainers and support staff be accommodated, have their meals, coffee-breaks and recreation?

Means and facilities

- What physical facilities are required/available?
- What training media and support services are required/available (e.g., printing, audiovisual aids, interpretation)?
- What facilities are required/available for accommodation, catering and coffee-breaks?
- Is transport required/available?
- What recreation facilities are required/available?

The organizer

- Who is dealing with the participants' administrative matters (registration, main travel and daily transport, reception, payment of or collection of fees, board and lodging, refreshments and social events)?
- Who is responsible for training personnel (interview, briefing, selection and coordination of trainers)?
- Who is providing training support services (printing of hand-outs, preparation of physical facilities and audiovisual training aids, translation and interpretation)?

3. Budget

An approved training budget (see an example of the budget form below) is another major output of the planning phase. It is based on the resources requirements identified during the preparation of the master plan. In most cases, a management training programme is organized as a separate economic activity with its own budget. A training unit within an enterprise may also charge for its training services. It is therefore good practice to accompany the master plan with a training budget. Such a budget contains training costs and participants' costs.

Training costs

- Cost of trainers: salary, travel and allowances.
- Cost of training support staff or services: course secretariat, audiovisual aid technicians, translation, interpretation, printing, etc.
- Tuition fees to be paid to other institutions.
- Rental of training facilities and equipment.
- Stationery, postage, telecommunications, if not included in overhead charges.

Participants' costs

- Main travel and daily local transport.
- Excess baggage allowance (for training materials).
- Transport for study visits/tours.
- Subsistence allowance (for accommodation, meals and incidental expenses).
- Board and lodging, if no subsistence allowance is paid.
- Allowances for books.
- Social events, receptions.
- Some companies compute the value of lost work time of the employee to participants' costs.

A sample budget is shown below for the TQC Corporate Management Workshop conducted in Osaka for 14 line managers of the design and production departments of the Sukiyaki Corporation.

Training budget

Programme: TQC Corporate Management   *Place:* Osaka
From: 15 Oct. *To:* 20 Oct.   *Duration:* 5 days
No. of participants: 14   *Programme director:* Prof. Y. Kondo

Training costs

Lecturer:	Programme director	for 2 weeks	=	204 000	
	QC manager	for 1 week	=	102 000	
External lecturer:	Prof. H. Kume	for 2 days	0	52 000	
		Travel from Osaka		0	
	Prof. Ishikawa	for 1 day	=	34 000	
		Subsistence allowance 10 000 x 2 days	=	20 000	
	(by Shinkansen)	Travel from Tokyo	=	16 300	428 300
Support staff:	Secretary	for 2 weeks	=	76 500	
	Audio technician	for ½ day	=	22 200	98 700
External tuition:	Guided visit to the Sushi Plant		=	48 000	48 000
Printing:	Modules 2, 4, 6		=	30 000	
Training aids:	Computer software CAI		=	120 000	150 000
Miscel-laneous:	Post, fax, telephone		=	10 000	10 000
	(A) Total training costs				735 000

Participants' costs

Travel costs:	Main travel from Tokyo (2), Kyoto (4), Nagoya (3), Mito (2), Kobe (3)		=	132 600	
	Transfer from railway station by taxis		=	26 000	
	Daily transport by Sako minibus		=	52 000	
	Study visits to Sushi plant in Nagoya		=	33 500	244 100
Subsistence allowance:	14 participants x 5 days x 9 600		=	672 000	672 000
Accommo-dation:	14 x 6 nights x 14 000		=	1 176 000	1 176 000
Catering:	Main meals: Participants pay				
	Refreshments/other: Closing dinner		=	12 000	12 000
	(B) Total participants' costs		=		2 104 100
	(C) Overheads: 15% on (A); 10% on (B)			110 250 + 210 410	320 660
	(D) Grand total				**3 159 760**

8.2 Preparing and organizing programme activities

The curriculum, together with the master plan and the approved budget, is the starting point for preparing and organizing programme implementation. On the basis of the three inputs, the organizer will prepare all information outputs required for the successful execution of the programme, illustrated in figure 8.4.

Following the checklist in the master plan, we are going to analyse each activity from number 58 to number 95 (see Appendix 1). All other activities (before number 58) have been discussed in Chapter 7 on programme design and at the beginning of this chapter.

Figure 8.4. The organizing stage of the programme implementation

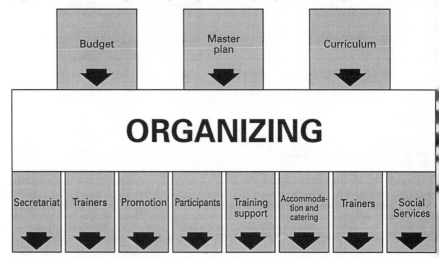

(A) Management

Activity 58: Programme director

The nominated programme director is responsible for all preparatory activities, for programme execution, and for expenditure within the budget. He or she directs the secretariat and staff involved in preparation and organization, selects, briefs and monitors the trainers, prepares the programme schedule.

Activity 59: Secretariat duties

The secretariat supports the programme director and professional staff in all administrative matters. Participants' needs should be the first concern of the secretariat.

(B) Trainers
Activity 60: Selection of trainers

Trainers should be selected on the basis of their professional reputation. Some audiences find it difficult to accept lessons from a management trainer who is junior to them, if that person is not a reputed genius. If you cannot afford to pay a management consultant's high training fee, look for a successful manager who would appreciate sharing experience with other managers, perhaps free of charge.

Activity 61: Briefing of trainers

A trainer needs to know, for example:

- The number of participants, their position, their experience in the subject-matter.
- The general objective of the training event.
- The subject to be taught, breadth and depth of coverage, skills to be developed, level to be attained.
- The teaching provided by the other trainers.
- Date, time, place, arrangements for travel, accommodation, training facilities.
- Contract conditions, if any.
  The participants expect the following from the trainer:
- Outstanding professional experience on the subject presented.
- A written summary of the lecture and any other materials which need to be reproduced and distributed to participants.
- Appropriate skills in teaching methods and in the use of audiovisual aids, etc.

Activity 62: Contract preparation

The contract between the trainer and the organizer should contain a description of services to be rendered, including the preparation of papers and teaching aids, the dates and duration, fees and allowances, travel arrangements and accommodation, if applicable.

Activity 63: Questionnaire

A questionnaire (see Appendix 2) has been prepared in order to collect information from visiting speakers on:

- what activities they plan to do with the participants (group work, role-playing with video play-back, study visits, etc.);
- what training support services they need (interpretation, visual aids, teaching equipment, printing hand-outs, rooms for group exercises, etc.).

Questionnaire 1 should be sent to trainers at least six weeks before the training event takes place.

Activity 64: Analysis of Questionnaire 1

Questionnaire 1 should be returned at least three weeks before the training event to the programme director who should *personally* check whether the required equipment or services are available. The programme director should confirm to the trainer that the requested facilities and teaching aids are available and ready.

Activity 65: Collecting hand-outs

The secretariat is responsible for collecting from every lecturer the training materials to be printed and distributed to participants. Lecturers should send this material to the secretariat together with Questionnaire 1 at least three weeks before the beginning of the course. The programme director must check the materials for relevance and quality, together with the questionnaire.

Activity 66: Payment

The secretariat should ensure that payments of external lecturers are ready on the day they have completed their assignment. The programme director may authorize the payment on satisfactory completion of their work.

(C)   Promotion

Activity 67: Printing of programmes

Programme description or publicity pamphlets should contain the following essential information:

- the title, dates and place of the training event;
- the general objective;
- to whom it is addressed;
- the content, hand-outs, methods;
- names, qualifications and jobs of speakers;
- a description of the organizer;
- fees and/or allowances;
- instructions for registration, travel, accommodation, etc.

Publicity pamphlets for short programmes of one to three days' duration may contain a detailed schedule of activities. For longer programmes, the detailed timetable, prepared by the programme director, is distributed at the beginning of the seminar and should indicate:

- the title of the lecture or activity;
- the name of the lecturer or session leader(s);
- the starting and finishing times of the activity;
- the type of activity (lecture, group work, video projection, visit);
- the room number.

Appendix 6 provides guidelines for preparing good publicity for a training event.

Activity 68: Mailing of programmes

The secretariat ensures the programme publicity reaches, in time, the target population, their organization heads or sponsors if participants cannot afford to pay the fees. The programme director is responsible for establishing the mailing list for publicity materials. Personal networking of contacts by the organizer is time-consuming, but may prove more effective than a standardized, often obsolete, mailing list.

Activity 69: Press/radio/TV briefing

Depending on the location of the target audience, daily press, radio and television networks may be more efficient than mailing programmes for spreading information about the training event.

(D)   Participants
Activity 70: Identification of candidates

Candidates for an in-company training programme are normally identified by their chiefs, who make recommendations as to who should be trained in what skills. Candidates for an "open" course are more difficult for the organizer to locate. In this case, good publicity and personal networking of contacts is the most appropriate solution.

Activity 71: Informing candidates

Candidates registering for an in-company training programme should receive first-hand information from the organizer through a personal interview or a briefing session. Candidates for an "open" course receive the information materials described in Activity 67. The secretariat deals with any additional queries.

Activity 72: Receiving registration

The secretariat is responsible for registering and transmitting candidatures to the programme director for selection or confirmation.

Activity 73: Selection of participants

Participants for a company staff development programme should be selected by a selection committee which includes heads of concerned services, the personnel manager, a union representative and the training director. The committee establishes the selection criteria and procedures, which should be based on corporate growth strategies as well as on the career development expectations of the individual. Participants who register for a sponsored course are normally selected according to criteria established by the sponsor.

Paying participants for a commercial open course are normally welcomed until the break-even number is reached, where the fees cover the fixed training costs. If more participants register, a selection can be made. Once all participants are selected, the secretariat should issue a list of participants to be distributed to participants as well as to the trainers.

Activity 74: Collecting fees

The secretariat is responsible for collecting fees. On registration, participants should pay a non-reimbursable advance of the fee. The remainder should be paid before or at the beginning of the course.

Activity 75: Reception of participants

Participants should get the impression on their arrival that they are expected. The secretariat should attend to each participant personally and make the necessary arrangements for them, such as:

- handing out programme materials, a name card, and lists of participants and speakers;
- briefing them on where and when training sessions will take place, and on accommodation, catering and transport facilities;
- payment of allowances or meal coupons;
- introducing trainers and other participants.

Activity 76: Payment of allowances

Some sponsored courses provide participants with an entitlement of allowances, such as:

- reimbursement of travel expenses;
- daily subsistence allowances to pay for accommodation and meals, if not provided; and
- an allowance for books, if available.

(E) Training support services

Activity 77: Inspection and selection of facilities

The selection and inspection of facilities are the responsibility of the programme director. He or she should study the layout of the lecture room(s), cloakrooms, lavatories, safety exits, and parking facilities, check if the air-conditioning (if any) is working properly, if the outside noise level is acceptable, and if the electricity outlets for teaching aids are in order. The seating and table arrangements need to be tested; there are various patterns depending on the type of activity, e.g. conference, film projection, group work, role-playing, etc.

Activity 78: Booking of facilities

The secretariat should confirm in writing the reservation for the inspected facilities. The letter should confirm the verbal agreements, including:

- the dates and hours;
- the exact description of facilities, room numbers;
- the seating capacity and arrangements;
- air-conditioning and power requirements;
- technical and cleaning services, if any; and
- payment conditions.

Activity 79: Preparation of facilities

On the eve of the training event, facilities are prepared under the supervision of the secretariat or a trainer who ensures that the rooms and furniture are cleaned, seats and tables are properly arranged, air-conditioning/heating/ventilation is working, notebooks, pencils, name tags, and also flip charts, chalk and eraser, etc., are provided.

Activity 80: Preparation of training aids

Following the trainers' instructions in Questionnaire 1, training aids, such as transparencies for overhead projection, flip charts, colour slides or even video films are prepared by the visual aids teams.

Activity 81: Preparation and maintenance of equipment

The audiovisual aid technician sets up, tests and maintains in good working order all the available equipment requested by the trainers. The equipment may include:

- public address and simultaneous interpretation system;
- teleconference system via cable or satellite;
- computer-assisted learning hardware and videodisc player;
- video projection systems;
- overhead projectors and screen;
- black or white boards;
- flip charts;
- sound recording system;
- spare electrical extension leads and spare plug adaptors as well as spare bulbs; and
- in some countries, voltage-regulating equipment.

The technician works under the supervision of the programme director and should be on call at any time during the training sessions.

Activity 82: Translation

Do not underestimate the cost of translation in international conferences or seminars. You need to know the standard translation rate per page or per 1000 words, and the number of pages or words to be translated to estimate the cost. If you need interpreters, you may hire the same persons who translated the text. But not every translator can do the job of an interpreter!

Activity 83: Printing

It is the responsibility of the programme director to ensure printing of all training materials. The most cost-effective choice of reproduction methods depends on:

- availability of equipment and paper quality;
- availability of outside printing services;
- budgetary provisions;
- number of pages to be printed from one original;
- the type of original (text, illustrations, photographs, colour);
- the required print quality; and
- the available time or the required urgency.

The programme director should make sure photocopy equipment is available for last-minute printing, even during the course. If often happens that a trainer wants a hand-out to be printed ten minutes before his or her presentation begins.

Activity 84: Interpretation

Interpretation can be of two kinds:

Simultaneous interpretation normally requires two interpreters for each language. It also requires special facilities such as an interpretation booth for each language and a simultaneous interpretation network of microphones and earphones.

Consecutive interpretation uses up half of the available lecturing time. This should be borne in mind in preparing the timetable of speakers. It has the advantage of being less costly because it may require only one interpreter and no special equipment.

Both types of interpreter usually ask to study the hand-out of the speaker at least one day in advance.

Activity 85: Study visits

Trainers or programme directors may request to support or complement their lecture with a study visit, in order to provide participants with the opportunity of direct observation. Study visits should be scheduled preferably in the afternoon, when participants' concentration for classroom lectures is as a rule lower than in the morning sessions. A good combination is theoretical exposure in the morning with practical field observation and discussions in the afternoon.

(F)   Accommodation and catering

Activity 86: Inspection and selection of facilities

The selection of accommodation and catering facilities is also the responsibility of the programme director who should personally inspect the facilities. The venue of a residential course should satisfy such needs as:

- training facilities (conference, lecture, group activity rooms);
- training support services (printing, audiovisual aids, interpretation, etc.);
- accommodation/catering; and
- recreation facilities (e.g. swimming pool, tennis court, gymnasium).

An organizer would perhaps choose a first-class hotel or a recreation/health/ conference centre for top managers. For younger middle-level managers, a university or training centre campus would be a good choice.

Accommodation should be adequate to the status of participants without raising feelings of discrimination among them. Sometimes, and with prior notice, participants may agree to share twin bedrooms, if the budget is tight or if the choice is between a single-room accommodation in a lower standard hotel or twin-bedroom accommodation in a higher standard hotel, for example.

Encourage participants to stay in the same place, so as to facilitate transport between accommodation and the training facilities, enhance punctuality of attendance, and improve communication and teamwork.

During intensive residential courses where training and accommodation are in the same place, evening team assignments after dinner are common practice.

Catering may include breakfast (if not combined with the accommodation), lunch, dinner or official dinners if provided by the organizer. Even when meals are not included in the programme, the programme director should be aware of the quality and price ranges of nearby convenient restaurants, self-service cafeterias, snack bars and the like so as to provide a choice for participants. Particular attention should be paid to vegetarian requirements or any other specific dietary preferences.

Activity 87: Rooming list

The secretariat should prepare the rooming list which will be distributed to participants, the hotel and the trainers in order to improve communication.

Activity 88: Booking accommodation

The secretariat books the inspected and selected accommodation (hostel, hotel, recreation campus, etc.) specifying:

- dates;
- number of single and twin bedrooms;
- rooms for non-smokers (available in some hotels); and
- price and payment conditions.

Activity 89: Booking of meals

Lunch or dinner bookings should be made or confirmed once participants have arrived. The secretariat should take care of special requirements for vegetarians and non-smokers.

Activity 90: Coffee breaks

Coffee- or tea-break services are usually provided in or near the lecture rooms. For a small group of participants, the secretariat may prepare it. For a large group, a catering service may be hired.

(G) Transport

Activity 91: Travel arrangements

The secretariat may be faced with the task of arranging participants' travel from their home town to the place of study. If this involves issuing air tickets, the secretariat should use the services of a good travel agency. In many cases, the secretariat's task is limited to informing participants how to reach the training facilities, and the cost of the taxi fare, for example. In some cases, road signs or instructions at the airport or railway information desk are helpful.

Activity 92: Daily travel

If participants are accommodated in a hotel which is not near the study place, the secretariat should arrange daily transport by bus to ensure punctual attendance. If good public transport is available, a good briefing of participants on arrival should be adequate.

Activity 93: Study visit travel

For nearby places, study visit transport by bus is common practice. For a small group of a dozen persons, for example, a combination of train and taxis may also be convenient, if good public transport is available and if a guide accompanies the group.

(H) Social and recreation services

Activity 94: Official receptions

The secretariat may organize official opening or closing ceremonies combined with social dinners. Foreign guests may appreciate dinners accompanied by local traditional or cultural performances. Prominent personalities and important keynote speakers are invited to address the guests at official receptions. Make arrangements for a photographer and inform the press and local television networks. This will add publicity and importance to your course or conference.

Activity 95: Social activities

If there are free weekends during the course, the secretariat may organize recreation activities such as an outing by bus to a tourist attraction or arrange bookings for golf and tennis. Well-planned social activities may strengthen team building and the spirit of collaboration between trainers and participants, but also between bosses and their subordinates in a company staff development programme.

8.3 Executing the programme

When all preparatory work has been completed with the help of the master plan and Questionnaire 1, the training programme is off to a good start.

The secretariat is organized; trainers are briefed and ready; the promotion campaign has resulted in the enrolment of participants; the training support staff has prepared the required facilities and printed the necessary materials; accommodation, catering, transport and social services are ready to receive the participants. These are the required inputs for programme execution which produce the three final outputs illustrated in figure 8.5.

Figure 8.5. The programme execution stage

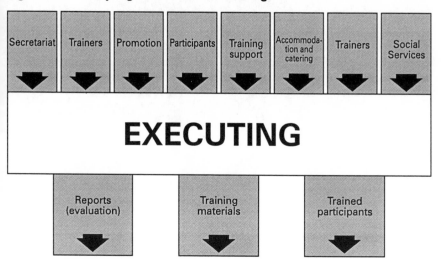

Programme execution includes three main activities:

● the starting-up activities;
● the actual training operations; and
● the concluding activities.

To avoid last-minute improvisation and accidents which disturb the smooth running of training activities, it is recommended to use checklists to monitor each of the three main activities mentioned above. An example of such checklists is shown in Appendix 4.

The start-up checklist should be distributed to trainers as well as to support staff at least one day before the course begins. Persons responsible for each activity are indicated by the training director. The checklists for training operations should be handed to all responsible persons indicated on the list, at the latest on the opening day of the event.

The checklist for the concluding activities should be given to the staff responsible for making the arrangements for closing the training event.

Thus, after the programme design stage, careful programme implementation planning, preparation and organization of the programme activities and programme execution are all of crucial importance to the effective management development process.

Appendix 1: Programme master plan

1. Training event: ....
2. Date: .... 3. Place: ....
4. Objective: ....
    ....
    ....
5. Participants: ....
    ....
    ....
6. Number: .... (expected) .... (confirmed)

Approval of master plan

7. Client: ....
    signature: .... date: ....
8. Sponsor: ....
    signature: .... date: ....
9. Organizer: ....
    signature: .... date: ....

Guidelines

1. Write the official title of the course, seminar, etc.
2. Give starting and ending dates.
3. Specify the location, city, country.
4. Summarize the objectives of the course.
5. Describe the target population (financial auditors; front-desk managers).
6. State the expected or confirmed number of participants.

Approval of master plan

After consultation, the master plan should be approved by:
7. The client organization/department which commissioned the course.
8. The sponsoring organization/department which pays the costs.
9. The training organization/department implementing the course.

Input data checklist

Implementation procedure policy

1. Is it an independent training event?
2. Is training combined with corporate organizational changes?
3. Is it a one-time course?
4. Will the course be repeated?

5. Out-of-company training?
6. Training within company?
7. Outside working hours?
8. During working hours?
9. Residential?
10. Non-residential?
11. With external trainers?
12. With company trainers?
13. Business-oriented training service?
14. Non-profit-oriented training?
15. Charge to participants?
16. Charge to organization?
17. Other:

Curriculum checklist

Yes   Source of information

18. Are objectives stated?
19. Is the target population defined?
20. Are the prerequisites or admission criteria stated?
21. Is the detailed syllabus available?
22. Is written content available?
23. Are the learning activities/methods indicated?
24. Are required training aids indicated?
25. Are evaluation instruments available?
26. Other:

Constraints

27. When and how long are participants available?
28. Travel distance/time/cost to attend:
29. Number of participants who with to attend:
30. Maximum capacity (seating) available:
31. Participants' heterogeneity of languages:
32. Heterogeneity of age:
33. Heterogeneity of experience:
34. Heterogeneity of hierarchy:
35. Are participants motivated to attend training?
36. Are participants motivated to pay for training?
37. Other:

Estimated available resources

Cash allocation:

Shortlist of potential trainers (names)

38. In house .... subject: .... cost: ....
.... subject: .... cost: ....
.... subject: .... cost: ....
38. External .... subject: .... cost: ....
.... subject: .... cost: ....
.... subject: .... cost: ....

Training support staff/services

40. Programme director .... cost: ....
41. Secretariat .... cost: ....
42. Audiovisual aid technician .... cost: ....
43. Translation/interpretation .... cost: ....
44. Printing .... cost: ....
45. Drivers/messengers .... cost: ....

Training facilities

46. Conference hall .... cost: ....
47. Lecture room(s) .... cost: ....
48. Public address system .... cost: ....
49. Simultaneous interpretation .... cost: ....
50. Blackboard   Whiteboard   Flip chart   Overhead projector
Video projection (which system) ....
Sound/slide projection (which system) .... curtains? ....
Film projection (which system) .... curtains? ....
Sound recording (which system) ....
            Total cost (50) ....
51. Power supply: voltage: .... cycles: .... stability: ....

Accommodation and catering

52. Name, type of accommodation: ....
53. Rooms: type and number: ....
54. Name, type of catering: ....
Average cost of: breakfast: .... meal: ....
55. Coffee break facility:
56. Transport: ....
....
....
57. Social and recreation facilities: ....

Checklist of planning outputs

This checklist is intended for the organizer responsible for the preparation activities prior to and during programme implementation.

Activity	Person responsible	Target date	Done/date/ initials
Management 58. Directs the programme 59. Runs the secretariat			
Trainers 60. Selects trainers 61. Briefs trainers 62. Prepares contracts 63. Sends Questionnaire 1 (see Appendix 2) 64. Collects Questionnaire 1 65. Collects hand-outs 66. Pays trainers			
Promotion 67. Prints programmes 68. Mails programmes 69. Press/radio/TV briefing			
Participants 70. Identifies candidates 71. Informs candidates 72. Receives registration 73. Selects participants 74. Collects fees 75. Receives participants 76. Pays allowances			
Training support services 77. Inspects/selects facilities 78. Books facilities 79. Prepares facilities 80. Prepares training aids 81. Prepares/maintains equipment 82. Arranges for translation 83. Prints hand-outs, etc. 84. Arranges for interpretation 85. Organizes study visits			

Activity	Person responsible	Target date	Done/date/ initials

Accommodation/catering
86. Inspects/selects facilities
87. Prepares rooming list
88. Books accommodation
89. Reserves catering
90. Arranges coffee break
      services
 	
Transport
91. Arranges travel
92. Arranges daily group
      transport
93. Organizes study visit
      travel
 	
Social/recreation facilities
94. Arranges receptions
95. Organizes social activities			

Appendix 2: Questionnaire – For visiting trainers

Date sent: ....
Programme: ....
Place: .... Date: ....
Trainer's name: ....
Address: ....
....
Telephone/fax: .... (office) .... (home)

Please return this form at least three weeks before your lecture to enable us to prepare what you have requested. We shall confirm availability of training resources and arrangements.

Please remember to send us together with this questionnaire your lecture hand-outs to be printed and the text or illustrations to be reproduced on transparencies.

Thank you for your cooperation.

Training Director

Trainer requirements

Programme: ....
Lecturer: ....
Date: .... Length of lecture: ....
Title/topic of lecture: ....
....
Language of lecture: .... Language of hand-outs: ....

Method or activity
Conference/lecture
Syndicate/small group
Individual learning
Projection
Study visit

Training resources required

Hand-outs (list papers to be reproduced by title; identify the type of paper, i.e. background paper, summary, case, questionnaire, etc.).
Transparencies to be produced
Black- or whiteboard
Flip charts
Overhead projector

Slide projector (silent)
Slide projector (sound)

Teaching aids

Video (specify VHS, VHS-C, BETAMAX, U-MATIC. System: PAL, SECAM, NTSC, etc.).
Film (specify 8 or 16 mm, silent, magnetic sound, optic sound)
Computer hardware (specify)
Other (i.e. teleconference)

Appendix 3: Checklist 1 — Start-up activities

	Done	Person responsible
Trainers Arrival confirmed, transport and welcome arranged Timetables and participants list issued Questionnaire 1 checked Printed hand-outs/visual aids available Name badges issued Keynote/opening/closing speakers selected Accommodation/catering provided Other		
Participants Arrival confirmed, transport and welcome arranged Participants registered, name badges issued Daily subsistence allowances paid Timetables, participants list, briefing materials Accommodation/catering provided Other		
Training support services Training rooms and seating in order Air-conditioning, heating, lighting, power supply OK Public address/interpretation equipment OK Blackboard/whiteboard/chalk/felt pens/erasers Flip chart installed; new felt pens available Overhead projector and screen installed/operating Slide projector/sound/curtains functioning Film projector/sound/blinds functioning Video projector functioning Printed hand-outs ready for distribution Instant photocopying available Interpreters ready and briefed Technician on duty Toilet facilities, classroom in order Other		
Other services Tea break services ready Transport services ready Photographer invited Press invited Other		

Appendix 4: Checklist 2 — Training operations

	Done	Person responsible
Trainers/participants Begins/ends session punctually Monitors participants' attendance Distributes hand-outs Uses teaching aids effectively Stimulates active participation Monitors participants' learning gain Monitors trainers' performance Other		
Training support services Hand-outs supplied Instant photocopying available Flip chart, felt pens renewed Black/whiteboard cleaned Power, air-conditioning, etc. functioning Public address/interpretation equipment functioning Teaching aids/equipment functioning Interpretation accurate Seating arrangements OK Reporting/secretarial services Other		
Other services Transport punctual Catering acceptable and punctual Tea breaks punctual Other		

Appendix 5: Checklist 3 — Concluding activities

	Done	Person responsible
Trainers Participants' learning gain recorded Participants' attendance recorded Trainers' reports prepared Training materials filed Other		
Participants Participants informed on learning gain Participants received summaries/reports Participants prepared course evaluation Participants returned library books Participants paid their bill Other		
Trainer director/secretariat Trainers/participants paid Trainers' evaluation collected Participants' evaluation collected Training materials classified/filed Record file prepared Summaries/reports collected Summaries/reports published/sent Thank-you letters sent Facilities/equipment returned Invoices paid Audit of training and cost completed Final course report prepared Follow-up actions decided Other		

Appendix 6: Guidelines for preparing good publicity

1. Good publicity does not mean expensive publicity, but rather that it should be simple, attractive, well presented. The outside cover of a pamphlet or brochure should be attractive enough to invite people who see it lying around to pick it up and read it.

2. Come to the point quickly. Who is doing what? For people with what type of qualifications, previous experience, responsibilities? Give the complete titles of the various sessions with subtitles if necessary for clarification. Make sure that the titles give a true indication of the content of the session. There is nothing more annoying than to go to a course or conference expecting one thing and then to get something entirely different. Nothing will destroy your reputation and that of the institution you represent more quickly than this type of deception.

3. Remember that time is precious. When your pamphlet or brochure arrives on a person's desk, the problem is to decide whether it's worth considering or not — whether it merits time spent on it or not. If the pamphlet isn't simple, clear, attractive, it is highly probable that it will go straight from the in-tray to the wastepaper basket.

   Say something about the speakers in your pamphlet — what is their "authority" for speaking on this subject? This will help *you* to sell the programme, and help people to make a decision.

4. How much notice should you give? This may depend to some extent upon the custom of the country. But clearly, whatever the country, if your first notice reaches its target two days or one day before the meeting, it is unlikely there will be a good response.

   The length of notice which is appropriate for an activity tends to vary with the level of the activity, the distance the participants have to travel and the cost. For international conferences, the date may be announced many months in advance. Many institutions which are engaged full-time in the organization of training and activities publish a programme for a complete calendar year and issue it at the beginning of the year. If your advance notice fixing the date is sent out more than three weeks before the actual date of the activity, you may need to send a reminder.

5. Make acceptance easy. Incorporate a "tear-off" reply coupon in your pamphlet.

6. Date, time, place, travelling instructions — make sure that all these are included and that they are correct. Add a small street map showing how to get to the meeting place.

7. If you have to organize a large number of courses, conferences, etc., you might like to consider the usefulness of a standard programme "cover". This can incorporate all the basic information which does not change in the short run — name of organization, officials, telephone numbers, address plus a map inside the back page. In connection with each separate activity you now have only to prepare an "insert" and staple it inside the cover. It is helpful if the document you send is immediately recognizable as another programme from... It is also better publicity for you.

TRAINING EVALUATION AND FOLLOW-UP

9

Mark Easterby-Smith

What kind of image does the term "training evaluation" conjure up in your mind? Perhaps it is a questionnaire, two or three pages long, which is handed out for completion at the end of a course, and which you leave on the trainer's table before saying goodbye to everyone and going home. Or maybe it is an awkward discussion during the final session where the trainer asks people for their views of the course, and where participants try not to say anything that will upset or embarrass the trainer. In the case of written versions, course participants rarely see or hear any more of the forms that they have filled in. The trainers will of course be grateful to receive the forms, but after participants have left they are likely to skim-read them in order to gain a general impression of reactions, and to see if there are any unanticipated problems highlighted. In some instances, the data will then be extracted from the forms and stored on a microcomputer; this is largely a clerical process and may be of rather less interest to the trainers (and to the participants who have by this time been forgotten).

Is this an unduly cynical view of evaluation, and is this all that there is, or should be, to evaluation? First, it is not a particularly cynical view. A survey carried out by a colleague and myself regarding evaluation practice in British and European companies showed that roughly 95 per cent of companies regularly used procedures like this at the end of their management training courses, and that they did very little else (Easterby-Smith and Tanton, 1985). Secondly, there should be much more to evaluation than this. For a start, the written "happiness sheet" system described above is usually used to demonstrate that current training arrangements are satisfactory, and that no major changes are required. It is very unlikely to identify major problems with the training programme, or to be able to show what else might be done instead. It is also something of a ritual: it signals that the course has come to an end, that it is time to go home, and that the *trainer's* responsibility has finished. This popular evaluation practice is very limiting, in the sense that it protects the status quo; in the worst cases it may even be contributing to the *ineffectiveness* of training.

In this chapter, therefore, it is intended to look at different ways of designing and implementing evaluation procedures, and to demonstrate what can and cannot be achieved through using methods that go considerably further than happiness sheets.

This is based on experiences of evaluation which go back nearly 20 years, and has involved looking at a range of courses and systems in many different settings (companies, business schools, training centres), and in a number of different countries. In addition this chapter draws on new ideas and procedures which have been written up in the literature recently.

9.1. Why evaluate?

The starting point must be to consider why one wishes to carry out any sort of evaluation: what kind of purposes are intended to be served by the exercise? There are four main purposes that are most likely to be covered by evaluation activities, and each of these is most likely to be the concern of different groups of stakeholders (i.e. the people who have some legitimate claim to find out what effects the training is having). Figure 9.1 shows these four purposes as partially overlapping circles. That means that in many cases particular evaluation studies manage to combine more than one purpose, even though one or other of them usually predominates. A gap in the middle of the four circles has been deliberately left, which is intended to represent the hollow ritual of using evaluations without having any clear idea of why they are being conducted. Let us discuss briefly what each of these purposes are, and explain which groups of stakeholders are most likely to have their interests served by evaluations designed along these lines.

Figure 9.1. Four underlying purposes for training evaluation

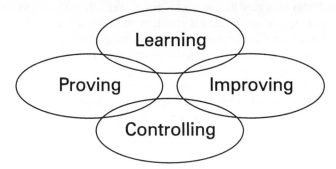

The notion of *proving* is most commonly seen as the ideal aim of the evaluation. Thus a study can be designed in order to demonstrate that a particular course has, or has not, had a particular effect on trainees, and that it therefore is, or is not, worth the amount of time and money that is being spent on it. This particular purpose is most likely to be the concern of sponsors, i.e. the people who have either authorized the training, or who have provided funding for it. The most likely sponsors are top managers, bosses, government departments, or international funding agencies. Let us now move on anti-clockwise to the next purpose: *controlling*. Once a particular programme or course has been approved by its sponsors the job is very often handed over to the experts to design, develop, and evaluate the programme. Particularly if a course is to be run by people other than the designers, then they will often be very keen to be able to monitor and check that the course is being delivered according to its specification. This general aim of controlling is usually incorporated in the evaluation procedures adopted by large organizations; it is also quite a common feature where programme managers or deans wish to check whether their various instructors and professors are performing up to the required standard. In order to do this they usually need quantitative rating scores which make it easy to compare the performance of individuals against each other — and this is inevitably a common feature of evaluation procedures that are intended as a device for exerting control.

Trainers and professors are understandably not too keen on evaluation devices used for this purpose — unless, of course, they consistently come out near the top of the pecking order. The more common concern of trainers and other people who are delivering courses is to find out how things have gone, and to see what the effect is of different innovations and adjustments which they might make to a course from time to time. This leads to the third general purpose for evaluations, which is to assist in *improving* the training and educational product or process. Evaluation procedures aimed at improving usually focus in some detail on the structure and design of courses, and leave space for participants' comments on how things might be changed and adapted in order better to suit their needs.

Finally, there is a group which is often completely overlooked when one considers the purposes of evaluation: this group comprises the trainees and participants themselves. It may be argued that once a trainee has been through a short course and has been trained, it is of no concern to her or him what future courses will look like. However, when a course is a long one — perhaps lasting a year or two on a part-time basis — it is possible for ongoing evaluation procedures to result in the course being adjusted in order better to meet the needs of participants as they emerge. Evaluation can therefore be used to improve things "in mid-flight", although it is always important to take account of likely defensiveness among trainers and their unwillingness to commit themselves to the additional work which would be entailed by major changes being introduced. It is also possible for evaluation to be designed in such a way that it facilitates the *learning* of the participants themselves. In some respects, that is what formal assessment and examination systems do: they provide targets and deadlines which are intended to motivate the students to work harder and to focus their efforts. Some assessment systems can be designed to contribute to the quality of learning as well as to its quantity. This is often an aim of open book exams or project assessments, as opposed to multiple choice tests or closed examinations. Even when a course is a short one and individuals are not being externally assessed, it is possible to design evaluation procedures which help individuals to clarify and summarize for themselves what they have learned (for example, through small group discussion or filling in "learning diaries" of each day of the course).

Thus far, it should be clear that evaluations may be designed to serve quite a number of different purposes, and that, as such, they may be more or less appropriate to serving the purposes and interests of different stakeholders. These different purposes can also be linked to some of the wider debates that have taken place in the literature about the most appropriate forms or models that should be adopted by evaluation. In the following section four models will be described, which represent "ideal" ways of designing and conducting evaluation to which people concerned with setting up evaluation instinctively try to adhere, and they are often to be heard apologizing when a particular study has failed to conform precisely to one particular model or another. So the reason for describing them here is to make it explicit that there are different models which may unconsciously underpin our thinking about evaluation, and to demonstrate that there are distinct alternatives which the individual should take responsibility for choosing.

9.2. General approaches to evaluation

Four general models of evaluation are identified in this section, and these, and some of their key features, are summarized in table 9.1.

Table 9.1. General models of evaluation

	Scientific	Systems	Illuminative	Interventionist
Main purpose(s)	Proving	Controlling; improving	Proving; improving	Improving; learning
Methods/features	Measures/pre-post tests; control groups; statistics	Rating scales; outcomes compared to objectives	Observation; progressive focusing; discussion	Short questionnaires and interviews; focus on stakeholders' questions
Usage	Very rarely used; largely myth	Most common model for training evaluation	Useful for new programmes; inside story	Adopted by consultants; effective lever for changing things
Weaknesses	Usually inconclusive; complex and expensive; often irrelevant	Picks up trivial outcomes; assumes objectives are real	Costly; difficult to use results	May be seen as biased

First, the *scientific* model is based on what is sometimes pointed out to be a misunderstanding of the way natural sciences work. There is similarity between this model and the way much agricultural research is conducted. Thus, typically, if one wishes to find out the effects of a particular fertilizer on yields of wheat, one would normally plant a patch of wheat with the fertilizer and compare this to a similar patch of wheat planted without the fertilizer (and for good measure one might also compare this to the effects of several other fertilizers), all of course grown in the same soil under exactly the same circumstances. In theory, the model looks like quite a good one. But in practice it does not work because trainees are not as plentiful or as standardized as are seeds and their conditions for learning application back on the job are quite different; they also have quite a lot of influence over what, how, and whether they learn anything from the training they receive.

The *systems* model is the most commonly applied and recommended for training courses. This usually takes the form of handing out questionnaires and rating scales to participants on courses, and occasionally following up on their reactions and thoughts after the whole thing is finished. Unfortunately, it is usual for evaluation to stop after the "reactions" stage, and it is rather rare for any systematic follow-up to take place. This is partly because of the cost of tracking down people who have left the premises, and partly because trainees become less positive about courses and their applicability once they have returned to their own workplace. The verdict, therefore, on the systems model is that it is a nice idea, that it can sometimes produce useful information for trainers, but that it usually results in a focus on the course and training process itself, rather than on its consequences and outcomes.

The *illuminative* model was developed partly as a reaction to what was seen as the sterility of scientific evaluation models. Illuminative evaluators rarely use measures or tests, preferring to talk to trainees and participants in depth, and to observe what takes place over quite a long period of time. It is of course quite a costly method, but it does have the value of providing radical perspectives on what is taking place — and this is often very valuable in the case of major new programmes.

Finally the *interventionist* approach is geared more towards answering the questions of stakeholders and producing information which can lead to changes taking place. It is more pragmatic than the other three models in the sense that it adopts whichever of the standard methods seem to be appropriate (i.e. observation, questionnaires or interviews), but it scales them down so that they are no more than the minimum required to answer whatever questions are at stake. As such it is quite a useful and cost-effective model for consultancy interventions in training systems that are already established.

It should be seen from the above that each of the four models has its own strengths and weaknesses. What is important is to be aware of where one's own natural preferences fit in, and hence to recognize the kinds of problems and circumstances to which they might be best suited.

9.3. What to look at

It is normally assumed that training evaluation should focus on what takes place within the training setting, with particular emphasis on the formal lectures and sessions run by the tutors and instructors. Moreover, if one adopts the systems model, as it has been suggested above, there are various reasons why trainers and evaluators would prefer to keep this as the main focus. However, there are many other factors which can have a significant bearing on the way training works, and on its consequences. For example, the process whereby people get to become members of a residential course can have a significant bearing on their feeling about participating in it. Some people choose, and compete, to get on to courses; others are sent by their bosses or their institutions. Sometimes people are sent on courses as a reward for doing particularly well in their work; other times they feel they are being sent to make up for some deficiency in their performance, or as a last chance before dismissal proceedings are instituted. One of the problems with a lot of courses is that participants are there for a number of different reasons; these reasons may well be of concern to an evaluator who is trying to understand how a particular course can be improved, or what its effects may be.

Figure 9.2 provides a sketch of the path that individual trainees might take, when moving from their jobs, into a residential course and then back into their normal jobs (this path is the squiggly line running from left to right).

Figure 9.2. Possible foci for evaluation studies

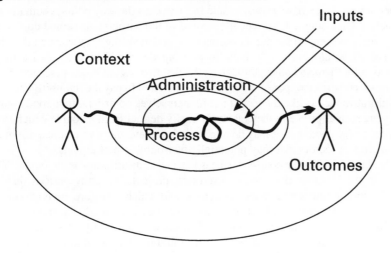

The remainder of the picture indicates relevant boundaries that are involved, and indicates some of the general areas into which the evaluation might choose to focus. The outer part of the figure is the *context* in which the training is taking place: in other words, it is the organization, the institution, or the domestic setting from which the individual trainee has come. Relevant contextual factors to investigate might include: why has the individual been sent on the course (reward, punishment, skill development, etc.); the wider culture and expectations of the organization itself; the needs that the individual perceives her/himself to have (and domestic pressures and expectations can be major elements in this too).

It is within the broader context that any *outcomes* from a training programme or process need to be evaluated and judged. What has changed as a result of the training? Does the person feel different, does he or she know something new, has he or she acquired new skills, has it resulted in changed relationships or new personal strategies? Although it may seem logical to start looking for areas of change which are closest to the apparent objectives of the course or training process, it is unwise to narrow the focus only to these. Very often the most significant outcomes from training and education have very little bearing on the formal content objectives of the course. For example, managers attending short courses on general management often come away with enhanced self-confidence, and an improved ability to present themselves and their ideas in public. These are very significant outcomes which are of relevance both to the individual and the sponsoring organization; but they may have little connection to the apparent objectives of a course which might, for example, be to increase knowledge of micro-economics and improve customer awareness.

The central part of the diagram contains three elements: the process, inputs and administration of the course. The *administration* can be seen as acting as a kind of membrane around the course as a whole. Factors such as nomination procedures, joining instructions, accommodation and meals, availability of handouts, access to telephones, etc., may have a considerable influence on the way courses actually run in practice. On a course I ran recently several of the participants turned up unclear about who was going to pay for their hotel bills, and therefore very worried that they themselves would eventually have to pick up the bill. This provided a major distraction for them and others throughout the first two days of the course, and it was only resolved when the sponsoring organization offered to pay the bill itself. Whereas administrative factors like these will not in themselves contribute to a good course, if they are seen as problems they may very easily detract from a course which in all respects is very good: thus it may be important for an evaluator to be clear about the administrative factors that may potentially be troubling participants.

The formal part of the course is what is labelled in the diagram as the *inputs*. This refers to the lectures, discussions, exercises, projects, or study periods that are initiated by the tutors and course designers, and which therefore are embodied in the formal course timetable. Evaluation questionnaires, particularly the end-of-course happiness sheet, usually place most emphasis on the quality of inputs and the performance of tutors involved. By now it should be clear what kind of purpose is being served by such questionnaires: it is largely one of controlling the teachers and professors, and ensuring that their ratings are sufficiently high to keep them on future editions of that course. The major drawback that I have noticed in evaluations with this emphasis is that tutors become very aware of the significance of their classroom performance; they become loath to try anything innovative or risky, preferring to use sessions and methods which they know have produced good ratings in the past. This concern with tutor performance may well divert attention from the educational aims of the programme or course.

Finally, there is the *process*, or experiences, of the participant going through the course. This refers not only to the things that they learn and do, but also the things that they are thinking about and feeling both within and outside the formal course structure. With a group of 30 people attending a one-week residential course, it is surprising just how much can take place. Personal enmities, rivalries, or attractions can be established; pecking orders and stereotypes can develop; individuals may receive bad news from the home or the office; many participants will sleep extremely badly in the unfamiliar setting; and, at any one time, one might expect about 10 per cent of them to be sick or otherwise "unwell". Competent tutors try to become aware of what is going on, and then try to deal with things which require action. Evaluation can certainly help to increase the tutors' awareness of these significant elements. If it is carried out in a sensitive way by evaluators (or tutors) talking to participants, it may help the resolution of some of the problems without any official action needing to be taken, and it may also contribute to the overall quality of learning.

It may seem that all of these five different foci are now producing an agenda far too complex for any evaluation to encompass. Perhaps the important point is to see them as a checklist from which to choose the most significant and problematic areas. One might, for example, gather a very small amount of data about each of them, and then decide to focus in rather more depth on one or two of the areas. What must be emphasized is that no evaluation is likely to be complete if it merely looks at inputs and one or two administrative factors; indeed, if it follows that format, it might produce results which are very misleading, because they provide such a limited perspective on what is a complex and multi-faceted whole.

9.4. Data collection methods

The majority of evaluation data is usually obtained in the form of *direct reports* (either spoken or written) from participants and others involved with a programme. Other methods, such as observation and examining records, have more specific uses, but they can also be used to supplement direct reports. Let us comment on these first before discussing methods for obtaining direct information.

The main value in having someone carrying out *observations* is that the observer, especially if he or she is an outsider, may be able to gain access to settings and situations which the trainer would not normally be able to access. In addition, if the observer is a complete outsider, he or she may be more likely to notice any peculiar customs or rituals which are normally part of the taken-for-granted experiences of trainers and participants alike. The evaluations which rely unduly on observation are likely to be expensive on resources, and this is therefore most likely to be justifiable in the case of new and innovative courses which have implications for far-reaching changes.

Records provide the second medium for gathering evaluation data, and here one can distinguish between existing records and those that are deliberately created for or by the evaluator. When a complete outsider is involved in evaluation, it is usually advisable to find out what has been written about the programme at different stages in its conception, design, promotion and implementation. Although promotional material, for example, may be written specifically to sell the course, it is still of interest to the evaluator because it can indicate some of the constraints and expectations under which trainers and participants will be operating. But records can also be created by the evaluator in the form of audio- or videotapes. These may have some superficial attraction because they provide a hard record of what takes place, but it should be recognized that this is a rather limited record. In the case of audiotapes, they will only pick up what is said audibly; they do not pick up expressions, background chatter, or people's thoughts — and tapes always have a habit of running out at the wrong moment. Videotapes have both advantages and disadvantages over audiotapes. The advantages are that they can pick up expressions and can enable one to identify who the speaker is, as well as much of the non-verbal communication that takes place in a training setting. The disadvantage is that video cameras are extremely intrusive, and they have a rather limited field of vision. Both audio and visual recording systems have a habit of breaking down quite regularly. They also have the problem of producing mountains of information which can totally bury the zealous evaluator unless he or she is very clear about what to look for and how to analyse it.

The third medium and, as indicated above, the most commonly used one, is that of obtaining information directly from the participants and other interested parties. These comments can either be written or spoken, and in each case they may be conducted in an open or closed way (an "open" question is one which gives people space in which to write, in their own words, their own comments, thoughts or reactions). *Written comments* usually have to be structured around an acceptable focus, such as formal aspects of the course, the nomination procedure, or what has taken place since the course was completed. It is less acceptable to ask people to comment on how they have been sleeping, whom they have been having arguments with, or what kind of informal chats they have been having with colleagues in the bar. To some extent one might be able to obtain some of this information by asking a few open questions at the end of a course, or some months after it. A useful open question to ask in a written questionnaire is: *What, for you, were the main high and low points in this course, and what do you think caused them?* Another open question which can be used in a follow-up study would be: *Could you please give two specific examples of things that you have done differently in the months following the course, where you feel there is a link between them and what took place on the course itself.* "Closed" questions, in contrast, provide a fixed number of alternative answers to any particular question and these normally have to be indicated by ticking boxes or ringing the appropriate number on a scale. The most common forms of closed questions are rating scales and attitude items. Some examples of these are given below:

Rating scale in an end-of-course questionnaire

Please indicate your views of the following sessions by ringing the appropriate number:

	No value							Very valuable		
• Time management	1	2	3	4	5	6	7	8	9	10
• Global markets	1	2	3	4	5	6	7	8	9	10
• Principles of marketing	1	2	3	4	5	6	7	8	9	10

Attitude scale in a follow-up questionnaire

Please indicate how important you believe each of the following issues will be to the multinational of the next few years:

	Not important		Very important	
• Business ethics	1	2	3	4
Environmental protection	1	2	3	4
• Globalization of competition	1	2	3	4

One of the points about attitude-type scales is that they normally require at least a couple of measures, because one will be hoping to find some kind of change over the period of the course. On the other hand, rating scales only need to be answered on one occasion, and so they may be rather more acceptable to the questionnaire-weary course participant. As can be seen, slightly different numbering systems have been used here for the answers to the rating and attitude scales. This is just to indicate that there are different ways of constructing scales and the final choice here is really a matter of personal preference. What is crucial about scales is that they should be quite unambiguous, and should not appear to be over-complicated. The difference between two nearest points should also be easily distinguished by a trainee.

Spoken reports may be obtained in either a structured or an unstructured way. When they are more structured, the interviewer may have a clear checklist of questions to which he or she requires specific responses, in a particular order. But, very often, they are less structured in the sense that the interviewer has a rough agenda to discuss, but will be prepared to wander into other areas if they appear to be of significance to the interviewee. Unstructured interviews in particular can take place very informally, and they may be no more than discussions over dinner or in the bar, or chance remarks made at coffee time. Clearly it is possible to cover a much wider range of topics in this way than in the case of written questionnaires, and the data provided may be rather less stilted and contrived. On the other hand, there can be considerable problems in recording spoken data sufficiently accurately (especially if the setting does not allow one to use a tape recorder), and it can be hard to collate the data, particularly if each interview has covered a slightly different range of topics. Ideally, one should take notes during the course of an interview/discussion, and if this is not possible one should note conversations down as soon as is practically possible afterwards (some evaluators have been known to rush off to the lavatory for this purpose as soon as they have reached the maximum capacity of their memory!).

When designing an evaluation procedure it is often a good idea to include several different methods of data collection because each method tends to have its own strengths and weaknesses, so a combination of methods may counteract the weaknesses of one with the strengths of another. Some methods will be more costly in terms of time and resources (such as observation or open interviews); other methods, such as closed questionnaires, will be less expensive to administer, but will also provide information that is far less rich. The final choice of methods is likely to depend on the overall purpose of evaluation, the context in which it is taking place, the resources available, and the personal preferences of the evaluator. Thus, it seems unwise to legislate for the ideal structure or procedures in an evaluation exercise.

9.5. Concluding remarks: Drawing the threads together

People often want to know how much data are needed in order to ensure that the evaluation is reliable or valid. The answer could be: as little data as you can get away with while still meeting the main purposes of the evaluation, as far as can possibly be done. Most evaluation systems collect huge amounts of totally redundant data, and it is always important to examine questionnaires and other instruments to see whether any items are definitely not going to be needed, in which case they should be removed. It is hard to justify end-of-course questionnaires more than one or two pages long unless, perhaps, it is a very new or unusual course. Similarly, it is not usually necessary to talk to everyone; a sample of participants and other informants should be adequate provided the sample is likely to express all of the major, and different, viewpoints. In addition, it is important that any questionnaires or data collection instruments are tried out in advance of any main data collection. This is not only to ensure that they are clear and understandable, but more importantly to assess whether the data that they yield will actually be usable. This is, of course, one of the key criteria to apply in choosing which questions to retain, and which to reject.

A second area of questions concerns the problem of sorting out just what the purposes of an evaluation are, given the potential number of stakeholders and interests that may be represented. A good approach to this could be to start off talking to everybody you can find in order to find out what they think the evaluation should be doing (many of them will not have thought about it at all until you ask them). Thus, many of these discussions involve helping stakeholders to clarify their expectations, and this is obviously something for which the evaluator can provide an input. The clarification of expectations is not just a one-off event, but a process which is likely to go on throughout the period of evaluation. The key point is that the clearer one is about the expectations and interests of stakeholders, the more likely it is that one will be able to produce some results and conclusions that will be of use to somebody, and upon which some action will be taken.

Finally, the question arises about which models of evaluation should be chosen. As ever, this is likely to be a function of the context and the apparent purposes of the evaluation, as well as the interests and abilities of the evaluator. There are always trade-offs to be made: time and resources are limited, and there are also limits to the amount of cooperation that one can expect from participants and other informants. Up to a point one can fudge the issue by using combinations of methods or techniques — such as combining quantitative and qualitative data collection instruments (Cook and Reichardt, 1979). But decisions about the basic emphasis of the evaluation will still need to be made. One of the most important of these, because of the implications about whose responsibility it would be to solve any problems highlighted, is the choice of whether the evaluation focuses primarily on the course itself, or on what takes place outside its framework. What happens to people before and after they attend a course may have a far greater bearing on its value than the actual design and the performance of the teachers involved. However, if the evaluator is to conduct a follow-up study, and identify these aspects as key problems, then it is the sponsoring organization rather than the training institution which must take responsibility for action. Ultimately, the evaluator must have an acute sense of the likely costs and benefits of different approaches, but above all it should be clear whom, and what purposes, one is serving.

Appendix 1: Course questionnaire

Name ....

Course number ....

Location ....

Please complete questions 1 and 2 immediately; question 3 after each session and the remaining questions at the end of the course.

1. What is your present job?

2. What do you hope to gain from this course?

3. Please rate the value of the individual sessions on a scale of 1 to 7:

	Very low						Very high
IT awareness	1	2	3	4	5	6	7
Competitive strategies	1	2	3	4	5	6	7
Training and learning	1	2	3	4	5	6	7
Job design	1	2	3	4	5	6	7
Organizational analysis	1	2	3	4	5	6	7
Management of change	1	2	3	4	5	6	7

4. On a scale from 1 to 7, please rate the following:

Hotel administration	Unsatisfactory	1	2	3	4	5	6	7	Satisfactory
Course administration	Unsatisfactory	1	2	3	4	5	6	7	Satisfactory

5. Can you suggest any areas where the course could be made more effective? Please tick as appropriate, then give details of the idea in the space provided.

> 1. Timetable

> 2. Sequence of sessions

> 3. Lectures and presentations

4. Practical exercises

5. Syndicate work

6. Hand-outs

7. Pre-course reading

8. Others (specify)

9. None

6. To what extent have the hopes you had for the course been met?

Not met   1 2 3 4 5 6 7   Totally met

Thank you for completing this form.

Appendix 2: End-of-course assessment

Could you please spend some time on the last morning considering your thoughts and feelings on the following aspects of the course by completing this sheet before you leave.

1. The design

   What has pleased you about the design of the course?
   Why?
   What did you not like about the design of the course?
   Why?
   What changes (if any) would you make in the design of the course?

2. Tutor assistance

   Please give your observations on the tutorial assistance you received. What alterations (if any) would you make to this aspect of the course?

3. Resources (such as visual aid equipment, hand-outs, library)

   Were the non-tutorial resources sufficient for your needs? What extra resources do you wish were provided?

4. Timing of the course

   Was it: Too long?   (Please tick the one
             About right?   you think is right)
             Too short?

5. Pre-course work

   Is there anything that you feel was missing from the pre-course papers and letter? If you do, what improvements do you recommend for future courses?

6. Please describe to what extent the needs that you identified at the beginning of the course were met for you.

7. Any other comments.

8. Your name ....

Thank you for your cooperation.

Appendix 3: Tutor report form

Name . . . .
Date . . . .
Course . . . .

. How do you feel the main sessions on the programme went; how (if at all) might they be improved?

Session	How did it go?	Improvements
IT awareness		
Competitive strategies		
Training and learning		
Job design		
Organizational analysis		
Management of change		

2. What were the main issues raised at the course review; what kind of action (if any) is needed?

Issue	What action needed?
1.	
2.	
3.	

3. Any other points or issues that you feel should be raised (e.g. administration, hotel, management, etc.)?

Issue	What action needed?
1.	
2.	
3.	

Thank you for your help.

Please return form to Training Administration within 3 days of the end of the course.

PART III

COMPENDIUM OF METHODS AND TECHNIQUES

SELF-DEVELOPMENT METHODS   10

Tom Boydell

Success in management development cannot be achieved without strong elements of self-development. No formal training programme can produce results until a manager-trainee is sufficiently motivated and organized to use self-development approaches. Besides, for very busy managers or those who cannot afford to attend formal training for different reasons, self-development methods may be the only way to improve their managerial competence. That is why we would like to start this part of the book devoted to training methods and techniques with the single most important method — self-development.

In this chapter we shall summarize the essence and some of the main elements of self-development. We will be using a number of exercises for *you* to try out, using *your* own experiences, reflecting on various aspects of *your*self. In that way, as well as being *about* self-development, it will, we hope, help with *your own* self-development.

Additionally, as a trainer, you will be able to use the exercises to help the managers with whom you are working on *their* development. Before using them with others, however, try them out on yourself. A good rule is never to ask someone else to try an exercise you haven't already done yourself, since it is only by doing it that you can begin to get a real feel for what it is about, what is involved, and what it feels like to do it.

10.1   What do we mean by self-development?

In the field of management learning, the term "self-development" as a separate method has been in use since the late 1970s. During that time it has come to take on a number of different meanings, some of which we will explore later. In broad terms, however, "self-development" has two main characteristics — development *of* the self, and development *by* the self. To illustrate these we will use a case-study in which you, the reader, will be involved.

At first we will describe a process, and by doing this we will in fact be using two important principles of self-development, which are that:

- it involves the developer working things out for him or herself; or

- the developer can be helped to do this by someone else providing an appropriate process.

Therefore, in order to start this first process, take a piece of paper and write down six or seven key developmental events in your life (i.e., things that have happened, experiences you have had, that in *your opinion* have led you to develop in some way). These events — which can be from your working life, your private life, or a mixture of both — may have been very short or long. As long as you can identify them as definite, separate happenings, then that is fine. When you have identified six or seven of these, draw up a table like table 10.1.

Table 10.1. Some key developmental events

(1) Events	(2) Outcomes	(3) Processes	(4) Feelings
1 2 3 4 5 6			

In the first column, write down your developmental events. Next, in the second column, list what were the effects of that event and in what way you developed. In the third column write down what you were doing during the event (e.g. thinking, sorting out new ideas, giving up old ones, trying out something new, taking a risk, stepping into the unknown, etc.). The important thing is for *you* to think back to each event and remember what you were doing; what processes were involved. Bear in mind, too, that there were almost certainly several processes with each event. Finally, in column 4, note the range of feelings you had with each event. What sort of things will go in this column? You may have had, for example, feelings of: excitement, relief, anxiety, fear, happiness, calm, sorrow, and anger. Try to note the most relevant feelings related to specific events and processes.

(A) The outcomes of self-development: Development of the self

Now look again at column 2. We cannot predict what you will have written; however, we can give illustrations from a number of self-development workshops, for example:

- a new sense of confidence;
- understanding yourself;

- feeling good about yourself or a positive self-image;
- understanding or tolerance of others;
- acquiring new skills;
- learning to speak up for what you believed in; or
- deciding what you wanted to do with yourself in the near future.

You will notice that these examples — and, probably, your own — represent qualitative changes: *new* skills, *new* ways of seeing things, *new* sets of feelings. It is less likely that they will be quantitative changes — to increase something you already had, such as knowledge on a familiar topic. Even if you have used words like "more confidence", this is likely to be a qualitative change. It is, in fact, a different way of being, rather than topping up an existing confidence level.

This is the first characteristic of self-development. It leads to personal change, to something *new* or *different* in the way you are. This is what we call *development of the self*.

(B) The process of self-development: Development by the self

Let us go back now to table 10.1. This time we will look at column 3 — processes. As before, these entries will vary from person to person. We have already given some possible examples, but for convenience here they are again, with some others:

- thinking, sorting out new ideas;
- giving up old ideas;
- trying out something new;
- taking a risk;
- stepping into the unknown;
- thinking about something that happened; or
- trying to achieve a goal.

Although different from each other, these are all quite active. The person is involved — mentally, physically, emotionally, in what is going on. It is through this involvement that they acquire the changes in themselves that lead to development of the self, as already discussed.

This active involvement, then, is the second chief characteristic of self-development. We call this *development by the self*. In summary, the active involvement of development *by* the self leads to changes that make up development *of* the self (figure 10.1).

Figure 10.1.   Development *by* and *of* the self

Development BY the self	⟶	Development OF the self

Figure 10.1, although simple, is very important because it shows that for someone to experience development *of* the self, they must be allowed, encouraged and helped to undertake processes of development *by* the self. This means that if the trainer does too much — prevents the learners from having to do some of the work *by* themselves — then they will not benefit from development *of* themselves.

Few trainers, of course, deliberately set out to prevent self-development. But it is very easy to get drawn into being *too* helpful, for example, by:

- giving the answer rather than letting the learners find out for themselves;

- stepping in when the learners have difficulties, solving a problem for them, rather than providing them with just enough guidance and structure to solve it themselves; or

- "doing the dirty work" for the learner; for example, by going to see the learners' boss on their behalf rather than coaching, persuading and encouraging them to take the risk and present their own case.

It was a realization of this danger, in fact, that led to the growth of management self-development in the 1980s. Before looking in further detail at both "of self" and "by self" development, we will now have a short look at how it came about.

10.2 How management self-development came about, and issues for the future

Management self-development as an identifiable school of thought and activity originated in the United Kingdom. After the Second World War the United Kingdom had a great shortage of skilled people. One of the solutions to this was seen to be systematic training — involving a careful analysis of job descriptions, job specifications, training needs, behavioural objectives and so on (Boydell, 1970 and 1985).

Systematic training was based on a number of assumptions — summarized in box 10.1 below — about people, jobs and organizations. However, after some ten years or so these assumptions began to be challenged. First, it was noted that they certainly did not seem to apply to managerial jobs, which involve the whole person in a complex, varying pattern of activities requiring discretion, and judgement — a far cry from breaking jobs down into simple pieces and then putting them together again. At the same time, the organization development school (see Chapter 3) began to challenge the previous assumptions about people being passive, requiring extrinsic motivation.

So, gradually, a new set of assumptions emerged (see box 10.2), out of which grew two main reactions against the rigidity of trying to apply systematic training to learning for management. The first of these was action learning (see Chapter 11), the other was management self-development as described in this chapter, which allows us to take account of individual goals, learning styles, aspirations, development needs, work situations and the like.

Box 10.1. Systematic training: Some underlying values and assumptions

- People are basically passive, needing extrinsic motivation.

- We can find ways of extrinsically motivating most people, but not everybody.

- People vary with respect to basic abilities; we can measure and remove this variation accurately, predicting job performance accordingly.

- Diversity should therefore be minimized in the interests of order.

- People need to be shown what to do and how to do it (training).

- The output from well-planned training is predictable, constant, with little variation.

- We can measure this performance reliably and consistently.

- Any variation in performance is due almost entirely to the individual.

- Jobs can be broken down into minute parts and then put together again for skilled performance.

- Learning is about changing behaviour in a predictable and constant manner.

- The purpose of one's job is to play one's part in a well-organized, smoothly running structure of interlinked parts.

- The purpose of one's life is not a meaningful concept.

- The whole equals the sum of the parts.

- There are two sets of people and situations — those to whom the above assumptions apply, and me.

Source: Pedler et al., 1990.

Management self-development therefore grew in importance during the 1980s (Pedler et al., 1990). After a time, however, two significant problems began to emerge. The first of these was that in a number of organizations, management self-development was used as an excuse for not providing proper management development at all. Managers were simply told that from now on they had to "develop themselves" and get on with it or be punished! This is, of course, a severe distortion of the approach we are advocating in this chapter. We have already seen that the trainer has a key role — demanding great skill and sensitivity — in encouraging, guiding and helping managers to develop themselves.

The second distortion was, in effect, in the opposite direction to the first. Managers were indeed being helped, guided, encouraged and so on, but in a somewhat self-indulgent, selfish way. The emphasis swung too far on to the needs of the individual, and the needs of the organization became neglected. For these two contrasting reasons, self-development began to get a bad name. So towards the end of the 1980s and the beginning of the 1990s, another approach emerged — the learning company (Senge, 1990).

Box 10.2. Integrated learning: Some underlying values and assumptions

- People are basically creative, active, intrinsically motivated, and want to do well. Extrinsic motivators at best make no difference, and usually make things much worse.

- While people do vary in basic abilities, we should note what they are good at and provide them with jobs that harness this.

- Diversity should therefore be recognized, respected, valued and appreciated in order to bring about creativity and richness in the company.

- People need a wide range of resources and opportunities to enable them to learn established ways and create new ones.

- The output from learning will vary; different people will learn different things in different ways.

- The only way to manage this variety is by producing a great range of opportunities (Ashby's Law of Requisite Variety).

- It is difficult to measure performance. In any case, we need to provide opportunities for a wide range of dialogue and feedback, not measurement.

- Variation in performance is mainly due to the managerial system, not the individual worker.

- Jobs cannot be broken into small parts. We need to work on continuous improvement of real outcomes and issues.

- Learning is about continuous improvement and forever striving to delight my customer.

- The purpose of my job is to delight my customer.

- The purpose of my life is to gain fulfilment by developing to my full potential.

- All too often the whole is less than the sum of the parts. However, it has the potential to be more.

- These assumptions apply to me and to everyone else.

The learning company — or learning organization — is still a new, emerging concept, and experiments are being made with different forms (see Chapter 18). But these have one thing in common: in a learning organization (a) self-development is encouraged *and supported* for all staff — not just for managers; and (b) systems and processes are set up to ensure that the development needs of individuals tie in with those of the organization, and vice versa.

Another very significant approach that has come to the fore over the past few years is that of Total Quality Management — TQM. While the roots of TQM might be said to lie in quality control, it broadened considerably in the late 1980s and now brings together self-management (i.e. the application of self-development) with empowerment of others; systematic, continuous improvement of work processes; and building mutually sustainable win-win relationships between customers and suppliers. TQM's initiators were statisticians, engineers and buyers. Now management trainers have another opportunity — and challenge — for making a significant contribution by bringing self-development back into a mainstream, commercial process. We will return to these points when we look at some of the methods available, in section 10.5.

10.3 Development of the self

(A) What do we mean by the "self"?

This idea of "self" is actually quite hard to define. So instead of a general, all-purpose definition we shall try to get at the idea through an expert — namely you, the reader. How are you defining yourself? It is possible that you pose yourself questions like the ones in box 10.3 below.

The self, then, can be seen as a complex cluster of attributes. Development of the self involves exploring questions about these attributes and your relationship to them. It is up to each individual to decide on what to work on — which aspect of *their* self to develop.

(B) Your higher and lower self

The idea of higher and lower self is very important when working with your development. We will introduce it by means of an exercise. Take a piece of paper and draw a line down the middle. Now think back over the past few months and try to remember three or four occasions when you were really pleased with yourself — when you did something really well, or handled a difficult situation, or whatever. The sort of events that afterwards you might have said "I really handled myself well today" or "I was on top form, at my best".

List these on one side of the sheet of paper. Then take each event in turn and think about it in some detail. What led up to it? What happened? Who else was involved? What did you do? What did you not do? What aspects of your self were you able to call upon, to bring into play, that made it go well? These aspects are part of your higher self. Obviously they will differ from person to person, but they might include:

- I was courageous.
- I took a risk.
- I used my sense of humour.

Box 10.3. Elements of the "self"

1. Gender: What does it mean to be a woman/man

    . . . in this company/organization?

    . . . in this society?

    How is the way I manage affected by the fact that I am a woman/man? What are the implications of this for my development?

2. Race, nationality, place of birth:

    (Questions as for gender, above)

3. Age; married or single; education; ambitions; career:

    Where am I in my overall life development? What have I achieved so far at home and at work? What do I still want to achieve?

4. Skills, inner qualities and characteristics:

    What skills/inner qualities do I possess/have I acquired? What do I want to acquire in the immediate future? Why?

5. Hobbies and interests:

    What sort of hobbies and interests do I have? Are they sufficient to provide a balance between work and leisure? Where in my life do I get a sense of creativity, fulfilment?

6. Values and ideals:

    What do I hold really important in life? What principles do I use to guide my behaviour? Where do these come from? How comfortably do they fit in with my work/home situation? What are the implications of this?

7. Others:

    As appropriate

- I was able to use my specialized knowledge, or skill.
- I was patient.
- I was considerate to someone.
- I put aside my own interests for a short time and gave my full attention to listening to someone else.

Whatever you wrote, these are parts of *your* higher self, which are there for you to call on when required. An important part of self-development is the ability to build up these positive attributes, to strengthen them. Unfortunately, as we all know, it is usually not as easy as that. It is often quite difficult to get in touch with these positive aspects of ourselves. Instead our negative side — our lower self — takes over.

To look at this aspect of yourself, now think of a number of occasions when you handled yourself badly; when things went wrong, and afterwards you thought "I let myself down there" or "If only I had ...". Write these on the other side of your sheet of paper and, again, analyse them. What led up to the event? What happened? Who else was involved? What did you do? What did you not do? What aspects of your self took over that made things go badly?

These, then, are parts of your lower self. They may include:

- I got aggressive; I lost my temper.
- I became impatient.
- I got so caught up with my feelings that I was not able to pay attention to the other person.
- I felt so nervous that I lost my confidence and was not able to do myself justice.

Again, these are all aspects of you — of your lower self. It is important to recognize them, not to deny them; but at the same time to tame them, not to allow them to control you. So self-development involves strengthening your higher self and taming your lower self.

Figure 10.2 shows seven main clusters of the higher self. It will be seen that these take the form of three complementary pairs, with an integrating or balancing element in the middle.

Figure 10.2. The higher self

Similarly, we can cluster the lower self in a similar way, and here a most vital aspect of the lower self can be seen. That is, the lower self is a distorted, unhealthy or inappropriate form of the higher self.

As an example, take being assertive, an aspect of initiating, involving speaking out, standing up for your own ideas. This, in general, is an admirable characteristic. However, if you go *too* far in this direction you become aggressive, bullying, domineering. Incidentally, it is very important to note that this is somewhat culturally determined. The line between assertion and aggression will depend to a considerable extent on local norms and expectations. So here we see this higher self attribute becoming distorted into the lower self. For this reason we often refer to the lower self as the "double" — negative version — of the higher self. In box 10.4, we can see some of the specific aspects of each higher self cluster, together with the related double.

Box 10.4. Aspects of higher self clusters

Cluster	Higher self	Double
Initiating	Having courage; taking risks; stepping into the unknown; making proposals; standing up for yourself; being assertive; starting things off; speaking up; challenging; confronting.	Being reckless, foolhardy; interrupting, dominating; bullying, being aggressive, over-forceful; being hurtful.
Responding and supporting	Receiving — taking in ideas, being open-minded; listening to others; considering other people's feeling; providing conditions for people or initiatives to flourish.	Being gullible, easily fooled; allowing others to dominate you; being over-protective so that others do not develop; taking on too many problems from others — martyr or saviour complex; being over-cautious or not looking after your own needs.
Finding meaning	Thinking theoretically; working out principles or concepts; seeing the total picture, forming an overview; grasping the essential elements from a mass of detail.	Being too theoretical, too abstract, out of touch with reality; dry, abstract, boring; making things too complicated or making them too simple.
Applying ideas and creating movement	Being practical; seeing and taking opportunities; trying things out, applying ideas to real problems; translating theory into practice; exploring alternatives; finding creative solutions; using humour to unblock a difficult or tense situation.	Being too practical in the sense of demanding examples, quoting exceptions; sticking to a narrow range of set responses; being all over the place, chaotic, disorganized, inconsistent; over-hilarious; never taking things seriously.
Looking forward	Having a vision, a view of the future; formulating goals; setting objectives; keeping going when things get difficult; constancy of purpose.	Escaping from the present into the future; having unrealistic aims; pursuing goals even when it should be clear that they cannot be achieved; having goals and plans that don't take account of other people's feelings.
Looking back	Reflecting; reviewing what has happened; learning from the past; keeping records, notes, minutes.	Nostalgia; living too much in the past; excluding others who do not share your own particular experiences; paralysis through analysis; collecting data for its own sake; "it's been tried before ..." (i.e. therefore cannot work).

Balancing	Sense of equilibrium, calm, of being in control of yourself; balance – bringing in the various other qualities when required, and taming or controlling the doubles; being in the present, centred, sensing what is appropriate.	This is a difficult task. It could be replaced by self-delusion; false sense of security; excessive balance leading to immobility.

(C) Modes of managing

The modes framework was started in the 1960s in the Netherlands, where aspects of Bloom's *Taxonomy of educational objectives* were related to broader aspects of development. Later Leary et al. (1986) and Boydell (1991) took this work further. Through intensive interviews in a number of diverse organizations they generated the seven modes of managing.

In fact this is a very general model; it can be applied to many spheres of activity. The modes are modes of being (e.g. being a manager, a teacher, a learner, a nurse, a gardener, a parent, and so on). It is indeed a description of the development of the self. Before summarizing the model, you might like to have a go at getting a picture of which modes you are using in your job. If so, complete the questionnaire in Appendix 1 of this chapter.

It is very important to note that the mode you are working out of depends on the situation you are in. Therefore when completing the questionnaire in Appendix 1, be careful to choose a particular aspect of your work or your life, and to concentrate on this when answering each question.

Mode 1: Adhering

In this mode my basic sense of self is one of self-protection. I am looking for safety and security in this world, so that I may be defended from its uncertainties and dangers. I therefore look for correct answers and ways of doing other things — either as a safe practice, or out of fear of being punished.

I operate from memory, thinking in terms of rules, checklists, procedures, recipes. I strive to operate these automatically, swiftly, correctly, to the letter; I try to do things by the book.

Mode 1 is useful when it is indeed important to do the "right" thing quickly and correctly. On the other hand, there are many discretionary jobs, tasks or situations in which there can be no predetermined, set procedure. In these, Mode 1 will prove at best inadequate, at worst a severe hindrance.

Mode 2: Adapting

The world is still uncertain or threatening, but now attack is the best form of defence. To protect myself I need to be able to "make out" in the world. I therefore want to tame, control, dominate the uncertain or dangerous environment, procedures, systems or people around me.

To do this I can string together a number of simple routines acquired in Mode 1. I am also prepared to bend rules and adapt procedures to make them work better. In so doing, I am making simple ad hoc experiments. As a skilful adapter, I thus generate quite a repertoire of gimmicks, twists, tricks of the trade, street skills.

Mode 2 is also very important as a developmental step away from Mode 1, for this is where I can start to do things "my" way — even if only by discovering and applying some simple tricks of the trade.

Mode 3: Relating

My basic orientation to the world is now that it is an attractive place, and I'd like to join it (rather than be protected from it — Mode 1 — or conquer it — Mode 2). My sense of self is that of a member of a group or society, accepted and respected by others.

Consequently I seek to find out what is acceptable; I try to tune in to the norms, conventions, OK ways of doing things. I want to demonstrate that I belong, by behaving in the appropriate way, by showing that I understand and agree with established explanations, theories, ideas; that I share the predominant values; that I have a repertoire of useful and praiseworthy skills.

If I am stuck in Mode 3, I am not going to be given the opportunity to influence things on a broader scale — policies, strategies and the like.

Mode 4: Experiencing

My sense of self now really emerges. It is no longer a mere reaction against others (Mode 2), nor is it simply defined by reference to a normative group (Mode 3).

To begin the process of knowing, being and valuing my inner self, I seek and participate in a variety of situations and experiences. More importantly, I reflect on these and make my own meaning from them. I am prepared to cope with the ambiguity of not having a source of right answers to call on. I am open to experience, prepared to learn from it. When the unexpected happens, when something does not make sense, or appears to go wrong, I am curious enough to reflect on it and come to a conscious, aware understanding of what this means. I thus generate my own understanding, my own meaning, from the experience.

Mode 5: Experimenting

I have now moved on from the somewhat frenzied, undirected experience-seeking of Mode 4. Rather than trying out a myriad of new things, I now see myself in terms of becoming really good at, or knowledgeable in, a few specific areas.

I am therefore now committed to deepening my expertise in a given field. To do so I am prepared to explore that field systematically, rationally, carrying out experiments in the sense of scientific (i.e. "knowing") method. I thus take active steps to seek further insights, to find out more, to increase my understanding.

I may well join with others in this research — although there is a danger that I will ignore those whose interests appear to lie in fields other than mine. Indeed, I may well see them as somehow imperfect, strange, even a hindrance ("those damned engineers/accountants/marketing folk/personnel types", etc.).

Obviously such expertise is useful, valuable. We need the outcomes of rational investigation to design or improve systems, processes, products and so on.

Mode 6: Connecting

In Mode 6 I sense my self as part of a much larger whole. To be myself, I need to achieve wholeness, balance, unity. I feel connected to other people, other departments, other groups, other societies. I see my ideas as connected to other fields of learning. I see connections between past, present and future. I see how what were "opposites" — male and female; good and bad; supplier and customer; manager and subordinate; management and trade union; teacher and learner; mass and energy; matter and spirit — are, in fact, essentially linked. They are parts of the same whole.

This is thus the mode of ecology and morality — be this physical, social or spiritual. This width of understanding leads to true wisdom, to Deming's notion of "profound knowledge", with great potential for influencing people and events.

The developmental threshold is therefore to take a realistic view of myself and my profound knowledge, and to decide what I can contribute to the world. What is my purpose? Why on earth am I here?

Mode 7: Dedicating

So now in Mode 7 I have recognized my purpose in life, and the task I want to achieve. Hopefully this task is not just for myself, but in some way makes a definite, identifiable, conscious contribution to the development of my field, specialization, art, craft, organization, area of expertise, hobby, community, affinity group or whatever I choose to commit myself to.

Although the modes appear in sequence, it is important to recognize that once a new one appears, earlier ones are still available. Thus, as I develop I have a larger repertoire or collection of modes available to me. Part of managing myself is being aware of the choice of modes open to me, and making that choice in consciousness of the advantages and disadvantages of each, bearing in mind the needs, opportunities and constraints presented by the situation in which I find myself.

To summarize the modes, you will see that the modes represent a progression in development, away from being controlled by others and what they want of you (Modes 1-3) to being managed by yourself (Modes 5-7).

Now that you have completed the questionnaire in Appendix 1, what does it tell you about yourself and your development? The question to ask yourself is how you feel about your own mode profile — which modes you are mainly working in. Your scores will tell you this, and by reading the descriptions, which summarize their advantages and disadvantages, you can begin to get an idea about which mode would seem most appropriate.

10.4 Development by the self: The process of self-development

In the first part of this chapter we took a preliminary look at how self-development happens, by asking you to reflect on some of your own experiences. We will now look at this process in more depth, as it provides the key to helping people with their development.

Let us start by considering a number of dictionary definitions of development, such as:

- "bringing out what is latent or potential in";
- "bringing to a more advanced or more highly organized state";
- "working out the potentialities of"; and
- "advancing through successive stages to a higher, more complex, or more fully grown state".

When we talk of development, then, we are referring to a process of qualitative change; this process is not gradual and incremental, but involves definite jumps to a new state of being, such that the change can be seen as somehow leading to a "better", more mature condition than before.

Let us imagine, for example, that I am a child learning to get around; that is, we are considering the dimension of mobility. To start with, I learn that I can move a certain distance by rolling over sideways. I am pretty pleased with this at first, although it is frustrating when I really want to go forwards. Then, one day, I really want to get at something a few feet in front of me. So I stretch towards it, and thrash about, and suddenly realize that I can sort of slide along forwards, pushing back with my legs, dragging on my arms and elbows and with a bit of practice I get fairly good at it. But sooner or later even this loses its initial golden glow. There are a lot of things I cannot reach when I am down here crawling; and Mum and Dad help me to get up and move while standing up. So, I am walking! A bit later still, I also discover running — different again. We can show all this diagrammatically, as in figure 10.3.

Figure 10.3. Development of mobility

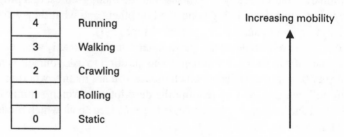

Here, then, we have an archetypal stage model of development. In this case development is in the direction of increased mobility — i.e. the more mature or fully grown state is that of greater mobility.

However, this maturity is not a simple quantitative change. Certainly, walking is faster than crawling, and crawling is faster than rolling. Clearly, crawling is not merely "advanced" rolling; it is a new, different form of movement, and is better than rolling. And in its turn, walking is not "better" than crawling, but is a different form of movement. In short, rolling, crawling, walking and running each represent significant qualitative changes in my mobility; they are stages in my development as a potentially mobile human being.

Another important characteristic of this development is that the stages or modes normally appear in a definite sequence. "You can't run before you can walk." If, for some reason, a particular stage is left out, this may lead to difficulties later in life.

The process of developing

In general, what can we say about the process of developing from one stage (i.e. increasing one's repertoire of modes of behaving) to the next?

For a start, since this new stage or mode is something different, a qualitative change, then it certainly can't be achieved by adding on more of whatever I can do already. Encouraging the baby to crawl faster will not help it to stand up and walk; indeed, it is quite likely to have the opposite effect, since the more satisfied it is with crawling, the less the urge or need to go one better by discovering walking. (This is an archetype of the process of professional deformation. By encouraging and rewarding a particular mode of behaviour, the individual's development — to the next mode — may well be retarded. Many organizations retard the development of their managers in this way.)

The key phrase in the preceding paragraph was "the urge or need to". For it is this that pushes us forwards, that makes us take our next developmental step (quite literally, in the case of walking!) across the threshold from our current stage to the next; from behaving in our current mode to the new one. Some of these urges or needs are:

- an external coercive power, forcing me into trying something new;
- a threat from which I cannot escape unless I change my mode of doing things;
- an external goal or reward that I cannot reach using my current mode of behaviour;
- a desire to make things work a bit better;
- a desire to please, or to conform with other people's expectations of me;
- a curiosity as to why things are done or organized the way they are;
- an experience, surprise or shock that forces me to see things in a different way, to adopt a new mode of behaviour;
- a curiosity, a need, urge or longing to find out more, to understand more, to explore something in depth, to work out a better way of doing things;
- a need or longing to see "whole pictures", to identify, feel and fulfil my part of

a wide whole, of a totality;

- a need to achieve wholeness and balance in what I do and the way I do it;
- a yearning or longing really to encounter another person;
- a desire or need to make something of my life, to give it purpose, that "my living shall not be in vain";
- a desire for spiritual understanding.

These, then, are some of the forces that may propel us towards and across the threshold of our development — pushing or pulling us into taking our next step into a new mode or way of behaving and being. It is immediately clear that there is a wide qualitative variety here — the nature of the various forces just listed is very diverse.

So development takes place through some combination of inner urges and/or external crises. If we can force these — or be helped to face them — we cross over these thresholds, and in so doing we create a "happening", usually associated with strong feelings, where our old view of the world and of ourself within it is no longer valid — but where we have not yet formed a clear new picture to replace the old one.

We now have to reflect on what has happened, come to terms with it, make sense of it. Again at this stage we may very well need help. And hopefully, with this help, we construct a new, valid picture of ourselves and the world; we have moved on, developed (figure 10.4).

Figure 10.4. Development cycle

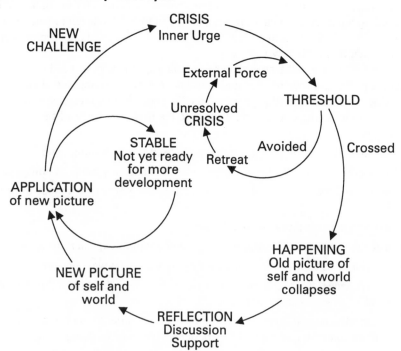

10.5   Self-development methods

In a sense it is almost a mistake to talk about self-development *methods* as such. The real issue is how to build self-development processes into any methods used. This is a very important point. What we are saying is that almost any "method" can be made developmental, provided it is used in a way that incorporates the principles and processes described in this chapter.

What, then, should we be doing if we want to enable our learners to develop themselves? If we are in a "classroom situation", either on regular courses, special self-development workshops or biography workshops, which specifically look at one's whole life development, we should try to relate what we are doing to the individual's own work or life situation. We can look for ways of using their own experience, their own issues, their own selves to introduce and explore topics. We can ask them to describe their own real-life situations and work with these, instead of using abstract case-studies.

If we do none the less use case-studies or other external material, then we should follow this up with extensive discussion on its significance and implications for their actual real-life circumstances.

The basic idea of development through the modes of managing means that, in general, we need to move away from teaching "right answers" and towards helping people to explore things for themselves, to experience a wide variety of new situations, new questions, new puzzles, new challenges. We will need to decide whether to provide these challenges through structuring appropriate exercises and experiences, or whether to encourage the learners to decide for themselves what issues, questions, challenges they want to work on, through processes of self-managed learning (Canning and Martin, 1990; Megginson, 1988).

We can thus find ways to combine inner urges and external forces to provide an appropriate crisis to trigger the developmental crisis that in a sense starts the cycle of figure 10.5. At the same time we will need to ensure that the learners either cross the threshold *or* choose, out of real freedom, not to. We must not force them beyond a threshold for which they are not ready. This requires sensitivity on behalf of the helper; very often the support of other learners is invaluable here. So working in pairs or small groups is strongly recommended.

Assuming they cross the threshold and get into new areas, working with new ideas, experiences, pictures of themselves, it is essential to provide the opportunity for reflection. This means we must provide adequate time for learners to think about what is happening, to discuss it, share it, compare it with others. Again, working in pairs or small groups is very helpful. At the same time we may need to structure the reflection, by posing questions that help the learner to make sense of what is happening to see its implications. There are also a number of simple but powerful techniques for reflecting on experience, some of which are described in Boydell, 1985. We have seen that development often involves strong feelings; we will therefore need to ensure the right conditions for learners to work through these.

In the final stage of the development cycle, we will need to provide plenty of opportunities for trying out their new picture of the world, for practising with it, reinforcing it or testing it. Of course, many of the developmental thresholds that people experience arise straight out of everyday life — at work or elsewhere. We can enable them to develop through these either by incorporating them into our classroom situations, as just described, or in other ways, such as by setting up self-development groups, or by coaching, or by mentoring. David Megginson (1988) describes these very clearly and relates them to the modes of managing, in boxes 10.5 and 10.6.

Another approach to providing support is through co-counselling, whereby learners form pairs, or speaking partners, and contract to meet regularly over a period of time (Boydell, 1985).

Project work can be extremely developmental. In the past the most systematic way of doing this has been through action learning (see Chapter 11; also Pedler, 1983 and 1990). More recently, the use of various continuous improvement tools by quality circles, quality improvement teams and the like has played a significant part in bringing together the development both of the individual and of the organization.

This integration is also to be found in a new general of integrated packages (Leary et al., 1989), combining a range of materials (workbooks, audio, video) and methods (private study, coaching, mentoring, self-development groups, action learning, quality improvement project), all in a structured programme built around the participant and his or her job.

10.6   Conclusion

Self-development, then, is more about process than method. However, certain methods are available that have been devised with these process in mind. In management learning, self-development emerged in the 1980s. Ten years ago it was a fringe activity, favoured by a number of practitioners who were seen as somewhat eccentric. It is now in the mainstream of management development, as it is increasingly being recognized that in order to manage complex, changing, diverse organizations, above all one must learn to manage oneself.

Box 10.5. Three ways of helping

Dimension	Instructor	Coach	Mentor
Focus on helping	Task	Results of job	Individual person developing through life
Timespan	A day or two	A month to a year	A career or a lifetime
Approach to helping	Show and tell; give supervised practice	Explore problem together; set up an opportunity for learner to try out new skills	Act as a friend willing to play the part of an adversary; listen; question to enlarge consciousness and listen more
Associated activities	Analysing task; clear instruction; supervising practice; immediate feedback on errors; consolidation	Jointly identifying the problem creating opportunities for development; developmental reviewing	Linking work with other parts of one's life; clarifying broad and long-term picture; identifying one's life-purpose
Attitude of ambiguity	Eliminate it	Use it as a challenge; encourage learners to puzzle things out	Accept it as being an exciting part of the nature of the world
Intended outcomes for the learner	Accurate performance of specified task at appropriate times; learner knows just where he or she stands	Improved results; increased capacity for independent work and performance; learner knows what he or she can achieve	Questioning of previously held assumptions about work and life; enlarged consciousness; learner knows where he or she is going
Potential outcomes for the helper	Satisfaction; control of standards	Satisfaction; learners who are self-motivated and developing	Questions for self-fulfilment
Benefits for the organization	Performance that is standardized, accurate and predictable	Performance that is both goal-directed and oriented towards improvements, creative solving of new problems	Conscious, questioning approach to the mission of the organization

Box 10.6. Instructing, coaching, mentoring and modes of managing

Model of stages of development

A. Stage*	B. Nature of next developmental step	C. Style of help needed to move on	D. Styles that people at this stage use
1. Adhering to rules and procedures	Start querying, modifying standard procedures, seeking explanation.	Instructing	Instructing
2. Responding by adapting, modifying and controlling rules, procedures, people	Seeking explanations. Building understanding that goes beyond skilful manipulation of authoritarian use of power. Being open to feedback.	Coaching	Instructing
3. Relating to norms and conventions	Questioning/challenging accepted ways and reasons. Are reasons given valid? Can you find a better way? Seeking wide experiences to explore own ideas.	Mentoring	Instructing Coaching
4. Experiencing things and learning from experience	Deepening interests. Seeking views of others to explore how these relate to yours.	Coaching Instructing	Instructing Coaching
5. Experimenting and deliberately trying to find out more	Broadening out again. Seeing the whole picture. Building cross-connections with views of others.	Mentoring	Instructing Coaching
6. Connecting, linking separate parts, ideas, people together	Seeking your special purpose. Asking "why on earth am I here? What am I doing with life?"	Mentoring	Instructing Coaching Mentoring
7. Integrating yourself with the world and dedicating yourself to your life task	This may be enough for most of us.	Reflecting	Instructing Coaching Mentoring

* Columns A and B adapted from Leary et al. (1986).

Appendix 1: Questionnaire on stages/modes of managing

Below are 70 statements about yourself and/or the way you manage. For each statement, allocate points from 0 to 8 as follows:

0. This is not at all like me/I am rarely like this/I do not at all agree with this statement.
1. This is hardly like me/I am rarely like this/I slightly agree with this statement.
2. This is a bit like me/I am occasionally like this/I slightly agree with this statement.
3. This is somewhat like me/I am sometimes like this/I somewhat agree with this statement.
4. This is like me/I am like this/I agree with this statement.
5. This is quite like me/I am quite a lot like this/I definitely agree with this statement.
6. This is a lot like me/I am very often like this/I agree quite strongly with this statement.
7. This is considerably like me/ I am nearly always like this/I very strongly agree with this statement.
8. This is very considerably like me/ I am always like this/I very strongly agree with this statement.

At the end of the statements you will find a table made up of boxes. Each box contains the number of one of the statements 1-70; write in the points that you have scored yourself for that item (i.e. 0-8) in the appropriate box.

The statements

1. I like to base decisions on established rules and regulations.
2. I will bend the rules if necessary to get the job done.
3. I try to keep reasonably well-in with the powers that be.
4. I like a job that gives me lots of variety and different experiences.
5. I think that I have a contribution to make to the way that things are done around here.
6. I keep open-minded and take into account any other views that other people may have, especially those that seem to differ from or contradict my own.
7. I feel that I know the answer to the question "why on earth am I here?"
8. I like a boss who tells me what I have got to do and how to do it.
9. You cannot afford to let feelings get in the way of doing a good job.
10. I try to find out about the way we do things — who decided it, when and why.
11. To be an effective manager you have got to be prepared to step out of line, to stand up for your way of doing things.
12. I like to manage things by working out carefully what I am going to do, how I am going to do it, when, and so on.
13. As a manager, your main responsibility is to manage yourself.
14. I am committed to a particular idea or philosophy of life.
15. When I am doing something unpleasant, I try to switch off my feelings and wishes, and just concentrate on the established rules or procedures.
16. I admire people who can get what they want out of others.
17. I like to have an explanation of the reasoning behind the way we do things.
18. Experience is the best teacher.
19. I base decisions on logical, rational thought.
20. It is important to get other people's opinions before coming to your own decision, because what you finally decide may have an effect on them.

21. There are some issues and principles to which I am prepared to give priority over my own personal success and ambition.
22. I like to do things by the book.
23. As a manager you cannot have too many scruples — it is a case of the ends justifying the means.
24. As a manager, I think that theories of motivation and so on can be helpful in understanding what is going on.
25. The way I learn best is through experience.
26. I like to pass on my ideas to other people.
27. You should take feelings as well as facts into account when making decisions.
28. I wonder if I am making a really useful contribution to the world.
29. When something goes wrong, or I make a mistake, I either refer back to the procedures or ask for instructions.
30. If I did not agree with what I was being asked to do, I would do what I thought was right, as long as I thought I could get away with it without anyone knowing.
31. If I did not agree with what was expected of me, I would still do it rather than risk rocking the boat.
32. I like to think things out for myself rather than rely on other people's decisions or explanations.
33. I like to be given really large-scale, "meaty" projects.
34. When making decisions, I try to put myself in the place of the other people who are involved and affected, and imagine how they will feel.
35. I know what it is that I have to give the world.
36. I am at a loss when something new or unexpected turns up.
37. You have got to stamp your own image on the way you do things.
38. As a manager, it is important to set an example to others by respecting commonly accepted standards of behaviour, dress and so on.
39. I am beginning to understand myself.
40. I want to experiment and explore, to find out better ways of doing things.
41. I base decisions on intuitive feelings for what is involved.
42. I have a degree of dedication to some more important cause than my own development.
43. A manager's job is to issue instructions and see that they are carried out.
44. I think that it is important to be clear-cut and decide things one way or the other.
45. I sometimes have ideas that I think would not be acceptable around here, so I keep them to myself.
46. I look for new experiences, even though these may be difficult and involve uncertainty and risk.
47. It is important to be systematic and methodical.
48. A manager's job is to enable everybody to manage themselves.
49. I am prepared to make personal sacrifices for something I feel to be very important, other than my own career or development.
50. I look to others for instructions as to what to do.
51. A manager's got to do what a manager's got to do.
52. When a change occurs I go to others who are also involved and ask them what they are going to do.
53. When something goes wrong, or I make a mistake, I try to learn from it and decide what went wrong and how to do it better next time.
54. I like to become really proficient in certain specific areas — "our resident expert on ...".
55. I place importance on thinking about what I can do for my subordinates' development as well as for my own.
56. A manager's job is to create a better world for others to live in.
57. I like to have clear-cut guidelines.
58. Procedures and so on are OK, but you have to ignore or modify them in practice, otherwise nothing would be done.

59. I find myself wanting to challenge the status quo, but do not bother because there is no real point and it will only make life difficult.
60. Sometimes I feel as though my face no longer fits around here.
61. It is important to think things through carefully.
62. When I am doing something, I am aware of the effect that my own feelings, wishes and prejudices are having on me, and try to take this into account before coming to a final decision.
63. I believe that I have a real contribution to make to society.
64. When I have finished this questionnaire, I would like to be given an interpretation of my score with instructions on what it means and what I should do about it.
65. When I have finished this questionnaire, I would like to be able to use it on others to find ways of supervising and controlling them.
66. When I have finished this questionnaire, I would like to compare my scores with those of other people.
67. When I have finished this questionnaire, I would like to try out another way of finding out about myself.
68. When I have finished this questionnaire, I would like to work out ways of getting more insights into myself, and then compare these results with those.
69. When I have finished this questionnaire, I would like to get together with some other people, share our experiences and try to work out how to help each other with our development.
70. When I have finished this questionnaire, I would like to think about what it means in terms of the extent to which I am able to make a useful contribution to society.

☐ ☐ ☐ ☐ ☐ ☐ ☐
1 2 3 4 5 6 7

☐ ☐ ☐ ☐ ☐ ☐ ☐
8 9 10 11 12 13 14

☐ ☐ ☐ ☐ ☐ ☐ ☐
15 16 17 18 19 20 21

☐ ☐ ☐ ☐ ☐ ☐ ☐
22 23 24 25 26 27 28

☐ ☐ ☐ ☐ ☐ ☐ ☐
29 30 31 32 33 34 35

☐ ☐ ☐ ☐ ☐ ☐ ☐
36 37 38 39 40 41 42

☐ ☐ ☐ ☐ ☐ ☐ ☐
43 44 45 46 47 48 49

☐ ☐ ☐ ☐ ☐ ☐ ☐
50 51 52 53 54 55 56

☐ ☐ ☐ ☐ ☐ ☐ ☐
57 58 59 60 61 62 63

☐ ☐ ☐ ☐ ☐ ☐ ☐
64 65 66 67 68 69 70

TOTAL

☐ ☐ ☐ ☐ ☐ ☐ ☐

STAGE MODE

1 2 3 4 5 6 7

EXPERIENTIAL AND ACTION LEARNING

11

Alan Mumford

When managers are asked to indicate the most useful of the different learning experiences to which they have been exposed, the majority of them answer "learning from the job". However, many job experiences are not used for effective learning. They arise in an unstructured, unplanned way. They are recognized, if at all, only by the individual manager and are not exploited by a trainer or developer. They are normally only partially understood and partially effective. Managerial work is fraught with stress, interruptions, long working hours, interpersonal issues, uncertainty, and heavy responsibilities. Managers rarely, if ever, have the opportunity to sit back and reflect on their experiences in order to learn to cope better with similar or new situations in the future. In most cases, time does not allow for it. Instead, good and bad experiences accumulate, and sometimes obliterate one another. Because there is a lack of opportunity for reflection and change, managers tend to apply solutions to new problems which are similar to the ones applied previously. They do not have the possibility of gathering enough information to attack their problems from a completely different angle.

However, this is not a question purely of training. It is also very much a question of managerial organization. Pascale and Athos (1981) report the following about learning in Japanese companies:

> There isn't a logical difference between how American and Japanese managers think about decision-making but the weight of experience in decision-making can be very different. The Japanese tap into their experience to inform their understanding. They regard their day-to-day corporate experiences as a learning lab from which they may acquire wisdom.

This may account for some of the success that Japanese companies have had in terms of innovation and efficient production systems. Indeed, major western companies realize when they try to achieve "just-in-time" production, with "zero defects" and "no inventories", that this is achieved first and foremost through an attitude of mind among their managers, which incessantly reflects on the way in which work is done, constantly using their analysis to search for continuous improvements.

Learning from experience requires more than the allocation of time. It requires the presence of people (peers, trainers, consultants, etc.) who have coaching skills that can help managers to really learn from their experiences. The main concern of this chapter is how to learn from experience on, within, and around the job.

Unfortunately, this whole area has often been seen by many trainers as one which does not concern them. Such trainers ignore the vast potential for increasing learning productivity which could be secured if we helped managers to learn more effectively in the real world through structured and purposeful learning at work.

This chapter is about enhancing the learning effects of experience. It attempts to describe ways in which the trainer can make use of managers' experiences in general through different approaches in a training setting, on the assumption that the trainer does not influence the work situation of the managers, but helps managers to learn from the situation they are in.

The fact that we have called this chapter "Experiential and action learning" may require an explanation. There is no clear distinction between the two terms in real life. Action learning tends to be a construct of experiential learning in the form of programmes which have certain characteristics. For example, a characteristic of an action learning programme is that it is oriented towards organizational change. In return, experiential learning — using real-life experiences to change behaviour or attitudes — also uses elements of action learning. However, when describing experiential learning we have in mind not a set of techniques or a type of programme, but a broad concept of utilizing real-life experiences for learning purposes. It may appear in a number of different forms on or off the job, or it may be achieved using a number of different techniques, and it may be of different durations. Experiential learning may be recognized in the actions of a session at a training course, as well as a several-months-long training programme. Action learning, on the other hand, is seen as a type of learning programme which corresponds to a set of criteria. Action learning comprises a set of logically interconnected activities which are structured specifically for achieving personal learning and organizational change.

11.1   Defining the process

Clearly, there is a great potential in turning experience into learning and using learning to cope better with new experiences. Before we discuss how learning from experience can be successfully carried out in practice, let us describe the term "experiential learning".

The most used theory of experiential learning is that of Kolb's learning cycle (figure 11.1).

The cycle is particularly useful for understanding experiential learning, its inner process. Accepting Kolb's model as a definition of what the learner does during an experiential learning cycle, we can illustrate how the trainer may interact with the learner during a cycle.

Figure 11.1. Kolb's learning cycle

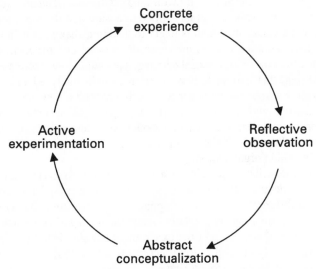

If the aim of the training is to achieve change in behaviour, the *concrete experience* should be selected from realities and problems encountered in the job which are of concern to the learner, and which are likely, when reflected on, to lead to a change in behaviour. For example, in the case of a manager encountering faulty deliveries of products going out of his or her department, one concrete experience to be selected might be a particular faulty product delivery. The trainer would then ask the manager to describe the circumstances of the faulty product delivery.

At the *reflective observation stage* of the learning cycle, the manager takes a detached view of what has happened, analyses the actions that led up to the experience, the interpersonal relations that were at play and environmental factors that influenced the actions, such as corporate strategy, budgetary regulations or personnel policies. The trainer is able, in a training situation, to assist managers to ask themselves "the right" questions and help them to avoid letting personal emotions or preconceived opinions distort their objectivity. For example, the trainer may facilitate a process whereby the manager's own assumptions that "it is all the fault of the system" are challenged, and the experience is analysed from the perspective that "some of the things went wrong because of the way I, as a manager, handled them".

Having analysed what has happened, and identified the factors that surrounded the experience, it is natural for the learner to establish his or her own concept of reality for future use. This stage is called "*abstract conceptualization*". Schein (1987) points out in his book on "process consultation" that managers often know that something is wrong, but do not know what to do about it. They often lack the appropriate skills to conceptualize, or to develop a general picture of the nature of the problem, which could be of help for solving similar problems in the future.

In our example, the manager might decide to keep in mind for future action that the way in which he or she listens to all collaborators when production matters are discussed might have something to do with faulty deliveries. This is a stage where, in a training setting, methods can be applied to ensure that the manager is able to conceptualize the situation, which is likely to lead to a change in behaviour.

Active experimentation is what managers do most of their time, consciously or unconsciously. In terms of experiential learning, it is useful to see "active experimentation" as the stage that leads up to new experiences to be analysed and conceptualized. The trainer assists the manager to experiment with a new approach, or new ideas of managing, which leads to a different experience, serving the purpose of giving the manager a better understanding about what different styles of management lead to in terms of results. The experimentation is of use, not only to the manager, but also to the whole organization.

Although we described experiential learning by giving concrete examples based on Kolb's tidy cycle, the reality of a manger, of course, consists of numerous circles, each one at a different stage of development at any one time. Many circles are incomplete, some are conscious, others escape the manager's conscious analysis. The major strength of well-thought-out experiential learning is to help the manager to develop, particularly the ability to reflect and to conceptualize, and to make use of new perspectives when encountering new problems.

11.2   Approaches to experiential learning

We suggest four approaches to experiential learning, based on research carried out by Honey, Robinson and Mumford, where a number of directors were asked to describe their learning experiences and to look at forthcoming activities, to see if they could identify learning opportunities within them. The intention was to produce practical guidelines on how directors and senior managers could learn more effectively from their work experiences. This study showed (through different dimensions) a similar picture and concluded that the people under survey used four different approaches; individuals learn differently from apparently similar experiences. Some individuals used one approach exclusively — few used all four. The four approaches were found to be "intuitive", "incidental", "retrospective" and "prospective".

(A)   The intuitive approach

This involves learning from experience, but not through a conscious process. The person using intuitive learning claims that learning is an inevitable consequence of having experiences. If questioned, he or she is able to talk in detail about a variety of different experiences, describing what happened and what was achieved. However, someone using the intuitive approach finds it difficult, and unnecessary, to articulate what they learned or how they learned it. They are content that learning occurs "naturally".

Since people using the intuitive approach put their trust in learning as a "natural", effortless process, they find it difficult to accept that there are advantages to be gained by making the process more deliberate and conscious, either for themselves or for other people.

(B)   The incidental approach

This involves learning by chance from activities that jolt an individual into conducting a "post-mortem". A variety of things can act as a jolt: for example, when something out of the ordinary crops up or when something has not gone according to plan. Mishaps and frustrations often provide the spur.

When people using incidental learning are particularly affected by something, they are inclined to mull over what happened in an informal, unstructured way. People using incidental learning tend to use the benefit of hindsight as a way of rationalizing, even justifying, what happened. One difference of the incidental approach from the intuitive approach is that people using it find it easier to conduct post-mortems by talking things over with someone else.

(C)   The retrospective approach

This involves learning from experience by looking back over what happened and reaching conclusions about it in a more structured way. The retrospective approach reviews mishaps and mistakes, but in addition lessons are drawn from routine events and successes. Learning is extracted from a diverse range of small and large, positive and negative experiences.

People using the retrospective approach conduct reviews, sometimes in their heads, sometimes in conversation and sometimes on paper. The sequence looks like this:

Something has happened ➝ It is reviewed ➝ Conclusions are reached

The outcome in the retrospective approach is that considered conclusions are knowingly reached. An individual, by reviewing, acquires knowledge, skills and insights or has them confirmed and reinforced.

An example of using a retrospective approach is a time management seminar that was held for a group of airline managers. In order to get an idea of how time was spent on communication, they were asked to bring copies of all the written communications they had sent or received in the last two weeks. In the training session, they reviewed critically their own correspondence. In doing this, they were instructed to assess the importance and the relevance of the various pieces of correspondence in relation to the goals and strategies of their organization and the time they spent on the correspondence. Their analysis showed that a significant proportion of their time was, in fact, spent on communication that was unimportant both for the organization and for their own jobs. It led them to take a closer look at the way in which they generally communicated in their daily work. It also helped them to become more conscious of their roles as managers in their organization.

(D)   The prospective approach

This involves all the retrospective elements, but includes an additional dimension. Whereas retrospection concentrates on reviewing what happened *after* an experience, the prospective approach includes planning to learn *before* an experience. Future events are seen not merely as things to be done, which are important in their own right, but also as opportunities to learn. The sequence in prospective learning is:

| Plan to learn | → | Implement the plan | → | It is reviewed | → | Conclusions are reached |

An example of using a prospective experiential learning approach is what Arie P. De Geus (1988) did as head of planning for the Royal Dutch/Shell Group of companies. Shell oil managers were made to take part in a hypothetical exercise where the price of oil was assumed to have plummeted to US$15 a barrel as opposed to US$27, the price at the time in question. They were asked to describe how the Government, their competitors and they themselves would behave in such a situation. At first, the managers regarded the exercise as being purely theoretical and not entirely relevant. They were used to optimizing based on a certain amount of control of the industry, and what had happened in the past. Hence, they were used to practising retrospective learning. However, they carried out the exercise, and developed mental models of the scenario. When the oil price went down to nearly US$10 a barrel a few months later, the organization had already visited the "world of US$15 a barrel", which, according to De Geus, helped "during panicky times".

11.3   From approaches to methods

Having discussed the process of learning from experience and described four possible approaches, we shall look at four different methods of enabling managers to learn from their experience:

1. Questioning

2. Confronting

3. Encouraging

4. Supporting

These methods can be applied in a situation where the trainer acts as a sort of development consultant to an individual or to a group. They can also usefully be included in training activities where the trainer enables managers to apply the methods to one another.

The four methods can be seen to form a process of change within an individual which takes place in an experiential learning setting. By being *questioned*, the learner discovers more about the nature of the problem. By being *confronted* with the facts, opinions or feelings of others, he or she recognizes a need for change. *Encouraging* the learner may mean making him or her want to go through a process of real change. By being *supported* the learner receives ideas, and may be supported in the form of materials or people to effect the desired change.

(A) Questioning

If a manager is to learn from experiences by reflecting on them and subsequently by changing behaviour, it is important for the trainer to understand the power of open questioning. Margerison (1988) distinguishes between open questioning and solution-centred questioning.

Solution-centred questioning is often used by trainers, consultants or peers who are so keen to see the problem solved that they suggest their own solutions in the form of questions, such as "Why don't you try talking to the trade union about it?", or "Why don't you throw away your expensive quality control system and motivate the workers to exercise continuous quality checks?" Margerison maintains that the solution-centred approach, unless requested, often leads the learner to defend against the solution. We suggest that it may also have the opposite effect, namely that the learner "buys" the solution, because it is an easy way out. Both effects, however, are unacceptable in an experiential learning programme.

Open-ended questions, however, encourage the learner to actively analyse his or her experience and search for answers. This is essential for effective experiential learning to take place. Open questions are questions that cannot simply be answered by "yes" or "no" and take such forms as "Why did you decide not to talk to the trade union about it?" or "What are the exact benefits of your quality control system?"

Open questions serve two main purposes. The first is to engage the learner in uncovering hitherto unseen aspects of the problem. The second main purpose derives from the first one. It is to assist the learner in identifying the causes of the problem — causes due either to behaviour or to environmental constraints. Open questioning deals with the learner's process of reasoning and actions rather than actual solutions.

(B) Confronting

It is normally by being confronted with the fact that something is not working out that managers are encouraged to attend a training programme based on experiential learning. Because management is such a personalized process, where the managers' style is a function of their perceptions of their own role, their organization and of their peers and subordinates, the effect of confrontation is often to make them realize that the reality may be different from their perceptions of it.

For example, a classic management dilemma is that of motivation and control. The manager wants the benefit of a motivated workforce but, out of fear that the final product will not be up to standard, also directs and personally controls the work to ensure that it is carried out satisfactorily. Suppose that the manager was attending a training programme which was based on experiential learning methods. Suppose also that the department for which the manager was responsible was receiving complaints from customers about substandard service. The manager's "experience", to be used as a basis for learning, is of customers complaining of substandard service. His or her perception of a manager's role is to direct and control while encouraging the employees to do their utmost in their job. In this case, an appropriate means of confrontation would be to try to find out from the employees what prevented them from rendering high quality service to customers, and presenting their views in the form of statements or questionnaires. In certain cultures the answer might well be that managers' well-intentioned style of giving direction and controlling the output is, in the eyes of the employees, partly *why* their service was not up to standard. What the manager thought would be motivating was, for them, demotivating. It is quite likely that a manager would be subconsciously aware that what he or she thinks is good has a different effect on co-workers. However, it may take a training situation with appropriate methods of confrontation and subsequent encouragement and support to enable the manager to acknowledge that the facts do not confirm his or her own perceptions and then to do something about it.

There are several ways of confronting managers with information that will help them change performance. Some sources of information are at the workplace, others arise during the training. Here are some examples of sources of information from their daily work:

- performance figures (production, profits, sales, etc.);
- customer surveys or individual customer statements; and
- corporate culture surveys.

In a training session, confrontation can be created through feedback from other participants on one's own behaviour and/or analysis of the experience.

Confrontation can be painful. It can also be constructive. Painful confrontation results when undesired information is communicated without providing the feeling of psychological safety, as Schein (1987) puts it. Robin Snell (1990) suggests that "managers who suffer distress may not learn from it. They may instead sink in psychological withdrawal, burnout, cynicism, or chronic disillusionment, dwelling on bad feelings rather than concentrating on improvement."

Managers who "suffer distress" in an experiential learning session do so because they are confronted with disquieting information without being provided with constructive help so as to be able to receive the information positively. The trainer may usefully draw on the experience of other managers in the group to help the participant to see the information as being a source of personal improvement, rather than as a threatening fact.

Management is often a lonely job, in the sense that the manager is responsible to the organization for a certain result, and obtaining this may conflict with the needs of the employees. Confrontation should be constructive and take place in an atmosphere of empathy where it is implicit that any mistake is human and that it is more important to learn from the mistake than to avoid making it.

Experiential learning sessions, where managers learn to turn disquieting information into a means of improvement, enables them to realize immediate benefits. An example would be when poor results from a corporate climate survey are taken as symptoms of a situation that needs improving, and are consequently acted upon by discussing the results with subordinates.

(C) Encouraging

One of the basic principles of action learning is that managers, when working in sets, consult with one another on the problems they encounter in the implementation of their projects. They thus provide encouragement to one another through constructive criticism and ideas for improvement. They frequently find that they share the same kinds of problem. As Revans, the originator of the term "action learning" pointed out, they are "comrades in adversity" (Revans, 1982). Encouragement is also an important element of a process of learning from experience, because when managers change behaviour, it often creates difficulties in their environment. Think, for example, of a manager who decides to become more team-oriented. Breaking down old barriers vis-à-vis co-workers, which have been created by a past authoritarian style, may take a lot of courage and insistence, simply because past perceptions of the previous management style linger on. Changed behaviour towards a more participative style may arouse suspicion, even resistance.

For managers who have been questioned about their problem and thereby acquired additional perspectives on it, and who have then been confronted with information that may have contradicted their individual perceptions, it is important for them to get the feeling that "I can do it, I can successfully change to meet the challenges of using new skills". In a training situation, encouragement can be created by learning about someone else's experience, to see how they can cope, or by having other participants work on one's own situation.

(D) Supporting

In one of the projects of the International Labour Organization, the project manager in the field was experiencing interpersonal conflict and resistance to the introduction of new schemes within his project team. An external management trainer was brought in to help. The trainer soon realized that the team consisted of highly capable people who felt that their work was being hampered by two major factors. One was that the project lacked clear objectives. The other factor was the authoritarian leadership style of the manager. The trainer concluded that an intervention was required which was a mixture of consultation and training. Consultations with the group were arranged, where the team members and their manager were confronted with the effects of their bad relations with one another. Information was collected from each member of the team. The joint analysis of the information by the team led to a consensus that not only did the situation have to be improved, but also that it was possible to change it, and that the manager would have to lead the way.

The manager recognized the need to change his style, but admitted to the trainer that he did not know how. He also expressed fear of losing face if he were to "experiment" with different styles in front of his team. The trainer, with Headquarters' approval and funding, invited him to participate in an open training seminar on team-building skills, together with managers from other organizations. He accepted willingly, knowing that the seminar would provide him with a skills base for improving his behaviour with his team. This is an example of support that can be provided during an experiential learning process.

The support took three forms. The first was the fact that the trainer demonstrated that he understood the problems faced by the team. Hence it had an element of empathy. The second was to offer an appropriate form of skill building to the manager. The third form of support was to get the approval of Headquarters and to obtain funds for participation at the training seminar.

Table 11.1 below illustrates how the four methods — questioning, confronting, encouraging and supporting — can be applied in training. It suggests appropriate training methods, the type of appropriate group, examples of use, and the purposes of each method.

Table 11.1. Four experiential learning methods

	Questioning	*Confronting*	*Encouraging*	*Supporting*
Types of groups	Large groups (lectures) Small groups of 3-6 persons (consultations) One-to-one	Large groups (lectures) Small and large groups (discussions) or simulations One-to-one Individual (tests)	Small groups (discussions, consultations) One-to-one communication	Small groups One-to-one communication
Examples	Direct questions between learners Open questions to group from the trainer	Exposition of results from surveys or studies Feedback on behaviour Assessment tests Examples of other (and better) practices	Descriptions of alternative practices and the results thereof Descriptions of process of change Descriptions of consequences of change	Transfer of ideas for implementation Action plan preparation
Purposes	To reach a better understanding of the problem To identify causes of the problem	The learners recognize the need to change behaviour or attitude	The learners wish to go through a process of change	The learners receive the necessary inputs to effect change

11.4 Experiential learning: An example of application

In October 1990 the World Association of Industrial and Technological Research Organizations organized a training workshop for directors of technological institutes from Africa, Asia and the Caribbean in Arusha, United Republic of Tanzania. Sponsored by the British Commonwealth, the aim of the workshop was to identify causes of performance problems within the directors' respective institutes. Following the definition of learning which says that learning is successful when "a learner knows something he or she did not know earlier, and can show it", participants identified unexplored causes of their institute's performance problems. If they gained different perceptions of the realities of their respective institutes and their problems, experiential learning had taken place.

The elements of the process used at the workshop were the following. After a lecture on effective management, the participants, in small groups, formulated criteria of organizational sustainability:

- Collaboration

- Organizational structure

- Use of information

- Leadership style

- Understanding customers

- Strategy formulation

- Definition of the organization's purpose

- Use of technology

- Use of innovation

- Attitudes towards change

- Problem solving

The participants then established a systems model of an organization and its environment. They worked in plenary sessions and in small groups to define the important characteristics of the links between different organizational and environmental elements.

Workshop output

A joint effort by the participants produced the following description of linkages that were considered vital for organizational sustainability.

On this model the participants superimposed linkages between the different elements. For each linkage they formulated a set of characteristics that were considered essential for the good functioning of the linkage. The outcome of their work is summarized in box 11.1.

Box 11.1. An example of workshop output

Linkage	*Characteristic*
1. *Purpose — technology:*	*Appropriate, relevant*
Explanation:	The technology has to be appropriate and relevant to the organization's purpose, and vice versa. The technology chosen should be the most suitable for achieving the organization's purpose.
2. *Purpose — management:*	*Understanding*
Explanation:	It is essential that all members of management fully understand the purpose of the organization.
3. *Purpose — people:*	*Compatible (job satisfaction), understanding, acceptable*
Explanation:	If the organization is to achieve its purpose, it should be understood by the people and compatible with their personal ambitions. In this lies their genuine acceptance of the purpose.
4. *Purpose — environment:*	*Relevant, understanding, acceptable*
Explanation:	The purpose has to be relevant to the explanation of the environment. Then it may become accepted. The purpose also has to be clear to the environment.
5. *Management — people:*	*Appropriate, free innovation, leadership style, trust, teamwork, delegation of authority and responsibility*
Explanation:	The terms are self-explanatory. The terms most frequently used in the workshop were "trust" and "delegation".
6. *Management — technology:*	*Understanding, commitment*
Explanation:	The management has to fully understand the technology of the organization, to take it into account in their strategic planning and be committed to the technology.
7. *Management — environment:*	*Understanding, commitment*
Explanation:	Management needs to understand the expectations and the potential of the environment, to be fully committed to managing in a way that responds to the environmental realities.
8. *People — technology:*	*Compatible, activity, technology generation*
Explanation:	The technology has to be right for the people's competences. It has to be a natural part of their activities. They have to use it effectively and take an active part in generating the technology.

Linkage	Characteristic
9. *People — environment:*	*Communication, understanding of solution, trust, acceptance*
Explanation:	There needs to be proper communication between the people of the organization and of the people in the environment they are supposed to serve. There needs to be proper understanding and trust of technological solutions by the users.
10. *Technology — environment:*	*Free innovation, appropriate, acceptable, relevant*
Explanation:	The technology must be based on innovation in an inspiring environment. To be accepted it must be appropriate to the needs of the environment.

At this stage, there was a common understanding about what helps create organizational sustainability. In other words, they had created a picture of the type of organization they should be striving towards by changing their own organizations. The time was ripe to assess their organizations against this somewhat "idealized background" which they had constructed. In so doing, they would identify causes of present organizational problems.

All the participants then, in turn, made a presentation in plenary of how they perceived their organization's problems. Fellow participants were given the task of exploring, through questioning, the problems as they were presented. They were instructed to find out about the nature of the problem by asking open questions to the presenter. An extract from the problem descriptions that emerged from the rounds of questioning appears in box 11.2.

The exploration of the nature of the organizations' performance problems enabled participants to identify causes. While the nature of the problems had been explored through questioning, causes were identified in discussion in plenary. As causes were identified, they were charted on a board for everyone to see. The causes were identified against the "ideal" organizational model that they had constructed. Although causes of performance problems were identified for each organization separately, they were put together in the final presentation, to obtain an overall picture of the most common causes of problems.

Having discussed causes in groups, the "helpers" among the participants consulted with the presenters by suggesting how some of the problems could be solved. By helping one another through questioning, discussion and consultations over their respective experiences, a high degree of experiential learning took place.

11.5 Action learning: Programmes for making the most of experiential learning

Action learning was the first management development process to focus primarily

Box 11.2. Examples from a round of questioning

Organization A	Its relevance to industry is unclear. There is a lack of organizational identity among their scientists vis-à-vis the institute.
Organization B	The overall purpose of the organization is not clear. There is friction between the mother organization and the Ministry, which hampers its performance.
Organization C	The organization has a poor image vis-à-vis the public.
Organization D	They do not involve industry sufficiently in their development activities, especially the SME sector. They have at times been applying the wrong solutions to problems in industry.
Organization E	They have limited information about the overall needs in the environment. They have no documented plan of action.
Organization F	There is a problem of poor management-people relations, hampering the implementation of solutions. There is insufficient communication between management and their environment.
Organization G	They have problems keeping staff on board. There is poor compatibility between the skills of the people they employ and what the organization tries to do. There is a lack of delegation in the organization, which leads to insufficient involvement of the people in the development work.
Organization H	They perform inadequate market surveys/research. They have inadequate manufacturing facilities.
Organization I	They have defined a purpose which is unrealistic in relation to the available human and financial resources. They also suffer from an inappropriate organizational structure.

on real work and real problems, as distinct from traditional education and training activities which dealt only occasionally with real work, or more frequently with simulations. Professor Reg Revans was the initiator of early examples of action learning, and the force behind its introduction in the United Kingdom and in promoting it in the rest of Europe, the Americas, Asia, Australasia, and various parts of Africa. There is now however a further stream of development which stretches the concepts of action learning beyond their original dimensions, providing a different focus for, and different initiatives in the creation of, improved learning from experience.

(A)   A definition of action learning

Some trainers assume that action learning is only another phrase for "learning from experience". It is not uncommon to come across training and consultancy companies who, in the presentation of the programmes, claim that they make use of "action-learning methods". What lies behind the phrase is traditional training methods such as case-study, simulations or action-plan formulation. In reality action learning is not simply a method, or a set of methods whereby the manager learns through action.

Revans has written many volumes about action learning, without committing himself in any single one of them to a total view of what action learning is. It is a typical Revans paradox, in fact, that in his *ABC of action learning* (1983) he offers a definition of what action learning is not. In this work Revans comes closest to capturing most of what his work has actually been about:

Action learning is a means of development, intellectual, emotional or physical, that requires its subject, through responsible involvement in some real, complex and stressful problem, to achieve intended change to improve his observable behaviour henceforth in the problem field.
The essentials of action learning are as follows:

1. Learning for managers should mean learning to take effective action. Acquiring information, becoming more capable in diagnosis or analysis has been overvalued in management learning.

2. Learning to take effective action necessarily involves actually taking action, not recommending action or undertaking analysis of someone else's problem.

3. The best form of action for learning is work on a defined project rooted in reality and of significance to the managers themselves. The project should involve implementation as well as analysis and recommendation.

4. While managers should take responsibility for their own achievements on their own project, the learning process is a social one; managers learn best with and from each other.

5. The social processes should be achieved and managed through regular meetings of managers to discuss their individual projects; the group is usually called a "set".

6. The role of people providing help for the members of the set is essentially and crucially different from that of the normal management trainer. Their role is not to teach (whether through lectures or case simulations) but to help managers learn from exposure to problems and to each other.

One of the reasons why action learning as a term is not used as loosely as other terms in training and development is that action learning has become almost a movement. Practitioners in several countries meet at conferences to elaborate on uses of action learning.

Some trainers and organization developers who have operated according to the basic rules of action learning would go as far as to say that action learning is a philosophy of carrying out training programmes and organizational interventions. It has become a philosophy for certain people, because the sheer experience of running action-learning programmes has also influenced their way of thinking about other types of training intervention. In fact, many trainers and consultants we have met developed their organization consultants' skills by running action learning programmes. However, to avoid feeling too much bound by the action-learning approach, they have kept and modified elements of the approach for other types of programme, using other names for these programmes.

(B)   A case for action learning

As a result of research work (Mumford, 1988), a new model of management development has been created. This is shown in table 11.2. For our purposes the basis for the model can be simply stated. It is that when most management developers have talked about management development, they have essentially focused on type 3. While the reasons for this focus are understandable, namely the ineffectiveness of much so-called "learning on the job", the failure to recognize and deal effectively with type 1 has been a major weakness in management development processes.

Table 11.2   Model of management development

Type 1 "Informal managerial"	— accidental processes
Characteristics	— occur within managerial activities — explicit intention is task performance — no clear development objectives — unstructured in development terms — not planned in advance — owned by managers
Development consequences	— learning is real, direct, unconscious, insufficient

Type 2 "Integrated managerial"
— opportunistic processes

   Characteristics
      — occur within managerial activities
      — explicit intention is both task performance and development
      — clear development objectives
      — structured for development by boss and subordinate
      — planned beforehand or reviewed subsequently as learning experiences
      — owned by managers

Development consequences
      — learning is real, direct, conscious, more substantial

Type 3 "Formal management"	— planned processes
Development characteristics	— often away from normal managerial activities — explicit intention is development — clear development objectives — structured for development by developers — planned beforehand or reviewed subsequently as learning experiences — owned more by developers than managers
Development consequences	— learning may be real (through a job) or detached (through a course) — is more likely to be conscious, relatively infrequent

Source: Mumford, 1988, p. 115.

Conceptually and practically our position is that we can improve some aspects of type 3 through action-learning processes. We can take many of the crucial elements of action learning back into type 2 situations, the critical difference being that whereas type 3 processes are essentially initiated, directed and probably controlled by management development specialists, in type 2, managers initiate, direct and control their own learning from real work experiences.

If we start with type 1 activities, we will, as argued earlier, actually be dealing with the most frequently encountered learning experiences for managers. However, as suggested at the beginning of this chapter, these informal and accidental experiences, though powerful, are often not very well understood or used as learning experiences. By far the biggest increase in effective management development would be to engage managers to improve these processes, and to convert them into type 2. Managers are unlikely either to recognize these opportunities for what they are, or to work on them effectively unless they are given help, and this is where the management development adviser and trainer can and should come in. The great leap which is required here is not that of managers jumping from type 1 to type 2, but rather that required of advisers and trainers, in order for them to grow in their own work to provide managers with the help they need.

(C) Action learning and other approaches

Revan's own theory of learning can be repeated here as an equation:

$$L \text{ (Learning)} = P \text{ (Programme knowledge)} + Q \text{ (Questioning)}$$

Action learning is concerned with the Q part of the equation. The simplicity of the equation, and the attractiveness at least to managers of the basic idea of "learning from experience", should not delude us into thinking that action learning is exclusively founded on real work with all its complexities, turbulence and difficulties. Action learning also involves complex relationships and requires depth of understanding, although it is based on a fundamentally simple proposition.

The major difference between action learning and many other programmes where reality-based problems are dealt with, is that action learning aims purposely at learning from solving problems that entail taking risks and resolving uncertainties. Action learning acknowledges that most management problems are open-ended and that there is rarely one right solution to the problem. Thus, managers tend to learn how to cope better with managing successfully in situations of complexity and uncertainty. In this respect, action-learning programmes represent a counterweight to programmes which are based on providing rational, "correct" solutions to practical issues. Action-learning programmes concentrate more on enabling managers to learn to develop *their own ability* to solve problems. Therefore, improvement of skills in solving organizational issues of an interpersonal nature often represent important benefits to the participants. George Boulden and Alan Lawlor, two experienced action-learning practitioners, stress that action learning is not "the final solution". It is a means of learning about learning (Boulden and Lawlor, 1987).

Action learning is characterized by learner-based development programmes. Box 11.3 gives an indication of how it relates to business school programmes, pre-packaged courses and group dynamics laboratories.

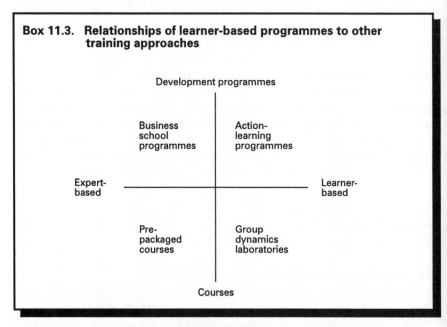

Box 11.3. Relationships of learner-based programmes to other training approaches

Box 11.3 may require some explanation of terms. By "expert-based", we mean training based on the transfer of knowledge and skills from a source, e.g. the trainer or invited specialists, and which normally aims to transmit the same skills and knowledge to all participants. An example is training in specific time-management techniques, a certain approach for creative problem-solving, or procedures for budgeting. "Learner-based" learning, on the contrary, allows the learners to assess their competence level and choose for themselves. An example is where a manager designs and implements his or her personal project for achieving improvements in the organization. Self-development is an approach that is also relevant to this category. By "courses", we mean training events aiming to achieve a specific, limited set of skills. They may also aim to provide participants with specific knowledge, such as technology advances or international law. "Development programmes", apart from tending to be of longer duration than courses, have more overall objectives, such as increasing participants' general management skills, or making them more effective agents of organizational change.

An example of an action-learning programme

Den Norske Kreditbank, one of Norway's major banks, experienced a drop in organizational performance. Several symptoms were evident. Their newly acquired technology did not live up to its expectations, organizational changes had been introduced which allowed less flexibility in the handling of clients, and there was increasing disagreement about what the criteria for good management practices should be.

They had tried different measures to boost performance. More than 100 staff members had attended extensive sales training courses, productivity groups had been set up, and most of the managers had attended various types of training courses and seminars. In spite of these efforts, there were only marginal improvements in the ways that people went about their work.

A Regional Director, Mr. H. Anonsen, decided that a different approach was needed. He started looking for a type of training that would "get under the skin" of his managers and thus create a lasting impact.

Labor Ltd. — an action-learning firm — caught his interest by offering a programme where the managers develop their skills by tackling real company problems. "We will not teach them any management skills", they said. "What we require is that you give your managers the freedom to implement changes while solving the problems which they are assigned to. We will ensure that learning takes place."

The participants had worked with actual problems in their departments. They had learned to act as consultants to each other, not by advising, but through open questioning: "Why is this a problem in your department? What prevents you from solving it?", etc. A peer pressure had been developed among the group to solve their problems. They were thus forced to search for the real problem's causes, which, some of them painfully realized, were due to their own shortcomings as managers. Once they realized where they had gone wrong, they were able, with the blessing of the top management, to put it right.

No management skills had been taught, nor had there been any cases, simulations or role-plays. In the words of Björner Christensen, Managing Director of Labor Ltd.,

"It was not a matter of providing skills, but to enable them to reflect on their performance with the help of other managers. The projects gave them the opportunity to practise their insight and to see the immediate effects of their actions."

Thirteen months later, most of the 15 managers in the programme had not only significantly improved ways of managing their departments, they had also introduced changes that saved the bank the equivalent of several million United States dollars in expenditure.

Is it that simple? Not quite. There is more to action learning than we can describe here. But the basic principles remain valid. Managers learn best from acting and reflecting on what has happened, and doing it better the next time. What action learning does is to help them appreciate this way of developing their skills. It is, in effect, a means of learning how to learn.

(D)   The process of action learning

Box 11.4 contains an outline for running action-learning programmes as suggested by Pearce (1983).

Box 11.4. How to begin an action-learning programme

Starting action learning is similar to starting training activities, but there are some significant differences:

- the programme participants will need real problems/opportunities to work on;

- important people will need to be prepared intellectually and emotionally to accept that the programme will bring about changes to the way things are done;

- people who do not consider themselves as participants on the programme will be involved, i.e.:

    (a) the person(s) who own(s) the problem/opportunity,

    (b) individuals and groups who are significant in the problem/opportunity, and

    (c) departments which have a bearing on the problem/opportunity;

- line management will need to be involved in deciding the forms of the programme because it involves them and their business. It cannot be left to functional experts.

Box 11.5 outlines stages in setting up an action-learning programme.

Box 11.5. Steps in setting up an action-learning programme

1. Decide you really want to do it.
2. Start explaining why and what you are doing.
3. Gain some support and commitment.
4. Agree on the people and problems/opportunities that will be aimed at.
5. Produce a basic outline of the programme, i.e. objectives, estimated (or fixed) timings, costs, resources, activities, etc.
6. Try to produce a cost/benefit analysis (in operational terms and as far as possible in financial terms).
7. In some cases, produce a prospectus explaining the programme.
8. Agree on a budget (try to get an allowance which the participants can manage).
9. Recruit resources internally and/or externally, i.e. set advisers, etc.
10. Get participants and problems.
11. It is particularly important that you spend a lot of time and energy briefing *everyone* you possibly can, but particularly: participants, the problem/opportunity owners, participants' bosses, your personnel/training colleagues, and your boss(es).
12. Bring the appropriate people together for a start-up activity. Involve participants' advisers and try to involve problem/opportunity owners, and participants' bosses.
13. GO!

Box 11.6 shows a typical "own job" action-learning programme.

Box 11.6. Outline of a typical "own job" (Type 1) programme

Setting up the programme (time likely to be taken 2-6 months)

1. Getting delegates (usually quite time-consuming).
2. Course organizer/set adviser interviewing each delegate and his or her sponsor (usually boss), plus any other interested parties, such as personnel specialists, training managers or management development advisers.
3. Agreeing the project that the delegate will treat on the programme, i.e.:
    (a) current job;
    (b) selected parts of job, e.g. an area which requires special attention because it is a problem or because it has never been properly tackled for whatever reason;
    (c) a special part-time project devised by more senior management. With this option it is vital to ensure that the project is real and sufficiently important.
4. It is useful if each delegate is asked to do a simple write-up to create a benchmark and to show the stage reached. It can help later to judge progress.

Box 11.7. describes what should occur during an action-learning programme.

Box 11.7. What should happen during the programme

1st meeting

Preferably dinner on the first evening and short session afterwards. It would be useful if sponsors could attend this session. Next day the set works a full day with the set adviser(s). At this first meeting the agenda runs as follows:

(a) the set adviser to describe action learning, the aims of the programme, the format of the programme, the role of the set adviser, the facilities available, i.e. budgets, etc.

(b) each delegate to describe their job/project as they see it, what they are trying to achieve, and how they hope to achieve it.

Questions suggested by Professor Revans are useful at this stage: What am I trying to do? What is preventing me from doing it? What action am I going to take?

2nd to 5th meeting (one day every fortnight, i.e. months 1 to 3)

1. Working on projects
2. Working on delegates' needs/skills; supporting and criticizing
3. Visiting one another's companies — as a set and individually
4. Dealing with whatever arises.

6th or 7th meeting (i.e. months 3 or 4)

Invite clients and/or sponsors to the set for lunch and an afternoon meeting, to:

(a) explain what has happened;
(b) answer their queries;
(c) show progress; and
(d) learn from one another.

7th/8th/9th meeting (i.e. months 3½ to 5)

1. Continue working on projects, particularly on action
2. Continue working on members' needs of skill/knowledge
3. Visits as appropriate.

10th meeting (5th month)

1. Review activity: (a) programme successes and low-spots
                         (b) personal progress
2. Decide how to handle unfinished business, i.e. how to continue with activities which still need handling, by working in pairs, etc.

For organizers — go back to zero.

(E)   Roles and functions in action learning

Figure 11.2 shows schematically the different roles and functions in an action-learning programme. It should be noted that although the figure describes participation from different companies, many action-learning programmes are run with people from the same company in a project set. A participant may work on a project from his or her own job, or try to solve a problem in another department or company. What is important is that he or she develops skills in tackling organizational problems by exploring different perspectives of the problem.

Figure 11.2. Typical exchange of participants between two of the four nominating companies

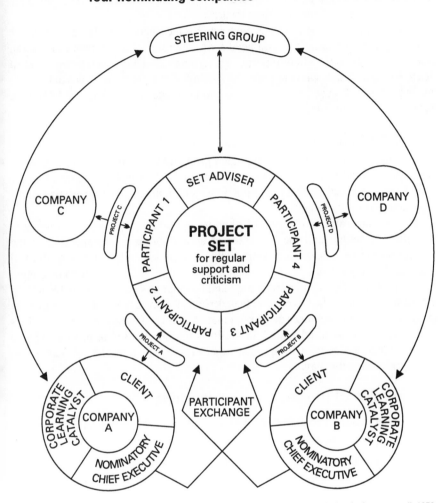

Source: Boulden and Lawlor, 1987, p. 28, adapted from ALP International Ltd., "The self-developing manager", 1978.

Client and sponsor

Projects however must have a "client" — in most cases probably one person but in some cases more than one. The client is the person who has a specific interest in the end result of the project. A manager participating in the programme ought to have a clear and direct need to carry out the project, but in all cases except those where the participant is also the chief executive, the participant will no doubt have to get agreement from someone else before the recommendations in the first part of the project are accepted for implementation in the second part.

As with the project itself, the client has to be chosen carefully so that he or she is the person who is actually most interested in solving the problem. This person is also sometimes called the "problem owner".

Unless the client is the chief executive who has the authority to allocate resources to solving the problem, there is a need for a "sponsor". The sponsor may be the executive to whom the client reports, or a resource allocator, such as the chief of finance or personnel, who supports the solving of the problem. It is vital for the outcome of an action-learning programme to negotiate sponsor support before the decision is taken to solve the problem.

The participant

As with any management development programme, the prime issue is that the participants should only be on a programme in the first place because there are identifiable needs for personal development which, in the mind of a participant, the programme is likely to help.

The special features of action learning mean also that the participant needs to be helped to understand the processes of action learning, and specifically the differences between how things work in this process as compared with traditional teaching. Many managers arrive on such a programme still expecting to be taught, and in the early stages show frustration and unhappiness when these expectations are not met. As individuals they have to understand the process and also to participate in it in a way which facilitates the development not only of themselves but of others in the *set*. "Fellows in adversity" or "fellows in opportunity" in most groups do engage successfully in helping each other. There are, however, obstacles and difficulties along the way.

The roles of the set in action learning

- To assist members to define the purposes, time-scale and desired end results.
- To assist others by testing and clarifying ideas.
- To ask the questions others will not ask of themselves.
- To provide additional motivation for each individual to take action.
- To share ideas on resolving difficulties encountered by others.
- To offer information derived from their functional and managerial experience.
- To monitor progress.
- To share time effectively and appropriately.
- To manage themselves and review the effectiveness of that management.
- To take charge of their individual and group learning.
- To establish ways of reviewing and improving their learning.

Sometimes in a set, a participant may want to take too much time for his or her own problem at the expense of others; others adopt too low a profile; some are insensitive in the way they present advice, or unduly sensitive in receiving it. They must recognize that they are involved in a mutual learning process, that they are not involved in "teaching" each other anything. The best action-learning groups seem to produce effective personal feedback of the kind sought in the past from other training processes. It is more effective because it revolves around real issues and real problems. Each participant brings and discusses a project or problems, and reviews progress on it.

The set adviser

Action learning is a process in which the learner is the centre of attention, not the tutor or teacher. When the process is working properly, there will very rarely be any occasion on which the set adviser delivers knowledge. There will be temptation to do so, but if the set is to be enabled to work properly by carrying responsibility for its own learning, the temptation has to be resisted.

This is not to say that the set should be left to wallow in their own ignorance, or that the adviser should remain dumb. The appropriate intervention is to ask how they can obtain the knowledge they may well need, and to encourage the set to work out their own solutions. These may be to read material before the next meeting, to arrange a meeting with a functional specialist — or even to arrange a separate and content-oriented session with a tutor.

These principles are not easy for advisers to follow, nor always easy for the set to accept. Actual and potential set advisers should read the guidance offered by Casey (1983). In summary, Casey's suggestions based on his own experience as set adviser includes four distinctive tasks:

1. To facilitate giving.

2. To facilitate receiving.

3. To clarify (to the participants) the various processes of action learning.

4. To help others to take over tasks 1, 2 and 3.

The crucial things which trainers need to accept if they want to take on an action-learning role are given below:

Roles of set advisers

1. *To facilitate group processes*
- Develop understanding of different roles in a group.
- Help the set understand what is happening, and why.
- Help the set recognize those things which may constrain progress for the set and for individuals.
- Help the set recognize positive forces for growth and development in the set.

- Confront the set or individuals with unresolved problems
- Encourage the set to review both task and process achievement from time to time.

2. *To facilitate learning*
- Discuss and subsequently identify individual and group learning processes.
- Encourage participants to keep a learning log.
- Encourage participants to set learning goals for themselves as a group and as individuals.
- Encourage the group and individuals to review learning achievement.

3. *To encourage management processes in the group*
- Advise the set to define measurable objectives.
- Help the set develop its own targets for the use and sharing of time.
- Help the individuals within the set to share the management of the group, e.g. chairmanship.

(F)   Features of action learning

Victoria Marsick (Marsick and Watkins, 1990) suggests that managers are normally helped to learn from experience by:
- working through a process of finding the right problem to be addressed;
- examining a problem from multiple perspectives;
- learning to challenge taken-for-granted norms;
- learning a process of consultation;
- gaining insight into the dynamics of the groups in which they work; and
- gaining insight into oneself as a manager.

Something participating managers often find out when exploring the nature of the problem to be addressed is that the problem needs to be reformulated. As Marsick points out, typically 90 per cent of the project problems get redefined, particularly when the issue is complex (which it often is in management) and it involves stakeholders throughout many parts of the organization. Because action learning aims to develop participants' skills in finding and dealing with causes of problems, what seems to a manager to be a fairly straightforward solution, may, when explored, uncover a maze of obstacles, each one having a number of causes. Action learning is based on dealing with open-ended problems, which cannot be said to have one "right" solution. In management, open-ended problems are, as Boulden and Lawlor suggest, affected by human values and attitudes as well as by technical considerations. For example, a decision to formulate a company's vision or business idea is more open-ended than deciding on the type of electronic mail system to install.

Action learning involves negotiation of solutions. The participants often find that they have to negotiate at the problem-finding stage as well as at the solution-implementation stage. This may account for the fact that many projects get redefined when the participant discovers that more of the problem comes from interpersonal issues in the organization than was originally anticipated. Kjell Wold, Director of Labor Ltd., claims that most of the managers attending the company's programmes recognize that it is their own ways of dealing with interpersonal issues which are at the root of the problems they select to solve in the programme.

Marsick gives an example of an electricity company that wanted to move its staff more into customer service orientation as the company marketed a new package of services instead of one product. The company thought difficulties with implementation resided in its service representatives, but as the group interviewed staff throughout the company, they found a host of other key problems that also had to be addressed, such as a major conflict between the marketing and distribution divisions that called for high-level reorganization.

There are three criteria which should be applied to the selection of problems to be worked on in an action-learning programme:

- the problem should be of real concern to the client organization, or its unit;
- it should be open-ended, i.e. there should not be one, "best" solution to it;
- it should be of a nature which enables maximum personal development to take place with the participant.

Whereas most conventional learning methods take place within the limits of what is acceptable in terms of ideas in the organization, action learning encourages participants to challenge taken-for-granted norms. In analysing an organizational problem, the participant tries to see it from different perspectives, and tries to ask well-founded questions about why things have come to be the way they are.

Someone once said that "the person who knows only one side of a matter doesn't even know that side". The action-learning participant may try and see the problem from the perspective of, say, employees, customers, other departments or national authorities. The role of the peers in the action-learning set is also to help the participant to discover additional perspectives of analysis. In doing that, the participant may well be questioning norms that until then have been tacitly accepted in the organization. As Peter Way (1989) puts it, action learning "questions the culture of an organization and may try to change it". We shall give an example.

In a chain of food stores, although lower-grade staff working in the shops are constantly in contact with customers, it is not normally the case that floor assistants have a say when it comes to deciding which products to purchase from the wholesalers. In other words, there may be many requests from customers for specific food products which these employees are not encouraged to communicate to management. It is a tacit norm, which is not questioned for two reasons. One is that management assume that their own monitoring system gives them adequate information about the types of food that might be in demand. The other reason has to do with organizational rank and perceptions of lower-level employees as not being able to provide useful information, or to suggest good ideas.

This is the type of norm that an action-learning participant might question. He or she might obtain information from employees and from management, to see if this is a real obstacle to improved product selection, and get an idea of the attitudes involved at the various levels. If more active participation by lower-level employees appears to be a useful measure, and if attitudes of perceived incompetence are at the root of the problem, he or she might negotiate a course of action with management and employees.

In an action-learning set, members consult with one another. They confront each other, they question one another to develop perspectives on their problems, and to search for ways of solving them. As the programme proceeds, the set becomes in itself a kind of small-scale learning organization, where a high level of learning from one another is achieved. When the participating managers learn to appreciate the fruitful group dynamics of their set, they gain understanding into ways of practising participative management, which is useful for application in their jobs.

GROUP WORK AND DISCUSSION METHODS

12

Tor Hernes

There is hardly a training session which does not involve group activities. Case-studies, role-plays, process consulting, problem-solving, even lecturing — all contain group activities as an important training element. This chapter aims to review the most essential group training methods. Generally they can be classified into three basic sets: undertaking problem-solving tasks in groups, learning in groups and group processes.

Group training methods may apply to: (a) in-company work groups set up to learn new skills or to solve problems; (b) groups that meet once under the direction of a manager or a trainer; and (c) groups of participants in a training intervention who are involved in anything from answering a 15-minute quiz to a long-term skills development programme.

The purpose of establishing a group is that the mere fact of being together and interacting in a certain way enables managers to achieve more than the sum of what they are able to produce individually (the synergy effect).

In many group-learning situations synergy is not always guaranteed. Cases arise, for example, where a member's views or experience are not used because the group climate does not encourage differing opinions to be put forward. As a result the group misses out on valuable contributions, since its members are unable to add their experiences.

On the other hand, a group which treats different (rather than converging) opinions as important issues and explores them together may become a breeding ground for ideas, innovation and learning.

The degree of synergy that can be obtained depends largely on the way in which the group members interact. In training we are concerned with two basic forms of synergy:

- Learning synergy — the degree to which each member learns from taking part in the group; and

- Task synergy — the degree to which synergy facilitates problem-solving.

Achieving synergy leads not only to the better accomplishment of a task, but to improved satisfaction for group members, motivating them to learn and recreate the same conditions in their workplace and become better managers.

12.1   Group processes: Principles and features

(A)   A definition of groups and their objectives

In the context of learning and working together, a group could be identified by the following characteristics (Adair, 1987):

- A sense of shared purposes — group members share the same tasks, or goals, or interests.

- A definable membership of two or more people.

- Group consciousness — members think of themselves as belonging to a group, they have a collective perception of unity; they consciously identify with each other.

- Interdependence — the members need each other's help to accomplish the purposes for which they have joined the group.

- Interaction — group members communicate with one another, influence one another, react to one another.

Because training in groups can have a variety of effects, it is important for the trainer to be able to distinguish between the different objectives that are at play. These objectives can be classified as follows:

- Learning objectives (i.e. to enhance the skills, knowledge and attitudes of group members).

- Task objectives (i.e. to accomplish concrete tasks).

- Process objectives (i.e. to enable group members to work and communicate better as a group).

These three basic objectives are interlinked and overlap (see figure 12.1).

Learning objectives

A group's *learning* objectives normally reflect the overall objective of the training intervention and are related to attitudes, skills and knowledge. They may apply to an individual and/or to the group as a whole.

In the case of individual learning, these objectives relate to management skills (technical, interpersonal, strategic, etc.). Individual learning takes place when one member learns from working with the other members of the group. This often tends to be the objective of open training programmes which are attended by people who do not normally work together and who might be from different units or organizations.

Group learning also becomes the training objective when the group as a whole needs to learn ways of dealing with a given situation. It is used mostly in tailored training interventions in which people belonging to the same work unit are confronted with a common problem. A typical situation is where a department within an organization does not satisfy its clients. A logical starting point for a training intervention is to confront the department, as a group, with the way it is perceived

Figure 12.1. Group training objectives

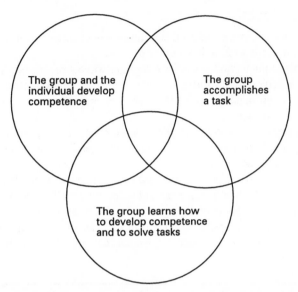

by its environment and how its substandard performance may affect its future. A learning situation is created, first, when the department is made to appreciate its weaknesses and, second, when it engages in a process where the members diagnose problems and work out solutions together.

The overlap between learning objectives and process objectives arises when the objective calls for the group members to develop their interaction skills. In such a situation, learning objectives relate to the individual members, whereas process objectives relate to the group as a whole.

Task objectives

These objectives concern the accomplishment of the identified group task. They describe what the group is expected to do, be it to solve a problem, prepare an action plan, or reach a conclusion on a case-study.

There will always be a certain element of learning in a group that is engaged in solving a problem together. The mere fact that a member recognizes other ways of accomplishing a task after working with the group constitutes a form of learning. However, the primary objective is to improve effectiveness. This is why quality circles and task forces, for example, are based primarily on task objectives.

When task work is taken a step further and allows for reflection by group members (together or individually) and they relate ways of solving the problem to their own situation as managers, the task objectives become, at the same time, the learning objectives. Task objectives focus on how, in terms of quality and quantity, the group will accomplish a given task. In addition, task objectives focus on the way the task is accomplished — such as using available information, external resources and problem-solving procedures and techniques.

Process objectives

Before a group can successfully enter a situation of effective learning or problem-solving tasks, it needs to function well as a group.

Most people, if put to work on an issue together without prior group training, may well find themselves living through power struggles, unproductive discussions, haphazard decision-making, lack of active listening, excessive courtesy and, consequently, frustration.

In group training, the process (i.e. the way members of the group work together while learning or solving problems) is an important objective. The process objective, in many ways, forms the very basis for the previous two objectives, because it aims at enabling the group to make maximum use of the individual members' capacities to achieve the overall objective. It is an aid to learning and problem solving.

Process objectives reflect certain characteristics of group behaviour, on which there are many different views. To give the reader an idea of the parameters that may be reflected in a set of process objectives, we list in box 12.1 the elements of group rating used by Schein (1969).

Box 12.1. Elements of group rating

- Goals (clarity, commitment)
- Participation (Does everyone participate? Is everyone listened to?)
- Feelings (Are they expressed freely and received with empathy?)
- Group problem diagnosis (Are problems carefully diagnosed? Does the group attack causes rather than symptoms?)
- Leadership (Does it at all times meet the group's needs?)
- Decisions (Is there consensus and support?)
- Trust (Do group members have confidence in and respect one another?)
- Creativity and growth (Is creativity encouraged? Is the group flexible?)

Some training interventions focus mainly on the process objective, such as certain team-building programmes as well as sensitivity training. In organizational development programmes where management development constitutes one of the objectives — such as in action-learning programmes — the intervention could start with the process to develop the capacity of the participants to work effectively in a group and consultatively with one another.

The three objectives at work

When carrying out group training, the function of the trainer is continuously to maintain the balance of the three objectives. He or she should be conscious of the role of each objective at the different stages of the intervention and should use them as criteria for training evaluation. Below are some general experiences encountered when using the three objectives in practical training situations:

- Without a well-developed group process, members are not able to learn fully from one another.
- The group process is improved when members learn how the group functions.
- Learning occurs not only as a result of accomplishing a task, but also from finding out what went wrong (or well) and why.
- Over-attention to problem-solving may detract from the quality of the process; a broader vision of the process and learning effects may be lost.
- When a group has to accomplish a task under pressure (of task complexity or time-limits), focus on member interaction may develop automatically.
- Short-term objectives may well become long-term learning objectives. After the group's task has been achieved, individuals reflect and look back on what was learned while working together.

(B) Critical success factors of group work

Whether or not a group is to succeed is determined by a number of factors. The usual critical factors of success are:

- the environment;
- the task;
- the group; and
- the facilitator.

These factors apply equally well to a group problem-solving exercise at an open seminar as to an in-company task force.

The environment

The group and its objectives are created in response to a set of needs and expectations in the environment. The environment may be the managers' organizations which may expect a change in behaviour or attitudes as a result of the training, or it may be the training process itself, i.e. the other participants, who expect the group to produce certain results.

The success of the group's work is measured by the extent to which it satisfies the needs and expectations of the environment. The motivation for a group to solve problems or to learn effectively is made up of two essential elements. The first is the group members' individual needs: "What do I need to learn?", "What problems are important for me to solve?" The second element is determined by the expectations of the environment: "Is the work of the group important to us?", "Do we have confidence in the ability of the group to resolve the issue?"

If the members' needs correspond to those of the environment, the basis is laid for productive group work. Otherwise, the group exercise may be of little value: the group's solutions will not be implemented and the group learning will not be used after the intervention.

The client's expectations give the group a sense of purpose. However, they may also fix limits for the group's work. It is important for the trainer to clarify the expectations of management, trade unions, employees, other departments, etc., when formulating the problem to be dealt with.

In many cases, the expectations may not be expressed in words. The environment may not know exactly what it can expect from the group's work. In such a situation trainers need to use their judgement based on their knowledge of the norms and values of the organization. For example, in a task- and relations-oriented culture, the learning of interactive skills in groups is regarded as a key factor. In a power culture, on the other hand, interactive skills training may prove counterproductive. In the best case, managers trying to apply their acquired skills are likely to become very frustrated from lack of response. The environment, being confronted with a behavioural pattern which is different from what it expected, may regard such training as a waste of time.

In open training courses, a task which is to be accomplished simply because the trainer says so is not likely to be carried out with the same degree of motivation as one which the group feels to be important to part of its work.

The task

The basis of any group training, whether the overall objective is learning-, task- or process-oriented, is the allocation of a task. The task may be set by the trainer or by senior management. It may also originate in the group itself.

The nature of the task given to a group determines the outcome of its work. It is in fact useful for a management trainer to regard the group as an organization built around the task. The following task-related success indicators could be useful for trainers to take into consideration when planning the group process:

- *Commitment* — the extent to which the task is embedded in the needs of the individual group members (i.e. the degree of "ownership" that the group member feels towards the group's task).

- *Means* — who can perform the task? How is it to be performed? What additional resources will be required?

- *Clarity* — how well is the task defined in terms of objectives, time-limits, presentation and quality standards? Is the task construed in the same way by everyone in the group?

The group

There are several different schools of thought about what constitutes an effective group. The most important characteristic of a group is its purpose. In the case of a task group, for example, decision-making capability is a major effectiveness criterion. In a learning group, the group's ability to pay attention to development needs and to learn is important. In a process-oriented group the degree of interactive listening, openness and quality of communication between the members is a major criterion. Group characteristics can be divided into the following seven sets (Mumford, 1986):

- Background
- Participation pattern
- Communication
- Cohesiveness
- Atmosphere
- Standards
- Structure and organization

The *background* of a group includes its past successes and failures in pursuing common objectives, the way it solves a problem, the accumulated group knowledge as to what works and what does not work, leadership, procedures and roles which have been applied in the past. The background also relates to the environment and why the group was formed in the first place.

Trainers — often task-oriented and focused on the present — may fall into the trap of ignoring the events and processes within the group which could belong to the past, but which dramatically influence the present. For example, if a case-study was the last group experience, it may not readily switch to another method — such as role-playing.

The group *participation pattern* can also say something about the way in which people relate to each other and the dominant leadership pattern. The group may also vary from a cacophony of everybody talking with one another to disciplined monologues by individuals.

For example, when much of the interaction in the group revolves around one person, decisions and conclusions are largely influenced by this person. Referring continuously to one person may give the members a sense of security. It may also be a kind of common delegation to the one who appears most able. This may suggest that the other members are not much concerned with the outcome of the exercise. Or it may be the result of imposed authority by one person.

It is important for the trainer to interpret a group's participation pattern and to make the group realize what effect this has on its performance.

Communication is a key factor in the success of group work and is characterized by how well the group members interact and understand one another's views. Too often in groups there are people more concerned with expressing themselves than with listening to each other. Often people are too busy preparing their next statement to listen to what other people are saying. Communication is also about understanding the *implications* of what a person means. For example, in a group decision-making process, a person saying "I don't agree with our course of action" means that he or she would have preferred another strategy. However, the implication may also be that he or she will not support it actively when it is implemented.

The role of the trainer is to sensitize the group to the importance of good communication and to make the group understand what this means in practice.

When an individual has a definite sense of belonging to a group, it is a sign of a certain group *cohesiveness*. It is sometimes referred to as the "we-feeling" of the group, the extent to which the members talk in terms of "we" and "us". In a training situation this sense of commitment to the task of the group rather than to one's personal goals is vital.

In *A passion for excellence*, Tom Peters and Nancy Austin (1985) suggest the following connection between the sense of belonging to a group and the corresponding learning effects:

> . . . we observe (and commend to you) that educating is **NOT** principally about jamming techniques down the neophyte's throat, whether the neophyte is a new hire, new manager or new vice-president. The prime education is "you belong", "you can contribute". Once that message is genuinely transmitted, and absorbed, then the "technique-learning process" can be shortened by 60 to 90 per cent, for there is suddenly a will to learn.

The *atmosphere* in a group is something which is intangible, but relatively easy to sense. It is very much reflected in the degree of openness among the members and the confidence they have in one another. A free and open atmosphere makes people feel good about being together; it prevents members from feeling restrained and dominated.

It is quite astonishing how many groups produce a result which is inferior to what the members would have produced individually, just because they paid undue attention to maintaining a courteous and harmonious atmosphere. By being frank (but constructive) about the way they perceive the functioning of the group and individual contributions, groups can create an atmosphere of trust and mutual understanding.

The failure of groups to resolve problems better than individuals is sometimes referred to as "groupthink". The effect of a groupthink process is that members make a trade-off between whether to voice objections — and risk the irritation and resentment of the group — or bow to powerful pressures to comply with what seems to be the group consensus. Jack MacAllister, Chief Executive Officer of US West is cited in the book *The renewal factor* by Robert H. Waterman (1987), as saying "I go bananas if I come up with an idea and everyone says 'That's great!' ... If it's a team that's based on agreement, covering up, not creating any waves, that kind of teamwork leads to bankruptcy."

The *standards* of a group basically define the dos and don'ts of the group. They form a code of conduct which can be broken down into various categories, which to some extent function differently:

- *Work standards* define how the work is carried out, such as its intensity, quality and speed. This is an important aspect in solving problems, for example, where the depth of analysis and the use of assumptions tend to vary from group to group. The trainer should be aware of the differences in standards which exist between and inside groups, and how this may affect the outcome of the intervention.

- *Attitudes* denote the values and beliefs that tend to be shared in the group. For example, different managers tend to have different ways of perceiving their managerial function. Where some managers may view their role to be one of "walking around", listening and involving employees and customers, others may insist that their essential role is to "direct and control". In group training, the trainer can usefully bring such differences in values out into the open, to enable members of the group to learn from their differences rather than let them become a source of misunderstanding and conflict.

- *Interpersonal behaviour* is a standard that changes as the group spends time together. For example, the use of action-oriented learning methods for small-scale entrepreneurs suggests that the sharing of ideas between group members starts at a distinctive low at the beginning of the intervention, when they are reluctant to help potential competitors. However, given the opportunity to take up issues that the entrepreneurs feel are important to them, the group can develop into a close-knit learning team where openness is a major feature.

Structure and organization affect the way decisions are reached in the group. They can be formal, with an appointed group leader or facilitator, or informal, where authority may be related to factors such as professional knowledge, social status or simply powerful personal characteristics. The formal structure, which may be hierarchical in more traditional work groups, is less prominent in training groups.

The facilitator

The functions of the facilitator can be divided essentially into two types:

- those that link the work of the group with the environment; and
- those that facilitate the work of the group.

Acting as the agent between the *group and the environment*, the facilitator designs interventions that help the group to fill certain needs in the environment. In the case of in-company training groups, the facilitator ensures that the mandate and the final outputs of the group's work correspond to the expectations in the environment. More specifically, this includes:

- identifying the problem areas to be solved by the group or the skills to be developed in the group;
- organizing the group with a view to the competence which is required and representing the different organizational functions; and
- preparing a work plan and monitoring system for the intervention.

Facilitating the work of the group basically implies adopting a mode of action which will enable the group to attain the objectives of the session. There are a number of possible roles that a facilitator can adopt in working with the group. A parallel between the roles of facilitators and consultants could be drawn. Figure 12.2 shows the different roles of a consultant. It applies to consulting styles with individuals as well as with groups.

An important success factor is that the facilitator should be able to distinguish between the task and the process. While solving a problem a group will always encounter difficulties, such as a lack of technical competence in the group, inappropriate problem-solving procedures or an inadequate group process. The facilitator must be able to define which of these three types of problem is at play in the group.

Figure 12.2. Description of the consultant's role on a directive and non-directive continuum

MULTIPLE ROLES OF THE CONSULTANT

Reflector	Process specialist	Fact finder	Alternative identifier	Collaborator in problem-solving	Trainer/ educator	Technical expert	Advocate

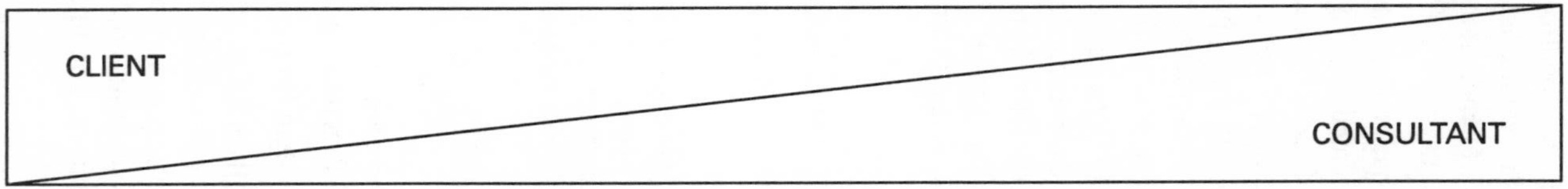

CLIENT

CONSULTANT

LEVEL OF CONSULTANT ACTIVITY IN PROBLEM-SOLVING

Non-directive

Directive

Raises questions for reflection	Observes problem-solving processes and raises issues mirroring feedback	Gathers data and stimulates thinking	Identifies alternatives and resources for client and helps assess consequences	Offers alternatives and participates in decisions	Trains the client and designs learning experiences	Provides information and suggestions for policy or practice decisions	Proposes guidelines, persuades, or directs in the problem-solving process

Source: Kubr, 1996, p. 61, (adapted from G. Lippitt and R. Lippitt: *The consulting process in action* (La Jolla, California, University Associates, 1979), p. 31.)

It is often tempting to intervene with suggested solutions when the group does not seem able to progress. If the difficulty is a lack of ideas, suggestions from the facilitator may be a good thing. However, if the group stalls because there is a problem in a group process — lack of communication, for example — putting forward ideas would have little effect on the group's work.

The trainer/facilitator should always take time to explain to the group what role he or she is adopting. This avoids misunderstanding in the group about what to expect from the facilitator. Table 12.1 suggests how the different facilitator roles are likely to influence the achievement of various objectives.

Table 12.1. Facilitator roles and objectives achievement level

	Task objectives	Learning objectives	Process objectives
Reflector	L	H	H
Process specialist	M	H	H
Fact finder	M	M	L
Alternative identifier	H	L	L
Collaborator in problem solving	H	L	L
Trainer/educator	L	H	L/H[1]
Technical expert	H	L	L
Advocate	H	L	L

Key: Probability of achieving objectives: H-high, M-medium, L-low.

[1] If the learning experiences are related to interpersonal processes, then the probability of achieving the objectives is high; if, on the other hand, they are concerned with task issues, the probability is low.

12.2   The elements of group training

The activities (which we will call "elements" to distinguish them from the more general operations within the group) that take place in group training can be categorized and analysed in their progress towards the expected outputs (Stuart, 1984 and Mouton and Blake, 1984). They are as follows:

- *Generate ideas* — In a group, ideas form the basis of innovation and therefore of the original solutions. Many groups contain people whose main strength is to think of ideas which sometimes go beyond the group's framework. These people do not always take an active and continuous part in all group activities. However, they often introduce ideas and suggestions which can provide a basis for solutions to problems.

- *Share experiences* — Whether a group is set up for the purpose of members learning from each other or to solve a problem, the sharing of past experiences should be encouraged. As with idea generation, it is important that the group has the capacity to listen to and understand individual experiences, and to use them in the context of its work. When a set of experiences is presented, it is important for the other members to ask questions rather than to pass judgement about the relevance or usefulness of the experiences. Similarly, individual group members should learn to be disciplined in the sharing of experiences, to select relevant experiences, be concise and to judge the amount of time spent in relation to the contribution made.

- *Consult* — The effective use of a particular member's knowledge or skills is an essential element of a group's work. This knowledge can be allowed to emerge naturally in the course of the work, or it can be formalized by the trainer by, for example, showing the group how to work as consultants to each other.
  It is often helpful to hold a separate training session in which the members learn to use open questioning as a tool for helping others. This technique, extensively practised by organization consultants, includes as a central element the planned use of open "why", "how", "where" and "when" questions. Open questioning opens up an effective dialogue between the specialist and the problem owner, and it involves the latter fully in solving the problem.

- *Challenge* — Devil's advocates tend to become the least popular and at the same time the most useful of a group's members. They may challenge not only statements made by others, but also the way the group functions. There are essentially two factors which determine the extent to which challenge can be used effectively to enhance the group's work. The first is the intention of the person doing the challenging. Is it to further personal interests? Is it to put someone else down in front of the rest of the group? Or is it done out of sincere concern for the quality of the output? When the rest of the group is in doubt about the intentions behind the challenge, they should have the ability to question the challenger about this.

  The second factor is the group's ability to use challenges. There are essentially three ways in which a group can react to a challenge:
  - emphasize points of agreement and continue as before;
  - accept that there are differences, but not do much about them;
  - define the differences, explain their causes and use them productively in its work.

  An effective group will tend to use option three, since it may contribute to the successful outcome of its work.

- *Test* — It is important for the manager to ask the right questions in order to make the best decision possible. This also applies to training groups. Testing is a means of sounding out, anticipating snags, identifying faults. When done by a group member, it is a way of inviting the rest of the group jointly to explore an issue which is important to the quality of the group's work. Testing is also done between members, such as when individual statements are probed for clarification or elaboration.

- *Build* — When the members constructively respond to one another's ideas to help the group to progress, they are building. The degree of building in a group determines not only the quality of the outcome, but also the amount of time it takes to reach the outcome. Building is likely to occur when each group member is continuously aware of the objectives of the work, and assumes responsibility for making contributions that are relevant to the objectives. Building is closely linked to the group's listening ability. It does *not* take place when one person dominates the discussion or tries to alter its course.

The motivation and commitment of individual members towards the group depends greatly on its ability to build. Let us for a moment regard the group as an organization. The management trainer is well aware that one of the motivational factors for someone to perform well on the job is the extent to which that person is able to see the effects of his or her contribution. In a training group, the degree of building is what enables a person to feel that they are having an impact on its outcome.

- *Combine* — The outcome of a group's work is the combination of the ideas, the experiences shared and the suggestions and comments made. It is each member's responsibility to be constantly combining what is said and done by the other members in order to obtain the whole picture, which will enable the group to reach its objective. Combining is also one of the main tasks of a facilitator, who helps the group relate present things to the past. Combining is also about relating the communication that is taking place between the members to the task they are working on.

- *Feedback* — In order to keep all elements in balance, an effective group needs feedback. Feedback should confront the group with the way it is progressing, the interpersonal processes, and the quality of the task accomplishment. Feedback is given to individual members (group members observe each other) and to the group as a whole (a group observer is appointed). An important part of feedback is also to describe the consequences of certain behaviour or group process.

The most effective and impartial feedback is provided by people who are not taking part directly in the group's work. Good feedback could be summarized as follows:

- it is concise and unambiguous;
- it distinguishes between task and process;
- it is impartial and entirely objective;
- it relates to the overall objectives of the group;
- it explains the consequences of certain behaviour or group process; and
- it differentiates between output and input criteria.

In some cultures it is acceptable to give corrective feedback to specific members, while in others this is not acceptable for fear of loss of face. It is important for trainers to realize this when working in a new cultural context.

12.3   Group work methods

In this section we shall attempt to describe different methods of group training in the light of the following:

- practical application;
- relevance to the three types of group training objective (learning, task work and process);
- trainer's skills and functions;
- use of different group process elements; and
- prerequisites for success.

(A)   Learning from materials

When books, training manuals and other printed or audiovisual material are used in group training, it is assumed that group techniques are employed to utilize group synergy. The use of materials in the group may serve two different purposes:

- as background information, a catalyst, or a framework for discussion and experience sharing; and
- in solving problems related to the content of group members' own situations. Most training material is not tailor-made for the target group, hence its direct learning effects are minimal unless the group members get the opportunity to relate the material to their own situation.

Learning materials can be advantageous when they contain examples, advice or information which are immediately useful to the group participants.

The two most important trainer skills in facilitating learning from materials are:

- identifying materials that could be useful and effective for the group members; and
- enabling group members to use one another's experiences and knowledge effectively while interacting over the materials.

(B)   Learning from each other

Whenever they are in a group, managers learn from each other. Interpersonal learning takes place when people share particular experiences with each other or demonstrate different ways of participating in the group. Interpersonal learning means learning from somebody's mistakes as well as from their successes.

When a group encounters a particular problem, a specific need for knowledge arises. The group is thus open to learning from particular members. However, interpersonal learning can be formalized and facilitated by the trainer. It is important to know "who knows what" in the group. The trainer should be able to identify any particular experience or knowledge in the group which is important for other group members. The group should be encouraged to identify interesting resources within itself.

Once these sources of knowledge or skills have been identified, the mode of learning may take either of the following forms:

- *sharing* (members describe their experiences); and
- *consulting* (members act as consultants to each other).

In the case of interpersonal training, the trainer has to be very sensitive to what the group members want and/or need to obtain from each other, how the knowledge obtained is going to be used, and how the group itself can learn to assess and use interpersonal learning techniques.

(C)   Group exercises

When a group is involved in an exercise (case-studies, role-plays or simply agreeing on a series of questions posed by the trainer), the objective is partly learning-oriented and partly task-oriented. An important aspect of using group training in problem-solving is the organization of the group. Members learn different things in different group compositions. The trainer should take into consideration the following factors when organizing the group.

- *Organizational belonging.* When the members come from different organizational settings, the cross-fertilization effects are likely to be greater. Members will also feel more free about expressing themselves and sharing experiences.

- When the members come from the same organization, the interaction in the group may be more restricted, but more relevant to each member's work situation, and the long-term effects of the training are likely to be greater, as some kind of peer pressure will probably persist after the training.

- *Background.* Put two engineers together to tackle an exercise and more often than not they are going to present a solution which is structured and technical in nature. Add a psychologist to the group, and the engineers are soon likely to be confronted with the way they solved the problem and challenged to think differently. The learning effects of the exercise process are influenced by the different backgrounds of the members. The trainer should appreciate such differences and their impact, and help the group recognize the usefulness of such differences.

- *Managerial position.* Managers at different levels perceive organizational problems differently. A divisional director, for example, may be more concerned about external customer relations and marketing strategies than a first-line supervisor, who is under continual pressure to meet production targets and solve interpersonal conflicts. Putting people from different levels in the same group is useful when the objective is to learn about organizational processes. Where solving common professional problems is concerned, however, more is gained from putting people from similar managerial positions in the same group.

In general, when formulating an exercise, the trainer should pay attention to:

- the clarity and conciseness of formulation;
- the time-limits;
- the quality and quantity criteria;
- the form of presentation;
- the use of resources (literature, specialists, etc.); and
- how exercise objectives relate to overall training objectives.

(D) Task forces

A task force is a temporary group of selected people who are brought together on a full- or part-time basis to solve a problem and sometimes implement recommended solutions. Task forces may represent a "vertical" slice of an organization, meaning persons of different rank, but from the same functional area, a "horizontal slice", meaning persons of the same rank, but from different functional areas, or a "diagonal slice", meaning persons of different rank and from different functional areas.

As the name implies, a task force is oriented towards achieving a set of task objectives. There is ample evidence, however, that they also provide an effective way for managers to learn how organizations are changed. Trainers, therefore, may contribute considerably by helping task force members to make the most of the learning effects and the company management to organize task forces in such a way that the learning element is fully utilized.

It is important that the task force consist of people who can and want to do something about a particular problem, that they be given the opportunity to learn and work effectively as a team, and that the task force be given enough time to accomplish the work to be done.

(E) Problem-solving

When applied to real-life problems, problem-solving has a double effect. First, there are the direct benefits of solving the problem. Second, the participants learn the process of how to solve problems by going through successive steps of diagnosis and decision making. There are a number of different procedures for group problem-solving. The following is one procedure which has been applied in training owners of small-scale enterprises.

Step 1.   Defining the problem.

Step 2.   Describing the problem (when, why and how it occurs).

Step 3.   Assessing the extent of the problem (what it represents in terms of money, time and other resources).

Step 4.   Ways in which the problem has been solved before.

Step 5.   Brainstorming for solutions.

Step 6.   Identifying the best combination of solutions.

Step 7.   Formulating an action plan.

Step 8.   Implementing the action plan.

Although problem-solving is primarily aimed at task objectives, it is also well suited to process objectives. It is while solving a problem and deciding on which solution to adopt that a group really demonstrates the quality of its group processes.

The most important group training elements for problem-solving are: "generate ideas", "challenge", "build", "combine" and "test".

The trainer plays a somewhat withdrawn role during problem-solving. It is important that he or she be sensitive to the fact that the group is solving *its* problem and that the solution belongs to the group. In addition to the required group process skills, the trainer should have sound knowledge of problem-solving procedures and techniques and be able to recognize the types of problem faced by the group.

(F)   Group dynamics training

Group dynamics training helps groups to analyse and improve the processes they use to make decisions, solve problems, resolve conflicts and generally work effectively together (Armstrong, 1986). Team building and interactive skills training focus almost exclusively on process objectives.

Team building helps a management team to work better together. Bill Critchley and David Casey (1994) suggest that team building is done within a set of three axes. The first axis is "the mode of working" of the group. In a management team there are three main modes, namely "unshared certainty", "cooperation" and "shared uncertainty". In the "unshared certainty" mode the group functions as an assembly of specialists, each content to be doing his or her little bit. A management team asked to deal with an open-ended issue, such as formulating a strategy, needs to go into the "shared uncertainty" mode. It is in this mode that the team will recognize the usefulness of the "build", "test" and "feedback" group training elements.

The second axis represents the processes divided into three groups: the polite social processes, the task processes and the feelings processes. The authors maintain that a management group becomes a proper team when the task and feelings processes are accomplished simultaneously with the "shared uncertainty" mode from the first axis.

The third axis represents interpersonal skills. When interpersonal skills in the group (empathy, listening, communication, etc.) converge towards the "shared uncertainty" mode and the combination of task and feelings processes, the group forms an effective management team. It is important to maintain a very delicate and deliberate balance between the work the group has decided to pursue and the degree of sharing of feelings that the group is prepared to accept in order to accomplish that work.

Interactive skills training aims at increasing the effectiveness of an individual's interactions with others. It may include sensitivity training groups (sometimes called T-groups) which aim to increase an individual's sensitivity (the ability to perceive how others are reacting to one's behaviour), diagnostic ability (the ability to perceive the state of relationships between others), and action skill (the ability to demonstrate the behaviour required by the situation). T-groups are a form of "laboratory training" which focuses exclusively on group processes.

The members of a sensitivity training group represent a sort of microcosm of the organization; they develop explicit and implicit codes of conduct. How do people feel about the decision the group just made? Did it arise from genuine consensus or from steam-rollering? Why is Robert always silent? The purpose of looking at behaviour is to understand that things occur between people in groups, and in what way they prevent or facilitate sound decision-making.

Perhaps the most important element of sensitivity training groups is feedback (i.e. making public the reactions of one person towards another, such as, "when you interrupt me, I feel discouraged", or "you seem to evaluate my ideas negatively rather than to see what is constructive about them"). Group members thus get an idea of the impact of their behaviour on others. In relation to management development, one of the most important elements of behavioural learning is to appreciate the effect of one's behaviour to motivate others.

An example is the use of the managerial grid developed by Blake and Mouton (1985). While solving a series of exercises in groups in the course of a seminar, participants observe each others' interactive skills and position one another in a managerial grid, where different positions indicate the degree of a manager's task orientation versus concern for people. Five principal managerial styles are described in a managerial grid:

- Impoverished management — the exertion by the manager of minimum effort to complete the work required to maintain membership of the organization.
- Task management — the manager is demanding in task efficiency and obedience and pays little attention to human satisfaction.
- Country club management — high human satisfaction, but low production output or quality.
- Middle of the road management — reasonable task performance and morale.
- Team management — high performance is achieved by the integration of task and human requirements into a unified system.

During a grid seminar, participants usually work in groups of between six and eight people. They learn how to assess managers in various situations using the grid. Eventually each individual assesses his or her own style without communicating with the other group members. Subsequently the group members take turns in assessing each other's style. It is important to note that much of the behavioural learning of the individual group member lies in self-assessment with regard to one's style, and then being assessed, maybe to exhibit another style, by the others in the group. Two styles are used to describe the individual: a predominant style and an alternative style. Whereas the predominant style is the one used by the individual most of the time, the alternative style is what he or she resorts to when exposed to situations where the predominant style is not appropriate.

There are a number of evaluation formats possible for interactive skills training. Typical reactions, such as defensiveness, assertiveness, use of authority, flexibility, conflict-solving ability, non-verbal expressions, etc., can all be formatted by the trainer and thus adapted to the group's situation. The feedback, which is the main group training element, can be provided, either by the trainer or by the group itself.

A useful technique is the "fishbowl" exercise. In such an exercise one part of the group is seated around the other part, which is solving a particular problem. The observers are given a set of instructions for observing the interactive skills practised by the group inside the "fishbowl". The observers may also be asked to evaluate the problem-solving procedure. At the appointed time, the observers feed their observations back to the group for discussion. In the next round, the observers go into the "fishbowl" and the other group takes over as observers. The trainer may usefully serve as observer of the quality of the feedback and the interaction between the groups while discussing the observations.

The advantage of the "fishbowl" is that by acting as observers, the participants are made to appreciate the impact of certain behaviour on the performance of the group. As soon as this is understood, they are in a better position to improve their own skills.

We have briefly outlined the nature of group dynamics training for managers, and the examples mentioned above describe essential elements of the approach. A wide range of methods and approaches is available for achieving process objectives with groups. For example, real-life "in action" sessions with outside observers can be combined with mini-lectures to describe the theory of group dynamics. Simulations can be run to illustrate specific aspects of group dynamics, such as conflict resolution. Assessment forms can be given to the group members to allow them to evaluate the dynamics of their group.

(G) The nominal group technique

We have so far described techniques which are based on interaction between group members. One problem with member interaction is that not all viewpoints are given the attention they deserve. Interaction, especially in groups where frankness of opinion is limited, also prevents members from speaking their minds. Yet another potential problem of interaction is that it limits opportunities for reflection without being distracted.

In a nominal group, individuals work in the presence of others but do not interact verbally. Thus, it is a complementary method to group interaction, which eliminates the above-mentioned disadvantages. Typically, some written output is normally obtained from each participant (van de Ven and Delbecq, 1971).

The following example illustrates how the nominal group technique may be used to diagnose employees' perceptions of their company's strengths and weaknesses. Employees are organized in groups of six to eight, and asked to respond to two questions: What are the strengths of the organization that have helped us to reach our present state of effectiveness? What are the problems of the organization that are preventing us from reaching our potential effectiveness? The consultant proceeds with the nominal group process as follows.

1. All groups are asked to respond to the two questions by *writing their views* on cards. There should be *no verbal interaction* among group members during this phase. Although the time allowed may vary, a limit of *20 minutes* is generally satisfactory.
2. At the conclusion of this listing phase, each group is asked to select one member to serve as note-taker.
3. Using *large sheets of paper* and a magic marker, each note-taker asks for members of his or her group to *read off one strength* from his or her list. If anyone else has the same strength, a checkmark is placed by the item. The process continues, *one item at a time until all strengths are recorded.* The process is structured *to discourage discussion of each item until all items are recorded.* When all the strengths have been recorded, the same process is followed for the problem areas identified by the group members.
4. When both lists are complete, *discussion is allowed* to synthesize, clarify or add items.
5. Next, each group member is again given a card and asked to *vote for the five strengths* he or she thinks are most significant and the *five problems* that are most crucial and should be given highest priority.
6. After the votes have been counted, each group reports its top five strengths and weaknesses *to the group as a whole.* The consultant then explains that these data will be classified and the results presented to the participants and top managers so that the organization can proceed to develop strategies and action plans in order to build on strengths and overcome the problem areas.

The nominal group technique has advantages and disadvantages. The main advantages are that viewpoints are brought out into the open without being influenced by group pressure to conform. Hence, a broader range of viewpoints is obtained than with interaction. A second advantage is that in the absence of interaction, group members are given the chance to reflect on their own ideas as well as those of other members. This may enhance creativity in the group.

In our opinion, the method has two important limitations. One relates to achieving task objectives. The method encourages decision by vote. Hence an idea that receives, say, only one out of eight votes is not likely to be adopted. This is potentially risky when one is training managers to make decisions that are sensitive to highly divergent views. There are numerous examples in the management literature about faulty decisions being made by majority vote and the overlooking of the "odd one out", which later proved to be the right one.

Another limitation is related to learning objectives. The trainer should be aware of the risk that, by not interacting, participants may not learn effectively about group processes and group performance. However, this can be avoided, or even turned into an advantage, if the trainer makes the participants aware of the differences between nominal work and interaction, and asks them to analyse the differences in terms of group output. Such an exercise should enable them to pinpoint some of the weaknesses of their day-to-day interaction with subordinates, such as listening to minority views.

(H)   Discussions

Discussions are used mainly to facilitate an exchange of views and ideas. They are not regarded as effective for achieving change in behaviour or attitude, although they help to increase knowledge and problem awareness among the participants. For example, a discussion involving sales managers and production managers may enable them to gain insight into one another's problems, especially when led by a trainer who helps them to understand each other's views and to avoid defensive argumentation which easily develops between two functions that are sometimes at odds with each other.

The fundamental aim of discussions is to gain insight about one another's views. Discussions are not normally meant as a means of arriving at a decision. The expression of one's own views and the registration of those of others are regarded as being more important than moving towards a decision. The interaction, in a discussion, is focused on a topic where there is no pressing need to resolve conflict.

Leading a discussion is done in four stages: getting off to a good start; leading in to the discussion; guiding the discussion; and summarizing the discussion. Box 12.2 sets out in more detail the elements of leading a discussion. The most effective trainer style of a good discussion is probably the questioning approach.

There are mainly two types of question used by the facilitator of the discussion. The general question is addressed to the group as a whole and is intended to stimulate thinking by all the members of the group. The second type — the direct question — is addressed to a particular individual to elicit his or her viewpoint in order to enrich the discussion. Some hints follow on the use of questions.

* Questions should be brief, clear and simply worded.
* Direct questions should be distributed at random and among all group members.
* Each question should, as far as possible, cover one point only.
* Questions should be related to the ability and/or experience of the person to whom they are addressed.
* Give the person sufficient time to think before expecting an answer.
* Do not use rhetorical or leading questions to get out of a difficult or awkward situation in the group. It is likely to make the situation worse.

12.4   Conclusion

We have discussed group work and discussion methods in the light of three different types of objective: learning (for the individual and the group); task achievement; and group process improvement. We have identified areas where objectives overlap, such as in the case where the learning objective is to improve participants' ability to work effectively in groups (process). Besides some difficulty in distinguishing

Box 12.2. How to lead a discussion

1. Get off to a good start
   - Start the meeting on time.
   - Try to make the group feel at ease.

2. Lead in to the discussion
   - State the general purpose of the discussion.
   - Announce the topic clearly and concisely.
   - Explain the discussion procedures and define its limits.
   - Introduce the topic.

3. Guide the discussion
   - Encourage participation by all members.
   - Control the over-talkative member.
   - Draw out the shy member.
   - Don't allow one or two members to monopolize.
   - Deal tactfully with irrelevant contributions.
   - Avoid personal arguments.
   - Keep the discussion moving.
   - Keep the discussion on the subject.
   - Summarize frequently.
   - Use audiovisual aids.

4. Summarize the discussion
   - Review the highlights of the discussion.
   - Review the conclusions which have been reached.
   - Make clear what has been accomplished by the discussion.
   - Restate any minority viewpoint.
   - Get agreement for any action proposed.
   - End on a high note.

between objectives, it is nevertheless useful to keep in mind the three different types of objective as a mental checklist when designing training interventions.

In this chapter we have considered the use of groups in a broad sense. We have expanded the term from classroom groups to cover groups that are set up within organizations, such as task forces. This has also expanded the trainer's role from course facilitator to process consultant assisting managers in action-oriented learning programmes. Another reason for taking this broad view is that the nature of the group dynamics is similar to — and hence transferable from — the "traditional" training group to the organizational problem-solving group.

We have also looked at different approaches to group work, and discussed them in the light of the various elements of group interaction, such as "generate ideas", "share experiences", "consult", "challenge", "test", "build", "combine" and "feedback". The elements suggested are not meant as any kind of rigid list. Each trainer has his or her own notions of what the elements of group work are and uses them to develop further group work methods in training.

SIMULATION METHODS 13

Tor Hernes

Simulation is a powerful training approach — particularly for achieving behavioural changes. It permits trainees to act as if they were in a real situation. It also allows them to experiment with skills away from their jobs. It enhances learning effectiveness and presents certain advantages over experience-based training.

Many aspects of managerial work can be modelled using simulation — from the manager's personality and work tasks to the organizational environment. This chapter discusses the merits of using simulation, the types of training for which it is effective, various ways of modelling managerial work, and how different patterns of modelling apply to simulation in the learning process. We also pay attention to the practical application of the method.

13.1   Simulation: Definition and features

A simulation is a training exercise where a model of reality is used. A manager's reality is influenced by many factors, some related to managerial skills, background and personality, others to responsibilities, subordinates, colleagues, and the norms and rules of the organization. It is important to be aware of the various factors that have a bearing on the manager's work in selecting or designing simulations. We suggest looking upon them as a learning exercise where one or a combination of three parameters of the manager's work — such as the behaviour, the task and the environment — are simulated.

There could also be a parameter which is not simulated and is reality-based. De Geus (1988) provides an example where, as head of planning for the Royal Dutch/Shell Group of companies, he ran an exercise in which managers were made to assume entirely different market conditions from those prevailing at the time (see Chapter 11.2 (D)). They were asked to identify an appropriate corporate strategy for those market conditions, assuming they were imminent. The overall aim of the exercise was to increase the responsiveness of the company. In this case, the participating managers also applied their own *behavioural* skills. Their *task* was also reality-based, since they worked as managers with overall organizational responsibilities. The internal *environment* of the company was reality-based, in the sense that they assumed the company's basic characteristics, such as its staff, financial condition, products, etc. However, the company's external environment was simulated to allow for the principal learning objective, i.e. to develop managers' mental preparation for changing market conditions.

In a role-play, however, the task may be the only real parameter, as the environment is not real and the characters are simulated by the participants acting according to a script or a character description.

A simulation, unlike theoretical learning of skills, is based more on reality since it involves action on the part of the learner. It is less reality-based than an in-house project team, since it always includes parameters which are not part of the learner's day-to-day reality.

Thomas Keiser and John Seeler (in Craig, 1987) define simulation as "an operational model using selected components of a real or hypothetical process, mechanism or system".

It would be useful to be able to classify simulations according to certain criteria — the area covered, for example. This could be the organization (e.g. "total enterprise" or "top management"). Participants would be able to see how the different functions linked up in areas such as policy-making, product development and customer relations. Another area could be functions such as production control, sales and personnel management, where participants experience simulated functional problems. A third possible area of coverage could be specialized areas, such as legislation or computer operations (see also ILO, 1972).

Another way of classifying simulations would be by the nature of the model, such as card games, computer-based simulations, role-plays, video-assisted simulations, outdoor simulations, etc.

Linda Standke (1978) suggests that the most useful way to classify simulation games is according to whether or not they attempt to simulate reality. She maintains that "for understandable reasons, simulation games — ones where the game's rules and roles are drawn from real life — tend not to have non-predictable outcomes. Non-simulation games, by contrast, involve temporary suspension of real-life rules and roles and the substitution of game rules and roles." Following Standke's classification, we shall discuss simulations using the three parameters mentioned at the beginning of the chapter. Table 13.1 provides a framework.

A simulation may be a combination of the different positions given in the table. Take, for example, a role-play which is aimed at improving personnel managers' interviewing skills for recruiting and selecting new employees. Let us assume that the main focus of the role-play is on interviewing style. More specifically, the managers are able to learn to appreciate the effect of different interviewing styles, for example, how closed questions reveal much less about the interviewee than do open questions. In order to learn to appreciate the effect of different styles, the managers are made to experiment with them and assess the outcome. Participants take turns posing as interviewees. Taking into account the behaviour, the task and the environment, this role-play can be described as follows:

Table 13.1. Simulation of managerial parameters

	Degree of simulation	
	← Low (reality-based)	High (far from reality) →
Behaviour	The participants adopt the appropriate behaviour based on their assessment of the situation	The participants adopt a behaviour based on prescribed parameters
Task	Tasks and managerial functions as in a participants' daily work	Tasks and functions entirely different
Environment	The simulated environment is close to the manager's actual environment	The simulated environment is completely different

- The behaviour (style) is exposed to a high degree of simulation in order to learn the effects of different types of behaviour and thereby identify a style which is the most effective.

- The task is reality-based, i.e. managers perform a function which they normally carry out in their jobs.

- The environment — in this case the interviewees — is simulated close to reality.

13.2 Main objectives of simulation

There are basically three main objectives in using simulations: to change attitudes, to develop skills and to identify needs and problems.

Any training intervention, whether reality-based or theoretical, will have a minimal impact if the participants are not ready to change, are unable to appreciate new ways of tackling problems and are unwilling to implement what they learn. This is what is implied by attitude change, to which simulations can contribute, provided that the managers' environment encourages change.

If organizational factors are conducive to change, simulations can be a useful means of making this happen. Prior to designing an intervention, it is important for the trainer to analyse exactly what is preventing attitudes from changing — for example, interpersonal conflicts, a manager's short-term orientation, or the failure of previous attempts to solve similar problems.

Simulations can also help to develop a range of different skills. In this regard, it is useful to distinguish between the various behavioural skills — for example, interpersonal, problem analysis, decision-making and specialized operations (Kepner and Tregoe, 1981).

If the objective is immediate performance improvement, behavioural skills are not readily developed through simulations alone. However, they do provide an opportunity to develop and test skills in a modelled situation where failure does not have serious consequences. For example, role-play results in feedback from someone who is objective and open, and thus allows different ways of interacting with people to be tried out and objectively evaluated.

For specialized operational skills, which include the use of management information systems, budgeting, trouble-shooting systems, application of staff regulations, etc., simulations provide an excellent approach allowing the participants to acquire skills through trial and error without serious economic and/or safety consequences for the organization.

Needs identification is the third objective of using simulations. Kubr and Prokopenko (1989) suggest that valuable information on several aspects of management skills, knowledge, attitudes and shortcomings can be obtained in a situation that is close to actual practice. They propose that simulations provide reliable data on training needs as a by-product of the training process, and hence at a low cost. They also suggest that during simulations, participants tend to be open about their knowledge and skill gaps, readily asking for help and advice. Thus, simulations can provide the trainer with valuable qualitative information on where and how to focus future training efforts.

13.3   The merits of using simulations

We shall discuss the advantages and disadvantages of using simulations in relation to, on the one hand, working with reality and, on the other, learning from theory.

(A)   The advantages of working with reality

By "working with reality" we mean that the training is intended to have a direct bearing on job performance and that managers learn or solve problems by dealing with real issues in their own organization. When managers diagnose real issues that concern them and their organization, and come up with appropriate solutions which are then implemented, and the fruits of their efforts are evident, then both the managers and the organization are likely to experience an impressive learning cycle.

A major advantage that simulations have over reality is that they allow managers to try out the skills without risking anything other than corrective feedback. The types of risk faced in the everyday life of a manager are the cost of failure, time loss, health risks, etc. Simulations provide an opportunity to experiment with different approaches to solving problems, a luxury which they cannot afford in everyday life. As Douglas McGregor suggested in *The human side of enterprise* (1960), "the acquisition of manual skills requires practice, or experience accompanied by feedback". He also maintained that "(managers) cannot learn unless (they) receive cues which tell (them) about the success of (their) efforts". Organizations where this is done systematically and thoroughly are unfortunately still rare. Hence, in the absence of the ideal reality, simulations represent an advantage over reality-based training which McGregor sees as a prerequisite for managerial training.

Simulations have the advantage over reality that they can take people momentarily out of their usual frame of reference. They can help managers to think differently about things, see problems and opportunities from a different angle altogether, look beyond the immediate and less significant obstacles and thus solve issues that have more far-reaching consequences. They may help avoid reactions such as "... we've seen this before ... there are only two solutions to this problem, and they don't work ...".

One example is a production company that was experiencing a drop in sales. An experienced consultant was called in to help them diagnose and solve the problems it was facing. The company management suggested to the consultant that they run an interdepartmental task force programme. The consultant discovered that although they were trying to remedy a drop in demand from customers, they were intending to launch a programme that did not involve their customers. While agreeing to the concept of a task force, the consultant persuaded them to ask a cross-section of the company to take part in a simulation involving real customers, where the task of the "company" was to market and sell itself as an "organization" to these customers.

The fact that the exercise was close to their real-life situation provided a close-to-reality simulation of the environment for the organization's staff. The participants were given tasks to simulate that were different from their jobs. The purpose of this was to reinforce the learning effect of understanding how their organization as a whole responded to its customers. There were two immediate effects of the simulation. One was that task force members realized the importance of looking at their actions through the eyes of the customer. The other was that they realized that they were all in the same boat together — that sales, for example, were not just the responsibility of the sales department, but of everyone in the company. The simulation made it possible for the task force to attack the causes of substandard performance immediately — with the support of the director who took part in this simulation as one of the task force.

Another argument in favour of simulations is that they are more readily replicable throughout organizations and between them. Although they are not likely to produce tangible changes in behaviour, they represent a relatively cost-effective way of providing managers with a set of basic skills, knowledge and attitudes. Reality exercises require skilled trainers or consultants who are competent in organizational change processes. Simulations, once produced and tested, can be run by people who are trained as trainers and who possess group process skills.

(B) The advantages of learning from theory

When taking part in a simulation, the participants are in effect provoking different reactions, either from other participants or, for example, from a computer programme. Given the pattern of reactions that they provoke, the participants change behaviour and thus influence the outcome of the simulation. Learning from theory, on the other hand, is an exercise in which the outcomes are often given in advance.

The relationship between theory-based learning approaches and simulations may be illustrated using Kolb's learning cycle (concrete experience — reflective observation — abstract conceptualization — active experimentation) discussed in Chapter 11.

All of a manager's actions (from day-to-day work and dealing with people to overall strategic planning and decision-making) trigger different responses. Depending on the attitude of the manager and the encouragement received from the environment regarding learning and performance improvement, the manager reflects on concrete experiences. At first, single events appear most important for reflection; then, with time, a more generalized pattern of events may crystallize, which leads to the stage of abstract conceptualization. The manager may choose to let things go on unchanged or do something about them.

This reflective observation may be considered in two parts. The first involves thinking about one's own actions and the responses of the environment. Here simulations play an important role as they help the manager understand concrete relationships between adopted behaviour (active experimentation) and response from fellow participants (concrete experience).

In the second part the manager's reflections take a more holistic perspective in the sense that the manager relates his or her own experiences to established concepts of managerial behaviour. This is the part where theoretical learning plays an important role. It gives the manager access to other managers' experiences in different organizational cultures.

Thus, theory and simulations complement each other — both are important in management learning. Experience suggests, however, that to have an impact on performance, the order of training activities is important. When used as a means of confirming and relating personal experiences, learning from theory is best done after the managers have been through a simulation exercise.

(C)   Simulations — strong and weak points

Table 13.2 suggests how simulations relate to reality- and theory-based learning methods in terms of the influence of three factors (direct impact, change of attitudes, and concepts and integration) on training efficiency (Boydell, 1985).

As shown in the table, direct impact on training performance is best achieved through reality-based training, while theory-based training is best for developing new conceptual knowledge and integration of totality. Simulations are the most effective for changing attitudes, have some potential in direct impact and help to develop conceptual knowledge. It is interesting to notice that if theory-based training has low potential in direct impact and attitude changes, and reality-based training is inefficient in conceptual learning, the simulation method has certain potential in achieving results in all three dimensions.

Table 13.2. Relationships of simulations to reality- and theory-based learning methods

	Direct impact	Attitude change	Concepts, integration
Reality-based training	H	M	L
Simulations	M	H	M
Theory-based training	L	L	H

Key: Probability of achieving objective: H - high, M - medium, L - low.

13.4 Criteria of successful simulations

Two main sets of criteria permit the success of simulations to be judged. The first has to do with the way the simulation relates to participants' needs and attitudes and to the training programme. These criteria are made up of the following four components:

Challenge — the degree to which the simulation encourages the participants to apply their skills, creativity and intuition actively in solving problems;

Relevance — the degree to which the topic of the simulation is relevant to the needs of the participants and their organizations;

Realism — the extent to which behaviour, tasks and environment are recognized by the participants as realistic to their kind of problems; and

Objectives fit — the extent to which the simulation contributes to the attainment of the overall training objectives.

The second set of success criteria relate to the trainer's ability to keep the components of the first set *in balance* with each other.

(A) Challenge

The simulation should challenge the participants to apply themselves, make them want to seek new and innovative solutions, create a desire to use skills that they have not used before or to use them differently. For example, in a simulation for owners of small enterprises where the theme is personnel management and where the general tendency among them has been to treat personnel in an autocratic way, a simulation where they can apply human insight will challenge them to take a different view of dealing with people.

Another way of introducing challenge is to make use of quality criteria, time-limits or group pressure. An example would be a sales promotion simulation where the customer is instructed not to "buy" a product unless a certain number of predetermined criteria have been satisfied. The sales managers are forced to keep trying harder in their preparation and presentation of the product. If they work in groups, a certain amount of pressure will soon build up for the group to arrive at a suitable result.

(B) Relevance

A game of Monopoly can be fun, especially when in good company. However, it may not reflect the needs of a manager who is constantly facing a mixture of operational, strategic and interpersonal problems. A relevant simulation is one where the theme reflects the needs and interests of the participants. The degree of relevance is important in motivating participants to become actively involved.

Douglas McGregor included in his assumptions for the famous "Theory Y" that commitment to objectives is a function of the rewards associated with their achievement. In the context of a simulation, the rewards would be the skills or knowledge acquired for application back on the job. Participants should thus be aware that taking an active part in the simulation is a means of increasing satisfaction through improved managerial performance. While the satisfaction to be derived from performing well in the simulation and thereby obtaining rewards during training is useful, it must under no circumstances stand out alone or as a more important objective than the ultimate job performance rewards.

The overall concerns and needs of the participants should be reflected in the needs analysis. If the analysis does not provide sufficient information to design the simulation, the attitude of the participants while taking part should indicate to the trainer whether the simulation is relevant or not. Moreover the needs and concerns of the participants are not necessarily the same. For example, whereas their *concerns* may be current interdepartmental relations, their *need* may be to put their work into the perspective of the organization and its mission as a whole. A general rule which applies to the design of simulations is to enable the participants to appreciate the linkage between their concerns and their needs. Although the ultimate objective of the intervention is to fulfil a set of organizational or individual needs, it has to be assessed *via* the participants' concerns.

(C) Realism

The realism of a simulation may sometimes be difficult to distinguish from its relevance. Whereas the relevance of the simulation reflects the relationship between its content and the participants' needs and concerns, its realism is addressed to the organization being simulated and the extent to which participants are able to recognize their work situation reflected in the simulation.

Among the first questions a participant asks him or herself when taking part in a simulation are: "Do I recognize this situation? Are the tasks and the environment realistic?" The degree of realism determines whether the attitude of the participants is going to be "it's just a game" or "this gives me the opportunity to learn new ways of tackling my problems".

The trainer may find the following points useful for attaining realism in simulations:

● the task should be a recognizable action of managerial work;

● the environment should produce effects that are readily understandable and recognizable by the managers;

- participants should be able to see clearly the cause-effect relationships of their actions; and
- the reward system of the simulation should be compatible with those used in real life.

The participants should also be aware of the elements in the simulation that are not possible to model realistically, such as the time factor, and also that certain elements are missing. This helps to avoid the problem of disregarding feedback on behaviour because certain conditions did not appear realistic to the participants.

(D) Objectives fit

Since simulation is normally part of a programme, its purpose is to contribute to the overall training objectives. Unfortunately, when it comes to designing the programme, simulations are sometimes suggested because "they are good", not because they contribute to attaining the broader training objectives.

In setting simulation objectives it is important to make sure that they are realistic, attainable and concisely formulated. It should also be clear how they contribute to the attainment of the overall objectives.

(E) The trainer

The function of the trainer is to ensure that the above-mentioned four success criteria are observed. Although there is no single recipe to make sure that all criteria are met, it is possible to suggest a set of characteristics in the trainer that facilitate effective simulations. For example:

Group process skills. The trainer needs to be experienced in running group processes, to diagnose what is happening in a group, analyse symptoms and causes, distinguish between task and process, and help to improve the group's functioning.

Learning process skills. The trainer should be able to tell at any stage during the simulation if the desired type of learning is taking place, identify attitude changes and skills acquisition, and perceive the extent to which learning is going to be applied on the job. The trainer should also be able to assess which stage in the learning cycle the individual learners have reached.

Understanding how organizations work. The trainer should understand organizational learning — i.e. how organizations learn and the ways in which the learning is applied in decision-making — and the relationships between management training and organizational learning. This will help the trainer to formulate a suitable training contract with the organization and the participants and implement a programme where simulations contribute significantly to the attainment of objectives.

Understanding the nature of managerial work. The trainer should be able to understand and appreciate the participants as managers (the degree of fragmentation of their work, superficiality, crisis management, interpersonal conflict, strategy formulation, concern for personal career development) and their relationship with the organization (e.g. reward systems, political influence, organizational norms and values).

Innovation. The trainer should realize that the design of an effective simulation involves a great deal of creativity, the ability to think of as many options as possible, and to apply each one in the light of the four success criteria: challenge, relevance, realism and the set of objectives.

Ability to state specific objectives. If the simulation is to contribute significantly to the attainment of the overall training objectives, the trainer must be able to state in concrete terms what specific objectives should be achieved from the simulation.

13.5   Different aspects of simulations

As has already been mentioned, a simulation is an operational exercise where parameters such as personality, task and environment are simulated to a lesser or greater extent. In this section we shall discuss the merits of modelling each of these parameters to achieve successful simulation.

(A)   Personality

The most common form of simulation in which human behaviour is simulated is role-play; participants are required to act according to a script or a character description. They have to decide what would be appropriate behaviour in a given situation, which is not necessarily the way they themselves would tackle the situation in real life.

When the people are "real", meaning that the participants are not bound by a script or character description, they are free to apply their own perceptions of the situation and their own skills and knowledge.

A list is provided below of some points which may help the trainer to choose whether the participants should pretend to be someone else in the simulation or whether they should be themselves.

Acting as someone else

- This helps people to appreciate another person's situation and problems. It may be useful when the objective is, for example, to sensitize managers to the work of supervisors, where the managers are asked to act according to the description of a supervisor's values, background, knowledge and attitudes.

- It allows a person to perceive the environment differently. A male personnel manager, for example, when made to act the role of a woman applicant for a position with the company, may more readily appreciate the environmental constraints on women in the organization.

- It helps the participants to think of new solutions to problems by adopting the viewpoint of a different persona.

- It makes the simulation easier to reproduce and disseminate to a larger population, because there is a higher degree of universality of design and implementation. The outcome of the simulation is also more predictable.

Acting as oneself

- This helps to develop existing skills in the simulation. It gives the manager the opportunity to test present skills in an environment where failure does not affect his or her career.

- It makes it more likely that skills are going to be applied in the job after the training and relates what happens in the simulation to the actual situation in the organization.

(B)   The task

The task is modelled in such a way that new skills are required in order to carry it out. In a business game, for example, managers make decisions based on simulated company and market information. Although the information is not real it can be treated as such, and new managerial skills and behaviour may be needed to deal with it.

Should the task be modelled or not? Let us take as an example a team-building exercise for managers. The object of the exercise is to improve the skills of making decisions in teams. The trainer has two options:

- to ask participants to make decisions that are representative of managerial work, say, by suggesting an organizational environment where they are called upon to make a series of realistic decisions together. Learning about how to make decisions in teams would then be done in the framework of the type of work they normally do; or

- to ask participants to make completely different types of decision, say by playing a card game, building a toy structure together, or doing an outdoor exercise which they do not normally do in their work environment.

Keeping the second example in mind, we suggest that the following factors be considered by the trainer when faced with the choice between using realistic (first option) and modelled (second option) tasks:

- *realistic tasks* are more directly linked to their work and hence allow for the direct application of the skills learned after the training; they also create a stronger incentive to learn managerial skills from the exercise;

- *modelled tasks* allow for more intellectual simulation, as the participants are allowed to diagnose a situation without being influenced by their usual concerns; the participants are more readily encouraged to innovate in solving issues; but the tasks run a greater risk of not being treated as a serious learning exercise by the participants than do realistic tasks.

If the two types of task are used in succession, the use of modelled tasks before starting realistic task exercises helps to prepare the participants to solve the latter successfully, by giving them a broader vision for later conceptualization.

(C)   The environment

The environment may be the immediate departmental environment, the organizational environment or the business environment with its customers, competition and legislation. It can be modelled in two ways: one is to give written or verbal information before or during the exercise about environmental conditions, such as consumer tastes, competing producers or products, legislation, company policy, and organizational structure, etc.; the other is to make the participants experience it rather than informing them about it; for example, in the use of computer-based training to enhance the strategic decision-making skills of managers. The knowledge that the participants acquire about the environment comes from responding to specific actions.

Furthermore, the environment may be the only real parameter, while the people and tasks are simulated. Imagine, for example, an exercise where people from the organization act as customers to the company. They simulate the customers and the task in the real environment of their organization.

Some points which may help the trainer to choose between the use of a real or modelled environment are listed below:

Modelled environments are readily replicable; enable the participants to learn how other environmental parameters affect performance; reduce the participants' fear of failure; and allow for manipulation of parameters.

Using a real environment demands more knowledge and design skill from the trainer; requires far more involvement from the organization; and stands a better chance of making a direct impact on organizational performance.

13.6   Major forms of simulation

There are many different forms of simulation. We shall discuss only five of the most important: role-plays, simulation games, reality-based simulations, technology-assisted simulations and outdoor simulations.

While discussing the practical applications of each of these we will pay special attention to the nature of each simulation form, its advantages and disadvantages, required trainer skills for each specific form, and its practical applications.

(A)   Role-plays

Role-plays focus on human behaviour. They permit learners to enact situations which they face on the job, or that they expect to face in the future, or that they perceive as job-like (Laird, 1985). Role-plays are simulations performed with people only and are normally done in three stages.

- *Preparation*. The trainer explains why and how the role-play is to be run. The participants are given time to study their roles and, if necessary, to plan a strategy of behaviour. The trainer sees to the physical arrangements necessary for the exercise. The observers learn their instructions.

- *Playing.* Two or more players perform the role-play. The players may stay in the same roles throughout or change roles during the exercise. The observers monitor the behaviour of the players, and they record events and behaviour that are important for analysis.

- *Evaluation.* The players, the observers and the trainer discuss the ways in which they perceived the role-play, how it affected the outcome, and why it happened that way, in a free and open exchange of views.

Role-plays can be staged by the trainer. The advantage of such predesigned and "packaged" role-plays is that the outcome is frequently predictable. Another way of running role-plays is to ask the participants to stage them. The trainer simply sets the task to be reconstructed and asks them to typify a situation that they know. An example is when a management team is asked first to enact a case of mediocre decision-making, and then, in the next session, to enact the making of a consensus-based decision. The mere fact that they have purposely to present two extremes of their ways of working together, gives them valuable insight into their behaviour and its effect on team performance.

The advantage of learner-staged role-plays is that they tend to bring out reflections that are more directly connected to the real situation. A disadvantage may be that the learning effects are at the mercy of the participants' staging abilities. Such role-plays can be very entertaining and good fun. The effects of this can be both negative and positive: negative in the sense that the performance may become more important to the players than the learning; positive in that the role-play is retained longer in their memory.

Some practical hints on the running of role-plays are listed below:

- Role-plays should not go on for too long; ideally they should last from between five to 15 minutes.

- The physical arrangements should be kept to a minimum to avoid the risk of distracting attention away from the role-play.

- The role-play should be kept simple, i.e. with a limited cast and covering a few events; instructions to the players and observers should be concise and brief.

- The playing should not overshadow the real issues involved — the players' experimental behaviour rather than theatrical performance should be reinforced. Use humour, although not in excessive doses.

The most important trainer skills determining the success of role-plays are as follows:

- the ability to help the players and observers to understand what has gone on in the role-play and what the consequences are;

- sufficient organizational and management skills to help the participants relate the process in the role-play to their work in organizations; and

- sensitivity to the concern of the participants about playing roles in front of others. Ability to overcome shyness.

Role-plays, by focusing mainly on the behavioural aspects of management, enable managers to learn about the effects of their behaviour on peers and subordinates, to understand other people's behaviour, and to appreciate why they behave in the way they do.

As many as possible of the participants should be allowed to play the simulation, because they are likely to devise different strategies for solving the problem. After the simulation, an evaluation should be carried out in plenary to assess the impact of the differences in strategy adopted by the different players. Thus, each participant will have the possibility of learning, both from trying to solve the problem in action and from having analysed the strategies of fellow participants.

In the evaluation, it is useful to ask the group to analyse the simulation from different perspectives, such as:

- *Organizational structure.* The effects of people being put close to one another. For example, what are the possible effects on customer treatment of salespeople working close together?

- *The decision-making process.* The effects of making the decisions without sounding out the consequences beforehand. For example, how should the decision to change the office layout have been made in order to avoid this kind of problem?

- *Organizational culture.* The norms that people adhere to when working together. For example, what does the behaviour of the two salespersons who share an office tell you about the way in which people in this organization behave towards each other, and what are the effects of this?

- *Managerial style.* The personalized way of a manager to elicit information from people and to influence their work behaviour. For example, did the sales manager go about the discussion in the best way possible?

The above suggestions illustrate the usefulness of analysing behaviour from different perspectives. Broadly speaking, the perspectives are organizational structure, culture, processes such as decision-making and managerial style.

If the trainer makes it clear to the group what perspective is taken, the group will learn not only how to analyse specific situations such as the ones experienced in the simulation, but also about the different perspectives that can and should be taken in organizational analysis.

(B) Simulation games

The terms "games" and "simulations" are sometimes used interchangeably. Games are almost exclusively simulations in that they are operational models. A simulation, on the other hand, is not a game as long as it does not contain a competitive element. According to Keiser and Seeler (1987), there is a distinction between games and simulation games. To them, a game is "a structured activity in which two or more participants compete within constraints of rules to achieve an objective". A "simulation game combines the characteristics of games and simulations in a game based

Box 13.1. An example of a role-play

The role-play described below is for two people. We only provide extracts from the role-play in order to illustrate the essence of how it works. It involves one manager and one employee. The learning objective is to enhance managers' ability to identify causes of performance problems through effective interpersonal communication. Before role-playing, the manager and the employee are given narratives of the personalities they portray.

The manager's narrative tells how she has the feeling that the younger salespeople in her deparment (she is responsible for sales) do not exhibit the same level of enthusiasm for their work as they did six months ago. She decides to find out why this is so, and invites one of the salespeople to look for clues as to the possible causes of this apparent decline of morale.

The employee's narrative tells how, since they moved from a large open-plan office for the whole department to smaller offices, each one shared by two salespeople, he has found work less motivating. In the new system, each office is shared by one senior salesperson and one junior salesperson.

In the simulated meeting the conversation between the sales manager and the salesman ran as follows:

Manager: I've noticed that you haven't been your old enthusiastic self recently. Is there anything wrong?

Salesman: Well, frankly, it's somehow difficult to work. It doesn't work out too well with my room-mate.

Manager: Carlos, the senior salesperson in your office?

Salesman: Yes, he interrupts my client calls, tells me what I do wrong, and tries to coach me. I know I'm relatively new, but I need to learn from my own mistakes.

Manager: What have you done to try to improve the situation?

Salesman: I've told him that it would be better if I called on him when I feel that I need his help, but he says he's trying to help me because he can't stand to hear me make mistakes.

Manager: How does that affect your work?

Salesman: It annoys me. I need to be able to learn on my own. And because I get annoyed, I make more mistakes.

Manager: Have you done anything else?

Salesman: Yes, I've tried coming in early to make my calls. I've also tried staying at the lunch hour, but it's difficult to get clients during both those times.

Manager: So you've been trying to work around the problem.

Salesman: Yes.

Manager: It is possible that others have similar problems due to the way we changed our office structure. How do you think Carlos finds this situation?

Salesman: He said the other day that he was afraid of letting me make mistakes, because that might backfire on him.

Manager: I appreciate your openness. Perhaps we should have a department meeting on this. Before then, I will also see Carlos and some of the others separately.

on a simulation". Simulation games are normally exercises where the environment is modelled by use of information sheets, cards or a computer programme. Simulation games are often called business games.

The players may assume functions, in which they are normally free to exercise skills and knowledge without being bound by a script or a detailed character description. The task is usually realistic, as it tends to be related to managerial-type problem-solving and decision-making.

In a simulation game, the players are normally given the task of running a company in a given situation, or of managing a selected company operation. The term "games" in simulation games denotes the competitive element. Teams or individuals compete against each other. Where technology is used, such as in the case of computer-based simulation games, individuals or teams compete against the computer programme.

Craig (1987) defines simulation games as a combination of three elements: the *roles* assumed by the participants, a *scenario*, and an *accounting system*.

The roles define the parts played by the participants. They correspond to the more or less real or hypothetical situation which the simulation represents. Roles can be played by a group or by an individual.

The scenario depicts the situation which the simulation represents. It includes background information, such as a simulated company's annual report or an overview of market conditions. The scenario also includes the rules of the game, time-limits, etc.

The accounting system provides the players with feedback on the progress of the game. It can be in the form of written information on cards, feedback from team members, feedback from a nominated referee or feedback from a computer which calculates the effects of decisions and actions.

There are thousands of simulation games on the market. They have been designed for different purposes. Most simulation games fall into one or a combination of the following categories:

- Decision-making games, where the object of the game is to enhance the decision-making capabilities of the manager.
- Group interaction games, where the participants gain insight into the interaction between individuals and groups of individuals in an organization.
- Systems games, where the players develop insight into the internal functioning of organizations as well as the influence of market forces, society and legislation.

The trainer is often faced with the choice of using an existing simulation game and/or designing one specifically for his or her own purpose. When faced with the choice, the following factors should be taken into consideration:

- The environmental and task parameters of the existing game should be reviewed carefully — will they be realistic, relevant and challenging to your group?
- Is the existing game appropriate in terms of depth of analysis?
- What exactly are the objectives of the intended simulation game, and how do they correspond to the overall programme objectives?

- To what extent is it important to use reality-based parameters in the simulation?
- Can the simulation be done using a simple scenario (in which case it may present a greater potential for achieving an effective intervention)?

When ready-made simulation games are used, there will always be some misfit between the way the participants perceive reality and the way it is presented by the game. Incompatibilities that appear small to the trainer may in practice present the participants with an important obstacle to active involvement and learning.

The advantages of using simulation games is that they allow participants to make and correct mistakes in a realistic simulation while providing them with an incentive to apply themselves in competition with each other. Another advantage which simulation games have over other methods is that they are readily replicable. They often include detailed instructions for use, which may even allow them to be run by groups of managers without the assistance of a trainer. It is thus a relatively cost-effective means of training.

Their most important disadvantage is that they cannot fully replicate reality while allowing the participants to apply a range of skills to problem-solving. This invariably creates some degree of superficiality, which presents an obstacle to the application of skills on the job. However, it should be pointed out that a certain divergence between reality and the game may, if used skilfully by the trainer, help the participants develop new and hitherto unexplored ways of dealing with work issues.

Some practical hints for running simulation games are listed below.

- Ensure that the learning process is always more important to the participants than the competition.
- Help the participants to use the game as a means of analysing the reality on the job, cause-effect relationships and possible solutions.
- Be aware of the incompatibilities between the game and reality. Point them out and discuss them with the participants.
- Monitor the functioning of groups and ensure equal participation and consensus decision-making.

The degree to which the trainer's skills determine the success of a simulation game depends on how active the trainer is in adapting and running the simulation. In the case of a simulation game that arrives ready-packaged with questions and answers, the programme and activities' sequencing will not require much more than basic trainer skills. Such a simulation may even be run by a group of managers without the help of a trainer.

A simulation game that is to be designed by the trainer, or significantly adapted for a specific use, requires more advanced skills, particularly in instructional design, understanding the organization and learning process, organizing and facilitating.

(C)   Reality-based simulations

Reality-based simulations are used to enable attitude and skill changes in a few people, and these are expected to produce direct effects on job performance. They

Box 13.2. An example of a simulation game

The business game, *Decision Base*, was developed by Learning Methods International and has now been used by more than 200,000 managers worldwide.

Decision Base is a simulation game which falls into the category of systems games, where four, five or six companies compete on the same markets for a period of ten years. Each company is managed by a team of three to four people, with different areas of responsibility. The game is non-computerized. It provides concrete illustrations of a number of strategic and fnancial relationships which influence a company's competitiveness and ultimate survival.

The aim of the game is to help participants to understand the strategy and finances of the company. In terms of physical structure, the game consists of a board, which is a graphic representation of the placement and the movement of capital between the main functions of the company, such as purchase, finance, production, overheads, etc. Other elements of the game are cost carriers (little cylinders which carry the capital in the form of coins), customer cards (distributed to the companies once a year to indicate demand for their product) and market cards (indicating how the sales investments are distributed). Each team is made up of a marketing director, a production manager, a finance manager and a marketing manager. The trainers, in addition to being responsible for organizing the game, may act as consultants to the company managers.

The starting-point of the game is a consultant's report addressed to each of the companies, which states that "without strategic innovation at all levels, your company will perish within three years".

A great deal happens during the ten years the teams manage their companies. First, the participants learn how their companies function, and they adopt a strategy by trial and error. After a few years, they can see the results, and since they have learned to interpret financial information, they have a decision-making base which is sufficient for developing a more successful strategy.

As in real life, there is no right answer. The way it ends depends solely on what the competing companies do. The winners are the ones who know how to adapt the operations of their company to changing conditions, within and beyond the control of the company.

are normally conducted as in-house exercises designed by the trainer, in cases where the environment and the task parameters are interchangeably real or modelled. The objectives of reality-based simulation are related to the ways in which managers function in a specific organizational environment. The aim of such an intervention is to facilitate organizational change through concrete measures.

There are two different types of reality-based simulation. The first is when the *environment* is reality-based and the task is modelled (for example, managers take on the role as consultants to a real organization). It is an effective means of developing managers' views of their role in organizational processes and of giving them a vision of how a specific organization (their own, for example) functions in relation to the internal and external environment.

The second type is when the *task* is reality-based, in that the managers perform activities that are representative of their work, while the environment is modelled. An example is when a learning organization is modelled. The participants are asked to form an organization according to a certain set of criteria, and are then instructed to assess the effectiveness of their fictitious organization (for more information on the "learning organization", see Chapter 18).

Reality-based simulations can be less predictable than simulation games and role-plays. They are close to reality, therefore the process, duration and sequence of activities must be flexible and guided with considerable intuition by the trainer. The trainer needs to be able to modify the simulation during implementation, and even alter parameters and intervene when necessary. For this reason, reality-based simulations require more resources for implementation and monitoring than do other simulation forms.

In reality-based simulations the simulated parameters are brought into close contact with reality. Imagine, for example, a personnel manager who in an exercise has to deal with personnel issues brought by fellow participants, who are from the same organization.

The advantages of reality-based simulations is that, owing to their proximity to reality, they stand a good chance of producing direct behaviour changes. The major disadvantage is that they demand substantial resources as well as skilled trainers to design and implement them. They are suitable for organization-development type programmes where there are expectations of direct, tangible results.

Some points which should be taken into account when designing and running reality-based simulations are listed here.

- They require knowledge and understanding of the specific organization involved; an organizational analysis and possibly a climate survey should be undertaken prior to designing the intervention.

- They require the collaboration of the organization and the commitment of senior management; substantial negotiating thus needs to be done before a simulation is run.

- They may produce effects that are unappreciated by the organization, because it may be confronted by concrete signs of weakness from its own members.

- Because they aim at solving problems that exist in real life, they create expectations from the participants that the organization will follow up on their findings and recommendations.

(D)   Using training technology in simulations

There are two purposes in using technology in simulations. The first is using it to explain the scenario. In an interpersonal skills training programme, for example, the scenario may serve as an introduction in the form of a video-recorded situation where interpersonal skills are used with varied success. In a programme for production managers, the scenario may be a video recording from their respective production plants.

The second use is as a means of feedback. In a computer-assisted simulation, for example, the programme tells the players about the quality of their decisions. Another example is where video is used for a group to review their performance in solving a task.

The types of training technology can be broadly grouped into three categories: computer technology, video and interactive video.

Computers assist in representing the real world. They allow the participants to experience events and explore environments which in any other way would be too expensive, dangerous or time-consuming to reproduce. The advice to trainers when evaluating computer-assisted simulation is to assess in particular the degree of realism in the programme. The programme should have an augmented feedback feature which signals to the user not only when his or her decisions are likely to turn out badly, but also when things have turned out badly, and why.

Videos can be produced to convey a message to the participants or to demonstrate the application of a set of skills, which serve as a useful introduction to a simulation. Video production requires expertise and a relatively large investment in terms of money and time. When used to record events, however, video only requires basic operating skills and a far smaller investment of time and money.

It is important, therefore, for the trainer to be very conscious of what the video is to be used for and what can be achieved by using it. The instructional effects of video are often greatly exaggerated, except when used as a means of behaviour feedback.

Interactive video uses a combination of computer and video technology. Interactive video is basically an extension of computer-assisted training, but with the possibility of augmented visual facilities. The main question to answer when choosing between computer-based training and interactive video is whether the added visual motion effects are going to make any difference to the simulation.

When choosing between video-assisted training and interactive video it is important to know if the interaction is going to make a difference to the outcome of the simulation.

(E)   Outdoor simulations

Outdoor simulations are used more and more by companies for training their managers. They are a means for managers to get out of conditioned ways of seeing themselves in teams and how they function, and of perceiving the individual in the organizations. In outdoor exercises they have to meet challenges by making decisions other than those made at work. This helps them to develop a better view of what goes into decision-making and the role played by the environment and subordinates.

Outdoor projects demand good qualities of leadership, teamwork and managerial skill, and when combined with review and discussion are a powerful training medium. Outdoor activities must be used appropriately since the activities themselves, be they canoeing, climbing, or any other, are not a means to an end. They need to be linked with behavioural concepts, discussions and reviews to make the most of them as important learning events.

The idea of using the outdoors is to take the managers out of their usual setting and have them perform skills in a totally different environment. In outdoor simulations, the tasks given to the teams are simulated and may entail sailing a boat, building a structure, climbing a mountain together, or organizing a football team.

The environment to which the managers are usually accustomed is obviously modelled. It does, however, in many cases present unexpected and non-negotiable challenges to the participants which resemble in nature those in dynamic organizations competing in a changing market and environment.

The most common purposes of running outdoor simulations are to facilitate team-building or to develop the team management skills of individual managers.

An example is when a management team is made to sail a boat together. The simulation aspect of it is that the boat is defined as the organization, the crew represents those who work in it. In order to perform the exercise, they are automatically obliged to define their respective competences and organize the work accordingly. Once the responsibilities have been divided between them and they have agreed on a course, they depend on each other to reach their destination. Moreover, in a boat there is physical proximity, which enables them to get to know each other personally: to learn to listen and to understand each other while making fast progress towards their destination.

Outdoor simulations, like all training methods, have their pros and cons. They allow more scope for reflection than indoor training. However, some people may resent the loss of comfort and the presence of physical challenge. The outcome of the exercise may be subject to weather conditions, and there are certain limitations in using traditional training aids.

CASE METHOD $\qquad$ 14

John I. Reynolds

Case method has become an effective tool for management development, just as it has been a method of teaching management problem-solving and decision-making for three-quarters of a century. Although a simple definition fails to capture the essence of the method, case method can be described as interactive rather than didactic, and problem-centred rather than theoretically oriented. Case method has more in common with other interactive methods like role-playing, simulation and action learning than it does with lectures and presentation methods.

A working definition of case method will serve to get this chapter started. A group is taught by "case method" when participants have studied a case situation prior to discussing what should be done and how it should be done. The trainer in a case-method class is seen more as a facilitator and encourager of discussion and participation than as a repository of the "correct answer". The focus of class attention is on understanding the case situation, analysing the important interrelationships involved, predicting the probable outcomes of various courses of action, and choosing and defending the preferred decision. It is important for participants to reason well, i.e. along lines consistent with the best thought, about the situation portrayed in the case at hand, as well as to examine carefully the expected consequences of proposed actions.

14.1   History of case method

It is generally accepted that case method was first adapted to teaching business administration by the Harvard Business School (HBS). From the first days of HBS, the Dean sought to develop an innovative alternative to courses "made up only of lectures read from manuscript". He looked for inspiration to the Harvard Law School, which had developed a system of "case method" in which the students were continually challenged to study and discuss cases drawn from the law courts, the purpose being to derive principles from cases, rather than merely to memorize principles in a vacuum.

At first it was very slow going. In contrast to law, where "cases" were being brought to trial daily and written up for the archives by court reporters, business administration had no such ready-made backlog of material. Over the years HBS evolved and supported a substantial case-writing effort, which led to a large and multi-faceted library of cases. What evolved was a recognition that a satisfactory 'teaching case" had these characteristics:

- it was a short, written description of an actual business situation;

- it stopped short of presenting the actions taken by the manager in the actual situation, thus leaving open to the students the choice of actions to be proposed;

- the best cases included enough detail for students not only to gain the experience of relating facts to one another effectively in problem-solving, but also how to judge among important and unimportant details;

- cases drawn from real-life situations were to be "released" for teaching purposes by a principal of the cooperating firm. This served the dual purpose of quality assurance, i.e. being sure that the case-writer had captured the essence of the real-life experience, and of ensuring that no problems would later arise between the case-writing university and the cooperating firm.

"Case method" incorporated more than merely the preparation and teaching of a single case. "Case courses", involving writing and scheduling series of cases sequentially, each building upon the material mastered by the students in previous case discussions, was the first step, suggested by the practice. In this way, complexities are added only after proper groundwork has been laid out for them.

In the beginning, almost by definition, there was no "science" of administration. The expectation of early adherents of case method was that students would learn to derive generalizations about administration from a series of individual cases which appropriately reflected the environment of administration and frequently occurring management problems. Following these developments, important progress was made in systematizing the solution of such problems.

As these scientific solutions began to enter the literature of the field, "case method" expanded to accommodate the *technical note*, which described principles and/or analytical techniques found useful in handling management situations. In addition, of course, case-method teaching institutions have always, like Harvard, gathered the broadest and deepest libraries of management literature they can afford. Good case-method teachers stay closely in touch with state-of-the-art theory, and thus are able to recognize and encourage students' progress.

Another type of written material often useful in case method is the *industry note*, which provides more background information about an industry than could easily be incorporated in the pages of a single case. Therefore, particularly when a teacher expects to teach a series of cases based on the same industry, or even within a single firm in the industry, he or she will write or choose an appropriate industry note to provide the background information. An industry note gives an overview of such facts as the important products, raw materials, labour inputs, production processes, markets and competitive structure of the industry.

All three types of written material mentioned above, the *teaching case*, the *technical note* and the *industry note*, are meant to be issued to and used by students.

Teaching notes, which often accompany cases, are issued only to teacher-trainers. These are messages from the case-writer to other teachers who may be using the case, and may be merely short explanations of how the case came to be written, how it has proved useful in teaching particular concepts, or descriptions of student interpretations of parts of the case.

Over the years a number of written materials similar in purpose or in form to the cases described further in this chapter have been used with substantial access in management development. *In-basket exercises* and the *incident process* have both been used with substantial success in management training. *Case histories*, which are very like teaching cases except that they continue to describe the decisions and actions of the real-life managers, as well as the final outcomes of the situations, have been used successfully by the ILO, particularly in a series of construction management programmes. These case histories are written by and presented for discussion by experienced manager-participants in international and/or interregional workshops. The explicit purpose of these workshops is to share and compare experience to facilitate the transfer of experience from one region to another.

14.2   Case method and other methods

Case method and simulations. Compared to simulations, the case method is rather static. The analysis does not alter the nature of the case, whereas in simulations, events are acted out to provide new, often unexpected, scenarios. Simulations are more action-oriented, in the sense that participants act and get a response, which leads to new actions. Case method leaves more time for analysis. If we relate the two methods to Kolb's experiential learning cycle (see Chapter 11), we can say that simulations place more emphasis on "experience" and "active experimentation", while case method is more focused on "reflective observation" and "abstract conceptualization".

The two methods also tend to have slightly different learning objectives. Simulations enable the learner to understand how he or she reacts to a given situation, and the types of response that are triggered off by certain types of behaviour. Most simulations give the learner the experience of being in a given situation. Learning takes place primarily as a response to personal style or skills. Thus, it tends to be intuitive and directly behaviour-oriented.

Case method enables learning *about* situations to take place. Because it involves a high degree of analysis, sometimes of complex scenarios, learning is created through gaining understanding of a particular type of business situation, but from the point of view of a detached observer. Therefore, the type of learning created through case method is the ability to analyse a given situation rationally.

In conclusion, simulations tend to be more effective for an immediate change of managerial behaviour, while case method allows for a better overall understanding of how to solve organizational problems, and thereby aim at longer-term effects.

Case methods and lectures. Case method is based on group work, which is largely uninterrupted by the trainer. The participants make out their own answers to the case. Lecturing is based on the lecturer having answers to a given type of problem. The lecturer challenges existing practices or advocates new ways of doing things. Although case method may expose participants to new types of problem, the answers are worked out by the participants, using their existing knowledge and analytical skills. The answers they arrive at, and hence the learning they achieve, are largely subject to the quality of collaboration in the groups.

There are two important differences between case method and lecturing that come out of the above analysis. First, lecturing can, to a greater extent, be controlled to ensure that the same knowledge is conveyed to all the participants. With case method, this is left more to the discretion of the participants. As a result of the interactive relationship between lecturer and participants, a lecture can also be adapted to participants' response at any time.

The second important difference concerns the type of learning that is created. Because lectures provide insight into a limited defined topic, they are suited for brief interventions aiming to get a message, or a set of messages, across. Thus, they allow learners to benefit from an external body of knowledge and skills. Case method, on the other hand, is more suited to developing learners' capacity for independent analysis. Thus, whereas the *content* of the message is important in lectures, the *process* of reflection is more important in case method.

The two methods can be combined very effectively to get the most out of both. For example, a lecture can be given before the case is run, to illustrate new and different ways of analysing management problems. The participants will examine the case under the influence of the lecture. They will benefit from going through the process of analysing the case as well as having acquired different analytical methods from the lecture.

Case method and experiential learning. In case method, participants learn from someone else's experience, i.e. those whose actions are described in the case. Therefore, their interpretation of the actions in the case is intellectual and detached, as opposed to the emotionally involved way that they would have interpreted their own experiences.

It has been suggested that managers reason differently when they have to solve the problem themselves than when someone else has the responsibility for solving it. This enables us to draw up an important distinction between the case method and experiential learning. Because the case is someone else's problem, and because the participants are not distracted by the memory of everyday hassle while solving it, they are not acting out an entirely realistic situation. Experiential learning, on the other hand, requires that the managers bring their personal relationship to the problem-solving, because managers should analyse and understand their behaviour in a given situation. As a result experiential learning could be directly applicable back on the job, when similar situations arise. Hence, it is better suited for creating immediate behaviour change than case method.

There is nothing in the case method that obliges the manager to solve certain problems after the training, the way experiential learning does. The problem in the case remains hypothetical to the manager, and it is very much up to the individual whether to project the case problem on to his or her own situation or not. Therefore, it is most likely to have an impact on the analytical parts of a manager's job (the interpretation of financial results, assessing production layout, or getting an understanding of the company's business environment, etc.), rather than on behavioural aspects.

An important part of a manager's job is to analyse information. Case method also helps to develop analytical capacity, particularly effective for scanning and interpreting information. The type of competence in question is what Kolb calls "perceptual competence" — perspective taking, perceptivity and search for meaning.

14.3   Case method components and problem-solving

Managers typically follow several fairly well-accepted steps or processes in problem-solving, in roughly the following order:

- identify the problem;
- set objectives or goals;
- define possible courses of action;
- predict consequences; and
- choose and implement the course of action whose expected outcome is most desirable.

This "general-purpose problem-solving format" is shown in figure 14.1, which will serve as a road map for describing the necessary components of a successful case (Reynolds, 1980). The case contains the material shown in the left-hand box in the diagram, labelled "A". This box represents all the information about the problem situation, including past and present.

For each step, there is a process of interpreting ambiguities, selecting important information, discarding unimportant information and searching for more information. Mintzberg (1990) found, in a study of chief executives, that only 13 per cent of the mail they received contained information of specific and immediate use. Apart from this fact, the managers they studied put importance on getting as much "soft" information as they could, such as gossip, hearsay and speculation.

Because the "real world" of a manager contains a wealth of unstructured information, much of it appropriate at different times and for different decisions, the challenge to the case-writer lies in simulating this fact. The extent to which ambiguities and unimportant information are left in the case depends on the exact learning objective of the case. If the objective tends towards learning about the nature of decision-making, a realistic number of such elements should be left in. If, on the other hand, the learning objective tends more towards understanding about a particular organization issue, then too much irrelevant information may detract from

Figure 14.1. A general-purpose problem-solving format

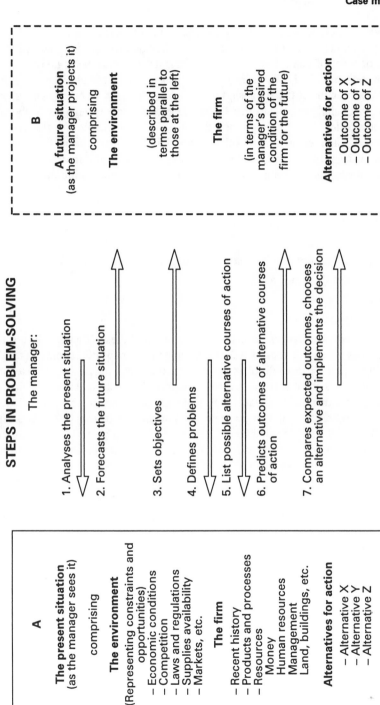

Source: Reynolds, 1980, p. 18

277

achieving the objective of properly understanding the issue.

What emerges in a case is a carefully crafted description of a manager in the midst of a set of conditions, both environmental (outside the organization) and organization-specific. For cases involving the general management of the firm, nearly every component of the suggested list in Box A is likely to be relevant in some degree. Particularly in courses that focus on general management (variously called "Business policy" and "Strategy formulation and implementation") effective cases tend to be much longer than in other fields. This field has long resisted research efforts to simplify and codify what the manager should do; it therefore remains a bastion of case method in many management development institutions.

14.4   Types of cases

Cases can be broadly divided into three categories:

- problem or decision cases;
- appraisal cases;
- case histories.

Problem or decision cases are the most common of these. They are descriptions of situations which stop short of a decision being made or an action being taken. The participants practise the skills of analysing situations, making decisions based upon their judgements about what would be the outcome of various courses of action, and planning the actions they will take. They make use of the information provided with the case, they select what appears important and analyse it from different perspectives. Because the real-life situation of a manager contains potentially vast amounts of information to be compiled and analysed before a decision is made, a case should reflect this reality by containing information of varying degrees of importance, clues and ambiguities. Thus, the participants spend much of the analysis trying to figure out "what the real problem is about", by selecting important items of information. Having defined the problem as they perceive it, they recommend decisions or actions which are appropriate, given parameters such as time, human resources, skills, etc.

Appraisal cases do not require suggestions for action from the participants, as is done with problem/decision cases. They are used more to develop managers' capacity to understand and to interpret seemingly complex situations.

One type of appraisal case is in-company human behaviour situations. Participants, when appraising such a case, gain understanding of the complexities of human behaviour. The following excerpt is an example of a case on human behaviour which is well suited for appraisal by participants (Gillette and McCollom, 1990):

> The scene is a hospital staff meeting. It is 15 minutes after the starting time, and still the members have not turned their attention to the work at hand. The hospital administrator looks to the chief medical resident to get things started, but she is busy in conversation with one of the staff nurses about a patient treatment. After another five minutes have

passed, the administrator attempts to pull the group together. As he starts, he feels a gnawing insecurity growing that he is not going to be able to get the group to accomplish what needs doing in the 45 minutes left. Sure enough, side issues, personal bickering, and drifting attention all lead to an incomplete discussion. As the administrator tries to schedule a follow-up meeting, half the members leave, including the chief resident, complaining that they are late for other work. The administrator feels defeated.

Another type of appraisal case is organization-environment cases, sometimes called "issue" cases. A description of the circumstances surrounding an oil spill; a selection of published material about a public protest over a nuclear power plant; excerpts from the records of a legal battle between two corporations; these are all examples of such cases.

Appraisal cases focusing on organization-environment are a useful means to train process management. Rummler and Brache (1991) argue that managers do not understand, at a sufficient level of detail, how their companies get products developed, made, sold and distributed. They suggest that a better way to manage in organizations is to regard them as horizontal flows of interactions between production, marketing, finance, etc., which are constantly monitored and improved upon to create optimal quality for the end customer. Process management requires that the manager aims at improving the interface with other departments rather than just trying to manage his or her department "the best way possible". The background materials process management case may include process charts showing interrelationships between the customer and the company and interaction between a company's departments.

Case histories provide the description of any relevant problem and its rationale. They tend to be elaborate narratives that have been produced as a collaboration between researcher and organization. They are usually broad in coverage, including internal as well as external conditions to the organization. Case histories illustrate problem situations and their solution by highlighting successful and unsuccessful practices. They are used with difficulty in management development programmes, due to their extent, and the time needed to review them. However, they do have a certain value for longer-term educational programmes as a source of issues to be explored from a variety of perspectives.

There is a difference in the style of presentation between problem, decision and appraisal cases as compared to case histories. The first type must necessarily contain clues and leads which, if pursued, lead to discoveries and conclusions. Therefore, there is a balance between information that is essential, just useful or of no use in the case.

A case history, on the other hand, is written for the purpose of fruitful and enjoyable reading. Thus, the emphasis is on giving facts that are interesting, rather than indicative of clues. The objective of a case history is much less the achievement of learning than presenting the reader with an illustrative story.

There is still room for a great many simple, short cases in nearly every management discipline, not only to serve as vehicles for managers practising new ideas and concepts, but also to explore many nuances of decisions for which generally accepted principles are set forth in the literature. Trainers are exploring problems and decisions where many environmental parameters are quite different from those on which western optimal-decision models are based, especially in regions out of reach of well-known business schools. One needs only to think of the western models that are based on assumptions of scarce labour and abundant raw materials to realize that they ill fit conditions in many parts of the developing world or economies in transition.

14.5   Case method: Advantages and disadvantages

There are several advantages and disadvantages of using case method. Its most significant contributions lie in its fundamental emphasis on practical application, and on learning through involvement and doing. The main pros and cons are as follows:

(A)   Advantages

1. The focus is on "doing" as a way to improve skills development. A high degree of involvement of experienced managers and mutual learning are likely to take place.
2. Learners enhance written and verbal communication skills. This occurs when managers make group presentations to other learners.
3. Mastery is developed in solving mysteries. Participants are invited to unravel the mystery implied by managerial dilemmas and to develop their analytical skills more effectively.
4. Because cases provide concrete illustrations of points, issues or managerial principles, the method helps to bridge the gap between practice and conceptual abstraction.
5. Cases deal with real organizational situations because they are derived from experience. This tends to provide additional motivation among participating managers to apply themselves in the search for solutions.
6. Cases imply artificiality. While bringing realism into the programme, they allow, as do simulations, the participants to take stands which do not concern them personally. They thus have the opportunity to explore the logic of a situation and learn new principles without having to change their own behaviour. Thus, case method is, in this respect, less threatening than is experiential learning.
7. Case method promotes constructive change in the management of firms by stimulating organizational analysis.
8. Otherwise abstract and boring material becomes enjoyable. Case method offers a good alternative to theoretical and textbook-oriented learning content.
9. The method makes effective use of reference points. When participants explore management situations in the case, they go through a process of association, i.e. they draw an analogy with their own practices.
10. Case method can help unlearn skilled incompetence, the unlearning of outdated

skills or ineffective behaviour. Particularly when managers prepare their own cases, drawn from their own situations, they are able to confront and question each other on their respective practices.

(B)   Disadvantages

1. Case method results in reduced trainer responsibility when the case is ready-made. It allows trainers to get away with little preparation. Running the case becomes an objective in itself more than achieving behavioural changes.
2. The method may be viewed as static. The approach cannot reproduce the "messy" reality that is characteristic of problem-solving realities in organizations. Moreover, the cases focus on something that has happened and that requires analysis, or a hypothetical decision at the most.
3. It does not allow double-loop learning to take place. The term "double-loop learning" denotes learning through correction of underlying assumptions of an organization.
4. The learners' ability to make effective generalizations may be reduced. There is a danger that a superficial interpretation of a case may lead to poor decisions by the participants in the job after the training has taken place.
5. Individual accountability for learning may be diminished. Because it is based on group work, it is likely that some group members will be more active and thus be able to learn more effectively from the case than others.
6. Non-critical norms may be promoted. One of the general dangers of group work is that group members shy away from being critical of one another, of themselves and of the way the group is operating. A norm of non-criticism may come to pervade the group's interaction, which again may prevent the group from breaking new ground in their analysis of the case.
7. The analysis may foster "safe play" — consensus and groupthink. It describes a learner tendency towards what is perceived as the "norm" in the discussion. Individuals who have totally different ideas about the issues of the case do not bring out their ideas for fear of being labelled as deviant.
8. The case approach may foster quantity and not quality interaction. There is a risk that some trainers may reward to a larger extent extrovert participants providing quantities of, in the trainer's view, agreeable answers, than reflective participants who keep a low profile with their, qualitatively speaking, more thoughtful answers.

The extent to which a trainer regards case method to be advantageous or disadvantageous, depends also on his or her personal views on decision-making processes. Some trainers base their training on the notion that decision-making is rational, i.e. that the group will arrive at an answer when the correctness of the answer is persuasively argued by one or more group members. Trainers who believe that this is a reflection of management decisions in practice, will tend to regard the objective analysis of case method as a great advantage and as an important contribution to the development of managerial skills.

Another view of decision-making is to consider it as a process of judgement, an opinion-based interaction among members of a group, where the "correctness" of a decision is subject to individual interpretation. This perspective makes power, coalitions, politicking, status and personality the central elements of the decision-making process. It is assumed that a problem does not have one right solution, but that it may have a wide range of possible solutions, the comparative value of each being subject to individual interpretation and preferences. Because there is an interplay between people in the process, the final decision may not be "optimal". In fact, it leads to companies making decisions that are visibly ineffective. Trainers and consultants with the latter perspective on decision-making tend to be more wary of the learning effects of the rational, objective thinking that the participants undertake in case method.

14.6   The process of case method

The main stages of a case method process are:

- Briefing (describe procedure, timing, provide specific information, etc.) of participants.

- Case analysis. The participants, organized in groups of normally 4-6 people, study the contents of the case, formulate decisions to be taken in relation to the case.

- Group presentations. The groups present their answers in plenary, using overhead projectors or flip charts.

- Analysis of answers. Differences and similarities between the groups' answers are analysed and discussed, either in plenary or in the small groups.

The most important part of the learning takes place in the case analysis, where the participants study the case in small groups. A participant is expected to take three stages of preparation during the case analysis:

1. One quick reading through the case, to familiarize oneself with the situation and plan the analysis, ticking marks in the margin at points which merit attention.
2. A slower second reading, taking notes, studying exhibits carefully to understand what they mean and what further information can be gained by working with more than one idea at a time.
3. A discussion in the small group with fellow participants, in which each participant tries out his or her ideas and preliminary conclusions, with each individual then continuing to polish the preparation for class.

It is at the case analysis stage that group dynamics plays an important role in achieving learning effectiveness. An example of a case analysis process where participants analyse a human relations case involving a manager, a supervisor and employees is presented below.

Stage 1. A "search for the villain". This means that many observers try to find the single person who is at fault. They may brand almost anyone in the case as the culprit. They sometimes blame people who don't appear as such: "The company policy should have spelled this out", "The union must be somewhere behind this complaint", or "The supervisor just asked for trouble".

Stage 2. A desire "to play God". This occurs after the search for the villain is thwarted by deeper analysis or, as in a group discussion, by more sophisticated participants. Unfortunately, at this stage, many analysts conclude that the problem could have been avoided or resolved quickly had the employee done this, the supervisor done that, the upper-level manager another thing. There is a mistaken tendency at this stage to prescribe corrective behaviour in a self-righteous tone.

Stage 3. A demand for "more facts". As frustration with what was originally a simple solution sets in, participants are likely to ask for more information. "Surely", the reasoning goes, "analysts can't be expected to solve a problem from which so many facts have been omitted." It is typical to want to know what went on between the supervisor and the employee before this problem arose. Other frequent questions are "How old is the employee? What has company policy been in the past?" and so on. It is at this stage of probing for more information that a true understanding of the situation will begin to blossom. They see that for every act there is a reason which is not always obvious. Only by finding and controlling the causes, however, can employee behaviour be anticipated and possibly improved.

Stage 4. Enlightenment. This is the natural outgrowth of stage 3. Participants begin to examine the total picture of human behaviour within the facts presented in a particular case-study. They begin to see the whole web of circumstances in which the compromise, give-and-take, mutual understanding, and reasonable expectations must develop. It is at this stage that managers consciously and objectively re-examine their knowledge base and their past experiences with similar situations. For instance, they ask "Was my own behaviour sensible at the time? Did it achieve the results that I expected? How did I feel at the time? How did this affect my behaviour? What effect did this have on the other person's behaviour?".

At this point, one of three activities may take place. Sometimes the small group takes responsibility for presenting a jointly arrived-at recommendation in class, with one major spokesperson and the others adding support when needed. A more frequent pattern is for the participants to return to individual status when it comes to the class session. Each person, therefore, is representing an individual point of view.

The worst approach is when the most directive trainers treat the case merely as an excuse for giving a lecture based on the case facts. However, it is equally bad when the least directive trainers merely call on one after another of the participants, avoiding giving any feedback at all. Neither of these extremes is very effective in management development contexts. Participants need more feedback than the trainer in the latter case gives them, and in the former case the participants will soon be discouraged from preparing the case before class. A better teaching style is somewhere in between. In case method, a good rule of thumb is that the trainer should not be speaking more than 25 per cent of the time, and even less is desirable. Several variables determine how directive the trainer should be; see figure 14.2

Figure 14.2. Determinants of responsibility for direction of discussion

Variable	More teacher direction	More student direction
Time in course	Early ⇒	Late
Teacher's purpose	To illustrate a specific concept ⇒	To encourage students to develop concepts
Students' level of preparation	Students unprepared ⇒	Students well prepared
Students' stage of experience	Inexperienced students ⇒	Advanced and "post-experience" students
Nature of case	Unstructured or hidden structure ⇒	Fairly obvious structure

Source: Reynolds, 1980, p. 38.

Most successful trainers use a combination of devices, some of which are mentioned below, to keep the discussion moving, and provide needed information, encourage widespread participation and give evaluative feedback. The "plot" of a case class session might be conceived of as something like the diamond-shaped diagram in figure 14.3.

At the beginning the scope of the discussion is narrow, containing only the ideas of the opening speaker. As other participants introduce their ideas, conflicting with or amplifying the opener and as the trainer asks probing questions or seeks clarification, the discussion becomes broader in scope and more complex.

About midway through the discussion a class that is going well will seem to start to converge, as in the bottom part of the diagram. Some competing ideas, having gained no support, will be forgotten. Other suggestions, after argument, will be explicitly set aside. Consensus will develop about objectives, certain ways of stating the problem and certain alternatives that are worthy of consideration.

At this stage, the trainer should make a judgement about whether consensus is agreeable or not. As in management, it is tempting to support a process that moves towards consensus, especially if consensus tends towards the trainer's own preferred conclusions. Consensus is positive in the sense that there are more people for a decision than there are against. However, consensus also means rejecting points of view that come from completely different perspectives and, although they do not fit the prevailing norm, may be perfectly legitimate, even enlightening.

Whether to emphasize conformity or diversity is a choice that the trainer has to make. Where a group moves towards conformity of conclusion (or tries to), there is a learning effect in reinforcing one another's views and getting the feeling of having got to the "crunch" of the case together. The nature of the commonly agreed answer can then be explored for further mutual learning.

If, on the other hand, the *differences* in the respective conclusions are emphasized

Figure 14.3. Content of a case discussion over time

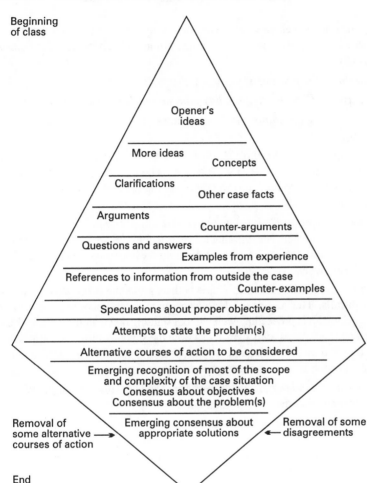

Beginning
of class

Opener's
ideas

More ideas

Concepts

Clarifications

Other case facts

Arguments

Counter-arguments

Questions and answers

Examples from experience

References to information from outside the case

Counter-examples

Speculations about proper objectives

Attempts to state the problem(s)

Alternative courses of action to be considered

Emerging recognition of most of the scope
and complexity of the case situation
Consensus about objectives
Consensus about the problem(s)

Removal of
some alternative ⟶
courses of action

Emerging consensus about
appropriate solutions

Removal of some
⟵ disagreements

End
of class

Source: Reynolds, 1980, p. 40.

by the trainer in the discussions, the learning effects may change slightly. First, it will reinforce the notion among the participants of the open-ended nature of management issues, which may in itself constitute an important element of managerial learning. Secondly, exploring the differences in perspective between participants may for some cases enable more productive learning, as the differences in conclusion are likely to enlighten the participants further about the different aspects of the case.

Good case method trainers view their responsibility as facilitating this process. It is unsatisfactory for participants to fail to be aware of some course of action. It is equally unsatisfactory if they reach closure too quickly because of failing to recognize the complexity of a situation.

14.7   The trainer's role in case method

In the interaction with either small groups or plenary, there are certain functions that the trainer needs to carry out. Here are some points to keep in mind for facilitating case method:

- *Requesting clarification* of prior statements.
- *Rephrasing what a participant has said*, to see if the meaning is clear.
- *Asking probing questions*, preferably neutral, that force participants to expand their argument.
- *Reporting and interpreting illustrative experience.* This includes translating unfamiliar jargon, correcting misconceptions about known facts and the situation, and occasionally introducing a workable assumption that may smooth over a gap in case data.
- *Giving a "lecturette": Introducing concepts and techniques.* There are times when a technical note is not available, yet a technique, unfamiliar to the participants and which can be described in five minutes or so, will help in performing a useful analysis.
- *Providing evaluative feedback.* This is both an important function and one fraught with pitfalls. The trainer needs to know how much encouragement to give a participant who is proceeding well without shutting down all the others' thinking. And the trainer needs to recognize that even the slightest hint of disapproval may shut off not only the participant who is speaking, but also others who are trying to develop a similar line of argument.
- *Writing on a board* or other public recording device. This is a very powerful tool to influence what the class pays attention to.
- *Answering questions*, or, more appropriately, seeing that such direct questions as "What do you think, sir/madam?" get turned back to the class for treatment. The quickest way to finish a class is for the trainer to state his/her own opinion about the best solution.
- *Summarizing.* Some case method instructors make a practice of taking the last few minutes of a class to tell the participants what actually happened in the case situation, and how it came about. This is damaging to future class sessions, since participants rarely feel the need to work out a plan if the trainer is going to tell them. None the less, there will be times during a class session when it may help for someone to summarize the progress the group has made. If the trainer can encourage a participant to make this summary, all the better.

The successful case method trainer must accept a facilitative, rather than a directive, role. Participants must be given every possible opportunity to demonstrate their degree of prior preparation; they can only do this while speaking, and the trainer must let it happen.

14.8   How to organize writing a case-study

Effective cases must always have a focus which is selected by the trainer for the purposes of advancing the participants' learning. Evidently, the trainer must be comfortable not only with the concepts of the field he or she is teaching, but also with the practical applications in field situations. In many business schools, case method teachers spare themselves a lot of work by adapting published case books, which contain dozens of cases in a subject area, already arranged in a suggested sequence for teaching. However, even if good cases are available from an institution, sooner or later every good case-method trainer will want to do the field research to write a case.

Often the temptation is very great to "armchair" a case, by which is meant to sit in one's armchair and think about all the characteristics of a situation which would serve one's training purposes. There are doubtless many fine cases which have had such authorship. But it takes a very experienced writer to make an "armchair" case both internally consistent and believable. A much better plan is to go into the field, as the questions, make the observations and discipline oneself to capture the essence of the manager's situation in a few pages of prose and some diagrams or numbers.

The place for armchair research in fieldwork is at the very beginning, when the trainer has defined the types of situations needed for several parts of a course. Where, within a reasonable distance, is there an organization in which the manager may be facing two quarrelling subordinates, with a need to mediate their quarrel in such a way as to get them to work side by side in some dangerous endeavour? Perhaps the foreman in a nearby foundry is facing or has recently faced a problem of this sort. Or a coal-mining venture half-a-day's drive away might prove fruitful.

Although the next paragraphs speak of the researcher in the singular, in fact some cases, and particularly series cases dealing with various aspects of the same firm at one point in time, can best be written by teams of case-writers. These team members work cooperatively but conduct separate interviews, view different worksites and pursue case vehicles useful for teaching different concepts. Sometimes whole platoons of case-writers will fan out from case-writers' workshops organized by an institution to foster case-writing skills among their staff as well as to add to the volumes of cases appropriate to their region.

Almost always the first useful step, once one has made the initial contact, explained what is needed in the way of a case-study, and received permission to proceed, is to spend some time merely getting a "walk-through" of the workplace. This is particularly true of groups of case-writers, each of whom may have a slightly different planned case focus. In fact, host firms are often happy to arrange a "facility visit" to further the teaching of students, even before fully understanding what is entailed in case research.

Following a walk-through, it is usually very helpful to sit and talk with the responsible manager, to let him or her explain the situations one has been observing, and to express in the manager's own words what problems, if any, are facing the firm (or a smaller segment of the organization). A skilled trainer, being objective about the situation, is likely to see things somewhat differently from the manager, but this is neither necessarily good nor bad news about the possible case. The trainer's purpose is to report as objectively as possible what can be seen in the field situation, in the written history or accounts of an organization, and in the testimony of anyone he or she interviews, including the responsible manager. Potentially different interpretations make a particularly rich opportunity for participant discussion of the case.

In any event, what finally results from a case research contact is one or more written cases, each of which will contain information of the types mentioned below.

14.9 The structure of cases

A general case structure normally consists of three major parts, opening, case body and closing. The contents of these three parts are described in table 14.1.

Table 14.1. A general case format

Opening (First few paragraphs)	Name and title of responsible manager Name, location and product line of organization Date Synopsis of decision or problem setting
Case body	Company history, if relevant Environmental facts, if relevant Expanded description of the decision or problem situation Organizational relationships Other case characters Products and processes Financial data Marketing information Human interaction facts etc.
Closing (Last paragraph or two)	Scenario to establish a sense of urgency about the problem or decision

Source: Reynolds, 1980, p. 95.

The key to this format is the opening section, which is often as short as a single paragraph. In simple prose it should set the scene for the participants. By quickly introducing the responsible manager by name and title it tells the students what role they are to play. By giving a date it establishes the environmental context. By identifying the product line of the company it quickly tells whether they have relevant previous experience. Finally, by stating the decision setting, at least as seen by the manager, it helps participants prepare for analysis of what is to follow.

Cases often contain certain conventional considerations, as well. Balance sheets and operating statements are usually given in their conventional form. Charts, graphs and tables often prove to be good ways of presenting large amounts of quantitative data (even in situations where the organization has not itself prepared such methods of presentation). The training purpose intended for the case will determine how much or how little organizing of the data one does beforehand, and how much is left for the students to do.

The same can be said about the decision to include or exclude information. The field is always rife with information, in the form of myriad details. What is desired is a compromise between the "stripped-down" case, one that gives only the minimum information needed to exercise a manager through a single analytical technique, and a case that has "everything but the kitchen sink". The stripped-down case is often as uninteresting as a mere "example", while the latter has few if any clues as to how to proceed. A good rule of thumb is to include enough material so that the trainer could work out a rich analysis of the situation, plus a modest amount of other relevant material so that the case is more interesting than a mere example.

Just as there are clues in the real world which may, if identified, change considerably the way a decision is made, a representative case might contain clues which are not too obvious, and which show the participants that being inquisitive, even about seemingly unimportant and obscure information, may be crucial. A clue is a piece of information which, presented as a hint, may guide a course of inquiry. Organizational literature contains numerous examples of opportunities that were missed by companies because managers were not able to identify the potential offered by the ideas, facts or critiques being communicated to them. In organizational communication — oral as well as written — there are messages which are not stated explicitly, sometimes because cultural norms do not allow them to, sometimes because questions are not asked in a way that encourages frank, explicit answers. In cases, this is reflected by putting clues into the text.

A very important part of any case is its cut-off point. Usually this raises no problems when a case is written over a short period, using only material available at the time of the research. But cases based on a situation remembered by the manager, or taken from the files of the organization, often have a fuzzy cut-off point. Keep in mind that no data should be included (even though it might be available by the time the case is written) which could not have been known to the manager at the date of the case. This will provide a consistent cut-off point.

A final element is the last few paragraphs of the case, which is almost the only point where invention enters into field case-writing. Frequently it is useful, even when the situation has not presented such a sense of urgency, to invent a context in which the manager would feel a pressing need to come to a decision. It goes without saying that one would set the scene appropriately to the nature of the situation. If the manager needed three weeks to prepare the paperwork to solve the case problem, the urgency might be suggested by describing a board meeting to be held in a month's time. The need to act to avert a violent outburst by a subordinate, however, might be suggested by referring to a phone call which alerted the manager to the fact that the subordinate had just left the plant, a few minutes away by car, "headed towards your office". The purpose of this invention is to "hook" the participants with the need for action, rather than merely "talking about" the situation.

A typed version of the case should be presented to the host organization for "sign-off". Failing this step the trainer is severely handicapped in making use of the case, and particularly in publishing and sharing cases among training institutions. Probably more frequently than not, the best way to facilitate this process is to disguise the case.

The simplest disguises merely invent fictitious names for the firm and the manager, while leaving all other facts as they were found in the field. Where a city (or even a country, in some parts of the world) has only a single organization in a particular line of business, it is usually better to invent a fictitious country than to change the industry. Where the financial figures are a matter of concern to the person releasing the case, one can often disguise them by multiplying all figures by a constant. In this way, although the scale of the enterprise is changed, the important ratios and relationships are preserved. In instances where the scale of the enterprise is itself something that participants should question, other means of disguising may need to be found. Except for some micro-level cases in personnel or quantitative control techniques, any attempt to disguise the industrial area of a firm is sure to introduce distortions that one cannot control.

A case cannot be considered ready for use until it has been tested and found to work satisfactorily. Frequently one finds that a few of the facts left out of the case must be put back in to give learners a proper understanding of the real situation. In other instances some rewriting is called for. A case should never be considered finished. There are always improvements that can be made, especially where the training organization itself has compiled a case in response to a customer need, and has not had the opportunity of spending vast resources on thorough research and testing.

LECTURES AND PRESENTATION METHODS

15

Aamir Ali

It is a matter for pleasant wonder that though we have at our disposal all the electronic gadgetry of our age — videocassettes, TVs, tape recordings, computers, sophisticated software, films — the old-fashioned lecture still remains a staple diet. There is something about the human voice, about one human being communicating with others, which no artefact can rival.

In all training courses, though one may use all the aids available and to good effect, the lecture remains an important method. It is also an essential complement to other methods. Lectures are usefully applied in combination with discussions, for example, as a way of communicating ideas, points of view or concepts. A lecture, delivered on a subject area of which you have unique competence, is an excellent opportunity to let others share your personal experience with you.

The lecture has one important advantage over other methods. The speaker can look at the audience, judge their reactions, and modify the lecture accordingly. Things can be repeated when necessary; points can be omitted or treated more lightly when considered less important. There are few lectures which do not give an opportunity for some exchanges with the listeners. It is the two-way communication, the visual contact with the audience and the opportunity to adapt personal experiences to the presentation, which make lectures special in relation to other training methods.

We have all been exposed to lectures that are boring, too long or uninteresting. We have also attended lectures that captured our attention, made us ponder, gave us insight into other ways of doing things. In this chapter we shall discuss factors that prevent the first type of experience taking place, and factors which make lecturing an effective, even indispensable tool in a process of achieving behavioural change with managers. We shall discuss why we select lecturing among other training techniques. We shall also describe characteristics of the lecture, which, once it has been selected as a method, enable it to give maximum benefits to the audience.

15.1 Definitions

There are different ways of defining a lecture. One could say that the lecture is a talk given by one person, excluding the use of visual aids and excluding discussion with the audience. A second way of defining it would be to say that the lecture is the verbal part (one-way and two-way) of a presentation. A third way would be to say that the lecture is "everything" that goes into communicating a concept, a theory or a method, which is an integrated process of one-way talk, questioning, discussion, written presentation of text on overheads, flip charts, etc.

In this chapter we shall use the latter definition, i.e. regarding the lecture as a method where the talk by one particular person is the essential element, but where the integration of different means, verbal and written, is used to achieve effective communication. The reason why we emphasize the process that is used to supplement and to support the "talk" is that one of the key success factors of management development is *variation*. Variation is more easily achieved when the lecture is conceived as an integrative process of supportive elements built around the "talk" itself.

15.2 Elements of the lecturing process

Below we have attempted to break down the lecturing process into a number of elements, and to suggest the different functions of each element. The elements we suggest are: expositions, anecdotes, discussions, examples and questions.

Expositions

Expositions are the part of the lecture where the essence of a concept, a theory or an idea is communicated. It is the part of the talk where maximum attention from the audience is necessary and also where the main message of the lecture is put across. This is the purpose of the exposition: to make your point. Other elements, such as anecdotes, examples and elaborations are used to support the exposition.

An example of an exposition is where, in a lecture on creative problem-solving, the steps in the process (e.g. problem definition, search for causes, brainstorming for solutions, combination of solutions) are described. The use of illustrations, examples and anecdotes, on the other hand, would be used to help the participants understand how the creative problem-solving process works *in practice*.

Expositions can be done in a variety of ways. They can be done verbally, by visualization or, as is most often done, by a combination of the two. Expositions are done explicitly from the lecturer to the audience.

Anecdotes

Use of brief accounts of interesting incidents related to the topic of the lecture can prove helpful. The function of the anecdote is to add colour to the talk. If the theme of the lecture is theoretical or conceptual, anecdotes from life in an organiza-tion enable the participants to relate the contents of the talk to a setting that is familiar to them. In addition to "colouring" the lecture, anecdotes serve another important function, namely that of credibility. In our experience, managers tend to be very concerned that the trainer understands their world, and that the lecture is directed towards a type of problem that they feel is relevant to their work. This is particularly important for the trainer who is not immediately recognized by managers as having been a successful manager. It would be useful for the trainer to collect a sizeable collection of anecdotes, analyse them and keep them for adding interesting points to the lecture.

Discussions

Discussion opens up two-way verbal communication. It enables participants to ask for clarification, to expose their own views, to obtain additional views or ideas from the lecturer. Discussions can be deliberately included in the programme, such as at the end of each part of a lecture. An alternative is to give the lecture as a sort of continuous discussion with the participants, with elements such as anecdotes and expositions put in at appropriate moments. The extent to which discussion can be effectively used varies of course with the size of the audience. Audiences above 20 people make fruitful dialogue between lecturer and participants difficult.

Examples

Examples that are relevant and illustrative add considerable value to the lecture. Whereas anecdotes tend to be personally experienced incidents, examples illustrate the application of a general concept to a particular situation. The primary function of the example is to enable the audience to better understand how the content of the lecture applies to specific managerial situations.

A lecture may contain an example on how rigid accounting methods may impede company performance. The message of the exposition may be that unless the accounting system is analysed in the light of how it affects operational performance, it may, in some cases, be counter-productive. The *example* could show that in a production company, machines were put down as investment, whereas tools were marked as expenses. Tools were required to reduce set-up time and hence production time. However, as tools were put down as expenditure, the acquisition of tools was discouraged. Several machine operators had to share the same toolkit and wait for one another to finish. Thus, production time remained high, which meant that customers had a longer waiting period from the time of ordering until the finished product was received. Consequently the company suffered a loss of competitive edge in the market.

Questions

Questions asked by the lecturer serve either of two functions. One is to clarify the relationship between the audience and the theme of the lecture. The most common questions to ask the audience are their knowledge of the subject of the lecture, their opinions about it, or their expectations of the lecture. By starting with consulting the audience, the lecturer demonstrates to the audience that he or she intends the lecture to be a process of active two-way communication.

Another, more specific, type of question is subject-related. We may consider such questions in three different categories:

The *open* question — addressed to the entire group and to nobody in particular. It is often a question which opens a discussion such as, for example, "what do you see as being the greatest advantage of implementing company-wide Total Quality Management programmes?"

The *direct* question — addressed to a particular individual. The direct question is helpful for getting more information from a participant or from getting other views in the discussion.

The *probing* question — this is a form of active listening whereby the lecturer probes into the views of the participants by reflecting back to them their own ideas and feelings. An example is "so you're saying, Linda, that the Total Quality Management concept does not seem appropriate to your company. Could you explain why this is so?" Probing questions clarify points and issues, encourage participation, and let participants know that you really are listening to what they have to say.

15.3   Why lecture?

Learning is more effective through seeing than through hearing. We are told that only 11 per cent of our knowledge is derived aurally as compared with 83 per cent visually. We are also told that on average people retain only about 25 per cent of what they hear; a motivated student might retain 50 per cent. Not very encouraging figures for someone preparing a lecture. However, we should be aware that these figures relate to experiments based on listening only. They are likely to be very different for a lecture where visual aids are used, and also where the audience is engaged in two-way communication.

With all these handicaps, why use a lecture at all? Is it ever useful? Indeed, yes. It is effective for:

- Conveying organized information. When there is an accepted body of organized knowledge, it can be most usefully transmitted through a lecture.

- Outlining and explaining concepts. It is useful for deepening the understanding of ideas and values and for the exposition of concepts.

- Stimulating people to think in new ways. Developing as a manager has very much to do with gaining new perspectives on one's self, and on one's environment, with colleagues, systems and organizational policies. Some of the most effective lectures challenge people's present thinking, especially when given by people who hold quite different views about organizational problems, and who can demonstrate that their thinking is legitimate.

Below we suggest advantages and disadvantages of the lecture method compared with other methods.

Lecturing versus video or computers

Lectures are adaptable to the specific characteristics of a group of listeners. A lecturer can clearly communicate enthusiasm and express views and experiences in a personalized way, e.g. through eye contact. A skilled lecturer can readily modify the style of presentation, the way the content is put across and the duration of the lecture according to the needs and expectations of the group. Video productions and computer programmes do not offer this possibility, apart from, perhaps, interactive programmes, where different messages from the user trigger different responses on the screen. A comparative advantage of using videos or computers is that they ensure that the same content is transmitted to all the listeners. This may be of importance in, for example, multinational projects or companies, where there is concern that a message on central issues is transmitted in the same fashion to employees in all the countries.

Technology-assisted training takes more time to produce. B. Geber (1990) reports that whereas one hour of classroom instruction takes about 30 hours to develop, one hour of CBT (computer-based training) requires about 300 hours. Once developed, of course, technology-based instruction is far less costly to replicate to large numbers of learners. One last advantage it has over lecturing is that it is more convenient for learner-directed training. A computer, for example, can be switched on at the learner's convenience. A lecture only takes place when the learner and lecturer are both present.

Lecturing versus small group work

Small groups normally have fewer than eight people in them. Experience from working with groups of managers in training situations suggests that learning in one group may be far richer than in another group in the same session. Although the groups present their answers to an exercise in plenary, thereby allowing the less active group to get a glimpse of the more active use of knowledge in the other group, the time in which the groups share experiences is relatively short. It therefore sometimes seems that a good, communicative lecture would have been more beneficial, at least to those who worked in the less active groups. Thus, lectures help to create greater evenness of learning.

15.4   When to select to lecture

In results-oriented management training the question is more often *whether* to lecture than *what* to lecture on. When it comes to brief expositions lasting less than ten minutes to spark off a discussion or to provide participants food for thought when solving case-studies, the choice is clear — lecturing is the best means. However, choosing lectures instead of another method of delivery for sessions lasting three-quarters of an hour or more, requires serious consideration. A 45-minute lecture that fails can do serious damage to a training session, in most cases more than if the participants were organized in small groups and asked to elaborate on an issue. The points listed below may be of help to the trainer when considering whether or not a lecture on a certain topic should be included in the programme:

- Source of competence — does the lecturer represent a unique source of experience which is of particular interest to the participants? Will the lecturer, by virtue of background and personality, be able to communicate effectively with the participants?

- Lecturing skills — does the prospective lecturer possess the skills necessary to capture the attention of the audience? If this is not the case, a round-table discussion with the specialist as resource person might be more appropriate, i.e. instead of giving a talk, the specialist answers questions put by the participants.

- Breaking the monotony and pausing for reflection — participative, action-oriented programmes tend to become quite intensive for the participants. A lecture where they can sit and listen and reflect is a welcome break, and may break up a certain monotony.

15.5 Preparing a lecture

Like any other human activity, a good lecture needs good preparation and this means hard work. Even if it is a subject that you know thoroughly, one that you have at your fingertips, you still need to prepare. A lecture is not a one-way street with one person active and the others passive. It is a form of communication, and the listeners are an essential part of the exercise; listening can and should be an active exercise and it is the lecturer's responsibility to see that this is so.

The presentation has to fit the needs of the audience and the occasion; every lecture is a different, a unique exercise. Even if it is the same lecture, for the same purpose, to the same type of audience, each time it is a different performance.

How do you set about preparing a lecture? There are two things to get quite clear right at the start:

- First, what is the purpose of the talk?
- Second, what is the nature of the audience?

Purpose

The purpose can be to inform, or to persuade, or to inspire, or to entertain, or any combination of these. If the lecture is part of a training course, the purpose may be to inform, to instruct, to stimulate. If it entertains as well, so much the better, for this will help the listeners to pay attention and to remember what is said — but entertainment will not be the main purpose of the performance.

Throughout the preparations, this specific purpose must remain the beacon light. Too often lecturers get carried away by their topic and stray into byways that are fascinating but not directly relevant. It will be the clear definition of the purpose that provides the framework of the lecture. Whatever the purpose of the lecture, it has to match what the audience expects in terms of content and message.

Peter Delisi (1990), a consultant with the Digital Equipment Corporation, tells of a lecture in which he challenged an audience from a large aerospace company to envisage expanded use of management information systems (MIS) in the years to come, in particular the use of information technology (IT). The result was disappointing. Delisi writes that "the audience seemed only concerned with the more mundane uses of IT. It was almost as though they were saying "'what does this have to do with the report I have to get out at 3.00 this afternoon?'"

It seems that while the lecturer had a legitimate purpose for his lecture, that purpose was at a futuristic level which did not strike the listeners as being of immediate use for dealing with their present situation. The purpose of a lecture is best identified by listening to the concerns of people who are representative of the audience before preparation of the lecture is undertaken.

Audience

It may or may not be possible to judge the audience at a management training session: its interests, managerial functions, educational backgrounds. Yet the fact that they are there to hear you, that they have been invited or chosen to come, already gives an indication. It may be possible to find out more about them, especially if it is an organized group.

Surveying the audience should yield information, not only about the participants, but also about their preoccupations. The preoccupations of individual managers tend to be largely a function of their organizational responsibilities. Personnel managers, line managers, sales managers, managing directors and after-sales managers each tend to have different priorities, which should influence the way the lecture is presented and what points are highlighted. For example, a managing director is concerned with overall organizational performance. Therefore, a lecture on, say, organizational culture that is given to a group of managing directors should not leave out the possible relationships between an organization's culture and the criteria of overall performance, such as profitability and growth.

Your effort must be to try to establish a relationship with your audience even before you speak to them, even before you see them. Imagine yourself as one of your listeners. What are the aspects that you are likely to find useful and interesting? How much do you already know? What additional elements do you need to know?

The theme and outline

What is going to be the theme of your talk? What is the thread on which it all hangs, the axis on which it turns? You have to decide this — it should preferably be something that can be expressed, like the purpose, in one short sentence — and keep this in mind throughout your preparation. The theme will, of course, be a function of your purpose and your audience.

Next, prepare an outline. This will be forming in your mind during your preparations and be based on the purpose and the theme you have defined. Basically, the outline will be in three parts, like any other composition, literary or musical: a Beginning, a Middle and an End. Or, to put it another way, the Introduction, the Body and the Conclusion.

It is useful to flesh these out with divisions and subdivisions. Merely to arrange them in sections under numerical headings such as I, II; 1, 2; or (a), (b), etc., gives a form to the outline and clarifies your thoughts. The form and the shape of the final product are of vital importance. The audience must be able to follow the talk from one step to another, from one point to the next. The whole of it must have a coherent shape, as does a picture: it may have many separate details but forms a harmonious whole. An outline helps to form that shape which must finally exist clearly in your mind.

Selection of material

In preparing your outline, selection becomes of major importance. If you have far more information than you can use, it is obvious that you must choose what you are going to use and what you will reject. This has to be based on the purpose, the audience, the theme and the time available.

A common temptation is to try and put in too much, to believe that the more information you can cram into the talk, the better. This is a temptation firmly to be resisted. Overloading your lecture does not make it more effective, but less so. It is better to select a few important points and focus on them, rather than to throw in so many issues that it distracts — and detracts — leaving the listener confused. If you have, for example, 30 minutes for the body of your talk, it is unlikely that you can deal with more than four or five major points.

In any case, you must end up with enough information to cover the subject "in the round", so that the core of information you propose to impart is surrounded and cushioned by information which you are not going to use directly — but which is essential for you if your lecture is to be worthwhile. You must have vastly more information than you will use; or put in another way, you will use only a fraction of the information you possess. As John Gunther, the well-known writer once explained, "I always try to get ten times as much information as I use, sometimes a hundred times as much." What is true for the writer is true for the lecturer.

Overstepping your time does not demonstrate how much you know about the subject and how clever you are; it only demonstrates your lack of preparation or judgement. It is particularly difficult to be ruthless in rejecting matter which you have gathered together with much expense of time and effort, but it is well worthwhile. It is a good idea to work out the timing of your talk and the amount of time you will accord to each item.

The introduction and the conclusion

The introduction and the conclusion are both important. The introduction — the first few minutes of the talk — will set the tone and will gain or lose the interest of your listeners. It should tell them what your purpose is and what you intend to say. It should arouse curiosity; it should establish a sympathetic relationship between you and your listeners.

The conclusion sums up the lecture. It reminds the audience of the basic message of the lecture, and of the most important points that have been put forward, either by the lecturer or by participants. As your listeners leave the room, these last words are likely to be the ones still echoing in their minds.

15.6 Delivering a lecture

You can have the most interesting information to impart, you may have assembled your material over many weeks, you might have prepared the most excellent outline — but if your delivery is not appropriate you will get little across and your listeners will gain little except boredom. If preparing your material and organizing it is half the battle, delivering it is the other. Both are equally important.

The style of delivery to adopt may also be largely a question of culture. Cultural values vary from country to country, as they do from organization to organization. A confrontational style laden with technically convincing arguments may succeed much better in a group of efficiency-oriented production managers than in a group of managers from a public educational institution. Here are some points worth reflecting on when considering the style of delivery of the lecture:

- *Provocation* — to what extent you should allow yourself to challenge the way in which the participants view and carry out managerial practices at present. Some people or cultures may accept and even invite challenges to their existing thinking. In others, people may more readily see it as being offensive.

- *Talk/discussion* — certain groups may wish to listen attentively to someone, then reflect on what has been said, then offer their views. Other groups may reject this, and wish to see the lecture as a verbal, two-way communication.

- *Expert/non-expert role* — in some cultures a lecture that is delivered with authority and persuasion is considered the only appropriate way of lecturing. In such a culture, manifesting oneself as not being the expert, but presenting one's knowledge rather as being complementary to the expertise of the audience, may lead to loss of respect among the participants. In other cultures, a style that suggests indisputable expertise on the part of the lecturer, may, regardless of the contents of the lecture, be rejected by the audience.

The style of the lecturer reflects to some extent his or her attitude towards the theme of the lecture and towards the audience. The combination of style and content determines the climate that develops between the lecturer and the listeners. A climate of two-way respect, openness and confidence sets the stage for a good learning experience. This allows conflicting points of view to be seen as constructive rather than antagonistic. A climate lacking mutual understanding and respect in either direction does not enhance learning, whatever might be the content of the lecture or the oral skills of the lecturer. The climate which develops between the lecturer and the audience is not something tangible which can easily be described. Rather, it is what gives you, the lecturer, a feeling of communicating effectively with the audience, the feeling of giving them something that they appreciate.

Stage fright

The commonest difficulty that most of us have is nervousness, or stage fright. The thought of standing up in front of an audience, of seeing those many faces turned to you, wondering if they're going to get bored and show it, wondering if you'll forget what you want to say and be struck dumb — all these are frightening thoughts It is quite human to have them, very uncommon not to have them.

With experience, the nervousness diminishes. If your lecture is part of a course and if it is one of several you are giving or if it is to a small group, there may be no noticeable nervousness at all. If, however, it is addressed to a large unknown audience, the nervousness will be greater.

So the first thing to remember is that you are not the only one who feels nervous, it is a natural and universal reaction. Indeed, if you don't feel nervous, then there may be something wrong — a real cause for being nervous! And there is an advantage to feeling nervous: it will incite you to prepare more thoroughly. The better prepared you are, the better your lecture will be.

It is easy to say that one should relax before a lecture, but this, like much good counsel, is easier said than done. It appears more unnerving to walk in to give a lecture for the first time to a group when the group is already present in the room than if you, as a lecturer, are there when the group arrives. If it is practically possible to be in the room before they enter, the trainer may reduce nervousness by spending some time in the room before the participants arrive, so that he or she has the opportunity to get "a feel" for the premises before giving the lecture. It may also help to sit for a while in an audience chair and think through the lecture from the perspective of a member of the audience before they arrive.

Monotony

A monotonous sound or occupation sends you to sleep. Speak in the same tone of voice, at the same speed, with the same rhythm and you may be contributing to the fight against insomnia but not getting any message across.

If you want to hold the attention of your listeners, vary the tone, the speed, the pitch, and use pauses. These variations must, naturally, match what you are saying

The lack of variation in tone is a common fault; people who speak in quite a lively fashion in private conversation may use a stilted monotone in a public lecture In normal speech, you would use a range of 12 to 15 tones. If you are using only five, ou are being monotonous. If you suspect that you do not vary your tone as much s you should, use a tape recorder and listen to yourself. Then try the same text again, triving for more variation.

Tempo and pace

The speed of speech must vary in accordance with what you are saying but, by nd large, an average rate of speaking is 120 to 160 words a minute. If you are too low, say 100 words a minute, or too fast, say 200 words a minute, your audience vill have difficulty in following you. If you are speaking to a large audience, speak little slower than you would normally.

A judicious pause now and then has been called a "miracle worker". It can be nost effective if properly used: to emphasize a point, to mark the beginning of a new dea, just to give yourself and your audience a little breathing space. Sometimes lervousness leads a lecturer to fill in his or her pauses with padders, such as "er" r meaningless phrases like "you know". Practise avoiding it and gradually you will lrop the habit. Lecturers sometimes spoil a perfectly good remark by adding another ne before the participants have had the chance to reflect on it.

Use your eyes

If you want your listeners to feel that you are talking to them and not to the eiling or the wall behind them, you must look at them. If it is a large audience, this vill mean turning your head and eyes from time to time, but gently, smoothly, not s if you were watching a tennis match.

Looking at your audience has other advantages. It helps to hold their attention. You can judge whether they are interested or not. You can adapt your presentation, nake special efforts to capture — or recapture — their interest: a sudden pause, a hetorical question, a reference to someone or something in the room.

Gestures

The body, the hands and the face speak a language of their own, often no less ommunicative than the voice. How you hold your body, what gestures you make, vhat expression you have on your face, all carry eloquent messages. You have to nake sure that they carry the messages you want to convey.

Sometimes it is difficult to know what to do with your hands, or even just how o stand. The sensible answer is to adopt the posture that comes most naturally, using your hands and gestures as you would normally. Again, this is easier said than done. As soon as you become conscious of your hands, it means that you are finding it lifficult to be natural; you may then tend to fidget. The remedy is to work out what s natural to you, then practise that consciously, as an actor would. In other words, ecome natural through artifice.

Vitality

The most important feature in holding the interest of the listeners and getting a point across is the vitality and the enthusiasm that you yourself have. If you are enthusiastic and have a real interest in what you are saying, your audience may respond in the same fashion. We say *may*, because there is a point at which an increase in vitality detracts from the message of the lecture, and where the participants get the feeling that the vitality is a sign of the lecturer becoming so engrossed with the subject that what *they* want to hear is of less importance. Lecturers sometimes become increasingly enthusiastic when there is a drop in attention from the audience and, because they become insecure, they react by becoming more intense in their presentation. This is a very easy trap to fall into. One way of avoiding it is to decide, before giving the lecture, to stop at certain points for a brief reflection on one's own performance in relation to the signals received from the audience.

As any experienced lecturer would confirm, the audience gives clear signals about how they find the lecture without saying anything. Although the communication from the lecturer to the audience is verbal and physical, the communication in the opposite direction will, in most cases, be physical. There are many signs which tell you how the lecture is being received. Signs of attentiveness by way of posture or stares, posing questions to themselves, nodding or shaking heads, taking notes, etc., are means by which the listeners respond to the talk without saying anything. Being able to interpret at any particular moment how the lecture is being received, and being able to respond to the signals, is one of the most important skills a lecturer can possess. Indeed, this skill is a characteristic which distinguishes a good lecturer from someone who is simply a good speaker.

Visual aids

The lecture is a process of combining verbal presentation and visual aids optimally. The talk and the display of text or figures should be planned and carried out as two complementary elements of the same process. Examples of visual aids are flip charts, overheads and writeboards. Visual aids serve the following functions in relation to the talk:

- They reinforce visually what has been said (most people retain better what they see than what they hear).

- They provide additional illustrations (for example, showing an overhead slide of an organization chart to explain interrelationships between the departments of an organization).

Visual aids, if they are to be used effectively, have first and foremost to be used with flexibility.

Every lecture is a different, unique exercise. Two lectures given on the same theme, conveying the same message, may require a different performance, simply because the reactions of the audience will differ. Therefore, although a certain overhead slide, for example, was used repeatedly during the previous lecture, it may be used only once in the next lecture to a similar audience. There is a definite danger in structuring the lecture too rigidly. The lecturer who knows his or her material well, and who communicates well with the audience, monitors constantly during the ecture the reception of the various parts of the talk, and chooses the appropriate use of visual aids accordingly. Quite often there are questions that are asked which, when answered by the lecturer, illustrate a point that was meant to be dealt with later in the lecture. The skilful lecturer assesses the clarification achieved by answering the question and may consequently go over the point quicker when he or she gets to the point where it was programmed in the lecture.

It is therefore important not to load the lecture with too many points, not to programme them too rigidly and to build flexible use of visual aids into the lecture.

Here are some general rules about the use of visual aids:

- They must fit in with the lecture; the aid must fit the message you are conveying and the words you are using.

- Do not use too many types of aid in any one lecture. Probably two is as much as you can handle in a normal 45-minute lecture.

- Make sure that all your equipment is in good working order, that the slides are in the right order, that the machine is ready to turn on when you want it without fussing around.

The use of visual aids is discussed in more detail in Chapter 16 — "Audiovisual, computer and communication technologies".

Words and language

We all have a tendency to use elaborate language when describing anything complicated, particularly if it is our special subject. We convince ourselves that we cannot be simple or use simple language when dealing with such erudite matters. Not true. "Speak properly, and in as few words as you can, but always plainly", advised William Penn, the Quaker leader, "for the end of speech is not ostentation but to be understood."

Or, as John Kenneth Galbraith, an outstanding scholar with the gift of communication, wrote in his *A life in our times* published in 1981: "... there is no idea associated with (economics) that cannot, with sufficient effort, be stated in clear (language). The obscurity that characterizes professional economic prose does not derive from the difficulty of the subject. It is the result of incomplete thought; or it reflects a priestly desire to differentiate oneself from the plain word of the layman; or it stems from a fear of having one's inadequacies found out." Or, as Wittgenstein put it, "Everything that can be thought at all, can be clearly thought. Everything that can be said, can be clearly said."

AUDIOVISUAL, COMPUTER AND COMMUNICATION TECHNOLOGIES   16

Barry Smith

In common with most other training, management development currently uses some technology-based delivery systems. In the future, greater use of such systems can be expected. This chapter will outline the technologies available for management development, and will attempt a brief evaluation of their appropriateness and effectiveness. It will also examine the use of basic as well as advanced visual technologies in the management development process, and some future trends in this area.

16.1   Basic visual aids

Approximately 80 per cent of the information that humans absorb is received via the sense of sight. This physiological "fact of life" has several inescapable consequences for every training and development professional. The first is that failure to use visual information inputs will greatly reduce the efficiency of information transfer. The second consequence is that failure to utilize the sense of sight will almost certainly provide the opportunity for vision to become occupied with other distracting information.

In order to avoid the double bind of limiting input capacity and encouraging interference with learning, it has long been recommended that teachers and trainers should fully utilize visual modes of information input to learners. This section will review the strengths and weaknesses of boards, charts, and overhead slide and video projectors, and make some recommendations for their effective use.

Boards

Boards are of four main types — chalk, white, magnetic, and paper. A chalkboard is any flat surface, usually painted black, brown or green, on which chalk will leave a mark. A whiteboard is a metal or plastic surface which can be marked by special whiteboard pens, giving a more visible image than the chalkboard and eliminating chalk dust. A magnetic board is any ferrous metal surface to which magnets will adhere. This allows the posting of words, diagrams, etc., on paper or card. Finally, a paper board can be constructed simply by attaching large sheets of paper to any convenient flat wall so that they may be written on with oil pens. Chalk and whiteboards are common because they are infinitely reusable at minimal cost. However, they are bulky to transport, can be messy and remind people of school classrooms. Paper or magnetic boards are often preferred for remote or outdoor locations.

Planning boardwork

No matter what type of board is used, the same principles of use apply. The board is visible to the learners throughout the session, so you should put on the board any material that the learners need continuous access to. Typically, this material will be the key learning points of the session you conduct, so the logical use of the board is to record progressively the key points of the session as the points are made. By the end of the session, you will have recorded on the board a summary statement of the important points covered. Such a record is invaluable to learners, and almost guarantees that the learners have received the key learning points in their logical order.

To achieve this type of boardwork, a board plan is required. The board plan is created in conjunction with the session plan. Once you have decided on the key points your session will cover, you should visit the training site to check facilities. What boards are available? What size and shape are they? Can they be readily divided into subsections? In addition to the key content words, you should think about how you will indicate structure (e.g. divisions, headings, numbering, colouring, etc.) and whether you can effectively use diagrams.

If you are using magnetic boards, you will also have to make up the necessary cards and attach magnets to them. This is a little extra work, but the cards are almost infinitely reusable, and so may be worthwhile preparing for a session that you will deliver several times.

Using boards

Preparation
1. Ensure that your notes, the chalk (or pens), and erasers are conveniently placed near the board.
2. Clean the board to remove potentially distracting visual information.

Dos
1. Write (or print) legibly.
2. Write quickly (if possible).
3. Allow time for learners to copy the key points that you have written on the board.
4. Use signposts (divisions, headings, colours, numbers, dashes, etc.) to indicate logic, structure and relative importance in your boardwork.

Don'ts

1. Don't talk to the board. It will muffle your voice and stop you maintaining reasonable eye contact with the learners.
2. Don't obscure your boardwork by standing in front of it.
3. Don't use invisible colours. Avoid dark chalks on dark chalkboards and light pens on whiteboards.

The board as a visual record

A quite separate use of the board is also important. In any training session involving discussion, it is useful to develop a progressive visual record of the key content points introduced. Such a record cannot be planned in detail, but at least its structure may be predicted before the session.

As the learners produce important points during the course of the discussion, these points should be noted on the board. The words written on the board should be as similar as possible to the words used by the learner, with minimal revision or rewording by the trainer. In this way, the board record becomes a form of public recognition to the learners, and they are more likely to remember their own words.

As the record of the discussion builds up, it begins to perform a useful directing function within the discussion, and removes from the trainer some of the pressure to lead. With the record in front of them, learners can see at a glance what has been covered, so that unnecessary repetition is avoided. Any learner who loses the thread of the discussion will probably be able to pick it up again simply by reviewing what is on the board. This reduces the need for the trainer regularly to summarize and integrate material. Finally, a review of what is on the board will often suggest logical ways to move the discussion forward. Overall, a visual record of a discussion helps the trainer to be less directive in the group.

Charts

A chart is basically a board that is produced before the session is delivered. This allows for careful artwork and a very professional result. A possible problem, however, is that learners are distracted by material on the chart which has not yet been covered in the session. As a consequence, the use of charts is usually limited to special applications, such as the presentation of drawings that are too complicated to reproduce on a board, but which are required for the whole session, or for the presentation of material which is greatly enhanced by high quality artwork.

Overhead projection

Apart from boards, the major method of presenting visual information during a training session is the overhead projector (OHP). It can be used like a board in the sense that a transparency (OHT) can be written on while it is being projected. Usually, however, the OHP is used to project OHTs which have been carefully planned and produced in advance to convey particular points. The OHP can produce high visual impact, saves writing time for the trainer during a session, allows control of what learners see and when they see it, and allows scope for the trainer's visual creativity.

Basically, an OHP is not suited to keeping information in front of learners for a complete session. The screen is often too small, and the bright light can cause eye strain over prolonged periods. Consequently, OHPs are best adapted to providing visual material needed only for short periods.

Making OHTs

Some general rules for the design and production of OHTs are:

- Use one OHT for one idea.

- Use graphs, diagrams, or cartoons (as appropriate), with or without accompanying print.

- Use print that is at least 6 mm (¼ inch) high. Ordinary typing or typeset material is usually too small.
  Use about four words per line, and up to six lines per OHT.

- Use colour as appropriate to enhance meaning.

- Word processing and desktop publishing programmes can be used to create very professional paper masters via a laser printer. The image on paper is then transferred to acetate via a photocopier.

Using OHTs

- To reduce glare, use a coloured background rather than clear OHTs. Cover any unused portion of the OHT with a paper mask.

- Attach each OHT to a cardboard frame (or mount) or place it in a purpose-designed clear plastic envelope. This preserves the OHT, reduces buckling due to heat from the OHP and allows you to write reminder notes on the frame.

- Point to an item on the OHT by laying a pencil or similar pointer on the OHT. If you hold the pointer, the shadow on the screen will not be steady.

- Use progressive disclosure to help concentrate the learners' attention on the point you are now talking about and progressively disclose points as you require them.

- Build up complex images by using overlays. These are additional OHTs which are hinged (by tape) to one edge of the foundation OHT. Additional parts of the total image can then be added simply by flipping overlays on to the foundation OHT.

- Turn off the OHP whenever possible, to reduce glare.

- Allow adequate time for learners to think about or to copy material from the screen, before adding any necessary extra information verbally.

- Do not stand between the OHP and the screen, or between the learners and the screen.

Slide projection

Slides have a distinct advantage over the OHP in being able to present "real" scenes. In some situations, a camera can record what the unaided eye cannot see. Slides, however, are not good for projecting printed material, because the room must be darkened to see the image clearly, making note-taking very difficult. Slides may require a rather complex production procedure, and take days to be ready compared to hours or minutes for an OHT. Finally, OHTs in a session are flexible in regard to order and repetition, while slides are limited to a relatively linear presentation.

Video projection

A recent innovation involves viewing of images via a video projector. These images can be sourced from videotape, from a CD, or from a computer. Words and diagrams (as on OHTs) and still pictures (as on slides) can be created and stored in a computer with the appropriate software, and any image can then be viewed via the video projection system. Exciting and informative visuals can be created, given time, skill, and availability of the necessary technology.

16.2   Managers and technology: Setting the scene

Many managers now depend almost totally on computers and communications technologies. One particular field of technology that will affect managers is the one which may be used in the delivery of management development or training activities. Managers will react to both the material and the delivery technology according to their individual predispositions and the circumstances at the time. Trainers should be aware that these two reactions are linked. Unfortunately, some managers will "throw the baby out with the bath water" by rejecting content if they do not like or cannot accept or are threatened by the technology of delivery. Technology-based delivery systems must always address and clear this hurdle before any useful learning can occur.

The same comments apply to trainers choosing and using technologies for the delivery of learning materials. Where detailed evaluative information is lacking (as is usually the case with recent technologies), the personal predispositions of the trainer often become important factors in the choice and use of training delivery technologies. The trainer is then in a position to be able to:

- hold the organization back from the effective use of appropriate technologies;
- commit the organization to the use of inappropriate or ineffective technologies; or
- facilitate the adoption of appropriate/effective technologies.

Given personal predispositions and frequent lack of reliable information, decisions on the choice and use of training delivery technologies are of critical importance in management development.

Technological literacy

Several generations of present-day managers and trainers grew up in an era when the most complex technology they had contact with was the family car. A considerable number of present-day middle managers are significantly limited in their ability to understand or to be comfortable with the technology they are now expected to use in their jobs.

Many trainers also face a similar problem. Training is usually perceived as a relatively "human" side of organizations, and consequently attracts a high proportion of people who are interested in and motivated by the human contact component of the training job. Such trainers are frequently neither interested in nor competent with technology in general or with technological delivery systems in particular. Their reward system and their self-concept of competence within the training profession are threatened by the very presence of technology in the delivery of training.

Finally, all of the problems outlined above are exacerbated by the incoming tide of technologically more competent graduates presently leaving education systems worldwide. Most recent school-leavers have the advantage of long exposure to technology (particularly computers) throughout their school careers, and have developed at least an acceptance of technology and its costs and benefits. While the advent of new starters who are more adapted to technology is a benefit to organizations and to the new starters themselves, it is a problem for older workers, who often feel pressured by subordinates to adapt to technology at a faster rate than is comfortable, or even possible.

In summary, some current generation managers and trainers, for a variety of reasons, have difficulty in adapting to technology. The problem may be partly motivational, and may also have an understanding (or technological literacy) component. Future managers and trainers may demand use of appropriate technology of which they are aware, and be vocally dissatisfied with doing things in "old technology" ways. This will constitute a considerable challenge to today's less technologically oriented managers and trainers.

16.3 Technologically delivered input in traditional courses

This section will briefly review two major types of technological delivery systems that can be incorporated into traditional management development courses.

Film and video

For the purposes of this section, film and (pre-recorded) video will be regarded as equivalent. Although the physics of the technologies are totally different, they are now almost indistinguishable from the point of view of the learner. Large, high-contrast screens for improved video projection are now virtually as effective as standard 16 mm film projection. The cost of video equipment is generally higher, but the cost of programmes on videotape is usually lower.

The decision to incorporate film or video into a course should not be taken lightly. First, both media suffer from learner expectations (fostered by movie and television experience) that activities on the screen are lightweight entertainment. Secondly, the trainer is handing over the course to the producer/director who almost certainly will have made the video or film to achieve a different set of objectives to those specified for the course. The degree of overlap of the two sets of objectives must justify the time and other costs incurred in using the video or film.

To maximize learning from a video or film, several steps should be followed:

- *Analyse the audience and the desired outcomes.* Identify characteristics of the audience that may influence their reception of the video or film. Possible variables include age range, work experience, existing knowledge and skills, language comprehension, and relevant attitudes (e.g. to authority, to humour). In addition, rigorously identify the outcomes you want this video or film to achieve for this audience.

- *Assess the video or film.* Read the blurb. Talk to others who have seen it. Most importantly, view the video or film in full. A comprehensive checklist is provided in box 16.1 below (Smith, 1988).

- *Establish effective viewing conditions.* In particular, check that:
  — the physical condition of your print of the video or film is good:
  — your equipment is working well and the sound is satisfactory;
  — illumination is appropriate, without glare or reflections;
  — screen size and position suits the audience;
  — everyone is comfortable (seating, ventilation, temperature, noise).

- *Introduce the video or film.* Use the introduction to set the learners' expectations about what will happen; what they are expected to note in particular; what they should ignore; how it relates to past and future content; and, most of all, what is special about the film, i.e. the reason why they should watch the film attentively.

- *Debrief after the video or film.* Have a pre-planned strategy to regain the attention of the learners, and to refocus their attention on the objectives of the course. Discussion, including highlighting the key points of the video or film and how they contribute to achieving the objectives of the course, is often effective.

When to use video or film

When used as a component of a course, video or film can:

- give the learners "real" visual information that cannot be easily imported into the classroom, e.g. too large, too small, too dangerous;

- allow non-invasive (and repeatable) observation of human interactions;

- give learners access to geographically remote experiences;

- give every learner a "worker's-eye view" of a demonstration, so that they see exactly what they will see when they are doing the job themselves;

Box 16.1. Checklist 1: Assessing video or film

Does the video or film:
1. Assist in achieving the learning objectives of the session?
2. Achieve the objectives more effectively than any other method?
3. Fit into the context of the total training course?
4. Appear relevant to the needs of the viewers?
5. Grab and hold the attention of the viewers?
6. Build on existing trainee knowledge and skill?
7. Use terms, explanations and examples that the viewers will understand?
8. Appear to be realistic?
9. Present the data needed by viewers (not too much or too little)?
10. Contain any distractions, e.g. inappropriate equipment, old-fashioned objects, accents, recognizable actors?
11. Allow appropriate note-taking by viewers, and provide appropriate written materials?
12. Periodically summarize important content?
13. Lead to some action by viewers, e.g. discussion, individual work practice, action plan?
14. Come with a trainer's guide?
15. Have acting, camera work, and editing of an appropriate standard?
16. Have acceptable technical quality?
17. Play on the available equipment?

If the video or film is to be used for modelling:

1. Does the programme display the complete behaviour required?
2. Are *key* components of the behaviour obvious?
3. Are any inappropriate behaviours visible or audible?
4. Does the programme make it clear to viewers that the model is an "expert"?
5. Can viewers identify with the model?
6. Does the model's environment approximate the real one?
7. Does the programme display the positive outcomes of the appropriate behaviour?

- import an expert, who may be perceived to be a more valid source of information than the on-site trainer;
- start a segment of the course with a memorable, motivating "common experience" which serves as a focal point for subsequent analysis and discussion;
- present a "model" performance for learners to imitate, practise, and eventually incorporate into their own behaviour.

Computer-based learning

Computer-based learning (CBL) will be discussed in more detail in the next section on technology-based delivery of training packages. However, CBL is also used to deliver component parts of traditional courses. When used for this purpose, the trainer is responsible for choosing and integrating the computer-delivered material into the rest of the course. To achieve this, a procedure parallel to the one outlined for video or film is appropriate. To assist with Step 2 — Assess the courseware (to use the appropriate CBL term), Smith and Delahaye (1987) have provided detailed procedures, described below in box 16.2.

Box 16.2. Checklist 2: Evaluating CBL courseware

1. Are the course objectives fully and clearly defined?
2. Are prerequisite knowledge and skills stated?
3. Is the target audience clearly defined?

Content
1. Is the content presented clearly and logically?
2. Are the structure and relationships of the content emphasized?
3. Is the content consistent with the objectives?
4. Are new terms explained?
5. Are the terms used appropriate to the topic and the target learners?

Design
1. Does the programme use effective teaching or learning strategies?
2. Does the learner skip content that is already known?
3. Does the programme use the most effective display modes (colour, graphics, sound)?
4. Are displays clear?
5. Are displays understandable?
6. Are displays attractive?
7. Does the programme use the most effective learner response modes?
8. Are detailed typing and complex keying minimized?
9. Does the programme contain appropriate previews and reviews?
10. Does the programme require sufficient activity by the learner?
11. Is feedback to the learner constructive?
12. Is feedback to the learner motivational?
13. Can the content and design be modified to suit local needs?

Course management
1. Does the programme include diagnostic and evaluative testing?
2. Does the programme keep records of trainee responses?
3. Does the programme produce summary statements indicating the trainee's progress?
4. Does the programme suggest future learning activities for each trainee?
5. Does the programme provide both screen and printed-out options for presentation of progress records?

Using the programme
1. Is the programme "user friendly"?
2. Are "help" procedures available at all times?
3. Is the programme reliable in normal use?
4. Can trainees exit the programme whenever they wish?
5. If non-computerized materials are included in the course, are they readily available, directly related to the course objectives, effectively presented, and motivational?

When to use CBL

CBL is particularly useful when:

- learners possess an appropriate level of computer literacy;
- there are wide variations in the existing knowledge and/or learning ability of the trainees;
- learners are widely spread geographically;
- learners require the learning at unpredictable times, or in very small (and

therefore uneconomic) class sizes;

- there is a critical requirement for standardized learning, both in terms of content covered and standard achieved;

- learners appreciate regular feedback and control of their own pace of learning;

- the major task is to transmit information. Although CBL will later be shown to be potentially very flexible, the majority of the courseware available heavily emphasizes the transmission of information.

16.4   Technological delivery of complete courses or packages

The previous section discussed technologically delivered components of trainer-controlled management development courses. This section moves to the qualitatively different field of complete (package) courses controlled and primarily delivered by technological means such as video or computer, and even books.

Clearly, such courses were designed by a trainer, but they are intended to stand alone, requiring little or zero support from a "live" trainer while the trainee/s are using them. This necessitates an altogether more thorough and detailed design and production effort, since the finished product must be suitable for many trainees and in different situations.

Video-delivered courses

It could be argued that, in the absence of a live trainer, the next best thing is a video in glowing colour and hi-fi sound. In relation to delivery of the basic message, this is probably true. The trainee can see all the graphics; observe all the facial expressions and gestures; hear all the tones of voice, inflections and pauses in addition to the actual words; and, by virtue of receiving this "complete" set of incoming information, can even develop the feeling of "being there".

However, there are also differences which must be noted. A significant disadvantage is that communication is one-way. The trainee cannot ask questions of the video, so extra effort must be expended to ensure that the video message is thoroughly adapted to the target audience and is as clear as possible to that audience. Some of the advantages include:

- trainees at different times and locations all being exposed to exactly the same key points in the same message. This may be useful if standardization of learning is important;

- at the push of a button, trainees can have the "instant replay", an opportunity which is often forgone in classroom training sessions through shyness, concern for image, difficulty in questioning, or obvious rush by the trainer;

- trainees have some control over the pace of their learning, in terms of length and timing of the sessions;

- the learning material is available whenever they need it. New starters in a job can thus be trained singly whenever they need the information, rather than having to wait until sufficient trainees have accumulated to make a full course viable.

Actual delivery of training via video occurs in several modes. An early version was simply to broadcast the material to trainees sitting in front of their television sets. These approaches are basically a one-way classroom, since trainees are committed to broadcast times and session lengths.

With the advent of relatively inexpensive video recorders, a significant alternative is available. The programme is delivered via a videotape, which is usually posted to the trainee. A variety of courses are available to anyone who subscribes, ranging from formal education topics to hobby material to professional updating services to management development activities. Much material is also available within organizations, created or purchased for the development of staff.

Some video training is individual-based, allowing the trainee to do some learning when and if there is a quiet period during the day or shift. Other video training is group-based, so that the material can be discussed by a group of trainees after viewing.

A relatively recent combination of the two systems outlined above involves the broadcast of learning material at times when no other material is going out; for example from 3 a.m. to 4 a.m. The trainees record such broadcasts on their prepro-grammed video recorder, and then study the material at a time suited to their other commitments.

When evaluating a video course or package for use in your organization, you should ensure that:

- the objectives of the course are clearly stated and appropriate to your purposes;
- the course content, structure and language are suited to your audience;
- the course presentation is pseudo-personal, rather than impersonal;
- the course grabs and holds attention, and appears to be realistic;
- the course involves learners in appropriate activities, and periodically summarizes important points;
- the course uses appropriate non-video material, such as manuals, to ensure a permanent record of learning.

Another self-contained application of video training is the organizational news or magazine type of programme. Dick Smith (a self-made millionaire via the Australian electronics industry) suspected that his employees were not reading the monthly printed news and product information bulletin produced by his organization, so he decided to check it. In the middle of a standard in-house news item, a single sentence was inserted which said "To get $10, ring ..." (which was a head office telephone number). He reports that he did not have to pay out any cash to callers. Following this field research, he decided to de-emphasize information transmission in printed form, and to create a video magazine. The monthly programme conveyed important news, had "real" faces explaining important decisions rather than relying on the power of impersonal signatures, showed employees other parts of the organization, and publicly rewarded effective performance.

Many other organizations are using similar magazine programmes, especially when staff work in many geographically separate locations. In particular, banks, finance and insurance companies are using video extensively, with larger companies establishing well-equipped video studios and employing full-time professional staff to create the programmes. A similar news magazine targeted at managers is obviously a potentially powerful management development device.

Another use of video magazine programmes which is relatively unexplored relates to organization development applications. Team-building and climate-setting messages can be carried through the organization in a powerful, timely, and relatively personal way by the use of video. Models and "champions" can be widely seen throughout the organization, and may be able to create or change the organization's culture via a planned and sustained sequence of video inputs. Alternatively, the video magazine can provide significant reinforcement and follow-up after more traditional organization development interventions.

In summary, video can provide stand-alone training for managers in a variety of ways. Home study broadcast courses, employer-provided videotaped material to be studied on or off the job, and organizational news programmes can all contribute to the specific and/or general development of managers.

Computer-based learning

Computers are the other major technology capable of delivering stand-alone training courses. As outlined previously, trainees require a basic level of computer literacy (involving knowledge, skill and attitude).

What does the computer do?

The computer can either deliver the learning material to the learner (called computer-assisted learning, or CAL), or it can manage the learning process for the learner (called computer-managed learning, or CML), or it can do both. Note that in the mass of abbreviations that characterize this technology, instruction (I) and training or teaching (T) are synonymous with learning (L), so that CAL = CAT = CAI, and CML = CMT = CMI. CBL is the broad term to cover any form of learning that is delivered or managed by a computer. In many applications, the material to be learned by the trainee is actually determined by the computer programme and displayed on the computer screen. The trainee responds to prompts (often in the form of questions), and the programme in the computer uses this information to produce the next piece of material to be learned. This process is CAL.

Independent of how the information to be learned is generated, a computer can be used to test the trainee's learning at the completion of a unit, give feedback on results to the trainee, store the results of many trainees for reporting to a trainer or a course coordinator, and direct the trainee to the next learning experience appropriate to that trainee's knowledge level. This process is called CML.

Finally, a computer can be programmed to perform both CAL and CML functions. The technology teaches, tests, and diagnoses the next learning exercise, as a trainer would when working in a one-on-one learning environment. Of course, the computer can seldom be programmed to take account of the variety of cues, conditions, or resources that an effective trainer would be aware of.

How are CBL programmes structured?

CBL material designed to convey information is either linear or branching in structure. Linear programmes present information in segments (called frames) that are sufficiently small in size for the vast majority of trainees to be able to learn each frame without error. The trainee simply proceeds through the frames in sequence. Although systematic and comprehensive, the linear approach often produces boredom in the learner, and this is likely to apply particularly to managers. The alternative structure (branching) is usually preferred by experienced learners. This approach provides much more information per frame, and then poses a question. Based on the answer given, learners proceed to the next frame, are returned to the previous frame, or are diverted into appropriate remedial frames to repair the gaps in their learning.

Types of learning available via CBL

CBL can provide a variety of learning activities. In increasing order of sophistication, they are:

- *Data reduction.* The computer performs various processes and calculations which simplify and clarify data and relationships to be learned (e.g. tabulating, simple statistics).

- *Drill (practice).* The computer is used to practice certain principles or procedures already known to the trainee. Examples are spelling, maths, language and typing programmes.

- *Tutorial.* This is basically a drill programme, with provision for the computer to give information or explanation when the trainee reaches certain stages of the programme.

- *Simulation.* This type of learning is qualitatively different from the foregoing types of CBL. The programme is always based on a model of some process, equipment, or procedure. Trainees are expected to learn the model through the business simulation, and then transfer their learning to the real world.

- *Problem-solving.* Some programmes teach problem-solving processes, including the critical skills of situation assessment and diagnosis of needed information.

Advantages and disadvantages of CBL

The literature provides extensive lists of the advantages and disadvantages of CBL (e.g. Smith and Delahaye, 1987; Dean and Whitlock, 1988). Some of the major advantages include:

- learning individualized for content and pace;
- immediate and regular feedback;
- time savings for equivalent quality of learning;
- lower administration costs.

Among the disadvantages most often mentioned are:

- high development costs;
- learner resistance to computers;
- lack of contact with people.

CBL technology

The first major CBL applications occurred on large mainframe computers, mainly because minis and micros had not yet arrived. The Plato system is one example of a mainframe CBL system which is used worldwide to deliver and manage a wide range of education programmes suited to all levels of study. In addition, Plato has more recently been used to deliver training that is specifically job-related; for example, significant cost savings occurred by using Plato for pilots' training before learners moved on to a flight simulator.

With the advent of micro computers and their common availability, most programming effort was directed towards courses that would run on the home/desk/office computer. Many workers (including managers) were first exposed to CBL via one of the special training programmes that are supplied with, or are available for, most of their application packages (e.g. databases, spreadsheets, CAD, statistics packages, etc.). As the processing capacities of micro computers has increased, so the size and complexity of CBL programmes has also increased. The relatively inexpensive availability of large hard disk memories and high capacity CD-ROMs has been important to these developments, and has also allowed increased user friendliness to be designed into modern CBL materials.

Many universities now require students to have access to their own micro computer, and some university correspondence courses are now CBL-distributed on floppy disk, with assignment work also submitted and feedback provided on floppy.

A variation on the theme which has the effect of reducing time delays and postage costs is to link computers to a network. At a minimum level, this can be a bulletin board arrangement, where various computer users can leave messages for one another. At a more sophisticated level, micros can be linked to a mainframe to increase processing power, or they can be linked to transmit real-time messages in a network controlled by a trainer or tutor. Such systems are used (and rented out by) major computer companies, both for staff development and for customer training. Universities which specialize in distance education often have such a system.

The main development of this type of networking is seen in the extensive e-mail and Internet systems now available. Although these are primarily communication technologies, learning applications are obvious. E-mail greatly facilitates "learned discourse" between colleagues and associates who are geographically spread. Internet allows an individual access to an amazing array of resources on a global scale, many of which can affect the development and learning of the recipient. These systems are so large that they require very careful management, otherwise the point of overload and therefore ineffectiveness can quickly be reached.

Norton (1984) reports on CBL training for employee-relations professionals, and particularly commented on the extent to which computer literacy training was necessary for these workers. It was found necessary to devote half of a four-module course to computer keyboard skills, computer terms and definitions, and basic commands, before moving on to the use of computers in the human resource management area. Daniel reports that once managers are computer literate and competent, CBL based on simulation appears to be the most acceptable learning method because of its similarity to "real-life" situations (Daniel, 1988).

Interactive video

The final type of technology that is well adapted to delivering stand-alone management training courses is interactive video. Basically, this is CBL which extensively uses video disk to store information, which is then reproduced under computer control. In this way, still pictures, moving pictures, and realistic sound can be used to provide information to the learner. The input then appears to most learners to be more personal, more visually interesting and realistic, and is much more flexible than even the best computer-generated material.

Some of the advantages of interactive video training compared to either video or CBL are:

- disks are virtually indestructible (compared to videotape);
- disks have a very large capacity for information, especially if still pictures are being used;
- disks produce better quality pictures and sound than tape;
- material on disk can include a narrator who can establish an atmosphere of one-to-one communication, thus reducing a major criticism of CBL — lack of personal contact;
- there is virtually instant access to any material on a disk, which facilitates branching programmes;
- computer-generated images can be used with or superimposed onto the disk material;
- the computer still provides all the diagnostic, testing, recording and reporting functions available in CBL.

The major difficulties inherent in interactive video are that the equipment itself is relatively expensive, the design and production of programme materials is complex, and a high level of design and technology skills are required from both designer and user. It should be noted, however, that problems one and two are rapidly being reduced by further technological developments, and problems three and four are becoming less crucial as more designers gain experience primarily through the creation of video games.

Although costs are high, they may be justified in a number of circumstances, such as when:

- there is a large number of trainees using the material over an extended period of time;
- the wide geographical spread of trainees makes normal courses very expensive;
- there is a critical requirement for standardized on-the-job performance; and
- there is a critical requirement for training to be available whenever a trainee needs it.

A separate use of interactive video which can also be training related is as an electronic information retrieval system, optimized for the display of "real-life" data (pictures, sounds) rather than the printed word. A series of menus allows the user gradually to refine the request for information. Such a system can provide data, list procedures, or lead the operator through a diagnostic algorithm related to solving a particular problem.

Examples of interactive video in use

In relation to information retrieval, interactive video is frequently used at conferences, exhibitions and in shopping centres, so that specific information can be provided to meet the needs of the enquiry. A major Australian car manufacturer uses interactive video training throughout its dealer network. The system is primarily used for providing product information to customers and salespersons, but is also available for management training.

A particularly interesting example of the use of interactive video is reported by Sellers (1988). IBM used this technology to train redeployed managers in sales skills. The programme presented sales situations from the disk, to which the trainees had to respond. The stimulus and response could be videotaped for later analysis and critique. Successive situations were chosen for each trainee depending on how they responded to the previous stimuli. Given the record of responses, trainees were found to become their own harshest critics.

In summary, though interactive video is presently limited by the complexity and cost of equipment, designing and producing interactive programmes, the potential appears to be enormous. However, the more sophisticated the hardware becomes, the more difficult and costly it is to create programmes. Until relatively inexpensive make-your-own video disks become available, interactive video is not likely to see much use in management development, unless it can be justified by large numbers of trainees.

16.5 Other uses of technology in management development

In this section, we will examine video as a feedback device, training incorporated into computer operating systems, expert systems, and telecommunication.

Video for feedback

The continual improvement of human behaviour occurs largely via a process of incremental refining (called shaping by learning experts). Essential to this process is the provision and acceptance of feedback on previous performance. Most of us acquire some feedback by analysing what we "saw" and can remember of our previous behaviour and performance, but this is seldom systematic or unbiased.

Video feedback, in its glorious colour and true-to-life sound, is systematic, unbiased, relatively complete and undeniable. These characteristics make it a potentially powerful medium for behaviour change, which is frequently a prime objective of management development.

However, being videotaped usually increases stress. The key to dealing productively with this stress seems to be the creation of an atmosphere of support among the learners. Key elements involved in this are:

- perceived willingness by the trainee to receive feedback on his or her own performance;
- clear ground rules about what is expected of learners;
- every learner receives video feedback, so that everyone faces the same circumstances.

The equipment necessary to record the performance can be hidden or obvious. Hidden equipment (behind one-way screens, or mounted out of the way with remote control) is expensive, and often distracting to learners who are prone suddenly to start wondering what the "invisible equipment" is doing. Obvious equipment with an operator can also be distracting whenever the operator moves. Many users have found that the best approach is simply to have the equipment (for example, a camcorder to minimize size) present and visible in the room, so that it tends to become part of the furniture. At the appropriate time, it is turned on and left to run itself. The resulting videotape is relatively uninspiring (no pans, zooms, etc.), but has the overwhelming advantage that it has minimized the learner's distraction and stress.

In summary, video feedback is a potentially powerful tool for behaviour change. Learner stress must be accommodated, feedback must be given caringly, and disruptions caused by the equipment must be minimized.

Training incorporated into computer operating systems

The creation of computer programmes seems to have followed a historical sequence. Initially, individuals wrote programmes without bothering about any form of advice from the training programme designer on how to use them.

As competition to sell software became more fierce, a common marketing "carrot" was to offer training in the use of the programme. Initially, this training was often planned and run by computer programmers, and developed a well-deserved reputation for being a very poor learning experience. When this problem was recognized, trainers were hired to design and often run the training, and technical writers were employed to improve the manuals. Sometimes the two functions were combined to provide a self-teaching package, usually paper-based but incorporating appropriate activities on the computer. Eventually, some of these materials were converted to a CBL format, so that the learner could use the computer to learn about the programme.

There is still, however, a problem. What does the learner do if he or she is using the programme (the real one, not the learning one) and comes across something new? Turning off the current work so that the learning programme can be loaded and run hardly seems acceptable. The solution is to have the learning programme completely integrated with the operational programme, so that any time users experience a problem, they can instantly become a learner, find out what they need to know, then instantly return to productive work again. Help screens are beginning to play an important role in this respect.

This integrated training approach is best suited to mainframe plus multiple terminals environments. In this context, the memory occupied by the learning programme in proportion to total memory and in relation to the number of users who can access it is relatively small, so that benefits outweigh costs. With early micros, however, the learning component of a programme occupied so much memory that the operational usefulness of the programme was significantly curtailed. The advent of relatively inexpensive hard disks has reduced this problem.

Very often, decisions on the purchase of computer hardware and software are made exclusively on the basis of the technical performance of the products. It is now being widely recognized that if the training is integrated into the actual operating system, allowing users to acquire whatever knowledge and develop whatever skills they need when they need them, then the training criterion for purchase decisions should have been well met. This approach to training for computer programmes is also particularly well suited to managers. It allows them to learn exactly as much as they need and exactly when they need it.

Expert systems

Typically, expert systems are created where complex knowledge that has often been built up over years of experience is likely to be lost (e.g. due to retirement) or now needs to be spread more widely to other specialists who do not have the experience to make the necessary decisions for themselves. Additionally, the decisions involved will normally be complex, yet capable of a single best solution, and the consequences of the decision will be significant.

Compared to other technologies, expert systems are more in the promise stage than the performance stage, especially in relation to a multi-faceted and multi-option system such as management. Managers will, however, be in contact with a variety of technical occupations where expert systems are currently in use, so some knowledge of them is appropriate. A review of expert systems by Barker (1989) is a good starting-point for a beginner. It explains that expert systems are a subset of the developing field of artificial intelligence, and require:

- a knowledge base, containing the facts and rules of the content area;
- an inference mechanism, which is the logic or "intelligent" part of the system, choosing the rules to apply and information to incorporate into the decision; and
- an interface with the user.

The interface component is usually fairly straightforward. The inference mechanism is the reserved realm of the expert programmer, but several can be purchased as shell programmes. Construction of the knowledge base also requires expertise of a different kind — someone who can extract the relevant knowledge from the expert and formulate it into the facts and rules of the system.

Barker concludes with a statement that is relevant to all technology-based training, but is particularly relevant to expert systems. "Expert systems have much potential, but then include the possibility of wasting a lot of people's time and money."

Telecommunication

In relation to management development, telecommunication has two aspects to be considered. It can be a training delivery system, and it can provide a whole range of "interpersonal" contacts which otherwise would not have happened and from which the participants learn something. As a delivery system, it ranges from fairly basic two-way audio communication, through a variety of one-way still and moving picture transmissions, up to relatively sophisticated two-way video and audio with graphics systems that can be transmitted worldwide via satellite. The possibilities appear to be very extensive indeed. A variety of applications have been recorded, and will be briefly summarized here.

Audio-conferencing has been used in the banking industry in the United States (Waller, 1982), the training of trainers in the United Kingdom (Rushby, 1987), education in Wisconsin and Alaska (Winders, 1989), and the development of salespeople through peer feedback (Bertrand, 1989). Video-conferencing has been used extensively in law training in the United States (Zimmer, 1988) and in many organizational environments. Kastiel (1986) reports that about 20 companies had installed their own on-site, permanent video-conferencing networks, and were using them for stockholders' meetings, the introduction of new products, and customer training (Texas Instruments and Computerland), and marketing and merchandising applications (J.C. Penney). Winders reports that many American hotel chains have teleconferencing facilities to clients, hairdressing demonstrations have reached 350 hairdressers in seven cities in France, and millions of illiterate adults are being taught to read in India. Satellite systems are bringing education to remote students in British Columbia, Alaska and Australia. Many education institutions that are geographically close to one another have been linked and share resources via optical cable (for example, the LIVENET system in London, and the UNINET system in Sydney).

The applications of video-conferencing are highly varied, and are widespread around the world. But few of them have been directed at management development in the sense of running courses, although the incidental development that occurs through the interactions on the network may often constitute significant experiential learning. One development which may well be used for class-type management development is IBM (Australia)'s recently installed Interactive Satellite Education Network. The network will be used for developing IBM staff, for training the staff of IBM customers, and will be available for hire. It consists of 11 classrooms in six cities, all interacting in video and audio with a trainer in a studio and to some degree with each other. In addition, it incorporates individual learner keypads to answer test items. The costs of hire in the early 1990s was approximately A$16,000 per day, which compared competitively with the transport and accommodation expenses involved in having a significant number of learners at a central venue.

Some of the claimed advantages of video-conferencing are presented by Arnall (1987), Jennings (1987) and Bertrand (1989). They include:

- the benefits of interactive contact, providing feedback to all parties;

- a claimed one-third higher retention rate than for seminar-type training;

- quality control of training, with all learners having access to the best trainer;

- immediate dissemination of information, independent of geographical spread;

- marked reduction in the (perhaps unproductive) costs of travel and lodging in management development activities;

- taping of the proceedings to provide a permanent record of the event, to be reviewed later by those who could not attend, or to serve as an official history or legal record of what occurred.

Other important types of telecommunication, as mentioned earlier, are the Internet and e-mail. These are now being used extensively by business, education and private users, and the growth rate in numbers of subscribers is phenomenal. Users report that when the systems are working they are very effective, but when they are "down" they are very frustrating.

In summary, telecommunication technologies play a significant role in modern business. Video-conferencing, e-mail and the Internet will be increasingly important in the future both in organizational decision-making and in training and development activities, especially as the costs decrease as new technology is put in place.

16.6   Conclusion

It has become all the more evident that the combination of computers and telecommunication will make managerial work "in the office" obsolete for at least some people. These people will work from wherever they choose, being available for instant contact as required. In these circumstances, the information provision and training functions will become critical, because there will be fewer meetings or informal chats, and very little helping each other out with problems at the office. Such independent work will have to be very well supported with self-directed learning activities, and advanced technology, including artificial intelligence and expert systems.

This chapter has examined the technologies currently used in management development, and has also previewed technologies which are likely to be used in such training in the future. Emphasis has been placed on video and computers, singly and in combination, as the prime advanced technologies for the foreseeable future.

A final comment is critically important. Technologically delivered learning has developed something of a "whiz-bang" reputation over the years, primarily because trainers get carried away with the potential of the hardware, and launch into grandiose training efforts without understanding the demands of the hardware. The crucial fact of life is that the greater the potential of the hardware, the greater are the resources required to produce software that utilizes the potential of the hardware. Good interactive video learning programmes require highly developed and rather scarce design, programming, and video production skills for somewhere between 200 and 800 hours of preparation to create each hour of learning. Investment in training technology is therefore a relatively expensive business, not only the costs of the hardware, but more significantly to acquire and retain the skills required to produce the software to optimize the hardware. Don't let this frighten you away from technological training delivery systems — but do be sure you know what you are letting yourself in for, and that the resources are available to allow the technology to function at the level where it can produce the necessary rate of return on investment.

HOW TO MAKE THE BEST USE OF AVAILABLE METHODS AND TECHNIQUES

17

Joseph Prokopenko

The most important and effective training methods and techniques have been discussed in previous chapters. Here we would like to help the management development professional in selecting the best method to apply to a particular learning event.

Until the 1970s the armoury of teaching and training methods suitable for management education was quite modest. For years the case-study was the only real participative method being used other than the more academic, classical methods. Today the management trainer can count somewhere between 70 to 100 methods and techniques described in books and training manuals.

However, we are still far from knowing exactly how managerial competence is best acquired and developed, but we now know much more about the learning process than we did two decades ago. Management training is endeavouring to see the manager's job in its entirety by taking into account many factors which influence the operation of the enterprise in the contemporary world. This has emphasized the need for continuous improvement not only in content, but also in the overall methodology of the management training process.

During the past 20 years, more new methods have been developed, tested, and adapted to different learning situations than ever before. Some of them have become irreplaceable tools in the trainer's hands; others have remained marginal. Some are simple and can be used by virtually any trainer (or by the managers themselves) without any special preparation; others are fairly sophisticated, and it is not advisable to use them without extensive preparation of both trainers and course participants.

Many of the traditional management training methods seem to have very deep historical roots. The lecture method may be seen simply as the institutionalization of the process of one person telling others about something, or how to do something. The seminar process was perhaps first explicitly embodied in the Socratic method of teaching where questioning promoted discussion. The process involved in the use of case-studies can be seen in embryonic form in the Bible's parables; and the way in which the Harvard Business School borrowed the case method from the Law School to introduce it to management development is an interesting example of how innovations actually occur (through adapting an existing method, rather than by designing a new one from scratch).

Even such a relatively new method as the business game appears to have ancient origins which can be traced back to war games. The popularity of games and case-studies can be accounted for by the fact that they compensate for the abstractness of other methods, and in reaction to methods in which the learner is predominantly passive. The expansion of the family of experimental methods can be seen as a reaction to the way in which other conceptual methods concentrate on the theory of management techniques and neglect people's feelings, values and emotions.

We are now in an era in which more and more systematically designed, new and innovative management development methods are appearing, based on modern learning theories. This means that the task of creative trainers at present is more complicated and challenging. Their task is not only to select the best available training methods, but also to be able to create new combinations or design innovative ones.

However, if we put aside the few cases of trainers and consultants who, often for commercial purposes, want to amaze their clients with "miracle methods of training", we find that the overwhelming majority of trainers are seriously concerned about finding and using the most effective methods available. They want to assess the methods' advantages and disadvantages in relation to others. They try to match the method with the training objectives and the specific conditions in which learning is to take place.

In this chapter, by training methods (or learning methods, technologies, or techniques) we mean the methods used to convey learning to the learner. These could also be considered as devices to stimulate and direct learners towards behavioural changes.

Before discussing the selection of different training methods we shall make a few comments, which should be kept in mind during the selection process.

- *There is no one best training method.* Different methods enjoy varying degrees of effectiveness, depending upon training objectives, the trainee's background and motivation to learn, and the trainer's skill.

- *Any single learning event may utilize a number of training methods.* Most training programmes have several learning objectives. Therefore even a single lesson could demand a combination of several methods, for example to develop skills and knowledge, and to change attitudes.

- *A variety (combination) of methods improves trainees' motivation to learn effectively.* A variety of techniques means a variety of stimuli to the learner and, therefore, a variety of trainee responses, enhanced interest and motivation to learn.

These principles explain why the range of training methods and techniques is normally much larger than the number of learning objectives. From a total of more than 40 training methods two to four properly selected methods should be sufficient to achieve any single learning objective. The general process of training methods' selection could be as shown in figure 17.1.

Figure 17.1. The general process of training methods selection

This chapter will be devoted to a discussion of the main factors and criteria to be considered in selecting training methods.

17.1 Factors affecting the selection of training methods

There are many factors affecting the choice of training methods. The most important are the learning objectives, content and subject area, trainee numbers and background, available time, finance, facilities and other resources, including trainers' skills and motivation. Finally, factors related to principles of learning (such as learners' readiness and motivation, their involvement in the learning process and the design of the learning event itself) are also of crucial importance in selecting training methods. Figure 17.2 presents these factors classified into five major groups. The factors will be discussed in detail in the following sequence:

- Learning (training) objectives
- Training content and subject area
- Human factors
- Time and material factors
- Principles of learning and method selection factors

In addition to these factors and selection criteria we would like to consider some new trends in management development methods and techniques which would certainly influence the selection of future approaches.

(A) Learning objectives

Normally management development needs in the light of organizational problems or tasks and individual manager's capabilities are the starting point for designing learning objectives. These are defined in terms of changes to be effected in three major learning outcomes — improved knowledge, skills and activities. It is assumed that in a positive organizational environment these changes should lead to improved managerial performance.

Figure 17.2.   Factors affecting the selection of training methods

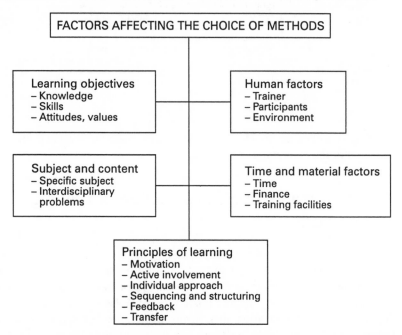

An example of a learning objective could be: "The participant will be able to define the term 'conflict management' and outline a process for handling conflict".

In designing learning objectives the focus should be the learner. The objective should therefore be stated in terms of what the learner will know, do and become (changed attitudes, behaviour) as a result of the training programme.

A properly defined set of objectives will tell the designer the type of learning situations and learning outcomes that should be built into the programme. Objectives broken down into skills, knowledge and attitudes will indicate that certain training methods are more applicable than others.

The classic relationship between training objectives, learning processes and training methods and the general goal of management development (management effectiveness) are given in figure 17.3.

As can be seen from this model, a preliminary analysis of needs will help to identify training objectives. Methods will then be selected with regard to their ability to impart new knowledge, influence attitudes and develop practical skills.

Figure 17.3. Links between management development objectives and training methods

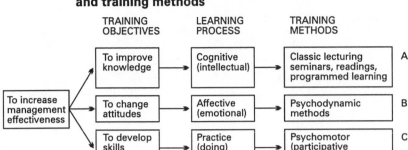

In this connection Hawrylyshyn (1967) has developed a simple but interesting model based on the experience of the Centre d'Etudes Industrielles in Geneva (see figure 17.4). In this model six participative methods are related to the general skills which a manager should possess whatever his or her special field of work or level in the hierarchy may be.

Each method in the model can serve various purposes; however, a method reaches its peak of effectiveness only in connection with a specific purpose. This can be well demonstrated with the case method. Pertinent data are given to the trainee in the description of the case. She or he has to diagnose and analyse the problem, consider alternative solutions, discuss those solutions and modify them after hearing colleagues' views. The trainee does not have to make decisions or implement them; consequently, he or she is not trained in the skill of decision-making and there is no reliable feedback on the correctness of solutions.

The main lesson to be drawn from this model is that if training is intended to improve multiple skills (which is usually the case), a combination of teaching methods must be used. A similar type of analysis could be made to determine which methods are most likely to affect the managers' attitudes or impart a specific kind of knowledge.

For example, let us consider a typical management activity cycle (left column) with each element requiring its corresponding broad skills (right column):

Management activity cycle	Required skills
1. Perceiving problems or opportunities	Sensitive perception
2. Gathering data and assigning priorities	Source of relevance
3. Problems and opportunities analysis	Diagnostic skills
4. Formulating alternatives	Creativity
5. Choosing from among the alternatives	Decisiveness
6. Implementing decisions	Leadership, communication, motivation

Figure 17.4. Effectiveness of participative methods

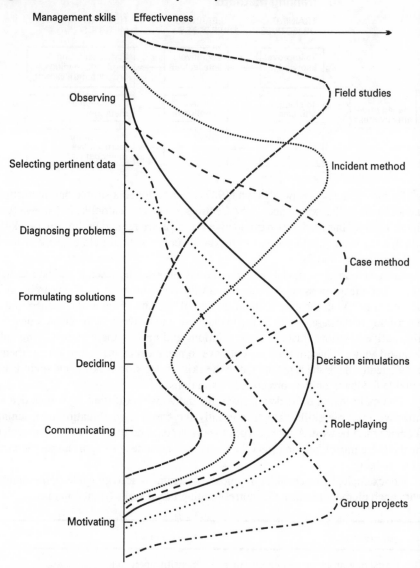

Source: Hawrylyshyn, 1967.

Using the model (figure 17.3), it is possible to recommend a broad set of training methods or to look for a specific one, even before identifying the precise training method needed to acquire the skills in each of the six elements of the management cycle. Thus, for the first element of the cycle we need a combination of methods from blocks B and C. To develop a sense of relevance, methods from blocks A and would be useful; for the third element (diagnostic skills), there is a high probability of finding the appropriate techniques in block A and perhaps in block B; to develop creativity, block A would be the most likely place to look. Finally, for the last two elements of the management cycle, training methods from all three blocks would be desirable.

The next step should be selecting methods focused more precisely on specific learning objectives from the previously selected broad sets. Let us take the example of using specialist knowledge and experience in the preparation of management decisions on complex business matters. It is of little use lecturing about the value of specialists to a manager who overestimates his or her own individual judgement and is not willing or perhaps able to use the specialist services which are available. Teamwork in syndicates, participation in business games or practical projects might make such managers aware of their limitations so that they begin to change their attitudes towards teamwork and the importance of specialists. The manager's interest in new knowledge and skills will undoubtedly be awakened. On leadership style, communication abilities, and behaviour in general, a manager may get more direct and stronger feedback from other participants in sensitivity training or as a member of a team working on a group project than in years of work in a managerial position.

To implement this fine-tuning of training objectives and methods, in addition to the information provided in the previous chapters, the reader could use Appendix 1 which gives a brief description of more than 40 training methods suitable for the development of knowledge, skills, attitudes, or interpersonal skills, as well as the degree of trainee participation and involvement in the learning process, assuming that the trainer has at least average skills in using the methodology, and that the quality of the environment (training facilities, equipment, time, trainees' motivation) is suitable. Obviously, as can be seen from this appendix, knowledge, skills and attitudes are interrelated, and this should not be overlooked when choosing training methods. Furthermore, they are related to certain specific management functions or subject areas or, in many cases, to multi-functional situations and interdisciplinary problems.

(B) Training content and subject area

The content and subject areas of training are also important factors to be taken into consideration in the process of selecting methods. The choice may be influenced by whether the subject-matter is abstract or not, by its level of complexity and even by the comprehensiveness of the materials and content.

Various subject areas (production management, finance, personnel, industrial relations, general management, etc.) have their own specific features. For example, operations research techniques are based on the extensive use of mathematics and statistics. It is usually taught through a combination of lectures (using audiovisual aids) and exercises during which the technique is practised. This may be supported by reading assignments. In certain cases lectures may be replaced or supplemented with programmed books.

In programmes concentrating on the behavioural aspects of management —

communication, leadership and motivation — training methods may be selected and combined in ways which give the participants numerous opportunities to analyse human behaviour and, at the same time, directly influence their own attitudes and behaviour. These programmes use case-studies dealing with the "human side of the enterprise", business games emphasizing communication and relations between participants, role-playing, sensitivity training and various other forms of group discussion, assignments and exercises.

It is often desirable to choose from several methods if we want to deal with a particular subject or problem. Thus, the analysis of a balance sheet can be taught through the case-study method, a combination of case-study with role-playing, a lecture, as a classroom exercise or by reading a text or a programme book on the subject. This is possible because the principal methods are versatile enough to be used in teaching a number of different subjects. Lectures, discussion and case-studies are being used in virtually all subject areas. However, in management training the main problem is not how to deal with specific subject areas and functions, it is much more important to:

- *understand and explain* the relationship between various sides and functions of the enterprise and show the highly complex, integrated nature of the management process;

- *help* the participants to avoid a one-sided and oversimplified approach to multi-dimensional situations;

- *promote* general management skills, which essentially lie in an interdisciplinary approach to management, and to combine and coordinate the various functions of management.

(C)   Human factors

In choosing training methods, the "human factors" are normally understood to be the trainer, the participants and the environment from which they come to the programme.

The trainer

The professional capability of the trainer is one of the key factors determining the choice of training methods and techniques. First, the trainer should have sufficient skills and knowledge of the subject-matter and, second, he or she should be comfortable in using the most effective training methods and techniques appropriate to the training objectives. To put it bluntly: *the trainer has to have a clear and significant message to pass, and his or her personality has to be acceptable to the trainees so that effective communication links can be established quickly and easily.* If these contributions are filled, a well-chosen and properly used method is likely to ease and stimulate learning. If they are not, unfortunately the method may become an end in itself.

Trainers have to assume personal responsibility for choosing the best methods for a particular training assignment. They ought to be able, therefore, to make a ational appraisal of their own abilities and to try to employ methods likely to enhance — not reduce — the expected impact. Role-playing, for example, is an exercise requiring some knowledge of psychology, a lot of experience with various types of human problems in management and the ability to react quickly in discussions. That is why a trainer who does not possess these qualities, but has an analytical mind and experience in solving business problems, might give preference to the case method.

The participants and their work environment

To be effective in the learning process the selection of training methods should also be based on such factors as how many trainees will be in the programme, their expectations, and their capability of learning through the training methods chosen by the trainer. In other words, the following factors should be considered:

- the intellectual level and educational background of the participants and their learning capabilities;
- the participants' age and practical experience; and
- their social and cultural background.

For example, in training programmes intended for supervisors or small entrepreneurs who often have only a basic education and have been away from school for a long time, lectures should be replaced by short talks and extensive use of visual aids. Emphasis should be placed on concrete examples and not high-level theories; simplified case-studies instead of long and complex cases; simple programmed books instead of the traditional textbooks.

With regard to the participants' practical experience, a distinction must be made between young people with little or no management experience, who have learned about management in a university or business school, and participants with practical experience, either in a managerial position or in specialist work in a functional department.

For the former, much of the information will be new and it will be difficult to link the teaching process with any previous experience. However, students are often more open-minded and receptive to new ideas than the latter group. In training people with experience, only additional knowledge should be imparted, and it is not only possible but essential to appeal to the participant's experience by relating the training to it. However, some of the participants in this group may take the attitude of "knowing it all". If so, the trainers' main problem may be how to change this complacency into awareness of what they need to learn to do their job better. In such cases, practical assignments, case-study discussions or simulation exercises are more likely to help participants realize that there are gaps in their knowledge and skills and that training may be the answer.

Experienced managers have a better capacity to learn directly from each other, provided a favourable atmosphere is created and methods are used which stimulate this learning. Discussion groups, working parties, syndicates, consultancy assignments and practical projects carried out by groups of managers are well suited for this purpose.

The complexity of the problem may be increased by social and cultural factors. It must be remembered that many of the participative teaching methods were developed in the United States — a country with its own particular social and cultural characteristics. High achievement, motivation, little respect for formal authority, priority given to action before contemplation — these and many other cultural factors may be absent in the country to which one or another method of training is to be transferred.

A number of experts with considerable experience in developing countries have also confirmed that, in general, any participative method may be used in any environment provided that it is instilled gradually, with foreknowledge of the cultural setting, and that the necessary modifications and adjustments are made to the method to avoid hurting national pride and traditions.

(D)   Time and material factors

In selecting the correct training methods, one should also consider the available time, finance and training facilities, including training equipment and materials. The most important questions to be answered by the trainer before finalizing the programme design are:

● How much time is available for both programme preparation and implementation?

● What training facilities and equipment can be afforded in relation to certain training methods?

● What are the total training costs associated with the methods chosen and is it worth spending this amount to achieve the expected learning objectives?

Normally, all three of the above-mentioned resources limit the trainer (and often the participants) and may in fact influence the type of training method and technique to be selected. For example, preparation time, which affects the cost of the training materials as well, varies for different training methods. As a rule, complex case-studies and business games require long and costly preparation, which includes designing and testing with trainers or experimental groups, and making necessary revisions.

The length of the course also predetermines the kinds of methods which can be used. The longer the course, the better the chances are that the trainer will be able to use business games, complex cases and practical projects. This is not to imply that participative methods should be eliminated from short courses; however, only methods which are not time-consuming and which are liable to pass the message across quickly can be used in these courses.

The time of day chosen for courses is more important than many course designers would imagine. For example, in the period after lunch (14.00 to 16.00 hours) it is advisable to have the more enjoyable sessions, with more participation and demonstration, rather than lecturing or seminars.

The training facilities may be a limiting factor in some institutes, or in courses given outside the institute, e.g. in small towns. Factors such as the number of rooms available for group work or the accessibility of audiovisual aids should be anticipated and the methods altered well in advance.

Thus, we should look at what we can and cannot afford in relation to our total budget and to the learning environment (physical, social and organizational). The importance of the culture and structure of the organization should also be remembered — this may favour some training methods. For example, some senior managers may not support external courses as a way of developing their subordinate managers, while others may see such courses as an essential part of the developmental process. We must also obtain data on the *past effectiveness of certain methods*, and on their *current effectiveness in other organizations* using them for similar learning situations (Harrison, 1989).

17.2 Principles of learning and methods selection factors

Another important stage in selecting the training method is finding which methods correspond best to the principles of learning built into specific training events. Among the many different schools and theories of learning, three major groups emerge: the pragmatic, the behavioural and the so-called logical. Their relationship to the key skills and major groups of training methods is presented in figure 17.5.

Figure 17.5.   Three groups of thought on the management learning process

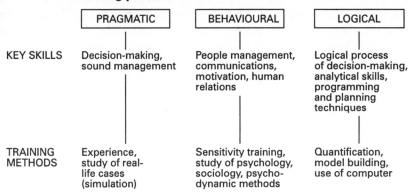

	PRAGMATIC	BEHAVIOURAL	LOGICAL
KEY SKILLS	Decision-making, sound management	People management, communications, motivation, human relations	Logical process of decision-making, analytical skills, programming and planning techniques
TRAINING METHODS	Experience, study of real-life cases (simulation)	Sensitivity training, study of psychology, sociology, psycho-dynamic methods	Quantification, model building, use of computer

It is interesting to note that these three groups of thought on management learning (pragmatic, behavioural and logical) have very close correlations with the main general learning objectives — developing skills, attitudes and knowledge. You may see the same close similarity between training methods (compare figures 17.3 and 17.5). Thus, the design of the learning event itself and its structure (a balance between pragmatic, behavioural and logical approaches in the design) provide an important source of information on where to look for adequate training methods, and which group of methods should be selected for further analysis (see Appendix 1).

Another important consideration in method selection is to link the main principles of the learning process with the training methods. Here again we narrow the field of choice by selecting those methods that best correspond to the specific learning event.

The following are among the main principles of learning most often mentioned: drive and stimulus (motivation), response and reinforcement, active involvement, individualized approach to learning design, proper sequencing and structuring of the learning process, feedback to evaluate learning effectiveness and, a matter of critical importance, the transferability to practical use back on the job of new skills and knowledge. Some selected aspects of the relationship between principles of learning and teaching methods are discussed below.

Motivation

The motivation to learn is enhanced if the presentation of the material is interesting, if its applicability is emphasized and if the benefits to be drawn from its application can be appreciated. To a certain extent this could be obtained through any method, including a good lecture. However, many participative methods are directly concerned with applying theoretical knowledge to real-life situations. The diverse ways in which they can be combined and sequenced can add to the enjoyment of learning and minimize participant fatigue. For example, when deciding on whether to use case-studies or in-basket exercises, prior discussion with some of the participants may well reveal that they would prefer in-basket exercises, and would find case-studies too artificial and time-consuming given that there are going to be 20 course members and only a day or two to cover the course content. The in-basket exercise may take just as long, but offers absolutely transferable learning. Therefore it emerges as the more satisfactory because it is most likely to stimulate the learners and help them achieve and reinforce correct responses.

Active involvement

The principle of active involvement is perhaps the main *raison d'être* of participative training methods. As a rule, the deeper the involvement, the higher the motivation, the more the participants are able to retain and the better they are equipped to apply what they have learned. It should not be overlooked, however, that the method itself, although considered to be highly participative, does not ensure that each person will be fully involved. The involvement level depends on the organization of simulation exercise preparation, trainer style and other factors. The participants may also be passive if they consider the material to be of poor quality or the performance of the trainer to be below the expected level.

Individual approach

Training programmes should take into account the fact that individuals have different training needs, different capabilities and learn at different paces; they also have their own personal style of study and application and may need individual attention. The overall course design and methods of teaching therefore have to provide not only work in groups and teams, but also the opportunity for individual reading, thinking, exercising and the application of knowledge.

This can be done through compulsory individual assignments (reading, exercises, projects); the use of training aids for individual learning (videotapes, computer programmes); the breakdown of group assignments and projects into tasks for small homogeneous groups or even for each individual; and voluntary additional activities for the more capable participants.

Sequencing and structuring

Some methods are better suited than others to introduce new topics and ideas, to sequence them correctly or explain the structure of a vast, complex area. That is why in certain situations the trainer cannot do without lectures, reading assignments and seminars to explain the subject (or managerial function), its structure and its main elements.

Feedback

Different types of feedback have to be provided in learning: feedback, for example, on competence and behaviour (from the other course participants, from the trainer and from the trainees themselves), feedback on what was actually learned, and on the ability to apply it effectively on the job.

Direct feedback on the soundness of decisions is an integral part of business games, for example, whereas in case discussions the only feedback on the individual's analytical abilities is the opinion of other participants and of the discussion leader. Strong feedback on behavioural patterns is provided by participation in role-playing, business games and sensitivity training (group dynamics). Exercises, consultancy assignments and application projects provide feedback on the practical relevance of learning.

Transferability

This principle requires that training, besides enhancing managerial competence, should also help the individual to transfer what he or she has learned to live situations. Some training methods, like lectures, study of literature or discussions do not pay much attention to this transfer. On the other hand, in many participative methods the element of transferability is strong. For this reason simulation and practical application projects are considered by some trainers as the most effective methods as far as transferability is concerned.

Figure 17.6 is an attempt to rate the potential of some training methods to the practical application of the above-mentioned learning principles. A simple three-point rating scale has been used and the rating is based on the opinions of experienced trainers and management consultants, as well as objective testing.

Figure 17.6. Application of some principles of learning in teaching methods

Method

Principle	Training on the job	Lecture	Group discussion	Case-study	Business game	Role-playing	Application project	Reading assignment
Motivation	Good	Average	Average	Average	Good	Average	Good	Weak
Active involvement	Good	Weak	Average	Good	Good	Good	Good	Average
Individual approach	Good	Weak	Average	Average	Average	Average	Good	Average
Sequencing and structuring	Average	Good	Weak	Average	Average	Weak	Average	Good
Feedback	Good	Weak	Average	Average	Good	Good	Good	Weak
Transfer	Good	Weak	Weak	Average	Average	Average	Good	Weak

Rating: ■ Good   ■ Average   □ Weak

Source: ILO, 1972, pp. 3-9.

The need to properly sequence and combine the various training methods in order to secure the greatest impact on learning emerges from an examination of training methods from the viewpoint of the principles of learning. It also explains why there is a growing interest in methods with high motivational feedback and transfer potential.

17.3   Some trends in training methods selection

We shall briefly review actual and expected changes in management skills profiles resulting from changes in managerial practices and the business environment in order to answer the question about present and future trends in management training methods and their applications.

We shall consider the expected changes in managerial profiles using the Ashridge Management College classification system, which makes a distinction between action-oriented management skills and techniques ("doing"), and the more qualitative aspects of management (managers' attitudes, perceptions, drive and values, or "being") (Barham et al., 1988).

The "being" dimension includes "inherent" qualities such as the values and attitudes of the manager. For example, it is crucial for the future manager to have drive, vision and a clear idea of how to shape and manage the organization of the future. Future managers should be able to manage ambiguity, understand whether people are ready to accept change, and appreciate the opportunities, pressures and constraints facing people and organizations.

Flexibility and adaptability, important qualities for the future manager, imply being open to new ideas and concepts regardless of their origin and being adaptable because of the changing and unpredictable environment.

As to changes in leadership patterns, the tendency towards decentralization, the strategic integration and the demands for local autonomy will produce more and more points at which multi-functional horizontal leadership will need to be exercised.

The "doing" dimension (implementation skills) of the manager's profile will stress technological literacy, the ability to use increasingly sophisticated information systems, analytical, financial and marketing skills, decision-making and communication as well as motivation and human resource development skills. Influencing people and managing interpersonal interaction will also be important issues in future management. The skill to take decisions in an uncertain environment will be of particular importance. Managers must understand such risk management skills as statistical and analytical methods, the concept of probability, the company's risk acceptance profile, the value of further information, and the need to reassess decisions constantly.

As can be appreciated, some corresponding changes in management development policies, approaches and methods will be necessary to accommodate the expected changes described above. The main change in methods would probably be to develop multi-dimensional managers (not just generalists lacking depth) who understand the complex interrelationships between functions. A combination of depth of function and breadth of management is likely to be the major objective of future management development methods and systems.

The changes in management training approaches fall into three phases: the fragmented approach, the formalized approach and the focused approach. The fragmented and formalized approaches correspond to the directive managerial style in vertical (hierarchical) organizational structures. The focused management development approach is more appropriate for the non-directive, democratic, decentralized style of management in organizations with a horizontal (flatter) structure.

The fragmented approach is characterized by unsystematic training of managers, which does not link training needs to organizational objectives, and the emphasis is only on knowledge-based courses in which lecture and seminar methods dominate. The organization takes little responsibility for training and expects little in return.

The formalized approach is characterized by some linkage to human resource development needs and to an appraisal system. There is more concern to link training programmes to individual needs. However, while individual training needs are recognized, there may often be little freedom of choice to vary the course programme and methods. The formalized approach has begun to supplement knowledge-based training with training which is more concerned with developing new skills and a values base, while training activities are increasingly becoming part of a continuous process. This approach, while still based on the lecturing and seminar methods, uses increasingly different participative and values-developing methods.

The focused approach to management training makes development intrinsic to the organization. The approach moves the emphasis away from formal training towards personal development and recognizes that the organizational environment has an important part to play in development. Training and development are focused both on the strategic goals of the organization and on the needs of the individual. The approach represents a switch from teacher-centred to learner-centred training, from emphasizing "training" to emphasizing "learning". Organizations which adopt the focused approach are often called "learning organizations". Learning here is not fragmented, and becomes a continuous process, where on-the-job learning has become a way of life. The continuous questioning and the very close monitoring of the environment and its operations constitute a quite effective learning device. The focus of training and development on organizational goals and learning is matched by a corresponding focus on the learning needs of individuals.

The new emphasis on the individual in the learning organization is reflected by a trend away from structured, taught courses to a learner-centred approach, where on-the-job training is regarded as the best form of development. This means that courses will be more problem- and learner-oriented, with corresponding changes in the role of the trainer. Thus, general trends in changing management training approaches can be briefly described as moving from:

- a fragmented to a formalized and focused approach;
- teaching to learning systems;
- knowledge-based to skill- and value-based learning;
- management training to management development;
- training departments to learning organizations.

These changes will certainly result in more emphasis being placed on new, more participative methods for management training and development that allow the development of integrative skills, the ability to communicate and coordinate, and the development of all kinds of entrepreneurial skills and personal attitudes. However, the most important need at present is for an integrative approach which combines a detailed understanding of management disciplines and cultural, political and economic diversity.

Integrative management development methods have to allow the convergence of two important management needs. One is related to innovation, creativity and responsiveness to an ever-changing environment. The other concerns growing complexity, which can be handled only in an integrative way. Thus, a plurality of development methods will be required. Neither lectures, nor free-form discussions, nor even conventional case-studies are likely, alone, to be effective learning tools. The new learning systems should be developed for the needs of the future.

Some of the attributes of this system are suggested for discussion. The future learning system should be integrative in method: methodologies and techniques used at each stage of the management process need to integrate functions, areas of concern and level of analysis. Training methods should be more participative, with more effective use being made of the knowledge and experience of each participant.

An important requirement of future training methodology is that it should be more relevant to practical needs. This means that a more systematic effort should be made at the implementation phase of the training process. Key developments from the international business environment should be distilled into effective training methods. There should be a new approach to the case-study method, which has traditionally been oriented towards the past. New methods should look to the present and the future.

Traditional training methods will be less and less acceptable, because future learning will not take place exclusively in the classroom. Training will increasingly take place partly at the workplace and partly at the institution using, for example, the action-learning methodology, which is based on real job issues and a questioning, problem-oriented approach. In this type of programme, managers and other participants address their real needs. Trainer's advice is always available, but it is led by (rather than leading) the learning needs of the individuals and the organization (Prokopenko, 1988).

In addition to many traditional and new training methods, structured practical experience is likely to be of even more importance in the future than it is now. There is growing concern with the early identification, rewarding and development of high-flyers (promising young managers). Thus, practical experience structured in advance will become a more significant component of management development systems, as will familiarity with new instructional and communication technologies, including computers.

Another important present and future management development tool is management consulting, which is particularly crucial in transferring training programme results into practice and also in analysing problems and training needs. It is an excellent means of keeping trainers in contact with reality while providing a valuable service to companies. It can also be the most enriching part of the professional development of the trainer.

The latest progress in management development methods is networking, which facilitates and expands horizontal communication, the exchange of information and cooperation between management development institutions. The role of the trainer is also changing: as the focus of courses broadens, mainly as a result of the growing emphasis on learning and self-development, a wider range of skills will be demanded of the trainer that will include facilitating group events, individual counselling, providing learning resources and constant support to line management.

In the present conditions of rapid change, managerial obsolescence has become a matter of major concern. One of the remedies for this is cyclical retraining of managers. It is becoming clear, however, that formal retraining is not enough and not always possible. Managers themselves must continue to learn so that they can foresee and understand changes, innovate and act correctly in completely new situations. Thus, management *self-development* should be their principal skill, which again is linked to a specific attitude — never to stop learning.

That is why good management training programmes do not deluge the participants with enormous amounts of detailed information (which tomorrow will be obsolete), but place emphasis on helping them *to learn how to learn*.

It is no exaggeration to say that the two above-mentioned features of management training — concern about its relevance to a continuously changing real-life situation and emphasis on learning how to learn — are becoming the determining factors in the selection, use and further evolution of training methods and techniques.

Appendix 1: A Brief guide to management training methods

Training method	Description	Skills building	Know-ledge	Atti-tudes, values	Inter-personal skills	Level of trainee participation			Best application in man-agement development
						High	Medium	Low	
Action learning	Process of learning by solving open-ended problems in organizations with emphasis on acquiring skills for ana-lysing and solving future problems	■		■	■	■			Problem identification Problem-solving Team-building Motivation Organization development
Action maze	A case-study or incident that has been programmed, involving a series of decision points with options at each point, the choice of which leads to the description of a new situation with new alternatives	■					■		Decision-making Problem-solving Trouble-shooting Organization development
Application project	A task (often practical) laid down by the trainer, often providing opportuni-ties to develop and use practical and cognitive experience, creativity and initiative. Trainees learn from design-ing and taking action	■	■	■	■	■			Problem-solving Project management Creativity Integrative skills
Behaviour modelling	A model or ideal enactment of a de-sired behaviour presented through an instructor, a videotape or a film. This is usually followed by a practice ses-sion on the behaviour. The aim is to modify the behaviour of managers by increasing their behaviour repertoire			■	■	■			Managerial behaviour Motivation skills General leadership skills Organization development

Management development

Training method	Description	Skills building	Knowledge	Attitudes, values	Inter-personal skills	Level of trainee participation			Best application in management development
						High	Medium	Low	
Brainstorming	A relatively unstructured form of discussion where creative thinking is emphasized rather than practical analysis			■	■	■			Creativity Problem identification Organization development Listening skills Team-building
Business clinics	Meetings of a group of people with common interests devoted to the analysis and treatment of real and relevant problems in a special field, and reaching their own solutions	■		■	■		■		Problem identification Problem analysis Analytical skills Organization development
Buzz groups	Small discussion teams with specific tasks (normally ideas, products) which should be completed in specific time-limits. The group then share their ideas between themselves			■	■	■			Developing a learning-centred agenda Devising ways to reach common objectives Problems and solutions identification Organization development
Case-study	A written or oral presentation of an event, incident or actual or imaginary situation for a small group to identify and analyse problems and solve them	■		■	■	■			Problem-solving Decision-making Industrial relations Listening skills Problem identification Organization development

Training method	Description	Skills building	Know-ledge	Atti-tudes, values	Inter-personal skills	Level of trainee participation			Best application in man-agement development
						High	Medium	Low	
Coaching (mentoring)	Long-term assistance to a young manager by an experienced senior by providing practical advice on management, business and behavioural issues. Normally these are trusted and open relationships, helping the younger manager to grow in maturity	■		■	■	■			Behavioural skills Specialized knowledge
Colloquy	A modification of the panel using 6-8 people, of whom 3-4 are experts. The audience (3-4) asks questions, expresses opinions and raise issues to be treated by the experts. A moderator directs the proceedings. This provides an opportunity to establish a rapport between the audience and the experts		■					■	New information Listening skills Discussion skills
Conference	Used to discuss problems, suggest solutions, exchange information between a group of 5-50 persons representing different organizations or departments with common interests and backgrounds		■	■				■	Presentation skills Listening skills New information Problem analysis and solving Organization development

Training method	Description	Skills building	Know-ledge	Atti-tudes, values	Inter-personal skills	Level of trainee participation			Best application in management development
						High	Medium	Low	
Critical incident	Participants are asked to describe an important incident related to their work lives, which brought about changed behaviour or conditions. This is then used as a base for analysis. Sometimes such incidents are suggested by trainers, but they should be relevant to participants' own problems	■		■	■	■			Analytical skills New experience Listening skills Problem identification Organization development
Debate	A presentation of conflicting views of two people or two teams of people for the purpose of clarifying the argument between them			■	■		■		Listening skills Analytical skills Presentation skills Assertiveness Self-confidence
Demonstration	A resource person performs an operation or a job, showing others how to do a specific task. The participants could undertake the same task	■	■					■	Job structure Job orientation Skill development
Discussion	A group of 5-12 people have a relatively unstructured exchange of ideas and opinions focused on the attitudes and values they hold relative to a specific issue or problem	■		■	■	■			Values and attitude changes New information Listening skills Team-building Evaluation Organization development

Training method	Description	Skills building	Know-ledge	Atti-tudes, values	Inter-personal skills	Level of trainee participation			Best application in man-agement development
						High	Medium	Low	
Exercises, struc-tural experiences	Planned exercises or experiences, re-peated performance of a skill, usually using some instrument or guide, fol-lowed by a discussion of the partici-pants' feelings and reactions. Confront participants with important decisions or information; could also be a test of knowledge and skills. Could be used for job enrichment, job rotation and job enlargement	■		■		■			Practical skills Sense of relevance Result orientation Independence
Field trip (Study tour)	The group travels to offices, factories and other establishments that provide sights, equipment or operations not possible within the classroom. The re-sults can be used as the basis for dis-cussion, reports and other practical ex-ercises		■	■				■	New information Developing sense of relevance
Forum	A form of free and open discussion with the moderator's assistance in which any participant is permitted to talk any time the attention of the group can be secured. Could be accompanied by a brief speech before discussion			■	■		■		Presentation skills Listening skills Sensitivity skills New information

347

Training method	Description	Skills building	Knowledge	Attitudes, values	Inter-personal skills	Level of trainee participation High	Level of trainee participation Medium	Level of trainee participation Low	Best application in management development
Games	An activity characterized by structured competition between a few teams to provide an opportunity to practise specific skills (e.g. decision-making); gives an insight into the attitudes, values and interests of the participants. Decisions are made and actions are taken by participants (6-12) with different managerial roles	■	■	■	■	■			Behaviour modelling Team-building New information Sense of relevance Organization Development Problem-solving Decision-making Skills assessment
Guided reading	An important assignment to be accomplished either in or out of class hours. Reading management books, articles and hand-outs in accordance with the programme and involving an element of test and reinforcement		■	■				■	New information Self-development
In-basket exercises	A form of stimulation that focuses on the "paper symptoms" of a job. Participants respond to material, files, letters or documents managers might have in their in-basket. Action taken on each item helps trainers to sort out their priorities, and develop their understanding of different activities and decision-making skills	■		■		■			Priority setting Communication skills Decision-making Sense of relevance Understanding an organization, its culture and structure Coping with pressure

Training method	Description	Skills building	Knowledge	Attitudes, values	Interpersonal skills	Level of trainee participation			Best application in management development
						High	Medium	Low	
Incident process	A case-study in which an individual or small team analyses the case (incident), uncovers a problem and critical facts, clarifies them and makes a decision for action	■		■	■	■			Diagnostic skills Fact-finding and setting of priorities Decision-making Industrial relations Team-building
Individual study	Learning factual and conceptual information, working at the trainee's own pace, often alone and probably at odd times. Could be structured or unstructured; combines both reading and experimental learning		■	■			■		New information Self-development Specialized functions
Instruction	A relatively precise formula for teaching a person to do a job or specific operations by presenting factual information and ensuring repetition and retention	■						■	Skills development
Lecture/talk	A one-way, organized, formal talk given by a resource person to a large audience for the purpose of presenting background information about a series of events, facts, concepts or principles. Could be accompanied by questions and discussions by participants		■	■				■	New information Attitude changes

Training method	Description	Skills building	Knowledge	Attitudes, values	Inter-personal skills	Level of trainee participation			Best application in management development
						High	Medium	Low	
Management consulting	Process of providing professional and independent assistance to help in problem identification and solving and to improve general management competence and abilities	■	■	■	■	■			General management Functional management Problem identification Problem-solving Team-building Organization development
Nominal group techniques (NGT)	Groups of people "nominate" problems through data collection techniques, tapping individual judgements and arriving at decisions which cannot be made by one person		■	■			■		Organization development Problem identification Sense of relevance
Observation	Structured observation of senior, more experienced managers' actions in different job situations, and learning from their successes and mistakes		■	■				■	Sense of relevance New information Organizational understanding
On the job	Combination of training and non-training events on the job, closely related to management activities, using career development, job rotation, job enrichment and job enlargement methods	■		■	■	■			Practical skills Relevance Organizational understanding Broad management functions General management

Training method	Description	Skills building	Know-ledge	Atti-tudes, values	Inter-personal skills	Level of trainee participation			Best application in management development
						High	Medium	Low	
Organization development	Planned and purpose-oriented development of the human side of organizations as well as the norms, culture and psychological climate, using behavioural science to improve the general organizational performance and management of human relations skills	■		■	■	■			Human resource management Human relations skills Organizational understanding Team-building Cross-cultural management Communications
Panel	A group of 3-8 experienced people present their views on a particular topic or problem. A moderator assists with questions and discussions among the panel members, often without participation		■	■				■	New information Attitudes and values
Programmed learning	Learning factual information at the trainee's own pace, usually alone. The material appears in small, carefully sequenced segments, which elicit a response from the learner, who immediately finds out whether or not his or her response was correct. This facilitates cumulative learning. Computer applications are broadly used		■	■				■	New information Attitudes and values

Training method	Description	Skills building	Know-ledge	Atti-tudes, values	Inter-personal skills	Level of trainee participation			Best application in management development
						High	Medium	Low	
Question-and-answer session	Small groups of participants develop questions to which they wish resource persons to respond extemporaneously. Could be separate activities or part of other training techniques		■	■			■		New information Attitudes and values Analytical skills Diagnostic skills
Role-playing	The spontaneous dramatization of a situation or problem followed by a group discussion. Trainers are asked to enact, in the training situation, the role they will be called upon to play in their job. The trainer acts as a coach, staging and reinforcing the desired role performance	■		■	■		■		Communication Attitudes and values Behavioural modelling Building self-confidence Sensitivity skills Organization development
Seminar	A group of people gathered together to study under an experienced leader, doing research, identifying and analysing problems, exchanging results through reports and discussions		■		■	■			Planning Self-awareness Attitudes and values Problem identification
Sensitivity training (T-groups, group dynamics, human relations training, family group)	A group of people assist each other with self-disclosures and feedback. The learning, assisted by a trained psychologist, focuses on group process and interpersonal relations, creating an effective group to change behaviour so as to contribute towards more effective leadership styles, and improve awareness of their actual and possible behaviour			■	■	■			Team-building Self-awareness Behaviour modelling Communication Human relations skills Leadership skills Organization development

Training method	Description	Skills building	Know-ledge	Atti-tudes, values	Inter-personal skills	Level of trainee participation			Best application in management development
						High	Medium	Low	
Simulation	A learning environment or a model that simulates a real setting in which the skills are required, with the focus on attitudes and values being related to the situation presented. Given basic data about the situation, participants make decisions and follow through to the next sequence, to decide again what to do. This cycle continues until the learning objective of the simulation has been achieved		■		■	■			Planning Organizing Team-building Trouble-shooting Problem-solving Organization development
Symposium	A series of related meetings with speeches (3–6) by people qualified to speak on different phases of a single subject or problem		■					■	New information New concepts
Syndicate	A small group of trainers assigned specific tasks as part of a large training design. The chairman usually presents the syndicate's report or findings to the larger group (or other syndicate) and it is commented on by them and a trainer	■		■	■		■		Team-building New information Communication skills Problem-solving Organization development

Training method	Description	Skills building	Know-ledge	Atti-tudes, values	Inter-personal skills	Level of trainee participation			Best application in management development
						High	Medium	Low	
Transactional analysis	A method to improve face-to-face communication, analysing the emotional and behavioural states of a person, or the interaction between two persons	■		■	■	■			Understanding one's own behaviour Communication Improving relationships Leadership styles Appraisal methods Behaviour modelling
Workshop	A group of persons with common interests and experience which works in much the same manner as a seminar, emphasizing free discussions, practical methods, skills and applications of principles. It allows considerable flexibility in the combination of concepts and practice	■	■				■		New information Skill development Communication Problem-solving Organization development

Source: Prokopenko and North, 1996, pp. A-38 to A-43.

PART IV

MANAGEMENT DEVELOPMENT PROGRAMMES IN PRACTICE

TOWARDS A LEARNING ORGANIZATION

18

Olle Bovin

Management training and development have normally been perceived as a separate function within the organization. Learning has been seen to be the result of the particular efforts of trainers and consultants to improve the skills, knowledge and attitudes of managers.

The concept of the learning organization brings a new dimension to the discussion on training and development. Instead of speaking of these as a separate function, the whole organization is treated as a learning system, where individuals learn from the activities taking place in the organization and where the organization as a whole learns from actively participating individuals.

Learning organizations require changes in people's roles, in management styles and in the way in which human beings are seen as resourceful agents of change. They also require trainers and consultants to review their roles. In this chapter, in addition to exploring the concept of the learning organization, the different forms that learning organizations may take and how they influence ways in which trainers and consultants work will also be discussed. The rationale behind learning organizations and why it is important for companies to develop in this direction as well as examples of measures that can facilitate the development and running of learning organizations will all be presented here.

18.1   The changing business environment

The fall of the Berlin Wall, the rapid political changes in Central and Eastern Europe, unexpected currency and world stock market fluctuations, increasing global competition and a changing and more demanding market are all creating a new situation for industries seeking to participate in the global game. This period of uncertainty and unpredictability had already started during the mid-1970s at the time of the first oil crisis. However, although we were facing a new era in the way businesses were run, very little changed with regard to the education of managers in companies and in business schools. It was only in the late 1980s that companies and business schools discovered that new approaches would have to be taken in order to ensure value and return on the time and money invested in the process of enhancing the ability to manage.

The rapidly changing market situations and new customer demands have increased the pressure on nearly all corporations to become more flexible, more responsive and faster in developing and introducing new or better products and services.

A major shift that could be characterized as "managing the firm from outside in" versus "managing the firm from inside out" was predominant up to the mid-1970s and early 1980s. This shift implied that there were a number of parameters for success that had to be changed and that were likely to have an impact on nearly every part of the firm.

Since the industrial revolution and the introduction of modern, industrial methods, most activities in any company have been focused on improving and enhancing internal processes and procedures. In fact, basically all management research and academic contributions, even today, have been primarily focused on how to run a business and how to improve within quite stable external parameters.

In business planning and budgeting the "escalating method" has been predominant. This way of planning and developing can also be named a "strategic fit". It means that we define objectives and make a plan for the future based on history and the resources available, then we decide how much and when we want to invest in order to reach the strategic objectives.

The current situation and the future business environment demands a radically new concept on how to accomplish goals. It demands a fundamental change from the type of organization that slowly changes its procedures and practices with a changing environment, to the type of organization that responds readily to rapid changes, either internal or external. The rate at which organizations learn may become their only sustainable source of competitive advantage. The structure of competitive organizations is changing, too. The emerging organization consists of networks rather than of bureaucracies. Interest in rules and procedures diminishes, and is taken over by the identification of tasks and the establishment of teams.

Because of very rapid changes and the restructuring that is going on in business with mergers, acquisitions, management buy-outs, etc., it becomes a necessity for companies to have a very clear picture of where they want to be and how fast they want to get there, without primarily asking "what resources do we have?" to get there, but rather, "what do we need to do?"

This is a fundamental change, because it means the ability to mobilize total resources inside the company and effectively utilize resources outside the company that will play the major role in achieving new strategic changes. This way of thinking and acting will drastically change the way people are managed in the company.

The need to look for and use creativity and to quickly identify competences and utilize them will be profound. The task is not to build structures, but rather to mobilize forces, to respond quickly and accurately to external factors and to take bold actions in the company to satisfy customers or beat the competition. As de Bono (1980) points out, managers are well trained to be reactive, i.e. to solve problems they are faced with. What they are much less prepared for is to be proactive, that is, to identify potential opportunities in a new situation. First of all this means monitoring the borders of the organization, and searching actively for information that uncovers malfunctioning practices vis-à-vis customers, suppliers and business partners. Secondly, it means engaging the people of the organization in solving the problems and searching for opportunities of improvement. For a number of managers this in itself is a totally new task.

Naturally, management development and people development have been planned and have performed to make the members of a business organization better and better at their jobs within current acceptable structures, and most programmes have been heavily focused on how to improve what already exists. In management education institutions and in universities, all management education has been focused on "scientifically" describing how to do business in, for example, finance and accounting, marketing, manufacturing, R & D, etc. It is heavily functionalized with very strict borders drawn between the functions in the company.

The areas of people development, the use of competence, customer responsiveness and increased competitiveness have been especially difficult to teach and to develop. We must therefore examine to what extent the principles and methods we have been using to develop our people and our organizations are appropriate to the new company behaviour.

18.2 The changing organization

People who engage in change and development must see a fundamental return on their investment with regard to time and money, and these benefits must be brought into the development process. We must ensure that there is a high return for the individual, for the specific business and for the whole corporation.

Organizations differ from individuals. Organizations represent structure, control and collective action. People in general represent emotion, creativity and a need for freedom in order to express their maximum capability. Thus we have a basic incompatibility in the nature of the relationship between individuals and organizations. Individuals pursue goals that relate to their own well-being and to that of their immediate environment. As Kolb put it, the direction that learning takes is governed by one's needs and goals. We seek experiences that are related to our goals, interpret them in the light of our goals and test implications of these concepts that are relevant to these felt needs and goals.

Organizations, on the other hand, pursue overall goals related to things like short-term profit, long-term survival or the achievement of social objectives (particularly for public institutions). The apparent contradiction between individual and organizational goals has been handled inadequately by organizations in the past.

Management development in the last two or three decades tended, on balance, to be more introverted, functionalized and internally focused on the efficiency of the organization and how to make the internal process work better. By far the largest number of companies in the world were either national or newly international in their nature of operation. Consequently, and rightly, they focused upon national and internal issues. In fact, the 1980s represented the true development of the global market- place. Not only was the knowledge that managers were assimilating too internally focused and not necessarily relevant to global issues, but it was not sufficiently converted into true, practical, results-oriented applications within the company. On examining many companies, it is evident that internal organizational structures and their responsiveness to the external environment stimuli have not been appropriate.

Let us now look at the classic business process of a typically highly regarded 1970-80s company and see how that process is inappropriate for today's environment (see figures 18.1 and 18.2).

Figure 18.1. The classic business process of the 1970s and 1980s

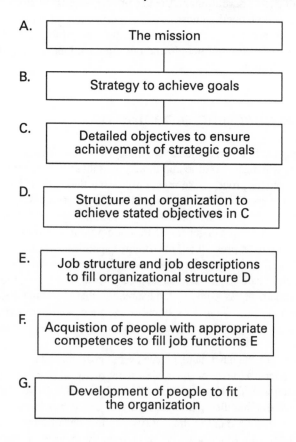

Referring to management development within the above construct, if the people in step F had a competency set that did not fulfil the company profile required in the job description E, this is typically where training and development would be focused.

The truly advanced organization is beginning to realize that this business process is inappropriate. The root cause of this discrepancy lies in the exceptionally swift change in two basic business elements in the 1990s. One key factor is the changing demographics. Both the gross numbers of people and the specialist skills available to organizations today are diminishing. Skills are in shorter and shorter supply and will become even more scarce in the 1990s in relation to industry's needs in many countries. Thus, organizations are starting to realize that they currently have large human assets which must be more efficiently utilized.

As human resources are becoming an increasingly precious asset for organizations, the competition among companies for competent people increases in intensity. People with sought-after competences select the companies that offer, more importantly than a good salary, an organizational culture where employee involvement, teamwork, personal creativity and responsibility are central features. More and more companies realize that in order to attract the kind of competences they need, they have to change managerial roles from positional power towards team leadership based on empowerment.

Another element refers to the increased nature of competitiveness in the global marketplace. This requires that all internal business investment be closely scrutinized in order to achieve maximum efficiency. Thus, high levels of return on investment are needed.

The convergence of these two elements means that the future focus of organizations will be the maximization of currently available human potential and the efficient control of investment in people development in order to ensure value added to the company.

Thus, the A to F business procedure presented earlier changes (see figure 18.2).

This business and development process is quite different. Once abilities are recognized and developed in step D, the organization structure in E, which is actually the outcome of the follow-up process, is driven by the objective to maximize individual competences and to organize team competences to ensure maximum effect. The result of E is the "new" organization.

The "new" organization now takes another step and the cycle is repeated. This embodies the true focus to attain maximal return upon investment for people development. Once individual competences have been "discovered" or identified, the operational team concentrates upon developing and using the top innate competences within each member of the team.

There is a key difference between a high level of innate competence and a developed or trained capacity. People have certain natural better-developed skills and tend to converge towards those skills when approaching and solving organizational problems or tasks. People enjoy doing what they are best at. However, organizations have tried to make the "complete manager" of every manager in the organization.

Figure 18.2. The business process of the future

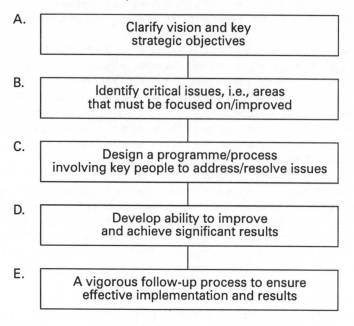

A. Clarify vision and key strategic objectives

B. Identify critical issues, i.e., areas that must be focused on/improved

C. Design a programme/process involving key people to address/resolve issues

D. Develop ability to improve and achieve significant results

E. A vigorous follow-up process to ensure effective implementation and results

For example, if the average organization finds that the competence of one of its managers is below the acceptable level in the area of time management, the organizational response would be to send the manager on a time-management course. Thus thousands of dollars are invested in raising a low level of competence to the level of mere acceptability. Such managers will never be brilliant time managers. They will waste time on developing their time-management skills. They will, in addition, be concerned about the time they are spending on developing their time-management skills. They may even worry and be under stress because of their perceived lack of ability in the area of time management.

Meanwhile, such a manager is a superb supervisor and coach for his or her team. The organization therefore is consistently depressing innate top competences in order to raise incompetences to a level of acceptability.

This process is inappropriate for learning organizations. Development should concentrate on raising his or her already excellent leadership skills to an even higher level. The low level of competence in time management should be backed up by organizational restructuring so that it presents no liability to the company. This approach is equally important when putting teams together.

A classic mistake, made over and over again, is to build teams of people with similar competences and similar backgrounds and coming from the same part of the organization. In such teams there is a tendency for opinions to converge, e.g. a group of engineers may tend to solve a problem in a systematic, rational and mechanistic way. Staying ahead in today's markets means doing the opposite; using the differences in people to foster innovation. This means putting together teams that are diverse in their composition, in order to encompass the complexities of the organization's environment.

An example is Japanese car manufacturers, who are undoubtedly successful in getting large shares of overseas markets, who have psychologists and anthropologists working with their engineers to conceive cars with characteristics that match the various tastes of prospective buyers. Another example is the policy of some companies to ensure the participation on project teams of groups made up of people of different race, sex and age. Utilizing top competences also means emphasizing people's diversities. Using individual competences and managing for diversity is not just a necessity, but a great opportunity for the leading-edge companies of the future.

It is difficult for the organization of the 1970s and 1980s to accept this construct. Of course it is difficult to link and utilize top individual competences in appropriately balanced teams in order to achieve real change and results. It takes time, it takes expertise and it takes involvement.

18.3   The learning organization

What we have described above as the organization that responds readily to markets, empowers its people and is ready for change, is what we may label a "learning organization". What is a "learning organization"? What is the meaning of learning? What happens when the organization learns?

Pedler et al. (1989) offer a concise, although broad definition of what they call the "learning company": "an organization which facilitates the learning of all of its members and continuously transforms itself". They stress that the essence of the learning organization concept is not training, but individual and organizational self-development. This corresponds to what Barham and Rassam (1989) report as having been said by a manager at Jaguar: "changes can only be achieved by self-development. I believe that we are trying to do this, by moving from a directive to a development approach, bringing training to problems and discussing these problems on the spot." We discussed earlier the conflict of individual and organizational goals, which the vast majority of organizations have not been able to solve satisfactorily. In a learning organization, where learning for individuals lies in solving a problem, and where the organization learns from having the problem solved, the risk of such conflict is diminished.

In organizational learning, there is emphasis on two aspects: the learning done by individuals and the learning done by the organization. The difference between individual learning and what may be termed organizational learning may often be unclear. Despite the fact that "it is difficult to separate the mass of individuals and their learning from the organization as a mass and its learning" (Mumford, 1988), they should be distinct, as we shall discuss below.

Individual learning is perceived as a mixture of programmed training and learning from work. The programmed training is not very different from most of the training taking place in organizations. Learning from work is seen, in a learning organization, as a function of the nature of the work of the manager. Easterby-Smith suggests that for learning organizations to develop, use has to be made of structures such as job rotation, planned experience and transient project groupings.

As we shall see in the examples at the end of the chapter, the breaking down of barriers between units and functions also becomes essential. There is more emphasis on the roles that people have and the learning opportunities in those roles, than what can be offered in the way of training. Individual behaviour is powerfully shaped by the organizational roles that people play and, therefore, to change people's behaviour, the best way is to put them in a new context which imposes new roles, responsibilities and relationships. Expanded responsibilities for achieving results, as well as for one's personal learning, are key elements in a learning organization.

It is clear that an organization does not practise organizational learning simply by moving people around. It also needs to be able to monitor the performance of functions that managers are responsible for. We are bordering the issue of how the organization learns, as opposed to the way in which individuals learn.

There are several different definitions of how organizations learn. A central element in most of the definitions is that the organization learns by discovering and correcting deficiencies in its actions. This involves receiving information, then making decisions to change practices. It is probably true that all organizations learn. Most organizations know, for example, what the output is of a certain product per year. Some organizations know how satisfied the customers are, and are able to act when the level of satisfaction drops. Far fewer organizations are able to anticipate customers' future needs and to make the necessary changes to fulfil those needs when they arise.

The difference between one organization and another in terms of learning is not so much that one learns and the other doesn't. Rather it is the difference in *levels* of learning. The more nuanced the type of information an organization is able to receive (without risking information overflow) and the better it is able to respond to that information, the better it can be said to be learning.

How does an organization learn? It learns by correcting its actions based on information from its internal and its external environment.

Here are some examples of learning from the internal environment:

- new product innovations
- results from corporate climate analyses
- suggestions or critiques at meetings
- finance reports

An example of learning that stems from inside the organization is the system practised by Motorola, a successful high-technology communications company. In Motorola there is a standard which guarantees that any idea for improvement from an employee is responded to within 24 hours.

What the organization learns is sometimes written down in the form of policies, procedures, memoranda, etc. However, as suggested by Mintzberg (1990), much of what is learned by an organization is stored in the minds of its managers. Managers make up their own mental maps of how things are running and how they should be running, based on the experiences they have and the information they receive. Their personalized mental maps guide their actions, such as the kind of decisions they make, and how they make them.

The organization also learns from its external environment, such as information about:

- customer complaints
- opening up of new markets
- appearance of new technology
- competitors' actions
- changing consumer tastes

Organizations engage in different types of learning or, rather, as mentioned above, learning at different levels. A basic level of learning is that at which the organization only makes superficial changes in response to signals that it receives, such as abandoning a product that does not sell well. A higher level of learning would be one at which the organization actively searches for explanations *why* the product did not sell well. A higher level still would be reached when the organization undertook to examine its own internal processes leading up to launching the product. The latter would enable it to learn about itself and correct underlying causes of deficiencies.

Argyris and Schön (1978) make the distinction between what they call "single-loop" and "double-loop" learning. Single-loop learning takes place when the organization responds to information by correcting practices, but where the corrections stay within existing rules and norms. Double-loop learning is at a higher level, where the organization is able to search for underlying causes, such as by questioning existing norms.

Let us consider an example. A team of young designers from Honda were given the task of coming up with a car that would break with traditional trends, one that was fuel efficient and low priced. They called the project "Let's make an adventure". As a result of their own internal learning process, they challenged the existing idea (from Detroit) that a car should be "horizontally long and vertically short". Instead they started experimenting with the idea of a car that was "horizontally short and vertically tall", a type of "luxurious mini", which had "minimum space devoted to machine and maximum space devoted to man". The car became a success. But from the point of view of managers, trainers and consultants, perhaps the most important fact is that the team was encouraged to — and was able to — challenge existing norms. The organization can thus be said to have engaged in a double-loop learning experience.

There may be great differences between what the individuals learn and what an organization made up of the same individuals learns. There is a tendency, especially in organizations with more rigid structures less conducive to innovation and delegation, for people to want to keep what they learn for their own personal use, rather than to put it to the use of the organization. The organization as a system knows less than the sum of the knowledge of the individuals that make up the organization. There are many examples of products or services being developed by companies that turned out to be unsuccessful in spite of several people in the company knowing that the product or service had important deficiencies.

18.4   Characteristics of learning organizations

What takes place in a learning organization? What makes it different from other organizations? Below we sketch out some of the features of learning organizations, as proposed by researchers and consultants.

John Donegan, Development and Training Manager of British Petroleum, suggests four qualities that, for British Petroleum, characterize a learning organization (Donegan, 1990):

- Recognition that organizations must adapt to a future of constant change.
- Acceptance of the key role of people in this process of adaptation.
- Facilitation of the learning and personal development of all people in the organization through a truly empowering culture.
- The use of the combined energy, creativity and commitment generated among employees by this developmental climate to fuel an ongoing process of organizational transformation.

Pedler et al. (1989) have identified the four characteristics of a "learning company". They suggest that a learning company is one which:

- has a climate in which individual members are encouraged to learn and to develop their full potential: people perform beyond their competence, taking initiatives, using and developing their intelligence and being themselves in the job, and which
- extends this learning culture to include customers, suppliers and other significant stakeholders wherever possible: some total quality programmes for example have buyer-supplier workshops, invite customers to in-organization training and development programmes and so on, but which also
- makes human resource development strategy central to business policy, so that the processes of individual and organizational learning become a major business activity: e.g. as in IBM where the CEO is reputed to have said "Our business is learning and we sell the by-products of that learning", which involves
- a continuous process of organizational transformation which harnesses the fruits of individual learning to make fundamental changes in assumptions, goals, norms and operating procedures on the basis of an internal drive to self-direction and not simply reactively to external pressures.

An analysis of the above suggestions allows us to describe the characteristics of learning organizations in terms of different levels. At the level of the individual, the main emphasis is on learning opportunities. The main learning arena of the individual lies at a junction between learner-centred development and organizational transformation in which the individual takes an active part. As regards training, it is important that all members of the organization have access to training, regardless of what level they are at in the organization.

At the level of the individual's job, emphasis is on responsibility and meaningfulness. As stated previously, individuals enjoy doing what they are good at. They also have a need to make sense of what goes on around them, such as to understand how the organization makes use of individual contributions in dealing with the outside environment. Learning organizations tend to offer flexibility in the shaping of jobs. New functions are rapidly created in response to the combined needs of external markets and abilities of people.

At the level of the organization, an essential characteristic is readiness for change — the ability to respond to signals internal to the organization as well as from the external environment. Being ready for constant change means being able to readily mobilize the human resources to take on new challenges. There are two main elements which relate to organizational learning. One is an organizational culture where people are seen as indispensable agents of change, whatever level they are at. The other element is flexibility of structure, which allows teams across functions and departments to be mounted efficiently for special tasks or projects.

18.5   Organizational learning in large projects

Management of large complex projects is a management task that requires advanced management and leadership skills. Project management training has been mainly focused on project administration, tools for project administration and cost control and very little on the dynamics of a project. It is also known that major investments in the training of project managers have been made in a number of companies with very small return. A visible effect in increased profit margins or timely delivery as a result of the project management training is needed. With tougher competition, tighter schedules, global sourcing and an increasing mix of nationalities in project teams, a new approach has to be used in order to ensure a significant project output. Therefore, with very high demands on the project manager and the team members, it is becoming increasingly difficult to "train first" and then do the job. It is a necessity to find a way to:

- develop skills and competence;
- ensure that improvements are made; and
- achieve significant results

at the same time as executing the project.

When a project starts, a process has to be designed in which the three points mentioned above will be ensured. Project management resources as well as other resources are scarce in most corporations. Therefore, it becomes critical that the process ensures maximum utilization of skills and competence that exist within the project team. A focus on continuous improvement must be ensured from the project's start until it is finalized. Here a mental change is needed. It is not enough to deliver a project on time and meet the customer's requirements and profit goals. It is a must that each project performs better than was planned and better than the previous one. The experience we have gained so far in a number of large projects clearly demonstrates not only an interest and willingness on the part of the project managers and team members to engage themselves in continuous improvement, but also a significant ability to achieve results in the execution of projects while changing and improving the way things are done.

18.6   The training function in learning organizations

An interesting aspect of conceiving learning organizations is that of the relationship between training and management. Because learning (individual or organizational) is central, there is a close relationship between training and managerial roles. A change in the training function will lead to a change of managerial roles, and vice versa. Between managerial roles and training functions stands the aspect of learning. Who is responsible for individual learning? Who is responsible for making sure that it is put to the productive use of the organization? How is this done? These are some of the questions that are central in the conception of learning organizations. Below we present some suggestions.

If an organization is to achieve effective learning, at individual and organizational levels, managers will be faced with roles different from those they normally occupy. We have mentioned above that learning organizations tend towards teamwork, an active participation of people in decision-making and increased empowerment of people.

Peter Senge (1990) suggests that in a learning organization, leaders are responsible for the learning of their subordinates. He says that "in a learning organization, leaders' roles differ dramatically from that of the (traditionally) charismatic decision-maker", and that "leaders are designers, teachers and stewards". Senge goes on to explain that these roles require new skills: "the ability to build shared vision, to bring to the surface and challenge prevailing mental models and to foster more systemic patterns of thinking".

In the role of designers, leaders act as architects of organizations, not by drawing boxes and lines, but by "designing governing ideas of purpose, vision and core values by which the people will live". Implicit in this role is the creation of functional organizations, such as teams of task forces in which there is a culture conducive to good performance. In the role of teachers, leaders help their subordinates, as coaches, guides or facilitators, to understand the workings of the organization, such as causes of problems and patterns of individual behaviour.

In the role of stewards, leaders build the bridge between people's needs and aspirations and the achievement of the overall goals of the organization. They are trying to diminish the potential contradiction between the needs of the individuals and the interests of the organization.

An important aspect other than the managerial roles is that of the place of the training function within the organizational structure. This aspect contains two main elements, the first being the relationship between the training function and organizational units, and the second being the way in which training is incorporated into the organizational strategy.

In the more traditional type of organization, the training function takes much of the responsibility for developing the individual. What it means in many cases is that the training function offers what it thought was appropriate for building certain skills. The people in the organization are then able, in collaboration with their superiors, to select the programmes that they think are interesting. As it turns out, much of the training is selected by individuals to achieve their own private goals, rather than to improve the performance of their unit. The learning organization, on the other hand, has to respond to demands by making sure that the competences of its members are fully used. It is, therefore, an assumption of the learning organization that training is used as an additional means of ensuring readiness for change. The needs for training are determined by the individual in consultation with peers, based on the needs of his or her unit.

The second important element of the relationship between the training function and the organizational structure is the way in which the training is linked with corporate goals and strategy. Donegan (1990) argues that with the emergence of learning organizations, the opportunity now exists to place the training function firmly where it belongs — at the centre of the strategic management processes. Furthermore, it is now in a position to translate the values and directions of organizational change into an integrated human resource strategy which will facilitate the change.

This is in line with what Burgoyne (1988) calls step 6 on a management development stepladder: total integration between management development and corporate policy is achieved through management development processes, which enhance the nature of corporate policy-forming processes, which they also inform and help implement.

There is also a general tendency for companies adopting the characteristics of learning organizations to have a stronger representation of the training function at board level. This helps ensure that the management development aspect is incorporated from the beginning in strategic decisions of, say, markets, products or services.

18.7 The trainer and the learning organization

For many companies with their own training staff, moving towards a learning organization model would require that they revise the roles and the skills of their trainers. Learning organizations require more than programmed training. They require knowledge and skills in their trainers that help them to identify obstacles to learning and change, which may be in their culture as well as in the information systems they use.

Hence there is a need to develop the roles and skills of trainers towards a more sophisticated level. There is a need to develop trainers' consultancy skills. When consulting with responsible managers, for example, the trainer needs to be able to elicit from the manager some fundamental causes of the problems he or she is describing, then be able to translate the problem into training and non-training (i.e. consultancy or organizational change) components. This again requires that the trainers have a good understanding of how the organization functions as a social system.

It also requires that he or she understand the impact of training and consultancy in organizational change. Barham and Rassam (1989) suggest that as trainers will be seen more as internal consultants, their roles will be expanded from course instruction to include activities like facilitating group events, individual counselling, and the provision of learning resources and consultancy support.

In a learning organization, the trainer is seen more as an agent of change, i.e. someone who understands the nature of change and who can help facilitate change, rather than someone who merely espouses "the best practice" to managers.

The expansion of the roles and skills of trainers in the direction of internal consultants does not imply reduced focus on programmed training. However, what may change is the process of identifying needs for programmed training. The needs identification is done as a process of consultation and joint analysis with responsible managers. Changes in and around the company will to a great extent be used as a basis for selection of topics for programmed training. Programmes tend to be short, but with a broad range of topics, in order to be used in a flexible way. Finally, in companies with characteristics of the learning organization, there tend to be programmes focusing directly on topics like culture, teamwork and organizational change.

18.8 Approaches and programmes for learning organizations

Some examples of activities that can be considered common and appropriate to learning organizations have been selected from experience and the literature as follows:

- The training methods tend towards consultancy-type interventions.

- They attempt to provide managers with a perspective on the working of the organization as a system, vis-à-vis its people and the external environment.

- They emphasize managers' social interaction skills.

- They are mostly based on working with the managers' realities or highly realistic simulations. Hence, they tend to make more use of approaches like experiential learning and process consultancy rather than more traditional training methods.

Approaches that are specific to learning organizations have a primary objective to enable managers to set up and manage learning organizations successfully — i.e. organizations facilitating maximum learning for the individual, while being able to readily transform themselves. In order to achieve the objective of developing managers' ability to run learning organizations, the training should include certain elements. The organizations could generally increase their ability to learn through learning about organizational learning; promoting experimentation; and regulating awareness.

Learning about organizational learning would, in the context of training, mean that managers are given the means to understand the concept of organizational learning. At the same time, managers have to get a good grasp of what it entails. It will, for many of them, change the way they look at their jobs, and the way they relate to their organizations.

Promoting experimentation allows managers to test behaviours and systems and the effects they have on organizational learning. The description by Senge (1990) of learning laboratories given in the next section serves as an example, in that he describes highly realistic simulations for management teams, where they can practise in a low-risk setting away from their daily work.

Regulating awareness is a motivational factor. It means making managers appreciate the importance of building and maintaining learning organizations.

Learning laboratories: Practice fields for management teams

One of the most promising new tools is the learning laboratory or "micro-world": constructed microcosms of real-life settings in which management teams can learn how to learn together. The vision guiding current research in management learning laboratories is to design and construct effective practice fields for management teams. Much remains to be done, but the broad outlines are emerging.

First, since team learning in organizations is an individual-to-individual and individual-to-system phenomenon, learning laboratories must combine meaningful business issues with meaningful interpersonal dynamics. Either alone is incomplete.

Second, the factors that are obstacles to learning about complex business issues must be eliminated in the learning laboratory. Chief among these is the inability to experience the long-term, systemic consequences of key strategic decisions. We all learn best from experience, but we are unable to experience the consequences of many important organizational decisions. Learning laboratories remove this constraint through system dynamics simulation games that compress time and space.

Third, new learning skills must be developed. One constraint on learning is the inability of managers to reflect insightfully on their own assumptions and to enquire effectively into each other's assumptions. Both skills can be enhanced in a learning laboratory, where people can practise surfacing assumptions in a low-risk setting. However, a note of caution should be made: it is far easier to design entertaining learning than it is to have an impact on real management practices and firm traditions outside the learning laboratory. Research on management simulations has shown that they often have greater entertainment value than educational value. One of the reasons appears to be that many simulations do not offer deep insights into the systemic structures which cause business problems. Another reason is that they do not foster new learning skills. Also, there is no connection between experiments in the learning laboratory and real-life experiments. These are significant problems that research on learning laboratory design is now addressing.

Process consultancy as training for learning organizations

Labor Ltd. — a Norway-based action-learning firm — uses an approach which they call the "learning organization". The method is used in open programmes, with managers coming from different organizations, as well as for in-house programmes (see Chapter 11).

The basic feature of the approach is to assume that the group of participants (normally between 12 and 20) forms an "organization". This "organization" is given tasks and objectives which it has to achieve within certain time-limits. As with any group of people trying to complete a task while under pressure, a series of complications arise, such as who should be in charge, what work method should be adopted, etc. There are also interpersonal issues that arise, such as unresolved disagreements, power struggles, digressions from the theme of discussion, lack of listening, etc. Frustration builds up, for some members because the task is not getting done, for others because of the way they work together.

The facilitators help the group, not by telling them what to do in order to work better, but by enabling them to put their finger on what is not working well.

The group is confronted with a dilemma to which learning organizations are sensitive, namely, how to respond to the individual group member while at the same time responding to externally imposed change. The externally imposed change is simulated by the tasks that are given and by the limitations of time which are characteristic of business environments. The extent to which the group responds to the individual is registered, either as the individuals express their feelings, or, if they don't, as observations by the facilitators.

In this way, the participants learn primarily about things that hinder or facilitate group performance and secondly about the management of groups. Although they experience all this in their companies, it is not easily observed through the maze of activities, priorities and interruptions of everyday work. In the "learning organization" method, group performance and group interaction become visible, as transparency is created by the facilitators, i.e. people can see what keeps them from accomplishing specific tasks. In fact, some participants have said that "we have these problems in our workplace every day, but we don't seem to be able to do anything about them".

There are three particular aspects of management which are illuminated in the method. One is decision-making, such as who makes decisions, and what are the effects of the way in which decisions are made. Emphasis is on participation in the decision-making process, e.g. is it balanced, and are the views expressed by members taken into account, or is there a bias which is manipulated towards the preferences of certain members? A second aspect is that of clarification of expectations, that is, the clarification of the needs of individual members in relation to the overall task of the group. The focus is on the potential incompatibility between individual needs and organizational goals. As we have stressed previously, learning organizations strive to diminish this incompatibility. A third aspect is that of leadership in learning organizations. The exercise brings out perspectives on the functions and skills of leaders in learning organizations.

The approach is essentially a training exercise, because the principal aim is to develop the participants' skills and attitudes. The group works on solving problems that are created by the facilitators, and not on their own, daily work problems, which differentiates it from a consultancy intervention. In the case of in-house training interventions, they sometimes work on issues that concern their own organization. One example is where they have to elaborate together a set of the five most important criteria of good leadership for their company. However, the element of process consultancy is central to the approach, because it makes the participants aware of what impedes and what facilitates performance in an organization which has to respond to imposed change.

The ABB case

This is a description of a training consultancy programme that was run by International Leadership (Switzerland) for Asea Brown Boveri (ABB). It illustrates a type of programme which helps project managers develop project organizations that respond readily to customer needs while learning and inspiring the best from their people.

Over a three-year period just before the time of writing a "Project Performance Process" (PPP) had been developed and applied in large power plants in ABB (order value of 150 to 500 million US dollars and a delivery time of 18 to 36 months). In the Thermal Power Generation segment of the ABB business, power generation solutions are sold throughout the world. This is a highly competitive market, with major players in the United States, Europe and the Far East. Very often the specifications for implementation were aggressive, particularly with regard to the time-scale. As an example, a project would involve the installation of a 200 to 300 megawatt power plant producing power from gas and steam turbines in a combined cycle.

In the PPP, the following takes place:

When a contract is signed and the project manager and team members — normally about 15 to 20 people — are appointed for the project, each team member is interviewed by a consultant from International Leadership. The interviews aim at drawing out from each individual what they see as the critical issues in executing the project. Using their previous experience and knowledge of the current project, they then identify the issues that must be focused upon, or the specific areas where things must change or improve, in order to ensure an excellent project performance.

The interviews are also aimed at ensuring that the inputs from the team members will be the steering mechanism to ensure the true focus in the design of the project performance process. Interviews with several hundred project team members demonstrate that tremendous knowledge and experience exists even after only a few years in the business. However, the mechanism to use that knowledge and experience, most specifically to make significant changes in the organization in order to enhance project efficiency, is not sufficiently capitalized on. The majority of interviewees express a significant interest in participating in an improvement process throughout the projects.

When the interviews have been carried out, a summary of critical issues is made. Five to seven major areas of focus are defined with project management and business management, such as customer responsiveness, partnership with major suppliers/partners, improvement of profit, procurement and engineering efficiency, etc. Those major areas will then form the content of a seminar week, which is the start of the Project Performance Programme. This seminar week can be seen as an "extended kick-off" prior to which the project team members have acquired a basic knowledge of the project such as the scope and supply, delivery time, major contractual issues and project budget. During the seminar week the project team sets the scene to run the project successfully over the next 18 to 36 months.

Issues are addressed, action plans defined and commitment made to resolve the issues. During the seminar week, improvement tasks are identified whereby each individual decides upon a specific area within the project where he or she wants to improve and achieve specific improvement goals, such as schedule, specifications, purchase, cost, project management, etc.

The underlying theme is that the project team, at the beginning of the process (about six to eight weeks after the contract is signed), define all the parameters for success and put into place a review process through which excellence in execution will be secured. In the beginning of the PPP process, there is a strong focus on building the team, clarifying roles, identifying interrelationships, ensuring total knowledge of the project, a shared overall knowledge about the major issues to be resolved and an individual and joint commitment to resolving them, as well as to improving and achieving results better than planned.

The clients are invited to clarify their needs and issues for the team to establish customer-commitment. These commitments were made in groups, networks and parts of the overall group, with individuals and with consultants. This process gave maximum potential to giving total accountability to individuals and small teams of people. This, in fact, embodied a consensus-building process.

Every two to six months a project performance review would take place. The whole team, wherever they might be located, would be brought together and deviations from commitments would be reviewed with regard to potential implications and solutions.

Learning and improving while adhering to commitments are underlying themes. In the process following the first six to eight months, every new step in the execution of the project, such as construction, site works, commissioning and turnover, is regularly planned, equal to the start up of the project. Key people are identified, critical issues defined and a programme/process is designed to resolve issues and reinforce commitments to meet the project improvement goals.

In a number of projects, this intense focus on individual competence and motivation achieved significant improvements with regard to delivery on time, meeting customer requirements and reducing cost.

Some of the principles of the process run like this:

1. Every work objective would be regarded as a development opportunity to achieve both individual competence enhancement and the achievement of real measurable results for the organization.
2. Each individual or work group objective would be assessed at the beginning of a process and again after the application of inputs to achieve learning and competence enhancement.
3. Return on investment would be measured for each objective implemented throughout the process.
4. Learning and competence enhancement would be generated by networking small, inter-organization, geographic and intercultural networks of similar-level managers. Each of these teams or networks of managers would be focused on resolving critical business issues with high speed.
5. These independent groups and networks would be given both the time and resources to achieve objectives within their company responsibility area, as long as they could exhibit progression towards the forecasted return on investment identified at the commencement of the project.
6. Within this process, teams are allowed complete fluidity to utilize the top competences of each team member.
7. Leadership flows from one group member to another and is different under different stimuli and environmental conditions.
8. Teams would be allowed to act in a non-hierarchical manner within their organization and would be able to energize all levels of the organization, anywhere, in any function. This would ensure that objectives could be processed and achieved.
9. Continuous learning and competence enhancement, as well as the significant experience gained by intercompany, geographical and cultural networks would be actively transmitted around the whole of each interested organization.

This process facilitates the development of the truly organic organization within which the human element is paramount. Thus, a set of human competences networked within the organization can be utilized to maximum effect.

The Hewlett-Packard case

This case describes how a training programme enabled managers in Hewlett-Packard to achieve results with their self-designed projects, assisted by trainers and consultants. It illustrates how individuals can achieve effective learning through networking and information sharing.

Hewlett-Packard is regarded as an advanced organization in terms of people development. Throughout the 1980s a new management development process was created. All high-level managers (about 400 in all) responsible for running business entities in Europe were identified. A team of about 20 to 25 of them were invited to a management development process lasting six to seven months. This process would focus on critical issues identified by management such as competitiveness, customer satisfaction, leadership, management of change, etc. Each programme had participants with a different mix of experience from different functions and locations. These managers were requested to identify a focused short-term project to implement within their own area of responsibility during the programme. The managers attended the first part of the management development programme, a one-week seminar. Approximately 60 to 70 per cent of the programme was delivered in a lecturing and case-study mode to the participants. The remaining 30 to 40 per cent of the programme was focused upon individual managment projects. Participants worked in small networks based upon group self-learning and information exchange. In addition, each individual received consulting sessions from both internal Hewlett-Packard experts and external consultants. By the end of the week, each manager had developed a cohesive, comprehensive plan for the project's implementation and described it in front of the group. To achieve maximum commitment to results, the outlines of all projects were circulated to the top management of the HP-European organization and to the groups who attended the programme. Six months later, after implementation, the group came back together for two days and reviewed the results of projects and any deviations from the planned process (reductions of costs, increased market share, reduced throughput time, return on investment, etc.).

18.9 Conclusion

People are the true competitive advantage of learning organizations. Organizational control must be loosened significantly to allow competence to develop to its highest level and for implementation to be achieved in the most useful way.

Unfortunately the hierarchical nature of organizations, with all its baggage of status and structure, does not facilitate such a process. However, the early evidence is promising. Organizations are realizing that in order to compete in a global context they need to be flexible. Such evolutions do not happen easily, and many behavioural and structural barriers must be broken to achieve the effective organization of the 1990s.

What we have described in this chapter as learning organizations is a vision of a desired form of organization. The organization which learns fully at all levels may never exist. However, striving towards a state of permanent, higher-level learning is in itself valuable as a driving force for managers, consultants and trainers. The development of learning organizations should be one of the highest strategic objectives of a trainer with true vision.

The trainer's role in such an organization becomes vital. It moves from being responsible for training to helping the organization to perform better, and to creating a culture and systems which facilitate maximum mobilization of people's competence. The trainer becomes an agent of change, and hence an indispensable source of organizational sustainability.

OPEN AND DISTANCE LEARNING

19

Roger Lewis

This chapter explores the processes of management development through the means of open and distance learning. In so doing, it has to tackle a number of terminological difficulties including the definition of "open learning" and its relation to "self-development" and "distance learning".

First, "self-development". This has been an important strand in management development for some time (see, for example, Pedler et al., 1978, Boydell, 1985, and Chapters 10 and 26). The term self-development suggests that individuals themselves drive forward the development process by identifying their own needs, devising learning programmes, and evaluating the outcomes. The close link between this and open learning will become clear: both terms imply a prime focus on the aspirations and choices of the individual rather than the provider of education or training.

It is in the interest of an organization for individuals to develop the capability to "learn to learn" so they can engage in a process of continuous reskilling and development throughout their working lives. Within this context, self-development can be seen as a necessary route for individuals continuously to maintain and refurbish their skills, supported by their employers. Self-development has become a key issue in many effective organizations. A far-sighted company, wishing to retain its staff and respond to a competitive environment, will see the business benefits of employees who are independent and enterprising. The encouragement of self-help and learning at the operational level leads to a dramatic and sustained increase in the quality of services and products.

Thus self-development — a relatively vague and unfocused concept in the 1960s and 1970s — re-emerges as part of wider organizational development. This has reduced dramatically the gap between the individual and the organization.

Two other forces have contributed to the sharpening of self-development as a concept: growth of competences in organizing learning programmes, and the increasing importance of the formal acknowledgement of an individual's learning — i.e. accreditation. The two strands come together for example in national vocational qualifications whereby individuals can gain credit for discrete management competences, gained and demonstrated in a wide variety of ways, and without any necessity to engage in a *formal* learning process. Individuals can put credits together in a growing portfolio and, when they are ready, submit these for a larger award such as a certificate or diploma in management.

19.1 Open learning and self-development

The term "open learning" was first used in the late 1970s to describe any provision of education and training that actively sought to identify, and then to remove, barriers preventing certain groups from learning. These barriers included those endemic in conventional delivery of management development such as time (courses beginning and ending at set times of the day or the year), place (courses requiring the learner to attend an institution frequently and regularly) and pace (all learners having to study at the same pace). More significantly, for the topic of this chapter, barriers of educational design were also identified. These included rigid course structures, limiting learners' choice of *what* can be studied and how it can be studied; barriers of preset entry requirements; no learner choice of qualification; and lack of awareness or lack of confidence that may inhibit an individual from even considering learning in the first place.

In the early phase of open learning the first set of mainly logistical barriers was addressed: schemes such as the United Kingdom's Open University and Open Tech were designed to lessen or remove barriers of time, place and pace. Hence the importance of distance learning: through the provision of learning packages (mostly in printed form), management development could be delivered more or less anywhere and individuals could study at any time and at their own pace (see Keegan, 1986). In a distance-learning scheme, the course content is provided largely through specially designed materials supplemented by a tutor with whom the learner has to communicate for most of the time across a distance, by letter or telephone (or increasingly by e-mail), with only occasional face-to-face contact. This form of open learning uses a *dissemination orientation*. It is characterized by a relatively inflexible syllabus and course structure.

As we shall see, distance learning and open learning are not synonymous. Some open learning schemes involve learners in easy and frequent face-to-face contact with the tutor and other learners and/or other supporters to learning, such as line managers. Instead of a fixed syllabus, transmitted by materials, more open schemes allow greater learner participation in objective-setting and ways of learning. In contrast to the dissemination orientation of distance learning, such schemes show a *development orientation*. More recently open learning schemes have thus tackled the barriers of educational design, focusing on widening learner choice of what is learned, how it is learned and how learning is supported. Thus open learning is now generally associated not so much with removing administrative barriers to learning as with providing increased choice to learners across a wider front: choice potentially over all aspects of the learning process and at all stages in the learner's career. Table 19.1 shows three stages: entry to learning, during the learning and at the end of learning, and typical choices the individual may have to, or be encouraged to, make at each stage.

Table 19.1. The three stages of learning choice

New learners		Learners leaving
Entry processes	*Learning*	*Final assessment processes*
Why do I learn? Who can learn? What do I learn? →	How? Where? When? Who can help? How successful is my learning? →	How successful is my learning? What do I do next?

The link between "self-development" and "open learning" should by now be more clear. Both terms suggest more a philosophy than a methodology of learning. Any provider of management education through open learning must be driven by a need to help the individual use those freedoms seen as necessary in a particular context if learning is to take place. In practice, of course, much learning is negotiated, not only between learner and provider, but also with a sponsoring employer. Negotiation is also a key part of management itself and the acts of negotiating a study contract, setting objectives, allocating resources and checking progress are thus particularly appropriate in management development.

In practice, total choice over all aspects of learning is usually impossible, not only for practical reasons but also because this may not necessarily be desirable for the learner. Total freedom in assessment dates has, for example, often been found to paralyse rather than to motivate the learner. Choice is thus relative. What is important in any given case is, first, over what aspects of learning choice is given; and, secondly, how much choice is given.

Each of the basic questions in table 19.2 can be unpacked into its component parts and set on a continuum (Lewis and Spencer, 1986). On the far left-hand side, choice is non-existent, on the far right, choice is total. Most schemes fit somewhere in between. It is possible to break each part down, as in the examples in table 19.3.

This framework can be used to analyse any open learning management development scheme. Two familiar models are examined briefly below: the open enrolment programme operated by many institutions, often using distance delivery; and the in-company provision where a company runs or commissions the provision of a management programme for its own employees.

Open enrolment

Who?	Relatively open; few restrictions placed on entry.
Why?	Choice to study lies with the individuals, although this may be influenced, for example, by their employer (who may also offer to pay or part-pay the fees if the learner demonstrates success).
Where?	Packaged materials make the course portable. Attendance at day or residential schools may limit this aspect of openness.
When?	This aspect of choice may be limited, since enrolment may only take place once or twice in the year for reasons of administration.

Table 19.2. The function of choice in designing open learning

No choice		Maximum choice
Who can help the learner?	No support outside course package	Variety of possible kinds of support (e.g. advice, guidance, counselling)
	Only professional supporters	Non-professional as well as formal support encouraged (e.g. mentor, friends, family)
	Support available in one mode only, e.g. face to face	Support available in a variety of modes, e.g. letter, telephone, e-mail, face-to-face
	Regular fixed attendance required	Learner can attend or not, as desired
Where?	Practical work requires fixed attendance	Practical work offered through kits and/or drop-in access and/or place of work itself
	One place only (e.g. at work)	Learner chooses place (e.g. home, work, while travelling)
	Support available only in one place (e.g. training centre)	Support available in many places

Table 19.3. Examples of the degree of choice in open learning design

	1	2	3	4
Objectives	Objectives set in advance: no choice possible	Compulsory "core" objectives, learner chooses any additional objectives	Learner negotiates objectives with tutor	Learner formulates objectives
Starting date	Fixed annual date	Limited number of starting dates	Wide choice of starting dates	Start any time
Assessment methods	Externally fixed methods of assessment; no negotiation	Some choice available as to method, but only in special cases	Learner chooses between wide range of assessment activity	Learner constructs methods of demonstrating competence

| Who can help the learner? | Again systems may limit the degree to which variety is possible. Often a tutor will be supplied; other support will be very much up to the learner to organize. |

In-company

Who and why?	Learners' choice may be limited; they may be put on to the programme by the employer.
Where?	If learning is taking place on company time, choice may not be given here, especially if fixed equipment is used (for example interactive video players).
When?	Specially designed courses can be mounted at a time to suit the company; it will thus not be necessary to await the start of an open course.
Who can help the learner?	Again, the tailored nature of an in-company management development course means that potentially a wide range of "helpers" can be provided and briefed — for example, an external tutor, an in-company trainer, a line manager, a mentor, a learning centre administrator. More formally provided support can thus be provided than is often the case in open enrolment schemes.

Conclusion

These are only two examples of the possible range of approaches. As we shall see, there are many alternatives, such as the way new management schemes of an open enrolment type are using computer-mediated communication to seek to overcome some of the individual isolation often present in distance delivery.

It is important also to acknowledge that many traditional courses have "open" characteristics, for example:

- choice of topic may be given within the course;
- learners may work for some time at their own pace;
- projects may be used for relating the course to the individual's circumstances; and
- assessment can — up to a point — be negotiated.

What is new about open learning is the explicit identification of learner choice as critical and the systematic attempt to increase it.

19.2   The benefits of open learning

Accounts such as that by Northcott (1986) show the increasing use of open learning in management education. Why is this mode of delivery becoming so popular? The different participants in the learning process would point to the different benefits provided by open learning.

The learners often stress the flexibility of open learning provision. Study can be fitted into busy lives. The anonymity of learning is another advantage for learners who dislike the class component of conventional education — for example, they may fear being "shown up" by others. Open learning give learners the feeling that the scheme is specifically designed for them; it allows room for substantial personal input. In addition, open learning schemes often put a premium on links with the work environment, via projects and activities carried out with the support of workplace staff, such as managers. The learning can be brought right into the workplace in a way harder to arrange with conventional delivery in an off-site lecture room; it is more readily perceived as "relevant", and can more easily be applied — important in an area where the development of competence is usually sought.

Companies also value the flexibility of open learning. Open learning can be used to match the higher rate of change in business units with changing programmes which are adequately responsive and flexible. The provision of a learning package attracts some companies. They can, for example, see exactly what they are getting: open learning is more transparent than conventional training. Learning packages of the highest national quality can be selected, and performance standards throughout the company can be made consistent. Packages make it easier for line managers to support the training and help their staff, thus contributing to a company-wide learning culture.

Open learning also has simple practical advantages to an organization: training can be provided immediately, for example, to just one new employee, or to physically scattered managers, and some training costs (for example travel and hotel bills) can be substantially reduced. Learners can study while working, upgrading their skills while still making an economic contribution.

Open learning has attractions, too, learning professionals such as trainers and lecturers. Freed from the burdens of routine instruction, they can focus on developing the skills of facilitation and assessment, and can take on new roles, such as adapting learning packages and accrediting prior learning. Open learning enables training professionals to respond to demands from both employers and individuals to support continuous lifelong development.

19.3   The disadvantages of open learning

A number of disadvantages of open learning as a mode of delivering management education are often quoted. Some of these are based on misconceptions. Open learning does not, for example, necessarily mean that individual learners are isolated (peer contact and tutorial support are possible); and open learning is not necessarily confined to the highly literate (media other than print can be used). In this section, more substantial potential disadvantages are considered.

In conventional delivery of management education, the trainer can adapt instantly to the varied needs of the particular group. These needs can include differing knowledge of the subject, degree of confidence, learning readiness, intellectual sophistication, experience of management. An open learning approach, particularly one relying heavily on standard learning packages, is not able to adapt so quickly.

The interpersonal skills of the manager can also be better developed in conventional delivery. These skills require interaction, either "for real" (in the workplace) or through simulation, by using role-play or other similar training devices. Clearly, when learners are physically gathered together, the interaction is easier to achieve than in open learning.

These potential disadvantages of open learning — lack of tailoring to the individual, interpersonal skill development — can be overcome with careful design and development, but the latter may require a significant investment. High quality learning materials, together with the required support, do not come cheaply. To derive the benefits of open learning quoted earlier may commit an organization, not only in terms of capital (for example interactive video players, computers) but also in time and effort. To benefit sufficiently from this, the organization would probably need to convert a substantial part of its conventional delivery to open learning to benefit from economies of scale. Attitude change can be the biggest obstacle of all for users of new learning methods.

An example which illustrates some advantages and disadvantages of open learning is EKOPLAN, a computer-based distance learning programme for owners of small businesses in Sweden and Norway. The programme, which is based at Stockholm University, lends personal computers to the learners. The learners communicate via modem with the central computer in Stockholm, which helps them to calculate financial ratios of companies, based on the figures they provide. The EKOPLAN programme can compute 28 different financial ratios for the company, and thus enable the business owners to identify their firm's weak and strong points. To go with EKOPLAN, there is a computer application called ECOMARK to teach marketing and about planning marketing operations. ECOMARK also includes training modules on the theory of marketing. Local study groups of small business owners have also been created within the programme, who in some cases have made use of local teachers as support. In essence, the EKOPLAN/ECOMARK system is a theory-based programme providing the learners with instruments from economic theory to analyse their companies. At the same time it is experience based, in the sense that the learners use their own company data in the calculations.

The evaluation illustrates potential advantages and disadvantages of technology-based open learning. The major advantages expressed by the learners were:

- The topic and the material provided were relevant to their needs.
- They appreciated being able to communicate with the central computer at any time of the day.
- The database provided by the central computer on economic theory was found very useful.

The major disadvantages were:

- The level of knowledge of economic theory assumed by the system designers was too high for some of the participants.

- Instead of helping them to analyse and solve problems in depth, the system only provided theory-based tools to solve parts of the problems.
- Disturbances on the telecommunications network created considerable problems for communication via modem.

19.4 Learning materials

Mention "open learning" and many people immediately think of substantial learning packages. This is especially so for distance schemes, where the materials are often used to carry a high informational content, leaving occasional face-to-face sessions to cover interpersonal skills. The presumption that the role of the materials is only to convey information is limiting: in practice, open learning materials carry out a variety of roles. This section explores the function of materials, how materials can be selected and adapted, and considers the role of different media.

(A)   The function of learning materials

Open learning materials differ from conventional resources such as textbooks, in that they are expected to perform a number of the functions a good tutor would carry out in a well-run seminar. In the absence of frequent and regular face-to-face contact with a lecturer or trainer, the materials may be expected to:

- arouse interest;
- make clear the learning objectives;
- organize the content in a manageable way;
- give learners chances to practise;
- provide feedback on this practice;
- explain difficult or unfamiliar ideas or processes;
- relate learning to practical contexts; and
- build learners' confidence and independence.

Thus packages designed for use in open learning usually include features such as the following:

- spacious layout and good use of illustrations (tables, diagrams, photographs, etc.);
- an attractive and direct writing style;
- an explicit statement of objectives;
- short sections for ease of study;
- plenty of questions and practical activities, together with helpful feedback; and
- the use of a variety of media.

Decisions about the choices available to the learner will partly determine which of these features are important within a particular package. Some examples are shown in table 19.4.

Table 19.4. Choices in open learning and their implications for materials

Area of choice	Implications for materials
Learner to choose selection of content within the package and the order in which it is to be learnt. Learner to choose medium for learning.	Diagnostic/pre-tests; quizzes, etc., to help the learner to use this choice. Provision of a number of media; learner guided to make appropriate personal choice.
Learner to choose location of learning.	Learning media must be portable to enable use in many different locations (home, work, travelling, etc.)
Learner to choose from a variety of supporters (e.g. tutor, trainer, line manager).	Materials need to refer to the full range of possible supporters and the context in which each may work.

In addition, the philosophy underlying the programme and its syllabus will affect the nature of the materials; for example a course on managing change could at one extreme be theoretically based with a high information load and at the other be intensely activity-oriented and practical in emphasis. Other factors affecting the nature of materials will include:

- characteristics and context of the learner group (e.g. their previous experiences of management study, the circumstances in which they are learning);
- support provided in addition to the learning materials themselves; and
- practical constraints (e.g. budget).

(B)   Selection of learning materials

Wherever possible it makes sense to use existing materials. There are a number of reasons for this. First, to use existing material means that a scheme can be set up quickly. Secondly, an increasing number of high-quality management packages are now available, using a variety of media, and these can either be used as they stand or adapted. Thirdly, to generate new material is time-consuming and expensive, requiring a wide range of skills and experience.

The sequence for selecting materials is summarized below:

- Analyse the target group and their needs.
- Decide the characteristics of learning materials needed.
- Search for suitable packages.
- Examine packages against relevant criteria.
- Buy in and use suitable packages.

(C) Adapting materials

Your search for a suitable existing package may not be totally successful. You may, however, find one that *nearly* meets your needs. Adaptation is the modification of a standard learning package to better suit the specific requirements of an organization, whether a company delivering to its own staff, or a provider offering a management programme to the open market. Adaptation allows an organization to benefit from an existing package, often expensively developed, while at the same time gaining added value relevant to a particular context. Adaptation might, for example:

- Improve content (e.g. by updating, by adding new concepts).

- Modify content better to suit a company's management development style and culture (e.g. by changing terminology; by introducing different activities or projects, enabling users to apply their learning more easily).

- Dress a generic package in a particular user's colours (e.g. by using a company's logo, by featuring the chief executive on video).

- Help a learner group, for whom the package was not originally intended, to use the package productively (e.g. by adding an introductory learning skills module to help adults gain confidence in returning to formal study; by building in references to extra supporters such as tutors and mentors).

Adaptation can thus cover a wide range of actions. Some examples are set out below:

- A major public utility is using a standard open learning text for its junior and middle managers; the text is changed in one respect only — the organization's name is printed on the covers of the material.

- A bank is using a pack on developing writing skills, in an adapted form. In the original, answers to self-assessment questions were printed immediately after the questions themselves; in the adaptation the answers have all been removed to the back of the book. A section of the original material has been entirely removed in the adapted version, since it was not relevant to the bank employees.

- A chain of pharmacists is using standard open learning material to help its managers interpret and use financial data. The standard pack is augmented by an additional booklet containing company-specific material and procedures as well as new assignments.

- A water authority selected management topics from a wide range of publicly available material and asked the publisher to present the content in a new, company-specific desktop-published form. The opportunity was taken to add some entirely new material.

The easiest form of adaptation is the addition of new components to an existing product. The components may be short and simple (a few pages) or more complex (a new videotape or piece of computer-based learning). One component from a pack can be removed and replaced with another component (for example an audiotape from a published pack can be replaced with a wholly new audiotape).

The most expensive form of adaptation is usually to change the core resources themselves rather than simply to remove or replace them. Open learning publishers are, however, growing more sophisticated in materials planning and are "designing-in" opportunities for later adaptation.

So far we have covered the physical adaptation of the materials themselves. It is often easier, however, to adapt programmes by altering the support provided with them. For example:

- more tutorial time can be provided than the original learning material envisaged;
- additional supporters can be added, for example a tutor can be supplemented by a line manager carrying out assessment of management competences in the workplace;
- as well as face-to-face sessions, a telephone hot line can be provided for learners to raise difficulties that require immediate resolution;
- electronic mail or computer conferencing can be used to conduct continuing learner-tutor and learner-learner contact.

Such developments can be supported by guidance notes to the various parties, for example an assignment booklet for learners, assessment notes for line managers, advice to tutors on how to supplement sections of the learning material found difficult by learners. These issues are explored more fully in the later section on support.

(D) Media

In traditional correspondence courses, print is the only medium used. This has undoubtedly hampered the more widespread use of open learning in management education: potential learners and companies have formed the mistaken belief that open learning is just another name for correspondence courses, that it is unsuitable for developing skills, and that it is a second-best form of learning. Increasingly, open learning materials for management development include a range of media. This is partly the result of increased sophistication in the design of learning materials generally; partly the requirements of clients, who are becoming increasingly demanding in their expectations of what open learning materials should include; and partly the need to help learners develop and apply competences as well as to acquire information. Finally, technological developments provide an opportunity to use a greater variety of media than was the case a few years ago. However, print remains the staple medium, although the standard management pack now includes other ingredients. Some of these are set out in table 19.5.

A mixed media approach helps cover the full range of management skills. For example, managers can be taught speaking skills by audio cassette; the computer can simulate real-life decision-making, allowing the learner to manipulate a number of variables.

Table 19.5. Items and functions of open learning

Item	Function
Course texts or "workbooks"	These contain the core learning material.
Audio cassettes	These can be used for interviews with experts, case-studies, real-life examples, discussions, taking the learner through complex operations such as reading financial statements, or as aids to revision.
Video/compact discs	These can be used to show case-studies of managers in their working environments and to model interpersonal skills.
A user guide	This helps learners to integrate the different components of the programme.
An assessment booklet	This contains assignments, work-based projects and advice on gaining qualifications.

Practicalities must, however, be remembered. While it may be the case, for example, that complex media such as interactive video may be best for teaching a particular skill, this is of no use if learners do not have easy access to the right equipment. Print remains the core ingredient in most open learning schemes for many good practical reasons: it is relatively inexpensive to produce, it is portable and can be used anywhere, and it does not require access to any physical equipment.

19.5 Support

(A) What is "support"?

"Support" is defined in *The A-Z of open learning* (Jeffries et al., 1990), as "help available to a learner in addition to learning materials". The entry points out that "an exciting feature of current open learning" (and management education is no exception) "is the use of a variety of types and modes of support to help learners apply their learning to work". The help can be varied and may include encouragement, counselling, assessment, feedback, advice, access to learning experiences; and it can be provided by a variety of means including face-to-face, post and telephone; by a range of people including learning professionals (for example, tutors), managers, mentors and fellow-learners. Of the two ingredients — learning materials and support — the latter is now generally regarded as the more important; the belief that learning packages can *on their own* bring about significant learning, prevalent in the United Kingdom in the early 1980s, is now discredited.

(B) What support will learners need?

It is important for practical reasons (notably cost) to provide only the support learners will actually use and to provide it in the most time-effective way. The tutor will, for example, often be the most expensive component of any support system so, wherever possible, a provider of management education will want to use the tutor only for those forms of support which cannot be provided by less expensive means. It is also important to provide support that is effective: a tutor is unlikely, for example, to provide the kind of immediate job-related help that a line manager is well placed to give.

The first task is, then, to identify what support learners will need and will use. How this shall be provided, and by whom, can then be explored. Decisions about the support needed may depend on a number of factors, similar to those considered in the previous section in relation to learning materials. These include:

- the characteristics of the target learner group (for example: Are they young and well qualified? Are they used to formal study? Are they likely to lack confidence?);

- the context in which they are learning (for example: Are they studying in a learning centre at work, with the full support of their managers? Are they studying entirely at home, unsupported by an employer?);

- the programme (for example: Is it largely of a learning theoretical/academic nature or is it seeking to develop competences for immediate application in the workplace?); and

- the learning materials (for example: Is access needed to computer and video players to use the materials? Is frequent reference made to workplace projects?).

The kind of support learners may need will also depend on the choices that are to be made available to them. Some examples of the choices, and implications for support needs, are set out in table 19.6.

Table 19.6. Choices and supports

Choice	Possible support need
Learners are given a choice of ways of showing their competence	Assistance in choice of most appropriate method(s)
Learners can choose their own supporters (tutor, line manager, colleague, counsellor, etc.)	Help in deciding who, in the learner's situation, is best placed to provide different kinds of support
Learners can choose when to study	Construction of a study timetable

The choices to be made available to the learner will have implications for the selection and training of the supporters. Academic staff may, for example, be required to act as catalyst, counsellor or facilitator; used as they often are to lecturing, they may need training in unfamiliar roles.

Once the required support has been defined, the next step is to decide how to provide it. There are a number of possible sources of support. Among them are people and non-personal sources. It is possible, first, to build support into the learning materials themselves. An encouraging tone can be adopted, for example, and help can be given with learning strategies. In setting a task, the learner can be given help in tackling it. The Open University incorporates such help systematically into some of its courses. Ancillary resources can be provided, such as learner guides, study guides, introductory cassettes, the main purpose of which is to support the learner through encouragement, advice and reassurance.

Help can also be provided via technology. Learners can, for example, access information databases, communicate with other course participants via electronic mail, and have multiple choice questions marked by computer. Such developments — seen as increasingly important by some providers of management education — are discussed more fully in the final section of this paper.

Learners may also be able to gain help from local institutions such as libraries, colleges, local learning centres or careers offices. The most important single source of support in most schemes is, however, people.

(C) Supporters

People from diverse backgrounds can be used to help the learner. These include a tutor (from the providing centre, such as a college or university), a counsellor (again, from the providing centre or maybe working in the learner's company), the learner's manager, other learners on the programme, peers at work, an in-company trainer, friends and family.

It is possible to set out some of the dimensions on a continuum. The left and right hand sides of table 19.7 show extremes: there are many possible intermediate points. Neither extreme is "right" or "wrong": everything depends on the nature of the learners and the scheme, as discussed earlier.

Table 19.7. Ranges of support

Professional (e.g. an academic, a subject-specialist)	Non-professional (e.g. a spouse with no qualifications in the subject of study)
Provided as an integral part of the course (e.g. a tutor whose services are included in the cost of the course)	Activated entirely by learners themselves (e.g. self-help group)
Available at set times (e.g. residential workshops)	Available on demand (in a learning workshop with additional telephone hot-line)
Provided in only one mode (e.g. postal contact)	Provided in a variety of modes (e.g. postal, face-to-face, electronically)
Supporter playing one role only (e.g. tutor who grades for award purposes)	Supporter playing many roles (e.g. tutor who assesses, gives feedback, encourages, and coaches in skill development)

(D)   Selection and training of supporters

The role of the supporter has implications for the way in which supporters are selected, briefed and trained, and then themselves supported. The organization responsible for running the programme clearly has most influence over, and responsibility for, sources of support provided as an integral part of the programme. Thus, for example, if each learner has a tutor, and the cost of those services is built into the price of the programme, it will be the responsibility of the providing organization to:

- decide what support the tutor is to provide;
- decide how the support is to be made available (medium, frequency, duration, etc.);
- calculate the cost of this support (and price it accordingly);
- draw up a specification for the tutor;
- recruit the tutor;
- brief the successful applicant;
- provide any necessary training;
- provide any necessary materials (for example a tutors' guide covering such things as assessment and running of workshops);
- provide ongoing support (for example a tutors' newsletter, occasional meetings, someone in the providing organization whom the tutor can contact by telephone);
- monitor performance; and
- arrange payment.

Other supporters may be outside the direct control of the providing organization but nevertheless be a key to the learners' success. Line managers in the learners' company may, for example, act as mentors or coaches. For such staff, the provider may prepare support materials or may persuade the employer of these staff to run or fund a training workshop. Some supporters may be even further beyond formal control, for example learner self-help groups (Stuart, 1984).

A new qualification, the Certificate in Open Learning Delivery (COLD), provides the framework for many of the above tasks. The Certificate is built around *Standards for performance in open learning*, published by the Training Agency (United Kingdom) after extensive consultation within the open learning industry. This framework enables a provider to:

- draw up a job specification, using relevant competences in the above Standards;
- select and recruit staff with the necessary capabilities;
- identify any training needs;
- design training events focused on particular competences;
- enable staff to achieve a national competence-based qualification (COLD is provided by three awarding bodies in the United Kingdom); and

- assess staff performance (for example, at annual appraisals).

Examples of COLD competence elements are given in table 19.8.

Table 19.8. COLD competence elements

Group 1
Find and select open learning package and programmes

1.1 Establish the learning and delivery requirements of a client

1.2 Specify the criteria for a package or programme for a defined group of learners

1.3 Select appropriate open learning materials for a defined target group

1.4 Specify the requirements for modification in existing materials to meet the needs of a given target population

1.5 Provide a plan for the achievement of any recommended modifications

Group 2
Design and develop open learning programmes

2.1 Define the target population of learners

2.2 Specify the requirements for a new programme for a defined target population

2.3 Demonstrate that open learning is an appropriate vehicle for acquiring the specified elements of competence

2.4 Develop learning objectives for each programme element

2.5 Specify the content and study requirements of the package

2.6 Select appropriate learning media

2.7 Develop effective open learning materials

2.8 Specify the guidance and support needed from all personnel concerned with each phase of delivery

2.9 Produce an assessment strategy for an open learning programme

2.10 Devise assessment activities for an open learning programme

2.11 Prepare a production plan

2.12 Allocate work to individuals

2.13 Manage the production process

2.14 Brief the technical production staff on design and layout requirements

2.15 Pilot the draft package to confirm that original requirements are met, amending as necessary

2.16 Prepare final draft ready for production

Group 3
Provide guidance and direction to learners

3.1 Agree with a potential learner his or her needs, expectations and goals

3.2 Agree to an open learning programme to satisfy learner needs

3.3 Agree to an action plan with a learner given an agreed open learning programme

3.4 Agree to a resource and tutorial support plan with a learner

3.5 Provide guidance to learners on approaches to effective learning

3.6 Provide guidance to learners upon completion of a programme

Group 4
Provide tutoring for individuals and groups of learners

4.1 Maintain tutor records of learner progress and difficulties

4.2 Monitor the learner's activity to assist progress

4.3 Provide additional assistance to a learner experiencing difficulty with the programme

4.4 Obtain and use feedback about the learner's experience of the programme to assist his or her progress

4.5 Obtain feedback of learner's experience of a programme to contribute towards future amendments in design or delivery

4.6 Provide feedback on learner activity to motivate and support the learner

4.7 Assess performance against stated criteria using prescribed methods

4.8 Plan tutorial sessions

4.9 Conduct tutorial sessions

4.10 Adopt a tutorial style for groups and individuals which maximizes learning opportunities

Group 5
Provide administrative services for an open learning scheme

5.1 Operate an information service for an open learning scheme

5.2 Enrol learners whose learning needs have been identified

5.3 Make arrangements for tutorial sessions

5.4 Store and distribute open learning materials

5.5 Maintain a booking system for equipment and other resources

5.6 Administer arrangements for the support of the learner

5.7 Maintain a record system for an open learning scheme

5.8 Administer arrangements for certification and accreditation

5.9 Deal with complaints

Group 6
Manage the resources of an open learning scheme

6.1 Allocate physical resources for an open learning scheme

6.2 Manage the premises of an open learning scheme

6.3 Control the acquisition and stock of all equipment and supplies

6.4 Operate effective employment policies and procedures for the directly employed staff

6.5 Operate effective employment policies and procedures for the use of contract labour

6.6 Maintain financial control policies and procedures

6.7 Maintain the operating standards of an open learning scheme

6.8 Produce systems for the evaluation of an open learning scheme

Group 7
Provide marketing services for an open learning scheme

7.1 Create a marketing strategy for open learning products and services

7.2 Prepare a sales plan for open learning products and services

7.3 Design a promotional strategy

7.4 Create an information system for open learning products and services

7.5 Establish product packaging requirements

7.6 Create a system for dealing with customer complaints

7.7 Evaluate market conditions and product performance

Group 8
Evaluate and validate an open learning scheme and its programmes

8.1 Plan the evaluation of an open learning scheme or any of its components

8.2 Evaluate an open learning scheme or any of its components

8.3 Validate an open learning package or programme

(E)   Marking and contact by post

Distance learning schemes often require the tutor to maintain contact with the learner by post. A vital role here is the provision of feedback via the marking of assignments. This requires the tutor to comment more rapidly and more fully than would probably be the case in a conventional learning relationship.

The tutor needs not only to spot mistakes but also to identify what caused them and to suggest to the learner ways of putting them right. Strengths in learners' work also need full recognition. Learners should be clear about the criteria used to measure their performance. Script marking is thus more elaborate than that in conventional classes. Through comments on scripts, tutors can facilitate learning; maintain an ongoing contact with the learner; advise on the next steps; and give an overview of progress through the course. The tone of the comment, especially in the absence of face-to-face contact, is critical.

Postal contact is often supported by brief telephone calls. The tutor can use the phone: to make routine contact, to chase up progress, to follow up the return of an assignment, to deal with specific queries. The telephone can also be used for direct tuition. Unfortunately there is often resistance to telephone use for a number of reasons, including poor line quality, cost, the absence of the visual element and (even in the 1990s or the start of the twenty-first century) tutors' and learners' lack of familiarity with this use of telephone technology.

The distance tutor must be prepared to work with open learning material; this may require a change of practice, for academics in particular are used to preparing their own lectures. Tutors need a thorough familiarity with the course packages so they can advise learners on the most productive use of these materials, referring learners to specific sections and preparing ancillary (but not replacement) materials where necessary. The greater the sense of ownership of the packages that tutors have, the better the results are likely to be — hence in one organization, course writers are contracted to act as tutors for a minimum period of two years.

All these tutorial skills — detailed marking, commenting in an appropriate tone, using the telephone, supporting the materials — may be new to tutors, or major extensions of what they currently do. This reinforces the importance of careful selection, training and support of such staff.

19.6 Management and administration

Management and administration are needed to ensure that the learning materials and support areas are integrated and delivered. General management skills are needed: policy-making, control, allocation of tasks and responsibilities, scheduling, communications, deployment of resources. Running an open learning scheme often requires sophisticated planning and careful scheduling; for example, time must be allowed and systems built for marketing, pre-entry counselling, enrolment, stocking and despatch of learning materials, tutoring, assessment, collection and analysis of feedback, and revision of course materials.

Two areas of particular concern are marketing and evaluation. Marketing is of two broad types: reaching the right audience for an open, or public programme; and reaching the right audience in an internal, closed programme for employees in one company. Marketing is often confused with simple selling or advertisintg. It in fact covers a full range of activities: identifying areas of need and demand, designing the programme to meet the need, ensuring ease of access to the learning opportunities, informing not only potential customers of the opportunity but also those who can influence them, collecting learner responses and modifying the scheme accordingly. A communications strategy is needed, within an organization, to gain support from all groups from top management down. This means highlighting for each group the relevant benefits (see the earlier section on benefits) and covering costs, relevance, flexibility and the accessibility of open learning.

Evaluation is a vital and related activity. Results from evaluation can flow into the marketing programme. One useful model — set out in figure 19.1 below — shows the need for evaluation at five points.

Figure 19.1. Evaluation of open learning

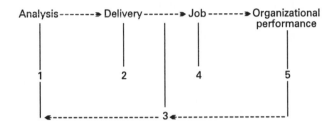

Evaluation at each of the numbered points ensures checks on:

● accurate identification of the development need;

● the delivery process of the open learning opportunity (e.g. number of assignments completed, learners' perception of the course materials and support, degree of use made of tutor contact);

● the extent of learning achieved (e.g. course results, competence tests, exams);

● the extent of the use of new learning within the job (e.g. better use of new technology, improved working methods, better communications, successful introduction of change); and

● the impact on organizational performance (e.g. increased productivity, less absenteeism, higher profits, quicker response to customers). Lewis (1989) can be consulted for a fuller discussion of this model.

To be effective, evaluation requires agreement on:

● identifying aspects of the scheme for analysis;

● setting a standard for each aspect;

● collecting and recording data;

● presenting the data and communicating results; and

● reviewing the standard as necessary (and moving round the loop again).

A further treatment of ongoing monitoring and evaluation — and their role in establishing a quality system — can be found in Open College (1990).

Responsibility for managing open learning programmes is sometimes split. Sometimes provision of a programme is undertaken jointly on the open market by an institution of higher education and an open learning organization. In this case, the former may be responsible for academic structure, selection of learners, writing the material and the award; the latter for marketing, enrolment, production, storage and dispatch of learning material and the systems for logging learner progress. In one scheme, a third institution is responsible for setting up and running a computer conferencing system and for training participants in its use. Such collaborative schemes of open learning are likely to become increasingly common.

19.7 The role of computers in open learning

The availability of inexpensive and accessible computers has aided the growth of open learning in a number of ways. The computer can, most obviously, be used to present course material to the learner. It can also support learning more generally. Managers can access a computer via the telephone for a variety of purposes: information (a notice board), mail (a letter box), discussion (a time-free seminar). The computer can greatly help the course organizer administer and manage learning. It can also be the means by which course material is stored, updated and produced.

Computer conferencing perhaps offers the most scope for cross-modular work, where participants share experiences, contributing from a particular specialization (for example, marketing or accounting). If such communication can be central to a course rather than just an "add on", a kind of "community of learning", often seen as possible only with face-to-face courses, should be achievable at a distance. The University of Lancaster's MA in Management Learning (started in January 1990) allows learners a unique tailor-made programme. With no pre-prepared materials, the learning programme is built around the development needs of each participant; computer linking allows the identification of resources suitable to help the individual attain unique learning objectives. The programme is built from an assumption that standard, pre-prepared course materials can have only a limited value in what is essentially a holistic, experiential learning process.

Hodgson et al. (1989) show the system in figure 19.2.

The counsellor may be outside the providing body's system (e.g. in the learner's workplace). The tutor will be an academic/learning facilitator — a resource to be called on by the learner where necessary, a professional partner rather than a teacher. The resources include names and addresses of specialists, references to useful books and articles, access to databases. A resource manager retains resource records and generally supports the system.

To play their part effectively, tutors will need not only to accept their changed role (facilitator rather than instructor) but they will also need technical fluency. This will probably entail professional development in the uses and purposes of information technology in open learning. One consortium sets out the requirements as: possession of appropriate equipment, familiarity with information technology (e.g. regular use of electronic mail), attendance at an induction day, three months' guided introduction to the facilities, and the capability to facilitate the expertise of conference members.

Figure 19.2. Schematic presentation of a computer-based programme

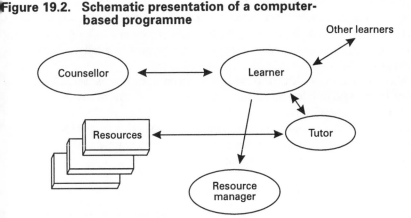

The computer to present material

The terms "computer-based learning" and "computer-based training" describe the use of the computer as a device for presenting course material directly to the learner. Presentation can be simple, for example the generation of text followed by questions to check understanding; or complex, for example simulation requiring the learner to assess variables and make a business decision. In between these extremes are many possibilities, such as branching options to take account of different learning styles or responses.

The computer has a number of obvious strengths as a presentation medium. Answers and responses to questions can be concealed (not the case in print, where the learner can "cheat"); feedback is usually immediate and is consistent and standardized to the level of detail required. Flexibility of the resource can be even greater when other media are added, such as video technology in interactive video, which enables information from the computer programme or from the video to be displayed in any combination.

There are inevitably also limitations to this use of the computer. The learner needs access to the necessary hardware; other media are more easily portable; high quality software exploiting more advanced uses of the computer is expensive to develop, requiring considerable expertise in learning systems design; and by no means are all learners "turned on" by newer methods of learning delivery.

The computer to support learning

The previous section stressed the power of the computer to generate feedback. This capability can be separated from the provision of the learning material itself. A learner could, for example, work through a book and video and, when ready, complete a test at the computer. In some open learning schemes, such as the Open University, learners answer multiple choice questions and send the answers, specially coded on paper, to the centre for processing. The learner then receives a simple "answer" (numbers right, numbers wrong) or more complex feedback; some systems print out letters to learners, providing a paragraph of response to each answer sent in. A computer-generated response of this kind can be very detailed, more comprehensive than a tutor would produce, and standardized.

Other forms of support can be provided by computer, such as names and addresses of other learners (to help learners to form self-help groups); careers advice databases; and reminders of work due.

The computer can be linked to other media to provide other support for learning. Modem connections to a telephone, for example, enable a central computer to send feedback direct to the learner's computer.

The management of open learning

The administration of open learning, as with the administration of any other form of learning delivery, is ideally suited to computerization. It helps with processes such as:

- enquiry handling (logging enquiries and their source; creating a database of enquiries);
- enrolment (entering details of learners, their addresses, qualifications);
- assigning tutors to learners (selecting a local tutor for the learner; automatically sending the tutor details of the newly enrolled learner, paying fees to tutors);
- chasing (for example, generating letters to learners who are late in submitting assignments; requesting fees);
- issuing results and certificates;
- marketing (for example, generating mailing lists); and
- evaluation (for example, the input and analysis of feedback forms from learners giving their views on course provision).

The computer can also be used directly by learners to help them manage their learning. In a learning centre, for example, the learner can "log in" to receive an analysis of performance to date and alternative routes for the next step. The computer can route the learner round a multi-media package, test readiness for learning, and inform the learner of any prerequisites. Data on learner performance, if appropriate, can be centrally recorded for later award of credit.

19.8 Conclusion

Northcott (1986) charts the "burgeoning of interest" across the world in open and distance learning for managers, since the early 1980s, caused by the need for managers to upgrade their skills, the convenience of open learning, the changing status of women and the increasing respectability of open learning as a training method. He examines eight case-studies drawn from Australia, Canada, Hong Kong, Norway and the United Kingdom. The largest provider of open learning for managers in the United Kingdom reports a 30 per cent growth in numbers each year from 1986 onwards. The extent of demand, stimulated in the United Kingdom by the Management Charter Initiative, can be met easily only by the influence of open learning delivery. The larger numbers requiring management training also have high expectations. They want user-friendly, convenient delivery.

New assessment methods also favour open learning: the provision of greater learner choice over how, where and when assessment takes place; modular rather than whole-course assessment; assessment that is competence-driven rather than information-based; and assessment separated from course design and delivery, incorporating recognition of prior achievement as well as formal learning. For the Management Charter Initiative, the "inputs" of learning are irrelevant; what is important is that the individual:

- identifies measurable targets for performance;
- is clear about the kinds of evidence needed to demonstrate effective performance; and
- has a coherent plan to collect the evidence, involving the support of teachers and colleagues where necessary.

All these developments form an excellent framework for the exercise of learner autonomy. The new qualification structures also fit well with the learner-driven, flexible philosophy behind open learning. As has been pointed out, open learning enables learners to progress at their own pace through different development schemes which are linked to particular criteria against which their success can be measured and accredited through professional qualifications. Technology will also have a role to play in responding to increased demand and to new assessment and qualification structures.

Underpinning this will have to be a commitment to the philosophy underlying open education — the supremacy of user choice; whatever the technology, this will continue to be the most important requirement in the art of the learning professional.

PLANNING, IMPLEMENTING AND EVALUATING A SUPERVISORY DEVELOPMENT PROGRAMME

20

Lester R. Bittel

Supervisory development needs the genuine support of top management and the active involvement of human resource professionals. This is essential because supervisors provide the critical link between high-level organizational policies and workplace realities. The supervisory position is also excessively demanding; yet at the same time it is characterized by ambiguities and uncertain authority. It is the rank-and-file employees — production and clerical staff, retail sales people and service operators, and an increasing array of highly trained, specialized knowledge workers — who actually carry out the work of all organizations. Without supervisors, however, to prepare, instruct, direct, translate and otherwise communicate higher management's concepts and operational strategies to the workforce, most of these vital ideas would never be implemented. Accordingly, an organization's policies and procedures stand or fall on the competence of its supervision. This competence, in turn, depends in large measure on the quality of training and development its supervisors receive. Few supervisors have the inclination, knowledge, or resources to provide their own development. Thus, supervisors are dependent upon the guidance, instruction, and structured support that only a well-conceived management development programme can offer.

20.1 Role definition and identification of competences

Supervisors are the men and women who maintain the tenuous interface between the management hierarchy and the vast body of employees who put their hands on, or apply their minds to, the real work of enterprise, both public and private. In most countries, supervisors are legally, as well as by job design, members of management. Their loyalties, however, are often divided. Seventy-five per cent or more have risen from the ranks of either blue-collar or white-collar labour in most countries. They rarely have the opportunity to establish the goals of the organizations they serve.

Their upward mobility is severely limited. As a result, the unique nature of the supervisory job and of a supervisor's origin creates a segment of management that is distinct from other managers (Bittel and Ramsey, 1982).

Role definition

Supervisors have been described, variously, as: " the persons in the middle" between management and the workforce; as the "keystone in the organizational arch — strengthening both management and labour" (Likert, 1970); and — in keeping with today's notions of participatory management — as "facilitators" who make resources and information available to subordinates while allowing them to plan and implement their own work. More definitively, the International Labour Office has proposed the following description:

Supervisors are usually first-line managers whose major function is working with and through non-management employees to meet the objectives of the organization and needs of the employees (Prokopenko and Bittel, 1981).

From a developmental viewpoint, it is often necessary to recognize the fact that there are *first-level* supervisors who manage only non-managerial employees; and there are also *second-level* supervisors who manage other supervisors in addition to non-managerial employees.

Responsibilities

Generally a supervisor's job involves five responsibilities:

- *Responsibility to higher management,* including planning the work of a department, coordinating that work with other departments, selecting and training employees, making work assignments, interpreting and implementing policies, keeping control of quality and costs, and maintaining morale and discipline;

- *Responsibility to employees,* including establishing a warm and friendly environment, protecting employees from arbitrary treatment from above, handling grievances promptly, distributing departmental amenities fairly, maintaining a safe and clean work area, and planning and coordinating work so that workloads are as predictable and stable as possible;

- *Responsibility to other supervisors,* including coordinating workflow between interdependent departments, exchanging information with associates about mutual needs and problems, providing support as members of the same management team, and coordinating policy interpretations to assure consistency and uniformity;

- *Responsibility to staff departments,* including complying with reasonable requests for information, conforming to standardized reporting formats and procedures, listening to counsel from staff members, and consulting with appropriate staff to utilize their special expertise; and

- *Responsibility in labour matters* (where employees are represented by a trade union), including becoming knowledgeable about pertinent aspects of the labour agreement, maintaining a conciliatory attitude in dealing with union representatives, respecting the terms of the agreement — even if in personal disagreement with them, effectively administering the grievance procedure, and representing the management viewpoint in matters of discipline as well as in participatory activities (Bittel and Newstrom, 1990).

Competences

From a developmental point of view, it is competences specification, rather than role definition and responsibility identification, that is essential. Competence specifications range from the general to the highly concrete. One large manufacturing company, for instance, specifies only seven "dimensions" of competence for supervisors: technical knowledge, administrative skills, ability to develop a plan for attaining goals, ability to deal with the managers to whom one reports, communications ability, capacity to deal with people outside the unit, and ability to deal with employees. Two researchers surveyed 314 supervisors in public employment and developed the "laundry list" ranking of supervisory competences shown in table 20.1 (Culbertson and Thompson, 1980).

Table 20.1. Ranking of competence dimensions among publicly employed supervisors

1. Motivating	12. Written reporting systems
2. Developing employees	13. Counselling
3. Communications	14. Functioning in the organization
4. Leadership	15. Time management
5. Planning and organization	16. Delegation
6. Human relations	17. Affirmative action/equal employment opportunity assurances
7. Performance appraisal	18. Safety
8. Disciplining	19. Termination procedures
9. Decision-making	20. Interviewing
10. Handling complaints and grievances	21. Hiring procedures
11. Management methods, such as management by objectives	22. Budgeting

In probably the most exhaustive research ever conducted into the identification of competences, AT&T isolated and ranked 14 principal tasks of supervision, as illustrated in table 20.2. This research began with the identification of a number of supervisors judged as "masters" in view of their outstanding performance and appraisals. The study not only listed the 14 basic competences but also the major tasks, decision points, skills, and related knowledge areas associated with each (MacDonald, 1982).

Table 20.2 in particular should be read critically by the trainer. It applies to one company culture at a given time. For example, in a company with autonomous work teams and thus a high degree of worker involvement, it is quite likely that the task competence ranked as number one for AT&T — "controlling the task" — might be ranked considerably lower. On the other hand, the task competence ranked 14th at AT&T — "representing the company" — is likely to be considerably higher for airline supervisors.

Table 20.2. Competences for master supervisors

Rank order	Task competence	Time spent on the process (%)	Frequency of performance
1.	Controlling the work	17	Every day
2.	Problem-solving	13	Every day
3.	Planning the work	12	Every day
4.	Informal oral communication	12	Every day
5.	Communication	12	Every day
6.	Providing performance feedback	10	Every day
7.	Coaching a subordinate	10	Every day
8.	Written communication/documentation	7	Every day
9.	Creating/maintaining motivating atmosphere	6	Every day
10.	Time management	4	Every day
11.	Meetings	4	Fortnightly
12.	Self-development	2	Weekly
13.	Career counselling a subordinate	2	Every two months
14.	Representing the company	1	Monthly

Trainers, in the traditional role of providing opportunities for skills development, would tend to rank their topics of training according to the competences employed by supervisors who are regarded as effective by their organizations. Trainers who act in the role of agents of organizational change would take note of the list, but they would at the same time assess the list from the point of view of organizational survival and competitive edge. They would review the appropriateness of the competences used by successful supervisors in terms of how the organization wishes to develop in the years to come.

For example, many organizations are trying to become more driven by market demand at the same time as they try and reduce the number of layers of management. This implies that in many cases, supervisors have to develop more interest in what takes place outside the organizations, such as the needs of the customers, who are the ultimate recipients of the organization's products and services. It also implies in many cases that the supervisors' team leadership skills have to be developed, in the sense that to a greater extent they allow their subordinates jointly to solve problems and propose solutions for implementation.

The implication for the trainer is that it becomes necessary to develop insight into the working of organizations, and especially the nature of organizational change. The reason is that the trainer as change agent has to help management to identify critical competences in terms of the demands that the anticipated organizational changes are likely to place on the supervisor.

Methods for establishing competences

Three methods for determining supervisory competences are in usage.

- *Traditional job analysis.* This is the most common method, and it can be carried out in three different ways:
  — interviewing supervisors and their superiors to obtain a list of: (a) tasks that supervisors perform; (b) related responsibilities as well as performance standards and measures; and (c) opinions from these individuals and from staff specialists about the skills needed to perform the tasks and discharge the responsibilities needed;
  — surveying supervisors and their superiors (seeking similar information) using one of the established lists of competences, with or without a request for some sort of ranking of importance (from 1 to 10, for example) and time allotments (in percentage of time spent, hours per day or week, or whatever). In some organizational cultures, it is acceptable to collect the views of supervisors' subordinates, to assess the level of their people management skills; and
  — studying existing job descriptions and specifications to obtain such data.

Once the data have been gathered, they can be sifted, ranked and consolidated by further interviews, surveys or group meetings of supervisors.

Another approach is to assign the interviews and surveys to a task force, with final refinement verified by consultation with incumbent supervisors.

- *Statistically verified research.* This is an expensive approach and requires: (a) a bank of extensive, detailed, and reliable supervisory performance histories as a basis for study; (b) development of a mastery model from this data; and (c) testing of the model against the ongoing performances of incumbent supervisors (Bittel, 1987).

- *Psychological testing.* Some large companies use standardized tests in validating their competence criteria for use in selecting supervisory candidates. Examples include tests for general mental ability, personality and motivational inventories, and the Thematic Perception Text, along with business games, simulations, and in-basket exercises. These tests should always be validated against successful performance on the supervisory job for which the tests are administered.

20.2   Needs assessments

Competences, when properly specified, form the basis of the standards (or criteria) against which: (a) supervisory candidates are evaluated; (b) supervisory performance is appraised; and (c) needs assessments for supervisory development are made. Typically, in making developmental needs assessments, the competence specifications are converted into interview, questionnaire and survey checklists, or are otherwise integrated into the analysis of performance data for evidence of deficiencies.

Traditional approaches

With or without validated competence specifications, developmental-needs assessments for supervisors may be conducted in several ways:

- *Capability assessments.* To establish the levels of capabilities already possessed by an organization's supervisory population, human resource analysts commonly use as sources:
  — performance reviews, from which specific, cumulative data identifying less-than-satisfactory performance against appraisal criteria are gathered;
  — critical incidents, compiled from formal records or through interviews with supervisors, their peers in staff departments, and their superiors; and
  — attitude (or climate) surveys, from which general indicators of unsatisfactory employee relationships are identified.

- *Internal sources of diagnostic information.* Routine operational data from within most organizations will provide a source of information for diagnosing supervisory training needs. Records that are most likely to be indicative include: employee absence, lateness, sickness, accident, grievance and turnover; production records and productivity measures; customer complaints; defects, errors and other quality measures; and unfavourable variances in expense budgets.

- *Needs inventories.* Most supervisory training needs assessments are made using standard needs inventory survey questionnaires, as illustrated in table 20.3 (Parry and Robinson, 1983). Table 20.4 is a useful guide for determining the significance of responses to an inventory needs survey (Bittel and Ramsey, 1982).

Most needs inventory questionnaires are addressed to supervisors, but valuable information can be obtained by also administering the survey to the supervisors' superiors. Results are likely to differ and will require interpretation; perspectives from above and below are different. Herein lies the very nature of supervisory work; striking the balance between superiors' expectations and subordinates' needs. The supervisor's superiors are normally concerned with results, such as deliveries on time, product quality to specification and low production costs. Thus, superiors tend to evaluate the supervisor's performance in terms of what they see in terms of results. The supervisor's subordinates evaluate the supervisor quite differently, because their needs and expectations are directed more towards their own well-being as workers, such as motivation, technical guidance, safety, work security, conflict resolution, etc. In any event, needs surveys do not yield entirely clear-cut or reliable results. Often, however, they produce the best information that the training professional can find. Needs surveys are relatively inexpensive and are fairly good at pointing to areas where needs are either very high or very low.

Table 20.3. Supervisory needs inventory format

Respondents are asked to rate each item according to a scale ranging from 3: "extremely important", through 2: "fairly important", to 1: "not relevant".

Ability to set realistic goals and standards, define performance requirements, and develop action plans for achieving and controlling results.

Skill in communicating effectively in face-to-face situations with subordinates, peers, staff and superiors.

Ability to conduct selection interviews in a way that produces the information needed to make sound hiring decisions. Skill in balancing daily activities between the demands of the task and of the employees.

Ability to challenge and motivate subordinates in a way that increases their job satisfaction.

Skill in orienting new employees and providing job training for all employees.

Ability to appraise performance objectively and to conduct effective two-way appraisal interviews.

Skill in writing letters, memos and reports that are clear, concise and compelling.

Ability to manage time of self and others effectively.

Skill in cutting and controlling costs and expenses. Ability to hold meetings, briefings and conferences that are well directed and results-oriented.

Skill in negotiating and in resolving conflicts. Facility in interviewing in depth, drawing out what is and isn't said, summarizing, and clarifying.

Ability to identify problems, to separate causes from symptoms, to evaluate evidence, to weigh alternatives, and to select and implement decisions.

Table 20.4. Needs inventory survey illustrating average levels of supervisory confidence for selected competences

Important job activities or tasks	Average percentage of respondents with high* degree of confidence to perform the task
Talk to employees on a one-to-one basis	88
Maintain harmony within your own department	80
Solve departmental problems as they arise	78
Conduct a group meeting in your department	79
Attain departmental goals as set by the organization	75
Plan and control the use of personal time	72
Enforce disciplinary rules	72
Conduct an effective performance appraisal	72
Sell your ideas to your superior	69
Motivate employees	68
Write clear memos and reports	68
Develop new ideas for improving productivity	67
Explain benefit programmes to employees	56
Use statistical techniques	51
Explain computer inputs and outputs for your department	47
Counsel an employee who abuses alcohol or drugs	39

* "High" means a 4-5 rating, where the scale is: 1-2: not confident; 3-4: somewhat confident; 5: very confident.

Influence of other factors

When training needs are determined, a distinct word of caution is warranted. An objective, systematic process for the identification of needs, or gaps, will minimize the constant danger of either: (a) jumping to generalized conclusions about needs; or (b) following whatever training fad is currently popular. Not infrequently, organizational structure or morale problems are confused with a lack of supervisory skill or ability. As the chart in figure 20.1 shows, training and development needs may be greatly narrowed through organization development (OD) programmes, more effective selection processes, and an improvement in supervisory morale generally (Prokopenko and Bittel, 1981). Care should be taken to separate structural causes such as these from symptoms that may properly be attributed to competence deficiencies.

Figure 20.1 brings out an important perspective on the role of the trainer in improving organizational performance. It suggests that what can be achieved by skills training may be limited. Indeed, experience from organizational change programmes suggests that there are factors in the system that put more severe constraints on a supervisor's job than the lack of training. Examples of such systematic factors are:

- bureaucratic administrative routines;
- ambiguous orders or messages from senior management;
- burdensome written reporting requirements; and
- ambiguous criteria of product quality.

Peters and Austin (1985), for example, suggest that by improving the organizational culture, the "technique-learning" process can be shortened by 60 to 90 per cent.

It can be very frustrating to design and execute an innovative training programme where most of the apparently lacking skills are included, and then find out that it produces little in terms of performance improvement. The question is: what can the trainer do to cope with this problem?

Much of the answer lies in expanding one's role from simply delivering training to helping the organization's management understand what hampers the individual performance of supervisors beyond skills development. This requires insight into two main areas: the functioning of organizations and the nature of managerial work. We discuss what this entails in Chapter 25, "The management development professional". We shall, in this chapter, limit ourselves to examplifying the nature of managerial work as it applies to supervisors. Mintzberg (1990) reports that a study of 56 American foremen found that they averaged 583 activities per eight-hour shift, which means an average of one activity every 48 seconds. These data suggest a working day of relentless interruptions. They may also suggest that before looking into the skills development needs of supervisors, it is advantageous to review the demands that are imposed on them by their immediate work environment.

The organization development (OD) element on figure 20.1 refers to changes that are made to systems, processes and structure in the organization to facilitate smoother operations. The selection element relates to recruitment and career patterns of supervisors. The motivation refers in part to the reward systems of the organization, in part to the organizational culture — the extent to which it encourages people to do their job the best they can.

Figure 20.1. Isolating training needs from other factors that contribute to supervisory performance

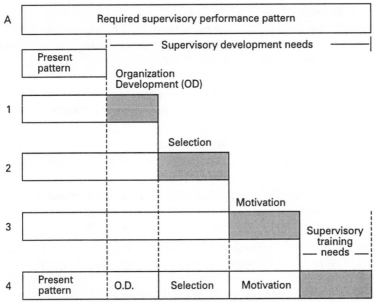

Elements that contribute to a required performance pattern, illustrating four factors that contribute to development: organization development, selection, motivation and training.

20.3   Programme planning

Planning for training and development programmes tends to follow a sequence that includes: (a) setting of objectives, usually a joint effort of line management and the human resource development professional; (b) determination of training needs, based upon prior identification of competence specifications; (c) establishment of policy guidelines; (d) design of the programme, including the choice of courses and topics; (e) selection of methods and approaches; (f) preparation of schedules; (g) briefing of management; (h) designation of participants; (i) programme implementation; and (j) programme evaluation and follow-up. Only those items that have aspects unique to supervisory training and development programmes will be discussed here.

Objectives

It is essential that developmental objectives be clearly stated at the outset. These objectives should be expressed in terms of incremental improvements in knowledge, skills or attitudes directly related to the acknowledged supervisory competences and the assessment of developmental needs. The more quantitatively these goals can be defined, the better, although many objectives can be expressed only in qualitative terms. Some examples of course objectives are:

- *Basic objectives of supervisory training*
  - To give participants essential knowledge of their responsibilities so that they may make decisions that are compatible with company goals and policies.
  - To give participants knowledge vital to good supervisory practices so that this may guide their day-to-day decisions.
  - To provide participants with the skills needed to direct the work of their departments and people in a positive and productive manner.
- *Introduction to supervision courses.*
  - To provide inexperienced supervisors with a basic understanding of management functions and of their specific responsibilities in carrying them out.
- *Advanced supervision course.*
  - To provide experienced supervisors with a review of job-related, fundamental management practices and to introduce them to a selected variety of important new concepts and techniques directly applicable to their work.

Whenever possible, objectives should also include a statement of how the acquired learning will be evaluated. These evaluation measures can include a number of methods, such as: (a) before-and-after comprehension testing; (b) feedback from supervisors after returning to their jobs; (c) evaluation of critical incidents by superiors; (d) routine performance-appraisal criteria; (e) measurement of performance-related data from the supervisor's unit, such as absence and turnover rates, grievances lodged, productivity and quality measures; and (f) identifiable achievements, such as reports prepared, problems solved, and conflicts resolved.

Policy decisions

The major elements of supervisory training policy usually cover such matters as: (a) participant selection; (b) role of professional training staff; (c) roles of line and staff managers whose supervisors are enrolled in the programme; (d) roles and responsibilities of participants; (e) hours of day and days of week that training will take place; (f) participant's pay while attending training sessions, during and after working hours; (g) selection of instructors and their pay, if not employees of the organization; (h) use of tests; (i) choice of training sites; (j) use of outside consultants or proprietary programme; (k) extent of participant travel and reimbursement; (l) tuition reimbursement for voluntary attendance at outside seminars related to, but not required in, the programme; (m) attendance requirements; (n) record-keeping for course completion; (o) awarding of Continuing Education Units (CEUs) or similar recognition; (p) integration with management or executive development programmes conducted by the organization; and (q) conformance with legal requirements and organizational policies.

Many of these policy items are treated in depth elsewhere in this book; the following, however, warrant more detailed coverage here.

Participant selection. There are two almost unrelated but important questions here. First, *should supervisors be chosen, or should they volunteer for the programme?* Ideally, selection should proceed from an indication on an individual's performance appraisal of either (a) an immediate competence shortcoming or (b) potential that can be developed for the good of the individual or the organization. In practice, however, supervisors may be nominated by their superiors for a variety of reasons. The choice may be viewed as a reward for long service. It may also be a veiled, but threatening, expression of dissatisfaction with the supervisor. Or it may represent the superior's eagerness to go along with the current political climate of the organization. All of these reasons are likely to be bad ones. A direct confrontation by the training professional may be difficult; a better approach is to advise the nominators about possible negative outcomes (at best, boredom; at worst, demotivation) and to stress systematic and productive ways for making the selections.

Trainers of supervisors should always look out for managers who are likely to approve supervisory training. Even the best of programmes will not produce change unless the supervisor's manager is committed to the programme and will support ideas for improvement which likely to result from the programme. It is advantageous to have a joint meeting with supervisor and superior prior to a programme, and thereby clarify with both of them their expectations and how they will cope with the type of changes that may result from the programme.

The second question is, *should supervisors from one department be mixed with those from other departments and with middle- and upper-level managers?* Most authorities agree that there is much to be gained by placing line supervisors from different departments and divisions in the same training classes, and including equivalent-level staff supervisors. The classroom interaction is likely to be democratic and vigorous, with valuable exchanges of on-the-job and course-related information and perspective. The choice whether or not to mix participants from different departments depends on the objectives of the training. If the objectives focus on individual enrichment and transfer of skills and knowledge between participants, it is advantageous to have supervisors from different departments attending. This allows for a wider range of views and experiences to be shared. If, on the other hand, the objective is to produce plans of action, it is worth considering participation of supervisors who work in the same department. This allows for more intensive follow-up of one another's action plans. It also allows for joint action plans to be developed. In general, there are risks involved in mixing participants from different levels of management. The learning experience can become threatening to lower-level supervisors and their participation in discussions inhibited.

Whether participation from different hierarchical levels will present an obstacle or not depends to a large extent on the trainer's group facilitation skills. With insight into group dynamics, an appropriate personal style and the ability to organize the groups for maximum participation, the trainer should arrive at balanced, frank discussions.

Integration with upper-level development. There continues to be a tendency to separate supervisory development from development programmes for middle- and upper-level managers. As a consequence, there is always the implication that supervisors (a) are not genuine members of management and that (b) their opportunities for advancement are limited. A better way is to establish a credible link between supervisory training and overall management development. The chart in figure 20.2 illustrates one such programme in the public sector. This integrated programme shows the normal progression of sponsored training from pre-supervisory to basic and advanced supervision, onward to middle management, and the ultimate possibility of entering a residential programme for higher-level managers (Bittel, 1987). This particular programme also awards a Certificate in Professional Development for supervisors who complete the basic and advanced supervision programmes.

Figure 20.2.   Integrating a supervisory training programme with a management development programme

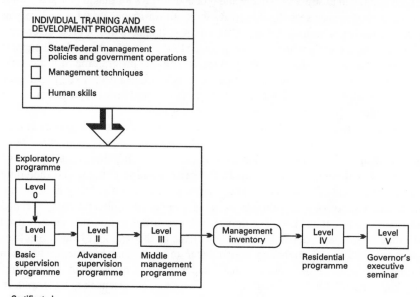

Certification. In many countries, a formalized system has been created to grant educational credits to individuals for completing courses that meet certain criteria. While these credits are not accepted by institutions of higher learning, they have acquired a great deal of credibility in management circles and are especially effective in recognizing developmental achievements among supervisors (Bittel, 1987).

Still another approach is to integrate a supervisory development programme with an opportunity for supervisors to obtain formal certification. The Institute of Certified Professional Managers in the United States conducts a full-scale, recognized certification programme based upon education, experience, and three certification examinations. The substance of the certification examinations parallels the range of subjects offered in comprehensive supervisory training programmes, and participant's and trainer's manuals are available for preparation purposes (ICPM, 1990).

Management clubs. In the United States and some other countries, there is a history of the formation of management clubs, with membership targeted primarily at first- and second-level supervisors. Some of these are entirely self-contained within a particular enterprise. Many others are affiliated to regional clubs or national and international organizations. Examples of this kind are the National Management Association, the International Management Council, etc. Club membership, on any basis, tends to strengthen a developmental programme and to reinforce the supervisor's status as a member of management (Bittel and Newstrom, 1990).

20.4   Programme design and formats

Many considerations in training programme design are not unique to supervisory development. Some features, however, warrant further discussion here.

Costs and budgets

Training costs are always a limiting factor, of course, and these must be measured against potential benefits. Few organizations actually charge the cost of time lost by supervisors attending training sessions against the training budget. Nevertheless, this factor can be large. For example, one study showed that the ratio of the cost of supervisory time — in participant-learning-hours (PLH) — was 1.5 that of all other training costs of the programme.

Format choices

Decisions must also be reached regarding the extent to which programmes should be conducted. Should they be:

- on the job or off the job? The great majority of supervisory training programmes are held off the job in classroom settings;

- on-site or off-site? Most full-scale programmes are conducted on company premises;

- during working hours or after? Most programmes are held during working hours, although this varies widely;

- continuous or on intermittent schedules, such as two hours a day for two weeks or one day a week for ten weeks? Schedules vary widely, but the intermittent approach prevails;

- using internal human resources such as faculty staff and deans or outside organizations such as vocational-technical institutes, independent consultants, or professional societies? Practices vary, but the most common practice is to use training staff for basic managerial and human relations courses. Subject-matter that has a significant technical or legal content is often delegated to staff specialists.

Programme configurations

Generally speaking, supervisory training programmes fall into three levels of progression and may be supplemented by any number of single-focus courses. The typical categorization of programmes is as follows.

- *Pre-supervisory, introductory, or orientation programmes.* Their purpose is to help newly appointed supervisors to adjust to the abrupt change from employee to managerial status. Very few organizations offer such training.

- *Basics, or fundamentals, of supervision.* This becomes the core programme and it may be offered to inexperienced or to experienced supervisors. It is typically designed to provide a solid foundation within 40 hours; or it may be presented in intermittent fashion in 120 hours over a period of one to three years.

- *Advanced, or refresher, supervision.* If an organization chooses to differentiate between the level of content, then the advanced course for more experienced supervisors will be more sophisticated both in content and approach.

Custom-designed versus packaged programmes

On the face of it, custom-designed programmes, developed internally or with the help of a consultant, would appear to provide the most effective training, since they can be designed to make a perfect fit with an organization's needs and culture. Unfortunately, these programmes can be very expensive to create, and their costs are often hidden in the ongoing salaries of the training staff.

On the other hand, there are any number of good packaged programmes that can be purchased off the shelf or through the services of a consultant-instructor. Most of these programmes are built on a framework of generally accepted, fundamental content and methodology. They do suffer, however, from their universality and the generalities that result from it.

Many communities, technical schools, community colleges, and universities offer comprehensive as well as specialized courses in supervision. Enrolment of supervisors in such courses is often the least expensive approach.

Schedules

There is little that is unique about the scheduling of supervisory development programmes. Most practitioners prepare and distribute a *programme calendar* which includes the following: (1) a listing of existing and proposed courses; (2) for each course a description of: (a) eligibility requirements; (b) course objectives; and (c) course structure (lecture, workshop, etc.); and (3) schedule information for the entire programme or each course, including (a) frequency of course offering: yearly, semi-annually; monthly; etc., or one time only; (b) schedule dates; (c) locations; (d) instructor or coordinator; (e) maximum enrolment; and (g) cost (if any) to be charged to the sponsoring department.

Methods and approaches

Supervisors respond most favourably to training and development methods and approaches that are participatory, interactive and experiential. Content is best when it is specific, rather than general, concrete rather than abstract. A great many supervisors, because of their level of education, their work backgrounds, and their job focus find it difficult to derive generalities or principles from the specifics of a situation. Similarly, the reverse is often true: they have difficulty in applying a generality or a principle to specific situations. As a consequence, learning approaches and course content should introduce theory slowly, always reinforcing it with illustrations of concrete applications. Whatever is presented must be able to stand the tests of practicality and credibility. From this awareness, several propositions have been accepted as guidelines for supervisory development.

- *In general, supervisors tend to prefer and to learn more effectively from specific, concrete examples, experiential and reality-oriented practice, and interactive exercises than from abstract, conceptual presentations or from reading assignments.* As adults, supervisors have moved out of the passive student roles into the roles of "doers". With this change comes the need to be treated with respect, to be in charge of their own decision processes, and to be seen as unique individuals. A supervisor's experience may be the biggest learning asset — or in some cases, a monumental liability. While past experiences are useful as comparisons and benchmarks, they establish habits and patterns of thought difficult to alter. This may cause learning problems. Nevertheless, to deny the learner's experience is to thwart the greatest potential available. Development begins to occur when the learner connects the educational experiences with "real life".

- *Discussions are more effective than lectures.* The lecture method encourages passivity rather than active involvement. It should be used sparingly and — as often as possible — be reinforced with small-group activities and other involvement techniques. In discussions, supervisors have the opportunity to think through the topic or problem as it relates to their own experiences, to voice their opinions, to ask questions, and to clarify thinking. This participation increases the probability that performance will actually be improved on the job after the training session is over.

- *Learning is enhanced with case-study analysis, role-playing, and simulations.* While it is a time-consuming approach, *case-study analysis* is especially useful in enhancing problem-solving ability, developing an awareness of interpersonal situations and providing supervisors with an opportunity to test the worth of their ideas by sharing them with other supervisors. As a natural outgrowth of case-study discussion, *role-play* can be instructive — provided that participants are seriously inclined and intensely interested in the outcome of the case. In the past, *simulation exercises* have been more appropriate for management development, but an increasing number are now available for supervisory training and are proving to be effective (Waddell, 1982). Interactive, computer-based exercises, in particular, can accelerate group experiences or provide an individual supervisor with an opportunity to gain group-related experience under self-study conditions.

- *Self-directed training approaches*. Generally speaking, most self-paced, self-motivated learning has not been effective for supervisory development. This includes such methods as correspondence courses, required-reading programmes and programmed instruction. It is not that these methods are not effective, *per se*; it is that they have proved of limited appeal to those who occupy supervisory positions.
- *Behaviour modelling, when professionally administered, can be unusually effective in improving supervisory skills in human relations*. Because behavioural modelling teaches skills, not theory, it has proved to be an effective method for improving the way in which supervisors handle interpersonal problems such as absences, grievances, and discipline (Byham and Robinson, 1976). The technique is an expensive one, however, whether custom-designed or packaged models are used. Furthermore, the success of its use depends largely upon the skill of the human resource professional who administers the programme, and the completeness with which each of its steps (as illustrated in table 20.5) are pursued (Bittel, 1987).

20.5   Programme content

Good supervisory training and development programmes reflect designated competences and assessed training needs.

A modular concept

Those subjects that seem most fundamental to supervision are shown in table 20.6. This list was compiled by the International Labour Office (ILO) and includes nearly all the perennial subjects.

The ILO envisions these 34 courses as modules that can be put together in sequences or clusters according to the needs and objectives of a particular organization. The modular design was premised upon allocating programme time according to the various training methods in the following proportions.

Training methods	*Percentage of time*
Lecturing	10-20
Films, group discussion, role-play	35-45
Case-studies, projects, problems	25-35
Homework, self-development	10-20
Needs analysis and course evaluation	5-8

Examples of basic programmes

There appears to be no standardized basic programme for supervisory development, but most programmes represent variations on this fundamental pattern:

Table 20.5. A behaviour-modelling system for use in supervisory development programmes

The problem-solving behavioural pattern that underlies
behavioural models for supervisor-subordinate relationships

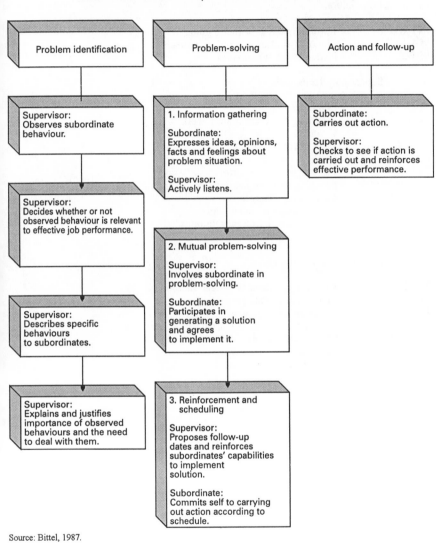

| Problem identification | Problem-solving | Action and follow-up |

Problem identification

Supervisor:
Observes subordinate
behaviour.

Supervisor:
Decides whether or not
observed behaviour is relevant
to effective job performance.

Supervisor:
Describes specific
behaviours
to subordinates.

Supervisor:
Explains and justifies
importance of observed
behaviours and the need
to deal with them.

Problem-solving

1. Information gathering

Subordinate:
Expresses ideas, opinions,
facts and feelings about
problem situation.

Supervisor:
Actively listens.

2. Mutual problem-solving

Supervisor:
Involves subordinate in
problem-solving.

Subordinate:
Participates in
generating a solution
and agrees
to implement it.

3. Reinforcement and
   scheduling

Supervisor:
Proposes follow-up
dates and reinforces
subordinates' capabilities
to implement
solution.

Subordinate:
Commits self to carrying
out action according to
schedule.

Action and follow-up

Subordinate:
Carries out action.

Supervisor:
Checks to see if action is
carried out and reinforces
effective performance.

Source: Bittel, 1987.

Table 20.6. Comprehensive listing of basic supervision courses: A basic modular programme for supervisory development

Course titles	
I.	Introduction
INTRO	Introduction and trainer's guide
M-I-1	The organization and the supervisor
M-I-2	Principles of supervision
II.	Supervisory techniques
M-II-3	Planning
M-II-4	Directing and coordinating work
M-II-5	Controlling work
M-II-6	Work study
M-II-7	Quality control
M-II-8	Finance and cost control
M-II-9	Problem analysis and decision-making
M-II-10	Introducing changes
M-II-11	Communication and records
M-II-12	Individual and group discussions
M-II-13	Management of time
III.	The main supervisory areas
M-III-14	Utilization of equipment and facilities
M-III-15	Maintenance management
M-III-16	Materials management
M-III-17	Energy utilization and auxiliary services
M-III-18	Office supervision
M-III-19	Purchasing
M-III-20	Marketing
M-III-21	Safety and health
IV.	Supervising people
M-IV-22	Leadership
M-IV-23	Informal groups and organizations
M-IV-24	Staffing
M-IV-25	Motivating employees
M-IV-26	Job evaluation
M-IV-27	Performance appraisal
M-IV-28	Salary and wage administration
M-IV-29	Training and development
M-IV-30	Behaviour in supervision
M-IV-31	Industrial relations
M-IV-32	Maintaining discipline and morale
M-IV-33	Complaints and grievances
M-IV-34	Supervising special groups

Source: Bittel and Prokopenko, 1981.

- *Nature of supervisory work.* Management-mindedness; people as implementers; responsibility for others; self-awareness; balancing of task emphasis and of people concerns.

- *Managing the supervisory job.* Planning, goals and schedules; organizing or distributing work and accountability; assignment and instruction; control and correction; problem-solving and decision-making.

- *Understanding human behaviour at work.* Human behaviour and motivation; interpersonal relations — with individuals and groups; attitudes and morale; goal conflicts between individuals and the organization.

- *Helping employees to meet organization standards and goals.* Leadership; authority and responsibility; communications — organizational and interpersonal; performance appraisal; employee training.

- *Preventing and resolving counterproductive situations.* Coping with change and conflict; grievances; performance deficiencies — absenteeism, alcoholism, and drug abuse.

Illustrative examples of programmes for basic supervisory development include:

- *For public-agency supervisors* (12 subjects, each consisting of three sessions of from two to three hours); role of supervisor, selection and utilization of personnel, job instruction training, position and pay management, performance appraisal, communications, discipline, health and sick leave, safety, career management, grievances, relationships with unions.

- *For manufacturing supervisors* (10 on-site workshops of two hours each, spaced over a period of six to ten weeks); supervisor's job, understanding the individual, attitudes/morale/communications, leadership, motivation, training, labour relations, accident prevention, managing your job, planning your career.

- *A university-sponsored open enrolment programme* (12 classroom sessions of two hours each, spaced over 12 weeks); the supervisor's job, communicating, leadership and authority, motivating employees, employee disciplining and counselling, performance appraisal, employee training and development, cost control, methods improvement, planning and scheduling, self-development, tying it all together.

Content of advanced programmes

Objectives for advanced programmes are typified by one organization's policy statement:

To provide opportunities for experienced supervisors to refresh or refine their self-awareness and their knowledge of supervisory goals and responsibilities; to acquire or further develop techniques for improving effectiveness of their leadership; to examine techniques for establishing and maintaining a departmental climate that encourages productive employee behaviour; to acquire new techniques for planning, controlling and improving the productivity of departmental operations.

A representative example of a comprehensive advanced programme is this one offered by a public agency in a 40-hour, open-enrolment course. Sessions are two hours each and spaced over a 20-week period: supervision and management awareness, behaviour analysis, interpersonal relations, self-confrontation, creativity, employee development and performance appraisal, performance standards, incentives and recognition, authority/strategies/decision-making, managing time, delegation, equal employment opportunities, labour-management relations, adverse actions, information sharing and communications, conflict resolution, planning an organization system, synthesis of management concepts, practical problem-solving, self-development.

Speciality courses

There are a number of courses that might be classified as either basic or advanced, or they might fall outside a particular organization's concept of what should be included in either. Typical of these "non-required", but frequently offered, courses are the following:

- *Information management.* Principles of data processing; computer operations; insights into computer language; record-keeping.

- *Budgeting and expense control.* How budgets are built; relationships to departmental operations; limitations.

- *Team-building.* Developing morale and initiative in small groups; participative leadership.

- *Job and work design.* Developing morale by focusing on the work elements rather than on people.

- *Understanding statistics and quantitative methods.* An overview stressing concepts, applications, interpretations.

- *Scheduling techniques.* Gantt charts; overview of PERT (programme evaluation and review techniques) and CPM (critical path method); short-interval scheduling.

- *Work-sampling workshop.* Methodology; applications; limitations; project experience.

- *Paperwork simplification.* Systems and procedures methodology; work simplification in the office; paperwork flow analysis; project experience.

- *Counselling workshop.* Non-directive interviewing; active listening; special problems — family, physical, emotional, absences, lateness, bizarre behaviour, substance abuse and so forth; referral; role-play or behaviour modelling.

20.6   Evaluation and follow-up

An evaluation of the effectiveness of training requires that the programme's results be compared against its objectives. *Needs assessment* has asked "What good *will* training do?" *Evaluation* asks "What good *did* the training do?" Accordingly, the needs assessment previously performed provides the criteria by which to measure the programme's success. One analyst suggests, however, that a supervisory development programme should be evaluated further against four levels of impact:

- *Level 1.* The extent to which the participants "enjoyed" the programme — in total and in each of its many variables — the setting, leadership, practicality of methods used, etc.

- *Level 2.* The extent to which participants assimilated the information or the learned skills during the training session.

- *Level 3.* The extent to which participants apply the acquired knowledge or skills back on the job.

- *Level 4.* The extent to which the programme measurably affects the operations, productivity, or profits of the organization and the quality of the products or services offered by it (Del Gazio, 1984).

Evaluation criteria

Validation criteria for supervisory training can be classified as (a) either subjective or objective and (b) either qualitative or quantitative. Objective, quantitative criteria are best, but such measures of results are often difficult to obtain. One authority surveyed over 300 companies offering supervisory training and found that subjective criteria were employed twice as frequently as objective ones, although almost all companies used two or more of the traditional criteria, which are shown ranked according to frequency of usage in table 20.7.

Follow-up

Much can be lost between completion of the training programme and the return of the supervisors to their jobs, so it is essential for the training coordinator to build bridges between the learning experience and the workplace. Several techniques are used.

- *Take-home action plans.* At the close of a period of training, supervisors are required to make a commitment to a specific plan of action. The plan is prepared in duplicate, with one copy to be delivered to the superior by the participant upon the latter's return from training. Typically, such plans cover:
  — *What will be done.* For example, "Tell Bill X about the number of errors he makes daily in his log entries", "prepare a work distribution chart for improving job assignments", or "delegate preparation of a weekly summary sheet to Mary J".
  — *When will it be done and how long will it take.* For instance, "complete by 15 April. Estimate it will take six hours of my time to do".
  — *How will it be done.* The specific plan or method to be employed, such as, "by analysing departmental records for the last six months", "by speaking

Table 20.7. Evaluation criteria for supervisory training programmes ranked according to frequency of usage

No. of mentions	Subjective criteria
156	Trainee's reactions, during or at close of programme
90	Reactions of immediate superiors of trainees
42	Trainer's evaluation of programme
41	Trainees' reactions, three to six months after programme
33	Reactions of higher management
30	"Informal observation"
392	*Total mentions*

No. of mentions	Objective criteria
41	"Department's records"
38	Review of performance appraisals of trainees, following training
28	Records — of absences, turnover, tardiness, or grievances in trainees' units, after training
22	Records — of production costs, quality, safety, and other factors — after training
19	Testing, at end of course
12	Testing, before and after
10	Attitude surveys among employees being supervised by trainees, following training
9	Formal programme-evaluation studies conducted by the company or by an outside organization
8	Accomplishment of specific objectives
187	*Total mentions*

to Jerry at least three times, preferably 15 minutes before the end of the workday", or "by conducting a work-sampling study".

— *Where will it be done.* For example, "at the mail sorting racks", "in the field", or "at home".

— *Who will be involved and who can assist.* For instance, "the employee and I", "the employee, the boss and I", or "with help from the personnel office".

— *Risk factors.* Which factors in terms of people, money, equipment or events can become obstacles to the successful implementation of the plan?

- *Reinforcement at the job site.* The supervisors' superiors often need coaching from the training professional so as to reinforce the learning that has been received. The following actions should be encouraged (Hoffman, 1981):
  - An interview with the returning trainee, covering: (a) the value received by the trainee; (b) methods that can be applied to the job; (c) laying plans for where the training can be applied; (d) securing a commitment to put the plan into action.
  - Periodic discussion with trainees regarding their application of what was learned, with a request for a demonstration that this is in fact occurring.
  - A request, at staff meetings, that supervisors present ideas related to their training that they think have worked well on their jobs.
  - When reviewing operational problems, questioning whether the concepts learned can be applied in the solution of these problems. Asking trainees to turn in periodic reports of how and where the learning has been applied.
  - Continuing to observe and to comment on the trainee's progress, complimenting for diligence in application and for improvement in performance.

MANAGEMENT DEVELOPMENT FOR SCIENTIFIC AND ENGINEERING PERSONNEL

21

Lester R. Bittel

The term *technical professional* embraces scientists, engineers, architects, health professionals and other extensively educated and usually disciplined individuals at work in fields associated with the various sciences and technologies. This chapter will often speak of *scientists* and *engineers* as being representative of technical professionals. Each group has its own occupational characteristics and singular needs for development as managers, whether in charge of professionals of their own kind or as managers of activities outside their fields of specialization. In view of an accelerating technology and the significant differences of those employed in its service or as its managers, there is an urgent need (a) to prepare individuals better to manage technical specialists and (b) to develop further their ability to apply their specialized knowledge, skills and experience to the broader areas of management.

21.1   Differentiating factors

In order to plan adequately for the development of engineers and scientists as managers, a further differentiation is helpful: engineers apply scientific information; scientists develop this information. Scientists have usually had a more advanced education than engineers and tend to perform more effectively in "open" work situations, while engineers are effective in more structured environments. Both types, however, perform work of a professional nature, which is described as:

(a) *being investigative in nature* — professional assignments always involve conducting investigations for the purpose of drawing scientific conclusions or solving technical problems, therefore it is often difficult to establish standards and monitor progress of professional work;

(b) *requiring individual contributions* — the technical professional is primarily concerned with the execution of technical work as an individual and only secondarily in cooperating with, or as depending on, the work of others. When the latter condition prevails, as with small-group work, management encounters considerable difficulty in obtaining performance coordination;

(c) *neither routine nor repetitive* — professional work does not necessarily follow a pattern or a cycle, nor does it always consist of specified responsibilities. More typically, professional work consists of a series of assignments, each having a definite beginning and an end; in many cases, each is quite different from the others with respect to the steps and the results achieved. Therefore, the professional position is neither defined nor limited by reporting relationships or by a responsibility for resources — human, physical or financial. Rather, it is defined and limited by the technical complexity of the assignments carried out. These conditions make managerial activities of planning, performance appraisal, progress monitoring and project control uniquely difficult.

Characteristics of technical professionals. Generalizations are dangerous, of course, but it has been observed by many authorities that those individuals who choose to become engineers and scientists are more likely to:

- view the job as intellectually challenging and be proud of their chosen field;

- rate challenge, advancement, and salary (in that order) as key factors in seeking an ideal job;

- feel that the degree of professionalism of their contribution is not appreciated by either the employer or the general public;

- have an insatiable appetite for the services of clerical and technical assistants and for more and better equipment and facilities;

- be more loyal to their profession than to the employer, and thus to be readily open to pirating offers from other firms; and

- have an enormous need to be right, and hence be overly sensitive to criticism.

Characteristics as managers. When technical professionals move into management, many display characteristics that are counterproductive. Two observers (Lewey and Davies, 1987), for example, noted the following behaviour among newly appointed technical managers.

- They over-apply their analytical skills, so much so that they become paralysed by a consideration of all the possibilities and — as a result — unduly defer their decisions.

- They are insensitive to, or hold themselves above, the realities of organizational politics. As a consequence, they are often unable to obtain the resources or to gain the support needed to advance their projects.

- They expect their own technical expertise to solve problems, rather than rely upon the knowledge and skills of their subordinates. Typically, this renders them weak in the human aspects of management.

- They have a tendency to respect logic over intuition and especially over emotions. As a result, they lack empathy for subordinates, do not consider feelings a data source, nor do they easily identify and reflect feelings, and they are ineffective in either motivational or leadership skills.

Obtuseness to shortcomings. A survey of 2,000 Canadian managers in high-tech organizations illustrates the problems encountered in delivering developmental programmes to managers there. The survey showed that: (a) over half of these managers had difficulty in understanding and implementing common-sense leadership techniques; (b) half considered their needs for leadership unique, but could not define this uniqueness; and (c) 45 per cent felt that they needed help but did not know how or where to get it (Philips, 1988).

Transition problems. In many instances, a technical specialist will accept a promotion into management but will be unable to let go of the technical work. There is also difficulty in dealing with the shift from individual achievement to becoming an "influencer" responsible for the accomplishments of others. Unfortunately, most companies neither encourage nor actively promote technical professionals who show an interest in management.

Changing relationships. It has also been observed that in technology-dominated fields especially, the preponderance of hierarchical organizational structures is waning. For example, technicians are being upgraded to para-professional status. There is also an increasing use of teams or small workgroups to solve training problems. This mixes together professionals of all grades, along with craftspersons and even unskilled workers. Hence, the management of professionals is further complicated by the disruption of traditional status and the existence of unstructured relationships (United States Congress, Office of Technology Assessment, 1988).

Fields of employment. An examination of employment demographics is also helpful in planning management development programmes for scientists and engineers. It is worth noting, for example, that in most countries, 50 to 75 per cent of engineers are employed in industry, while 10 to 15 per cent are employed by government and 10 to 15 per cent by universities and colleges. This employment pattern appears to have persisted into the 1990s.

Perceived dimensions. Effective managers of scientists and engineers (or of "technology") appear to require certain skills and attitudes. In general terms, these dimensions have been described as: (a) synergistic, combining technical and managerial capabilities to "help steer the organization safely through turbulent tides of technology"; (b) able to define the relationships of the activities of a technical group to overall organizational goals; (c) the ability to identify and exploit opportunities; and (d) skill in establishing a creative and productive atmosphere for subordinates.

The extent and complexity of the responsibilities — as well as the implicit knowledge and skills requirements — of a manager of technology is illustrated by the position description for a director of engineering (see box 21.1).

Motivational factors. It is well known that technical professionals have unique motivational patterns. The strongest of them are personal success and achievement, intrinsically rewarding work, and identification with important work (often as represented by the reputation of their employers). As a consequence, the outstanding motivator — one that distinguishes high-talent professionals from others — is the *challenge of the work itself.* The survey shown in table 21.1 is particularly useful in identifying those factors that engineers say contribute to challenging work.

Box 21.1. Position description for a director of engineering

Purpose: To provide overall technical and administrative control of corporate engineering activities.

Duties:
1. To provide overall technical direction and coordination of engineering design activities — mechanical, electrical, structural-civil and environmental.
2. To maintain overall cost control and all engineering design activities through administration of project budgets, cost reports and other similar tools.
3. To maintain top quality of engineering design work through procedures to eliminate errors and omissions in design, calculations, specifications and drawing.
4. To improve efficiency of engineering operations through use of techniques of standard specifications and computer-aided design and drafting.
5. To prepare schedules and ensure completion of work as scheduled.
6. To administer and implement engineering personnel policies such as job classifications, appraisal reviews, hiring procedures, labour utilization, and employee training and development.
7. To maintain liaison with engineers on project assignment and with project managers on programme schedules, costs, quality of work, and client problems.
8. To deal with clients as required.
9. To undertake business development and promotional activities as required.

Source: Bittel and Ramsey (eds.), 1985.

Table 21.1. Ratings of factors contributing to the value of the work itself for engineers

Factor	Percentage of survey group listing factor as primary
Creative work	18
Broad area	17
Diverse assignments	16
Select own assignments	9
Work with things	7
Work with people	6.5
Group participation	5.5
Specialize	5
Work alone	5
Supervisory responsibility	5
Routine work	3
Other	3

Source: Hinrichs, 1977.

Career expectations versus graduate education. There is always the question of which kind of post-baccalaureate, academic training best helps prepare technical professionals to advance into management. As an indication of the potential for technical professionals to move into management, generally, more than half of the engineers in an industrially advanced country are in development or production, 20 to 30 per cent in management and less than 10 per cent in research or teaching (Kaufman, 1974).

21.2 Career paths

The established career paths for technical professionals greatly affect the design and implementation of management development programmes for them. Two aspects of organizational career structures warrant special consideration.

Dual-ladder systems. For large, progressive, high-tech companies, a dual-ladder (or two-track) system is commonly employed for the career advancement of technical professionals. As illustrated in figure 21.1, engineers and scientists may be placed on, or opt for, advancement either (a) as technical specialists within their areas of expertise or (b) as managers of activities in technical areas. The intention is that both status and salaries will be equitable between the two ladders. Ideally, there is an opportunity to move back and forth between the two tracks, and career counselling is provided. The programme is given additional credence when someone at the top level of management, such as a vice-president or director of research and engineering, supports such programmes in name and presence.

IBM and Control Data have operated dual-ladder systems effectively for years. A unique aspect of the IBM system is that it requires employees to advance through three levels before they may decide whether to take the management or non-management ladder. The dual-ladder system may not be feasible everywhere. ITT, for example, was unable to implement its two-track system in Germany, where they encountered more traditional hierarchical organization structures. In Italy and Spain, on the other hand, it was less of an issue for ITT.

In reality most engineers and technical professionals have three options to pursue in career advancement, as shown in figure 21.2. They may (a) choose to remain within the narrower confines of their specialities, and the education and training provided by their employers will be of that nature; (b) choose, or be tapped, for promotion (and training) as managers of technical operations; or (c) choose to be moved into broader areas of general management, where their development will encompass skills in such areas as marketing, finance and strategic planning (Bittel, 1985).

Matrix-related assignments. In the last several decades, the use of matrix organization structures for managing projects of technological complexity has become common. As shown in figure 21.3, matrix organizations meld together two or more specialized line organizations. Typically, a project manager will assume

Figure 21.1. Dual-ladder system for advancement

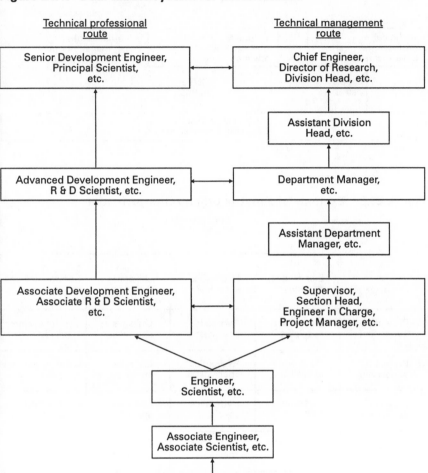

temporary authority over a group of professional specialists who have been assigned by their speciality managers to the project for a limited period of time. Such a practice, despite its implicit efficiency in the use of human resources, inevitably places a strain on the specialists, the project manager, and the manager of the specialists. Accordingly, this unique organizational arrangement calls for special attention in the development of project managers and of the managers of the specialists.

Figure 21.2. Three career paths for technical professionals

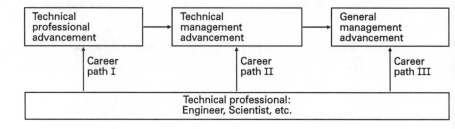

Figure 21.3. Example of a matrix organization structure

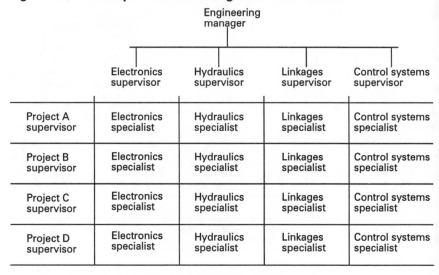

21.3 Policy considerations

Besides an organization's provision of (a) an equitable advancement system and (b) a demonstrable support of management development for its technical professionals, there are other matters of corporate policy that will influence programme design and implementation. These include:

- corporate attitudes towards integrated manufacturing training. Increasingly, the thrust is to bring together elite technical professionals with production workers, sales and marketing personnel, and other members of the organizational team that deal with interrelated changes brought about by technology;

- the extent to which managers are encouraged to take risks. This is an essential consideration of General Electric's New Managers' Programme. Other issues — such as values, culture and vision — are regarded by this high-tech company as integral parts of the developmental process (Komanecky, 1988);

- the degree of selectivity in the programme. At McDonnell Douglas, for example, participation in its High Potential Programme for managers is limited to 5 per cent of the managerial population (Settle, 1988);

- a stated need for greater integration of technology goals with corporate objectives. This intensifies the need for greater exposure of technology managers to strategic planning and a variety of managerial functions (Bittel and Ramsey, 1985);

- the position of development programmes for technology managers vis-à-vis those for all managers. Xerox Corporation, for example, employs a "building block" concept in constructing its programmes. *Awareness* is focused on pre-management training; *skills development* spans first-level manager and middle-manager training; *strategic direction* spans middle-manager training and executive education. Using this approach, most development for technology managers would fall under skills development and emphasize skills directed at their areas of operation;

- how compelling the incentives are to move into management or become proficient. Many human resource directors speak of the reluctance of professionals to accept positions of management. To become a "project coordinator" or "team leader" may be acceptable assignments; designation as a "manager" is felt by many to isolate them from their profession. Some companies counter this objection by guaranteeing a certain number of hours or days that a manager may devote exclusively to his or her professional work.

Corporate policy recommendations. In order to ensure that proper attention is given to the development of engineers, both as professionals and managers, it is recommended that the following commitments be made by the employing organization:

- Design infrastructures that encourage, support and sustain a policy of lifelong education, from the highest level of the enterprise through to line managers and to the practising professional.

- Involve engineers in the planning of curricula and programmes so as to instill the "personal ownership" that adult learning requires.

- Actively encourage managers to take part in career-long education — as participants, tutors and mentors.

- Educate managers in the best way to encourage the people they supervise to participate actively in professional development programmes.

- Reassess the structure and activities of the in-house training to encourage a cooperative and productive dynamic climate between the human resource staff that puts the programmes together and the engineers for whom the programmes are designed.

● Include — as part of the performance review and reward structure for managers — an evaluation of how effectively they support and encourage the educational development of the engineers they supervise.

21.4 Needs assessment

The needs assessment process for engineering and research managers follows closely the universal approach (see Chapter 6). However, the technical position dimensions and policy considerations discussed above demand that a distinction be made between (a) needs associated with management of the technology functions and (b) needs of all managers. Many companies, as indicated by the Xerox building-block approach, also draw a distinction between the needs of a manager of technology at the middle levels and those at the executive levels. For example, one observer found that the following subjects were generally irrelevant to middle manager competences: developing long-range plans, community affairs, finance and accounting, independence and risk-taking. The implication is that development criteria for managers of technology should not be overstated.

Desirable competences. A broad study by one researcher identified a number of desirable competences for *any* manager, but among them the following seem especially appropriate for managers recruited from, or who manage, a technical-professional population (Chenault, 1987):

● tolerance for values other than their own;

● tolerance for ambiguity, uncertainty, and turbulent environments;

● knowledge of how to promote collaboration as a cultural norm;

● management through relaxed, collegial interaction; and

● generosity demonstrated by giving public credit to the ideas and good work of others.

Commonly identified needs. A survey of the literature and a study of subjects presented in a number of effective programmes for managers of engineers, scientists and other technical professionals suggests the following, more specific listing of most-commonly encountered needs, besides professional university education:

Pertaining especially to R & D management

● work with informal groups;

● interdisciplinary communications;

● budgets and allocations;

● project selection and termination;

● project and programme control;

- project termination; and
- R & D management performance evaluation.

Managerial skills and knowledge necessary in addition to engineering education and experience

- budgeting and budget control;
- scheduling and time control;
- financial concepts;
- labour law;
- compensation practices and regulations;
- human behavioural processes; and
- motivational strategies.

Career-long needs for engineers

- managing human resources;
- leading and working effectively with others in a business environment;
- evaluating markets, assessing product lines on a national and global basis;
- allocating financial resources, assessing investments in capital needs, human capital and business opportunities;
- adapting to societal and regulatory constraints, interfacing with legal and social realities, appreciating other cultures and political systems; and
- interpreting technology to non-specialists and to the public.

For project managers in particular

- leadership;
- administrative ability; and
- power of persuasion.

For university-employed scientists and engineers

- support services and facilities for research, including accounting, purchasing and subcontracting, computer services and personnel administration.

For development of engineering managers

- investment decisions;
- budgeting and accounting functions;
- legal functions, especially product liability, patents and copyrights, contracts;
- product safety; and
- engineering and the environment.

For all managers of professionals

- professional responsibilities, including professional ethics and trade secrets;
- R & D policies;

- the patent system;
- project selection and termination; and
- launching new products.

In preparation for the transition from professional employee to corporate manager

- employment contracts;
- dealing with vendors and consultants;
- dealing with customers;
- selling projects to higher management;
- decentralization and engineering;
- corporate strategy for R & D;
- the art of negotiation; and
- engineering supervision.

For R & D management

- working with review boards;
- making committees effective;
- conflict management;
- technical marketing, including bid systems, proposals, technical forecasting, R & D contracting;
- legal aspects of R & D management, including federal procurement procedures, licensing, trade secrets, product liability; and
- professional practice liability, product protection, product liability.

A European survey of 263 organizations that employ technical professionals suggests that the main sources of problems among their managers were: people management, stimulation of innovation and change, and control of monetary expenditures. The survey also indicated that if sound management practices are acquired when managing relatively few people, subsequent increases in staff levels bring little in the way of increased problems. The implication is that there is a good case for providing appropriate management training early (Barclay, 1986).

21.5   Programme planning and design

Four areas of differentiation peculiar to the development of managers of technical professionals are considered here: programme objectives, programme planning models, instructional methods and instructional sources.

Programme objectives are usually formulated in terms specific to a particular organization. A more general statement of objectives would include the following factors:

- To develop the awareness of managers of technical professionals to changes in technology, human values and economic, social, political, and environmental conditions that affect the way they manage their areas of responsibility.

- To focus this awareness on the requirements of their particular industry, the needs of the company and the functioning of their departments.
- To assist in acquiring skills (or to expand present ones) in business, management and human relations.
- To develop critical thinking and conceptual and creative skills.

An astute view (Meadows, 1984) on the subject is that the traditional approaches of management development are no longer appropriate. Instead, the administrative mode of managing which emphasizes task differentiation and management control is being replaced by technology. Professional management which emphasizes task wholeness and innovative behaviour and which is more appropriate for the management of technical professionals is replacing administrative management. According to this view, a better set of objectives for management development would be:

- to explore roles and relationships;
- to learn to work with the issues (and technology) inherent in information processing systems; and
- to develop and use the knowledge resources of the enterprise.

This view implies that the emphasis in development should be on learning and not on didactic teaching.

Programme planning models. Management development can be represented as the unification of four areas or sectors of learning (see table 21.2). Sector A targets interpersonal skills like leadership, motivation, communications, conflict handling and so forth. Sector B covers basic management techniques, such as processes of planning, organizing, directing and controlling. Sector C focuses on developing operational skills that are specific to a particular function, such as accounting, data processing, engineering or research and development. Sector D is integrative and encompasses the areas of broader business considerations such as strategic planning, marketing and finance (Bittel, 1985).

With table 21.2 as a model, programme planning and design can proceed on the basis of the three career paths illustrated previously in figure 21.2. The matching of career paths with the planning model is shown in table 21.3.

Development for career path I is narrow in scope, designed to improve professional proficiency, and becomes broader only as the individual reaches a higher level of speciality. The development programme for career path II facilitates entry into management of a technology-related function and the acquisition and development of the skills associated with that position. The development programme for career path III (figure 21.2) is much broader in nature and emphasizes the integrative sector (D) of the model (table 21.2).

Bell Communications Research, Inc. in Piscataway, New Jersey, has developed and implemented a useful model for planning a curriculum for the development of individuals who manage professional people (see figure 21.4). The programme's

Table 21.2. Developmental planning model

SECTOR A	SECTOR B
Interpersonal skills	*Management processes*
Leadership	Planning
Motivation	Organizing
Communications	Staffing
Team-building	Coordinating
Conflict management	Controlling
Performance appraisal	Information management
Employee training	Problem-solving
Coaching and counselling	Decision-making
SECTOR C	SECTOR D
Operational techniques	*Integrative management*
Operational methods and controls that are specific to the function and to the industry	Company-wide operations and inter-dependencies
	Strategic planning
	External relations

Table 21.3. Career paths and development for technical professionals

	Career path I Professional specialization: emphasis on performance improvement and position enrichment	Career path II Engineering management: emphasis on performance improvement and career advancement	
Entry levels	Job-related technology	(A) (B)	Basic interpersonal skills Management process at supervisory level
Middle levels	Company-wide technology	(A) (B) (C)	Advanced interpersonal skills Management processes at mid-manager level, especially in staff departments Operations of the speciality function within the company
Higher levels		(A) (C) (D)	Selected interpersonal skills Operations of the speciality function in the industry Interdisciplinary coordination of all specialities within the company Management of technology

top priorities for new managers of this kind are: leadership, managing people, motivation, team-building, executive presentations and project management. The curriculum map considers three tiers of proficiency needs: (1) entry needs; (2) fundamental needs; and (3) enhanced needs (Katz and Rosen, 1987).

Figure 21.4. Model for planning a curriculum for training mid-level managers of technical professionals

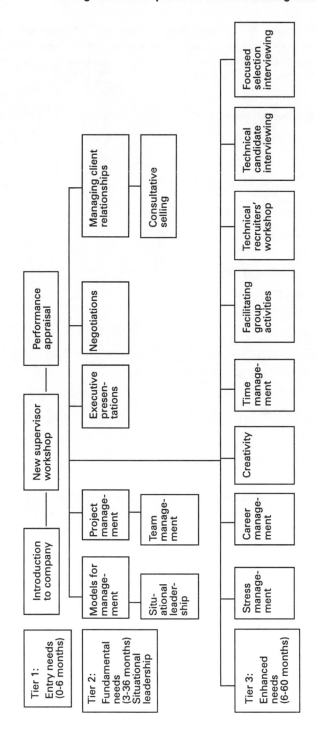

Instructional methods. As with most training and development, there is a potentially large range of training methods and approaches to choose from (see Part III). Those found to be most suitable for the management and development of engineers and scientists are the following:

- lectures;
- seminars and workshops;
- coaching;
- mentoring;
- sponsorship;
- job rotation;
- cross-training (similar to rotation);
- corporate colleges;
- simulations;
- interactive television (ITV);
- continuing and open education;
- instructional sources;
- internal staff;
- consultants;
- university courses and programmes;
- professional societies; and
- government agencies.

21.6   Programme examples

Business firms, academic institutions and professional societies demonstrate a variety of approaches and offer a number of different courses directed towards management development for scientists and engineers. A representative sampling of these programmes follows.

A programme for new managers of technology. General Electric prescribes a lengthy three-phase New Manager's Programme. It begins on the manager's first day, with a "starter kit" containing audio cassettes, booklets and various printed advice. The second phase takes place at what GE believes is the optimum "teachable time" — between the sixth and the twelfth months. This six-day course, held at GE's Management Development Institute, helps participants to learn how to create and lead competitive workteams; communicate candidly and effectively; design work and apply proven work-planning techniques; build networks outside their immediate work unit; solve problems; exhibit leadership; create ownership of employee performance; appraise differential performance; coach, counsel and provide constructive feedback; apply key corporate values in the workplace and in the market-place; and manifest excellence and integrity. Learning is presented in a highly participative manner, under the guidance of paired teams of a GE instructor and an adjunct. The third phase involves follow-up, and takes place six months later, when directors visit managers at their worksites and receive and offer feedback.

R & D management. Two typical programmes are reported here.

The American Management Association presents a three-day seminar, with certificates awarded. It features case-study analysis and includes:

- communications, motivation and leadership styles in R & D management;
- implementing and interfacing research objectives with corporate objectives;
- developing the long-range R & D plan;
- developing the information for R & D programmes and support activities;
- planning and controlling R & D projects and programmes;
- financial evaluation of research; and
- evaluating professional performance.

The Industrial Research Institute offers a three-day seminar "designed for experienced managers who supervise research and development". It features "interchanges" between participants under the guidance of a discussion leader, who is a top-level industrial research executive. Topics include:

- motivation, recognition and reward;
- project selection, control and termination;
- selling your R & D ideas and results;
- global management of R & D resources;
- multidisciplinary teams;
- entrepreneurship;
- technology transfer; and
- managing career development.

Management of technology (MOT). There is a powerful trend towards broadening the concept of simply managing scientists and engineers to that of *managing technology.* A very large, international, high-tech company leads the way in this direction. It is reported that the company encounters a major obstacle in that managers of technology there have a low tolerance for didactic presentation of ordinary management skills and accept as useful only issue-oriented discussions led by instructors of considerable scientific reputation. Accordingly, all its courses are taught by professors on loan from one of the major technological institutions. Three areas receive major attention in the company's MOT programme:

- the concept that management of technical professionals *is* different and requires special, more sensitive approaches;
- ways and means of shortening the product cycle-time; and

- how to manage projects more effectively.

To provide concrete direction for MOT programmes, the Task Force on Management Technology of the National Research Council (United States) suggests this definition: "Management of technology links engineering, science and management disciplines to plan, develop and implement technological capabilities to shape and accomplish the strategic and operational objectives of an organization".

For further guidance in programme planning, the Task Force developed the concepts and responsibility areas illustrated in figure 21.5.

Figure 21.5. Linkages and overlap of engineering and management issues, responsibilities and subjects within the scope of management of technology

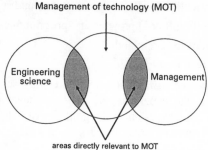

Management of technology (MOT)

Engineering science

Management

areas directly relevant to MOT

Discipline-based knowledge	RDE&M(d) Current operations issues,
Engineering systems	Technology support services and
Computing applications	issues
Manufacturing technology	Finance
Design (DFA(a), etc.)	Marketing
Risk analysis	Business policy/Strategy
Control theory	Control/Accounting
CAD/CAM(b)	Organizational behaviour
Quality assurance/Statistics	Human resources management
Operations research	Production and operations
MIS/DSS(c)	management
Reverse engineering	R & D Management
Awareness of available technologies	Managerial decision theory/
Strategic/Long-term issues relating	Statistics/Opertions research
to technology	Macroeconomics/International trade
Interfunctional issues relating	Microeconomics
to technology	

NOTES:
(a)   DFA: Design for automation or assembly.
(b)   CAD/CAM: Computer-aided design and manufacturing
(c)   MIS/DSS: Management information systems and decision support systems
(d)   RDE&M: Research, development, engineering and manufacturing.

Degree programmes in MOT are found in dozens of American universities and at all levels, from undergraduate through to doctorate programmes, although most stop at the master's degree level. A sizeable number of continuing education programmes directed at working scientists and engineers are offered by colleges, professional societies and other institutions. The Task Force emphasizes, however, that although there are areas of similarity, engineering management and technology management are not the same.

One such continuing education programme is found at the Graduate School of Business Administration at the University of North Carolina at Chapel Hill. Its Programme for Technology Managers takes place on campus for five two-and-a-half day periods. The curriculum consists of:

- management control and measurements;
- managing people and group effectiveness;
- financial management;
- operations management;
- marketing management;
- planning and strategy; and
- values, ethics and legal environment.

Instructors are drawn from the faculty of the university.

The most unusual, but perhaps the most practical and cost-effective approach to MOT training and development is provided by the National Technological University (NTU) operating out of Fort Collins, Colorado. This master's degree programme cuts across all the functions of an organization, from engineering and research and development to manufacturing and services. NTU is essentially a satellite network linking the faculties of 28 institutions of higher learning. Students enrolled in this degree programme must have several years' experience in industry or government. They take two courses each semester via satellite and meet in residencies at different sites seven times over a period of two years. In addition, each student works on a project over the entire length of the programme.

Project management. Skill in managing projects draws a very high priority in most management development programmes for scientists and engineers. One important study of 110 project managers in 20 high-technology firms shows, however, that the effectiveness of courses in project management is greatly dependent upon those selected to be project managers. The dilemma is that project managers, most of whom rise from the ranks of engineers and scientists, are expected to have a broad cross-functional perspective and to work mostly through and with people; the majority of formalized programmes, however, deal primarily with the technical side of the project management. Yet it is in people-skills that technical professionals most need to be assessed; or at least they should receive pre-course preparation in interpersonal skills. The study cites two successful programmes that provide their participants beforehand with training in written and oral communication, influencing skills, negotiating skills, conflict-resolution skills and group decision-making skills. Only in the project management course itself is the focus placed upon project planning and control skills.

Objectives. A good statement of objectives for project management training is suggested by Kepner and Tregoe (see Schlick, 1988). The programme described expects course participants to be able to:

- recall and describe the elements of project management;
- recall and describe the importance of people in project management;
- apply the steps and tools of project management;
- use basic people skills for project success;
- identify factors that affect project success;
- identify issues for designing a successful project-management system; and
- identify available computer software.

Content. A basic course in project management typically takes from three to five days and includes the following:

Defining project objectives
    statements of project objectives
    estimates of project's life cycle
    resource needs and allocations

Developing the project team
    specifying staff requirements
    staffing process
    communicating team members' roles and assignments

Creating the project plan
    project planning tools
    preparing project schedules
    establishing reporting and control procedures
    service and support facilities

Implementation
    obtaining plan approvals
    requests for proposals, subcontracting, etc.
    communications with interdependent participants
    ongoing documentation

Project and programme control
    expense control techniques
    project life cycles
    client and subcontractor liaison
    network control plans such as milestone charting, Gantt charts, PERT and CPM evaluations.

Conflict. Two researchers have established that conflict is a ubiquitous condition of project management. Their studies showed that at every stage of the project there is likely to be serious conflict over schedules, priorities, labour availability, technical issues, administration, personalities and costs — in that order of descending intensity. Based upon this reality, it would appear that skill development in conflict-handling would be a necessary adjunct to programmes in project management.

Video libraries. There has been a proliferation of video programmes in a large variety of management and business skills. Many of these programmes are prepared and sold by commercial producers, and are of high quality. The largest collection of videos designed for managers of technical professionals, however, is offered by the Association for Media-Based Continuing Education for Engineers (AMCEE), based in Atlanta, Georgia. AMCEE is a non-profit consortium of 33 of US leading engineering universities. Its objective is "to provide improved continuing education opportunities for engineers, scientists, and technical managers". The AMCEE Video Library of Management Skills, for example, lists 31 video courses in "professional management techniques — presented for engineering, scientific, and technical managers".

21.7 Evaluation and follow-up

As with many other areas, concrete measurement of programme effectiveness in the engineering and scientific management sector leaves much to be desired. The National Research Council, for example, laments the absence of hard measures to substantiate the economic value of such development. While many organizations do evaluate their programmes, most are weak in the final stage of *Kirkpatrick's Six-Stage Model for Evaluating HRD*: "VI-Impacts and Worth; Did it make a worthwhile difference? Has the need been met?" (see Brinkerhoff, 1988). Effective programmes, of course, are built upon a plan for specific evaluation of results.

Examples. Two companies, one a manufacturer and the other a public utility, provide examples of effective techniques for evaluation and follow-up of their development programmes for technical managers:

General Electric's New Manager's Development Programme provides evaluation and follow-up at the end of the course and six months later. Evaluation at the course's close is of a traditional nature, using questionnaires. Later, the company gathers data from subordinates and peers about participants' performance back on the job. This information is placed in a computerized data bank, containing each participant's performance and that of some 4,000 other new managers. Each manager is then advised of his or her ranking, and is also provided with suggestions for, and assistance in, improving below-average performance.

Other, more qualitative follow-up assessments of course content and structure are obtained by the course directors in focus-group sessions with course graduates (Komanecky, 1988).

Florida Power & Light trains its managers in methods for applying advanced quality control statistics to their daily work. Following training, instructors and professional specialists work with teams on projects, helping them to move towards solutions that they can present to senior management. This technique allows relationships that were built in class to continue afterwards, so that work and learning become "seamless" pursuits (Holpp, 1987).

TRAINING AND DEVELOPMENT OF WOMEN FOR MANAGERIAL JOBS 22

Valerie J. Hammond

Training and development of women for managerial jobs start with a clear statement of the objectives based on a full appreciation of the situation. The nature of the training will vary according to whether the objective is primarily to get women into management, to help them to establish themselves as effective managers or to enable them to move up into more senior management positions. The situation in which these objectives are to be met will be shaped by the cultural framework in which women live and work. Three elements can be identified: the accepted routes into management, the specific corporate culture and, finally, women's role and standing in society.

22.1   Diagnosing the cultural framework: Routes into management

Look first at the career paths and patterns of typical managers. Although there are and will be variations, a dominant picture is usually observable. Contrast the situation in Germany, for example, with that of the United States and the United Kingdom. In Germany the dominant pattern is for people to complete lengthy professional training and only then to enter management. A manager is therefore academically and professionally highly qualified. The predominant route in the United States is also through qualification, but more directly from university after obtaining an MBA degree. In the United States, management is therefore a primary career aim, and people can start on the management path at a younger age. In the United Kingdom the situation is less structured. Although the situation is changing, with more emphasis being placed on management education, many people are promoted into management from the "shop-floor", from management trainee schemes as well as from professions such as accountancy.

These different career routes have important implications for women. Experience will be assessed against the backdrop of the prevailing career path norms. Adachi, writing about management development for women in Japan, points out that generalized executive development calls for a combination of experience, training and education, specifically decision-making and interpersonal skills, job, organizational and general knowledge and specific individual needs (Adachi, 1989). However, women in Japan do not usually receive this development. They are not regarded as having management potential.

While considering these national norms, it is important to take account of any trends or foreseeable circumstances that will change the situation. For example, in virtually all industrialized nations the birthrate has fallen, so that there is an imminent decline in the size of the regular labour force; in some places this is already evident. This is forcing employers to seek new human resources, and women represent a pool of untapped labour. In this situation, the challenge for women is to be accepted for the whole range of jobs, including management.

In other parts of the world there are large numbers of young people and it may appear that women are not needed in the same way. However, women in the industrializing and developing nations are often the entrepreneurs and key workers. The issue here is similar to that in the industrialized world. Women must have access to and be given credit for their work in a wide range of jobs. They also need to have access education and skills to achieve this. Other pressures, such as rapid advances in technology and communications, the growth and spread of market economies as well as demographic shifts, are creating the possibility of many different patterns of working. The whole workforce may become more dynamic with people coming in and out of it, getting trained, switching careers, working full- or part-time at different stages, having several jobs at once, in Charles Handy's terms becoming "portfolio people". Many women already have experience of the type of flexibility and adaptability that will be required. However, if they are to have a role in management, women must secure appropriate training, and they may need to take the initiative in doing this.

Organizations have different accepted routes into management. The following questions may help to identify the routes for a given organization:

- At what age do people typically achieve their first management position?
- What is the "right" education for people who are managers?
- What qualifications do your managers usually have?
- What competences (skills, knowledge and attitudes) are expected in your managers?
- How are managers typically recruited?
  — from university
  — from specific areas of the company (which ones?)
  — from other companies
  — from all parts of the organization
  — in some other way (describe)
- What training and experience is required before managers are promoted? Note down the typical career routes and any important key steps. How do people get these?

The trainer may review the answers to these questions and consider how women's experience matches these norms, then compare with women's experience in their organization.

22.2   Corporate culture

Look now at your corporation, at the culture in which the women are to operate. Within the management career norms discussed above, there will be variations based on the ethos and values of the individual organization, division or department. The corporate values, whether these are explicit or implicit, affect all development activity in the organization; they should be identified, together with the effect on women, so that appropriate action can be included. For example, if the espoused values support a culture that emphasizes long hours, exclusive male activities and resignation of women from work on marriage (as is still implicit in many Japanese companies), then it will be very difficult for women to play a full role in management unless these values are challenged.

It is important therefore to understand the corporate culture. Sometimes this is expressed in a formal company document - a "mission statement"; it will also exist in the myths, stories, customs and rituals of the organization.

22.3   Building a profile of the organization

What clues are there about the organization and its values in the way it presents itself? The following questionnaire can be used within a women's training programme to generate material for discussion about their own perceptions and their role. It can help raise awareness about subtle organizational issues.

- Describe the buildings, furnishings, facilities, and the general environment.
- What does the corporate literature say about the organization? What does it highlight and what does it ignore? Is what is written about applied in practice?
- What impressions do visitors get? Think about those coming into the reception area, telephone callers. How do staff refer to customers and members of the public?
- How do people refer to their employment - with pride or something else? How long do people stay?
- What do people have to do to get promoted? Is it to do with being competent, getting results, exhibiting loyalty, having long service, having experience in particular departments or functions, or something else?
- Who are the outstanding people - past and present?
- Briefly describe any anecdote or story that typifies the organization.

- List any customs that the organization observes, or privileges or awards that it gives, and describe under what circumstances.

The answers will illustrate important implications for women. Is this an organization where the customs and values are readily apparent to women and do they find them attractive?

22.4   Women's role and status in society

Consider now women's role and status in your society. Is equality enshrined in law and is this a recent or a long-standing state of affairs? What in practice does it mean? Are women enfranchised? Do they own property and have responsibility over their own affairs? Are women accorded special roles in society (for example, revered as matriarchs, as in Italy)? Are women generally as well-educated as men? Do the majority of women work and, if so, are they in all types of jobs and positions? Are there many role models for women in management? If not, in what types of work do women predominate and what determines this?

An appreciation of the underlying values concerning the situation and status of women may help in shaping the training for women as managers, so that it can take account of the current situation and be more effective. A practical example which demonstrates this point comes from Portugal, where the Commission on the Status of Women introduced a programme of management training for rural women craft workers. The training was designed around the needs and experience of the women. Nevertheless, the trainers reported that a key learning point for them was that training in such situations must be organized on a different basis than the calendar year and be made more relevant to village life, where people live under the rules of seed time, watering, harvest and winter fallow ground. An obvious point, perhaps, but one which needs to be translated appropriately to ensure training always fits the real life needs of the trainees.

22.5   Training objectives

Next, we need to identify specific objectives for training women. As mentioned earlier, these might apply to three quite distinct stages: helping women to enter management, enabling women to establish competence in management jobs, and helping women to progress up the management ladder into more senior jobs.

As with the cultural profile, it is possible to build up a woman's experience profile to determine where efforts are needed (see box 22.1).

The results of the women's experience profile can be used to decide the focus for your training and development activities.

If women are not applying for first line or trainee management positions or are not successful in the selection process, then the focus should be on getting women into management.

> **Box 22.1. Women's experience profile**
>
> - Check the cultural profile. Are women presently employed as managers?
> - What is the proportion of all trainee manager jobs (where these exist) that are held by women?
> - What proportion of all junior manager jobs are held by women?
> - What proportion of middle managers are women?
> - What is the proportion of senior managers who are women?
> - Do women apply for management jobs with the organization in sufficient numbers?
> - Are women as successful as men in the selection process?
> - Do women and men follow the same career paths and do they have access to the same training and development opportunities (check if women are usually employed in some management jobs rather than others, and how the career progression from these jobs compares)?
> - Check career progression rates. Are women and men treated similarly with regard to promotion?

If women are successful in achieving first line management positions but are not performing as well as expected, then the focus should be on giving specific skill development and on broadening their experience of what is required.

If women are successful in junior management jobs but are leaving or are not being promoted to middle and senior management positions, then the focus should be on career planning, personal and organizational development.

So far we have discussed the cultural aspect that influences the choice of development programmes for women. We have also reviewed the different career stages at which interventions might be helpful. It might now be useful to examine some of the other factors that govern choices.

22.6 Women-only training?

The first major choice concerns the participants: should they be only women or mixed - women and men. It is probably a truism to say that it depends upon what one wants to achieve. When the overriding aim is to build women's confidence and to develop specific skills where they may need special tuition, then women-only training is the best route. Where the need is to build strong mixed teams, then it is important to develop women and men together. However, in this case it is important to ensure that women and men are each given proper recognition for results, and that differences in styles and approaches are noted but not devalued. It may require sensitive and careful coaching on the part of the tutoring or facilitating team to bring out the skills of the whole group.

Real equality of opportunity implies that men, as well as women, have to become much more aware of their own behaviours, attitudes and assumptions and the impact these have on others. There are already signs that men are beginning to address these issues for themselves. For example, both Sweden and Norway have Royal Commissions on the Role of Men through which they identify training as well as employment and social policies that need to be changed. In the United Kingdom and the United States development groups for men are starting to emerge. Awareness training, which deals with equal opportunities in the widest sense, is now offered in many countries.

There have been a number of interesting initiatives aimed at helping men and women in management to work more effectively together. For example, the chief executive of an insurance company in Sweden wanted to know why they had so few women managers. He set up task forces, one comprising women managers and the other his top management team - all men. The women discussed and reported on their experience of working in the company and identified where and what they thought were barriers. The men, in their task meetings, discussed why they found it difficult to work with women. The two groups then met for open discussions, to find and implement ways to go forward. This is a rare example of truly frank exchanges between men and women working together.

When Oxfam, the voluntary aid agency, wanted to encourage their women to reach senior positions, they set up a training exercise involving women and men. In one-to-one situations, women explained their view of the organization and described their experience of working within it. Significantly, the men were obliged to listen, and not to comment or interrupt but to be ready afterwards to discuss what they had learned. The result here was that men learned that women contributed different and useful perspectives. They also experienced in a small way what it was like to be at a meeting where one's contributions were not admitted.

Multiracial programmes

Even if it is decided that the participants are to be women only, there are more choices to be made, for example multiracial versus one race. This will depend on the general situation in society as well as the level of integration. The best rule to follow is that learning is most effective where the safest environment can be created in order for the learner to take the most risks. As with relations between the sexes, it is ultimately essential for the races to work together and have an appreciation of each other.

A useful example is provided by the Tall Poppies organization in New Zealand. Any management programme that is attended by Maoris has to include a Maori spiritual dimension, thus sharing the Maori heritage with white New Zealanders. In South Africa the women's management programme at the University of Pretoria similarly seeks to integrate black and white experience, this time paying particular attention to the imagery and content of training exercises. These are positive ways of valuing diversity, and ultimately they must benefit the organizations. The general point here is to give special attention to the likely needs of the whole group when multiracial training is being considered.

Single-grade or multi-grade groups

Similar arguments apply when considering whether a training programme should be offered to women who are all on the same grade or to a group drawn from different levels in the organization. In this case, it is usually preferable to have participants who are from the same level. Typically they will share similar responsibilities and face similar challenges. They will feel confident in sharing problems, and the value of this openness probably outweighs the benefit of the chance to network with senior people (who are themselves somewhat disadvantaged in this situation).

Faculty members

Another choice concerns the faculty staff, particularly whether these programmes are best taught by women or by a mixed team. The guiding principle here is that the trainers should be people who have resolved their own attitudes and beliefs about women's development and feel comfortable with women. Men can teach on these programmes very effectively as long as they are sensitive to the subtle issues involved.

Approaches to management development

The trend in management development is to relate it as closely as possible to the work experience, and this suggests that the emphasis should be towards on-the-job approaches to learning. Care should therefore be taken to ensure that women are included in task forces, special projects and assignments. All these can be important developmental experiences and often count significantly in promotion decisions.

Off-the-job training includes a variety of forms, including open and distance learning, taught courses and those that are more experiential in nature. When any of these approaches are used, there needs to be great care in helping the transfer of learning to the real work situation. Mentors or counsellors can play an extremely valuable role here, especially as women often experience feelings of isolation as they are promoted up through the organization. In Sweden there are formal mentoring programmes, where a senior person is assigned responsibility for guiding the career development of one or more younger people. Where women are concerned this has an added benefit. Women often find it difficult to find mentors, partly because there are few senior women and also because mentoring of women by a man can sometimes be open to misinterpretation. Where mentors are appointed by the company, it formalizes and clarifies the relationship.

22.7   Examples of management development for women

Getting into management

Self-development programmes are a useful way of helping women to enter management. These programmes aim to increase women's self-confidence and their awareness of career possibilities, and at the same time to encourage them to take responsibility for themselves.

Such training typically involves making a detailed and personal assessment of one's strengths and weaknesses and of preparing a personal action programme. A major component is training in assertiveness and communication skills generally. Guidance is also usually given in setting and achieving personal objectives and in designing (and later carrying out) personal action plans.

This type of training can be designed for a wide range of women. Young entrants to the workforce can all benefit, whether they are women in unskilled or semi-skilled work who now realize that they would like a more responsible job, or young graduates who have to find their feet quickly in the management world. Older women, especially those who have been out of the workforce for a few years having a family, or those whose circumstances mean a dramatic reshaping of their economic aspirations, also benefit.

Experience suggests that it is important that the learning processes used for this training supports and reinforces the messages, i.e., that the women can take responsibility for their own development. For this reason, although these programmes can be run as short courses, they appear to be more effective when run over several weeks or months. Often they are called self-development programmes and engage the learner in the design and delivery of the learning.

Self-development groups for women managers

One project in the United Kingdom reported by Boydell et al. and supported by the then Manpower Services Commission (a Government agency) followed the evolution and work of 16 groups of what were loosely termed "self-development groups for women managers" (Boydell et al., 1986). In practice, some of these groups comprised women who were managers, but more involved women who wanted to become managers. Some were already at work, others were planning to return to the labour force after a period at home looking after children.

Each group was given funding to provide for a facilitator to work with them for around 50 hours, with the time-scale and programme left open for negotiation. Most groups comprised about eight women, each working with one or two trainers. They met on average once every three or four weeks, usually for two to four hours at a time. The emphasis was on using practical issues as a vehicle for learning. Around 33 per cent of the time was spent on real issues to do with work, for example how to cope with a boss who constantly blocked suggestions and ideas. A further 33 per cent was spent on personal aspects concerning the individuals. Relationships, personal finance, dilemmas of balancing work and the family were some of the issues discussed. The rest of the time was devoted to real issues other than work, social issues for example, and to more formal syllabus items dealing with management models and frameworks. With regard to methodology, unstructured approaches like group discussion worked best. This was used not only for reviewing and studying work and other issues, but also for understanding the working of the self-development group itself. This was an important vehicle for learning, and provided the opportunity for the frank personal feedback which is often denied to women. Exercises and lectures on formal management topics and skills accounted for less that 20 per cent of the total activity.

At the end of the programme, many of the women had demonstrated enhanced levels of confidence in practical ways. Several applied for and achieved promotions. Others embarked on more formal studies, confident that these were appropriate to their new-found ambitions. Some went on to form and run self-development groups for women in their organization or locality. Specific outcomes mentioned by individuals included feeling more confident, able to be more assertive, thinking more logically, being less reliant on others for approval, being able to take on more responsibility, and having increased understanding and empathy with subordinates.

The project showed that in successful groups, participants share responsibility for decisions and actions and may run sessions themselves. It is important therefore to preserve and even enhance the self-development aspects. People from a wide variety of backgrounds can facilitate the discussions. It is not necessary to be an "expert" in self-development. It is important to be able to allow participants to work on their own issues and to be able to work in a loosely structured group setting.

There are issues that need to be addressed when groups of this type are sponsored or run by the employer. Self-development by definition is wide ranging and discussion will undoubtedly include matters far beyond the workplace. This is a characteristic of many different forms of women's development and reflects the inter-relatedness with which women typically approach their lives. Women's development frequently touches issues that need to be handled sensitively. For this reason, employers should not expect feedback on individuals from self-development groups.

A self-development programme in a corporation

In one bold experiment with self-development processes, the British Broadcasting Corporation has embarked on a programme which it is making available to its 8,000 women staff in non-management jobs. The programme, which is followed by 100 women at a time, is based on a self-development journal which each woman completes in her own time and more or less at her own pace. There are three time pegs, in the form of workshops: one to introduce the whole process, the second to give practical tuition in assertiveness skills, and finally the third to review progress and decide what happens next. The workshops are scheduled over a three-month period. However, the journal itself is the main vehicle stimulating questioning, personal discovery, discussion and recognition of the individual's own achievements — something which women often tend to overlook.

The journal is a practical workbook, both attractive and designed with humour. The learning is drawn directly from the experience of women in the corporation. Each individual can build a personal resource bank of information about skills, abilities, qualities, aptitudes and experience to use when applying for jobs, reviewing progress, setting new goals and so on. This is achieved by self-completion of inventories and questionnaires.

The journal includes short factual input to set the context for subjects, including setting goals, getting support for objectives, accessing and using information, increasing visibility and managing one's self. It gives practical examples, sets exercises to be completed at the depth and level the individual feels to be appropriate, offers questions to create dialogue and raise issues, suggests activities, and provides the framework for action plans.

This approach overcomes the disadvantage of some forms of "distance learning" by encouraging involvement with other people. Many of the activities it suggests require discussion with, or make enquiries of, others. In this way, the programme is building and reinforcing the behaviours that develop and sustain self-confidence.

In view of the emphasis on taking personal responsibility, it will be interesting to see how the corporation copes when hundreds of women have completed the programme and start to use their increased confidence and assertiveness to achieve more challenging career goals. It seems sure to unleash an enormous amount of demand, energy and talent.

Because approaches like this build confidence they are also useful for women who are not currently in the workforce; at home, perhaps, looking after children or elderly parents, as well as women who are at work but want to change career direction.

The important factor about these development programmes is that they must given recognition to the woman's current situation and to her current strengths and talents. Typically these are either not recognized or, even worse, are devalued by society at large. Often it is a case of re-evaluating skills, including ones gained in the domestic arena, in terms of core behaviours that do have wider currency. For example, managing the household requires budgetary control, negotiating and communicating skills, the ability to delegate and so on. It is by recognizing and building on these and other skills that women can gain confidence. Often this is the first, and necessary, step to achieving the appropriate formal qualifications or experience in line with social and cultural expectations.

22.8   Getting established in management

Once a woman achieves her first management post, it is important to ensure that she receives the appropriate training and development. Research shows that at this level women typically get the basic skill training that they need for the current job. Development also takes place on the job through interaction with colleagues and bosses. In many countries and companies there are still very few women managers, so that women do not have easy access to role models. Young women at this stage can feel very isolated at the professional level and feel that they are not making the progress they expect and that they are not taken seriously enough by male colleagues. At its worst this can result in women leaving the company, and this sets in motion a spiral which leads other women to believe this is not a woman-friendly company and therefore not one to join. To break this spiral, far-sighted employers are looking more closely at the experience of their women managers.

As mentioned, some employers are appointing mentors and making managers accountable for the development of all their staff, women as well as men. Others are encouraging women to set up networks. This can help women to share their experience and learning, and help create a pool of women who can be role models and mentors in their turn.

At this stage, however, it is generally important to ensure that women are integrated into the company, and it is to be expected that most of their training and development will be as part of mixed programmes. The following are two examples of programmes aimed at learning more about women's experience and needs at this level.

Sharing experience within the corporation

In an international engineering company with very few women managers, the company decided to bring the women together to learn more about their experience and to see how the company could be more "women friendly". The participants were mostly young graduates, but also included one or two women who had been with the company for several years and had been promoted through the ranks. As preparation for a two-day workshop, the women completed a questionnaire which was assigned to help them share their expectations and experience of the company. It was felt important to hear what they expected from the company, as this would inevitably influence their satisfaction with their actual experience.

The questionnaire was completed and analysed in advance of the workshop, which involved about 25 women. The results were presented to them for discussion about issues. This is a useful approach since the anonymous data laid open a wide range of issues and appeared to encourage participants to talk frankly about their experience more quickly than would otherwise be the case - important when time is a scarce resource. In this example, the women classified their issues into topic areas for discussion and action; the company wanted recommendations. The groups were helped in this by a process of "active enquiry". Senior women from other companies were present during the day and were consulted as "experts" by the groups. This helped to expand the vision which might otherwise have been limited by a one-company perspective. Having analysed the issues and possible solutions, they were then able to talk with senior management about ways in which company practices and procedures might be developed for the benefit of all employees. The company chairman attended, and thus gave witness to his support, asking for a fuller written report at an early date.

In another large telecommunications company, groups of women managers attend workshops to review their experience and to compare it with that of senior managers. They are also able to raise issues about company policies and procedures which may have an impact on women's ability to reach their potential. Through these workshops, women have shared their knowledge of flexible working by variable hours, working at home, sharing jobs and so on. Although these conditions are technically available to all, the fact that local management is allowed to exercise its own discretion means that for many women these options effectively do not exist. The workshops publicize what is possible so that women can decide what they should do.

Moving up to middle and senior management

As already mentioned, women typically receive basic skills training. Where they tend to miss out is on the broader development programmes. These may be programmes based on formal qualifications or shorter executive education. In both cases, the training usually has important "rite of passage" connotations as well as the actual input. It is important that companies check that women are put forward for these programmes.

It is also useful to check whether women managers who have followed "non-standard" career routes — perhaps being promoted into management from technical roles or via a "shop-floor" route or after a career break — have a firm foundation of skills and knowledge necessary for senior management. Women may be successful managers but nevertheless feel that they lack (as may indeed be the case) the theoretical framework that underpins management action. In these cases, intensive programmes like the Smith Management Programme offered at Smith College, in Massachusetts, are useful.

22.9   A general management programme for women

In the Smith Management Programme, which is offered to women only, major management disciplines including finance, marketing, computing, economics, organizational behaviour as well as skills such as negotiating and making presentations are tackled in periods of three weeks over each of two summers. Learning is consolidated by a project that is carried out in-company between the two summers. The programme is taught by a mixed group of faculty members, drawn from major American business schools. The pace is intensive but each woman is able to get as much help and feedback as she needs from both fellow participants and the tutorial team. Contact is also maintained when the women are back at their company. To develop experience of mentoring others, those women coming back in their second summer are given responsibility for the integration of the women who are there for the first time.

Examples of personal development programmes for senior women managers

For many women, promotion to higher levels of management is associated with re-evaluations of life style and behaviours. Some women feel an oppressive choice between further promotion and family life, particularly when they have children. Others perceive that the skills and aptitudes that have brought them thus far may not be sufficient for further promotion. They are unclear about the competences required of senior management and whether they have them. They become more aware of power and influence and the need to exercise these. They want to know how to develop appropriate strategies. At the same time, they are often concerned about values - their own and those of the organization. In order to move forward at this stage, when women typically find themselves more socially isolated than at earlier stages in their career, some women find it helpful to reconsider their chosen career path.

In programmes like Business Leadership for Women, offered at Ashridge Management College, women have the opportunity to re-evaluate their career, to build on strengths in terms of skills and knowledge, to create strategies for handling development areas, to set and find support for challenging new goals. A key tenet of this programme is that although it focuses on and develops leadership behaviours in the context of organizations, and particularly organizations undergoing change, it also emphasizes personal development and sets all action in the context of whole-life planning. Thus, a woman who arrived believing she had a choice between promotion or starting a family decided she could do both. This she achieved, and she was able to use her experience and position to institute flexible working and child-care policies in the company. In this way she ensured that other women do not feel the pressures of having to make a similar choice unless it is their wish to do so.

The Ashridge programme is based on original research work involving round-table discussions with a wide variety of women in leadership positions. The aim was to learn from them what experiences had been helpful in their development and what it would be useful for other women to know. Comparative data on the styles and meaning of leadership was also collected from women in the United Kingdom and the United States, as well as from a sample of British men.

The resulting programme is based on a series of core blocks that deal with raising self-awareness — giving direct and realistic feedback on behaviour, communicating and negotiating skills, visioning, managing strategically, developing power-and-influence strategies, developing a wide range of leadership behaviours and skills for analysing and understanding organizations, and personal planning. The programmes are attended by women from a wide range of organizations and from many different parts of the world, giving access to great cultural diversity. The diversity is used as part of the learning process and its benefit is retained when the women form their own network at the end of the programme to help the transfer of learning to their work situation. The women keep in touch and become their own resource and mentor network.

A remarkably similar approach was used by the Asian Institute of Management to study successful women managers in Indonesia, Malaysia, the Philippines, Singapore and Thailand, with the aim of documenting their career strategies, managerial practices and experiences. Using questionnaires and extended interviews, they were able to develop role-model case-studies from each of the five countries. They also used the knowledge gained to develop a workshop on career strategies for women managers. This consisted of five modules: setting career objectives; environmental assessment and job analysis; career management; potential problem analysis; and formulation of individual career plans. The case-studies formed the core of the workshop, augmented with exercises and games.

Elements of personal development programmes

These examples support the rule that training and development for women in management should be designed for the specific population in mind. However, it is also true that there are some components that recur, at different levels and depth, in most programmes. These include understanding the organization, developing and having confidence in one's own management style, communicating effectively, managing oneself and taking care of one's own career development.

Understanding organizations

Understanding the organization has been discussed briefly in section 22.3, "Building a profile of the organization". It is useful to include this, as women often believe that doing the job well is what counts, and tend to overlook or ignore the way organizations actually function. A critical look at organizational culture can help women to make more informed choices.

From this type of analysis it is possible to go on to examine organizational power and particularly the sources of power that are available to individuals. Women typically underestimate the extent to which they have power or, by their actions, they give it away. There are many models of power. Choose one that you feel comfortable with or use the following simple one, which is based on only four types of power:

Formal authority	the right to make decisions conferred on the individual by higher management
Expertise	specialist knowledge and skills, usually acquired through professional training
Resource control	control of physical, financial or information resources in the organization
Personal skills	the ability to persuade and build good relationships

Then ask the women to review their own use of and potential for power. To do this they should draw a circle in the middle of a plain piece of paper and put their own name inside it. Around this first circle they then draw others showing the names of people who have an important effect on their work - customers, suppliers, colleagues, subordinates, bosses and so on. Each circle should be linked with a line to the one in the centre.

Then ask the women to write along each line the type of power that flows between themselves and the other person.

- What type of power does each person have?
- What is their power based on?
- Who depends on whom and for what?

Usually both parties have some power, so look at two-way flows.

Discuss whether women are clearly signalling their source of power. For example, they will not be able to capitalize on "expert power" if they have not ensured that they are recognized for their specialist knowledge and skills. This can lead into a session on the need to be clear in promoting their own ability, not being falsely modest, taking risks when necessary and using their skills.

Management style

Developing a personal management style is likely to become more important as old authoritarian styles give way to more flexible and adaptable organizations. Women are generally credited with being concerned about individuals and group processes as well as in getting the job done. However, a warning comes from Rosabeth Moss Kanter (1977), who links a focus on the task with authoritarian behaviour and says that women do this because they are uncertain about power. This emphasizes the need to clarify power issues, to encourage women to delegate more and to build participative teams.

With regard to relationships, it is worth spending time on discussing the role of networks, both formal and informal. Women can benefit from using these actively both for professional contacts and information, and for more informal support. Women need to be part of the networks that exist and carry influence, and they may need to create their own. As mentioned earlier, they must develop their own contacts and mentors.

Communication

Communicating effectively is an important area for women's management development. It may include formal and informal presentations, personal appearance, language, style and so on. Assertiveness is essential for effective presentation and it is therefore a skill that every woman manager should acquire.

Assertiveness has to be practised, and a substantial amount of time may need to be allocated to this topic. Usually women need first to distinguish between assertive and other behaviours such as passive and aggressive styles which seem to be more commonly used. For example:

- an aggressive person wants to win, even if this means disregarding the rights and feelings of other people, over-values herself and attacks or accuses others;
- a passive person lets other people walk all over her;
- an assertive person stands up for herself but recognizes the rights of others. She communicates clearly and honestly, sharing her opinions and intentions.

A typical session would ask participants to check their own levels of assertiveness by getting them to think about their reactions and behaviour in different situations, for example, how they would handle the following:

- sending poorly cooked food back in a restaurant;
- confronting a senior colleague who put forward your idea at a meeting without giving you credit;
- making your point at a meeting where the chairperson seems intent on avoiding you;

Usually women will think of other situations where they know they find it difficult to be assertive. This can lead to role-playing and practice in being assertive. This means:

- stating their needs, wants, opinions and feelings directly;
- making statements that demonstrate that the point of view of the other person is understood - even if one disagrees with it;
- pointing out the difference between what has been agreed and what is happening;
- making clear to the other person the effect their behaviour is having;
- making sure the other person understands the consequences of not changing their behaviour; and
- finding out the needs, wants, opinions and feelings of the other person.

Techniques to enhance assertive behaviour are well documented by many specialists in books, videos and other training packages.

Increasing personal effectiveness

Personal effectiveness involves getting women to critically review factors such as time management and stress. Ask women to carry out a personal audit showing how they spend their time - at home as well as at work. Use a 24-hour clock to ensure everything is included. Women need to check they are not falling into a "superwoman" trap, trying to do everything, being overly accessible, not delegating and so on.

It can be useful to get women to:

- identify, and write down, their key objectives; and
- keep a diary to record how they use time.

They can then check whether their behaviour is actually helping them to meet their objectives and, if not, to take appropriate action.

Stress management is a topic that always has a large response from women when it is offered as a workshop choice. Perhaps this is not surprising given the exceptionally busy lives most career women lead. It is always worth including relaxation techniques and also reviewing other stress-related behaviours such as diet and eating patterns.

Career planning

Finally, programmes for women managers can usefully include time on career planning and ensure that this is whole-life planning. Almost all senior women who are also married emphasize the importance of a supportive partner, so it seems clear that career planning must be an open activity, taking into account the widest needs of both parties. It is only in this way that women can avoid being thrown off course by unexpected issues or by paying a high price for success in terms of a broken personal life. This does not, of course, mean that everything has to be pre-planned with no spontaneity. It means that there need to be generally agreed goals and objectives, so that both parties can respond to opportunities and challenges in a positive way.

22.10 Conclusions

Women's management development programmes need to be designed to meet the specific needs of a given population. There are, however, some general principles that can be applied: such programmes should be based on women's real-life experience; they should be led by people who are themselves well-versed and sympathetic to women's issues. The aim should be to increase women's awareness of their own strengths and styles while enabling them to develop and increase their range of management competences. The women should understand the culture and the informal, as well as the formal, processes of their organizations and they should be equipped to take charge of and plan their career strategies. In this way, women will be more able to reach their potential for the benefit of their organizations, as well as for their personal fulfilment.

However, as has been intimated, to be completely effective, women's management development must be accompanied by appropriate awareness and development on the part of men, by changes to human resource policies and procedures and by shifts in the culture of organizations. One of the benefits of the current rapid pace of change is that it is providing the possibility for such shifts and therefore for women to play a part in the reshaping of organizations to meet new challenges and opportunities.

MANAGEMENT DEVELOPMENT FOR PUBLIC SERVICE ORGANIZATIONS 23

Harald Stokkeland, R. Weitz and L. Lawson

Throughout the 1980s concern was expressed and much attention paid to productivity in the public sector in general and the public service sector in particular. We begin this chapter by discussing some of the common features and how they influence management training for the sector. First, both the size and the growth of the service sector — private and public — account for the importance of the issue. Secondly, there has also been a growing understanding of the relationship between public service sector productivity and social and economic development in society in general. Not only does low productivity in the public service sector hamper development in other sectors of the economy, but it also promotes social injustice and inequality, and may cause serious political problems.

A third area which should be taken into consideration is the specifics of service sector management as compared to other sectors. In a recent study, lack of authority and autonomy, accountability, productivity measurement, difficulties in assessing outputs and outcomes in services, resistance to change and lack of competition were highlighted as problems facing managers in the public service sector (Prokopenko, 1989). To this list could be added the lack of consumer or client orientation which is the focus of the "Service Management" tradition (Normann, 1984).

Management development approaches must aim at addressing these specific public service factors and criteria. It is evident that the development measures required go far beyond traditional training.

23.1   The nature and characteristics of public services

The aim of public services is to improve the quality of life of the general public. Many different types of goods and services are required such as fire protection, transport, post and telecommunications, education, health care, water, electricity and gas, recreation, etc. Whereas a private service company is governed by commercial interests, a public service company responsible for the provision of public services is heavily influenced by political and social priorities. At the consumer end, the objectives of a public service organization are social rather than commercial.

The aim is to provide necessities to the public at large, some of which the public does not pay for directly. Where commercial companies usually focus on opportunities and innovation, public service organizations focus more on control and structure. This increases the time it takes an agency to carry out the routine and necessary steps to execute their programme missions. Such problems are particularly common in large government agencies because of their multiple layers of management review and approval (Usilaner, 1980).

This is changing in many countries. Heavy, bureaucratic structures are loosening up to give way to more functional, service-oriented structures. The shift in corporate thinking (see Peters and Waterman, 1983) made many companies change from product-oriented to customer- and market-oriented approaches. Some public service organizations have followed suit. Public service professionals are having to reassess their approach to meet the demands of an increasingly aware general public for service satisfaction. Arguably, for the first time, they now consider themselves accountable to the public they serve.

This shift in thinking has led many public service organizations to take measures to improve the quality of their services. These not only include internal efficiency improvement measures, but also the "front line" contact with the public. For example, in the United Kingdom, certain police authorities are experimenting with psychology, behavioural and communication training for their officers. Another example is France Telecom which, through frequent and systematic consumer surveys, is exploring the public's present and possible future needs for services.

In spite of such initiatives, public service organizations on the whole retain their bureaucratic nature. Even though attempts are made to improve their accountability vis-à-vis the public, they remain largely monopolistic, with the environment in which they operate staying fairly stable over time. These two factors — a high degree of monopoly and, as a result, lack of competition — make public service organizations resistant to change.

23.2 Management in public service organizations

(A) Managerial practices

Kooiman and Eliassen (1988) point to two major differences which have been identified between private and public sector managers in Sweden. The first difference is to do with goal orientation: private leaders attempt to maximize or satisfy rather clear and definable objectives, while public managers have to face the notion of public interest, which is not only subjective but also more vague and contradictory. Secondly, public managers work in a more stable, bureaucratic environment than private leaders.

Bearing in mind that the pattern of activities of public service organizations is moving towards the same mode as commercial firms — i.e., becoming more adaptable and efficient — it seems highly desirable that they should move from

Table 23.1. Bureaucratic versus managerial control

	Bureaucratic control	Managerial control
Managerial focus	Norms	Results
Breadth of orientation	Narrow	Wide
Managerial latitude	Rigid	Flexible
Budgetary orientation	Spend completely	Spend efficiently
Adaptation to change in environment	Little	Much

bureaucratic towards managerial control as well. To facilitate this is one of the most important tasks facing the effective training department.

(B) Managerial competence

The public service will always need managers who can harmonize political and economic objectives, balance the mix of resources and cope with the administrative constraints inherent in the public service environment. Such managers will need to develop flexibility and openness to new ideas and concepts, "breadth plus depth" or multi-dimensional skills and competences, leadership, ethics and extreme sensitivity to issues of morality, value systems and social codes, global orientation, decision-making capabilities under uncertain conditions, communication skills, ability to discriminate, technological literacy, adaptability, etc. Senior civil servants will need to play a greater role in introducing new technology, providing a less authoritarian leadership, rapidly recognizing and concentrating on new problem areas and using modern IT devices.

A key issue is also the question of delegation and hence the issue of trust. In organizations where bureaucratic control mechanisms are at work, the level of trust between manager and subordinates is correspondingly low. This presents an obstacle to delegation of initiative to lower levels, which again stifles the organization.

There are examples of training programmes which try to remedy the absence of dynamic leadership skills in public sector organizations. In Norway, for example, a three-month course for senior public servants covers management by change; power and management; the leader's function; and the leader's responsibility for information and service.

Another interesting example is a 12-week training programme in Finland which seeks to "rekindle the entrepreneurial spirit of government managers". The programme has been specially designed to motivate managers to meet the demands of "the rough and tumble world" of public management in the 1990s, when they increasingly have to compete with the private sector (Savoie, 1990). A rationale of the programme is an observation that "a long career in administration seems to condition some to passivity at work". The Finns argue that "strong central control and direction must be substantially cut back, so that they can adjust their operations to capture emerging opportunities and deal quickly with pressing problems".

23.3　Implications for management development programmes

Many public managers spend most of their lives operating inside public institutions that resist change. As a result they themselves become inflexible and resistant to change, frequently because they fear the unknown — or perhaps even the known (if they think that an attempt at performance improvement will cost them their jobs or status). This static environment is the main reason why training alone is unlikely to yield positive results. Public servants know only too well that initiatives to change may cost them more in terms of hard work and frustration than will be given to them in return. Changing the practices in the system and organizational structures requires the application of non-training solutions as well.

Actual organization performance could be improved by using results-oriented, participative approaches that combine classroom training with the practical implementation of on-the-job projects as well as organization development programmes. An action-learning programme, task forces, experience-based training and action plans contain elements of both training and non-training solutions which lead to concrete measures being taken to effect changes in organizational practices and cultures.

Some non-training activities which aim at improving organizational efficiency and removing the obstacles which prevent managers and their subordinates from doing a better job could be, for example, the following:

- developing a more specific corporate vision, mission statement and strategic objectives;
- changing the organizational structure, routines or systems;
- introducing new technology;
- delegating formal responsibility further down the organizational hierarchy;
- interdepartmental projects;
- changing the reward system to emphasize results and not positions;
- introducing systems to monitor and assess managerial performance, etc.

Once it has been decided to run a training programme, the issue of training approaches becomes of crucial importance. Richards (1989) argues that "management development initiatives are required to enable public managers to develop not just the competencies, but also the self-confidence and attitude needed to manage and not just to administer public bureaucracies". That senior government officials prefer to learn from one another's experiences, successes and failures rather than from outside experts should be taken into account.

Corfield and Penny (1983) give an interesting account of how action learning helped managers in a family and community services department overcome some of their inertia to change. The department exhibited the typical features of a bureaucracy: centralized decision-making, formal communications and emphasis on formal rules and relationships. It had already invested considerably in a management and supervisory training course, which had failed to bring about the desired change on the job. One result of this disappointment was that the organization at large became the scapegoat in the eyes of the managers. Typical comments were "management training should start at the top", and "how can I become a better manager if the Office Head won't let me?".

From discussions with managers, the trainers observed "an unwillingness to act until a finite solution, guaranteed to succeed, could be formulated". The managers showed a certain amount of apathy and were prepared to live with a system which they knew suffered from major deficiencies.

A decision was taken to launch an action-learning programme, where the managers would engage in joint problem-solving with the assistance of the two trainers as set advisers (for a description of roles and functions in action-learning programmes, see Chapter 11). Examples of problem areas which the managers themselves identified and tried to tackle during the programme were:

- improving the performance of a deputy;
- developing and building a team of residential child-care workers;
- attempting to change the functioning of a management team;
- changing the role relationship between the staff of a residential unit and fieldworkers; and
- setting up and running a pilot project using a patchwork approach to service delivery.

Weeks later, two main conclusions were drawn about the training. First, through the interaction with one another and with trainers, the participants were able to articulate their problems, receive feedback and perceive their problems as managers differently. Secondly, they seemed better able to come to terms with and deal with the inter-personal and organizational barriers which were blocking the way to greater effectiveness.

23.4   Management development approaches

In many countries public employees have access to a range of management training programmes and facilities to meet their training and development needs. For example, training institutions for senior civil servants and for managerial and technical staff exist in several countries, and paid educational leave arrangements are also available to public servants in 30 or more countries.

Unfortunately, however, a large number of existing institutions still provide formalistic and low quality training without much care being taken to fit the training programme to participants' development needs. Training methods still emphasize the lecture and the provision of abstract knowledge, without giving due attention to the development of skills, abilities and attitudes. Too many programmes are standardized and not flexible enough to take into account the needs and problems of participants and their respective public service organizations.

Only a few public administration institutions use participative training approaches which focus on practical problem-solving. Fewer still systematically plan exchange programmes between public administration and private businesses, including practical work and assignments in other organizations, in order to share the best experiences and work cultures (Prokopenko, 1989).

With the aim of reducing these gaps in public administration education and training, making the training more participative and closer to the needs of the participants and their organizations, and introducing learning into the process of public administration improvement, a dual-focus training approach has been developed and tested in the field by the World Health Organization. This approach is described in the following sections.

23.5 An example of a management development programme

The Dual-Focus (D-F) approach to solving public service managers' performance problems in the water and sanitation sector has been used by the World Health Organization for many years. The original impetus for using a different approach to human resource development (HRD) came from the fact that traditional training, which often took place within an academic context, was not having a strong enough impact.

The D-F approach combines organizational changes and result-oriented training. These are the five key characteristics of the D-F approach:

- needs and results orientation;
- creative problem-solving;
- action learning;
- service management; and
- organization development

Besides these five characteristics, the approach has also been very much influenced by more specific concepts introduced as participative "tools" throughout the programme.

(A)   Needs and results orientation

The structure of the D-F programme is determined by a critical water and sanitation consumer needs assessment which provides the context and relevancy of the training, evaluation and follow-up components of the programme.

The overriding theme used throughout the D-F approach is the basic value of *participant*-generated goals and responsibility. Processes and tools are chosen that will offer critical and strategic thinking experiences within the context where a project team has taken *responsibility*. The needs of the teams are transformed into the objectives of the programme.

(B)   Creative problem-solving

The problem-solving aspect of the D-F approach is probably the most important one. It relates to real performance problems and is based on a procedure which differs significantly from traditional training. Numerous "creative" problem-solving techniques and tools have been applied throughout the programme — from "brainstorming" to more structured ways of eliciting creative ideas. These problem-solving techniques involve extensive use of group work and cooperation.

(C)   Action learning

The principles of "action learning" are actively used in the D-F approach. The "action learning" ideas go beyond "learning by doing" and include "learning by exercising responsibility". This means (i) real work with real problems; (ii) that the problems are of great importance; (iii) they are unclearly defined; and (iv) they cannot be solved by simple routine techniques. Another important aspect of action learning is the notion that people in similar situations learn from one another. These general ideas of "action learning" are integral parts of the D-F effort.

(D)   Service management

A fourth characteristic of the D-F approach is "service management", which considers management as a service function (see Normann, 1984). "Service management" orientation is the first step towards establishing the proper position of the company's operations department, *the front line in meeting the users' needs*.

(E)   Organization development

Another characteristic of the approach is "organization development" (OD). In the water and sanitation sector as well as other public service organizations the more common term is "institutional development". This means that an organization has acquired special status and legitimacy for providing public services and meeting normative customer expectations.

23.6   Strengths and limitations of the Dual-Focus programme

(A)   The strengths

One of the strengths of the D-F concept is that it relies heavily on the "gospel" and philosophy of action learning. It promotes innovations and innovative combinations. It ensures that the people responsible for implementing the programme are always on the move, searching for suitable tools to serve the programme objectives. Both the participants and the facilitators learn a lot. It includes:

- a systematic follow-up programme;

- a *multidisciplinary* and *multicultural* approach - both in terms of the mix of facilitators and the mix of participants;

- an opportunity to create new tools related to actual working experience, involving the facilitators and the participants in the design work; and

- an approach wherein concepts are offered as *possible* improvement vehicles which participants can accept completely, or in part, or reject altogether, rather than as absolute truths.

(B)   The limitations

The limitations of the D-F concept are linked to resource and time constraints, which force you to make choices and to use strategies and tools that are not always successful. Furthermore, there is a tendency for the two different main groups of tools (directed towards individual and organizational problem-solving) to exist in isolation from one another.

TRAINING AND DEVELOPMENT OF ENTREPRENEUR-MANAGERS OF SMALL ENTERPRISES

24

Arturo L. Tolentino

A competent entrepreneur-manager[*] is one of the most important requirements for the success of a small enterprise. The total performance of the business is mainly determined by the attitudes, decisions and actions of the entrepreneur-manager. The definitions of small enterprise vary between countries and regions, and are usually based on such criteria as number of employees, size of investment in plant and machinery and volume of production or sales. The definition adopted by a particular country is usually based on the specific national context (e.g. the size-structure of enterprises in the industry sector in which the business operates), and on the use and objectives for which the definition is formulated (e.g. for policy and legal framework, promotional and administrative purposes and so on). One characteristic, however, that clearly distinguishes small enterprises from medium-sized and large ones is the management structure and system of the enterprise. Small enterprises are closely linked with the practice of entrepreneurship, where the strategic and operational management decision-making rests primarily with one or two people who, more often than not, own the enterprise. The independence of the small enterprise is sometimes also a criterion, i.e. not being a subsidiary or production unit of a larger firm. In the European Union, for example, an enterprise cannot have 25 per cent or more of its control in the hands of a larger enterprise for it to be considered as a small enterprise. However, with the globalization of the economy, small enterprises are increasingly participating in networks of relations with other firms of various sizes.

---

[*] The term *entrepreneur* is used in business literature to refer to an individual who creates a new business venture, assumes the personal and business risks associated with the new business and continues to actively manage its operation. Small business *managers*, on the other hand, are those that assume the management responsibility of an ongoing small business by, for example, buying the business, inheriting it or being hired to run it. In this chapter, the term *entrepreneur-manager* is used to refer to both of these groups. As discussed in the various sections, their training and development needs, preferences and constraints are different, and must be consciously considered in designing and delivering specific interventions.

There is very close and intimate identification between the entrepreneur-manager and his or her small business. The development of the competences of entrepreneur-managers is closely linked to the development of the small business, and the development of the business invariably requires the development of the competences of the entrepreneur-managers. This very close identification of the person and the business leads to the particular and specific nature of the resulting management style, systems and practices in the small business. Different stages in the life cycle of the enterprise require specific competences and capabilities of the entrepreneur-managers, which must be considered in formulating and implementing training and development interventions. The entrepreneur-managers also have particular orientations, preferences and constraints that must be considered in designing and delivering training.

24.1   Competences required of entrepreneur-managers of small enterprises

The management structure and independence of a small enterprise put the entrepreneur-manager in the most critical position in the running of the enterprise. The success and failure of the business depend entirely on the person's competences. Various studies on mortality, survival and growth of small enterprises support this; most failures of small businesses are due to poor entrepreneurship and management.

(A)   The roles and functions of entrepreneur-managers of small enterprises

Entrepreneur-managers of small enterprises perform two distinct yet closely intertwined functions: entrepreneurship and management. In small enterprises, these functions are so embedded in each other that it is very difficult to distinguish them. It is only for the purpose of analysis that these two groups of roles and functions are discussed separately here.

Entrepreneurial functions

There are many theories of what makes a person an entrepreneur. At one extreme is the view that an entrepreneur is born already endowed with the entrepreneurial traits of enterprise and business acumen. At the other end is the view that any person can become an entrepreneur when in a situation that provides the opportunities for (or requires) the practice of entrepreneurship. Experience and studies of active entrepreneurship and small enterprise development promotion show that, in reality, entrepreneurship is somewhere in between these extremes. This has led to programmes for entrepreneurship education, training and development, and the creation of a conducive and enabling environment for the start-up and growth of enterprises.

Entrepreneurship is the quality which enables people to start a new business or vigorously and innovatively to expand an existing one (Harper, 1983). Entrepreneurs are known to exhibit (always or at any particular time) some or all of the interrelated characteristics shown in table 24.1. These qualities enable them to seek out business opportunities, conceptualize and initiate business projects, gather the physical, financial, and human resources needed to start the business, set goals for themselves and their enterprises, and guide the enterprise and its people to accomplish the goals.

Table 24.1. Profile of an entrepreneur

Characteristic	Traits
Self-confidence	Confidence, independence, optimism
Task/result oriented	Persistence, perseverance, determination, tenacity, drive, energy, initiative
Risk-taking	Risk assessment and risk-taking ability; likes challenges
Leadership	Leadership behaviour; gets along well with others; responsive to suggestions and criticism
Originality	Innovative, creative, open-minded, resourceful, versatile, knowledgeable
Future-oriented	Foresight, vision, perceptiveness

Entrepreneurs, as people having an internal locus of control (Ward, 1993), provide the driving force behind small businesses, based on their belief that their behaviour and action, rather than outside factors beyond their control, determine the outcome of any endeavour. They believe that environmental factors can be influenced and managed. These beliefs are the source of the self-confidence in their exercise of leadership of small businesses. They provide the insight and the vision, being perceptually alert and having a great ability to see opportunities and threats in the environment. This ability to recognize business opportunities and develop them makes them the source of innovations — in products and services, in new processes and in doing business — in the enterprise. They provide the links between the small business and its environment, relying on informal networks of family, friends and business people that support entrepreneurial activities. Networks are vital to perceive opportunities, test ideas and acquire resources to create the new enterprise. They help the entrepreneur and the small business to keep abreast of current trends, to get to know new technologies, to assess changing customer trends and to develop new ways to manage and solve problems (Tjosvold and Weicker, 1993).

Managerial functions

The traditional functions of managers are planning, organizing, leading and controlling (see Chapter 1). Under these general functions are specific activities and techniques, which in a small business are usually performed by one or two people:

- *planning:* defining the goals and objectives of the business, deciding on the best route and ways of achieving them, allocating and budgeting the resources required in the performance of the work and tasks involved, and preparing contingency plans;

- *organizing:* structuring how and where the various functions, work and tasks are to be done and how they will interact and relate with each other; coordinating the activities of the various units of the organization; and assigning responsibilities and authority to people and groups for carrying out specific duties and tasks;

- *leading:* motivating and enabling people in the business to achieve goals through good communication, creation of an organizational climate for good performance and development of their capabilities, skills and competences; and

- *controlling:* making sure that performance is according to plans and expectations, through the establishment of standards of organizational and individual performance in key result areas, monitoring and measurement of actual performance, comparing actual performance against expectations, and taking corrective action whether to adjust performance level or to modify standards where necessary.

With the advent of new forms of enterprises and new forms of work organization, new managerial functions and required competences also arise. The highly dynamic and competitive globalized business environment has given rise to lean production systems that operate based on core competences and networks, and which are flexible and adaptable. Organizations are becoming less hierarchical, with less rigid job specifications and differentiations, and are transforming themselves into learning organizations that are constantly learning and applying the knowledge and insights gained from earlier experiences to improve their operations and practices (see Chapter 18). Production workers are organized in self-managed cells, making their own decisions on task distribution and work schedules. Production systems are increasingly knowledge-based, making human resources the key asset and determinant of enterprise competitiveness.

Due to these changes in the business environment and in the organization and operations of businesses, managers and supervisors are now more process-management focused. Their roles now include:

- *enabler:* developing the competences of people and creating the work organization and environment that will enable them to achieve high performance;

- *facilitator/coordinator:* creating linkages and relationships between individuals and work units that will facilitate the performance of the tasks and activities of the whole organization;

- *communicator/negotiator:* making clear to those concerned the organizational goals and targets, and ensuring acceptance and commitments;

- *change manager:* preparing people and the organization for the constant process of change that production and organizational flexibility require; and

- *internal consultant:* providing individuals and work teams with advice and assistance in problem-solving and effective improvements.

(B) Peculiarities and specificity of small business management

Entrepreneur-managers are so intimately identified with their small businesses that business development is almost synonymous with entrepreneur-management development and vice versa. Because of this close identification, the cultural background, personality, preferences and behaviour of the entrepreneur-manager and the characteristics of the small enterprise (e.g. size, sector, technology level) strongly influence each other, leading to very specific and particular management practices. That is why it is not appropriate to make sweeping generalizations on the training and development needs of entrepreneur-managers and their enterprises. Any training and development intervention must be based on careful needs analysis and the understanding of the particular requirements and situation of the target individual or group. This is particularly important when undertaking small business management development in a specific country, industry or community.

Table 24.2 gives some characteristics of small enterprises and their possible implications in the management style and practices in the firm (El-Namaki, 1989). The personality and behaviour of the entrepreneur-manager are reflected in the management systems and practices in the firm. Entrepreneurial traits such as creativity, achievement motivation, perseverance and risk-taking ability are combined with personal idiosyncrasies such as the approach to control, attitude to structure and standards, view of the environment and need for recognition. These will strongly influence the way the business is organized and managed. Professional and technical background and personal preferences dictate the priorities and task assignment, and determine entrepreneur-managers' degree of involvement and time allocation in the performance of the various managerial and operational business activities.

With small enterprises there is close involvement of the business with the family, the immediate community and other social and business networks of the entrepreneur-manager. Cultural traits and values of the entrepreneur-manager's family and community strongly influence managerial practices and systems, particularly in the area of personnel management and interpersonal relations. For certain communities, culture, traditions and religion have a direct impact on the culture and values of the enterprise. At the extreme, especially for very small enterprises, the separation of business and family concerns is often blurred.

The small size of the business brings with it advantages such as simple structures and processes that allow for greater flexibility, adaptability and dynamism, and

Table 24.2. Major management implications of characteristics of small enterprises

Observed characteristic	Implications for management styles and practices
Close link between the personality and behaviour of the entrepreneur and the small business	High degree of centralization, personalized management style, strong personal loyalty considerations, lack of succession plans, shortage of time for management and other tasks
Close link of the small enterprise to the family and/or immediate community	Strong influence of the family and community culture, informal approach to personnel recruitment and development and to management control
Small size of business operations	Simple and flexible processes and systems, multi-functional role of the entrepreneur-manager, informal communication and record keeping, close relationship with the workers, strong reliance on on-the-job training, easier integration between policy and practice, shortage of management and other resources
Narrow financial resource base	Stress on operational issues of management, preoccupation with finance as a functional decision-making area, limited strategic planning
Limited internal technological base	Dependence on knowledge of particular individuals, need for continuous technology acquisition and transfusion from the outside

Source: El-Namaki, 1989.

disadvantages like lack of resources and a limited supply of managerial and technical competences. While the small size of the business offers some degree of independence and a higher degree of control, it also presents greater business and personal risks to the entrepreneur. These size-related advantages and constraints lead to the entrepreneur-manager managing practically all of the functional areas (e.g. marketing, finance and production) and even performing some of the jobs on the production floor. While this requires and enables the entrepreneur-manager to have a holistic view of the business and to have more centralized control, it exerts tremendous demand on his or her time and makes it very difficult to be away from the business for an extended period of time. Supervision and control are informal and personal, communication is direct, and business records are often minimal or non-existent. The small enterprise generally relies on the technical knowledge of the entrepreneur-manager, of a technical partner or key employees, thus limiting its capacity for innovation and upgrading of process and product quality. Financing of the enterprise is mainly based on the resources of the entrepreneur-manager and his or her family and close associates, as well as funds generated by the enterprise's operation, which makes the financial resource base narrow and often causes the management to focus on the short-term operations of the enterprise, limiting or discouraging long-term strategic orientation.

While planning management development interventions, particular attention must be given to the peculiarities of the personality of the entrepreneur-manager and of the management systems and practices in small business. To be successful, the problem identification and needs analysis, programme strategy and approach, design and content of specific training approaches, the mix of training and non-training interventions, and the methods of programme delivery must all be compatible with the background and culture of the target individual or group.

24.2 Training and development needs of entrepreneur-managers

(A) Needs at various stages in the life of the small enterprise

The knowledge, attitudes and skills needed by the entrepreneur-manager will vary at different stages in the life of the small business. The competences required to conceive of and start a small business will be different from those needed to make the enterprise survive, be profitable and grow. At the stage where the business is transforming from a small to a medium-sized enterprise, the attitudes, management style and competences required will be totally different. A concise (but admittedly incomplete) list of the training and development needs of the entrepreneur-manager and his or her small business is presented in table 24.3.

Conducive and enabling environment

A conducive and enabling environment for small business creation and development allows entrepreneur-managers to emerge and flourish. Such an environment not only encourages the start-up of new businesses and nurtures their development, but it also provides the learning environment, stimuli and opportunities for entrepreneur-managers to continuously pursue self-development and enhance their capabilities.

The formation of the entrepreneur-manager starts with the "enterprise culture" of the person's immediate family and community, and of society at large. Entrepreneurship is a behavioural pattern shaped by the attitude of society towards business, and nurtured by a culture that values and regards success in business highly. This enterprise culture sees entrepreneurship as a desired way of achieving economic, social and political success, and provides the social, financial, technical and market support networks that facilitate people's entry into business. Young people growing up in this culture are immersed in business operations in their formative years. In communities and societies where this opportunity exists for young people to be exposed to the practice of entrepreneurship and to actual business operations, entrepreneurship education and education for enterprise programmes are often incorporated into the educational system.

It is now widely recognized that a conducive and enabling environment is crucial to the development of small enterprises (Tolentino, 1995). The overall macro- and micro-economic framework and the legal, regulatory and political environment influence the rate of new business creation as well as their survival and growth. A healthy economic and business climate based on market principles is of critical importance for a growing and dynamic small enterprise sector. Small enterprises are, after all, just like any other participants in the economic life of a country. They will develop when the overall environment is favourable to the growth of the whole economy. Creating an enabling environment for the development of the small enterprise sector therefore implies first of all the creation of a favourable overall policy framework for the development of all enterprises and of entrepreneurship. Such an environment must provide the possible rewards and gains for potential entrepreneurs to venture into private business, market opportunities for business viability, and a policy and regulatory regime that makes it easy for people to start and operate businesses, and that also offers a "level playing-field" to enterprises of all sizes.

Small enterprises, because of their size and particular characteristics, have certain constraints that may require them to seek assistance and support from outside sources. They are also often subject to policies and incentive schemes that are biased towards large enterprises. To offset these disadvantages, small enterprise promotional programmes and support schemes are often necessary, and the establishing and strengthening of the supportive institutional framework (governmental as well as private) are required. This network of support programmes and institutions provides services that help to build the capabilities of the entrepreneur-managers to deal with specific business concerns, such as access to markets, development of internal management systems, improving productivity, technology upgrading and so on.

Awareness and pre-start-up preparation

A small enterprise is created through a process that brings together human potential and environmental potential in a business undertaking. The human potential (for example, entrepreneurship or managerial competence) combines with the environmental potential (which includes real market opportunities, availability of inputs, technology, capital, encouraging policy and so on) and results in a value-creating and profit-making enterprise. The process leading to a successful small business is initiated and pursued by the entrepreneur who perceives the opportunity, thinks of a business idea to take advantage of the opportunity, and mobilizes the necessary resources to bring this venture into reality.

At this stage in the development of the business, the training and development of the potential entrepreneur is aimed at developing entrepreneurial skills, behaviour and attributes; developing self-awareness of the capability for starting and running

Table 24.3 Needs of entrepreneur-managers and their small enterprises

Enterprise development phases

Conducive and enabling environment	Awareness and pre-start-up preparation	Business start-up	Survival and strengthening	Growth and expansion
1. A supportive policy and regulatory environment which provides: rewards and incentives for entrepreneurial ventures equal treatment and level playing field for large and small enterprises positive encouragement and support to small enterprises 2. A supportive network of institutions providing assistance in matters such as: market development and linkages entrepreneurship and management development product design and improvement technology and process improvement access to finance access to needed information 3. A networking among enterprises of various sizes 4. An enterprise culture that provides: community support and encouragement on entrepreneurial ventures a network of business community contacts and linkages the opportunity to be exposed to the practice of entrepreneurship	1. Motivational and behavioural reinforcement for the practice of entrepreneurship, enhancing entrepreneurial traits and skills 2. Opportunities for exposure to and familiarization with the entrepreneurial and managerial tasks and rewards involved in setting up and running a small business 3. Access to information on products and market opportunities 4. Access to information on resource possibilities and availabilities 5. Access to information on relevant promotional and incentive schemes as well as existing legal and regulatory system	1. Refinement and validation of the market opportunity and product ideas 2. Need-based training on how to start a business covering: reinforcement of entrepreneurial motivation basic business techniques and systems and how to manage a small business in general building networks and exposure to the real world of business how to prepare a business plan/feasibility study 3. Competences and capabilities on how to access and use: market information technical information resources credit and finance 4. Information on sources of managerial, technical and financial assistance 5. Information on relevant laws and regulations.	1. Continuing management development, particularly on the various functional areas of managing a small business 2. Know-how on improving quality and productivity 3. Improvement and upgrading of the various internal management systems, e.g. marketing, finance and production systems 4. Technology and process upgrading 5. Assistance in product improvement 6. Access to additional fixed and working capital 7. Information on the business trends and other developments in the business environment	1. Improvement in capability for strategic management 2. Access to new markets, domestic or export, and know-how on how to conduct business in these markets 3. Access to new technology and processes 4. Access to additional credit and finance 5. Ability to operate in a broader business environment 6. Developing entrepreneurial and managerial capabilities to manage the transition from a small enterprise to a medium-sized enterprise, which involves more functional specialization, managerial decentralization and a greater degree of delegation.

a business; developing real insights into the business development process, its rewards and pitfalls and competence requirements; and expanding exposure to the business world to sharpen the capability to identify business opportunities. An example of a pre-start-up training programme addressed to youth is the Know About Business (KAB) programme of the ILO International Training Centre in Turin. The purpose of the KAB is not necessarily to have young people begin their careers as entrepreneurs or self-employed people immediately. Rather it is to give them an awareness of the opportunities, challenges, procedures, characteristics, attitudes and skills needed for entrepreneurship and self-employment (Manu et al., 1996). The specific training and development interventions required to prepare those venturing into business will be dictated by the needs and requirements of particular target groups (e.g. displaced workers, women, unemployed graduates or youth in their formative years). The issues addressed by the education programme for preparing youth for entrepreneurship are as shown in figure 24.1.

Business start-up

At the business start-up stage, the potential entrepreneur validates and refines his or her business ideas, and makes the decision whether to undertake the particular business venture being considered. If the decision is affirmative, resources and linkages are mobilized to set up the business. At various phases of this analysis-decision-action process the entrepreneur-manager requires specific competences and capabilities. The training and development needs often involve reinforcing the entrepreneurial attributes, inculcating basic knowledge of business systems and of how to manage a small business, developing networks of know-how and "know-who", and developing skills for preparing, analysing and evaluating business plans.

In the choice of particular training and development interventions to be used at this stage, the following issues must be considered (Kubr and Prokopenko, 1989):

- Potential entrepreneurs and founders of new small businesses come from various social environments which may lack the opportunity for business experience and the enterprise culture discussed earlier.

- The people concerned may have very different individual backgrounds with regard to education, technical skills, practical experience, family circumstances and so on.

- The standards to be achieved are very difficult to establish, since they depend on a number of factors and forces influencing the development of business in the given environment.

- In addition, many different views exist on whether and how training can help potential and new entrepreneurs; the different conceptual approaches to training and non-training interventions have considerable influence on all stages of training programme design and delivery.

One possible pitfall is taking a maximalist approach, where training programmes aim to impart the maximum possible knowledge and skills before the business

Figure 24.1. Business education for youth – the key issues

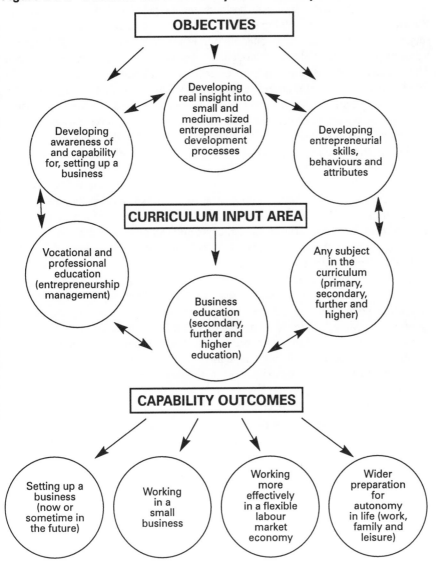

creation process starts. As a result, the amount of knowledge provided exceeds the knowledge actually needed, and the instruction remains essentially theoretical. Motivation and reinforcement through practical applications are missing. On the other hand, programme graduates will inevitably encounter numerous problems which were ignored or not anticipated in a generalized course.

To avoid such pitfalls, practitioners of entrepreneurship development suggest that training programmes and strategies be such that training is related to competence needs as they occur during the business start-up process, and that the learning situations that arise while solving problems and difficulties encountered at various stages be exploited as capability-building opportunities. The potential entrepreneur learns by doing as he or she goes through the various steps of setting up the business. This approach makes it possible to discriminate effectively between common training needs of all programme participants, which can be met through courses, workshops, group discussions and briefing sessions before and during the formal training programme, and individual needs which can be met in several ways (special courses, self-study, action learning, counselling and so on) at the appropriate points of the enterprise creation process. This will also allow the effective use of a combination of training and non-training interventions. Training can be made to fit individual learning needs and the pace of learning that a participant is able to follow. Furthermore, training can be better focused, not only on the profile of a particular individual, but simultaneously on needs related to specific business ideas and projects. The link between the concepts and techniques on the one hand and real business situations on the other is also highlighted, leading to enhanced learning motivation and retention.

However, before adopting this pattern of tailor-made and action-oriented training, it is necessary to ascertain its feasibility from the viewpoint of time, costs and the competence and flexibility requirements of trainers and counsellors. Generally speaking, trainers' experiences and competences are very important factors affecting the design of training and assistance programmes. In many cases it will be a limiting factor: a programme that is too demanding in terms of methodology and trainers' time and experience will have to be simplified to be realistic.

Survival and strengthening

Creating a business is one thing; making it viable and profitable is another. Small business mortality is very high during the first and second years of operations. This is the period when the entrepreneur-manager must fully apply his or her entrepreneurial and managerial competences to make the business competitive and profitable. It is also the period of maximum learning. The basic skills acquired from the start-up stage and the rudimentary business systems installed at the time the business was created are not sufficient to ensure the successful running of the small enterprise. New or enhanced competences are needed to improve the various systems (marketing, production, finance, personnel and so on) as well as quality and productivity. Processes will need refinement and upgrading. New networks must be stabilized and managed. In particular, the managerial competences of the entrepreneur must be developed and honed at this stage.

Again, the training and development interventions must be suited to the learning needs and learning capacity of the entrepreneur-managers. In addition to standard short courses on functional areas, training and non-training interventions must be provided that address entrepreneurs' needs for information on the business environment, further development of problem-solving skills, communicating, leading, negotiating and other "soft skills", and that also deal with problems and concerns specific to the industry sector.

Entrepreneur-managers have been found to rely on their network of family members, associates, competitors, customers, suppliers and other business counter-parts for information. Such sources of learning should be encouraged and utilized. In particular, learning from the experiences of other entrepreneur-managers (both in the same business sector and in other trades) must be maximized. In addition to structured formal exchange of experiences (e.g. having an experienced business person present his or her experiences in a classroom training situation), group-based approaches such as study visits, business clinics, action learning, benchmarking and the like could be explored. Joint programmes with industry associations, chambers of industry and commerce and other trade groupings should be utilized to catalyse and facilitate this peer learning process.

Growth and expansion

Significant changes in the scale of an enterprise require completely new competences of the entrepreneur-manager. Enterprise growth could involve any or all of the following: increase in size in terms of volume of business and employment, increased diversity of product types and product lines, expansion into new markets, whether domestic or foreign, adoption of new processes and higher technology (Tolentino and Theocharides, 1992). Correspondingly, new and better management systems must be installed; increased decentralization, delegation and specialization in functional decision-making are called for; and strategic matters will be of increasing concern to the entrepreneur-manager. The middle managers and supervisors who are assuming more managerial functions in the areas of marketing, finance, production, personnel and so on will require development of their competences in these areas. Providing short courses in these fields will help in building the competence base and the managerial talent pool of small enterprises, enabling them to go through the process of transition from a small to a medium-sized enterprise.

Some entrepreneur-managers find the transition process very difficult and painful. Being accustomed to direct, hands-on management of day-to-day operations, and to making all the decisions, the entrepreneur-manager could find it hard to adopt a more decentralized management style and to delegate decision-making and authority. Not having enough time to attend to the ever-enlarging and increasingly complex business concerns, entrepreneur-managers often feel as if they are losing control. At the same time, strategic matters demand more and more managerial time.

Training and development programmes that help entrepreneur-managers to be aware of and understand the transformations required (their own as well as that of their businesses) will go a long way in preparing them emotionally, behaviourally, as well as technically, for the change process. Equipping them with skills in analysing the strong and weak points of their enterprises, as well as of the threats and opportunities in the business environment, and developing competences related to strategic corporate planning, will also be useful. Training and development interventions aimed at developing the new managerial skills — such as facilitating, negotiating, team-building and networking — required by the new forms of enterprises and work organization will help them to prepare for the top management roles in the medium-sized or large enterprise that their businesses have become.

(B) Developing the competences required of entrepreneur-managers of modern small businesses who are supplying global production chains

Small businesses, even when they are catering only to domestic or local markets, are not exempt from the effects of the increasing globalization of the economy, structural adjustments and trade liberalization that are sweeping across the world. They are also affected by the rapid advance of production and communication technologies. These trends in the domestic and international environment require that the entrepreneur-managers continuously upgrade their abilities in order to enable them to adjust their businesses to the very dynamic, highly competitive environment.

There are many small enterprises that actively participate in the globalized production systems which are increasingly becoming a distinct feature of the national and international business structure. The rapid globalization of the world economy, and the technological possibilities brought about by the rapidly advancing communication and production technologies, have resulted in a flexible, network-based, lean and competitive production system that serves a market characterized by end-customers whose preferences are internationalized, demanding more product differentiation and specialization. Products and fashions not only spread rapidly across the globe, but also shift and change very quickly. The product variety is thus increasing and the product life cycle of specific designs becomes shorter. In response to such a market environment, domestic and multinational enterprises alike are resorting to production systems based on networks of suppliers and buyers, and other forms of inter-firm relationships which provide the flexibility, technical capability and access to specific markets that will allow them to achieve competitiveness and short-term and long-term viability. Modern small enterprises are increasingly joining these domestic and global enterprise networks, often as suppliers, subcontractors and franchises of large domestic and/or multinational enterprises.

To operate successfully in this new business structure of relationships, the entrepreneur-managers of modern enterprises are required to develop new competences and capabilities such as:

- constant awareness of market changes and technical trends;
- the ability to manage the production and work organization systems that are now more flexible than ever before;
- readiness to adopt and constantly modify production processes and technologies;
- the ability to use the "language" of the network, and communicate effectively and efficiently with business partners regarding specific aspects of the business, such as costs, prices, production and delivery schedules, quality performance and so on;

- the use of better record-keeping and more structured management information systems that follow standard norms and practices; and
- the ability to negotiate and, increasingly, use intercultural skills.

(C) Particular training requirements and constraints

In addition to addressing the particular and specific competence development needs of the entrepreneur-managers, the design and delivery of training and development interventions must always take into consideration their particular requirements and constraints when it comes to training. Among these are the following:

- Shortage of time for attending training is a serious constraint for entrepreneur-managers. Given the extreme demands on their time, and their extensive and intensive involvement in the operations of their business, they could not afford to be away for extended periods. It is very difficult and costly (in terms of business opportunity costs) for them to attend training activities that require them to be continuously away from their businesses for long periods.

- Being very pragmatic, entrepreneur-mangers are more used to and comfortable with learning by doing and through problem-solving, rather than through classroom training. Practical and immediately applicable tools and techniques are more appreciated than distant, theoretical and seemingly complex systems and concepts.

- Women entrepreneur-managers may have particular and specific requirements and concerns.

- In some cultures and religions, certain training practices and arrangements may not be appropriate.

- Because of limited financial resources, many entrepreneur-managers, especially those engaged in very small businesses, have limited capacity to pay for expensive training programmes. They would also be reluctant to pay high fees for programmes that do not promise immediate benefits and returns.

- Some entrepreneur-managers might not have the high academic background and preparation often required by some management courses.

24.3 Guidelines for effective training and development of entrepreneur-managers of small enterprises

Management development practitioners with rich accumulated experience in small business promotion and in the training and development of entrepreneur-managers have identified a number of guidelines for effective training and development interventions. The Committee of Donor Agencies for Small Enterprise Development (1996), which brings together the experiences of major international agencies in small enterprise development, has come up with the following lessons learned:

- The target groups for training, and their training needs, must be clearly identified when designing and implementing training programmes. Entrepreneurs' participation in training must be based on their perceived needs and discretion, not on compulsion or incentives (such as inducement by access to credit).

- Training should be demand-oriented, modular and based on the principle of "learning by doing". Participatory methodologies are essential for effective adult learning; "on-the-job" training that makes the trainees work on their own problem situation is the most effective.

- Training must take place close to the trainee's place of work or enterprise, and at time schedules that are appropriate (e.g. in the evenings or on weekends).

- The costs of training are often justifiably subsidized due to the "public character" or social benefits that the training provides; however, it is always important to ensure that trainees bear some of the costs of training.

- Course programmes must be gender-sensitive (see Chapter 22).

- Linkage between formal training and other small enterprise development support programmes and intervention must be established.

With respect to the design of specific entrepreneurship/small business management development programmes, the pointers in box 24.1 will help to make the training more effective (El-Namaki, 1989; Gibb, 1991).

24.4   Training and development approaches

The various management development approaches, processes, tools and techniques described in various chapters of this book can also be applied in the training and development of entrepreneur-managers, provided that they are adapted to the particular requirements and constraints discussed earlier. An important point to remember is that, because of the very close relationship between the entrepreneur-manager and his or her small business, the training and development interventions will necessarily involve elements of small business development. In fact, because of the pragmatic, action-orientation of entrepreneur-managers, as well as their keen interest in immediate applicability of techniques learned, enterprise development (especially of their own respective enterprises) serves as a very effective platform for their own training and development.

(A)   Individual-based approaches

Short training courses

Short training courses in general management and in specific functional areas which are offered at convenient times for entrepreneur-managers (e.g. evenings, weekly one-day or half-day sessions, weekend sessions) could be cost-effective for building their competences. The courses should be practical and results-oriented

---

Box 24.1. Pointers for effective small business management training

- Carefully recruit and select participants, and try to have some degree of homogeneity in terms of needs, learning capacity, business background, etc.

- Design the training based on thorough analysis of training needs of the participants, making sure to differentiate clearly between needs that can be met by training and those that require non-training intervention and assistance.

- Focus upon business problems and opportunities, and the related knowledge and skills needed to solve the problems or grasp the opportunities.

- Adapt inputs, training techniques and methods to the requirements of the particular group of participants.

- Use the right language and level of instruction, dependent upon the educational background and level of sophistication of the participants.

- Concentrate on the "know how" and not just on the "know what". Focus on the conversion of knowledge and skills into action, using illustrations and cases closely related to (if not actually drawn from) the real problems being faced by the participants; move from presenting general principles (e.g. of marketing) to specific applications (e.g. product labelling and display).

- Maximize the opportunity for peer-learning through sharing of knowledge, experiences and information.

- Use highly participative styles of teaching, building upon the learning-by-doing style to which the entrepreneur-manager is accustomed; use simulation, role-playing, critical incident analysis, problem-solving cases and other similar methods.

- Be as company-specific and as industry-sector-specific as possible.

- Be holistic and multi-disciplinary in approach, rather than concentrating on narrow functional specialization; even when the course is on a specific functional area, make sure to show the relationship with other aspects of the business.

- Be flexible in the learning approach used, and deal with learning problems as they arise and as articulated by participants, regardless of the original agenda of the training programme.

- Provide adequate material for participants to take away as memory aids and future reference which indicate key points for application and implementation.

- Whenever possible, use a combination of training and consultancy.

- Use the institutional and resource network (e.g. bankers, suppliers, public administrators, technology centres, small enterprise development organizations, etc.) in the environment that is relevant to the issue being discussed; this will help the participants to be familiar with resource sources and build a "know who" network; this will also facilitate access to post- training advice and guidance.

- Use convenient and accessible venues for training which provide environments conducive to learning, and that make possible the use of learning projects and exercises.

- Design the training structure and process so that the programme can be conducted at convenient and suitable times, accommodate the operational constraints of the participants.

rather than theoretical. They should be highly participative and incorporate opportunities for the participants to work on real problem areas of their enterprises. The content and methodologies should be flexible and easily adaptable to the specific training needs of the participants.

Combined training and consultancy approach

In the combined training and consultancy approach, general and functional courses are given in very short sessions and are aimed at providing knowledge and skills that can be used immediately. Participating entrepreneur-managers then carry out activities and applications under the guidance of the trainer or consultant. The cycle is then repeated, addressing different management development needs or areas that logically follow from the results of the application of learning from the earlier cycle. This approach is very effective when introducing new management systems and practices (e.g. new bookkeeping methods, new information systems, maintenance management, quality control and so on). Flexible learning packages and modular programmes such as the Improve Your Business Programme (see box 24.2) fit very well with this highly participative, hands-on approach.

(B)   Group-based training and development

Among the best sources of learning for entrepreneur-managers are their peers, clients and suppliers. Training and development interventions that bring together in a group entrepreneur-managers in similar or related businesses, and facilitate their sharing of experiences and expertise, are very effective, especially when combined with experts' inputs as required. Group-based approaches are more effective if the members share some common problem and interest and if they are prepared to work together, which may involve the sharing of some business information. They require a high level of confidence and trust among participants, the building of which must be an essential element of the techniques and approaches used. They are easier to implement when done in cooperation with small business associations, trade associations or employers organizations.

Study visits

Entrepreneur-managers are very observant and perceptive individuals. They can easily see how a certain management approach or technique can be applied in their businesses. Study visits and observational study missions are organized ways of exposing the participants to contrasting management practices, good and bad, and learning from the practices of others. In one design of the programme (Tolentino, 1986), participants coming from the same industry branch and from businesses of similar sizes were first given very short classroom sessions on key management and production practices (e.g. materials management, layout, quality control and production management). Visits were then arranged to three types of enterprise in the same business: smaller, the same size and bigger and better than their own. Discussions with the host entrepreneurs were also arranged for more sharing of experiences. The visits were then followed by group discussions by the participants to share their observations and lessons learned. Follow-up evaluations, the first one after six months and the second one after a year, showed significant transfer of management practices and techniques. The approach is best done with trade associations and small business associations or in conjunction with association-

---

Box 24.2.   The ILO's global Improve Your Business Programme

The Improve Your Business (IYB) Programme is a system of interrelated training packages and support materials for providing small enterprise owners and managers with training in basic business management skills. The IYB provides a comprehensive set of materials to institutions such as employers' organizations, small business development organizations and training institutions, as well as individuals who are involved in training for small enterprises. These materials deal with various topics related to small enterprise development, such as training, business extension, follow-up training, monitoring and evaluation.

In addition, to date, the following packages are available: Improve Your Business aimed at small enterprises managers who are aiming to strengthen and expand their business; Improve Your Business Basics aimed at entrepreneurs with only basic education; Improve Your Construction Business for that specific sector; and Start Your Business for those wanting to start their own business venture. A special monitoring and evaluation system has been developed for continuously assessing the programme's impact, business extension service guides provide follow-up training and consultancy, trainers' guides provide guidelines on how to plan and conduct training, and the IYB business games provide a practical and lively simulated experience of managing a small business.

The IYB programme has been used in more than 60 countries and has been translated into over 30 languages. It is estimated that more than 100,000 entrepreneurs have directly benefited from the materials. Several evaluations of the IYB have indicated that the majority of the entrepreneurs who have participated in the course were able to translate lessons learned into improved business performance.

---

building programmes, as it requires a high level of trust and willingness to share among the participants and host enterprises.

Inter-firm comparison and benchmarking

Inter-firm comparison is a process whereby key performance figures for a group of small enterprises engaged in similar activities are presented in a way that allows any enterprise to compare its own performance with other enterprises in the group and with the group's averages. The performance indicators are selected to be those that are of critical importance to the participating enterprises (e.g. labour, energy, materials, productivity and so on). The members of the group agree to collect data on their own performance, and have these compiled and put in formats that will allow easy comparison. The members of the group can then compare performance figures regularly (e.g. quarterly or every six months) on their own or during group seminars. Differences in performance indicators are analysed, causes identified and suitable remedies (which could include, among other things, training) considered. This process is very effective in developing entrepreneur-managers' problem-solving competence, while at the same time helping them establish a good business performance monitoring and evaluation system. Like other group approaches that involve sharing of information and ideas, inter-firm comparison requires high levels of trust and confidence among the participants. It is best to implement this approach in cooperation with associations of small businesses.

The broader approach of benchmarking can also be used by the group. In this process, the participating small enterprises identify and target key improvement areas within their respective enterprises, identify and study the best practices by others in these areas, and then implement improvements in their respective enterprises to enhance their performance.

Business clinics

Business clinics are arrangements whereby groups of small business entrepreneur-managers meet to get advice and share experiences on how to deal with the problems commonly faced by all of them. It can be a one-off exercise (e.g. an afternoon session) or the problem may require a series of meetings. The group may decide to meet regularly to tackle specific problems at each meeting. A business clinic can be combined with inter-firm comparison and benchmarking. Like study visits, it is best to organize this in cooperation with trade associations or the local small business associations.

Action-learning workshops

Participants in action-learning workshops get together in order to work collectively in solving problems faced by their small enterprises. (For a detailed description of action learning see Chapter 11.) As a rule, in the first phase, the workshop focuses on problem identification and on selecting those problems which are of common interest to most participants and should thus be examined collectively. The problems selected are then analysed in greater depth by the whole group or its subgroups. Drawing on their experience, the members of the group come up with possible solutions. The group could meet once a week and continue to have short meetings for some eight to twelve weeks. In between meetings, the members of the group could undertake information gathering and even experimentation and testing of some ideas. If the group's knowledge and experience are not enough, the group defines information and training requirements that are met by a consultant acting as facilitator, or experts invited for a specific purpose.

These various individual- and group-based approaches can be used in combination. An example of a training programme that combines study visits, action learning and some form of benchmarking is the ILO WISE (Work Improvement in Small Enterprises) Training Programme (see box 24.3).

Integrated sector-specific approach

An integrated and comprehensive package of training and development programmes, that focuses on a specific group of small enterprises and their entrepreneur-managers in a specific sector, is very effective in developing not only individual enterprises but also the linkages and networking among them. Such an approach is also capable of developing mutually beneficial linkages with larger enterprises and bringing the small enterprises into closer association with the support institutions in the environment. It is, however, a long-term approach and can involve

---

Box 24.3. The ILO WISE Training Programme: Higher productivity and a better place to work

The WISE Training Programme equips entrepreneur-managers of small enterprises with systematic approaches to raising productivity and working conditions in their enterprises. The content and coverage of a specific training event is flexible, depending on specific problems and opportunities found in the participants' enterprises, but in general the broad coverage of the training includes such topics as materials storage and handling, work station design, productive machine safety, control of hazardous substances, lighting, work organization and other topics related to improvement.

It is based on the action-learning approach, using local examples, practical activities in the participants' enterprises and the formation of groups for mutually supportive consultancies. The following steps are generally followed in preparing and delivering the training:

- recruitment and selection of participants;
- trainers visit participants' enterprises and develop course materials reflecting good practices;
- participants visit a factory where they identify areas for possible improvement, which are then discussed in groups;
- half-day workshops covering the main technical content;
- participants form consultancy groups and visit each other's factories, preparing improvement action plans;
- workshops to discuss how to implement the various action plans;
- implementation of selected improvements in participants' factories;
- final workshop to present and exchange experiences and to award recognition to the best applications and practices; and
- post-training follow-up.

---

any or all of the following: sectoral small business group and association building, studies of the problems and constraints faced by small enterprises in the sector (e.g. the policy and regulatory framework or technological and managerial issues), promotion of business linkages such as subcontracting and franchising, technology support services, and integrated and holistic management development programmes which focus on general and sector-specific management development requirements. The ILO FIT Programme (which began as the Farm Implements and Tools programme, but has expanded to cover many other industries) is an example of a micro and small enterprise development programme that uses this approach (see box 24.4).

Box 24.4.   The ILO FIT Programme

The FIT Programme focuses on the development of micro and small enterprises engaged in the manufacturing of farm tools and implements and food-processing equipment. It aims to develop innovative approaches to ensure more effective support services for small-scale metalworking and food-processing enterprises. The following are examples of the FIT's activities:

- Sectoral and sub-sectoral studies of the problems and opportunities facing the target small enterprises.

- Building and strengthening of sectoral associations which can play an important role in the provision of support services, especially in the area of technological upgrading and development.

- Provision of marketing tools such as guides on topics like rapid market appraisal and how to organize trade shows and exhibits.

- Bringing together and building closer communication between small enterprises and their clients, suppliers and resource institutions for more participatory product and technology development.

- Study visits to encourage small businesses to share valuable knowledge and experiences.

- Building linkages between small enterprises and larger enterprises through subcontracting and franchising.

PART V

DEVELOPING EFFECTIVE TRAINERS

THE MANAGEMENT DEVELOPMENT PROFESSIONAL 25

Brian Delahaye and Barry Smith

25.1 The structure of the profession

This chapter will focus on the roles, tasks and competences of the management development (MD) professional from three complementary perspectives: the MD professional as a trainer; as an organizer of training activities; and as an organization consultant.

The function and required competences of the MD professional are linked to the type of organization that is emerging now, and what Hennecke calls the "change-sensitive" organization (Hennecke, 1991). Contrary to this, "change-resistant" organizations deny the need for change despite the fact that the business environment changes rapidly.

The change-sensitive organization adapts to changing market conditions. It is able not only to predict customer needs, but also to counter moves made by competitors effectively. Change-sensitive organizations are usually innovative, able to anticipate changing customer needs and to create, at a fast pace, products and services which fit them. They are also able to retain and rapidly redeploy their people and their technology in the face of external threat. From this perspective, the primary task of the MD professional is to stay in close touch with the organization's changing reality and to help it move through change.

The MD professional has to be able to respond to the changing requirements of the organization. For example, the MD professional can play a key role in setting up a task force, assist with the formulation of objectives and apply his or her knowledge of group dynamics in helping the task force to work effectively. In addition, the MD professional of the change-sensitive organization has to be *pro-active* and assist the senior management to predict and create the types of management development systems which will help the company survive in a changing market. There are two main functions of the MD professional, which can be broken down into a number of activities (see figure 25.1).

The first one is to develop the competences of individuals, to provide them with skills, knowledge and attitudes which make them effective managers. In this function, the MD professional has the role of the principal trainer and the training organizer.

Figure 25.1.   Main functions of the MD professional

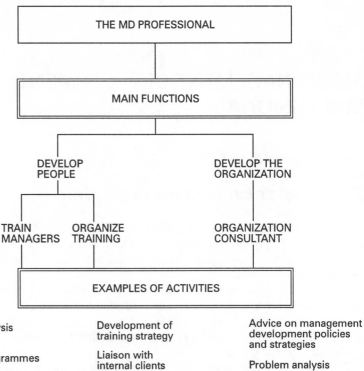

Needs analysis	Development of training strategy	Advice on management development policies and strategies
Design programmes	Liaison with internal clients	Problem analysis
Select methods	Liaison with external institutions	Proposing solutions
Prepare materials	Recruitment and administration of trainers and consultants	Team-building and problem-solving
Deliver training	Organize documentation, equipment, etc.	Organizing transfer of learning to the job
Evaluate	Financial management of training activities	Running assessment centres
Follow up	Evaluation and reporting	Advice on management development approaches

The second function is to help to improve the way the organization operates, so that it makes maximum use of the managers' available competences. This involves, for example, setting up action-learning programmes; organization development activities, such as advising senior management on recruitment, career structures, or how to improve the company's management information system; and raising awareness of factors that hinder managerial effectiveness. This function fulfils the role of an organizational change agent, influencing the system through an internal consultant process.

In this function, the MD professional works mainly as an internal consultant to the senior manager, assisting in identifying performance problems and their causes, working out solutions, including those related to managerial development.

Despite the fact that, in the above diagram, training and consultancy activities are shown as falling under separate functions, in real life there is much interaction between them. One example concerns activities which are partly training-based, partly aimed at effecting organizational change, such as action learning and task forces. All of them usually involve negotiation and direct consultations between the MD professional and senior management to obtain approval and support. Another example is training-needs identification, based on an analysis of performance problems, which is actually a consulting activity but is aimed at improving training effectiveness.

However, to understand better the structure of the MD profession, it is convenient to consider these three main functions separately.

25.2   The MD professional as trainer

A focus on the tasks and the competences of the MD professional as a trainer begins by examining the underlying processes frequently used in management development, and how the most appropriate processes can be predicted by analysing the character-istics of the learner, the content and the trainer. From this, a range of necessary trainer competences are identified and discussed, leading to a brief analysis of a career development plan for trainers. Finally, consideration is also given to the situation where a manager has to develop a subordinate, thus playing the trainer's role.

The process

While the content is usually the focus of any developmental experience, the process is an often invisible but highly important guiding mechanism that ensures the content is delivered in the most acceptable manner. The various processes available to the MD professional may be viewed as a continuum (see figure 25.2).

A description of each of these processes is available in this book. However, there are two significant issues that need to be addressed now. First, the MD professional needs to predict which of these processes is appropriate in a given situation. Secondly, the competences required to use each of these processes successfully need to be examined. These issues will be discussed below.

In any learning experience, there are four major variables — the process, the learner, the trainer and the content to be learned. Some information and methods on how to select the appropriate training process have been provided in Part III of this book. Here we would like to emphasize the other three variables (the learner, the trainer and the content).

Figure 25.2. The processes

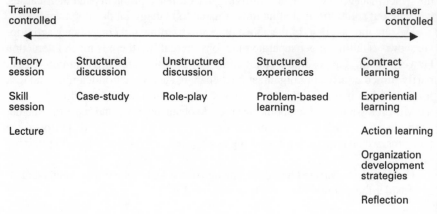

The learner

To examine this variable, we can use a concept called "learner maturity" which is made up of the following four characteristics:

1. *Content base.* With no previous experience in a particular subject, learners often prefer others to structure the learning for them. When familiar with some of the content, however, learners are capable of developing a structure themselves, and will probably have done so.
2. *Motivation.* The higher the learner's interest in and need to acquire the knowledge or skill, the more likely it is that the learner will prefer, and often successfully use, the learner-controlled learning strategies.
3. *Responsibility.* The learner has to accept responsibility for his or her own learning before the learner-centred methodologies can be used effectively.
4. *Learning skills.* The learner ought to be able to decide what end result needs to be achieved, what should be learned so the end result can be achieved and how it should be learned. The more a learner has acquired these skills the more likely it is that he or she will succeed with learner-controlled learning processes.

In addition, our recent research indicated that the learner's personality may also have an effect on his or her preference for the various types of learning processes as follows:

● *High-structure processes* (theory, skill, lecture, structured discussion, case-study). The learner preferring this style has a high need for security, and feels secure because the trainer is taking decisions about content and process.

● *Medium-structure processes* (unstructured discussion, role-play, structured experiences, problem-based learning). Learners who prefer these processes are looking for some security while feeling an urge to be independent. Hence they prefer the trainer to suggest to them what should be learned, although not as explicitly as occurs in the highly structured processes. The learners want the trainer to respect them as individuals and allow them to explore by themselves within the limits imposed by their level of confidence. They need encouragement from the trainer to "leave the nest" and need some direction in the path they should follow. They find security in the trainer assessing their learning.

• *Limited-structure processes* (contract learning, action learning, organization development strategies, reflection). Learners who prefer these processes want to take responsibility for their own learning. Support is provided by a trusting relationship with the trainer and cooperative peer group norms. Such relationships mean that there should be little competition among peers or pressure from the trainer.

As can be seen, the variable of the learner is quite a complex one. It is apparent that some learners will be more likely to prefer learner-centred processes, while others will opt for more trainer-centred approaches.

The content

If we go back to the basics of training needs analysis, we know that the design of learning experiences is based on a thorough examination of the working situation of managers. The results of this examination can be readily converted into learning objectives or outcomes for management development strategies.

An interesting study by Burgoyne and Stuart (1978) incorporates most of these commonalities of learning outcomes, and also establishes them in a hierarchy with ten levels ranging from simple and direct to complex and integrative (see box 25.1).

The reason the Burgoyne and Stuart hierarchy of management competences is highlighted is because it provides a tool to analyse the learning situation. If the learning outcome desired is at the beginning of the hierarchy (i.e. basic facts, or facts or knowledge of a technical nature) then the lecture, theory or skill session is appropriate; if analytical, then one of the discussion methodologies; if interpersonal skills or emotional resilience, then a role-play or an experiential strategy; if the development of good learning habits, then one of the self-directed learning methods, such as contract learning or action learning. Box 25.2 (Smith, 1989) shows the relationship between the learning hierarchy and the requirements of the teacher (trainer) and the learner.

On closer examination, the logic behind these interactions and the alignment of the learning processes and the learning hierarchy becomes more obvious. Basic facts and knowledge of a technical nature tend to be what could be referred to as "single issue" matters. The answers to any questions in this area are almost always the result of straight line analysis and, in general, are not in dispute. The MD professional should possess good cognitive, lecturing skills.

However, when the desired learning outcome is, for example, interpersonal skills, then the structured methodologies of a lecture or a theory session do not achieve a great deal. At the most the learner can "List the steps of ..." or "Describe how to ...". These do not produce the skills needed to carry out actively some interpersonal behaviour. To develop the actual behaviours of relating interpersonally with another, the learner needs to do and practice the skills. Hence, the role-play or experiential

---

Box 25.1. Learning outcomes

1. *Common basic facts* - e.g. the price of a commodity, the level of stocks, the name of a person responsible for some relevant function.

2. *Relevant professional understanding* - facts and knowledge of a technical nature which are essential inputs to managerial decisions (e.g. the technology of a product or production process, advertising or accounting practice).

3. *Continuing sensitivity to events* - those skills concerned with perceptiveness and data gathering, including getting both hard data (quantities, facts, figures) and soft data (other people's feelings, emotions, level of satisfaction or dissatisfaction).

4. *Analytical* - most simply described as a store of analytical problem-solving, ways of considering alternatives and decision-making procedures, skills or programmes, from which relevant ones can be summoned up to be used in current plans.

5. *Social skills and abilities* - contains a store of skills appropriate to plans, decisions and actions that are concerned with working with and through people, and the group and organizational processes that stem from the fact that they are made up of people.

6. *Emotional resilience* - covers those characteristics of the manager that help him or her to work effectively in stress-inducing situations.

7. *Purposeful action* - contains those goals and aims about which the manager is proactive - positively seeking to achieve.

8. *Creativity* - both in the sense of an ability to come up with unique new approaches to situations, and in the sense of having the imaginative breadth to immediately recognize and adopt useful new approaches from elsewhere.

9. *Mental agility* - refers to both general mental capacity for understanding and grasping complex situations, and the speed with which this is done.

10. *Balanced learning habits and skills* - there are four habits and skills that specifically emerge as relating to success or effectiveness:
    - being dependent (accepting the wisdom of an expert) and independent (making up one's own mind) as appropriate;
    - being capable of abstract as well as concrete practical thinking and being able to relate one to the other and move rapidly between them;
    - being capable of using various learning processes, such as input (receiving expository teaching), discovery (trial and error), and reflection (a process of analysing and reorganizing existing experiences);
    - having a broad understanding of what the skills of management are (e.g. recognizing that there are managerial skills or qualities in many or all of the categories discussed here).

---

learning would be more appropriate as we move along the continuum from trainer to learner control of learning.

What should also be recognized in this movement is the change in emphasis from content to process. It is achieved by the trainer gradually releasing control both of defining the learning outcome and of providing the information or experiences that will achieve the learning outcomes. Under the trainer-controlled methodologies, the trainer maintains a tight grasp of the content and the process in a relatively mechanistic or "one right answer" way. However, with the movement towards the learner-controlled end of the continuum, the trainer gradually relinquishes control of the content and relies more heavily on conscious management of complex, multi-option

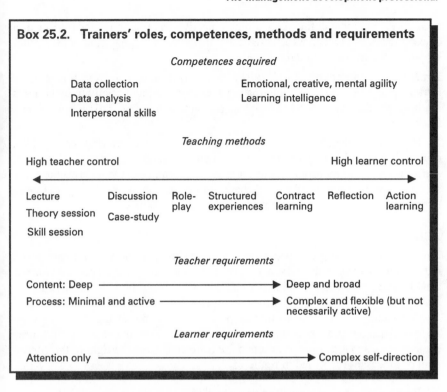

Box 25.2. Trainers' roles, competences, methods and requirements

processes to ensure that the learning outcomes are achieved.

This gradual shift in emphasis is illustrated in the following list of trainers' strategies that start with high trainer control and gradually shift emphasis to a more learner-controlled base.

Strategy 1. Trainer decides and defines the learning objectives and gives the information to the learners in a didactic mode (e.g. a lecture).

Strategy 2. Trainer decides and defines the learning objectives and gives the students specific guidelines on how to gather the required information (e.g. the traditional assignment).

Strategy 3. Trainer decides and defines the learning objectives but gives the participants few guidelines on how to gather the information. Alternatively, the trainer may provide a specific catalyst that generates information (e.g. a case-study).

Strategy 4. Trainer decides and defines the learning objectives and provides a less specific catalyst that generates information (e.g. a role-play).

Strategy 5. Trainer generally defines the learning objective and provides a general catalyst that generates information (e.g. sets a research problem in the "real" world).

Strategy 6. Trainer generally defines the objective only (e.g. problem-based learning). Learners may subsequently refine the objective.

Strategy 7. Learners define the learning objective and search for the information or experiences that will allow achievement of these objectives (e.g. contract learning) subject to the trainer's guidance/approval.

Strategy 8. Learners become involved in an experience, and from this identify learning objectives and further information or experiences, and finally reflect on this learning to identify general principles (e.g. action learning). This trainer is a facilitator only.

These steps cannot be viewed as a strict sequence as many overlaps can, and do, occur. However, the trend of the trainer gradually releasing control of the content and concentrating more and more on process is readily evident. The more the students assume responsibility, and therefore increase their risk-taking, the more likely that deeper levels of learning outcomes will be achieved.

The trainer

The trainer is the third consideration (with the learner and the content) which interacts to determine the most appropriate learning processes. The trainer needs a wide variety of multi-level skills and competences to be able successfully to manage the various learning processes.

Being able to identify the appropriate process is one thing. Being able to manage and facilitate the process is another. First, we will view the research on trainer competences, and then we will examine the competences in the light of the continuum of processes identified in figure 25.2.

Research on trainer competences

Numerous studies of the job requirements of the HRD practitioner have been published in the last ten years. The majority of these have attempted to cover the full spectrum of HRD activity rather than limiting themselves to management development. A relatively large number of them have reported similar outcomes, which suggests that the findings have a basic validity. As a representative of the group, one recent study will be summarized. McLagan (1989) identifies 35 HRD competences, which have been grouped under four headings.

There are 11 *technical competences* which include understanding adult learning, career development, computers, training and development and related subject matter, competence identification skills, electronic systems, facilities and logistics, objectives preparation, performance observation and research. There are nine *business competences* which include understanding business, industry, organization behaviour, organization development and organization functioning; and skills in cost-benefit analysis, delegation, project management and records management. There are eight *interpersonal competences*, including skills in coaching, feedback, group processes, negotiation, presentation, questioning, relationship building and writing. Finally, there are seven *intellectual competences*, including skills in data reduction, information search, model-building, observing and visioning, together with intellectual versatility and self-knowledge. It should be mentioned that different types of HRD jobs will require different mixes and different amounts of various competences. In the present context, the competences likely to be required of a "hands on" management developer will be the focus of attention.

Developing trainer competences

The continuum in figure 25.2 provides a reasonable conceptual model for developing the competences likely to be needed by a front-line MD professional.

Starting at the left end of the trainer-centred methods and gradually moving along the continuum to the learner-centred methods provides a relatively safe and practical path for the development of trainers. This path follows some of the basic principles of learning, because it allows the novice trainer gradually to assimilate new competences. A typical developmental path is described below.

Highly structured methods

The novice trainer is introduced to the highly structured models of the theory and skill session. These models have the advantage of having the principles of learning built into them and therefore the trainer does not have to be overly concerned with the macro-process levels. He or she can concentrate on the following micro-level skills:

- *Visual aids.* With these highly structured methods, we are concentrating on the assimilation of basic facts and knowledge of a technical nature. The chalk/whiteboard and the overhead projector are basic visual aids and even the novice trainer should be very competent in their use.

- *Questioning techniques.* Learning that is "discovered" by the learner is usually valued more highly and remembered longer. One method that significantly encourages this process is questioning techniques.

- *Feedback.* Feedback is a dynamic process and comes to the heart of learning. In the learning experience, this process presents the trainer with two responsibilities: first, to seek information on the development stage of the learner (i.e. feedback for the trainer) and, second, to provide the learner with information on the level of his or her achievement (i.e. feedback for the learner).

- *Setting learning objectives.* Learning objectives form the target for both the design of the learning experience and the learning experience itself. Structured learning processes — with their focus on relatively undisputed technical facts and knowledge — provide the ideal starting point for learning about setting objectives.

These four micro-level skills are vital at all levels of training, but they are most effectively learned while using the structured methodologies, which allow the novice trainer to practise these skills. It is necessary for the trainer to concentrate on the more learner-controlled methodologies later on.

Structured discussion

The structured discussion is the first learning strategy in the progression towards the learner-controlled methodologies. This requires additional competences and skills and provides new challenges to the developing trainer.

- *Confidence and trust in self.* First, the trainer needs the confidence to use the learning objectives as the major guiding tool available to direct learning. Secondly, the trainer must have sufficient trust in his or her competence in the basic skills of visual aids, questioning and assessing and giving feedback.

- *Managing groups.* One of the strengths of the less structured methods is the emergence of group dynamics as a source of energy. As with any type of energy, group dynamics in itself is neither good nor bad; *how it is managed* is the important issue. Social learning from a group is considered by many specialists to be a prime process of personal development. Interactions within groups can generate creativity and provide opportunities for the exchange of ideas and information and for personal comparisons of behaviour. Thus, the trainer needs to become competent in the management of group dynamics.

Unstructured discussion and case-studies

The next major set of competences are incorporated in the unstructured discussions and the case-study. The trainer has to continue releasing his or her hold on content, and must increasingly trust process as the tool to guide learning.

In addition, the outcomes at this level tend to be in the more complex area of analysis and interpersonal skills. This provides at least three additional challenges.

- *Converting the complexities into usable objectives.* These higher level outcomes need to be converted into learning objectives. Defining observable behaviours that will represent evidence of the achievement of these outcomes requires careful thought. Often, the result is a quite detailed list of objectives that are highly interdependent. So, for example, in an unstructured discussion on questioning skills, the trainer may define the required learning objectives as:
    — can differentiate between open and closed questions;
    — uses stems in open questions; and
    — demonstrates consistent use of the funnel sequence.
  It should be recognized that objectives within such a set are often highly interactive.

- *Observing complex behaviours.* This then leads to the second challenge — observing behaviours in each of the trainees to identify that development is actually taking place. This demands high levels of concentration as well as the ability to observe accurately and then compare behaviours over a period of time.

- *Setting enabling objectives quickly.* Because of the complex nature of the topics that demand the use of the unstructured discussion, the paths that can lead to the achievement of the learning objectives are often many and varied. This means that different groups can, and often do, follow different routes as they explore the issues. While the final learning objectives are defined before the session, the trainer must be able to formulate a sequence of objectives as the session progresses to enable the group to achieve the terminal objectives of the session.

Role-play and experiential learning

Role-play and experiential learning are used where the outcomes required are in the areas of interpersonal skills, emotional resilience, complex analysis and creativity. These outcomes constitute complex interpersonal developmental changes that can only be achieved by the learner performing complex behaviours and experiencing the accompanying feelings. These methodologies require the learner to take personal and interpersonal risks to some degree. They often have to demonstrate behaviours or disclose information about themselves that are not usually on public display. As a result, emotions are always engaged and are often close to the surface. Trainers' competences required with these methods include:

- *Comfort in the presence of emotional displays.* This includes the ability to empathize with the learner, while maintaining an adequate analytical distance to be able to judge when some form of intervention may be necessary.

- *De-roling skills.* The ability to defuse the emotional component of the experience sufficiently for the learner to be able to learn productively from it.

- *Promote analytical discussion.* These are basically the competences required for structured and unstructured discussions, although the source of data is not impersonal facts (for example, from a case-study) but emotionally charged experiences of recent origin. This trainer's repertoire of competences requires high levels of sensitivity, social skills, subtlety and, most importantly, emotional resilience.

Fully learner-controlled learning methodologies

At this end of the continuum, the trainer directs learning by managing the process only. The learner decides what content should be covered. Since learners follow individual paths to a variety of objectives, a wide range of competences is required of the trainer. While this "job enrichment" can be very rewarding, it can also be very stressful. Some of the additional demands a trainer may face are:

- *Assessing learning.* Keeping track of a number of learners, each of whom are going in very different directions.

- *Unpredictability of requests.* Not only are the learners travelling different paths, they are also progressing at different rates. In the highly structured methodologies, there is only one topic being covered at any one particular time, and learner queries tend to be confined to that topic. With the learner-controlled learning strategies, queries seem to come from all directions. The trainer needs to be able to answer these questions or at least be able to direct the learner towards the answer.

- *Having faith.* The trainer has to have faith that the learner will achieve. Learner-controlled learning strategies assume that the learner has the motivation and maturity to identify and explore the areas in which they need to develop.

- *Learning habits.* In addition to ensuring that the learners achieve the designated objectives, the trainer should ensure that the learner identifies and adopts appropriate learning habits. The overall aim here is to ensure that each learner is equipped with the learning skills required for that person to be capable of directing their own subsequent learning (see Mezirow, 1985; Boud et al., 1987; and Schön, 1987 on the skill of reflection).

As discussed above, the various methodologies require different competences from the trainer. Unless he or she can demonstrate these competences to a high level, then there will be difficulty in managing each of the strategies. This leads us to the area of career development of the trainer.

Career development

To advance along the continuum towards the learner-controlled learning strategies, the trainer needs progressively to develop a variety of competences. These competences are not discrete in themselves — rather they are cumulative. Therefore, the trainer needs to develop appropriate competences at each stage of the continuum. This, then, defines the ideal career path of the front-line trainer. If he or she starts with the highly-structured methodologies of the theory and skill session and the lecture, and practises them until the micro-competences have been acquired, the trainer will then be ready to move on to the next level of competences and so on.

Considering the parallels drawn previously, it is not surprising that, as the trainer develops the competences needed to manage each of the methodologies, he or she also progressively achieves the deeper levels of Burgoyne and Stuart's learning hierarchy. While a number of the levels can be developed to some extent at a variety of points on the continuum, the main outcomes that are achieved in the trainer's personal development are as follows:

Conceptual learning and skill	Relevant professional understanding, continuing sensitivity to events
Structured discussion and case-studies	Analytical and social skills and abilities
Unstructured discussion	Analytical and social skills and abilities
Role-plays and problem-based learning	Emotional resilience, proactivity, creativity
Fully learner-controlled learning	Creativity, mental agility, balanced learning habits

Thus, progressive development of the competences in the learning hierarchy provides the trainer with skills appropriate to the requirements of methodologies along the trainer control/learner control continuum.

The manager as a trainer

While we often think of the MD professional as someone on the personnel staff, the line manager is strategically placed in an organization to accept a significant role in developing managers for the organization. The daily interactions that usually epitomize the relationship between line managers and subordinates provide opportunities not available to the staff specialist in management development. The basis of these advantages comes from two of the most powerful influences on learning — modelling and shaping.

Modelling

We learn from watching others. This simple, but immensely important fact is often overlooked in organizations. Most of us are so adept at learning by modelling that we are not even aware we are doing it. This means that the manager can develop his or her subordinates simply by displaying the behaviours of a good manager for his or her subordinates to model. "Do as I say, not as I do" is *not* acceptable. The ways the line manager analyses problems, interacts with customers, and treats his or her staff, become models for the future managers of the organization. This places considerable responsibility on line managers but, unfortunately, many managers seem unaware of their power to influence in this way.

The probability that a person will copy a model depends on a range of factors, including:

- the perceived status of the model;
- the attractiveness of the model to the learner;
- the perception of the consequences of the behaviour to the model; and
- the consequences (outcomes) to the learner when the model is copied.

If a manager is attempting to influence subordinates by setting them a good example, he or she must pay attention to these factors, in addition to actually providing the appropriate behaviour to be copied.

Shaping

Technically, shaping is the administering of rewards for successively closer approximations to a desired behaviour. The manager is ideally located to provide these rewards to subordinates, and when an employee is seen behaving in a manner that is generally desirable, a reward is given. More rewards are then given when the behaviour comes closer to the specifically desired behaviour. There are, however, two issues that should be borne in mind.

First, the reward has to be of value to the employee. Fortunately, two of the most significant social intrinsic motivators are the need for *approval* and the need for *recognition*, and these are usually sufficient for most occasions when a manager is seeking to use shaping in the organizational context. In addition, they are readily available to the manager for use in day-to-day interactions.

Secondly, rewarding the learner every time the behaviour occurs is neither practical nor efficient. Of course, rewards must be given in some way since unrewarded behaviour will cease. It has been found that rewards are more effective if they occur less often than does the behaviour (i.e. on a ratio of 3:1 or 5:1 rather than 1:1) and if the rewards are also slightly unpredictable (i.e. if the reward does not occur every fifth time the behaviour occurs but, perhaps, on the fifth, then the eighth, then the sixteenth and so on).

To provide budding managers with opportunities and then gradually to shape their behaviours towards acceptable managerial competences should be the constant developmental role of line managers. Modelling and shaping are two techniques that all managers should use automatically to foster the management development goals of the organization.

Mentoring

A formalized method of management development which provides strong opportunities for both shaping and modelling is mentoring. This involves a relationship in which a skilled/knowledgeable/experienced person (usually a manager) helps another who is less so (Lawrie, 1987). The relationship can be informal, but when consciously implemented by organizations, mentoring always involves a formal recognition of the process. Typically, the mentor will not be the learner's immediate superior, and will often belong to a different segment of the organization. Meetings are usually scheduled, and a skilled mentor will have planned learning experiences arranged for the trainee, in addition to talking and reflection times.

Mentoring is obviously valuable to the learner (providing the mentor is doing a good job), but the process often encounters difficulties when used in organizations. The people who make the best mentors are also often the best managers, whose time is therefore very valuable to the organization. Even committed mentors often have difficulty in allocating sufficient time to their mentoring role. If the mentor is only providing help unwillingly, the learner often experiences a very unsatisfactory learning relationship.

25.3   The MD professional as organizer of training

This is a role which, according to Bennett (1988), "is primarily concerned with planning, organizing, controlling and developing the training activity or function. It will involve setting training goals, policies and plans; liaising with other departments and with senior managers about the contribution training can and should make to improving performance; ensuring that appropriate training activities are designed, developed, delivered and evaluated; acquiring and developing training staff; establishing effective lines of authority and communication within the training function; monitoring quality standards, and controlling activities against a total training plan."

As an organizer of training, the MD professional has a managerial role. The clients are the trainee-managers and the resources are trainers and consultants, who may either come from within the company or be recruited externally.

The training organizer needs to be able to think strategically at two levels: company strategy and management development strategy. A study carried out by Korn/Ferry International and Columbia Graduate School of Business (Lepage, 1990) among 1,500 senior executives from 20 different countries led to a list of recommendations for transforming the human resource function into one that can meet the demands of the future. The first item on the list is about the link between human resource planning and corporate strategy: "Corporations must expect their human resource experts to be *more* than specialized technical professionals with a superficial understanding of the company's products, strategies and objectives. Instead, human resource executives should think like any other executive, understanding which market segments are served by the firm and what products or services will be in demand. A grasp of the corporation's future problems will enable the human resource manager to collaborate with the CEO in identifying and training the executives who will solve these problems."

From this follows the second level of strategy, i.e. that of management development. It is necessary to be able to predict the kind of managers the organization will be needing in the future, secondly how to recruit and develop such managers. In order to do so, it would be useful to ask:

- What is our company culture likely to be, and what kind of leadership qualities are likely to internalize such a culture?

- What kind of organizational structure are we developing, and do we need project managers, or entrepreneurial managers to run profit centres for our structure, etc.?

- Where geographically will our markets be, and what type of managers do we want, with regard to language skills, ability to adapt to new cultures, international experience, etc.?

- What would be the most effective way of making sure that we get the kind of managers we need? To intensify recruitment efforts or to offer attractive career development schemes, or to increase experimental learning and job rotation for managers?

Organizing training means meeting the needs of a set of clients in the organization. While the MD professional should think strategically in the long term for the best interests of the organization as a whole, he or she also has to satisfy short-term needs of managers. It is also important to spend sufficient time clarifying with managers what has to be done after the training programme by them, their respective bosses and others around them at work.

Organizing training means liaising with internal and external training resources, such as suppliers of training material, trainers and consultants with particular knowledge of specific managerial disciplines, or managers who have experienced particularly interesting situations, in order to provide participants with practical, down-to-earth knowledge.

25.4 The MD professional as organization consultant

There could be different types of interaction between management development and corporate strategy. Burgoyne (1988) provides a ladder of six rungs, ranging from virtually no systematic management development to a complete integration between corporate strategy formulation and management development processes:

1. *No systematic management development.* Total reliance on natural, laissez-faire, uncontrived processes of management development.
2. *Isolated tactical management development* in response to local problems, crises, or sporadically identified general problems.
3. *Integrated and coordinated structural and development tactics* which impinge directly on the individual manager in assisting learning.
4. *A management development strategy input to corporate policy formation* through managerial human resource planning, and providing a strategic framework and direction for career development, education and training.
5. *Management development strategy input to corporate policy formation* and contributing to the forecasting and analysis of the manageability of proposed projects, ventures, changes.
6. *Strategic development of the management of corporate policy* as well as assisting in implementation.

Different dimensions of organizational structure to be improved require different interventions and thus qualities of the change agent. For example, a highly segmented, functional structure with little interaction between functions may require a higher level of understanding of other organizational functions, coupled with specialized technical knowledge. A matrix structure requires integrated knowledge of products and markets. A profit-centred-based structure requires entrepreneurial qualities of risk-taking and market understanding. The organization's systems determine how information flows and the ways in which decisions are made. The MD professional is in a good position to identify and to document weaknesses, and to suggest improvements, thus actually exercising the management consulting functions.

The staff dimension determines to a high degree the type of management competence that the MD professional should help the organization to develop. For example, engineering firms which have to become more oriented towards product quality and the customer may need managers who can change the thinking of engineers, and who are also able successfully to set up and manage systems for customer quality. The MD professional is in a position to influence not only the training, but also the selection and recruitment of managers who have a suitable profile for the type of staff in the company.

The style of managers is shaped partly through the management development process. The MD professional may influence the style which is appropriate to the organization's culture through career development, performance appraisal, counselling and job rotation. However, style is also affected by the overall organizational climate. To influence the climate, measures could be taken at the level of top management, such as by running a team-building programme engaging MD professionals as the process consultants.

It is also the MD professional's job to respond to skills specifications, and to change the company's idea of the type of skills needed by the managers. In this role, he or she influences senior management through consultations and negotiations, providing supporting evidence of successes and failures that can be ascribed to different skills, which have a bearing on overall company performance.

In order to act successfully as an organization consultant, the MD professional has to assume a set of functions vis-à-vis senior management and learner managers. Temporal suggests the following functions of the MD professional as a person taking active part in shaping the organization (Temporal, 1990):

- As *adviser* to top management on issues of culture, learning and development, and strategic processes.

- As *catalyst*, to help managers and the organization to develop, learn and change.

- As *information specialist*, to collect data on the latest business and labour market trends.

- As *innovator*, to assist in future changes and creating a vision, experimenting with new and creative ways of learning.

- As *leader*, to assist in setting up strategic goals, developing a centre of excellence and shaping future managers.

- As *learner*, to look for learning opportunities and personal growth in real situations.

- As *monitor analyser*, to evaluate learning experiences and processes, organizational successes and failures, and bottom-line consequences of management development.

- As *strategy maker*, to integrate management development policy and practice, corporate strategy and business planning.

Trainers whose function is to deliver training programmes focus much of their energy on improving the content and the process of the programme. A management consultant, however, has to take a view which extends beyond the training itself. Where the trainer is only responsible for changing the individual, the consultant may also be responsible for changing the organization, so that it benefits fully from the managers' developed competence. The difference between the two is important, because training without paying attention to the need for organizational change may sometimes be counterproductive.

Phillips and Shaw provide a descriptive illustration of the difference between roles on training and organizational change, when they identify the trainer roles from the three perspectives: training, learning and organizational change (Phillips and Shaw, 1989). some organizations find that the conventional combination of pure training on one side and consultancies on the other side does not provide the kind of flexibility of human resource development services that they require. Phillips and Shaw's classification responds to this concern, by suggesting four different types of functions that an MD professional might have: trainer, training consultant, learning consultant, and organizational change consultant (see table 25.1).

Table 25.1. Four MD professional functions

	Trainer (1)	Training consultant (2)	Learning consultant (3)	Organizational change consultant (4)
Primary contact	With trainee on training programme	With client, sponsor	With client, sponsor	With whole organization
Focus of work	Running training programmes	Providing tailored training	Facilitating self-development	Facilitating organizational change and development
Diagnosis in terms of	General organizational needs	Client's problem and associated training needs	Barriers to effectiveness in client's area of responsibility and related development needs	Barriers to desired direction of organizational change in client's area of responsibility and related development needs
Impact on organizational effectiveness	Diffused	Localized	Localized	Focused
Material worked with	Mainly simulated	Simulated and live	Mainly live	Live
Application	Requires transfer of learning to work situation	Requires transfer of learning to work situation	Learning and working are simultaneous	Learning and working are simultaneous

Many consultants have started as trainers. It is a natural tendency, especially in management development, to progress from training to the role of organization development consultant. More and more trainers are moving into the kind of work that has more to do with directly intervening in the organization than with the traditional activities associated with trainers (Jones, 1986).

In fact, an increasing number of companies require that the MD professional take a more active role in shaping the organizational structure and practices, and making sure that the development activities really help the organization to achieve its objectives and fulfil its mission.

25.5   Conclusion

This chapter has examined the development of the management development professional. The range of teaching and learning methodologies was analysed, and it was suggested that a study of the learner, the content and the trainer would assist in the identification of the most appropriate strategies. A brief review of studies of manager competences was conducted, highlighting the learning hierarchy of Burgoyne and Stuart. This hierarchy, together with the learning methodologies continuum, was also suggested as an effective conceptualization of the competences required of a front-line management developer. These ideas suggest the skeleton of a career development plan for the committed management developer. Finally, brief mention was made of the role of experienced managers in the development of novice managers.

The competence studies clearly indicate that management and development both require a complex array of functions such as a trainer, a teacher, an organizer and a management consultant. Close attention to competence studies, and emphasis on both content and process are a good starting point for improving management development overall, and for securing a rewarding occupation for those trainers who wish to become true management development professionals.

USING CONSULTING FOR
MANAGEMENT DEVELOPMENT

26

Milan Kubr

The theme of this chapter is the use of consulting as a management development tool with the focus on two target groups. The first target group comprises management development professionals of various profiles and backgrounds, who are keen to enhance their consulting skills and make better use of consulting approaches and methods in developing managers. Our second target group is made up of those professionals who work primarily as management consultants, and perceive the need to be versed in training approaches and techniques in order to contribute more to the development of their clients' skills and competences.

There seems to be little need to justify this double purpose. In the past 30 years we have witnessed a quite remarkable and very visible *rapprochement* of consulting, training and development. There are now many professionals who describe themselves as both trainers and consultants. More and more trainers and training institutions devote more time and energy to consulting and are keen to be recognized and solicited for their consulting as well as their training competences. Consultants, in turn, view the development of their client organizations' managers and staff members as an objective that is equally and, at times, even more important than providing solutions to specific management problems. A new breed of professional service organizations has emerged, which offers the services of experts who feel comfortable in both consulting and training roles, and are able to switch and combine these roles in order to enhance the overall impact of their intervention. Both consulting and training organizations appear to draw considerable benefits from this *rapprochement* and synergy. However, the principal beneficiary is the client — the manager who turns to consultants or trainers for help. He or she is getting help that is more complete and more professional and stimulates the manager's own initiative and learning, in addition to helping to cope with specific management and business problems.

This does not mean that the traditional dichotomy of training and consulting belongs to history. There are scores of trainers who, for various reasons, do not bother or do not dare to leave the classroom to delve into the troubled waters of business practice. And there are consultants who feel that training the client is equal to giving away precious know-how and losing future consulting opportunities.

The chapter is divided in three sections. Section 26.1 reviews the key characteristics of the training and consulting approaches, stressing both their common points and differences. The purpose is to show that if trainers want to become consultants, they should realize that they have certain qualities within themselves that make this change in roles easier, while some of the values and stereotypes that are common in trainers' circles may act as obstacles. The consultant will face similar questions in deciding what to learn and what to unlearn to be a good trainer.

Section 26.2 examines the transition from training to consulting. It makes a number of practical suggestions to trainers, training managers and programme designers involved in this effort.

Section 26.3 provides the opposite perspective — that of a consultant who feels that he or she should do a better job in training clients and fellow consultants. However, this section is confined to critical issues of the consulting-training relationship, and does not aim to provide all the information and know-how needed to become an effective trainer which is, indeed, the purpose of this whole publication. Therefore section 26.3 is meant to be nothing more than a special introduction intended for management consultants who want to sharpen their training skills.

Throughout the chapter, our objective will be to show that management trainers have a number of predispositions to becoming good consultants, and that the consultant's experience is most helpful in becoming a competent trainer. However, a word of caution has to be addressed to those professionals who believe that any consultant is also a trainer and that if you are a trainer, it will be very easy to start consulting. In both cases there are also competence gaps that need to be identified and filled, and certain barriers that ought to be understood and overcome.

26.1   Training and consulting

Comparing training and consulting, and drawing conclusions on their common characteristics and differences, is a daring enterprise. Any trainer or consultant reading this chapter can challenge our statements, pointing out that they are oversimplifications and in no way concern their particular case. This is due to several reasons. We should not overlook that "management consulting", as well as "management development" and "management training", are open-ended and only roughly defined concepts, embracing a wide and steadily changing range of philosophies, approaches and methods. They are based on a combination of science and art. In addition to well-defined, rigorous concepts and procedures, consultants and trainers use their individual talents and know-how. The scope for applying imagination, creativity and innovation is limitless. Thus, a trainer or a consultant can handle the same technical task totally differently when dealing with two different clients.

Therefore we strongly advocate an individualized approach, whereby trainers or consultants examine their own educational background, experience, skills and value systems, and define a personal path from training to consulting, or vice versa.

Notwithstanding that, in preparing their own individual development programme readers may wish to refer to some general characteristics of the training and the consulting approaches.

(A)   Object of intervention

The target groups for whom this guide is intended, i.e. management development professionals and consultants, work in the same field of activity and share the same object of intervention — the management and effective operation of businesses and other organizations. For example, both a consultant and a trainer may work on questions of corporate strategy and planning, or on the financing of investment. The difference is in the level of generalization. Consultants deal with particular, unique situations and problems in client organizations. They have to provide solutions, not general and theoretical answers. If the theory in the particular subject area does not provide an answer, or orientation on where to seek answers, the consultant must find a solution despite the lack of theory, or, if necessary, against the advice provided by textbooks and manuals. In contrast, management trainers operate at higher levels of generalization. They are used to dealing with concepts, categories and trends reflecting the state of the science and the art in their particular fields. If they choose to be more specific, e.g. by using case-studies, they exercise control over the selection of cases, as indeed over the structuring and the course of the whole programme.

(B)   Ultimate purpose and immediate objectives

The ultimate purpose pursued by both management training and management consulting is the same. They are professional services to management and the final criteria of their relevance and impact are high management standards and organizational performance and effectiveness. These are practical standards, measurable in economic and financial terms. In consulting, this ultimate purpose is translated into operational objectives to be achieved by specific assignments and projects. In training, operational objectives are normally expressed in terms of changed (increased) competence at doing certain jobs. As a rule this will be the final operational objective. Only if training can be related to particular organizational problems, which will be resolved during the training programme or as its direct consequence, can we use operational business results as objectives for training. As the reader knows, this is one of the issues with which management training has been struggling for years without finding satisfactory and generally applicable solutions. Training whose effectiveness can be measured by tangible results is the trainer's ideal, but only a fraction of training programmes achieves this ideal.

The ultimate purpose of both management consulting and training can be expressed in terms of change. The current theory and state of the art views both consulting and training as essential instruments for planning, facilitating and implementing organizational change. Consultants and trainers alike tend to espouse the same or very similar basic concepts and philosophies of change, with all the implications concerning intervention methods, expert's behaviour, the client's participation, ethical values and so on. However, a difference in roles remains — consultants are directly involved in making organizational change happen, while trainers aim to prepare people for coping with change and managing it effectively.

(C)   Client base

Both consultants and trainers serve the same wide client base — the managers of organizations, large and small, private and public, commercial and not-for-profit. For example, the same managers, or organizations representing the position and interests of management circles, would be seen as partners with whom the state, the needs, and the future policies of both consulting and training should be reviewed. As regards specific consulting or training services, the manager can be in different client roles.

As a client of a consulting firm, the manager is in control and decides what is to be done, what proposals will be accepted and implemented, etc. As an individual client of a training centre, the manager decides to participate in a programme, but often has no control over the curriculum, method of instruction, information that will be made available, and so on. This role pattern has been changing, however, with the progression of learner-controlled and action-oriented types of training, and training programmes tailored to practical needs of specific organizations.

The fact that consultants and trainers have the same clients can be a major advantage if a training institution chooses to move into consulting: many useful contacts with managers have already been established. It might turn into a barrier if the institution, through its training, has acquired the reputation of an educational body that is good at manipulating abstract concepts but irrelevant to current business practice.

(D)   Working environment

Most consulting takes place at the client's premises, with all the consequences involved: interruptions, noise, shortage of space, changes in work priorities and schedules, and so forth. This working environment is provided and controlled by the client, not the consultant, who must be flexible enough to cope with it. The trainer's typical place of work is a classroom or meeting room. It is a more pro-tected, comfortable and stable environment, where events and conditions are controlled by the trainer and disturbances can be eliminated.

(E)   Activities, processes and methods

In comparing training and consulting with a view to facilitating transition from one to another, the most important thing is to find out what trainers and consultants actually do. Comparing the trainers' and the consultants' activities, styles and the methods used will show similarities that make transition between the professions easier, as well as differences and gaps that will need to be filled.

This comparison can be approached in various ways. One way is suggested by

Phillips and Shaw (1989). As shown in figure 26.1, they compare the training cycle with the consulting cycle and point out similarities between the two. The arrows in the table show where the training cycle has potential for preparing trainers for consulting work.

Figure 26.1.   Comparison of training and consulting cycles

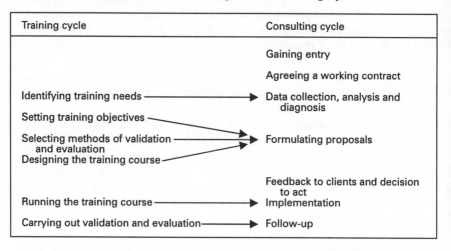

Another possibility is to compare the training and consulting styles or methods as shown in figure 26.2. In both training and consulting, the styles and methods used can be described and assigned a position in a continuum from directive and non-participative, through to non-directive and participative styles and methods. A trainer using non-participative methods will find it easy to master the same methods in consulting. Conversely, moving from directive training into highly participative process consulting may be a difficult task.

It is also possible to use more detailed competence models (see Chapter 1). These models can describe real competences of individual trainers, ideal competences of persons to be recruited or developed for particular jobs, etc. They can also use rating to measure the importance of individual competences for certain jobs, or classes of jobs.

To be meaningful, the comparison of trainers' and consultants' competences must be specific and detailed enough. For example, an important consulting competence is the ability to conceptualize (making syntheses and drawing conclusions from analytical data, separating essential from unimportant information, identifying important trends, visualizing alternative new solutions, producing scenarios, drawing up action proposals, etc.). An assessment of competences of a trainer who has done action research, designed new training programmes and written textbooks may show that the ability to conceptualize is one of his or her stronger competences. In contrast, a trainer who does no action research and uses programmes designed by

Figure 26.2. Continuum of training/teaching and consulting styles and methods

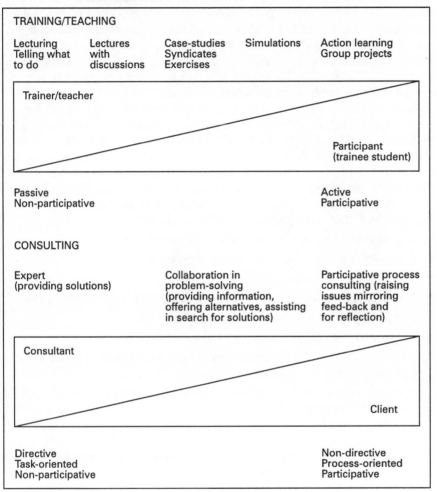

others may be an excellent communicator, but his or her conceptual skills may be quite weak.

In summary, general and vague comparisons of training and consulting cannot provide a sufficient basis for trainer or consultant development. It is necessary to identify specific competences and consider particular ways of developing them.

(F)   Professional cultures

Both the training and the consulting communities are more diversified and less cohesive than some other professional communities — for example, lawyers or accountants. Nevertheless, their life and work experience tends to be reflected in collectively shared values, beliefs, traditions and behavioural norms as in any other community. In short, there is a professional culture characteristic of trainers and teachers, and another one shared by consultants. These cultures include values concerning the trainer's or the consultant's mission, rights, social role, independence, commitment to the client, socialization patterns, and so on. The understanding of professional cultures reveals values that will facilitate or inhibit the transition from one profession to the other. Identifying these values, and determining whether and in what way they can be changed, will be essential.

Unfortunately, little research has been done into the value systems and behavioural norms of professional communities such as trainers/teachers of consultants. Bellmann (1983) and Phillips and Shaw (1989), have made some interesting observations. In introducing his observations, Bellman points out that "many of the abilities that make us fine trainers can block our effectiveness as consultants". He uses the term "untraining the trainer". In a similar vein, Philips and Shaw stress that, in becoming consultants, "trainers need to be willing to let go of a number of things they may well value", and provide the following summary:

● The pleasure of performing well in front of an audience.

● The security of a well-defined position in the training room.

● The advantage of working on "home" territory.

● The safeguard of being able to use theory and exercise to control situations.

● The predictability of a planned, sequenced workload.

● The relative simplicity of the trainer-trainee relationship.

● The luxury of working one step removed from the cauldron of organizational politics.

It is useful to be aware of the differences concerning issues such as the trainer's and the consultant's authority and power. The trainer is in charge and exerts control over the design and course of the training events, chooses the techniques and materials used and can even manipulate the subject matter (e.g. ignore or de-emphasize certain topics or aspects). The trainer has enough opportunity to influence the trainees' thinking by promoting particular views and even ideologies. Even if the training event is designed as a participative one, overall control of the programme concept and structure tends to remain in the trainer's hands.

In a typical consulting situation, the client is in charge. The consultant helps with planning, negotiating and implementing changes, without having any power to impose change and tell the client to do or not to do certain things. Relinquishing power and control and finding new ways of influencing the client's stance and behaviour may be difficult for trainers, in particular those who have become used to being regarded and treated like stars and unchallengeable authorities in their technical fields. In some cases, trainers who are recognized authorities in their fields (e.g. due to the renown of their publications) will retain this professional authority and power when coming to client organizations as consultants. It will be important to find out whether the client reacts to their proposals positively because they come from a recognized authority, or because they are practical and feasible by the client's standards.

Passing from training to consulting implies moving from a structured, predictable and more secure context to situations of uncertainty and reduced security. Trainees work on their own familiar territory and can create structures (course designs, training methods, audiovisual aids, classroom arrangements, etc.) in which they feel at ease and which will be available to them for a precisely determined or predictable period of time. Consultants work in unfamiliar and ambiguous surroundings, have to adjust to the client's planning (or complete lack of planning), and must be highly flexible and prepared to adjust their own time horizons, work plans and strategies many times during an assignment.

In most training situations, issues can be examined from the perspective of a particular discipline or subject. Comprehensive and interdisciplinary approaches are advocated, but rarely applied. Trainers specialize in areas such as production control, financial management, enterprise organization, international marketing, and so on. In consulting, there is considerable scope for applying specialist knowledge and approaches as well. However, they have to be applied in the context of the total business, bearing in mind that business practice is always multifunctional and interdisciplinary. Narrow perspectives and attempts to handle complex business and organizational problems by applying the viewpoint and methodology of only one discipline (e.g. systems analysis and design, or organizational psychology) can produce negative results.

However, the typical trainers' and consultants' attitudes to results are not the same. Consultants have to go persistently for tangible and measurable results in client organizations if they want to stay in business and be called again. In training, the results-oriented approaches and programmes have certainly gained ground, but for most trainers the principal measure of success continues to be their trainees' satisfaction. They aim to get high ratings as excellent performers in front of an audience. The excellence of classroom performance looms large in their value system.

26.2 From training to consulting

Following our review of common characteristics and differences of training and consulting, and of some problems to be faced by those trying to pass from training to consulting or vice versa, let us now discuss how a trainer or teacher can approach the path to consulting.

(A) Your profile as a trainer

Because there is such a variety of training approaches, and because consulting also uses a wide range of different modes and styles, it is useful to start by getting a deeper insight of your own values, skills, motivations and possibilities as a trainer.

This is self-diagnosis. A trainer who wants to become a consultant or make better use of consulting is well advised to engage in such a self-diagnosis, which can be a private exercise even if nothing similar has been foreseen by the management of the training institution. However, the managers of training staff and activities are aware of the growing interest in consulting and of opportunities that consulting competences will create for their institution. Furthermore, they are aware of the differences between individual staff members. Therefore they do not advocate standard approaches to skill development and are prepared to assist in self-diagnosis.

The main purpose of self-diagnosis is to identify one's own strengths and weaknesses. It is important to have a true picture of who you really are, how you are perceived by your trainees and colleagues when acting as a trainer, and what your real impact is. Through self-diagnosis assisted by your superiors and peers, and drawing extensively on the feedback from clients, you will be able to ascertain what you do well, with what training methods and styles you are most comfortable, and what makes you effective or ineffective.

Trainers have preferences for various methods, not only because they find them easier to use and less demanding on preparatory time, but because they fit the trainer's personality better. The same applies in consulting. The transition from training to consulting should help you to become stronger as a trainer, and to focus on those areas and styles of consulting that will give you a good chance to become a good consultant.

First, you want to become aware of your personal value system as a trainer. In the previous section, we made some comments on values that are fairly common among trainers. Are these your values as well? Are you prepared to give up your position of power as a trainer and face the ambiguity of a typical consultancy setting? Are you prepared and able to structure and plan your work in accordance with your client's wishes (and possibly caprices!) rather than on the basis of your own priorities? These and similar questions ought to be asked. You may be unable to produce answers before attempting to work in a different environment and trying out various consulting styles. Yet it is most helpful to be aware of your values, strengths and weaknesses when deciding to do consulting.

Turning to the subject matter or technical area of intervention (marketing, human resources, international finance, etc.), some trainers make an erroneous assumption that by giving courses on the subject they automatically qualify as consultants. It is useful to consider whether you are fully up to date and familiar with the state of the art, which will be necessary for practical interventions. Textbooks and course material lag, in many cases five to six years, behind practical developments. If you have not kept in touch with business practice, it may be that even your excellent theoretical mastery of the subject will not suffice for consulting. Remember that as a trainer you may have manipulated the subject matter, for example by completely leaving out a topic that was unfamiliar to you or unimportant by your judgement. You will not be able to do the same in consulting.

It is, then, essential to assess your particular style of training. Is it predominantly a directive style, a one-way communication of ideas and experiences whereby the participants are told what you want to tell them, and advised what is good for them? Or is it a participative style, whereby the trainees are encouraged and helped to identify and understand problems, ask questions and come up with solutions, without being told by the trainer what they should or should not do? Where would you see yourself on the continuum shown in figure 26.2? Are you able to move more or less freely from one end of the continuum to the other? Do you enjoy switching roles? What roles on the continuum of consulting styles would fit you best? Are you prepared to try out various roles? Remember that if you have no experience with unstructured, flexible and participative training/learning methods, you are probably not sufficiently prepared for process consulting. There are, however, many trainers who have paid considerable attention to recent learning theories, adult learning, organizational behaviour and theories of planned and assisted organizational change. Generally speaking, this is a good preparation for participative process consulting. But the risky step from theory to practice has to be made. You have to try out your skills, and sharpen them if necessary.

These observations do not imply that your training style fully predetermines your consulting style, and that you will fail if you try out any other style. They underline that you must become aware of the different approaches and styles, and of the effort that may be required in order to make a major move on the continuum of training or consulting styles.

(B) Opportunities for acquiring consulting skills

Trainers do not enjoy the same opportunities for acquiring consulting skills as consultants do. This may be due to the workload (student contact hours plus preparatory time), the policy and image of the training institution, the conditions of employment, and remuneration and other factors. Therefore trainers and training institutions that are keen to be more active and competent in consulting cannot wait until opportunities come to them, but must seek and create suitable opportunities for practising consulting. Let us consider a few alternatives.

Seminars and workshops providing an overview of consulting practices and basic training in consulting skills are useful and within the possibilities of any training institution. Either the institution can arrange such a training event for its own staff, or can make use of standard training opportunities offered by consultants' institutes, business schools, consulting firms or other training establishments. A sample outline of a short introductory workshop is shown in table 26.1. It is based on the following principles:

- The participants will be trainers and/or consultants.

- If possible, the programme will start by a welcome cocktail or dinner and informal discussions in the evening preceding Day 1.

- The purpose will be well explained; individual and group objectives set; daily reviews of progress achieved, arranged and used for immediate adjustments in the programme; and a final evaluation undertaken.

- Principal consulting activities and techniques will be briefly described and

Table 26.1. Introduction to consulting (workshop outline)

DAY 1	DAY 2	DAY 3	DAY 4	DAY 5
Workshop objectives and organization	Assignment planning and organization	Finding solutions to problems	Presenting recommendations	Assignment evaluation and follow-up
Training and consulting, development of consultants	Problem identification	Developing alternatives	Implementation of proposals	Final review of case and group process
Individual needs and objectives	Fact-finding	Formulating recommendations		
Case presentations	Interviewing	Oral and other presentations	Marketing and managing consulting	Participants' self-development plans
Client contacts, preliminary survey	Data analysis	Report-writing	Training and consulting fees	Workshop evaluation and closure
Assignment proposals		Issues in consultant-client relationships		
Managing change and consulting styles	Professional standards and ethics	Quality assurance	Current trends in professional services	
Group work and individual counselling	Group work and individual counselling	Group work and individual counselling	Group work and individual counselling	

demonstrated, and practised as much as possible through exercises, teamwork and role-playing.

- The workshop will be structured around a consulting case history, simple enough to be embraced in the workshop, and complex enough to provide for the practising of consulting skills and taking a participant through a consulting assignment step by step.

- There will be lectures, group discussions or syndicates on selected topics such as: training and consulting, current trends and issues in consulting and other professional services, consulting styles and underlying theories, professional standards and ethics, marketing of consulting, and managing consulting. These can be arranged in evening sessions.

- Evening time will also be used for group work, preparing for the next day's sessions and for exercises. Group dynamics will be encouraged.

- Individual counselling sessions with participants will provide advice and guidance on their particular development needs, objectives and self-development programmes.

- This design requires a minimum of two workshop leaders for a group of 14-20. Some sessions can be handled by invited speakers.

A one or two-week initial workshop can be nothing more than a solid introduction to consulting. It should help the participants to realize what ought to change in their behaviour as trainers, and how they should go about practising and developing specific consulting skills after the completion of the workshop, with the help of the organization that employs them and has sponsored their participation.

We are also reproducing in table 26.2 an outline of a model course on management consulting, produced by a working party of the Association of Management Consulting Firms (ACME) in the United States (ACME, 1991). Based on this or a similar outline, it is possible to develop various types of longer programmes on the principles, methods and organization of consulting. Handbooks and guides focusing on consulting practices and methods are a useful source of learning. Every training institution should have the basic works in its library and recommend them to the staff.

However, no trainer will become a consultant by attending a seminar or studying a guide to the consulting profession. Consultants develop by practising consulting in conditions that stimulate learning, and by successively undertaking sets of tasks through which they learn more facets of the profession. This normally includes a progression from working as a junior consultant under the guidance of a senior, through more independent work for clients, to identifying and selling new assignments and working as team leader or supervisor. Therefore a training institution must be prepared to make certain choices in respect of the linkage between consulting and training, and the type and amount of consulting to be practised.

A suitable point of entry can be provided by research into the problems, opportunities and trends concerning the client enterprises. Most training institutions do a

Table 26.2. A model management consulting course

Module One - Management Consulting

1.1   Definition
1.2   History and evolution
1.3   Types of consulting
1.4   Introduction to the consultant-client relationship

Module Two - The Management Consulting Profession

2.1   Management consulting today
2.2   Management consulting as a career

Module Three - Ethics in Consulting

3.1   Professional ethics
3.2   Examination and certification

Module Four - Process Skills

4.1   Client-consultant relationships
4.2   Human factors in consulting relationships
4.3   Questioning, listening and interpreting
4.4   Interpersonal and organization modification techniques
4.5   Ambiguity and paradox
4.6   Management of conflict

Module Five - Substantive Skills

5.1   Management theory
5.2   Basic quantitative skills
5.3   Hypothesizing solutions
5.4   Deliverables
5.5   Data collection techniques and tools
5.6   Information processing analysis
5.7   Developing solutions
5.8   Selecting solutions
5.9   Presenting results

certain amount of such research in order to develop up-to-date training materials (such as case-studies) and learn about practical problems and trends that ought to be reflected in the courses taught. Through this research, trainers have the opportunity to develop information and know-how that interest the clients. Consulting assignments may follow if the research findings are presented to the clients in a way that can arouse their interest (e.g. "our research has found that an obsolete organization of maintenance and division of labour causes financial losses to your firm(s)"). If such research is followed by a consulting project, this will be a good opportunity for involving junior trainers under the guidance of more experienced ones.

Another alternative is a consulting department within a training institution, on the condition that this department does not become isolated from the training function. Job rotation can be organized and trainers transferred to the consulting department for periods long enough to involve the trainer in all stages of sufficiently important and meaningful projects.

Most of the consulting normally undertaken by trainers is the direct product and consequence of training events. Typically, trainers suggest to the participants coming from business or governmental organizations that, if requested, they might be able and willing to help with follow-up and transfer to the participants' own organizational setting, as well as examining what specifically can be done in the unique conditions of their organization. On the other hand, it may be the participants who take the initiative, and ask a trainer who has gained their confidence for further advice and help.

Many trainers come to consulting in this way. Some trainers, and consultants alike, mount training events in order to market consulting, arouse clients' interest and find new consulting projets. This may lead to an extreme situation, in which the training function is turned into a vehicle for creating consulting opportunities and an appendix of consulting. This may be an undesirable development in an institution with a primary mandate to provide training.

Many training institutions have good experience with and learned a great deal from combined training/consulting projects. Such projects are normally negotiated with a business firm and designed for this firm. They may concern broad and complex issues of corporate strategy, performance and organizational change, or narrow issues in particular functional or technical areas. Some of these projects are designed as action-learning exercises (see Chapter 11). Participative training and consulting are used in most projects, and provide excellent opportunities for the training institutions to learn from working with clients on their business management problems. Teamwork is encouraged on both the clients' and the trainers' or consultants' side. In some management centres and schools these projects have become a significant component of service offering and an important source of income.

Finally, trainers should not overlook the fact that they can make a move towards consulting, and start developing consulting and counselling competences, while acting as trainers and designing and delivering training programmes. The less structured and the more participative training events are, the closer they are to consulting. In participative training, it is the trainee who searches for answers and solutions, and the trainer turns increasingly into a resource person, a counsellor and a provider of feedback. The transition from training to consulting can be smooth and hardly noticeable. Bellman (1983) has summarized his experience in the following terms:

Taking on these perspectives can have a major impact on your training. Some of the possibilities include:

- You will less often see training as "the answer" and more often accept other alternatives as legitimate change efforts (e.g. changing structure, clarifying objectives, transferring people or giving feedback).

- Your sessions will spend less time on theories, models and concepts and more time working out applications of the learning to the job.

- As leader, you will give fewer answers and ask more questions. There will be less total input from you and more input from the group, especially related to alternatives that might work back on the job.

- Your designs will take two steps toward reality and one step away from games. For example, in a role-play, participants could be playing themselves dealing with a real problem employee, rather than playing roles more removed from their situations.

- You will find that your investment in session ratings goes down and your interest in organizational change goes up. You will care less about how they feel about your session and care more about whether significant organizational issues were dealt with during the session. For example, you might feel particularly pleased with a session in which issues were discussed, people got uncomfortable and your ratings suffered.

- You will find yourself becoming more receptive to management actions and less receptive to participants who place all responsibility for change with their bosses. Your broader understanding of the organization will help you accept that everyone (higher management and your participants) has reasons for their present behaviour. Change is not easy for anyone.

- You will become less vocal in championing training solutions to problems as you face the fact that training is not as important as you once thought it was. Instead of being "the" solution, it becomes one of a number of alternatives an organization can pursue.

26.3   From consulting to training

This section looks at the relationship of consulting and training from the perspective of a consultant who feels that — thanks to a better knowledge of principles and methods of training, and a better use of training approaches and methods in consulting — he or she could become more useful to clients. In adopting this perspective we are aware that training is not a new thing to consultants. Most of them do some training of client staff as part of their assignments dealing with organizational change or helping to introduce new systems and methods. Many consultants regard consulting interventions as an important way of training the clients. Lyndon Urwick, one of the founders of the consulting profession, said years ago that "the only work that is really worth doing as a consultant is that which educates — which teaches the clients and their staff to manage better for themselves". Current theories of consulting are consistent in stressing that the consultant should work on the client's behalf and without the client's active participation only in those instances where, for valid reasons, the client cannot or does not want to be directly involved.

Practice, however, is often different. Many consultants have never been trained as trainers. They can deal with their client's problems, but lack the patience and skills to train the client for solving future problems without further help from consultants. In some assignment plans the time for training is intentionally eliminated to reduce costs. Finally, there are consultants to whom training is not a challenge, since they prefer to use their know-how and time for tackling new and difficult business problems.

As mentioned in the introduction to this chapter, this section does not aim to be a complete guide to the use of training by consultants and to developing consultants as trainers. We shall confine ourselves to several basic thoughts and approaches.

(A) The training dimension of various consulting styles

In the previous sections we have stressed that it is virtually impossible to arrive at any practical conclusions by dealing with consulting and training in general terms. Therefore, consultants who are keen to assess and increase the training effect of their consulting interventions should start by analysing their own consulting style and the role assigned to the client in this style.

Moving from non-participative to participative consulting, as shown in figure 24.2, is a way of increasing and strengthening the training dimensions of consulting. It is indeed difficult to speak about training if the consultant is asked to do an expert study or design an information system for the client organization without any (or with minimum) participation of the client's staff. If the proposed new scheme is accepted, staff of the client organization may be trained in using it, but they will hardly be able to understand and explain the full rationale behind the scheme, think of improvements, and change the scheme by themselves when it becomes obsolete. Due to the client's limited learning, the consultant will have to be called in again and possibly some of his or her tasks will be identical to tasks already undertaken in a previous assignment.

Generally speaking, the more the client participates in the consulting project, the better are the training and learning opportunities. However, this participation must have a technically meaningful content. If the client does simple and auxiliary tasks (because the objective was to reduce the cost of the assignment) and the consultant does all the difficult and conceptual work, once again, the training and learning effects are bound to be modest. Collaborative consulting provides opportunities for training and learning, but these opportunities must be seen and utilized by both the consultant and the client.

In process consulting, it is the client who does the work, while the consultant observes organizational processes, provides feedback, asks questions likely to stimulate the client's thinking and makes the client aware of alternatives. The consultant resists the temptation to provide solutions in order to speed up the process. However, he does provide information and technical inputs that the client needs to proceed with the job. In this mode of consulting, the client learns by finding the right solutions, with the consultant acting essentially as a catalyst and a facilitator.

(B) Sharpening the consultant's training skills

Once more we would like to advocate an individualized approach expressing the consultant's needs and possibilities, and would suggest starting by self-diagnosis. It may be useful to reflect on several recently undertaken assignments with a view to becoming fully aware of one's consulting style. What did you actually do in these assignments? What did the client do? Did you choose your intervention methods to get the task done and meet a tight schedule, or to transfer some expertise at every stage of the assignment? Were important opportunities for training the client and facilitating learning missed? Why were they missed? Was it due to the client (shortage of time, lack of interest) or to your attitudes and work methods?

Self-diagnosis will be enhanced if a senior consultant (team leader or supervisor) helps by providing his or her views and feedback on these issues, and if the clients are asked similar questions about experience transfer and learning from consulting assignments. This will depend on the consulting firm's philosophy and policy. If the firm regards transfer of know-how to clients as a major objective of every consulting project, partners and managers responsible for negotiating and supervising assignments will be interested in helping the operating consultants to become more effective as trainers and facilitators. If not, the seniors will be interested in selling assignments, meeting deadlines, getting proposals accepted by the clients and controlling costs, but training and learning will have little meaning to them. A consultant as an individual will be encouraged to become a better trainer if this is consistent with the firm's policy and practice. Consultants will have a more difficult task if they want to achieve this without support from their firm's management.

As mentioned above, to learn from consulting the client must collaborate closely with the consultant on tasks from which something can be learned. In consulting practice, there are normally many opportunities for increasing the client's involvement, even if originally this was not clearly spelled out and described in the assignment plan. If tactfully invited to work more closely with their consultant, most clients will be happy to accept. Thus, it is often possible to make the assignment increasingly collaborative as the project makes headway. The consultant practises training on the job. Because the project continues, there is immediate feedback showing what the client has learned and how he or she is prepared for the next task. The consultant, in turn, has a better opportunity to learn the client's substantive technical skills, and to become more competent at developing the client's know-how through collaboration of a common task.

In short, this is how most consultants sharpen their training, advisory and counselling skills. They do it at work, by collaborating with clients on tasks from which both the client and the consultant can draw some learning benefits.

There are, furthermore, various opportunities for arranging more formal and structured training events in connection with consulting projects. Numerous examples could be given. The client's staff may be trained for data collection and diagnosis, for operating a new information system developed by the consultant, and so on. A part of this training may be arranged off the job, in classrooms or meeting rooms at the client organizations, or in the consulting firm's own training establishment. Such training events provide an opportunity for trying out training techniques described in various parts of this book. Consultants who make frequent use of formal training in support of consulting projects may find it necessary to become versed in a wide range of training methods and techniques, possibly by participating in training of trainers programmes. Shorter and more selective trainers' training can be organized specially for consultants.

(C)   Human resources development consultants

The relationship and synergy of consulting and training has a special meaning to one group of consultants — those calling themselves human resources development (HRD) or business resource management consultants.   As distinct from their colleagues specializing in fields such as corporate strategy, finance or logistics, their field of intervention is the human side of the enterprise — personnel or human resources management and development, with special focus on issues of motivation, interpersonal relations, organizational behaviour and the training and development of management and staff. Their educational background is often in behavioural services. The leading professionals in this field are well aware of a wide range of intervention techniques available to consultants and trainers alike. In working for clients they usually provide combined consulting/training services with a strong emphasis on client participation.

It is useful to see HRD consulting as a bridge and link between consulting and training. For example, HRD consultants can help their colleagues specializing in various technical areas to broaden their portfolio of intervention techniques and become more effective in facilitating the clients' learning. To educators and trainers, HRD consultants can demonstrate the feasibility and advantages of integrating training with consulting in pursuing organizational effectiveness, renewal and excellence.

26.4   Conclusion

The message of this chapter has been that training and consulting have much in common and that the management development profession can draw tremendous benefits from making better use of consulting approaches and skills in management development programmes, both in-company and at external management development institutions. Consultants, in turn, can become more effective by regarding themselves not only as problem-solvers, but also as trainers and facilitators of their clients' learning. The principal beneficiary will be the client, who will get more complete and balanced professional services, helping to plan and manage organizational changes, rather than sets of fragmented, incomplete, overlapping and at times even conflicting consulting, advisory or training interventions.

SELF-DEVELOPMENT FOR THE TRAINER

27

John Wallace

"Self-development" describes a process in which individuals take the initiative, with or without the help of others, in diagnosing their own needs, formulating development goals, identifying human and material resources for their development, choosing and carrying out appropriate developmental strategies, and evaluating the outcomes. In practice, self-development usually takes place with various helpers, such as trainers, mentors, resource people and peers. In fact, trainers who use self-development strategies help each other a lot. Detailed conceptual and methodological material on managers' self-development has been discussed in Chapter 10. This chapter is for trainers, to be used for their own development.

27.1 The advantages and disadvantages of self-development

Malcolm Knowles — a pioneer in self-development — makes the telling observation that the advantages and disadvantages of self-development stem largely from the fact that most of us know only how to be taught; we haven't learned how to learn (Knowles, 1975). This observation leads us to the advantages of self-development, as well as to its disadvantages.

Self-development is *effective:* people who take the initiative in developing their competences learn more things, and learn better, than do people who sit at the feet of teachers passively, waiting to be taught. They enter into the process with more purpose and with better motivation.

Self-development is *natural:* it is in tune with the way people become competent. As people grow they develop strong needs to be independent, first, of parental control, and later, of control by teachers and other adults. Becoming mature is essentially a process of taking increasing responsibility for our own learning.

It is *timely:* participants entering self-development programmes usually know what is the best time for them and how much time they have to invest in such activities.

It is *relevant:* in our fast-changing world, much of what a person knows quickly becomes obsolete. As more and more organizations realize that their competitive edge depends on employees who are up to date, self-development will become the dominant mode for training.

It is suitable for *isolated settings:* most conventional approaches require the learner to go to where the training activity is taking place. A person using self-development, however, is more able to set up the development activities to suit her or himself.

Self-development *adds to the trainer's repertoire:* trainers who have successfully used self-development are better placed to use it with their trainees.

In summary, self-development is a powerful tool that needs to be used wisely. It is often less expensive than formal development, and can be used when *you* are ready, not just when the funds and facilities for conventional training are available.

27.2   The characteristics of self-development programmes

Two important characteristics of good self-development programmes are that they allow a person to complete whole learning cycles, and that their "scope" is quite flexible. They can be used for improving job performance, for developing a career, and even for the whole self. The idea of using complete learning cycles to enhance a trainer's career or job is illustrated in figure 27.1. The three cycles shown emphasize *your* plan, *your* activities, *your* evaluations. These should become more important than the plans, activities and evaluations set by other people (your boss, your organization, etc.) for you. This approach requires that you take charge of your own development.

The left-hand column of figure 27.1 shows a typical *learning cycle.* It starts with your problems and goals, and moves through a search for solutions. Then you try out some solutions, and reflect on what you learned. This, we believe, is how adults learn best. Adults do not learn well by storing up a lot of facts and theories for possible future use; instead they learn best by finding out what they need to know to solve immediate problems — from the birth of a first child, a pending promotion, buying a house, to finding a new job. Most experiences like these create learning opportunities, and each of these opportunities can be divided into these four steps: *goal-setting, solution search, implementation,* and *reflection.* Let us now apply these ideas to the use of self-development in improving your performance as a trainer, and in enhancing your career opportunities.

In the right-hand column of figure 27.1 is a job-oriented model of professional development based on the work of Chalofsky (1984). You start this process by looking at your current job, and comparing what you do well and poorly with what you *should* be doing. Step 2 involves setting priorities, because nobody can work on everything at once. In step 3 you ask yourself what skill, knowledge and attitudes

Figure 27.1. Models of self-development

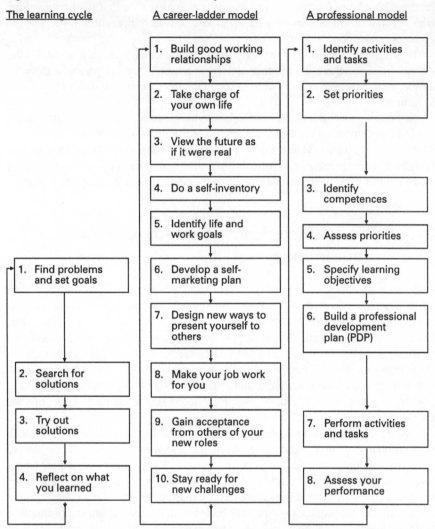

The learning cycle · A career-ladder model · A professional model

The learning cycle

1. Find problems and set goals
2. Search for solutions
3. Try out solutions
4. Reflect on what you learned

A career-ladder model

1. Build good working relationships
2. Take charge of your own life
3. View the future as if it were real
4. Do a self-inventory
5. Identify life and work goals
6. Develop a self-marketing plan
7. Design new ways to present yourself to others
8. Make your job work for you
9. Gain acceptance from others of your new roles
10. Stay ready for new challenges

A professional model

1. Identify activities and tasks
2. Set priorities
3. Identify competences
4. Assess priorities
5. Specify learning objectives
6. Build a professional development plan (PDP)
7. Perform activities and tasks
8. Assess your performance

you need to perform each task, and in step 4, you assess your current level of proficiency and identify gaps that need to be filled. Then you prioritize your learning needs and in step 6 you build a plan to fill those needs. Steps 7 and 8 involve actually carrying out the tasks to fill those needs and evaluating your progress. At each step you may validate your progress with your colleagues and professional peers to make sure that you are on the right track and to build commitment and support from your organization for your continued professional development.

Down the centre of figure 27.1 is a *career-ladder model* of professional development based on the work of Chadiris and Fornaciari (1985). Whereas the job-oriented model concentrated on your job description, this ten-step model concentrates on your curriculum vitae. Furthermore, whereas the job-oriented model emphasizes how proficient you are in a set of *competences,* the career-ladder model emphasizes the way you develop *working relationships* throughout your working life.

The first step is to assess your skill in interpersonal communication so as to ascertain which behaviour is enhancing and which is limiting your ability to build good working relationships. Next, you make a conscious decision to *take charge* of your own development, and in step 3 you "stretch your mind", suspend as many constraints as possible, and create a mental picture of your future. In step 4 you build a self-inventory, which you analyse in step 5. This inventory should contain both life-goals (Who I am and who I will be), and career goals (What I do and what I will do). The next step is to devise a marketing plan for yourself that has two essential elements: (a) a statement about the career that you *should* be in, and (b) a set of objectives and goals for building your career.

Step 7 involves pulling all this information together and risk "doing it", and in step 8 you let other people know what you are trying to accomplish. It takes skill to talk to other people about yourself, but it is vital that you let them know your career goals so that they can begin looking out for you. When opportunities arise, it is then more likely that they will think of you and let you know.

In summary, develop your ability to market yourself for the rest of your life. It is never-ending. It has end points and milestones, and consists of complete learning cycles, one after the other. You should first choose the scope of your programme. will it be your job, your career or your whole self?

27.3   The scope of self-development

Designing a self-development programme requires a series of four major decisions. The first decision concerns the *scope* of your programme. Will you concentrate on *your job, your career,* or *your whole self?* The next step is to *collect information* from other people, from events and from diagnostic instruments that will allow you to focus on the specific areas you want to work on. Third, you need to select methods for *finding solutions* to your development issues, and follow this with methods for building up your proficiencies. Finally, you will need to employ techniques to help you *reflect on what you have learned* and for building a new plan for your next learning cycle.

Let us start with the first choice: should you work on your job, your career, or your whole self?

(A)   Doing your job better

The first step is to identify what you do, and this can be based on a detailed job description that spells out the tasks you are expected to perform (although job descriptions, where they exist, seldom represent reality). First, you may need to make a list of what you do, and even to ask your peers and your boss to look at your list and comment on it. Appendix 2 can help you do this. Find the role profile there that best fits your present job, and list the "critical outputs" and the "critical competences" you find there on a separate sheet of paper. It might look like table 27.1. *A competence is an identifiable combination of knowledge, skills and attitudes that a person exhibits when he or she performs a certain job or range of jobs.* It is "what I do". A proficiency is "how well I do it". Make sure your list is "proactive" and takes into account not only what you should be doing now, but also what you should be doing in the near future. This will not only help you do your present job better, it can also assist you in determining the job changes that can provide future challenges.

Table 27.1. A method of setting priorities for developing job competences (weight scale 0-10)

My job	A	B		C	D	E
	Importance	*Proficiency*			*Gap*	*Priority*
		current	desired			
Competence						
Adult learning	9	7		10	3	27
Making presentations	10	8		10	2	20
Questioning skills	9	7		10	3	27
Listening and feedback	8	6		9	3	24
Training and development techniques	9	8		8	0	0
Group process skills	7	5		10	5	35
Subject knowledge	10	10		10	0	0

We have filled out the table for a typical classroom instructor seeking improved job performance. The list of competences is from the description of the role of an instructor in Appendix 2. Weights ranging from 1 to 10 have been placed in column A to reflect the current importance of each competence. Current proficiency in each of those competences is ranked in column B, and desired competences are given weights in column C. The difference between B and C is the gap to be filled. Multiplying column A by column D gives a priority for each competence. We see that this instructor should consider working hardest on listening skills and group process skills.

(B) Career development

Previously we discussed the steps in building a career development plan. Now let us go into more detail on the career opportunities that are likely to be open to you. Figure 27.2 illustrates many of the career opportunities of the typical management trainer. Let us trace several of these career paths, and illustrate how they can be used

Figure 27.2. Career patterns in management training and development

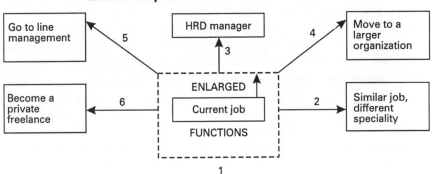

in the self-development process (each paragraph is keyed to the numbers in the figure).

1. A good place to start is by enlarging your current job. For example, many people who use this book are classroom instructors using course designs that were already in place when they took their present jobs. If you are in this situation, you can acquire new skills in training and development techniques by re-examining the course objectives and finding new ways to meet them. You can also build competence in needs identification by visiting prospective participants in their work places and re-evaluating the course objectives.

   At the same time, you can build skill in evaluation by finding out how past participants applied what they learned. By carrying out such activities, you can enlarge your job from that of an instructor to that of a learning specialist.

2. You could also start by moving from your current job to one that is similar, but more complex and specialized. Let's say that you are a supervisory trainer — a common speciality because there are so many supervisors to be trained — and you want to work with middle and senior managers, to increase your status and visibility. You might do this by designing courses on managerial skills that are needed at different levels of management. You could use such a project to increase your skills in management development techniques, your understanding of how managers learn, and your understanding of the management development field — three important competences. For this new course, you might want to carry out some needs-identification exercises, set up an evaluation scheme, and develop and test new team-building exercises, thereby using the project to strengthen a host of competences.

3. A move into HRD management will require that you develop many competences, including skills in cost/benefit analysis, motivation, working with groups of clients, scheduling programmes, marketing and defending your offerings, and providing leadership, to name only a few. For many management trainers, this

is a long-term career objective, for which self-development is an ideal vehicle. You might also consider moving to a smaller organization in order to have more management responsibilities.

4. If you already work in a small organization where you do many tasks, of which management training is only a small part, you may want to move to a larger organization in order to specialize, or to work with higher-level managers.

5. Many management trainers come from the ranks of line management, and look forward to going back to being staff or line managers. They find that management training and development is an ideal place to learn many interpersonal, planning, and analytical thinking skills needed at higher management levels.

6. Many managers who have moved into HRD and liked it find that they cannot advance in their organizations unless they go back to being line managers. Rather than leave the HRD profession, they become private or freelance consultants and trainers.

(C) Working on the whole self

The balanced self involves the widest scope, wider than a concern either with one's job or career. There are many ways to do this, and they have been the focus of philosophers and religious thinkers in all times and cultures. If you choose to work on this broad a scope, one way to start is by considering how to put more balance into your life in four main areas: health, skills, action and sense of identity.

A balanced concern for health — a sound mind in a sound body — is vital because making presentations to audiences of practising managers for hours at a time is a more demanding job than most people realize. Handling such stress requires staying reasonably fit. In turn, management trainers who take up a concern for fitness claim that they have more energy and enthusiasm for their work than they had before.

A balanced concern for action and contemplation is also vital in this field. Most trainers are "on-stage" much of their working time, during which they must know when to take charge of situations to keep things moving, and when to hold back and let the participants lead. In fact a crucial training skill is knowing when to push forward so that a group of managers gets caught up in an exciting activity, and when to hold back and let them lead. The successful trainer balances action and contemplation.

Health — physical and mental — provides a platform for developing skills. Motivation and courage are needed to translate these skills into action. As a result, a sense of identity develops — a feeling that it is "all right to be me". this self-acceptance is accompanied by self-knowledge, and by a sense of purpose. Thousands of self-help books with different approaches are available. Regardless of the approach, go through the learning cycle often: choose goals, find solutions, carry them out, and reflect on what you have learned. Let us now describe methods for each step in more detail.

27.4   The methods of self-development

This section describes general approaches and specific methods. They are arranged roughly in the order that they are used in a self-development programme, with the diagnostic methods first, the methods for carrying out a plan next, and those for reflecting on what was learned and for starting a new learning cycle at the end.

(A)   Methods for identifying problems and setting goals

The first two steps of a learning cycle are involved with self-assessment. The cycle starts with the gathering of data from three major sources: other people, events, and diagnostic instruments, and ends when we begin taking actions to develop ourselves. It involves comparing the information about how we actually are with how we want to be, and creating a plan to fill the gap. It is best to use at least two of these sources in order to get a balanced view of your strengths and weaknesses. Start with what people can tell you about yourself, supplement that with information about significant events that happen to you, and then seek out and use diagnostic instruments to complete the picture. First we look at the three sources, and then discuss specific methods in detail.

Feedback from people. Trainers get feedback from many people — bosses, colleagues, participants, family and friends. Indeed, we are bombarded with praise and criticism. Unfortunately, we can seldom do much with it. While participants get many opportunities to tell us what they think of our work in post-course evaluations — "happiness sheets" or "smile forms" — we seldom have the time, the resources or the incentives to do better.

Since we get so much feedback that we can do so little about, we need to separate the wheat from the chaff. This can be done by first drawing a diagram with the "important people" on it. Put yourself in the middle. Try to place the other people as they relate to your short-term and long-term goals. If, for example, your career goal is to become a better instructor or group facilitator, you would want to pay a lot of attention to feedback from participants. If, on the other hand, you want to move up in HRD management or line management, then you will want to pay more attention to feedback from other managers, perhaps including your boss. Having decided who can provide the most useful feedback, set about seeking and recording it.

Learning from incidents. This involves thinking about important things that happen to you — critical incidents — difficult situations where things went badly or well. To analyse a critical incident you need to answer five questions: What happened? How did I handle it? What was I thinking and feeling? What did I want to happen? How could it have turned out differently? Now look carefully at this information and pick out its meaning. Is the feedback positive, is it telling you about strengths you didn't know you had?

Using diagnostic instruments. You may wish to start your self-assessment with instruments like the one in Appendix 3, which can help you choose which competences of a management trainer to concentrate on. You might use the instrument to build something like table 26.1, discussed earlier. However, most of the information that you will need to orient you to your strengths and weaknesses will come from other people and from analysing incidents that happen to you. Diagnostic instruments are best at helping you to pinpoint specific things about yourself once you have used information from people and incidents to zero in on the areas you want to work on.

In summary, we have briefly reviewed the sources of information. The next task is to discuss specific methods for gathering and using the information to develop and carry out self-development programmes.

(B)   Methods for finding solutions

This section describes five methods for turning the results of self-assessments into self-development plans. It starts by helping you improve your reading skills, includes courses and formal education programmes, and ends with suggestions for creating a "self-development plan", and for setting up learning contracts to help you carry your plans to completion.

Active reading. Reading is one of the best ways to find solutions. After all, there are hundreds of books and thousands of professional articles with information about how others have succeeded and suggestions about how to avoid their mistakes. Self-directed learners take the initiative in using resources, rather than simply reacting to transmissions from the resources. They are proactive rather than reactive learners.

But most of us use resources such as books passively, or reactively. We start at the beginning and read to the end, letting the author tell us what he or she thinks we ought to know. Books like the one in your hands are not designed for a one-way transmission of information. We can use them effectively if we know how. Readers who know the questions that they need answered can turn to the table of contents and index of such books. These books then take on a different character; rather than being a one-way transmission of information, they are resources for self-directed learning. If you are a passive reader, try the active reading exercise in Appendix 4. It builds reading skills. Since the training field is blessed with a constant supply of new books, articles and papers, it pays to be selective. Develop a list that supports your objectives. Let the list be a habit that you acquire, and continue to add to it throughout your career.

Educational programmes. It used to be quite difficult to find educational and training programmes for management trainers. If your self-assessment indicates a need for more academic preparation, you can do two things: look for available academic programmes, and talk to deans of selected institutions about designing a programme to fit your needs.

When you choose a business school, examine its curriculum carefully, visit the school and talk to deans of education, business, arts and science, and human services. See if you can design a programme specifically for you. Don't overlook the possibility that there may be an "open university" or "university without walls" programme that can be designed to fit your needs.

Courses. Since many "faculty development budgets" are really only for going to courses and for attending professional meetings, it makes sense to include courses in your self-development plan; otherwise you would be locked out of potentially rewarding experiences. With a self-development plan, however, you are in a better position to choose exactly what you need, and to apply what you learn. So, include in your plan a list of the types of courses that you would like to attend, and rank those available according to criteria from your plan. The criteria would include: What do I want to learn? What qualifications do I want to obtain? What are the alternative ways of achieving my particular aims? Would another method be better than a course?

Packages and programmed texts. An increasing number of "packages" and programmed texts are becoming available. They are often in a box that includes a book (sometimes as a loose-leaf manual), audio and videotapes, and a variety of exercises, perhaps with supporting computer programmes. If used properly, they overcome some of the disadvantages of courses and educational programmes: they are often much less expensive both in terms of money and time than courses, and they can be used at your convenience; you need not wait until the next session is scheduled. In addition, materials in such packages can often be adapted to your own needs.

Their main disadvantage, however, is their high drop-out rate. Working through a package on your own, with no one to discuss it with, and with no immediate use in mind, is more difficult than many people imagine. So if you choose to use a package, build in support by linking it to something you are doing. For example, if you have a project that requires a needs analysis or an unfamiliar type of evaluation, look for a package on needs analysis or evaluation, and use it on your project. Try to get someone to work with you on the package, so you can stimulate each other.

Professional associations. Joining and taking an active role in professional associations is an excellent way to get in touch with people whose interests are similar to yours. Most such associations produce journals and newsletters containing useful contacts, ideas and information about people, courses and new publications. Participating in their meetings, special interest groups and conferences, as well as writing for their publications, can bring you from the periphery and put you in the centre of your profession. Professional associations are excellent sources of information about mentors, specialized courses and educational programmes, and are good places to test out your ideas and to write and speak about your projects so as to consolidate your learning.

The mission of many professional associations such as the America Society of Training and Development (ASTD) in the United States and the Association of Management Education and Development (AMED) in the United Kingdom includes the development of their members both as professionals and as leaders. If your plan includes taking on more managerial responsibility, consider taking leadership roles in your associations at local, regional and national levels.

Having decided what you want to learn, and chosen some methods to use, consider drawing up a plan that includes the amount of time you expect to devote, other people who would be involved (particularly your boss), and any money or other resources needed. This will help you get a clear picture of the implications of what you plan to do. The plan should include the goals of your programme, any subgoals and dates by which you expect to complete each goal. Some forms and suggestions for such plans are in Appendix 5. It would be important to build into your plan some insurance that you will actually carry it out. This insurance requires the support of several people, especially your boss and another trainer. Learning contracts are a good way to do this.

There are typically three parties and three conditions to a learning contract. The parties are the learner (you), your boss and another trainer. The first condition is that all three parties to the contract should be satisfied that the learner has the motivation to learn the material with a reasonable chance of success. Second, the trainer and the learner must be convinced of the boss's commitment to cover the cost of the training, and the time and facilities to consolidate the learning and transfer it to the job, so as to improve the performance both of the learner and of the organization. Third, the learner and the boss must be convinced that the trainer is capable of carrying the learning project to completion. When this triangular relationship exists, there is a good chance that the self-development plan will succeed.

A learning contract is usually divided into stages, each of which is a complete learning cycle. The learner is required to devote several days a week to the project until completion, which might take from six to ten months. The learner typically fills in weekly time sheets which are countersigned by the boss and passed to the designated project manager, who is usually a trainer.

Learning contracts are a promising way of guiding the self-development process. These contracts leave no necessary elements to chance: the boss's interest and commitment, the learner's willingness and capability, and the trainer's capacity to transfer specific knowledge and skill into an organization are all dealt with. They also provide the time and the money to carry such projects to completion.

In summary, we have discussed five ways of finding solutions to your development needs — ranging from active reading, formal education programmes and courses, to packaged, programmed texts and professional associations. These are typical parts of a self-development plan, which can be formalized in a learning contract to help ensure that it is carried out, with the support of your organization.

(C) Methods for building competences

Having decided on the competences you wish to improve, and some of the ways you may wish to use to improve them, it is time to put your plans into action. In this section we cover several methods for actually building competences that should be included in any written plan.

Strengthening the courage to act. Self-development requires the courage to try out new things and to take the initiative. To be successful in self-development we must take charge of ourselves, and this is often difficult. In fact a trainer's career consists essentially of developing others, often out of a stated desire to "give something back". But the other side of the equation is that it often takes more courage to manage than to train. Many management trainers admit that they lack the courage to manage. After all, it takes courage to be responsible for hundreds of subordinates and great amounts of other people's money.

Three ways of strengthening courage are: (1) using other people as sources of courage; (2) imagining the worst that could happen; and (3) getting inspiration from the example of others.

Other people are good sources of courage. You can share your concerns with them either in pairs or in larger groups. Indeed, giving courage and determination can be a great benefit of working with groups of trainers who are carrying out self-development plans. Hearing other trainer's problems, and seeing how they tackle them, can be inspiring.

One good way of using a group to help develop courage is to ask each member to tell the rest of the group what he or she is going to do, or try to do, before the next meeting. Then, at the start of the next meeting, each member reports back on what they have done.

How does this work? During the time between meetings, knowing that they are going to have to report back to their peers, to account for themselves, people are spurred into action. "I dare not go back and admit that I have done nothing", they might say to themselves. Looking bad in front of one's peers becomes more of a threat than anything that could go wrong in trying out the new action that was promised.

For example, in the maintenance management campaign carried out by the Ethiopian Management Institute (EMI), each industrial company nominated several managers to become trainers and internal consultants in their respective companies. After each company had produced a plan for improving equipment maintenance, EMI began holding weekly meetings with all the internal consultants during which they reported on the progress that their companies were making. Consultants who lacked the courage to influence other managers in their companies were helped and challenged by the example and exhortations of their peers from other companies. As a result of such work, several of these people became leading consultants in Ethiopia (Donarski et al., 1983).

Part of this process of finding courage, alone or with others, often involves *examining the worst that could happen as a result of your actions.* Suppose you want to do something that is new to you — using a case for the first time, having your participants work on projects, or running a complex role-play for the first time — and it appears risky. List the sources of your fear or concern. Are you afraid of appearing stupid, making a fool of yourself, making someone angry, or ruining previous hard work? Often these and similar fears lurk in our minds, but they are mostly unfounded, and it can help to bring them out into the open.

What should be done? First imagine that the activity went smoothly; then imagine that it went wrong. When you are imagining that everything is going well, try to picture what you will be thinking and feeling. Think about the others involved.

What they will be thinking and feeling as a result of your achievement. You might also write down your findings in a column on a sheet of paper. Next, repeat the exercise, but imagine that things have gone wrong, that your worst fears have come true. Write down what you and everybody else involved are thinking and feeling. Now compare the two columns, and decide rationally whether or not to act.

Other trainers and managers can inspire us. You might read about or talk to a trainer who organized a particularly risky exercise and be inspired to try something similar. One trainer, for example, is well-known for having participants find ways to handle environmental crises, and in the middle of the course, he brings in a real TV crew so that the managers must try to handle the media while struggling to contain environmental damage. Seeking out and working with courageous trainers is often a good way to build up one's own courage.

Learning projects are at the heart of self-development. These projects can be inside your organization, or with managers and trainers in other organizations, depending on your needs and the needs of the organization. First determine what you want to learn. Then try to arrange a special project that will help you meet your objectives. Managers in your own organization may already have some special assignments pending and may be looking for someone interested in growing professionally. The first step might be to talk with your boss and other colleagues to see if they can direct you to special assignments that match your self-development objectives.

Even if no one knows of any such assignment, the discussions are bound to bring to light problems that need working on. Choose one and prepare a proposal for a project that will benefit both yourself and your organization. If there are management services specialists or internal management consultants in your organization, they may be able to guide you. Once you have chosen a likely project, talk with your boss about how to "sell" it within the organization. If your proposal is a good one, you may reap a double reward: not only will you meet your own learning needs, but you will also get recognition from the managers who accept your proposal, and who will help you to carry out your project.

If you cannot find a project inside your organization, consider starting one elsewhere. When looking outside, look first at organizations whose managers you train, and second at community organizations that might not otherwise be able to afford your services. Are there volunteer organizations in your community that have management problems and training needs, but lack the resources to obtain professional help? Learning projects in such organizations can provide rich opportunities for you to acquire skills in designing and testing instruments, identifying target populations, conducting surveys, analysing data, and designing training programmes and evaluating their impact.

Also bear in mind that the courses you conduct are excellent sources of projects. Each time you give a course, introduce new approaches. Concentrate on using approaches that take you into the participants' place of work. Ask them to bring problems from their workplace; get them to work on each other's problems and to make presentations about what they accomplish.

Probably the fastest way to learn is to design learning projects as if you were competing for a prize in organizing "winning" training programmes. Such programmes have several characteristics: they tackle problems that affect the organization's standing in the industry; employees' needs and work situation are carefully analysed to ensure that they will be able to apply what they learn and that the application will make a significant difference to the organization. The successful completion of such a learning project often enables the trainer to write in his or her curriculum vitae that the programme, " . . . saved the organization X amount of money, and improved quality by Y per cent", etc. To find such opportunities a trainer must often seek the advice and cooperation of the best people in the management training field.

Mentors. Working for or with an expert in your field is an excellent and exciting way to learn. Quite often, all it takes is to ask an expert whether you can help with a project, if not on a high-risk effort in a private sector organization, then in a voluntary capacity, such as in a professional society or community social service activity. If possible, follow a long-term management development effort through so that you can learn how the expert approaches the whole process.

In summary, identifying and using methods of building courage, undertaking learning projects, and working with mentors, are at the heart of self-development. The activities that come before are preparations for the learning, and the activities that come after consolidate the learning and prepare a trainer for the next cycle.

(D) Methods for reflecting on your development

Learning requires that we think and reflect on problems and experiences, come up with possible explanations and ideas, perhaps discussing these with others. As a result, new ways of seeing things — ourselves, the world around us — emerge. This process of reflection completes one learning cycle and helps start the next. Without reflection, we do not consolidate our experiences, and thus we do not learn. It is often remarked, for example, that many years of experience at the same job is just one year of experience repeated many times. It takes reflection to break out of such a rut.

Since learning cycles can be as brief as a few hours, or as long as a few months, different methods of reflection are needed to suit these different cycles. For example, you could keep a journal or a diary at the end of each day to help you reflect on the events of the day. Or you might decide to write for a professional journal as a way of summarizing what you have learned from a major learning project. Diaries help us to complete daily learning cycles, while writing articles can help us to reflect on much longer cycles that may span six months or a year. Let us first look at methods of reflecting on daily learning cycles, and then move on to methods for longer cycles.

Backwards review. With this method, at the end of each day, you go over the events of the day, starting with the most recent and ending with events at the beginning of the day. It is important to do more than make a mental list. Instead, the major events should be recalled in some detail. Observe yourself in retrospect; consider what you were thinking, how you felt; compare what you did against what you wanted to do; listen again to what other people said; observe what they did.

If you carry out a backwards review regularly and with discipline, you will find that you rapidly gain insights about yourself and others, and that the mental discipline will serve you well in other endeavours.

A personal journal can be used in several ways: as a diary of major events that affect your personal development; as a place to record scores on your self-analysis instruments (such as those at the end of this chapter); to do self-development exercises; as a record of your thoughts and reflections; and for keeping critical incidents. The journal entries will help you focus on your next steps and to review your progress. Periodically, you can look back at it, looking for the patterns, themes, and trends in your progress.

An incident diary is similar to a personal journal, except that you must organize it to answer specific questions about your self-development. Whatever the issue, the diary should be organized so as to provide the following information: what happened, what you thought, how you felt, what you intended to do, and actually did, who else was involved, and how it worked out. For example, a trainer who is building up negotiation skills, group process skills, and presentation skills would have a section in the diary for each of these. Likewise, a trainer who is trying to build up courage and to handle conflicts better would have sections in the diary for situations where conflict-resolution and courage-building are called for. Of course, the critical incident diary can be part of your personal journal. Periodically, you would go back over the diary and see what patterns and themes emerge.

Writing for professional journals. Writing is often the best way to find out how much you already know and what you need to learn. It can open up doors so that others will seek to learn from you and that, in turn, can speed up your own self-development.

If you want your article to have a reasonable chance of being accepted, first study carefully the style of the articles that have been published recently to find out what the editors are looking for, what sort of material they want, what type of audience is being focused on, what length the article should be. Should theory come first, followed by examples from your experience, or should the theory be omitted? Do not be afraid to ask for advice and suggestions and, if possible, work with authors who already know the ropes. Do not be too disappointed if your early efforts are rejected. After all, your major aim is to use writing to consolidate and reflect on your experience and to improve your writing skills.

If you aim to use your writings to advance your career, to market yourself, consider writing about projects — both the successes and the failures — that you carry out with your clients. Case histories about such projects are a form of promotion, sometimes referred to as "diplomatic advertising", because both you and your client will be involved in carrying out the project and then writing about it. So it will advertise you both, diplomatically.

Carrying out and writing about such projects builds several skills. You would be doing research with clients and evaluating the effectiveness of how training is designed and delivered. You would be building skills in needs analysis, evaluating what the participants learned, whether they applied what they learned, and whether it made a difference in their organizations. As mentioned above, writing about "winning" programmes is a fast way to develop.

(E) Choosing the methods

Which of these methods should trainers use? Should they use them all, and how often should they use them? To answer these questions, we must first realize that the methods are not ends in themselves; instead they are the means to generate outcomes. Consequently, we need to choose desirable outcomes and decide how we would know when they have been achieved.

The assessment and planning methods (e.g. feedback from people and incidents, instruments, diaries and journals, etc.) help us choose desirable outcomes. A good way to know when an outcome has been achieved is recognition from others, such as: "I didn't know you could do that! Where did you learn it?" That is why we stressed methods such as learning contracts and professional development plans; their completion brings recognition that signals the achievement of a self-development outcome. So we need to use enough assessment and planning methods to set up the right projects to get recognition, no more, no less.

Doing something and reflecting on what was learned is at the heart of self-development. There is no painless, effort-free way. The more you put in, the more you get out. Simply reading about self-development, or setting up a plan, accomplishes little. That is why learning projects are important, and methods for building courage and finding mentors are useful aids in carrying out such projects. Writing a paper about what you achieved and giving a course or seminar about it helps you to reflect on what you learned, and brings the recognition that signals the end of one cycle and the beginning of the next.

Finally, support is usually necessary to keep the learning cycles going. It is often helpful to meet with other self-developers, to challenge each other to complete each step by devising plans, finishing projects and writing papers. Some organizations help provide such support. Let us consider how.

27.5   Creating the conditions for self-development

An organization can make it easy or difficult to pursue self-development. It can be difficult, for example, if the organization's professional development budget is earmarked to send people on courses, with nothing left over to help trainers analyse their own needs or to carry out learning projects. It is easier if the organization's professional development budget encourages project-based development, and the personnel appraisal system helps trainers to set new challenges and reflect on what they have achieved.

If you feel that your organization could benefit by supporting more self-development, there are several things you can do: circulate articles and papers about the benefits of self-development, hold brief seminars on the topic, organize courses for interested colleagues where they build self-development plans, ask your personnel department to organize a support system for interested employees, to name but a few.

Introductory seminars can be organized in two ways: as stand-alone seminars, or as a topic on self-development in a longer programme. either way, the objective would be to encourage several participants to choose to experiment with self-development. A one-day seminar might cover five topics: (1) what is self-development? (2) how trainers can use it to develop proficiency in a job and enhance their career prospects; (3) an overview of the methods; (4) the need for support systems; and (5) the next steps in terms of some of the participants starting self-development programmes. The seminar should combine the "medium and the message"; that is, the seminar leader should not just talk about self-development but, instead, should incorporate selected self-development methods. For example, the participants should be encouraged to describe critical incidents, and to fill out some diagnostic instruments. They should work in small groups on their own self-development plans. At the end of the seminar, arrangements should be made for those who are interested to meet other self-developers to build and carry out their own self-development programmes.

Workshops on self-development. These workshops should have several objectives and outputs. First, each participant should leave with a self-development plan that he or she is committed to carry out. In addition, the workshop leader might aim to set up self-development support groups that could meet periodically over several months to help participants stick to their plans. A third objective would be for the participants to practise several of the methods. Written cases or a "live case" could be used to illustrate how trainers can use self-development. The written cases would describe how other trainers have developed, and the participants could work in groups to "advise" the trainers in the case how to develop faster, or more effectively. A live case would involve inviting trainers who are using self-development techniques to come to the workshop to describe what they are doing, and then to ask the participants for advice. At each stage of the workshop, participants should prepare parts of their own plan, using elements from the cases as a guide. They would work in teams helping each other refine their plans, and practising the necessary skills in self-development groups. Towards the end of the workshop, the resources needed to support all the plans would be discussed and plans made to find those resources.

Organizing support systems. The purpose of a support system is to ensure that self-developers complete their learning cycles. The organizer of the system must encourage group members to carry out their plans, help them to find opportunities to organize innovative training programmes, provide settings where they can discuss the problems they encounter on projects, and set up sessions where participants present what they have learned from their projects. Some sessions should include line managers who have problems that might be solved with training; other sessions should include HRD experts who can serve as mentors.

27.6   Summary

Self-development — a process where trainers take the initiative for their own development — involves diagnosing personal needs, setting goals, identifying ways to meet those goals, carrying out strategies and evaluating progress. Self-development is often more effective than conventional training, since the self-developer is likely to be more motivated and the pace of learning could be attuned to the trainer's learning capabilities and available time.

A self-development plan can be either narrow or broad in scope; it can reflect a job, a career, or the whole self. A job approach concentrates on competences such as the ability to lead groups or to analyse training needs, while a career approach concentrates on groups of competences that are required to play roles in the training field, such as classroom instructor or HRD manager. Developing the whole self involves improving the balance between attributes such as thinking and doing, or being and becoming, while refining your sense of who you are.

Having chosen the scope of his or her programme, the trainer should plan a series of learning cycles, each containing four parts: identification of needs, planning, carrying out the plan and reflecting on what was learned. Some cycles can be completed in as little as a few hours; others take months or even years. In each part of a learning cycle the trainer uses various methods, starting with gathering information from other people, from events and from diagnostic instruments, organizing the information in diaries and journals, and using it to develop a plan that can be formalized as a learning contract.

Finding solutions might require reading, going to courses, enrolling in formal educational programmes, using packaged learning materials, or joining professional associations. Having found solutions to their problems, trainers should try them out, and then reflect on what has been learned. This reflection could be as simple as making entries in a professional journal or as complex as writing an article or presenting a professional paper.

None of this is easy, and it often requires the assistance of other people, inside and outside of the organization. To assist an organization in promoting self-development, it is often necessary to hold seminars and workshops and even to create support networks of people who are interested in self-development.

Appendix 1: Self-assessment questionnaire

Answer the following questions on a scale of 1 to 5, to estimate your chances of succeeding with a self-development programme.

	Never . . . Sometimes . . . Always				
1. I need to do things on my own	1	2	3	4	5
2. I am a self-starter	1	2	3	4	5
3. I manage my time wisely	1	2	3	4	5
4. I see things through to the end	1	2	3	4	5
5. I set realistic goals for myself	1	2	3	4	5
6. Other people support my plans	1	2	3	4	5
7. I am innovative and creative	1	2	3	4	5
8. I am willing to work long hours	1	2	3	4	5
9. When things go wrong, I start all over again	1	2	3	4	5
10. When the going gets tough, I persist	1	2	3	4	5
11. I accomplish what I set out to do	1	2	3	4	5
12. I am resourceful	1	2	3	4	5

Interpretation: Add up your score. The maximum possible is 60 points. A score of more than 30 indicates that you are likely to finish a self-development programme. A low score, on the other hand, may indicate that you need to take more responsibility for your own development, but that you may not yet be ready and willing to do so.

Appendix 2: Careers and roles

This appendix describes several of the most common roles in the management training field. Roles may be defined in terms of the tasks carried out, the outputs produced, the competences required, and the types of persons who fill these roles best. These descriptions are designed to help you in analysing the types of career paths you might wish to follow.

- *Needs analyst.* Defines gaps between idea (or desired) and actual performance and helps specify the causes of the gaps.

Critical outputs. Written and oral reports on problems of performance and their relationships to knowledge, attitudes and skills; also develops tools to assess the knowledge, skill, attitude and performance level of individuals and organizations.

Critical competences. Skilled in identifying competences in questioning, listening, giving feedback and analysing data. Skilled in performance observation and is a good researcher. Understands organizations and organizational behaviour.

Comments. People who play this role are also probably good at evaluating training programmes.

- *Management development marketer.* Sells management development approaches and programmes, learning packages and services to clients.

Critical competences. Cost/benefit skills, proficient in group processes, counselling, giving feedback. Can quickly learn an industry; good at negotiating; understands organizational behaviour; has good presentation and questioning skills; listens well; writes well.

Comments. A person who has been a group facilitator, instructor, or HRD manager has probably developed many of the skills of a marketer. Industry understanding, negotiation and presentation skills are vital. Programme administrators and theoreticians are unlikely to do well. Past experience as a line manager helps generate empathy with prospective clients.

- *Programme designer.* Prepares performance aims and training objectives, defines content, selects and sequences activities for a specific programme.

Critical outputs. List of learning objectives, written programme plans and designs, etc.

Critical competences. Understands how adults learn, can identify competences; builds models of how organizations develop; can prepare objectives; understands management development techniques; can write well.

Management development

Comments. This person is usually a good instructional writer and theoretician, but a poor programme administrator. Being able to prepare objectives and thoroughly understanding management development techniques is vital.

- *Transfer agent.* Helps managers apply learning back on the job.

Critical outputs. Action plans, job aids to support performance and learning; helps organize coaching and support in the job environment.

Critical competences. Understands how adults learn and how organizations behave; can select and implement the techniques for transferring learning to the job.

Comments. This person is usually a good group facilitator, instructor or marketer. Programme administrators, media specialists, etc., rarely have the skills for this role.

- *Programme administrator.* Ensures that facilities, equipment, materials, participants and components of learning events are present and that the programme runs smoothly.

Critical outputs. Schedules, facilities equipment and faculty; secures and records participants' attendance; manages conference centre; distributes course materials (pre-course, on-site, post-course); may organize follow-up.

Critical competences. Includes audio-visual (A/V) skills, facilities skills and records management skills.

- *Group facilitator.* Manages group discussions and processes so that individuals and group members feel the experience to be a good one.

Critical outputs. Discussions where issues and needs are constructively assessed; decisions where individuals all feel committed to action; cohesive teams; enhanced awareness of group process, self and others.

Critical competences. Understands how adults learn; is skilled in asking questions, listening, giving feedback and in negotiating. Is skilled in group process techniques and at observing group processes.

Comments. These people are also likely to be good instructors, marketers and transfer agents; they need to concentrate on strong group process skills and to understand training and development techniques.

- *Instructor.* Presents information and directs structured learning situations so that managers learn.

Critical outputs. Produces videotapes, films, audiotapes, computer-aided instruction and other A/V materials. Produces and uses case-studies, role-plays, games, tests and other structured learning activities. Delivers lectures and presentations, administers examinations and gives feedback. Assesses managers' learning needs. "Produces" individuals with new knowledge, skills and attitudes.

Critical competences. Understands how adults learn; can make presentations; skilled at asking questions, listening and giving feedback, understands training and development techniques; has group process skills.

Comments. The effective instructor must learn to use a variety of media because learners are increasingly used to learning from different media. A good instructor is probably also a good group facilitator, marketer and transfer agent.

Appendix 3: Diagnosing learning needs

Rationale. Self-development starts when you become aware of the need for development. You may want a better job or greater self-confidence; more self-esteem or greater competence in performing a role; or you may want simply to enjoy the pleasure of learning or to satisfy a curiosity.

Objectives. This exercise will help you (1) better understand the self-diagnostic process, and (2) practise this process. It is suggested that you use this instrument to find one or two competences where there is a big gap between what you are required to do and what you currently can do.

Instructions. In the first column, describe the requirements of your current job by writing a number from 1 to 9, where 9 indicates a high required proficiency and 1 a low requirement. In the second column estimate your current ability (or proficiency) in the same way. Find the gap between what is required of you and what you are capable of by subtracting the second column from the first column. For example, if you are a classroom trainer who is expected to be excellent at using group process skills, and you have very little experience in working with groups, you might put a "9" in the first column and a "1" in the second, giving a gap of "8". If you are uncertain about the competences that go with certain jobs in the training field, look at the role profiles in Appendix 2.

Proficiency			Competence
Required	*Current*	*Gap*	
_____	_____	_____	1. *A/V skill*. Selecting and using audio visual hardware and software.
_____	_____	_____	2. *Delegation skills*. Assigning responsibility and authority to others.
_____	_____	_____	3. *Facilities skill*. Planning and coordinating logistics efficiently and effectively.
_____	_____	_____	4. *Feedback skill*. Communicating opinions, observations and conclusions so that they are understood.
_____	_____	_____	5. *Group process skill*. Influencing groups both to accomplish tasks and to fulfil the needs of their members.
_____	_____	_____	6. *Industry understanding*. Know the key factors that define an industry or sector (e.g. critical issues, economic performance, indicators, distribution channels, information sources).
_____	_____	_____	7. *Management development field understanding*. Knowing the technological, social, economic and professional issues in the field. Understanding how to help managers learn for current and future jobs.
_____	_____	_____	8. *Management learning understanding*. Knowing how managers acquire and use knowledge, skills, attitudes. Understanding individual differences in learning.

Proficiency			**Competence**
Required	*Current*	*Gap*	
_____	_____	_____	9. *Management development techniques understanding.* Knowing the techniques and methods; understanding their appropriate uses.
_____	_____	_____	10. *Needs-identification skill.* Identifying the knowledge and skills required of managerial jobs, tasks, roles.
_____	_____	_____	11. *Negotiation skill.* Securing win-win agreements while successfully representing a special interest in a decision situation.
_____	_____	_____	12. *Skill at setting objectives and aims.* Preparing clear statements which describe desired outputs with clients and trainees.
_____	_____	_____	13. *Organization behaviour understanding.* Seeing organizations as dynamic, political, economic and social systems with multiple goals; using this framework for understanding and influencing events and change.
_____	_____	_____	14. *Performance observation skills.* Tracking and describing behaviours and their effects.
_____	_____	_____	15. *Presentation skills.* Verbally presenting information to achieve its intended purpose.
_____	_____	_____	16. *Questioning skills.* Gathering information from and stimulating insight in managers and groups through the use of interviews, questionnaires and other probing methods.
_____	_____	_____	17. *Relationship versatility.* Adjusting behaviour in order to establish relationships across a broad range of people and groups.

Interpretation. Now find your two or three largest gaps. Consider building your first self-development so as to close those gaps. Don't try to build proficiency in too many areas at one time. Read the chapter carefully and use the planning instrument in Appendix 5.

Appendix 4: Active reading exercise

This exercise will help you understand the proactive use of reading material and help you build skills in reading proactively. (Based on "Learning Resource L", in Knowles, 1975, pp. 105-107.)

Part 1: Proactive searching

1. Make a list of questions that you want answered, for your own self-development.
2. Pick up one or two books, including this one, and determine if they are likely to help you find the answers.
3. Look at the dust jacket or the back cover of the books and read what the publisher says about their purposes. What are the author's qualifications to write it?
4. Turn to the introduction, foreword, or preface and read the author's or editor's orientation to the book.
5. Turn to the table of contents and see how the author has organized the information into chapters, subsections and other content categories.
6. Put the books down, and look back at the questions you made in step one. If these books don't seem to have the answers, write down three more questions about things that you have become curious about from your preliminary examination of the books.
7. Review the questions and find some key words or phrases that you think might be in the books' indexes or tables of contents.
8. Look up these words and phrases. If they are not there, think of synonyms and see if they are there. Go on until you find some pages where some answers are likely to be.
9. Now turn to the parts of the books that deal with your questions and get the answers. If the authors refer to material in other parts of the books, follow their lead until you have all the information relevant to your questions.

Part 2: Reflection on proactive reading

1. How did you feel about using books this way? Is it different from the way you usually use books?
2. Is there any difference in the "quality" of the information you gained?

Appendix 5: Suggestions for self-development plans

1. What is in a self-development plan?

A self-development plan consists of groups of action items, often beginning with the phrase: "I plan to ...". The action items indicate when you plan to start and when you hope to finish.

2. What action items look like

An action item is written so that you — or someone else — will know when it occurs. One way to help achieve this is to use specific action verbs such as the following.

Mental skill		Technical skill	Attitude
State	Demonstrate	Compute	Choose
Name	Discriminate	Design	Volunteer
Describe	Classify	Execute	Allow
Relate	Generate (a solution)	Operate	Recommend
Tell	Apply (a rule)	Reorganize	Defend
Write	Solve	Adjust	Endorse
Express	Derive	Manipulate	Cooperate
Recount	Prove	Handle	Accept
	Analyse	Present	Decide to
	Evaluate	Remove	Agree
		Write	Support

As you work on the action item, ask yourself: Is the behaviour described observable? Will it be obvious to me or others when it happens? For example, will someone be able to say: "Where did you learn to do that?".

3. Implement your action items

As you develop action items, think of yourself in your actual job setting, carrying out the activity you have described.

If you have an idea of when you will be able to begin carrying out the actions, make a note of it. You could, for example, write (i) "as arises" (you know exactly when the opportunity will arise); (ii) "within two (or some other number) months"; (iii) "after two months".

You may find that you can't try out your ideas exactly as planned. It is still important to write your intention, as a tentative plan, knowing you may have to modify the plan after you have talked to your boss, other managers and colleagues.

4. Improving your action items

Ask yourself the following questions:

Can you be more specific?

What will you need to do, and who will you need to talk to at work, to find out which items are possible?

Who would be carrying out the actions, or helping with them (formally and informally)?

Are the skills for carrying them out available?

How much time will they take?

Are special materials or equipment required?

What is involved in obtaining them?

Will you be using a tool, system or aid?

Is continual monitoring or follow-up involved?

Who will do it?

Do you have the authority to implement the action? If not, who does?

How much support do you think there is for your idea?

Will you need to sell the idea to people? Who? How?

Who will this action affect?

How will it affect them?

Will anyone be the worse for the results? Will anyone be better off?

What in the organizational environment might interfere with your doing this? Who would support it?

PROGRAMMES FOR THE TRAINING OF TRAINERS

28

Brian Delahaye and Barry Smith

28.1   Training of trainers programmes in general

The overall aims of training of trainers programmes are to improve training skills and to increase understanding of what is involved in the training process. Whereas many programmes are linked to the training process, some also include sessions on how to interact with the organization. The general trend for training of trainers (TT) programmes is to include the following four major components:

- Theory and techniques of teaching adults.
- Personal skills of the trainer.
- Preparation of training materials.
- Training within the organization.

Most TT programmes last from four days to a few weeks. The shorter programmes deal with the most essential techniques, and provide useful "tricks of the trade" to the novice trainer. Longer programmes explore in more depth the philosophy of training and the overall process of designing and launching training programmes.

Below is an extract of a programme on training design, run at the ILO's International Training Centre in Turin, Italy. The programme teaches trainers how to develop training programmes using a systems approach to the training process.

28.2   Modular series on training design

Principles of rational organization of training

- Learner-centred integrated training organized according to a systems approach.
- Curriculum design.

Training policy and needs

- Training policy and needs: aims, needs, means and content.

Analysing initial training situation and activities

- Study of target population.
- Constraint and resources: preliminary studies through a training action.
- Analysing activities: methods and analysis practice.

Analysing activities and learning factors

- Components of an activity.
- Categories of cognitive operations.
- Analysing complex objectives.
- Specifying training objectives.
- Learning: types and modes.
- Learning: basic mechanisms.
- Motivation.

Methodology

- Training methods — Description of usual methods.
- Training methods — Principles and criteria for choice.
- Individualization of training.
- Training strategies adapted to the different categories of operations.
- Structuring the content: factors to consider and modes of organization.

Evaluation

- Introduction to evaluation: problems.
- Evaluation tests.
- Observation.
- Evaluation of results.

Management of training systems

- Study of the function of a training system.
- Personnel evaluation: trainers.
- Planning resources.
- Organizing practical work.

When describing and implementing TT programmes, it is important to keep in mind the following (Pun, 1990):

- There are many roles in the training and development profession (e.g. training manager, instructor, management consultant, etc.) and people working in, or preparing for, these roles may have different development needs.

- Participants will differ in terms of prior experience, education, development needs and career goals.

- Programme direction and content should be responsive to the trainer-participant's needs.

- Adult learners, with appropriate support and guidance, can manage their own learning.

28.3   Programme introduction

In Chapter 25, we suggested that the various learning processes can be viewed as forming a continuum from trainer-controlled to learner-controlled methods. We believe that the preparation of trainers should follow a similar, progressive developmental path. Such a programme of learning allows the novice trainer initially to practise important but fundamental competences in a relatively predictable and safe environment. Once these competences are mastered, the trainee trainer can gradually incorporate more complex competences into his or her repertoire by working towards the learner-controlled methods.

Based on these premises, the TT programme should consist of four interlinked modules which progressively lead the trainers towards an ability to run learner-controlled processes (based on a programme run at the School of Management, Queensland University of Technology, Australia):

Trainer controlled			Trainee controlled
Module 1	*Module 2*	*Module 3*	*Module 4*
Theory session	Structured discussion	Non-directive discussion	Process-management approaches
Skill session	Case-study	Role-play	Contract learning
		Structured experiences	Organization development/ group dynamic techniques

The competences developed in each module are as follows:

Module 1:   Use of basic visual aids (chalk/white board), questioning techniques, planning and writing objectives, planning sessions, use of planned and ad hoc assessment, use of principles of learning and recognition of training needs and analysis.

Module 2:   Planned and spontaneous questioning, using training objectives to direct learning, orientation to trainee input.

Module 3:   Comfort with emotions, complex on-the-spot analysis, de-roling and debriefing, care of the individual, validity of personal data.

Module 4:   Acceptance of total release of control of content, faith in use of process management, acceptance of self-direction of learners, acceptance of uncertainty and ambiguity, situational aspects in deciding appropriate strategies.

Before discussing each of these modules, two general comments need to be made. First, only brief descriptions will be provided of the content of each module. For more details readers are referred to Smith and Delahaye (1987) and other "train the trainer" texts. Secondly, we consider the process of feedback to be very important. Feedback is central to the very concept of development, and it is therefore important that the TTs not only receive feedback relating to their own development on the modules, but also learn how to give feedback to others appropriately. We are, therefore, very careful to provide a good model when giving feedback. Generally, at the end of each TT practice session we give feedback in a two-stage process by asking:

- What went well in the session?
- What are the one or two improvements that could be made next time?

While this often goes against cultural norms (in Western societies it is common to focus on failure in an attempt to encourage learning), TTs begin to understand that development is a gradual process that builds upon retaining strengths. Most people can only improve gradually and should therefore only be asked to focus on a few improvements at a time. In addition, TTs are always asked to assess their own performance before receiving feedback, and feedback is given in a caring supportive manner.

Module 1

Many people provide training in organizations. On-the-job training is usually the responsibility of line managers and supervisors, with or without guidance from an expert trainer. Off-the-job training is usually the responsibility of professional trainers, who often import specialized information and skills by using line managers and supervisors as session leaders. Consequently, managers and supervisors need to develop competences in session presentation. Such competence development is usually a significant part of the organization's management development activities, and is often called a session leader's programme. A somewhat different programme, more demanding in its final outcomes, is required for those who are starting a career as full-time, professional trainers.

The session leaders' programme

A sample programme is shown in table 28.1. It is a relatively short but intense learning strategy for eight participants. We have found that it produces a minimum

Table 28.1. Module 1 – Session leader's programme

	8	30	9	00	10	00	11	00	12	00	13	00	14	00	15	00	16	00	17
Day 1	Formal opening	Principles of learning	The skill session	Questioning techniques	Preparation for 20-minute skill session	Preparation continued	Conduct 20-minute skill session			
		·····Administration·····>			·····> LUNCH ·····>		1 2 3 4 5 6			
Day 2		Review	On the job train-ing	Training needs analysis Training objectives	The theory session	The lesson plan	Basic visual aids		Preparation for 20-minute theory session	
		7 8					1 2 3 4 5 6			
Day 3	Tests and testing	Preparation for 20-minute theory session	Conduct 20-minute theory session		Conduct 20-minute theory session (continued)		Review and evaluation			
			1 2 3 4			5	6 7 8			

acceptable level of competences for people — often called training session leaders (TSLs) — who will conduct sessions in training courses managed by a competent trainer. Therefore, the TSLs need to have a reasonable level of competency in such structured presentation processes as the theory and skill sessions. The learning objectives for this type of programme are as follows:

1. Design appropriate training objectives.
2. Plan and design an effective training session.
3. Given a training room, basic visual aids and a group of trainees, conduct an effective:
   - 20-minute skill session
   - 20-minute theory session
4. Demonstrate the effective use of:
   - basic visual aids,
   - questioning techniques, and
   - tests.
5. List the principles of learning and apply them in session planning and execution.

The design of the programme is based on three assumptions. First, the TSLs will learn best by "doing". Therefore, a considerable proportion of the time is invested in practice. Second, the TSLs are not overloaded with information. They are given enough input to carry them through the next practice segment. Third, each practice session by each TSL is recorded by a video camera. The feedback provided by the TSL observing this recording will enhance the TSL's development.

Throughout the programme, the TSLs are given some time to prepare their presentations. We try to allow a ratio of about 4:1 preparation to presentation and also ensure that we closely supervise their preparation, as we find some of the most important learning occurs during this period.

We made two other important decisions in designing this programme — one to do with the session on principles of learning; the other with the positioning of the input on the theory and skill sessions.

The session on principles of learning is the first informational input and this provides the "keynote address" for the programme. As such it becomes the reference point for many discussions during the three days — for example, to settle concerns on how an issue should be presented during practice sessions. The material on principles of learning is presented via the theory session model. This has two advantages. First, the climate is set for the whole programme by involving the TSLs in early activities; second, the TSLs rewrite the learning principles on the chalk/white board for the activity of the theory session model, thereby introducing them to the feelings of being in front of a group of learners. Then we introduce the TSLs to the skill session model because it is the most direct, logical and easily understandable. After introducing them to questioning techniques, we quickly have them involved in planning and presenting — activity tends to direct their nervous energy towards positive outcomes. Starting with the skill session model has at least two other advantages. It is a little simpler than the theory session model. Also, by its very nature, the topic taught by the TSLs in the skill session is more observable and concrete than the informational content of a theory session. Finally, the session on training needs analysis is suggested since developmental experience should be tailored very specifically to the needs of the trainees and the organization.

Trainee trainers

The individual who is to become a full-time trainer will be interacting with trainees for significant time periods and will need to use a wide range of training procedures. Therefore, such an individual should initially be trained to a high level of competence in the theory and skill sessions, as well as developing and refining the fundamental training skills, such as questioning techniques, which have to be "second nature" when the trainer progresses to the advanced training techniques.

The learning objectives for this programme are similar to those for the TSL programme, except that they are to a higher standard. The obvious difference is that the participants are required to present a 45-minute theory session. In addition, all the skills — for example, questioning and use of visual aids — should be to a highly professional level.

As well as being of a longer duration, there are two additions to this programme for trainee trainers (see table 28.2). One difference in the design of the course is the presentation by each participant of a ten-minute "speechless". In this presentation the trainee trainer is required to give ten minutes of information without saying a word. This forces the presenter to consider seriously the planning and use of visual aids. In addition, the experience reinforces the importance of the visual sense and most participants are quite surprised at how much information can be communicated and how much is remembered by the learners.

The second addition is the inclusion of a session on the evaluation of training. Also, the time for the session on training needs analysis is expanded. Both of these subjects are considered to be of high importance to professional trainers. As with the TSL programme, video recording and feedback are used for each skill and theory session presentation.

Competences developed

Module 1 is designed to develop in the novice trainer a number of basic competences. By the end of the programme, the participants should be able to design appropriate training objectives and plan a lesson using structured models (i.e. a skill session and a theory session) that are based firmly on the principles of learning. During their sessions, questioning techniques and visual aids should be used to enhance learning. These could be termed "threshold competences" in that the novice trainers would find it impossible to operate without them. In comparison, the concepts of assessment and feedback are more "watershed competences". When the novice trainers cease to concentrate predominantly on their own fears and wants,

Table 28.2. Module 1 – Basic "train the trainer"

	8|30	9|00	10|00	11|00	12|00	13|00	14|00	15|00	16|00	17
Day 1	Formal opening	Principles of learning	The skill session	Questioning techniques	Preparation for 20-minute skill session	Preparation continued	Conduct 20-minute skill session	1 2 3	4 5	6
		←·········· Administration ··········→				→ LUNCH				
Day 2	Review		On-the-job-training	Basic visual aids	Preparation for 10-minute "speechless"	Preparation continued	Conduct 10-minute "speechless"	1 2 3 4	5 6 7 8	Review training objectives
	7	8								
Day 3	Theory session		Tests and testing	The lesson plan	Preparation for 20-minute theory session	Preparation continued	Conduct 20-minute theory session	2 3	4 5	6
							1			
Day 4	Review		Training needs analysis	Preparation for 45-minute theory session		Preparation continued	Conduct 45-minute theory session	1	2	3
Day 5	Conduct 45-minute theory session (continued)						Review	Evaluation of training	Future needs of participants / Evaluation of course	
	4	5	6		7		8			

and change their focus to assessing the trainees' level of learning (via the use of tests and questions), they have crossed an important barrier or watershed. Such behaviour is an indication of a significant step forward in their journey to becoming professional trainers.

Module 2

Module 2 starts the progression away from the highly structured methodologies towards limited learner control. A sample programme is shown in table 28.3. The programme starts with the trainee trainers reviewing their actual experiences of using the structured methodologies of the skill and theory sessions. The focus is on several aspects in particular — first, what went well; second, any problems they encountered and a discussion on how these problems could be overcome; and third, a reminder of the important skills that will still be used in the discussion method (setting objectives, questioning techniques and use of visual aids).

To introduce the discussion method, the trainee trainers view a sample discussion on video. The sample discussion provides a good model and is subtitled at appropriate parts (e.g. "Open question", "Summarizing") and a copy of the session plan used by the discussion leader in the video is also handed out. Following this viewing, the course leaders then conduct sessions on:

- *How to plan and conduct a discussion.* In relation to the "planning" section, many issues are covered, such as setting objectives, using cues to start discussions, identifying key questions and structuring the discussion. For the conducting section, issues such as the introduction, key questions and follow-up questions, non-verbal behaviour, rewarding, visuals and seating are discussed.

- *Concerns about conducting discussions.* This session is designed to achieve three goals. First, the trainee trainers identify common problems in discussions and develop possible solutions to these problems. Secondly, they take part in a real learning discussion, observing techniques which they can subsequently model. Thirdly, the session tends to lower the trainee trainers' stress levels.

Since these sessions are conducted using the discussion method, and the participants will attempt to copy the discussion-leading behaviours they see, it is important that the course leaders highlight examples of what they are doing by periodically calling "time out" to discuss process matters. The success generated by the successful presentation provides a confidence boost for the case-study presentation, when the trainees will plan and present their own cases and debriefing discussion.

After practice discussion sessions, participants are ready to move to the next stage — writing and using case-studies. They are given information on how to write a case-study. The steps emphasized are:

- define theoretical principles;
- convert them into training principles;
- define the population of trainees;
- establish the situation;

Table 28.3.   Module 2 – Structured discussion and case-study

	8|30	9|00	10|00	11|00	12|00	13|00	14|00	15|00	16|00	17
Day 1	Formal opening	Review of training experience	Example video	How to plan and conduct a discussion			Concerns about the discussion method and how to overcome	Preparation for 20-minute discussion		Conduct 20-minute discussion
		← Administration ····				→ LUNCH				1
Day 2	Conduct 20-minute discussion (continued)		Review of discussion method	Writing a case-study	Conducting a case-study		Preparation for 30-minute case study			Conduct 30-minute case-study
		3	4							1
Day 3	Conduct 30-minute case-study (continued)							Review of case-study method		Future needs of participants Evaluation of course
	2	3	4	5	6		7	8		

- develop understanding of the symptoms;
- write the case-study;
- check with objectives and audience analysis;
- develop questions (base specifically on objectives); and
- prepare debriefing activity (gather and analyse data).

Then follows preparation time, and practice and feedback sessions using videos for feedback purposes. The important time for learning is during the debriefing (the discussion after the case-study has been read by the trainees) and it is this stage that the trainee trainers must manage. During the writing of the case-study, they are encouraged to maintain a strong link between the learning objectives, the data included in the case and the discussion questions. This strong link must be maintained during the debriefing, and the learning objectives must be the main focus of the discussion.

Competences developed

In moving away from the more structured models of the skill and theory sessions, the trainee trainers need to build sufficient confidence in their abilities so that they can direct the learning of trainees without having total control over the subject content of the session. This is an important progression in their development. In conjunction with this release of total control of content, there should be an increasing reliance on learning objectives to focus the direction of learning. At the same time, they should be able to demonstrate competences in the areas of planned and spontaneous questioning, and show that they can take a range of data from the trainees and reduce it to important key words that can be placed on a visual aid such as a chalk/white board. Finally, the trainee trainers should demonstrate behaviours which are oriented to the trainees' needs rather than their own.

Module 3

Up to this stage in their progressive development, the trainee trainers have been concentrating on cognitive data as the content for their sessions and on their trainees achieving the first levels (common basic facts, relevant professional understanding, continuing sensitivity to events and analytical competences) of the learning hierarchy. In Module 3, they progress to learning models that have the development of social skills and abilities, emotional resilience and purposeful action as their desired learning outcomes.

Now trainee trainers are dealing with learners' behaviours, attitudes and emotions in addition to the cognitive processing of information. Consequently, a range of extra competences are required of them. Additionally, they may be confronted with previously unknown or suppressed information about their own behaviour and attitudes and the way they affect others. This sometimes requires significant personal and interpersonal growth for individual trainee trainers.

In this module, we concentrate on the role-play, which involves a representative sample of the competences trainers need in order to deal with emotions, attitudes and behaviours. Other learning strategies which could be introduced into the module at the request of the trainee trainers (after all, they should also be developing into learner-controlled learners themselves by this stage) include games, structured experiences, discussion of personal and interpersonal behaviours (as in sensitivity groups) and instruments for personal feedback. An example of this programme is shown in table 28.4.

Once again the programme starts with a review of the trainee trainers' actual experiences of using the earlier models, with particular emphasis on the structured discussion and the case-study. The issues of trainees interacting in groups, setting objectives, and feeling comfortable with having significant responsibility for content input need to be highlighted. In addition, the steps in writing a case-study must be revised.

The trainee trainers are then shown how to write a role-play using the following steps in writing a case-study as a base:

- define theoretical principles;
- convert them into training principles;
- define the population of trainees;
- establish the situations;
- develop understanding of the symptoms;
- write the role-play (background statement and briefings for players);
- check with objectives and audience analysis;
- develop guides for observers (link specifically to objectives); and
- plan debriefing (de-roling, players' reports, observers' reports, analysis, and improving behaviour).

In writing role-plays we have found the need to emphasize two issues. First, trainee trainers often tend to use the "negative" emotions (e.g. anger) when writing a role-play. We usually point out that in role-plays it is easy to stir up the "negative" emotions, but this may have a detrimental effect on their trainees both during the role-play itself and the debriefing thereafter. In addition, extreme emotions are rarely encountered in the real work situation and, even if it becomes necessary to expose trainees to such extremes, it should be achieved with a gradual escalation of emotions over several role-plays. We therefore encourage the trainee trainers to be more realistic in the situations they establish in their role-plays, especially in relation to the level of emotion generated.

Second, we encourage the trainee trainers to include cues so that the role-play is more likely to succeed. For example, in a role-play in conflict, the individual in the role of the "aggressor" can usually continue with a destructive role for the ten or twenty minutes of the role-play without any problem. However, this is sometimes to the detriment of the individual playing the role of, say, the "negotiator", who finds it either difficult or impossible to resolve the conflict and therefore to demonstrate some examples of conflict resolution. In addition, the individual in the role of the

Table 28.4. Module 3 – Role-play and structured experiences

	8:30	9:00	10:00	11:00	12:00	13:00	14:00	15:00	16:00	17
Day 1	Formal opening	Review of training experiences	Writing a role-play	Practice writing a role-play	Conducting a role-play	Conducting a role-play (continued)	Observation skills	Plan and prepare for role-play		
		····· Administration ·····			·····> LUNCH ·····>					
Day 2	Conduct role-plays				Review role-play method	Identification of participants' needs	Planning for remainder of workshop	As planned by participants		
	1	2		3						
Day 3		As planned by participants								

571

"negotiator" does not experience any success, which adds an emotional negative to the problem of the lack of development of skills in that role-play. During the writing of the role-play, we encourage them to include cues which will promote some level of success during the role-play enactment.

Once they have written a role-play, the trainee trainers need to know how to conduct it and, in particular, the skill of observation. We do this by having the entire group involved in a role-play — either as participants or as observers. The role-play we use is based on group leadership theory (Limerick, 1976) and this has the additional spin-off of giving the participants some input on relevant group theory.

We conduct this role-play, de-roling and debriefing as a behavioural model for the participants. Once the objectives of the model role-play (i.e. describe the four major roles in a group) have been achieved, we then move onto the next session — observation skills. We do this via a group discussion and ask the trainee trainers to use any information (their experience in the recently completed model role-play, any behaviours they have seen the course coordinators perform, or any other informational base they may have) to comment on the competences a group leader needs to observe during a role-play.

When discussing how to conduct role-plays, we emphasize two issues:

1. *De-roling.* Role-plays are designed to display behaviours and emotions that can be used as data for discussion and learning. Trainees involved often experience and demonstrate a variety of issues and feelings. It is very important that the participants should be fully de-roled after being involved in a role-play so that they are no longer attached to the role or to the feelings generated in the role. We suggest a variety of techniques to assist with de-roling:

   - leader stands or sits close to the role-players immediately after the play;

   - leader requests or encourages full verbalization of the feelings generated in the players. Such expression of feelings is often not easy, and the leader may need to persist through a series of questions. It sometimes helps to ask the players to express feelings in their role names before asking them to express feelings in their real names.

   - removal of symbols, props or name tags that may be part of the persona of the role;

   - using "disclaimers" so that the players can avoid guilt feelings for not being a perfect success (e.g. "Many thanks to Kylie and Megan for doing that role-play. We included a number of barriers that stopped them from resolving that conflict as well as they most probably would have preferred but, even with this, they did a very good job.");

   - physically moving players from the role-play situation to a different area for the debriefing discussion.

The leader must watch most carefully for any signs that a role-player is not fully de-roled or is slipping back into the role. Any retention of, or returning to, the role is likely to inhibit learning by that trainee during the debriefing discussion. Most individuals come away from Module 3 workshops with a healthy respect for the importance of de-roling.

2. *Debriefing.* As with case-studies, most of the real learning occurs after the role-play. Information from players and observers is gathered and this raw data is then discussed to highlight key learning points and to achieve the objectives of the session. Further role-playing to practise the key points may then follow.

Once the segment on role-plays has been completed, the trainee trainers are given the responsibility of deciding how to use the unallocated time in table 28.4.

Sometimes individual trainee trainers write and run role-plays without the support and advice of two other trainee trainers in a triad as occurred in the previous two days of Module 3. Alternatively, they can be introduced to some of the other learning methods which require the same leader competences as the role-play. This is done experientially, with the trainee trainers being exposed to a game, structured experience or instrument and then discussing the experience to highlight what they learned about themselves and what they learned about the competences needed to utilize such methods.

Competences developed

Trainee trainers progress further in being comfortable with more reliance on process and less on content. They accept that emotions and attitudes are the personal data on which learning is based. They also recognize the need for comprehensive de-roling and complex analytical debriefing, which is formulated on the spot rather than planned in advance.

Module 4

In this final module, the trainee trainers learn that managing the process while relinquishing all control of content is an acceptable strategy. This is a significant threshold to cross as, until this stage, there is at least some predictability in what will occur, as the trainee trainer has had some idea of the type of content that will be covered. As the content will now be dictated entirely by the learners in the strategies that the trainee trainers will manage, feelings of security based on content control will no longer be present.

While it is often an attractive thought to immediately throw them into a complete learner-controlled strategy (as, for example, in the T-group situations of the 1960s), we have found a gradual escalation — from solid structure, to less structure, to no structure — to be more beneficial. Indeed, some writings in group theory (see, for example, Jones, 1973) and specific suggestions in managing contract learning (Knowles, 1984) give considerable support to this approach.

We do not have a specific programme as an example for Module 4. This should not come as a surprise as we are examining a complex issue, and it is most doubtful that one specific solution would cover all situations. Rather we will discuss the main principles involved when developing trainers at the Module 4 level.

We have chosen to discuss two different strategies in developing trainers in process management — contract learning and organization development/group dynamics. When preparing them to use these strategies we have at least one commonality — behaviour modelling. Trainers use contract learning to learn about contract learning. Organization development techniques are used exclusively when the trainers are learning to manage process by organization development interventions.

Contract learning

Contract learning is a very individualized approach to learner-controlled learning. The heart of the strategy is a learning contract between the learner and the facilitator. In this example, let us assume that the facilitator is the course manager. The contract is a form usually consisting of five columns — the learning objectives to be achieved, the target date, the resources to be used in learning, a description of the evidence to be presented that will indicate that the learning objectives have been achieved and the criteria to be used in making this judgement. While completing this contract may appear to be a simple requirement, the learners (in this case the trainee trainers) need some considerable support.

This support comes mainly in three forms. First, there needs to be a relationship with peers. This condition has high similarity with the process of action learning — for example, Revans (1982) refers to "comrades in adversity" and the need to view learning as a social activity. The second form of support comes from the relationship with the facilitator. This relationship needs to be one based on trust, and must guarantee reasonable access by the learner to the facilitator. The third form of support comes from some initial structure managed by the facilitator.

In conducting a contract learning strategy, the involvement of the facilitator is high in the initial stages, decreases in the middle and then escalates somewhat towards the end.

Initial stage. For the facilitator, there are two main objectives. The first objective is to establish and develop the relationships between the learners and also between the learners and the facilitator. The second objective is to provide a structure that allows the learner to identify possible areas for learning and development. We use the following steps that are taken, in the main, from the writings of Knowles (1980a, 1980b, 1983a, 1983b, 1984).

1. A relationship-building, climate-setting exercise. The trainee trainers divide themselves into small groups and exchange information on who they are and what resources they bring that could assist the group in learning.
2. The facilitator then introduces the concepts of contract learning and how this learning strategy will be used for this particular group.
3. The trainees are again asked to divide into small groups and discuss and list any concerns they may have about the strategy, the facilitator or anything else that may impinge on their learning.
4. The facilitator then responds to these concerns openly and honestly. Some issues can be resolved simply by giving information. Other issues, however, take time

and interaction to produce resolution.

5. A list of competences is generated by the trainees. In their case, the competences relate to the role of a trainer (e.g. use of visual aids, questioning techniques, training needs analysis, adult learning, conflict resolution).

6. Once the competences list has been drawn up, the trainees can then make two assessments — first, on their own level of knowledge or ability and secondly, on the importance of each competence.

7. Copies of the learning contract form are given out and the concept is discussed. We find it important to emphasize that the contracts are infinitely renegotiable. The contracts are first completed on the information the learner has available at that time. Of course, as learners develop and also uncover more information, their needs may change. This flexibility in planning should be recognized and encouraged. When the trainee trainers have no further questions, they set about drafting their contracts and negotiating these contracts with the facilitator.

Middle stage. At this stage the role of the facilitator becomes more that of an educational clearing-house or traffic policeman. The trainee trainers have identified their learning objectives, but may need assistance in locating various learning resources. The facilitator may direct the learner to a particular reading, or arrange an introduction to a practioner or some other "expert" in the area in which the learner is interested. Although it may appear to be a contradiction in terms, the facilitator may at times provide information.

Final stage. The final stage of the contract learning process involves two activities. The first activity is comparing the evidence provided by the trainee trainers with the objectives and criteria identified in the learning contract. This basically answers the question "Has the negotiated learning occurred?"

The second activity we conduct is not usually a component of traditional contract learning. We ask the learners to reflect on their learning experiences to identify their personal learning processes. Questions such as "What went well?", "How could I do it better?", "What are my learning strengths?", "What additional skills do I need?" are intended to assist the trainee trainers to become more effective self-directed learners.

Organization development

Another method of managing process is organization development (OD). It originated in the work on group theory by such writers and practitioners as Bion and Lewin, and a number of its values and techniques developed in the T-groups of the 1960s. OD emphasizes "process consultation" where the facilitator works with individuals and groups to help them learn about human and social processes and to learn to solve problems that stem from process events. As such, OD is used extensively in organizations to manage change and to develop managers. Often these two aims are achieved simultaneously in that, while acting as a third party or change agent to bring change into an organization, the facilitator presents a behavioural model for the organization's managers (see table 28.5).

Table 28.5. Module 4 – Example of an organization development

	8:30	9:00	10:00	11:00	12:00	13:00	14:00	15:00	16:00	17
Day 1	Formal opening	Examining change Encourage Hinder — Administration —	Prioritizing solutions to inhibiting forces	Discussion of solutions in large group	Discussion of action research Feedback from action	→ LUNCH →	Observation skills	Discussion on group theory and management of groups		
Day 2		Role-play on consulting	Steps in consulting	Use of questionnaires as data generators		Role negotiation (continued)			Establish dyads/triads	
Day 3		Introduction to resource materials, e.g. on various types of intervention	Preparation for trainee-conducted interventions				Conduct interventions and feedback			
Day 4		Conduct interventions and feedback 3		4	5		6	1 The role and skill of the OD facilitator	2	
Day 5		A. Semi-structured B. Unstructured — learners' responsibility							Review and evaluation	

Active experience is the appropriate strategy for learning to manage OD processes because of the complexities and interdependencies of OD concepts. This also means that the learning strategy is process-oriented and content cannot be specifically prescribed. In general, we divide the strategy into two parts:

1. *The semi-directed part.* This section lasts for 15-20 hours either over two or three days (as, for example, in a workshop format) or even over five weeks (as in a tertiary academic one-semester subject of three or four hours per week). We cover the basic intervention models of Action Research, Force Field Analysis and Small Group Information Sharing. In addition, the issues of observation skills, steps in an intervention, and the ethics of consulting are examined by the trainee trainers. As a link to the next part, we usually conduct a role negotiation to clarify changes in their roles (both as learners and participants) and the facilitators.

These models and issues are all examined using OD methodologies. The following is an example:

(a) We often commence with force field analysis by asking the trainees to think of some change (e.g. a new computer system) that could come into an organization with which they are familiar. We then ask them, individually, to identify what may stop or hinder that change coming into the organization. Then they are asked to identify what would encourage the change. Trainees are then asked to form small groups and make up two lists: forces that encourage change and forces that inhibit change — and to write these lists on large sheets of paper. These sheets are then placed on the walls for all to see and the large group is asked to make a composite list which is written on the chalk/white board.

(b) Trainees are then asked to concentrate on the inhibiting forces and identify, individually, the one force they consider important. When each has written down his or her choice, they are asked to pick a second inhibiting force — the one they consider the second most important.

(c) The total list is then prioritized by having the trainee trainers vote for their preference. We ask them to put up two hands for their first priority and one for their second. In this way, the facilitator can count the number of votes for each inhibiting force.

(d) The major inhibiting forces so identified are then given out to the small groups (one to each) who are asked to create solutions to them. Again, these solutions are to be listed on large sheets of paper that, when the lists have been completed, can be placed on the walls so that everyone can see them.

(e) The solutions are discussed within the large group.

From this exercise, which usually takes three hours, trainees learn force field analysis (the inhibiting/resisting and encouraging/driving forces); the action research model (using a cue to have the group generate data, the group collates/prioritizes that data, another cue based on that collated data to generate more data); group information sharing (give the individual time to write down ideas, share and extend these ideas in a small group, share and discuss these extended ideas in the large group); and, finally, using large paper, sharing information publicly and efficiently.

2. *The self-directed part*. The length of this section depends on the number of trainees and whether the facilitator wishes them to gain experience as individuals, dyads (in twos) or triads (threes).

Trainees are charged with the responsibility of changing their own social system (i.e. to provide learning experiences for the other trainees). Each trainee unit (i.e. an individual, dyad or triad) takes responsibility for a particular time period in the workshop course. We have found that 90 minutes is the minimum that can be allowed. Each trainee unit designs and then conducts an organization development intervention with the trainee group. They are referred to texts such as McLennan (1989), Harvey and Brown (1982) and Dunphy (1981) for ideas on types of interventions. Usually, we encourage the first unit to use an intervention that will identify the training needs (for example, goal setting) of the trainee group and the last unit to conduct an evaluation. When each intervention has been completed, it is discussed for specific learning points — still using the feedback process of discussing the good elements before identifying the two or three points that could be improved in the future.

General comments

The main assumption of the two examples of Module 4 discussed is that people learn by doing. Trainees experience the method — either contract learning or organization development — and are given feedback and time to reflect on their experiences. Both models are entirely process-oriented. The trainees decide on and produce and deliver the content, which inevitably produces useful learning, but is really only a vehicle for the demonstration and practice of appropriate processes.

Competences developed

In Module 4, the trainees accept that learning can be facilitated by managing the process rather than the content. By experience they recognize the assumptions on which learner-directed learning is based, and come to accept the uncertainty and ambiguity that is part and parcel of managing learner-directed learning strategies.

28.4 Conclusion

The modules discussed in this chapter provide a progressive and flexible development strategy for training trainers. Module 1 is designed to establish the basic competences required for structured or trainer-controlled learning strategies. We have found that little change is required to the format discussed. However, depending on the situation (and the training needs analysis), the make-up of the other modules can change.

Preparation to take on the role of a professional trainer should not be a hit-and-miss affair. A variety of competences are required, and various competences are associated with various training techniques. New trainers should initially acquire the competences they need to effectively use the relatively straightforward and safe training methods where control is in the hands of the trainer. As additional competences are acquired, trainers will progressively be able to extend the range of training methods they can utilize to suit any learning situation. Development of training competences requires active practice by the learners, preferably in a carefully planned programme which develops the competences in an appropriate order and with maximum safety and support for the learners.

BIBLIOGRAPHY

Action learning: Putting learning into action resource. 1990. (Bradford, United Kingdom, MCB University Press.)

Adachi, K. 1989. "Problems and prospects of management development of female employees in Japan", in *Journal of Management Development* (Bradford, United Kingdom, MCB University Press), Aug.

Adair, J. 1987. *Effective teambuilding* (London, Pan Books).

Adler, M.J. 1985. *How to speak, how to listen* (New York, Macmillan).

— ; Izraeli, D. 1988. *Women in management worldwide* (New York, M.E. Sharpe).

American Management Association (AMA). 1991. "A global response to management needs", in *International Management Development Review* (New York, AMA).

American Society for Training and Development (ASTD). 1979. "A self-development process for training and development professionals", in *Training and Development Journal* (Alexandria, Virginia, ASTD), May.

— . 1983. *Models for excellence: The conclusions and recommendations of the ASTD training and development competency study* (Alexandria, Virginia, ASTD).

— ; Futures Task Force. 1984. "HRD tomorrow", in *Training and Development Journal* (Alexandria, Virginia, ASTD).

— . 1989. *A self-development process for training and development needs* (Geneva, ILO).

Andrews, K.R. (ed.). 1953. *The case method of teaching human relations and administration* (Cambridge, Massachusetts, Harvard University Press).

Argyris, C. 1982. *Reasoning, learning and action* (San Francisco, Jossey-Bass).

— ; Schön, D.A. 1978. *Organizational learning: A theory of action perspective* (Reading, Massachusetts, Addison-Wesley).

Armstrong, M. 1986. *A handbook of management techniques* (London, Kogan Page).

— . 1995. *A handbook of personnel management practice*, 5th ed. (London, Kogan Page).

Arnall, G.G. 1987. "Satellite-delivered learning", in *Training and Development Journal* (Alexandria, Virginia, American Society for Training and Development).

Asplund, G. 1988. *Women managers changing organizational cultures* (Chichester, United Kingdom, John Wiley).

Association for Higher Education (AHE). 1989. *AHE Annual Report, 1988* (Dallas, Texas).

— . 1989. *AHE: Professional Education Resources Center 1989* (September update) (Dallas, Texas, AHE, North Texas).

Association of Management Consulting Firms (ACME). 1991. *Management consulting: A model course* (New York, ACME).

Barclay, I. 1986. "A survey of the activities, problems and training needs of the technical managers", in *Journal of Engineering and Technology Management* (Amsterdam, Elsevier Science Publishers B.V.), Jan.

Barham, K.; Fraser, J.; Heath, L. 1988. *Management for the future* (Berkhamstead, Hertfordshire, Ashridge Management School).

— ; Osbaldeston, M. 1989. "Developing managers for the future", in *Journal of European Industrial Training* (Bradford, United Kingdom, MCB University Press), Vol. 13, No. 4.

— ; Rassam, C. 1989. *Shaping the corporate future* (London, Unwin Hyman).

Barker, J. 1989. "The whys and wherefores of expert systems", in *Management Bibliographies and Reviews*, Vol. 15, No. 1.

Barnes, L.; Christensen, C.R.; Hansen, A.S. 1994. *Teaching and the case method*, 3rd ed. (Boston, Massachusetts, Harvard Business School Press).

Beaulieu, A., et al. 1988. "Foreman development with a difference", in *Training and Development Journal* (Alexandria, Virginia, American Society for Training and Development), Apr.

Beckhard, R. 1969. *Organization development: Strategies and models* (Reading, Massachusetts, Addison-Wesley).

Bellman, G. 1983. "Untraining the trainer: Steps towards consulting", in *Training and Development Journal* (Alexandria, Virginia, American Society for Training and Development), Jan.

Bennett, R. 1988. "The right role", in *Improving trainer effectiveness* (Aldershot, Hampshire, Gower).

Bennis, W.G. 1969. *Organization development: Its nature, origins and prospects* (Reading, Massachusetts, Addison-Wesley).

Bertrand, K. 1989. "On the line for confidence", in *Business Marketing* (Chicago, Illinois, Crain Communications Inc.), Feb.

Binstead, D.; Hodgson, V. 1984. *Open and distance learning in management education and training* (Sheffield, United Kingdom, Manpower Services Commission).

Bion, E.R. 1961. *Experience in groups* (New York, Ballantine Books).

Bittel, L.R. 1981. *The continuing education unit* (Silver Springs, Maryland, Council on the Continuing Education Unit).

— . 1983. "New dimensions for supervisory development", in *Training and Development Journal* (Alexandria, Virginia, American Society for Training and Development), Mar.

— . 1985. "A model of simulated management experience for engineering managers", in *Paper 75-WA/Mgt-5* (New York, American Society of Mechanical Engineers), July.

— . 1987. *The complete guide to supervisory training and development* (Reading, Massachusetts, Addison-Wesley).

— ; Newstrom, J.W. 1990. *What every supervisor should know,* 6th ed. (New York, McGraw-Hill).

— ; Ramsey, J.E. 1982. "The limited, traditional world of supervisors", in *Harvard Business Review* (Boston, Massachusetts, Harvard University Press), July-Aug.

— ; — . 1982. *The 1981 national survey of supervisory management practices* (Harrisonburg, Virginia, James Madison University).

— ; — (eds.). 1985. *Handbook for professional managers* (New York, McGraw-Hill).

Blackler, F.H.; Brown, C.A. 1980. *Whatever happened to Shell's new philosophy of management?* (Aldershot, Hampshire, Gower).

Blake, R.R.; Mouton, J.S. 1985. *The managerial grid III* (Houston, Texas, Gulf Publishing).

Blankskey, M.; Iles, P. 1990. "Recent developments on assessment centre theory, practice and operation", in *Personnel Review* (Bradford, United Kingdom, MCB University Press), Vol. 19, No. 6.

Bloom, B. 1964. *Taxonomy of educational objectives: The affective domain* (New York, Donald McDay).

Boak, G.; Stephenson, M. 1987. "Management learning contracts", in *Journal of European Industrial Training* (Bradford, United Kingdom, MCB University Press), Vol. 11, No. 6.

Bolt, J.F. 1989. *Executive development: A strategy for corporate competitiveness* (New York, Harper and Row).

Bostock, S.; Seifert, R. 1986. *Microcomputers in adult education* (London, Croom Helm).

Boud, D.; Keogh, R.; Walker, D. (eds.). 1987. *Reflection: Turning experience into learning* (London, Kogan Page).

Boulden, G.; Lawlor, A. 1987. *The application of action learning: A practical guide* (Geneva, ILO).

Boyatzis, R.E. 1987. *The competent manager* (New York, Wiley Interscience).

Boydell, T. 1970. *A guide to job analysis* (London, BACIE).

— . 1985. *Management self-development: A guide for managers, organizations and institutions* (Geneva, ILO).

— . 1991. *Modes of being and learning* (Sheffield, United Kingdom, Transform Development Consultants).

— ; Leary, M. 1996. *Identifying training needs* (London, Institute of Personnel and Development).

— , et al. 1986. *A guide to self-development groups for women managers* (Sheffield, United Kingdom, Sheffield City Polytechnic and the Manpower Services Commission).

Brearley, A.; Sewell, D. 1990. *The Ernst and Young management self-assessment system* (Manchester, Ernst and Young).

Brinkerhoff, R.O. 1988. "An integrated model for HRD", in *Training and Development Journal* (Alexandria, Virginia, American Society for Training and Development), Feb.

Broadwell, M.M. (ed.). 1985. *Supervisory handbook: A management guide to principles and applications* (New York, John Wiley).

Burgoyne, J. 1988. "Management development for the individual and the organisation", in *Personnel Management* (London, Personnel Publications), June.

— ; Pedler, M.; Boydell, T. 1994. *Towards the learning company: Concepts and practices* (Maidenhead, Berkshire, McGraw-Hill).

— ; Storey, J. 1989. "Management development: A literature review and implications for future research. Part 1: Conceptualizations and practices", in *Personnel Review* (Bradford, United Kingdom, MCB University Press), Vol. 18, No. 6.

— ; Stuart, R. 1977. "Implicit learning theories", in *Personnel Review* (Bradford, United Kingdom, MCB University Press), Vol. 6, No. 2, Spring.

— ; — . (eds.). 1978. *Management development: Context and strategies* (Farnborough, Hampshire, Gower).

Byham, W.C. 1972. "Assessment centers: The place for packing management potential", in *European Business* (Brussels, Belgium, Europe Information Service), Autumn.

— ; Robinson, J. 1976. "Interaction modeling: A new concept in supervisory training", in *Training and Development Journal* (Alexandria, Virginia, American Society for Training and Development), Feb.

Caffarella, R.S. 1988. *Programme development and evaluation: Resource book for trainers* (New York, John Wiley).

Campbell, A.; Winterburn, D. 1988. "Organizational development through management development: The United Biscuits example", in *Management Education and Development* (Lancaster, United Kingdom, Lancaster University), Vol. 19, Part 3.

Canning, R.; Martin, J. 1990. "The learning community", in M. Pedler et al. (eds.): *Self-development in organizations* (Maidenhead, Berkshire, McGraw-Hill).

Carnegie Council. 1980. *Three thousand futures: The next twenty years of higher education* (San Francisco, Jossey-Bass).

Carnegie, D. 1990. *The quick and easy way to effective speaking* (New York, Pocket Books).

Cartwright, S.R. 1987. *Training with video* (New York, Knowledge Industry Publications).

Casey, D. 1983. "The role of the set adviser", in M. Pedler (ed.): *Action learning in practice* (Aldershot, Hampshire, Gower).

— ; Pearce, J. 1977. *More than management development* (Aldershot, Hampshire, Gower).

Chadiris, B.J.; Fornaciari, G.M. 1985. "Self development", in W.R. Preacy (ed.): *Human resources management and development handbook* (New York, American Management Association).

Chalofsky, N. 1984. "Professional growth for HRD staff", in L. Nadler (ed.): *The handbook of human resource development* (New York, John Wiley).

Chenault, J. 1987. "The missing option in executive training", in *Training and Development Journal* (Alexandria, Virginia, American Society for Training and Development), June.

Christensen, C.R. 1987. *Teaching and the case method* (Boston, Massachusetts, Harvard Business School Press).

Constable, J.; McCormick, R. 1987. *The making of British managers* (London, British Institute of Managers).

Committee of Donor Agencies for Small Enterprise Development. 1996. *Report on work in progress in the production of guidelines for small enterprise promotion and development* (Geneva, CDASED), March.

Cook, T.D.; Reichardt, C.S. (eds.). 1979. *Qualitative and quantitative methods in evaluation research* (London, Sage).

Cooper, C.L. (ed.). 1987. *Developing managers for the 1980s* (London, Macmillan).

Copeland, M.T. 1958. *And mark an era: The story of the Harvard Business School* (New York, Little Brown).

Corfield, K.; Penny, M. 1983. "Action learning in the social services", in M. Pedler (ed.): *Action learning in practice* (Aldershot, Hampshire, Gower).

Craig, R.L. (ed.). 1987. *Training and development handbook: A guide to human resources development* (New York, McGraw-Hill).

Crainer, S. (ed.). 1995. *The Financial Times handbook of management: The state of the art* (London, Pitman).

Critchley, B.; Casey, D. 1994. "Teambuilding: At what price and at whose cost?", in A. Mumford (ed.): *Handbook of management development*, 4th ed. (Aldershot, Hampshire, Gower).

Culbertson, K.; Thompson, M. 1980. "An analysis of supervisory training needs", in *Training and Development Journal* (Alexandria, Virginia, American Society for Training and Development), Feb.

Dale, E. 1993. *Developing management skills* (London, Kogan Page).

Daniel, C. 1988. "Tomorrow's computer skills — today", in *Personnel* (Paris, France, National Association of Directors and Personnel Officers (ANDC)), April.

Darnton, P. 1987. *Audio techniques in training* (Carnforth, United Kingdom, Parthenon).

Deal, T.A.; Kennedy, A.A. 1982. *Corporate culture, the rights and rituals of corporate life* (Reading, Massachusetts, Addison-Wesley).

Dean, C.; Whitlock, Q. 1988. *A handbook of computer-based training*, 2nd ed. (London, Kogan Page).

de Bono, E. 1980. *Opportunities* (London, Penguin Books).

De Geus, A.P. 1988. "Planning as learning", in *Harvard Business Review* (Boston, Massachusetts, Harvard University Press), Mar.-Apr.

Del Gazio, E. 1984. "Proof that supervisory training works", in *Training and Development Journal* (Alexandria, Virginia, American Society for Training and Development), Mar.

Delisi, P.S. 1990. "Lessons from the steel axe: Culture, technology and organisational change", in *Sloan Management Review* (Cambridge, Massachusetts, MIT Press), Fall.

Donaldson, L. 1980. *Behavioural supervision: Practical ways to change unsatisfactory behaviour and increase productivity* (Reading, Massachusetts, Addison-Wesley).

Donarski, J., et al. 1983. "Training through consultancy to improve maintenance management", in *Journal of European Industrial Training* (Bradford, United Kingdom, MCB University Press), Vol. 7, No. 3.

— , et al. 1988. "Results-oriented maintenance management", in *Journal of European Industrial Training* (Bradford, United Kingdom, MCB University Press), Sep.

Donegan, J. 1990. "The learning organization: Lessons from British Petroleum", in *European Management Journal* (Oxford, United Kingdom, Pergamon Press), Vol. 8, No. 3, Sep.

Drucker, P.F. 1968. *The practice of management* (London, Pan Books).

Dunphy, D.C. 1981. *Organizational change by choice* (Sydney, McGraw-Hill).

Easterby-Smith, M.P.V.; Tanton, M. 1985. "Turning course evaluation from an end to a means", in *Personnel Management* (London, Business Publications).

Easton, G. 1982. *Learning from case studies* (New York, Prentice-Hall International).

El-Namaki, M.S.S. 1989. "Management training for small and medium industries: A cross-country analysis of characteristics, constraints and catalysts", in *Proceedings of the Second Tokyo Conference on Management Development of Small and Medium-sized Enterprises in Asia* (Tokyo, The Foundation for Asian Management Development).

Elliot, G. 1984. *Video production in education and training* (London, Croom Helm).

Ellis, D. 1993. *Handbook of management training* (London, Pitman).

Eraut, M. 1989. *The international encyclopedia of educational technology* (Oxford, Pergamon).

Erskine, J.A., et al. 1981. *Teaching with cases* (London, Ontario, University of Western Ontario, Research and Publications Division).

Farlow, H. 1979. *Publicizing and promoting programmes* (New York, McGraw-Hill).

Farnsworth, T. 1975. *Developing executive talent* (Maidenhead, Berkshire, McGraw-Hill).

Fawbert, F. 1987. *Using video in training* (Carnforth, United Kingdom, Parthenon).

Flesch, R. 1986. *How to write, speak and think more effectively* (New York, Signet).

Franklin, C. 1989. "How to determine training needs", in *Productivity Digest* (Houston, Texas, American Productivity and Quality Center), Aug.

Freeman, R. 1993. *Quality assurance in training and education: How to apply BS 5750 (ISO 9000) standards* (London, Kogan Page).

Gardner, J. 1983. *Training the new supervisor* (New York, AMACOM).

Gayeski, D.M. 1983. *Corporate and instructional video* (Englewood Cliffs, New Jersey, Prentice-Hall).

Geber, B. 1990. "Goodbye classrooms", in *Productivity Digest* (Houston, Texas, American Productivity and Quality Center), July.

Gibb, A. 1991. *Defining success in entrepreneurship development programmes: A guide to model approach* (Geneva, ILO).

—. 1996. *Training for enterprise: The role of education and training in small and medium enterprise (SME) development.* Paper presented in the Italian Presidency Conference of Ministers from the Member States of the European Union and the Countries of Central and Eastern Europe, Central Asia and Mongolia (Turin).

Gillette, J.; McCollom, M. 1990. *Groups in context: A new perspective on group dynamics* (Reading, Massachusetts, Addison-Wesley).

Gough, J. 1996. *Developing learning materials* (London, Institute of Personnel and Development).

Griffiths, P.; Allen, B. 1990. "Assessment centres: Breaking with tradition", in *Journal of Management Development* (Bradford, United Kingdom, MCB University Press), Vol. 6, No. 1.

Hamel, G.; Prahalad, C.K. 1994. *Competing for the future* (Boston, Massachusetts, Harvard Business School Press).

Hammer, M.; Champy, J. 1993. *Re-engineering the corporation* (New York, Harper Business).

—; Stanton, S.A. 1995. *Re-engineering revolution: A handbook* (New York, Harper Business).

Hams, P.B. 1987. "Management development for the new work culture", in *International Journal of Manpower* (Bradford, United Kingdom, MCB University Press), Vol. 7, No. 4.

Handy, C. 1976. *Understanding organizations* (London, Penguin).

—. 1987. *The making of managers: A report on management education training and development in the USA, West Germany, France, Japan and the UK* (London, National Economic Development Office).

—. 1988. "The new management", in *Open Learning in Transition* (London, National Education Council (NEC)).

—. 1989. *The age of unreason* (London, Business Books).

Harper, M. 1983. *Selection and training for entrepreneurship development* (Geneva, ILO).

Harrison, R. 1989. *Training and development* (London, Institute of Personnel Management).

Hardingham, A. 1996. *Designing training* (London, Institute of Personnel and Development).

Harvey, D.F.; Brown, D.R. 1982. *An experiential approach to organization development*, 2nd ed. (Englewood Cliffs, New Jersey, Prentice-Hall).

Harvey-Jones, J. 1989. *Making it happen* (London, Fontana).

Harzing, A.-W.; Ruysseveld, J.V. 1995. *International human resource management* (London, Sage).

Hawridge, D. 1986. *Computers in company training* (London, Croom Helm).

Hawrylyshyn, 1967. "Preparing managers for international operations", in *Business Quarterly* (London, Ontario, University of Western Ontario), Autumn.

Hennecke, M. 1991. "Towards the change-sensitive organization", in *Training Magazine* (Minneapolis, Lakewood Publications), May.

Hinrichs, J.R. 1977. *High talent personnel: A critical resource* (New York, AMACOM).

Hodgson, V., et al. 1989. *Information-technology-based open learning: A study report* (Lancaster, United Kingdom, University of Lancaster, Department of Psychology).

Hoffarth, V.B. 1989. *Corporate women managers in South-East Asia* (Manila, Asian Institute of Management).

Hoffman, F.O. 1981. "Getting line managers into the act", in *Training and Development Journal* (Alexandria, Virginia, American Society for Training and Development), Mar.

Hofstede, G. 1991. *Cultures and organizations: Software of the mind* (Maidenhead, Berkshire, McGraw-Hill).

Holpp, L. 1987. "Technical training for non-technical learners", in *Training and Development Journal* (Alexandria, Virginia, American Society for Training and Development), Oct.

Honey, P.; Mumford, A. 1983. *Manual of learning styles*, 2nd ed., 1986 (Maidenhead, Berkshire, Peter Honey).

Horton, T.R. 1986. *What works for me* (New York, Random House).

Huczynski, A.A.; Buchanan, D.A. 1991. *Organizational behaviour: An introductory text*, 2nd ed. (London, Prentice-Hall).

ICPM. 1990. *Preparation guide for certification examinations* (Harrisonburg, Virginia, Institute of Certified Professional Managers).

ILO. 1972. *An introductory course in teaching and training methods for management development* (Geneva).

— . 1986. *The promotion of small and medium-sized enterprises*, Report VI, International Labour Conference, 72nd Session (Geneva).

Iuppa, N. 1984. *Practical guide to interactive video program design* (White Plains, New York, Knowledge Industry Publications).

Jeffries, C., et al. 1990. *The A-Z of open learning* (London, National Education Council).

Jennings, L. 1987. "How do you determine the use of new technologies", in *Training and Development Journal* (Alexandria, Virginia, American Society for Training and Development), Aug.

Jones, A. 1986. "The role of the management trainer", in A. Mumford (ed.): *Handbook of management development* (Aldershot, Hampshire, Gower).

Jones, J.E. 1973. "A model of group development", in *The 1973 annual handbook for group facilitators* (San Diego, California, University Associates, Inc.).

— ; Woodcock, M. 1985. *Manual of management development: Strategy, design and instruments for programme improvement* (Aldershot, Hampshire, Gower).

Josefowitz, N. 1980. *Paths to power: A woman's guide from first job to top executive* (Reading, Massachusetts, Addison-Wesley).

Kanter, R.M. 1977. *Men and women of the corporation* (New York, Basic Books).

Kaplan, R.E.; Drath, W.H.; Kofodimos, J.F. 1985. *High hurdles: The challenge of executive self development.* Technical Report No. 25 (Greensboro, North Carolina, Center for Creative Leadership).

Kastiel, D.L. 1986. "Putting video-conferences to work for sales and marketing", in *Business Marketing* (Chicago, Illinois, Crain Communications Inc.), June.

Katz, S.N.; Rosen, L.S. 1987. "Managing training for a technical population" in *Training and Development Journal* (Alexandria, Virginia, American Society for Training and Development), Oct.

Kaufman, H.G. 1974. "The graduate management degree: Is it really the road to success?", in *New Engineer* (New York, MBA Communications), Feb.

Kearsley, G. 1983. *Computer-based training* (Reading, Massachusetts, Addison-Wesley).

— . 1985. *Training for tomorrow* (Reading, Massachusetts, Addison-Wesley).

— . 1986. *Authoring: A guide to the design of instructional software* (Reading, Massachusetts, Addison-Wesley).

Keegan, D. 1986. *The functions of distance education* (London, Croom Helm).

Keen, P.G. 1995. *Every manager's guide to information technology* (Boston, Massachusetts, Harvard Business School Press).

— ; Knapp, E.M. 1996. *Every manager's guide to business processes* (Boston, Massachusetts, Harvard Business School Press).

Keiser, T.; Seeler, J. 1987. in Craig, R.L.: *Training and development handbook: A guide to human resources development* (New York, McGraw-Hill).

Kepner, C.H.; Tregoe, B.B. 1981. *The new rational manager* (Princeton, New Jersey, Princeton University Press).

Kirkpatrick, D.L. 1983. *A practical guide for supervisory training and development,* 2nd ed. (Reading, Massachusetts, Addison-Wesley).

— . 1988. "Supervisory management development: Update from an expert", in *Training and Development Journal* (Alexandria, Virginia, American Society for Training and Development), Aug.

Knowles, M.S. 1975. *Self-directed learning* (New York, Associated Press).

— . 1980a. "How do you get people to be self-directed learners?", in *Training and Development Journal* (Alexandria, Virginia, American Society for Training and Development), May.

— . 1980b. "The magic of contract learning", in *Training and Development Journal* (Alexandria, Virginia, American Society for Training and Development), June.

— . 1980c. *The modern practice of adult education* (Cambridge, Massachusetts, Cambridge Book Co.).

— . 1983a. "Developing the training professional", in *Training and Development in Australia,* Vol. 10, No. 1, Mar.

— . 1983b. "Developing the training professional, Part 2", in *Training and Development in Australia,* Vol. 10, No. 2, June.

— . 1984. *The adult learner: A neglected species,* 3rd ed. (Houston, Texas, Gulf Publishing).

— . 1985. *Andragogy in action* (San Francisco, Jossey-Bass).

Kohl, D. 1984. *Experiential learning* (Englewood Cliffs, New Jersey, Prentice-Hall).

— , et al. 1986. "Strategic management development: Using experiential learning theory to assess and develop managerial competencies", in *Journal of Management Development* (Bradford, United Kingdom, MCB University Press), Vol. 5, No. 3.

Kolb, D.A. 1984. *Experiential learning: Experience as the source of learning and development* (Englewood Cliffs, New Jersey, Prentice-Hall).

Kolter, J.P.; Faux, V.A.; McAuthur, C.C. 1978. *Self-assessment and career development* (Englewood Cliffs, New Jersey, Prentice-Hall).

Komanecky, A.N. 1988. "Developing new managers at GE", in *Training and Development Journal* (Alexandria, Virginia, American Society for Training and Development), June.

Kooiman, J.; Eliassen, K.A. 1988. "Public management in Europe", in A.P. Kakabadse, P.R. Brovetto and R. Holzer (eds.): *Management development and the public sector* (Aldershot, Hampshire, Gower).

Kubr, M. 1971. *Principles for selection of teaching and training methods* (Geneva, ILO).

— (ed.). 1982. *Managing a management development institution* (Geneva, ILO).

— (ed.). 1996. *Management consulting: A guide to the profession*, 3rd ed. (Geneva, ILO).

— ; Prokopenko, J. 1989. *Diagnosing management training and development needs: Concepts and techniques* (Geneva, ILO).

Kurt, L. 1951. *Field theory in social sciences* (New York, Harper and Row).

Laird, D. 1985. *Approaches to training and development* (Reading, Massachusetts, Addison-Wesley).

Lambert, C. 1984. *The complete book of supervisory training* (New York, John Wiley).

Lawrie, J. 1987. "How to establish a mentoring program", in *Training and Development Journal* (Alexandria, Virginia, American Society for Training and Development), Mar.

Leary, M., et al. 1986. *The qualities of managing* (Sheffield, United Kingdom, The Training Agency).

— , et al. 1989. *First line manager development programme* (Hove, United Kingdom, Macmillan Intek).

Lee, C. 1990. "Talking back to the boss", in *Training* (Minneapolis, Lakewood Publications), April.

Lee, M., et al. (eds.). 1996. *Management education in the new Europe* (London, International Thomson Business Press).

Leenders, M.R.; Ersksine, J.A. 1973. *Case Research: The case writing process* (London, Ontario, Research and Publications Division, School of Business Administration, University of Western Ontario).

Lepage, R. 1990. "Developing the international manager for 1990 and beyond", in *International Management Development Review* (Brussels, Management Centre Europe), Vol. 6.

Lewey, L.A.; Davies, B.L. 1987. "When techies manage", in *Training and Development Journal* (Alexandria, Virginia, American Society for Training and Development), Oct.

Lewis, B., et al. 1987. *Computer-based training* (Carnforth, United Kingdom, Parthenon).

Lewis, R. 1986. *How to write flexible materials* (London, National Council for Education Technology (NCET)).

— . 1989. "What is 'quality' in corporate open learning and how do we measure it?", in *Open Learning* (Harrow, Essex, Longman Group), Vol. 4, No. 3.

— ; Spencer, D. 1986. *What is open learning?* (London, National Council for Educational Technology (NCET)).

Likert, R. 1970. *New patterns of management* (New York, McGraw-Hill).

Limerick, D. 1976. "Authority: An axis of leadership role differentiation", in *Psychologia Africana* (Pretoria, South Africa, Bureau of Scientific Publications), Vol. 16.

— ; Cunningham, B.; Trevor-Roberts, B. 1984. *Frontiers of excellence* (Brisbane, Australian Institute of Management).

Lippitt, G.; Langseth, P.; Mossop, J. 1985. *Implementing organizational change* (San Francisco, Jossey-Bass).

London, M. 1985. *Developing managers* (San Francisco, Jossey-Bass).

Lowden, J. 1988. "Managerial skills for entrepreneurs", in *Entrepreneurs: A blueprint for action* (Bradford, United Kingdom, MCB University Press).

Loucks, K. 1988. *Training entrepreneurs for small business creation: Lessons from experience* (Geneva, ILO).

MacDonald, C.R. 1982. *Performance-based supervisory development: Adapted from a major AT&T study* (Amherst, Massachusetts, Human Resources Development Press).

Mailleck, S.; Huberman, S.; Wall, S.J. (eds.). 1988. *The practice of management development* (New York, Praeger).

Management Charter Initiative. 1992. *MCI for managers and supervisors* (London, MCI).

Management development to the millennium: The Cannon and Taylor Working Party Reports. 1994. (Corby, United Kingdom, The Institute of Management).

Mangham, I.; Silver, M.S. 1986. *Management training: Context and practice* (London, Economic and Social Research Council).

Mant, A. 1981. *The dynamics of management education* (Aldershot, Hampshire, Gower).

— . 1987. "Developing effective managers for the future: Learning through experience", in C.L. Cooper (ed.).: *Developing managers for the 1980s* (London, Macmillan).

Manu, G.; Nelson, R.; Thiongo, J. 1996. *Know about business* (Turin, International Training Centre of the ILO).

Margerison, C., et al. 1987. "High-flying management development", in *Training and Development Journal* (Alexandria, Virginia, American Society for Training and Development), Feb.

— , et al. 1988. *Managerial consulting skills: A practical guide* (Aldershot, Hampshire, Gower).

— ; Roden, S. 1987. *Management development bibliography* (Bradford, United Kingdom, MCB University Press).

Markham, C. 1987. *Practical consulting* (London, Institute of Chartered Accountants).

Marsick, V.; Watkins, K. 1990. *Informal and incidental learning in the workplace* (London, Routledge).

Mason, R.D.; Kaye, A.R. (eds.). 1989. *Mindweave: Communication, computers and distance education* (Oxford, Pergamon).

McCall, M.W., Jr.; Lombardo, M.M.; Morrison, A.W. 1988. *The lessons of experience* (Lexington, Massachusetts, Lexington Books).

McConnell, D.; Hodgson, V. 1990. "Computer mediated communications systems — Electronic networks and education", in *Management Education and Development* (Lancaster, United Kingdom, Lancaster University), Vol. 21, part 1.

McGregor, D. 1960. *The human side of enterprise* (New York, McGraw-Hill).

McInnes, F. 1980. *Video in education and training* (London, Focal Press).

McLagan, P.A. 1989. "Models for HRD practice", in *Training and Development Journal* (Alexandria, Virginia, American Society for Training and Development), Sep.

McLennan, R. 1989. *Managing organizational change* (Englewood Cliffs, New Jersey, Prentice-Hall).

McNair, M.P.; Hersum, A.C. 1961. *The case method at the Harvard Business School* (New York, McGraw-Hill).

McNulty, N. 1985. *International directory of executive education* (Oxford and New York, Pergamon Press).

Mead, M. 1990. "From colleagues in crisis to the synergy of the set", in *Industrial and Commercial Training* (Bradford, United Kingdom, MCB University Press), Jan.

Meadows, I. 1984. "The management of professional work", in *Practising Manager* (Australia), Oct.

Megginson, D. 1988. "Instructor, coach, mentor: Three ways of helping managers", in *Management Education and Development* (Lancaster, United Kingdom, Lancaster University), Spring.

Meredith, G.; Nelson, R.; Neck, P. 1982. *The practice of entrepreneurship* (Geneva, ILO).

Merrick, C.M. 1979. *Management division history for ASME centennial — 1980* (Easton, Pennsylvania, Lafayette College).

Mezirow, J. 1985. "A critical theory of self-directed learning", in S. Brookfield (ed.): *Self-directed learning: From theory to practice* (San Francisco, Jossey-Bass).

Mintzberg, H. 1990. "The manager's job: Folklore and fact", in *Harvard Business Review* (Boston, Massachusetts), Mar.-Apr., No. 2.

Mitchell, G. 1994. *The trainer's handbook: The AMA guide to effective training*, 2nd ed. (Aldershot, Hampshire, Gower and New York, AMACOM).

Morgan, B.S.; Schiemann, W.A. 1984. *Supervision in the 80s: Trends in corporate America* (Princeton, New Jersey, Opinion Research Corporation).

Mouton, J.S.; Blake, R.R. 1984. *Synergogy: A new strategy for education training and development* (San Francisco, Jossey-Bass).

Mumford, A. 1980. *Making experience pay* (Maidenhead, Berkshire, McGraw-Hill).

— . 1986. "Learning to learn for managers", in *Journal of European Industrial Training*, Vol. 10, No. 2.

— . 1988. *Developing top managers* (Aldershot, Hampshire, Gower).

— . (ed.). 1994. *Handbook of management development*, 4th ed. (Aldershot, Hampshire, Gower).

— . 1995. *Learning at the top* (Maidenhead, Berkshire, McGraw-Hill).

— , et al. 1987. *Developing directors* (Moorfoot, United Kingdom, Manpower Services Commission).

Nadler, G.; Hibino, S. 1994. *Breakthrough thinking: The seven principles of creative problem solving*, 2nd (revised) ed. (Rocklin, California, Prima Publishing).

Newstrom, J.W.; Scannell, E.E. 1991. *Games trainers play* (New York, McGraw-Hill).

Nind, P.F. 1985. *A firm foundation: The story of the Foundation for Management Education* (Oxford, Oxford Print Associates).

Normann, R. 1984. *Service management* (Chichester, United Kingdom, John Wiley).

Northcott, P. 1986. "Distance education for managers: An international perspective", in *Open Learning* (Harlow, Essex, Longman), June.

Northrup, H.R., et al. 1978. *The objective selection of supervisors* (Philadelphia, The Wharton School, University of Pennsylvania).

Norton, J.H. 1984. "Computer literacy training for employee relations professionals", in *Personnel* (Paris, National Association of Directors and Personnel Officers (ANDC)), Nov.-Dec.

Odiorne, G.S. 1984. *Strategic management of human resources: A portfolio approach* (San Francisco, Jossey-Bass).

Ogawa, E. 1994. *Small business management today* (Tokyo, Asian Productivity Organization).

O'Neil, G. 1987. *Interactive video in training* (Carnforth, United Kingdom, Parthenon).

Open College. 1990. *The management of quality* (Open College).

Osbaldeston, M.; Barham, K. 1989. "Developing managers for the future", in *Journal of European Industrial Training*, Vol. 13, No. 4.

Parry, S.B.; Robinson, E.J. 1983. "Management development: Training or education?", in *Training and Development Journal* (Alexandria, Virginia, American Society for Training and Development), Mar.

Pascale, R.T.; Athos, A.G. 1981. *The art of Japanese management* (London, Penguin).

Pearce, D. 1983. "Getting started: An action manual", in M. Pedler: *Action learning in practice* (Aldershot, Hampshire, Gower).

Pedler, M. 1984. *Self-development groups for managers* (Sheffield, United Kingdom, Manpower Services Commission).

—. 1983 and 1990. *Action learning in practice*, 1st ed. and 2nd ed. (Aldershot, Hampshire, Gower).

—; Boydell, T. 1986. *Managing yourself* (London, Fontana).

—; —; Burgoyne, J. 1978. *A manager's guide to self-development* (New York and Maidenhead, Berkshire, McGraw-Hill).

—; —; —. 1989. "Towards the learning company", in *Journal of the Association for Management Education and Development*, Vol. 20, Part 1.

—; —; —. 1994. *A manager's guide to self-development*, 3rd (revised) ed. (Maidenhead, Berkshire, McGraw-Hill).

—; —; —; Welsham, G. 1990. *Self-development in organizations* (Maidenhead, Berkshire, McGraw-Hill).

Percival, F.; Ellington, H. 1988. *A handbook of educational technology* (London, Kogan Page).

Peters, J. 1988. *Customer first: The independent answer* (Bradford, United Kingdom, MCB University Press).

—; Austin, N. 1985. *A passion for excellence: The leadership difference* (New York, Random House).

—; Waterman, R. 1983. *In search of excellence* (New York, Harper and Row).

Philips, C.A. 1988. "The competitive edge: Business leadership superimposed on technological excellence", in *Canadian Manager* (Willowdale, Ontario, Canadian Institute of Management), July.

Phillips, K.; Shaw, P. 1989. *A consultancy approach for trainers* (Aldershot, Hampshire, Gower).

Powers, E.A. 1987. "Enhancing managerial competence: The American Management Association competency programme", in *Journal of Management Development*, Vol. 6, No. 4.

Prokopenko, J. (ed.). 1983. *Modular programme for supervisory development* (Geneva, ILO).

—. 1988. *Management implications of structural adjustment* (Geneva, ILO).

—. 1989. *Improving public service productivity: Problems and challenges* (Geneva, ILO).

—; Bittel, L.R. 1981. "A modular course-format for supervisory development", in *Training and Development Journal* (Alexandria, Virginia, American Society for Training and Development), Feb.

—; North, K. 1996. *Productivity and quality management: A modular programme* (Geneva, ILO; Tokyo, Asian Productivity Organization).

Pun, A. 1990. "Action learning for trainers' development: A design for post-graduate studies", in *Journal of European Industrial Training* (Bradford, United Kingdom, MCB University Press), Vol. 14, No. 9.

Putman, A.O.; Bell, C.R. 1984. "Projections, paradoxes, paradigms", in L. Nadler (ed.): *Handbook of human resource development* (New York, John Wiley).

Rae, L. 1995. *The techniques of training*, 3rd ed. (Aldershot, Hampshire, Gower).

Ramsey, J.E. 1982. *The 1981 national survey of supervisory management practices* (Harrisonburg, North Virginia, James Madison University).

Reid, M.A.; Barrington, H. 1994. *Training interventions*, 4th ed. (London, Institute of Personnel and Development).

Revans, R.W. 1971. *Developing effective managers* (Milton Keynes, United Kingdom, Open University Press).

—. 1980. *Action learning* (London, Blond and Briggs).

—. 1982. *The origins and growth of action learning* (London, Chartwell Bratt, Bromley and Lund).

—. 1983. *ABC of action learning* (London, Chartwell Bratt, Bromley and Lund).

Reynolds, J.I. 1980. *Case method in management development: Guide for effective use* (Geneva, ILO).

Richards, S. 1989. "The role of management development in public service modernisation". Paper presented at the OECD meeting on Management Development for Higher Civil Service, Paris, 26-28 June.

Robinson, B. 1990. "Telecommunications for interactive tutoring: The Open University experience in the 1980s", in *Open Learning* (Harlow, Essex, Longman Group), Vol. 5. No. 2.

Romiszowski, A.J. 1988. *The selection and use of instructional media* (New York, Nichols Publishing Co.).

Rosenbaum, B.L. 1982. *How to motivate today's workers: Motivation models for managers and supervisors* (New York, McGraw-Hill).

Rossett, A. 1991. "Overcoming obstacles to needs assessment", in *Training* (Minneapolis, Lakewood Publications), Vol. 28, No. 1, Mar.

Rummler, G.A.; Brache, A.P. 1991. "Managing the white space", in *Training* (Minneapolis, Lakewood Publications), Vol. 28, No. 1, Mar.

Rushby, N. 1987. "Teleconferencing: Students' interaction by telephone: The PACNET experience", in *Technology-based learning: Selected readings* (London, Kogan Page).

Sadler, P. 1986. *Recent trends in management development in Europe* (Brussels, European Foundation for Management Development).

—. 1984. "Educating managers for the 21st century", in *Royal Society of Arts Journal*, No. 132, May.

Savoie, D.J. 1990. "Public management development: A comparative perspective", in *The International Journal of Public Sector Management* (Bradford, United Kingdom, MCB University Press), Vol. 2, No. 3.

Schein, E.H. 1969. *Process consultation: Its role in organization development* (Reading, Massachusetts, Addison-Wesley).

— . 1978. *Career dynamics: Matching individual and organizational needs* (Reading, Massachusetts, Addison-Wesley).

— . 1987. *Process consultation,* Vol. II (Reading, Massachusetts, Addison-Wesley).

Schlick, J.D. 1988. "Developing project management skills", in *Training and Development Journal* (Alexandria, Virginia, American Society for Training and Development), May.

Schön, D.A. 1987. *Educating the reflective practitioner* (San Francisco, Jossey-Bass).

Sellers, P. 1988. "How IBM teaches techies to sell", in *Fortune* (Chicago, Time Inc.), June.

Senge, P. 1990. *The fifth discipline: The art and practice of the learning organization* (New York, Doubleday).

— . 1994. *The fifth discipline fieldbook* (New York, Doubleday).

Settle, M.E. 1988. "Developing tomorrow's managers", in *Training and Development Journal* (Alexandria, Virginia, American Society for Training and Development), Apr.

Shears, A.E. 1995a. *Suggestions on planning, writing and using case studies: A workshop and toolkit* (Geneva, ILO).

— . 1995b. *Train the management trainer* (Geneva, ILO).

Smith, B.J. 1987. "Structured diaries", in *Training and Management Development Methods* (Bradford, United Kingdom, MCB University Press), Vol. 1.

— . 1988. "How to use video in training", in *Journal of European Industrial Training* (Bradford, United Kingdom, MCB University Press), Vol. 12, No. 7.

— . 1989. "Educational considerations in the preparation of professionals", in *Occupational Educational Forum,* Vol. 17. No. 2.

— ; Delahaye, B.L. 1987. *How to be an effective trainer,* 2nd ed. (New York, John Wiley).

Snell, R. 1989. "Turning bad times into good times and good times into better ones", in *Industrial and Commercial Training* (Bradford, United Kingdom, MCB University Press), Mar.

— . 1990. "Congenial ways of learning: So near and yet so far", in *Journal of Management Development* (Bradford, United Kingdom, MCB University Press), Vol. 9, No. 1.

Standke, L. 1978. "Using games to help meet your objectives", in *Training* (Minneapolis, Lakewood Publications), Dec.

Stewart, N.; McGoldrick, S. (eds.). 1996. *Human resource development: Perspectives, strategies and practice* (London, Pitman).

Storey, J. 1989. "Management development: A literature review and implications for future research. Part I: Conceptualisations and practices", in *Personnel Review* (Bradford, United Kingdom, MCB University Press), Vol. 18, No. 6.

Stuart, R. 1984. "Using others to learn: Some everyday practice", in *Personnel Review* (Bradford, United Kingdom, MCB University Press), Vol. 13, No. 4.

Tanburn, J. 1995. *Pointers to success: A framework for evaluating the impact of the FIT programme* (Geneva, ILO).

Tate, W. 1995. *Developing managerial competencies: A critical guide to methods and materials* (Aldershot, Hampshire, Gower).

Taylor, B.; Lipitt, G.L. (eds.). 1984. *Management development and training handbook*, 2nd ed. (New York and Maidenhead, Berkshire, McGraw-Hill).

Temporal, J. 1990. "Living management development to the corporate future — The role of the professional", in *Journal of Management Development* (Bradford, United Kingdom, MCB University Press), Vol. 9, No. 5.

Theocharides, S.; Tolentino, A. 1991. *Integrated strategies for small enterprise development* (Geneva, ILO).

Thurman, J.; Louzine, A.; Kogi, K. 1988. *Higher productivity and a better place to work: Action manual and Trainers' manual* (Geneva, ILO).

Tjosvold, D.; Weicker, D. 1993. "Cooperative and competitive networking by entrepreneurs: A critical incidents study", in *Journal of Small Business Management* (Morgantown, West Virginia) Vol. 31, No. 1, January.

Tolentino, A. 1986. "The local study missions and the association building projects: Approaches to SME development", in *Promoting small-scale industry in South-East Asia: Selected support schemes in the Philippines, Thailand and Malaysia* (Vienna, UNIDO).

— . 1995. *Guidelines for the analysis of policies and programmes for small and medium enterprise development* (Geneva, ILO).

— ; Theocharides, S. 1992. *Strengthening existing small enterprises* (Geneva, ILO).

Torrington, D.; Hall, L. 1995. *Personnel management: A new approach*, 3rd ed. (London, Prentice-Hall).

Tracey, W.R. (ed.). 1993. *Human resources management and development handbook*, 2nd ed. (New York, AMACOM).

TVI. 1986. *A handbook for producers and users of tutored video instruction* (London, Further Education Unit).

Tyson, S. (ed.). 1995. *Strategic prospects for HRM* (London, Institute of Personnel and Development).

US Congress. Office of Technology Assessment. 1988. *Technology and the American economic transition: Choice for the future* (Washington, DC).

Usilaner, B.L. 1980. "Can we expect productivity improvement in the Federal Government?", in *Dimensions of Productivity Research* (Houston, Texas, American Productivity Center).

Utz, P. 1980. *Video user's handbook* (Englewood Cliffs, New Jersey, Prentice-Hall).

van de Ven, A.; Delbecq, A.L. "Nominal versus interacting group processes for committee decision-making effectiveness", in *Academy of Management Journal* (Ada, Ohio, Academy of Management), Vol. 14, No. 2, June.

Waddell, G. 1982. "Simulations: Balancing the pros and cons", in *Training and Development Journal* (Alexandria, Virginia, American Society of Training and Development), Jan.

Waller, E.P. 1982. "Teleconferencing — A new bank training technique", in *Training and Development Journal* (Alexandria, Virginia, American Society of Training and Development), Dec.

Ward, E. 1993. "Motivation of expansion plans: Entrepreneurs and managers", in *Journal of Small Business Management*, Vol. 31, No. 1, Jan.

Warr, P.; Bird, M.; Rackham, N. 1970. *Evaluation of management training* (Aldershot, Hampshire, Gower).

Waterman, R.H. 1987. *The renewal factor: How the best get and keep their competitive edge* (New York, Bantam Books).

Way, P. 1989. "Action learning for managers: An Australian view", in *International Journal of Public Sector Management* (Bradford, United Kingdom, MCB University Press), Vol. 2.

Wiggenhorn, W. 1990. "Motorola University: When training becomes an education", in *Harvard Business Review* (Boston, Massachusetts, Harvard University), No. 4, July-Aug.

Wilbur, J. 1987. "Does mentoring breed success?", in *Training and Development Journal* (Alexandria, Virginia, American Society for Training and Development), Nov.

Wilcox, J. 1987. "A campus tour of corporate colleges", in *Training and Development Journal* (Alexandria, Virginia, American Society for Training and Development), May.

Wills, G.S.C. 1988. *Creating wealth through management development* (Bradford, United Kingdom, MCB University Press).

Winders, R. 1989. "Interactive teleconferencing in education and training. Part 2: Applications", in *Interactive Learning International* (Chichester, United Kingdom, John Wiley), No. 5.

Ykl, G. 1981. *Leadership in organizations* (Englewood Cliffs, New Jersey, Prentice-Hall).

Zemke, R. 1991. "Do performance appraisals change performance", in *Training* (Minneapolis, Lakewood Publications), May.

Zimmer, M.B. 1988. "A practical guide to video-conferencing", in *Training and Development Journal* (Alexandria, Virginia, American Society for Training and Development), May.

Zuber-Skerrit, O. 1984. *Video in higher education* (New York, Nichols Publishing Co.).